797,000 books
are available to read at

Forgotten Books

www.ForgottenBooks.com

Forgotten Books' App
Available for mobile, tablet & eReader

ISBN 978-1-332-77373-2
PIBN 10441219

This book is a reproduction of an important historical work. Forgotten Books uses state-of-the-art technology to digitally reconstruct the work, preserving the original format whilst repairing imperfections present in the aged copy. In rare cases, an imperfection in the original, such as a blemish or missing page, may be replicated in our edition. We do, however, repair the vast majority of imperfections successfully; any imperfections that remain are intentionally left to preserve the state of such historical works.

Forgotten Books is a registered trademark of FB &c Ltd.
Copyright © 2015 FB &c Ltd.
FB &c Ltd, Dalton House, 60 Windsor Avenue, London, SW19 2RR.
Company number 08720141. Registered in England and Wales.

For support please visit www.forgottenbooks.com

1 MONTH OF FREE READING

at

www.ForgottenBooks.com

By purchasing this book you are eligible for one month membership to ForgottenBooks.com, giving you unlimited access to our entire collection of over 700,000 titles via our web site and mobile apps.

To claim your free month visit: www.forgottenbooks.com/free441219

* Offer is valid for 45 days from date of purchase. Terms and conditions apply.

English
Français
Deutsche
Italiano
Español
Português

www.forgottenbooks.com

Mythology Photography **Fiction** Fishing Christianity **Art** Cooking Essays Buddhism Freemasonry Medicine **Biology** Music **Ancient Egypt** Evolution Carpentry Physics Dance Geology **Mathematics** Fitness Shakespeare **Folklore** Yoga Marketing **Confidence** Immortality Biographies Poetry **Psychology** Witchcraft Electronics Chemistry History **Law** Accounting **Philosophy** Anthropology Alchemy Drama Quantum Mechanics Atheism Sexual Health **Ancient History Entrepreneurship** Languages Sport Paleontology Needlework Islam **Metaphysics** Investment Archaeology Parenting Statistics Criminology **Motivational**

A SPECIAL

VOCABULARY TO VIRGIL,

COVERING HIS COMPLETE WORKS.

By J. B. GREENOUGH.

BOSTON:
PUBLISHED BY GINN & COMPANY.
1885.

Entered, according to Act of Congress, in the year 1882, by
JAMES B. GREENOUGH,
in the Office of the Librarian of Congress, at Washington.

J. S. Cushing & Co., Printers, Boston.

PREFACE.

THE author, in preparing this Vocabulary to accompany his Virgil, or for use with other editions, has had two things in view: first, to supply as much information as was possible in regard to the history and uses of the Latin words, so that the book should not be a mere key to translate by, but should also furnish means for the study of the language itself; and, secondly, at the same time to give or suggest a suitable English expression for every passage.

In every language which is to be rendered into another, there may be said to be three classes of meanings to the words: first, the etymological meaning, *i.e.*, the idea that a word presented when it was first formed or used; second, the literal meanings, *i.e.*, the ideas which a word came to have to those who used it in its later development; and, third, the foreign meaning or translation, *i.e.*, the word expressing the nearest equivalent idea in the language into which one wishes to translate. Of course these three classes of meanings may happen to coincide; a word may not have deviated essentially from its primitive force, and this same force may happen to belong to some similar word in the other language. It is, however, oftener otherwise; words have often diverged very far and in many directions from the primitive conception underlying them, and it is rare that a word in one language exactly covers the group of ideas which belongs to the nearest corresponding word in another; and this is especially true in poetry. The author has aimed to keep these classes of meanings separate so far as space would permit. For this purpose the etymological meaning, where it may not be directly deduced from the etymology, has been given first in a parenthesis. Then follow the literal meanings, as nearly as possible in the supposed order of development, with such hints as could be given of the connection of ideas. Such renderings as seemed to be necessary in English, but which did not accord with the Latin conception, have been given in their connection as examples. In this way it is hoped the pupil or teacher may find a good English expression without losing sight of the Latin conception, which is, after all, the most important of the three classes of meanings.

Further, an expression rendered by a bare representation of its ultimate mechanical equivalent, often loses not only all its poetry, but also the whole conception as it presented itself to the mind of the original speaker.

Take such a case as *fors dicta refutet*; the poet undoubtedly means "may fate avert the calamity I suppose," but he is far from saying so, nor could *refuto* to a Roman convey any such idea. What he does say is, "May fate annul (make void) my words," *i.e.*, contradict, or prove false, the supposition which I make. For, in ancient times, it must be remembered any supposition or suggestion of calamity was regarded as ominous, and as tending to bring about the calamity supposed; a force which vaguely underlies the expression in English, "Oh, don't speak of it." It can hardly be hoped that the desired result has been attained in all cases, but the idea has been constantly kept in view. Nor is it supposed that the expressions given are the only suitable ones, but it is hoped that they will be found suggestive.

In regard to the etymology, which occupies more space than is usual in such books, the author has wished to show not merely the kinship of words loosely, but, if possible, the precise manner in which one word has been formed from another. The fact is often overlooked that the Latin language, as we have it, is the growth of many centuries, during which forms have grown up and given rise to new formations, while they themselves have disappeared. The new formations have given rise by analogy to others seeming to be formed like them from lost stems, which, however, perhaps never existed at all. For instance, the forms in **-bundus** and **-cundus** are unquestionably originally formations from stems in *-bon* and *-con*, which are themselves formations from stems in *-bo* and *-co*, and these in turn have been formed by adding *-bus* and *-cus* (*bo* and *co*) to simpler stems or roots. It has been attempted by hints and cross references to indicate these gradual developments, and it is hoped that the treatment will present to many persons new views of Latin stem-formation. It is not desired that all pupils should learn this etymological matter; but the author has been led to insert it on account of the want of any such means of information in an accessible form.

The actual quantity of vowels, where known, has been indicated, irrespective of syllabic quantity, in order to aid the proper pronunciation of Latin words.

J. B. GREENOUGH.

CAMBRIDGE, NOVEMBER 1, 1882.

ABBREVIATIONS.

ă. — Actually long vowels are marked without reference to syllabic quantity, and all vowels (in the words when first presented) not marked long are supposed to be naturally short, although the *syllable* may be long by position. The pronunciation will of course depend on the rules learned from the grammar.

[ ]. — All matter in square brackets is etymological.

[Gr. Αἴολος]. — A Greek word in brackets preceded by *Gr.* indicates that the Latin word is borrowed from the Greek one given.

[?]. — The interrogation in brackets marks a doubtful etymology; after a word or suggestion it indicates, as usual, a doubt, or a suggestion not yet generally received.

†servo. — A dagger marks *a stem*, or, in some cases, *a word* not found in Latin, but which must once have existed. Such stems and words are printed in different type.

DHA. — Capitals indicate Indo-European words or roots.

√fer. — The radical sign is used for convenience to indicate a root. By this is meant the simplest Latin form attainable by analysis; though, strictly speaking, a root is impossible in Latin, as roots had ceased to exist, as such, ages before Latin was a separate language.

as if. — The words *as if* indicate that a word is formed according to such an analogy, though the actual growth of the word may have been different.

wh. — whence is derived.

cf. — Compare, either for resemblance, contrast, or etymological kinship.

poss. — possibly.

prob. — probably.

unc. — uncertain.

(-). — A hyphen indicates composition.

(+). — The plus sign indicates derivation by addition of a termination; the process originally, of course, was one of composition.

reduced. — The word *reduced* indicates the loss of a stem vowel either in composition, derivation, or inflection.

strengthened. — The word *strengthened* indicates a vowel change by which the length of a root vowel is increased; as √div., †Dyau, √snu, †nau.

weakened. — The word *weakened* means that a vowel has descended the vowel scale; as from *a* to *o* or *e*, *o* to *e* or *i*, etc.

p. — present participle.

p.p. — past participle.

p.f. — future participle.

p. ger. — gerundive.

abl. — ablative.

dat. — dative.

acc. — accusative.

compar. — comparative.

superl. — superlative.

Italics. — Matter in Italics is for translation; in Roman, is explanatory only.

VOCABULARY.

VOCABULARY.

ā; see **ab**.
ab (**ā, abs**), [reduced case form of unc. stem: cf. Gr. ἀπό; Eng. *off, of*], prep. with abl., *away from* (cf. **ex**, *out of*). — Used of place, time, and abstract ideas, with words of motion, separation, and the like, *from, off from:* ducite ab urbe; a me abducere; defendo a frigore. — With words not implying motion, *on the side of, on.* — Of succession, *from, after, beginning with, since:* omnes a Belo; nascor ab; a primis mensibus. — Irregularly, *from (out of):* agnae ab ovilibus. — With passives, *by, on the part of.* — Fig., *from, in relation to, in accordance with* (cf. **ex, de**): spectare ab annis. — Adverbial phrase: ab integro, *afresh, anew.* — With **usque**, *all the way from;* see **usque**.
abāctus, -a, -um, p.p. of **abigo**.
Abaris, -is, [Gr. Ἄβαρις], m., a warrior in Turnus' army.
Abās, -antis, [Gr. Ἄβας], m.: 1. A mythic king of Argos, grandson of Danaus, possessor of a famous shield which was sacred to Juno, whence the use of his name in Æn. iii. 286; 2. A companion of Æneas; 3. An Etrurian hero.
abdĭtus, -a, -um, p.p. of **abdo**.
abdŏ [ab-do (*put*)], **-dĭdī, -dĭtum, -dere,** 3. v. a., *put away, remove.* — With reflexive, *go away, take one's self off, withdraw, retire.* — Also, *hide, conceal:* (with dat.) lateri abdidit ensem, i.e., *plunged the sword deeply into his side.* — With reflexive, *conceal* or *hide one's self by withdrawing, withdraw and hide, hide away.*
abdūcŏ, -xī, -ctum, -cere, [abduco], 3. v. a., *lead* or *conduct away* or *from;* *take* or *bring with* one: coloni abducti. — *draw back* or *away:* capita ab ictu. — *carry off* or *away, get away.*
abdūctus, -a, -um, p.p. of **abduco**.
Abella (**Av-**), **-ae,** f., *Abella* or *Avella;* a town of Campania (now Avella Vecchia) famous for its fruit.
abeŏ, īvī or **iī, itum, īre,** [ab-eo], v. n., *go from* a place, &c., *go away, depart, withdraw, pass away, disappear, vanish, go down.*
abfore; see **absum**.
abī, etc.; see **abeo**.
abĭcĭŏ, -iēcī, -iectum, -icere, [abiacio], 3. v. a., *throw from* or *away, throw down.*
abiectus, -a, -um, p.p. of **abicio**.
abiēs, -ietis, [?], f., *fir* or *spruce,* a coniferous tree. Also the *wood,* a favorite material for shipbuilding and the like. — *a ship* (made of the wood), *a spear-handle, a spear.*
abĭgŏ, -ēgī, -āctum, -ere, [abago], 3. v. a., *drive away, dispel, remove:* nox abacta.
abĭtus, -ūs, [ab-itus], m. (abstr. of **abeo**), *a going away, departure, retirement.*—Concretely, *an outlet, place of egress, way of escape, escape.*
abiungŏ, -xī, -ctum, -gere, [abiungo], 3. v. a., *unyoke, unharness:* iuvencum.
abiūrātus, -a, -um, p.p. of **abiuro**.
abiūrŏ, -āvī, -ātum, -āre, [abiuro], 1. v. a., *swear off, abjure, — deny on oath:* abiuratae rapinae.

ablātus, -a, -um, p.p. of **aufero**.
abluŏ, -uī, -ūtum, -uere, [abluo], 3. v. a., *wash off, out,* or *away:* caedem. — *remove filth from* any thing by washing, *cleanse, purify, wash.*
ablūtus, -a, -um, p.p. of **abluo**.
abnegŏ, -āvī, -ātum, -āre, [ab-nego], I. v. a., *deny* (with accessory notion of refusal), *refuse, deny:* medicas adhibere manus.
abnuŏ, -uī, -uitum *or* -ūtum, -uere (-uiturus), [ab-nuo], 3. v. a. and n., *make a sign with the head in token of refusal, refuse, deny, decline, forbid:* omen.
aboleŏ, -ēvī *or* -ui, -Itum, -ēre, [ab-oleo], 2. v. a. (properly, *outgrow,* but only used in the causative sense), *to destroy, cause to perish:* monumenta. — Pass., *die.* — Fig., *take away, extirpate, blot out, remove,* &c.: Sychaeum (from Dido's mind).
abolēscŏ, -ēvī, no sup., -escere, [ab-olesco], 3. v. n. (*outgrow*), *be destroyed, decay, waste, vanish.*
abreptus, -a, -um, p.p. of **abripio**.
abripiŏ, -rĭpuī, -reptum, -ere, [ab-rapio], 3. v. a., *snatch from* or *away, drag off, carry off, tear away* or *from.*
abrumpŏ, -rūpī, -ruptum, -rumpere, [ab-rumpo], 3. v. a. (in causative sense), *break off* or *away from, tear away, rend asunder, break away* (clouds). — Of discourse, &c., *break off:* sermonem. — Of law, &c., *violate, trample on:* fas. — Of life, &c., *tear* or *rend away, destroy, put an end to:* vitam; invisam lucem (*abandon*); somnos cura (*banish*). — abruptus, -a, -um, p.p., *steep, precipitous, violent:* procellae; abrupto sidere. — in abruptum, *precipitously.*
abruptus, -a, -um, p.p. of **abrumpo**.
abs, fuller form of **ab** (cf. **ex, uls**).
abscessus, -ūs, [abs-†cessus, √ced + tus], m., *a going away, departure.*

abscīdo, -cīdī, -cīsum, -cīdere, [abs-cædo], 3. v. a., *cut off* or *away, destroy.*
abscindŏ, -scĭdī, -scissum, -scindere, [ab-scindo], 3. v. a., *cut* or *tear off* or *away, tear apart, sever, rend asunder:* arva et urbes; *tear:* flaventes abscissa comas; *tear* or *rend away* from one; *deprive* one of: umeris vestem.
abscissus, -a, -um, p.p. of **abscindo**.
abscondŏ, -dī and -dĭdī, -dĭtum and -sum, -dere, [abs-condo], 3. v. a., *put away, put out of sight, secrete, conceal.* — Pass. in reflexive force, of the heavenly bodies: *hide, disappear, vanish, set:* Atlantides abscondantur. — Of places as objects, *lose sight of, leave behind:* Phaeacum arces. — Fig., *conceal, hide:* furto fugam.
absens, -entis, p. of **absum**.
absiliŏ, -iī or -uī, no sup., -īre, [ab-salio], 4. v. n. and a., *leap* or *spring away, fly off:* scintillae.
absistŏ, -stĭtī, no sup., -sistere, [ab-sisto], 3. v. n., *stand away* or *apart from; withdraw, depart* or *go away, fly from.* — Fig., *desist* or *cease from, leave off, forbear, refrain* (abs. or with inf.): moveri.
abstineŏ, -tĭnuī, -tentum, -tĭnēre, [abs-teneo], 2. v. a. and n., *hold* or *keep away from; hold* or *keep off.* — With reflexive, *restrain one's self, refrain, keep off* or *away.* — Without reflexive, *refrain, abstain* (abs. or with abl.): tactu (*refuse to touch*).
abstractus, -a, -um, p.p. of **abstraho**.
abstrahŏ, -xī, -ctum, -here, [abstraho], 3. v. a., *draw* or *drag away, carry off.*
abstrūdŏ, -ūsī, -ūsum, -ūdere, [abs-trudo], 3. v. a., *thrust away, hide, conceal.* — With reflexive or in passive, *hide* or *conceal one's self.*
abstrūsus, -a, -um, p.p. of **abstrudo**.
abstulī; see **aufero**.

absum, -fuī, -esse, [ab-sum], (instead of **abfui, abforem,** etc., **afui, aforem,** etc., are also found), v. n., *be away from, be absent* or *distant* (in place. or time) : hinc aberat. — **absēns, -ntis,** p. as adj., *absent, away;* with adv. force, *in one's absence.*

absūmŏ, -mpsi, -mptum (better than -msi, -mtum), -mere, [ab-sumo], 3. v. a., *take away* (to spend, or by spending, cf. **sumptus**); *devour, consume:* mensas. — Of persons, *kill, destroy,* &c.: me ferro. — Of property, &c., *devour, consume:* salus absumpta (*gone*); absumptae vires (*exhausted, all used*).

absumptus, -a, -um (less correctly -mtus, etc.), p.p. of **absumŏ**.

abundāns, -ntis, p. of **abundŏ**.

abundē [†abundŏ-(ab-unda+us)], adv., *copiously, abundantly, in profusion; in a very great* or *high degree, amply, in plenty,* &c. — With gen. = noun or adj., *plenty of, sufficient:* fraudis.

abundŏ, -āvī, -ātum, -āre, [†abundo-], 1. v. n., *flow off, away, overflow,* i.e., *be very abundant* or *numerous; to be in abundance; overflow* with ; *to have an abundance* or *superabundance.* — **abundāns, -ntis,** p. as adj., abundans lactis.

ab usque; see **ab.**

Abȳdus (-dos), -ī, [Gr. Ἄβυδος], f. and m., a town in Asia, opposite Sestos (now *Avido*), famous for its oysters.

āc, reduced form of **atque,** wh. see.

acalanthis, -idis, [Gr. ἀκαλανθίς], f., *the acalanthis* (perhaps *the thistle-finch* or *gold-finch*), a small bird (fabled to have been changed from a girl of that name by the Muses, with whom she contended in song).

Acamās, -antis, [Gr. Ἀκάμας], m., a son of Theseus and Phædra, a hero in the Trojan war.

acanthus, -ī, [Gr. ἄκανθος], m. and f. Masc., *the plant bear's-breech, bear's-foot,* or *brank-ursine,* of which the leaf conventionalized appears on Corinthian capitals. — Fem., *the acanthus,* a thorny evergreen tree in Egypt.

Acarnān, -ānis, [Gr. Ἀκαρνάν], adj., *of Acarnania.* — Masc., a native of that country. — Plur., the inhabitants, *Acarnanians.*

Acarnānia, -ae, [f. of adj. **Acarnanius**], f., a province of central Greece (now *Carnia*).

Acca, -ae, f., a friend of Camilla.

accēdŏ (ad-), -cēssī, -cēssum, -cēdere, (perf. ind. **accēstis** for **accessistis**), [ad-cedo], 3. v. n., *go towards, draw near, approach, come to, visit* (persons or things). — With acc.: scopulos.

accelerŏ (ad-), -āvī, -ātum, -āre, [ad-celero], 1. v. a. and n. Act., *hasten, accelerate.* — Neut., *haste, hasten, make haste.*

accendŏ (ad-), -dī, -sum, -dere, [ad-†cando (cf. **incendo** and **candeo**)], 3. v. a., *set on fire, kindle:* tantum ignem. — Fig., *inflame* a person or thing, *set on fire, kindle, excite, fire, rouse:* quos merita accendit Mezentius ira.

accēnsus (ad-), -a, -um, p.p. of **accendo.**

acceptus, -a, -um, p.p. of **accipio.**

accersŏ, see **arcesso.**

accēssus (ad-), -ūs, [ad-†cessus, cf. **abscessus**], m. Abstr., *a going to* or *near, an approach, entrance, access:* ventorum. — Concr., *an approach, an entrance.*

accidŏ (ad-), -cīdī, no sup., **-cīdere,** [ad-caedo], 3. v. a., *cut into.* — Of food, *consume.* — Of trees, *hew, cut, fell:* ornas.

accinctus (ad-), -a, -um, p.p. of **accingo.**

accingŏ (ad-), -xī, -ctum, -gere, (inf. pass. **accingier**), [ad-cingo], 3. v. a., *gird on, gird around* or *about:* lateri ensem. — Pass., *gird one's self about with, gird on, arm one's self with:* accingitur ense ; accingier artes (*have recourse to,* as arms). — With abl.

of means, *arm, equip, furnish, provide,* &c.: paribus armis,— gird, i.e. *prepare, make ready.* — With reflexive or in passive, *prepare one's self, get ready, make one's self ready,* &c.: se praedae accingunt.

accio (ad-), -īvī, -ītum, -īre, [ad-cio, cf. **cieo**], 4. v. a., *cause to come* or *go to* a person or place; *summon, call.*

accipiŏ (ad-), -cepi, -ceptum, -cipere, [ad-capio], 3. v. a., *take* a person or thing *to* one's self, &c.; *take, receive:* te gremio. — *receive* or *entertain* as a guest, &c.: Aenean. — Gen., take, *get, receive, attain,* take in, *take up:* vulnera tergo; vitam deorum; aequora (of ships); me annus (*I enter upon*); animum quietum; accipe daque fidem. — Mentally, *perceive, hear, observe, learn, receive intelligence* of anything: sonitum. — *take* or *regard* a thing in any way; *consider, interpret, explain.* — accipere omen; also, without **omen**: *regard a* thing *as a (favorable) omen, take as an omen.* — acceptus, -a, -um, p.p., *acceptable, welcome.*

accipiter, -tris, [stem akin to **ocior-** stem akin to **peto**], m., *a hawk.*

accisus, -a, -um, p.p. of **accido**.

accītus (ad-), -ūs, [ad-citus], m. (only in abl. sing.), *a summoning, summons, call.*

accītus, -a, -um, p.p. of **accio**.

acclīnis (ad-), -e, [ad-†clinus (weakened), cf. **clino**], adj., *leaning against* or *towards, leaning on:* arboris trunco.

acclīvis, -e, (-us, -a, -um), [ad+ olivus (weakened)], adj., *slanting upwards* (opp. to **de-clivis**); *inclining upwards, ascending, up hill.*

accola (ad-), -ae, [ad-†cola (cf. **incola**)], comm., *a dweller by* or *near* a place; *a neighbor, dwelling near by.*

accolŏ (ad-), -colui, -cultum, -colere, [ad-colc], 3. v. a. and n.,

dwell by or *near* a place, &c., with or without acc.

accommodŏ (ad-), -āvī, -ātum, -āre, [ad-commodo], 1. v. a., *fit* or *adapt; adjust:* lateri accommodat ensem.

accommodus (ad-), -a, -um, [ad-commodus], adj., *suitable, fit:* fraudi.

accubŏ (ad-), -uī, -itum, -āre, [ad-cubo], 1. v. n., *lie, lie down* or *recline, at, by* or *near:* iuxta accubat. — Of shade, *fall.*

accumbŏ (ad-), -cubui, -cubitum, -cumbere, [ad-cumbo], 3. v. n., *lay one's self down upon, lie on; recline* (at table): epulis divum.

accumulŏ (ad-), -āvī, -ātum, -āre, [ad-cumulo], 1. v. a., *heap upon, heap up, accumulate, load:* animam donis.

accurrŏ (ad-), -cucurrī and -currī, -cursum, -currere, [ad-curro], 3. v. n., *run to, come to by running, hasten to.*

acer, -eris, n., *the maple.*

ācer, -cris, -cre, [√ac + ris], adj., (*sharp, pointed, edged*), *sharp:* sonitus. —Fig., *violent, vehement, strong, passionate, lively, bitter, consuming:* dolor; metus. — Of intellectual qualities, *subtle, acute, penetrating, sagacious, shrewd.* — Of moral qualities, in a good sense, *active, ardent, spirited, zealous:* Orontes; acrior successu (*inspired*); — in a bad sense, *violent, hasty, hot, fierce, severe, fiery:* equus.—Of things: arcus (*powerful*).

acerbŏ, no perf., -ātum, -āre, [†acerbo-], 1. v. a., *to make harsh* or *bitter, to embitter, augment* or *aggravate* anything disagreeable, &c.: crimen.

acerbus, -a, -um, [ācer + bus], adj., (*pointed, sharp*). — To the taste, or to the feelings, *harsh, biting, salt, bitter.* — Of persons, *rough, repulsive, morose, violent, harsh, rigorous, hostile, severe.* —

Neut. plur. as adv., *harshly, sourly, morosely, grimly, violently:* tuens (*furiously, bitterly*). — Of things, harsh, heavy, disagreeable, bitter, troublesome, rigorous, grievous, sad.—Neut., *calamity, misfortune.*— Poetic, *painful, violent, sad; causing pain* (to others), *afflictive, distressing.*

acernus, -a, -um, [ăcer+nus], adj., *made of maple, maple-:* trabes.

acerra, -ae, [?], f., *an incense-box.*

Acerrae, -ārum, f., a town of Campania, near Naples (now *Acerra*).

acervus, -ī, [ăcer + vus], m., (*a pointed mound*), *a heap.*

Acesta, -ae, (-ē, -ēs), f., a town of Sicily, named after King *Acestes* (earlier *Egesta*, later *Segesta*).

Acestēs, -ae, [Gr. 'Ακέστης], m., a son of the river-god Crimisus by a Trojan woman Egesta, or Segesta. He received Æneas as a kinsman.

Achaemenidēs, -ae, [Gr. 'Αχαιμενίδης], m., a supposed companion of Ulysses, left on the island of Sicily.

Achāïcus, -a, -um, [Gr. 'Αχαιïκός], adj., *Achæan, Grecian.*

Achāïus, -a, -um, [Gr. 'Αχαῖος], adj., *Achæan, Grecian.*—Fem. as subst., *Achaia*, a country in the northern part of the Peloponnesus, on the Gulf of Corinth. — Less exactly, *Greece.*

Achātēs, -ae, [Gr. 'Αχάτης], m., the trusty squire of Æneas.

Acheloïus, -a, -um, [Gr 'Αχελωïος], adj., *belonging to the river Acheloüs* in Greece.

Achelous, -ī, [Gr. 'Αχελῶος], m., *Acheloüs*, a river of central Greece (now the *Aspropotamo*).

Acherōn, -ntis, [Gr. 'Αχέρων], m., a river in Epirus, which flows through the Lake Acherusia into the Ambracian Gulf (now the *Verlichi* or *Delika*). — Hence, *a river in the infernal regions.* — Also, *the infernal regions, the world below.*

Acherūns, -untis, m., *the infernal regions, the world below.*

Achillēs, -is, (-ī or -eī), [Dor. Gr. 'Αχιλῆς], m., the famous hero of the Iliad, son of Peleus and Thetis.

Achillēus, -a, -um, [Gr.'Αχίλλειος], adj., *belonging* or *pertaining to Achilles, of Achilles, Achilles'.*

Achīvus, -a, -um, [Gr. 'Αχαιϝος (not found)], adj., *Achæan, Grecian, Greek.* — Plur., Achīvī, -ōrum, m., *the Greeks.*

Acīdālia, -ae, [f. of adj. Acidalius], f., a name of Venus from a fountain (*Acidalius*) in Bœotia.

acidus, -a, -um, [lost stem †aci- or †aco- (cf. aciculus, aceo) + dus], adj., (*pointed, sharp*). — Of taste, *sour, hard, acid:* sorba.

aciēs, -eī, [√ac + ies], f., (*point*), *edge, sharp edge* of a sword, sickle, &c.: acies ferri; falcis.—Of sight, *keen look* or *glance, power of vision, the sight, the eye:* geminas flecte acies;— *brightness* of the heavenly bodies: stellis acies obtusa videtur. — *line* or *order of battle, battle-array* of land or sea forces; a similar *line of boys; an army drawn up in order of battle; the action of troops drawn up in battle-array; a battle:* acie certare; *an army:* eoas acies.

aclis, -ĭdis, [Gr. ἀγκυλίς], f., *a small javelin.*

Acmōn, -onis, [Gr. "Ακμων], m., a companion of Æneas.

Acoetēs, -is, [Gr. 'Ακοίτης], m., an armor-bearer of Evander.

aconītum, -ī, [Gr. ἀκόνιτον], n., *aconite, wolf's-bane* or *monk's-hood* (a poisonous herb).

Aconteus, -eī, [Gr. 'Ακοντεύς], m., a Latin warrior.

acquīro, see adquīro.

Acragās, -āntis, [Gr. 'Ακράγας], m., a mountain and town in Sicily, called also *Agrigentum* (now *Girgenti*).

Ācrīsionē, -ēs, [Gr. 'Ακρισιώνη], f., the daughter of Acrisius, i.e. *Danaë.*

Ācrīsionēus, -a, -um, adj., *pertaining to Acrisione:* coloni.

Ācrīsius, -ī, [Gr. 'Ακρίσιος], m., *Acrisius*, fourth king of Argos, father of Danae, unintentionally killed by his grandson Perseus.

Acrōn, -ōnis, m., an Etruscan warrior slain by Mezentius.

acta, -ae, [Gr. ἀκτή], f., *the sea-shore.*

Actaeus, -a, -um, [Gr. 'Ακταῖος], adj., *of Attica, Attic.* — Masc. pl., **Actaei,** *the Athenians.*

Actias, -adis, [Gr. 'Ακτίας], adj. f., *Attic, Athenian.*

Actium, -ī, (n. of **Actius**), [Gr. ἄκτιον, *sea-coast*], n., a promontory and town of Greece on the Ambracian Gulf, off which the great victory of Octavius over Antony was gained.

Actius, -a, -um, [Gr. ἄκτιος], adj., *of Actium* (prop. same word as **Actium**, but used as adj. from it).

Actor, -oris, [Gr. Ἄκτωρ], m., a Trojan.

actus, -a, -um, p.p. of **ago.**

āctus, -ūs, [√ag+tus], m., *a driving, impulse:* fertur mons magno actu.

āctūtum [n. acc. of †actutus (cf. **cornutus**)], adv., *with speed, hastily, immediately, speedily, instantly.*

acuō, -uī, -ūtum, -ere, [†acu-], 3. v. a., *make sharp, sharpen:* ferrum. — Fig., *spur on, incite, drive on, rouse, disquiet:* lupos; curis mortalia corda. — Of passions, *rouse, excite:* iras. — **acūtus, -a, -um,** p.p. as adj., *sharpened, sharp* (in all senses): saxum; hinnitus (*shrill*).

acus, -us, [√ac+us], f., (*a pointed thing*), *a needle:* acu pingere (*embroider*).

acūtus, -a, -um, p.p. of **acuo.**

ad [unc. case-form], prep. with acc., *to, toward, against* (cf. **in**). — Of motion, direction, and tendency in all senses: tendens ad sidera palmas; spectare ad; respice ad haec; canit ad auras (*on the air*); ad unum (*to a man*). — Of rest, *near by, near to, at, by:* errantem ad flumina; ad Troiam; ad lunam (= in the moonlight). —

Mere end, purpose, or reference, *to, for, in respect to, according to, on:* ad frena leones (*broken to the bit*). — Of time, *at.*

adāctus, -a, -um, p.p. of **adigo.**

adamas, -antis, [Gr. ἀδάμας, *unyielding*], m., *adamant*, the hardest of metals, supposed to be steel, used loosely for a hard material: solido adamante columnae.

Adamastus, -ī, [Gr. 'Αδάμαστος], m., father of Achæmenides, and Ithacan.

adc-, see **acc-.**

adcēdō, see **accedo.**

adcersō, see **arcesso.**

addēnseō, no perf., no sup., **-ēre,** [ad-denseo], 2. v. a., *thicken, close up:* acies. Others read **addensant.**

addīcō, -xī, -ctum, -ere, [ad-dico], 3. v. a., (*speak in favor of*), *award, adjudge,* — *deliver, make over, yield:* me huic classi (*surrender*).

additus, -a, -um, p.p. of **addo.**

addō, -didī, -ditum, -ere, [ad-do], 3. v. a., *put near, by,* or *to, add, attach, join:* cognomen (*give*); se sociam; noctem addens operi (*employ in*); addere gradum (*press the pace*). — So: quadrigae addunt se in spatia (*consume the space*).

addūcō, -xī, -ctum, -ere, [ad-duco], 3. v. a., *lead to, bring.* — To one's self, *draw back:* arcus (*draw*); artus (*draw up, contract*).

addūctus, -a, -um, p.p. of **adduco.**

adedō, -ēdī, -ēsum, -edere, [ad-edo], 3. v. a., *eat into, gnaw, eat up:* favos stellio. — Of fire, *consume, burn up.*

ademptus, -a, -um, p.p. of **adimo.**

ademtus, see **ademptus.**

adeō, -iī (-īvī), -itum, -īre, [ad-eo], v. n. and a., *go to* or *towards, approach, accost.* — With hostile intent, *go against, attack, set upon.* — Of things immaterial, *enter on, arrive at, attain, incur:* labores; sales; astra.

adeō [ad-eo], adv., *to that point, to that degree, so* (in space, time, or degree): usque adeo turbatur; non obtusa adeo gestamus pectora (to such a degree as is indicated by the context); nec sum adeo informis (*so very*); adeo consuescere multum est (*such power has habit*). — With weakened force, *in fact, just, precisely, really, indeed, full* (with numbers): haec adeo ex illo speranda fuerunt (*just this*); nec me adeo fallit (*at all*); iam adeo (*just now*); vix adeo adgnovit (*really he could scarcely*, &c.); nunc adeo (*but just at this moment*); teque adeo consule (*and precisely in your consulship*); totae adeo acies (*absolutely entire*); haec adeo (*this is just what*).

adēsus, -a, -um, p.p. of adedo.

adfābĭlis (aff-), -e, [adfā- (stem of adfor) + bilis], adj., *to be spoken to, courteous:* dictu (*in speech*).

adfātus (aff-), -ūs, [ad-fatus], m., *an address, accosting.* — Less exactly, *mode of address*.

adfātus (aff-), -a, -um, p.p. of adfor.

adfectŏ (aff-), -āvī, -ātum, -āre, [ad-facto, or †adfectŏ], 1. v. a., (*make for*), *strive for, aim at, grasp at, catch, seize:* viam Olympo.

adferō (aff-), -tulī (att-), -lātum (all-), ferre, *bring to, bring:* honorem. — In pass., or with reflexive, *come, arrive*.

adficiŏ (aff-), -fēcī, -fectum, -ere, [ad-facio], 3. v. a., *do to some one, affect, treat*. — With abl., *treat with something, give something to:* pretio (*to reward*).

adfīgō (aff-), -fīxī, -fīxum, -ere, [ad-fīgo], 3. v. a., *fasten to, fix to or in, fasten:* radicem terrae; flammam lateri.

adfixus, (aff-), -a, -um, p.p. of adfigo.

adflātus (aff-), -a, -um, p.p. of adflo.

adflīctus (aff-), -a, -um, p.p. of adfligo.

adflīgō (aff-), -flīxī, -flīctum, -ere, [ad-fligo], 3. v. a., (*dash against*), *dash down, overthrow.* — **adflictus**, -a, -um, p.p. as adj., *ruined, overwhelmed, wretched, miserable:* vita; res.

adflŏ (af-), -āvī, -ātum, -āre, [ad-flo], 1. v. a. and n., *blow on, breathe on:* me ventis. — *inspire:* adflata est numine dei. — *breathe something on one, bestow, impart:* oculis adflarat honores.

adfluō (aff-), -fluxī, -fluxum, -ere, [ad-fluo], 3. v. n., *flow to, towards,* or *into.* — Less exactly, *pour in, flock to, throng to.*

adfor (aff-), -ātus, -ārī, [ad-for], *speak to, address, accost.*

adfore (aff-); see adsum.

adfui; see adsum.

adgerŏ (agg-), essī, -estum, -erere, [ad-gero], 3. v. a., *bear to, heap upon:* adgeritur tumulo tellus.

adglomerŏ (ag-), -āvī, ātum, āre [ad-glomero], v. a. and n., *roll together, gather together, heap up.* — Of a band of men, *join, attach themselves to:* lateri adglomerant nostro. — *gather, crowd together, close up:* cuneis se coactis.

adgnoscŏ (ag-), -nōvī, -nitum, -ere, [ad-(g)nosco], 3. v. a., *recognize:* matrem.

adgredior (agg-), -gressus, -gredī, [ad-gradior], v. dep., *go to, approach.* — *attack, assault:* turrim. — *accost:* aliquem dictis. — *Seize upon, lay hold of* (cf. "go at"): hastilia. — Fig., *undertake* (with inf.).

adgressus (agg-), -a, -um, p.p. of adgredior.

adhaereō, -haesī, -haesum, -ēre, [ad-haereo], 2. v. n., *stick to, cleave to, hang on, adhere:* sudor.

adhĭbeō, -buī, -bitum, -ēre, [ad-habeo], 1. v. a., *have by* or *near, apply, turn, employ, adopt:* manus medicas ad vulnera; animos; hos castris socios (*secure*). —

Esp., *invite to a banquet, invite:* Penates.

adhūc [ad-huc, cf. ad-eo], adv., *to this point.* — Of place, time, or degree, neque adhuc (*never thus far, never yet*). — *still, yet, longer:* quis adhuc precibus locus ?

adiciŏ (adj-), -iēcī, -iectum, -ere, [ad-iacio], 3. v. a., *throw to* or *at.* — Fig., *add.*

adigŏ, -ēgī, -āctum, -ere, [ad-ago], 3. v. a., *drive to, force, send, hurl, plunge:* me fulmine ad umbras; alte volnus adactum (*deeply planted*). — Fig., *force, impel, compel, bring* (force), *drive.* — With inf., *oblige:* vertere morsus in exiguam Cererem.

adimŏ, -ēmī, -emptum, -ere, [ad-emo (*take*)], (*take at* or *by*), *take from* or *away:* lumen ademptum (*put out*). — Fig., somnos (*deprive of*).

aditus, -ūs, [ad-itus], m. Abstr., *a going in, approach, access.* — Concr., *an entrance, approach, means of access, way of approach.*

adiunctus, -a, -um, p.p. of **adiungo.**

adiungŏ, -unxī, -unctum, -ere, [ad-iungo], 3. v. a., *join to, fasten, yoke, harness, attach:* ulmis vites. — Fig., *place beside, attach:* lateri castrorum adiuncta classis. — Less exactly, *add, state further.*

adiūrŏ, -āvī, -ātum, -āre, [ad-iuro], 1. v. a., *swear to, swear.* — With acc., *swear by:* caput fontis.

adiuvŏ, -iŭvī, iūtum, -āre, [ad-iuvo], 1. v. a. and n., *give help to, aid, assist, help.*

adlābor (all-), -lāpsus, -lābī, [ad-labor], 3. v. dep., *fall to* or *towards, glide to* or *towards, approach* or *reach* (with smooth or sliding motion): viro adlapsa sagitta.

adlacrimŏ, -āvī, -ātum, -āre, [ad-lacrimo], 1. v. n., *weep.*

adlāpsus (all-), -a, -um, p.p. of **adlabor.**

adligŏ (all-), -āvī, -ātum, -āre, [ad-ligo], 1. v. a., *bind* or *tie to, bind, fasten, moor:* ancora naves. — Fig., *detain, confine.*

adloquor (all-), locūtus, -loquī, [ad-loquor], v. dep., *speak to, address, accost, pray to:* deos.

adlūdŏ (all-), -lūsī, -lūsum, -ere, [ad-lŭdo], 3. v. a. and n., *play with,* or *at; refer in jest, jest.*

adluŏ (all-), -luī, -ere, [ad-luo], 3. v. a., *wash against, wash* (of a river or sea).

admīrandus, -a, -um, part. of **admiror**, used as adj.

admīror, -ātus, -ārī, [ad-miror], 1. v. dep., *wonder at, be surprised, admire, marvel at, gaze with surprise* or *admiration.* — **admīrandus**, -a, -um, ger. as adj., *admirable, marvellous, wonderful.* — **admīrāns**, p. as adj., *admiring, with surprise, with admiration.*

admisceō, -iscuī, -ixtum (-istum), ēre, [ad-misceo], 2. v. a., *mix with, intermingle, unite with:* stirpem Phrygiam. — Less exactly, of persons, *add to, unite, intermingle, join.*

admistī, contr. perf. of **admitto.**

admissus, -a, -um, p.p. of **admitto.**

admittŏ, -mīsī, -missum, -ere, [ad-mitto], 3. v. a., *let go to, admit, allow to approach, let in.*

admoneŏ, -nuī, -nitum, ēre, [ad-moneo], 2. v. a., *give warning to, admonish, warn, remind, suggest.* — With inf., decedere campis. — Less exactly, *urge on:* telo admonuit biiugos.

admordeŏ, -momordī, -morsum, -ēre, [ad-mordeo], 2. v. a., *bite into, gnaw:* admorsa stirpe.

admorsus, -a, -um, p.p. of **admordeo.**

admoveŏ, -mōvī, -mōtum, -ere, [ad-moveo], 3. v. a., *move to, conduct, apply, bring to:* te ventus (*waft*); admorunt ubera tigres (*offer, give suck*).

admōram, etc.; see **admoveo.**

adnīsus (ann-), -a, -um, p.p. of **adnitor**.

adnītor (ann-), -nīsus (-nīxus), -tī, [ad-nitor], 3. v. a., *struggle to, towards*, or *against, lean against, support one's self by, lean on:* cubito. — Fig., *struggle for, strive, exert one's self.*

adnīxus (ann-), -a, -um, p.p. of **adnitor**.

adnŏ (ann-), -āvī-, -ātum, -āre, [ad-no], 1. v. a., *swim to, float to:* terrae.

adnuŏ, -uī, -ūtum, -uere, [ad-nuo], 3. v. n. and a., *nod to, nod.* —Act., *indicate by a nod, nod* (with inf.). — Neut., *nod assent, assent, agree:* petenti. —With inf., *grant, permit*, vellere signa. — So of approval, *approve, favor:* audacibus coeptis.—*promise* (by a nod).

adoleŏ, -uī, -ultum, -ēre, [ad-oleo], 2. v. a. (*add by growth;* cf. adolesco). — Fig., *magnify* (in religious language), *sacrifice to:* flammis adolere Penatis. — Transferred, *burn, kindle, light, sacrifice:* verbenas pinguis; honores; altaria taedis.

adolēscŏ (adul-), -ēvī, (-uī), -ultum, -ere, [ad-olesco], 3. v. n., *grow up, mature:* prima aetas. — Fig. (relig. term), *be kindled, burn, flame:* ignibus arae. — **adultus**, p.p., *grown up, mature, full grown, adult:* fetus.

Adōnis, -is, (-idis), [Gr. Ἄδων, Ἄδωνις], m., a youth beloved by Venus. He was changed by her into a flower, and supposed to be mourned by her at a yearly sacred day in spring.

adoperiō, -eruī, -ertum, -īre, [ad-operio], 4. v. a., *cover over, cover.*

adopertus, -a, -um, p.p. of **adoperio**.

adoreus (-ius), -a, -um, [ador + eus], adj., *of spelt* (a peculiar cereal used by the Romans as food, *Triticum spelta*): liba.

adorior, -ortus, -īrī, (cf. orior), [ad-orior], 4. v. dep., *rise up against* (perhaps from ambush), *attack.* — Less exactly, *accost.* — Fig., *enter upon, take up, undertake, attempt, essay* (with inf.).

adōrŏ, -āvī, -ātum, -āre, [ad-oro], 1. v. a., *pray to, worship, adore.* — Less exactly, *beg, intreat, implore:* vos adoro.

adortus, -a, -um, p.p. of **adorior**.

adpāreŏ (app-), -uī, -itum, -ēre, [ad-pareo], 2. v. n., *appear at some place, appear.* — Fig., *be visible, manifest, evident, apparent.*

adparŏ (app-), -āvī, -ātum, -āre, [ad-paro], 1. v. a., *prepare for, make ready for, put in order, provide.* — Fig., *prepare, be ready, make ready, be about* (with inf.).

1. **adpellŏ (app-), -pulī, -pulsum, -pellere,** [ad-pello], 3. v. a., *drive, move, bring to* or *towards.* — With navem (or alone), *bring to land, land.*

2. **adpellŏ (app-), -āvī, -ātum, -āre,** [akin to 1. adpello, but diff. formation], 1. v. a., *address, speak to, accost* (cf. **adgredior**).—*name, call, hail:* Acesten victorem.

adpetŏ (app-), -īvī or **-iī, -ītum, -ere,** [ad-peto], 3. v. a. and n., *fall upon, attack, assail:* ferro caelestia corpora.

adplicŏ (app-), -āvī or **-uī, -ātum** or **-itum, -āre,** [ad-plico], 1. v. a. and n. (*fold upon*), *join, fix, fasten, attach, gird on:* ensem. — Fig., *drive, force, bring to* (nautical term).

adpōnŏ (app-), -posuī, -positum, -ponere, [ad-pono], 3. v. a., *put, place at, beside,* or *near, serve up, serve, supply* (of food): pabula (for bees).

adquīro (ac-), -sīvī, -situm, -rere, [ad-quaero], 3. v. a., *get* or *procure in addition, add to, acquire:* viresque adquirit eundo.

Adrastus, -ī, [Gr. Ἄδραστος], m., a king of Argos, father-in-law of Tydeus.

adrectus, -a, -um, p.p. of **adrigo**.

adreptus, -a, -um, p.p. of **adripio**.

Adriacus, -a, -um; see **Hadriacus.**
adrigō (arr-), -rexi, -rectum, -rigere, [ad-rego], 3. v. a., *set up, raise, erect:* leo comas; adrectus in digitos (*rising on*); currus (*tipped up, with the poles in the air*); aures (*prick up*); adrectis auribus (*listening*); adrecti oculi (*staring*). — Fig., *rouse, excite:* animum (*encourage*).
adripiō (arr-), -ripui, -reptum, -ripere, [ad-rapio], 3. v. a., *snatch, catch, seize, grasp:* hanc terram velis (*make for*).
adscendō (asc-), -scendi, -scensum, -scendere, [ad-scando], 3. v. n. and a., *ascend, mount up, climb:* collem.
1. **adscēnsus, -a, -um,** p.p. of **adscendo.**
2. **adscēnsus, -us,** [ad-†scānsus], m. *ascending, ascent.*
adsciō (asc-), no perf., no sup., **-scīre,** 4. v. a., *take to one's self, receive, admit.*
adscīscō (asc-), adscīvī, adscītum, adscīscere, [ad-†scisco], 3. v. a. inch., *receive, admit, adopt.* — Fig., *take* or *draw to one's self, receive, take, adopt, appropriate.*
1. **adsēnsus (ass-), -a, -um,** p.p. of **assentio** and **assentior.**
2. **adsēnsus (ass-), -ūs,** [ad-sensus], m., *an assenting, assent, agreement, approval, assent to* or *belief in* any thing. — Esp. (with expression), *assent, approbation, sign of assent.* — Fig., *echo* (as answering in accord).
adsentiō (ass-), -sēnsi, -sēnsum, sentīre, [ad-sentio], 4. v. n. (*think in accordance with*), *assent, give assent, approve.* Also deponent.
adservō (ass-), -āvi, -ātum, -āre, [ad-servo], 1. v. a. (*watch over*), *guard with care, preserve, protect, defend.* — In hostile sense, *guard, watch over, keep in custody.*
adsideō (ass-), -sēdi, -sessum, -ēre, [ad-sedeo], 2. v. a. and n., *sit by* or *near.* — Act., *besiege, beleaguer:* muros hostis.

adsiduē (ass-), adv. [abl. of **adsiduus**], *continually, constantly, incessantly, persistently.*
adsiduus, -a, -um, [ad-†siduus ($\sqrt{sed}$ + uus)], adj. (*sitting by*). Fig., *permanent, constant, increasing, perpetual, incessant:* sal (of the waves); voces; fuligo.
adsimilis (ass-), -e, [ad-similis], adj., *like, resembling, similar.*
adsimulō (ass-), -āvi, -ātum, -āre, [ad-simulo], 1. v. a. (*make like*), *compare, liken.* — *copy, imitate.* — *counterfeit:* clipeum divini capitis; formam adsimulata Camerti (*assuming the form*).
adsistō (as-), -titi, no sup., **-sistere,** [ad-sisto], 3. v. n., *stand at, by,* or *near:* super (*stand over*).
adspectō, -āvi, -ātum, -āre, [ad-specto], 1. v. a. intens., *gaze at* (with some emotion). — Fig., of a place, *look towards, look out on, lie towards, lie opposite.*
1. **adspectus, -a, -um,** p.p. of **adspicio.**
2. **adspectus (asp-), -ūs,** [ad-spectus], m. Act., *a seeing, looking at; a glance, look; the faculty* or *sense of seeing, sight.* — Pass., *visibility, appearance.* — Of things, *appearance, look.*
adspergō (asp-), -ersi, -ersum, -ergere, [ad-spargo], 3. v. a., *scatter, cast, strew, spread:* pecori virus. — Less exactly, *strew, sprinkle about:* sapores. — Transferred, *bestrew, strew* (with something), *sprinkle, bedew.*
adspergō (aspargō), -inis, [ad-†spargo- ($\sqrt{sparg}$ + o)], f., *a sprinkling, besprinkling.* — Concr., *drops, spray.*
adspernor, -ātus, -āri, [ad-(or ab-) spernor], 1. v. dep. (*spurn from one's self*). — Fig., *disdain, reject, despise:* haud adspernanda (*not to be despised, not despicable*).
adspersus, -a, -um, p.p. of **adspergo.**
adspiciō (asp-), -exi, -ectum, -icere, [ad-specio], 3. v. a. and

n., *look upon* or *at, behold, see.* — Esp., *look with respect, admiration,* or *regard:* aspice nos (*regard*). — Neut., *look, glance:* aspice! (*see!*). — Act., *catch sight of, espy.*

adspīrō (asp-), **-āvī, -ātum, -āre,** [ad-spiro], 1. v. n. and a. Neut., *breathe* or *blow to* or *upon:* Auster in altum. — Fig., *be favorable, assist, smile on:* labori. — Of winds, *blow:* aurae in noctem (*blow on into the night*). — *aspire to:* equis Achillis (poet. dat. for ad). — Act., *breathe something upon:* ventos eunti (of Juno). — Fig., canenti (*inspire*). — *infuse, instil, impart:* dictis amorem. — Of odors: amaracus (*breathe its fragrance*).

adstŏ (ast-), **-stĭtī, -stĭtum, -āre,** [ad-sto], 1. v. n., *stand at, by,* or *near:* adstitit oris (*reached*). — Less exactly, *stand up, stand out.*

adstringŏ (ast-), **-inxī, -ictum, -ingere,** [ad-stringo], 3. v. a., *bind, tie,* or *fasten, to, bind.*

adsuēscō (ass-), **-ēvī, -ētum, -ēscere,** [ad-suesco], 3. v. a. and n., *accustom to:* ne tanta animis adsuescite bella (*become accustomed in your thoughts*). — Neut., *become accustomed, be wont* (with inf.). — Pass., *be accustomed* or *habituated:* silvis.

adsuētus (ass-), **-a, -um,** p.p. of adsuesco.

adsultus, -ūs, [ad-saltus], m., *a bounding towards.* — *an attack, assault.*

adsum (ass-), **-fuī** (aff-), **-futūrus** (aff-), **-esse,** [ad-sum], *be at, near,* or *by, be here, be there, be in, be present:* coram adest (*is here before you*). — Esp., with idea of assisting (cf. "stand by"), *aid, assist, defend, favor.* — In special sense, *come* (and be present), *approach:* huc ades (*come hither*).

adsurgŏ (ass-), **-rexī, -rectum, -gere,** [ad-surgo], 3. v. n., *rise up, lift one's self up.* — Esp., *rise up out of respect, pay respect,* (fig.), *yield the palm to.* — Of things, *mount* or *rise in height, increase in size, stand* (of high objects): turres. — *rise* (in the heavens): Orion. — *rise up* in or for something: querelis (*break out in*). — Of degree, *increase, rise:* irae.

adulter, -era, -erum, [ad-ulter; cf. **ultra,** etc.], adj.(*going beyond, abroad,* with special sense of illicit love). — Masc., *a paramour.*

adulterium, -ī, [adulter + ium, n. of -ius], n., *adultery.*

adultus, -a, -um, part.of adolesco.

aduncus, -a, -um, [ad-uncus], adj., *hooked towards one, curved inward:* rostrum. — Less exactly, *curved upwards.*

adūrō, -ūssī, -ūstum, -ere, [ad-uro], 3. v. a., *burn into, scorch, singe, parch, dry up.* — From similar effect, *nip, freeze, bite* (with frost).

ad usque ; see ad and usque.

advectus, -a, -um, p.p. of adveho.

advehŏ, -vexī, -vectum, -ere, [ad-veho], 3. v. a., *carry to, convey, bear:* advecta classis (by the winds). — Pass., *go by any conveyance, ride, sail, arrive, reach.* — With reflexive (rarely alone), *go to, arrive, reach.*

advēlō, -āvī, -ātum, -āre, [ad-velo], 1. v. a., *cover over, wrap, encircle, surround, deck:* tempora lauro.

advena, -ae, [ad-†vena ; cf. ad-venio], m., *one who arrives, a stranger, foreigner, new-comer, chance-comer.* — In adj. sense, *foreign:* exercitus.

adveniō, -vēnī, -ventum, -īre, [ad-venio], 4. v. n., *come to, arrive at, arrive, reach:* Tyriam urbem.

adventŏ, -āvī, -ātum, -āre, [ad-vento], 1. v. n., *come to often, frequent.* — Less exactly, *come, arrive.*

adventus, -ūs, [ad-†ventus; cf. eventus], m., *a coming to, arrival, approach, coming.*

adversātus, -a, -um, p.p. of adversor.

adversor, -ātus, -ārī, [ad-versor], 1. v. dep., *turn* or *act against, oppose, resist, withstand:* non adversata petenti (*refusing*).
adversus, -a, -um, p.p. of **adverto.**
adversus, prep.; see **adverto.**
advertō, -vertī, -versum, -ere, [ad-verto], 3. v. a. — Act., *turn towards* or *against:* pedem ripae. — Pass., or with reflexive, *turn, direct one's course.* — Less exactly, *direct, steer, sail:* classem in portum. — Fig., *turn, direct:* numen malis. — With animum or animo (*turn the mind* or *turn with the mind*), *notice, recognize, attend to, give heed, heed, give ear* (with or without object): animis advertite vestris. — adversus, -a, -um, p.p., *turned towards, facing, in front* · obluctus adversae arenae (*against the sand*); sol adversus (*opposite*); flumine (*up a river*). — Also, *opposing, unfavorable, hostile, adverse:* venti adversi. — in adversum, adv., *against.* — adversus, as prep. with acc., *against.*
advocō, -āvī, -ātum, -āre, [ad-voco], 1. v. a., *call to one, summon.* — Less exactly, *call to one's aid, call for:* arma.
advolō, -āvī, -ātum, -āre, [ad-volo], *fly to, come flying:* fama.
advolvō, -volvī, -volūtus, -ere, [ad-volvo], 3. v. a., *roll to* or *towards, roll up:* ulmos.
adytum, -ī, [Gr. ἄδυτον (*unapproachable*)], n., *the sanctuary of a temple, inner shrine* whence oracles were delivered. — Less exactly, of a tomb as a temple of the Manes: ex imis adytis (*recesses*).
Aeacidēs, -ae, [Gr. patronymic], m., *son of Æacus* (Achilles and his son Pyrrhus, and Perseus).
Aeaeus, -a, -um, adj., *of Æa,* an island of the river Phasis, in Colchis.
aedēs, -is, f. [cf. **aestas**, and αἶθος, *fire*], (lit., *fireplace*), *temple.* — Plur., *apartments, house:* cavae aedes (the interior rooms). So of bees, *hive, home.*
aedificō, -āvī, -ātum, -āre, [†aedific-, cf. **opifex**], 1. v. a., *be a house-builder, build.* — Less exactly, of other things, *construct:* equum.
Aegaeōn, -ōnis, [Gr. Αἰγαίων], m. a giant, called also Briareus, who attempted to scale the heavens.
Aegaeus (-ēus), -a, -um, adj. [Gr. Αἰγαῖος], *Ægean* (i.e. of the Ægean Sea, between Greece and Asia Minor): Neptunus. — Neut., with or without **mare**, *the Ægean Sea.*
aeger, -gra, -grum, adj., (-rior, -rimus), [unc. root + **rus**], *sick, weak, ill, suffering, weary, worn, feeble.* — Fig., *sick at heart, troubled, sad, dispirited, dejected:* mortales. — Transferred, *feeble, sad, sorrowful, unfortunate:* anhelitus; amor.
Aegeria, see **Ēgeria.**
aegis, -idis, [Gr. αἰγίς], f., *the ægis* (shield or breastplate) of Zeus, worn also by Pallas.
Aeglē, -ēs, [Gr. Αἴγλη], f., a Naiad.
Aegōn, -ōnis, [Gr. Αἴγων], m., a shepherd.
aegrē [abl. of **aeger**], adv., *weakly, with difficulty, hardly, scarcely.*
aegrēscō, -ere, [†aegrē- (stem of aegreo) + sco], 3. v. a., *grow sick, sicken.* — Fig., *grow worse, increase:* violentia Turni.
Aegyptius, -a, -um, [Gr. Αἰγύπτιος], adj., *of Egypt, Egyptian:* coniunx (Cleopatra, called wife of Antony).
Aegyptus, -ī, [Gr. Αἴγυπτος], f., *Egypt.*
Aemonidēs, see **Haemonides.**
aemulus, -a, -um, [†aemo- + lus, cf. **imitor**], adj. In good sense, *vying with, emulating, rivalling.* patriae laudis. — In bad sense, *envious, jealous, grudging:* Triton. — Transf., of things, *grudging:* senectus.
Aeneadēs, -ae, [Gr. patronymic from Aeneas], m., *descendant of*

Æneas. — Plur., *the Trojans*, his companions.
Aeneas, -ae, [Gr. Αἰνέας], m., *the hero of the Æneid*. See **Silvius.**
Aenēis, -idis, [adj. of Gr. form], f., *the Æneid*, Virgil's great epic.
Aenēïus, -a, -um, [borrowed or imitated form from Gr. adj.], adj., *belonging to Æneas, of Æneas.*
Aenīdēs, -ae, m., *son of Æneas.*
aēnus (ahē-), -a, -um, [aes+nus], adj., *of copper* or *bronze, copper, bronze:* falces; lux (such as bronze gives). — Neut., *copper* or *bronze kettle, kettle:* litore aena locant.
Aeolidēs, -ae, [Gr. patronymic from Aeolus], m., *son of Æolus.* — Esp., *Sisyphus, Ulysses* (as the son of Sisyphus). — Surname of Clytius, a warrior under Turnus. — Surname of Misenus (perhaps as son of 2. Æolus).
Aeolĭus, -a, -um, [Gr. Αἰόλιος, from Αἴολος], adj., *belonging to Æolus.* — Fem., *Æolia*, the country of the winds, a group of islands off the Italian coast (now *Lipari Islands*).
Aeolus, -ī, [Gr. Αἴολος], m.: 1. The god of the winds; 2. A companion of Æneas.
aequaevus (-os), -a, -um (-om), [†aequŏ-aevŏ (stem of **aevum**)], adj., *of equal age.*
aequālis, -e, [†aequŏ (reduced)+ ālis], adj., *even, equal, of like size:* corpus. — Of degree of amount, &c., *like, equal:* aevum. — In age, *coeval, of same age:* catervae. — Masc., *comrade, crony.*
aequātus, -a, -um, p.p. of **aequo.**
aequē (-ius, -issimē), [abl. of **aequus**], adv., *evenly, equally, justly.*
Aequi, see **Faliscus.**
Aequĭculus, -a, -um, [†Aequico+ lus], adj., *Æquian, belonging to the Æqui* (a people of Italy).
aequiparŏ, -āvī, -ātum, -āre, [†aequo-par (as if †parŏ)], 1.v.a., *make equal. — equal, match.*

aequŏ, -āvī, -ātum, -are, [†aequo-], 1. v. a. and n., *make equal, equalize:* laborem partibus iustis (*divide*); caelo aequata machina (*raised to*); nocti ludum (*prolong through*); aequare caelo (*extol to*). — *equal:* ducem vadentem (*keep pace with*); lacrimis labores (*do justice to*). —
aequātus, -a, -um, p.p., *level, uniform, even, regular:* aurae; aequatis velis (*before the wind*).
aequor, -oris, [unc. root (in **aequus**) + or], n., (*the level*), *the smooth sea.* — Less exactly, *the sea, the waves:* pascentur in aequore cervi; — *the surface* of other waters; — also, *a level plain, a field.*
aequoreus, -a, -um, [aequor+ eus], adj., *of the sea, sea-, watery:* genus (*tribes of the sea*).
aequus (-os), -a, -um (-om), (-ior, -issimus), [?], adj., *even, equal, level.* — Neut., *a plain, a level.* — Fig., *fair, equitable, just, impartial, kindly, favorable:* oculi; aequo foedere amantes (*with requited love*); aequius fuerat; aequo Marte (*on equal terms, in a drawn battle*); aer (*wholesome*). — Neut., *justice, equity.* — Of feelings, *calm, unmoved, tranquil, resigned:* sorti. — With reference to something else implied, *equal:* pars (to the other).
āēr, -ĕris, [Gr. ἀήρ], m., *the air* (nearer the earth than **aether**). — Less exactly, *cloud, mist.* — Poetically: summus ... arboris (*the top*).
aerātus, -a, -um, [aes (as if †aerā-) + tus, cf. **armātus**], adj., *provided with bronze, bronze-clad, bronze-plated:* postes; navis; acies (*mail-clad*).
aereus, -a, -um, [aes- (r for s) + eus], adj., *brazen, of bronze, bronze, copper:* cornua. — Less exactly, *bronze-* or *copper-clad:* clipeus.
aeripēs, -edis, [aes (as if †aeri) -pes], adj., *bronze-footed.*
āërius, -a, -um, [āēr + ius], adj.,

belonging to the air, aërial: **mel** (*from heaven*); **palumbes** (*of the air*). — Less exactly, *aërial, lofty:* **ulmus.**

aes, aeris, [?], n., *copper, bronze* (an alloy of copper and tin). — Things made of bronze, *trumpet, beak, cymbals, statues, arms,* &c. — Esp., *money.*

aesculus (esc-), -ī, [†aescŏ (perhaps √ed + cus) + lus], f., *oak* (of a particular kind), *Quercus esculus.*

aestās, -ātis, [stem akin to **aedes** + tas], f., (*heat*), *summer, summer air.*

aestifer, -era, -erum, [†aestu (weakened) -fer (√fer + us)], adj., *heat-bringing, burning, hot.*

aestīvus, -a, -um, [†aestu (reduced) + ivus], adj., *belonging to heat* or *summer, summer, hot.* — N. plur. (sc. **castra**), *a summer camp.* — Less exactly, *a summer pasture, cattle* (in pasture).

aestuŏ, -āvī, -ātum, -āre, [†aestu-], 1. v. n., *be hot, boil, be aglow:* **ager.** — *be heated, heat, be fired:* **umor.** — From similarity, *seethe, roll in waves, ebb and flow* (cf. **aestus,** *tide*), *fluctuate:* **nebulā specus** (*be filled with clouds of smoke*); **gurges; in corde pudor.**

aestus, -ūs, [root akin to **aedes** + tus (cf. **aestas**)], m., *heat, boiling, the sun.* — From similarity, *tide, sea, waves, roll* (of fire), *surge.*

aetās, -ātis, [†aevo + tas], f., *age* (young or old): **ambo florentes aetatibus; firmata** (*mature*). — Esp., *old age, age.* — Less exactly, *time, lapse of time.* — Fig., *an age, a generation.*

aeternus, -a, -um, [†aevo + ternus, cf. **hesternus**], adj., *everlasting, eternal, enduring, immortal, undying:* **ignes; vulnus; imperia.** — Adv. phr., **in aeternum, aeternum,** *for ever, eternally, unceasingly.*

aether, -eris, [Gr. αἰθήρ; same root as **aestus**], m., *the upper air* (conceived as a fiery element), *the ether.* — *the sky, the heavens, heaven.* — *the atmosphere, the air, the open air* (opp. to the lower world). — Personified, *the Sky* (Jupiter).

aetherius, -a, -um, [†aether + ius], adj., *belonging to the ether* or *upper air, heavenly, celestial.* — *of the air, of the sky:* **plaga; aura** (*of the air,* opp. to the world below).

Aethiops, -opis, [Gr. Αἰθίοψ], m., *an Ethiopian* (inhabitant of Africa).

Aethōn, -onis, [Gr. Αἴθων, *burning*], m., (originally, no doubt, a name of one of the horses of the sun), *a horse of Pallas.*

aethra, -ae, [Gr. Αἴθρα, cf. **aether**], f., *clear weather, clear sky.*

Aetna, -ae, [Gr. Αἴτνη], f., *Mt. Etna,* the famous volcano in Sicily (now *Monte Gibello*).

Aetnaeus, -a, -um, [Gr. Αἰτναῖος], adj., *belonging to Mt. Etna, of Etna:* **fratres** (the Cyclops). — Less exactly, *Etnaean, Etna-like, fire-belching:* **ignes; antra.**

Aetōlia, -ae, (f. of adj.), *a district of Central Greece;* see **Aetolus.**

Aetōlus, -a, -um, [Gr. Αἰτωλός], adj., *Aetolian, of Aetolia:* **urbs** (*Arpi,* built by Diomedes). — Masc. plur., *the inhabitants of Ætolia, Ætolians.*

aevum, -ī, [√i (increased) + vum (n. of **-vus**)], n., *age* (young or old), *life:* **integer aevi sanguis** (*fresh blood of youth*); **aequum** (*the same age*). — Esp., *old age, age.* — Less exactly, *any season* or *period of life.* — *an age, a generation* (in both senses as in Eng.).

Āfer, -fra, -frum, [?], adj., *African.* — Masc. plur., *the Africans, inhabitants of Africa.*

aff-, see **adf-.**

affore, see **adsum.**

affui, etc., see **adsum.**

Africus, -a, -um, [†afro + cus], adj., *African.* — Masc., *the S. W. wind* (blowing from that region). — Fem., *the country Africa.*

Agamemnonius, -a, -um, [Gr. Ἀγαμεμνόνιος], adj., *of Agamemnon:* phalanges (the forces under him at Troy).

Aganippē, -ēs, [Gr. Ἀγανίππη], f., a fountain in Bœotia, a favorite resort of the Muses.

Agathyrsus, -a, -um, [Gr. Ἀγαθύρσος], adj. Only in plur., a people in Scythia.

age, see **ago.**

agellus, -i, [dim. †agro + lus], m., *a little field* or *farm.*

Agēnor, -oris, [Gr. Ἀγήνωρ], m., a king of Phœnicia, father of Cadmus and ancestor of Dido.

ager, -rī, [√ag + rus, cf. *acre*], m., *a field.*—Plur., **totis turbatur agris.**—Collectively, *land, soil.*

agger, -eris, [cf. **adgero**], m., (*what is heaped up*), *a mound, heap, levee, dyke, rampart, wall:* **Alpini** (*the Alps*); **viae** (*the bed*); **tumuli.**—Less exactly, *a drift of snow.*

aggerō, 3. v. a., see **adgero.**

aggerŏ, -āvī, -ātum, -āre, [†agger], 1. v. a., *heap up, pile up:* **cadavera.**—Fig., *gather, increase:* **iras.**

agglomerō, see **adglomero.**

aggredior, see **adgredior.**

Āgis, -idis, [Gr. Ἆγις], m., a Lycian warrior.

agitō, -āvī, -ātum, -āre, [†agito, as if p. of **ago**], 1. v. a. Freq. of **ago**, *drive violently* or *frequently.*—*hunt, pursue.*—*drive, tend.*—Fig., *rouse, move, drive:* **gentes.**—*trouble, vex, pursue, drive mad* (esp. of the Furies), *persecute.*—Of abstract things, *engage in, pursue, press on in:* **fugam.**—*pass, spend:* **aevum.**—*consider, revolve, meditate, be moved:* **mens agitat** (with inf., *is moved to*).

agitātor, -ōris, [†agitā + tor], m., *a driver, charioteer.*

agitātus, -a, -um, p.p. of **agito.**

agmen, -inis, [√ag + men], n., *a driving, a march, line of march, course, flow* (of a stream), *falling, fall* (of rain), *movement* (of oars).—The thing which moves, *band, army, throng, flock:* **turba agminis aligeri.**—Phrase, **agmine facto,** *in column* (of attack).

agna, -ae, [cf. **agnus,** m.], f., *a ewe-lamb.*

agnosco, see **adgnosco.**

agnus, -ī, [cf. **agna,** f.], m., *a lamb.*

agŏ, ēgī, āctum, -ere, [√ag], 3. v. a., *drive, lead, drive away.*—Of living beings: **capellas**; **aliquem pelago** (*force upon*); **acti fatis**; **metus agit** (*inspires*).—*pursue, chase:* **apros.**—With reflexive (or without): *proceed, move, go.*—Imp., **age, agite,** *come, come on.*—Fig.: **Lucifer diem age** (*bring in*); **ratem** (*steer*); **nox acta horis.**—Of things: **tempestates actae** (*driving*); **venis acta sitis** (*coursing through*); **pinus ad sidera acta** (*towering up*); **se palmes agit** (*bursts forth*); **undam** (*roll*); **vias** (*traverse*); **testudo acta** (*worked, formed*).—With inf., *urge, impel.*—Of acts, *do, act, perform:* **id ago** (*aim at*); **gemitum** (*raise*).—Of time, *pass, spend.*—**nullo discrimine agetur** (*shall be treated*).

agrestis, -e, [unc. stem (prob. in t, cf. **eques**) + tis (cf. **Carmentis**)], adj., (*of the field*), *belonging to the country* (as opposed to the town), *country, rustic, woodland:* **calamus.**—Masc. and fem., *a rustic, a countryman.*—Less exactly, *rough, rude, wild:* **poma.**

agricola, -ae, [†agro-†cola, cf. **incola**], m., *cultivator of the land, husbandman, farmer.*

Agrippa, -ae, [?], m., *M. Vipsanius Agrippa,* son-in-law of Augustus, and his most distinguished general and supporter.

Agyllīnus, -a, -um, [Agylla (reduced) + īnus], adj., *of Agylla* (a town in Etruria, more commonly known by its later name *Caere,* now *Cervetri*).—Masc. plur., *its inhabitants, people of Agylla.*

āh (ā), interj. (chiefly of surprise, but used also in many other states of mind), *ah, oh*.

ahēnus, see **aenus**.

Aiāx, -ūcis, [dialectic or corrupted form of Aἴας, -ντος], m., *Ajax*, name of two heroes of the Trojan war: 1. *Telāmōnius*, son of Telamon and brother of Teucer, who contended with Ulysses for the arms of Achilles; 2. *Oīleus*, a less distinguished warrior, son of *Oileus*. He offered violence to Cassandra, and was punished by Pallas.

āiŏ [perhaps √ag, cf. **nego**], v. defect., only pres. stem, *say, speak*. — Esp., *say yes, affirm* (opp. to **nego**). — **aiunt**, *they say*.

āla, -ae, [perhaps for †axla, cf. **axilla**], f., *a wing*. — *the wing of an army, cavalry* (as the cavalry originally formed the wings). — *riders in a hunt, huntsmen*.

alacer (**-cris**), **-cris, -cre**, [?], (**-crior, -cerrimus**), adj., *active, lively, quick*. — *eager*. — *joyous, happy, cheerful*. — Transf., *lively, eager :* voluptas.

alātus, -a, -um, [†talā + tus (cf. **armātus, armo**)], adj., *winged*.

Alba, -ae, [f. of albus, *the white town*], f., *Alba Longa* (the supposed mother city of Rome).

Albānus, -a, -um, [albā + nus], adj., *Alban, belonging to Alba*. — Masc., *Mt. Albanus*.

albeŏ, -ēre, no perf. nor sup., [†talbŏ-], 2. v. n., *be white :* campi ossibus.

albēscŏ, -ere, no perf. nor sup., [†talbē -(stem of albeo) + sco], 3. v. n., *grow white, whiten, gleam :* fluctus; lux (*dawn*).

Albulus, -a, -um, [†talbŏ + lus], adj., dim., *white*. — **Albula**, f., ancient name of the Tiber, from the yellow paleness of its water.

Albūnea, -ae, [f. of †talbunŏ- (fr. **albus**) + eus], f., *a fountain at Tibur* (*Tivoli*) in a sacred grove. — Also, the grove itself (?).

Alburnus, -i, [?], m., *a mountain in Lucania* (now *Monte di Postiglione*).

albus, -a, -um, [cf. ἄλφος], adj., (no comparison), *pale white* (opp. to **ater**, *dull black*, cf. **candidus**, *shining white*): ligustra; scopuli ossibus. — Neut. (as subst.), *white*.

Alcander, -drī, m., a companion of Æneas.

Alcānor, -oris, m.: 1. a Trojan, father of Pandarus; 2. a Latin.

Alcathous, -oī, [Gr. Ἀλκάθοος], m., a companion of Æneas.

Alcīdēs, -ae, [Gr. Ἀλκείδης], m., descendant of Alcæus. — Esp., a name of Hercules, his grandson.

Alcimedōn, -ontis, [Gr. Ἀλκιμέδων], m., a famous wood-carver, mentioned only by Virgil.

Alcinous, -oī, [Gr. Ἀλκίνοος], m., king of the Phæacians (*Corfu*), whose gardens became proverbial.

Alcippē, -ēs, [Gr. Ἀλκίππη], f., a female slave.

Alcōn, -ōnis, [Gr. Ἄλκων], m., a Cretan bowman.

alcyōn, -onis, [Gr. ἀλκυών], f., *the kingfisher, halcyon*.

Alcyonē, -ēs, [Gr. Ἀλκυόνη], f., a woman who with her husband Ceyx was changed by Thetis into a kingfisher.

Ālectō, see **Allecto**.

āles, -itis, [ala (weakened) + tus (reduced)], adj., *winged*. — Subst., *a bird:* Jovis (*the eagle*). — Transf., *swift, winged :* Auster.

Alēsus, see **Halaesus**.

Alētēs, -is, [Gr. Ἀλήτης], m., a companion of Æneas.

Alexis, -is, [Gr. Ἄλεξις], m., a beautiful slave, loved by the shepherd Corydon.

alga, -ae, [?], f., *seaweed*.

aliās [unc. case-form of **alius**], adv., *elsewhere*. — Of time, *at another time :* non alias (*never before*, or *again*).

alibī [dat. or loc. of alius, cf. **ibī**], adv., *in another place, elsewhere*.

aliēnus, -a, -um, [unc. stem (akin to alius) + nus], adj., *belonging to* *another, of another, another's:* volnus *(meant for another).* — *strange, foreign:* custos; arva; menses *(unusual).* — Masc., *a stranger.*

aliger, -era, -erum, [†ala (weakened) + ger (√ger + us)], adj., *wing-bearing, winged.*

alīō [old dat. of alius, cf. eō], adv., *elsewhither, to another place, in another direction.*

ālipēs, -edis, [ala (weakened) + pes], adj., *with winged feet, wing-footed.* — Masc., *a horse* (as swift of foot).

aliquā [abl. f. of aliquis, cf. quā], adv., *by some way, in some way, somehow.*

aliquī, see **aliquis.**

aliquandō [†ali-quando, cf. **aliquis** and **quando**], adv., *at some time* (indef. affirmative), *some time, ever, once, formerly, hereafter.* — Emphatically, *at last, at length.*

aliquis(quī), -qua, -quid(quod), indef. adj. (and subst.) [†aliquis], *some, some one* (indef. affirmative, cf. **quisquam** with neg.). — Neut., *something.* — With **si** and relative words, *any, any one, anything.*

aliquot [†ali-quot], indec. adj., *several, a number, a few* (affirmatively, cf. **pauci,** *only a few*).

aliter [†ali + ter, cf. **forti-ter**], adv., *otherwise:* haud aliter (*just so*).

alitus, -a, -um, p.p. of alo.

ālituum, irr. gen. plu. of ales, from another stem alitu-; see **ales.**

alius, -a, -um, -īus, (stem alio, often ali), [√al + ius, cf. ἄλλος for ἄλyos], *other*(not all, cf. **ceteri,** *the rest*), *another, some other* (of many, cf. **alter,** of two): haec inter alias urbes. — Esp., alius ... alius (*one ... another*); alii pars (*some ... another part*). — Usually agreeing with its noun, rarely with partitive or equivalent construction: aliud mercedis (*a different reward*).

allābor, see **adlabor.**

Allēctō, -ūs, [Gr. 'Αληκτώ], f., a Fury.

Allia, -ae, f., a river near Rome, famous for a defeat of the Romans by the Gauls.

alligō, see **adligo.**

allium (āl-), -ī (-iī), [?], n., *garlic.* — Also plur., same sense.

alloquor, see **adloquor.**

allūdō, see **adludo.**

alluō, see **adluo.**

Almō, -ōnis, m., a Latin, son of Tyrrhus.

almus, -a, -um, [√al + mus], adj., *nourishing, fostering, bountiful:* Ceres; ager; vitis. — Less exactly, *propitious, kind, kindly, refreshing.*

alnus, -ī, [cf. *al-der*], f., *alder.* — *a vessel* or *boa*t (made of the wood).

alō, aluī, alitum (altum), -ere, [√al, cf. **adoleo, almus**], 3. v. a., *nourish, feed.* — Less exactly, *sustain, suppor*t, *feed, bring up:* Africa ductores (*produce*); volnus venis (of Dido, *feeds,* i.e., *is consumed by*).

Alōīdēs, -ae, [Gr. 'Αλωείδης, patr. of 'Αλωεύς], m., *descendant of Aloeus.* — Plur., Otus and Ephialtes, giants.

Alpēs, -ium, [a foreign word akin to albus], m. plur., *the Alps.*

Alphesiboeus, -ī, [Gr.], m., a herdsman.

Alphēus, -eī, [Gr. 'Αλφειός, cf. **albula**], m., a river of Elis which disappears under ground, and was fabled to reappear again in Sicily.

Alphēus, -a, -um, [Gr. 'Αλφεῖος], adj., *of the river Alphēus, Alphean:* Pisa (founded by a colony from Elis).

Alpīnus, -a, -um, [†alpi (lengthened) + nus], adj., *of the Alps, Alpine:* Boreae.

Alsus, -ī, [?], m., a Latin.

altāre, -is, [n. of adj., †altŏ- (reduced) + āris], n., *an altar* (higher than ara).

altē [old abl. of altus], (-ius, -is-

sīmē), adv., *highly, on high, high, —deeply, deep.*

alter, -era, -erum, -ius, [√al (cf. alius) + ter (cf. uter)], pron. adj., *other* (of two, cf. **alius,** other of many), *the other.* — Alter ...alter, *one*...*the other.* — alter ...alterius, *one of another* (reciprocally), *of one another.* — In order, *the second, a second:* **primus**...alter. — Opposed to both, *one or the other.* — Fig., *the second, next:* alter ab illo. — With negative: nec alter (*another, any other*). — Plur., of a number or set, &c.: alterae decem (*ten more, another ten*).

alternŏ, -āvi, -ātum, -āre, [†alterno-], 1. v. n., *do by turns, alternate.* — alternantes, p., *by turns, alternately.*—*wavering, vacillating.*

alternus, -a, -um, [alter + nus], adj., *belonging to the other, alternate, by turns, responsive, reciprocal.*—Neut. pl., *alternate strains, alternate acts, alternation:* alternis. — Masc. pl., *matched man for man.*

altrīx, -īcis, [√al + trix], f., *a nurse.* — As adj., *nourishing, fostering:* terra.

altus, -a, -um, [p.p. of **alo**], (*grown up*), adj., *high, lofty, great* (in all senses): montes; rex Iupiter. — Neut., *the heavens, heaven, the sky:* in altum (*on high*). — Also, *deep:* gurges; quies. — Neut., *the deep, the sea, the high sea, the main.* — ex alto (*from far, far*).

alumnus, -ī, m., -a, -ae, f., [†alŏ- (stem of **alŏ**) + mnus (cf. -μενος, Gr. p.)], (*fostered, nursed*), *foster child, nursling.*

alveārium, -ī, [†alveŏ (reduced) + arium, n. of -arius], n., *a beehive.*

alveus, -ī, [†alvŏ (reduced) + eus], m., *a hollow, cavity, channel.* — *a boat, skiff.* — *bed* of a river, *channel = (current).*

alvus, -ī, [√al + vus], f., *the belly, the body* (inner or lower part).

amāns, -āntis, p. of **amo.**

amāracus, -ī, [Gr. ἀμάρακος], m. and f., *marjoram.*

amarantus, -ī, [Gr. ἀμάραντος, *unfading*], m., *amaranth,* an unfading flower, prob. *coxcomb.*

amārē [old abl. of **amarus**], adv., *bitterly.*

amāror, -ōris, [unc. stem (cf. amarus) + or], m., *bitterness.*

amārus, -a, -um, [?], (-ior, -issimus), adj., *bitter:* salices. — Of smell, *harsh, ill-smelling, pungent.* — Fig., *sad, melancholy, unfortunate, unhappy:* amores; rumor. — *bitter, implacable:* hostis. — Of words, *bitter, severe, harsh:* dicta.

Amaryllis, -idis, [Gr. Ἀμαρυλλίς], f., *a rustic maid.*

Amasēnus, -ī, [?], m., *a river in Latium.*

Amaster, -trī, [?], m., *a Trojan.*

Amāta, -ae, [f. of **amātus**], f., wife of King Latinus.

Amathūs, -ūntis, [Gr. Ἀμαθοῦς], f., a town of Cyprus (now *Limisso*).

amātus, p.p. of **amo.**

Amāzōn, -onis, [Gr. Ἀμαζών, anciently supposed to mean *bosomless*], f., *an Amazon,* one of a fabled nation of Scythia, composed only of women. — Plur., *the Amazons.*

Amāzonicus, -a, -um, [†Amazon + icus], adj., *of the Amazons, Amazonian.*

Amāzonius, -a, -um, [†Amazon + ius], adj., *Amazonian, of the Amazons.*

Amāzonis, -idis, [Gr. Ἀμαζονίς], adj., *Amazonian, an Amazon.*

amb- (am-, an-), [†ambi, cf. ambo, Gr. ἀμφί, Germ. *um*], insep. prep. Only in composition, *around, on both sides, double.*

ambāgēs, -is, [amb-ūgēs (√ag?, cf. ambigo)], f., *a circuit, winding, circuitous way.* — Of speech, *circumlocution, a long story, long details.* — Less exactly, *obscurity, anything perplexing, mystery, mysterious expression, obscure oracle.*

Vocabulary. 19

ambedō, -ēdī, -ēsum, -edere, [amb-edo], 3. v. a., *eat around, gnaw, nibble, eat.* — Fig., *consume, devour.*

ambēsus, -a, -um, p.p. of **ambedo.**

ambiguus, -a, -um, [†ambigŏ (cf. **prodigus**) + vus], adj., *uncertain, doubtful, dark, mysterious, dubious, perplexing, ambiguous:* domus; proles; voces (*dark hints*).

ambiō, -iī (-īvī), -ītum (cf. **ambitus**), **-īre,** [amb-eo], 4. v. a. and n., *go around.* — Less exactly, *encircle, surround:* aliquid auro (*rim, edge*). — For a special purpose, *entreat, solici*t*:* reginam; conubiis Latinum (*gain Latinus's consen*t *to*).

ambŏ, -ae, -ŏ, [cf. amb-], pron. adj., *both* (of two together, cf. **uterque,** *both separately*). — Less exactly, *two.*

ambrosius, -a, -um, [Gr. ἀμβρόσιος, *immortal*], adj., *divine, divinely beautiful.* — Fem., *the food of the gods, ambrosia.*

ambūrō, -ūssī, -ūstum, -ūrere, [amb-uro], 3. v. a., *burn around, scorch, burn.*

ambūstus, p.p. of **amburo.**

amellus, -ī, [?], m., *starwort.*

āmēns, -entis, [ab-mens, *having the mind away*], adj., *senseless, distracted, frenzied, frantic, maddened.*

āmentum, -ī, [unc. root + mentum], n., *thong* (attached to a spear and unwinding, so as to give a rifle-ball motion to it).

Amerīnus, -a, -um, [simpler stem akin to **Ameria** + inus], adj., *of Ameria* (a town of Umbria; now *Amelia*), *Amerian.*

amīcē [old abl. of **amicus**], adv., *in a friendly manner, as a friend, kindly.*

amiciō, -icuī (-ixī), -ictum, -īre, [amb-iacio], 4. v. a., *throw around, wrap around.*—Transferred, *wrap, cover, conceal:* nube cava.

amīcitia, -ae, [†amicŏ + tia], f., *friendship.*

amictus, -a, -um, p.p. of **amicio.**

amictus, -ūs, [as if amic (cf. **amiciō**) + tus], m., *an outer garme*nt, *wrap, robe, covering:* nebulae.

amīcus, -a, -um, [unc. stem from √am + cus], adj., *loving, friendly.* — Of things, *friendly, favoring, favorable.* — Masc., *a friend.*

Amīnaeus, -a, -um, [Gr. Ἀμιναῖος], adj., *of Aminæa* (a district of Picenum, famous for its vineyards), *Aminæan.*

āmissus, -a, -um, p.p. of **amitto.**

Amiternus, -a, -um, [?], adj., *of Amiternum* (a Sabine town, now San Vittorino), *Amiternian.*

āmittō, -mīsī, -missum, -ere, [ab-mitto], 3. v. a., *let go, send off* or *away, abandon, lose:* arma; Anchisen (by death).

Ammōn, see **Hammon.**

amnis, -is, [?], m. and f., *a river, a stream, body* (of water): aquae (of water in a kettle). — Gen., *water.*

amo, -āvī, -ātum, -are, [√am, but prob. fr. a noun-stem, cf. **amicus**], 1. v. a., *love, be fond of, cherish, regard.* — Of things, *delight in, love.* — Fig., *keep close to :* litus (*hug*). — **amāns, -ntis,** m. or f., *a lover, loving man* or *woman.*

amoenus, -a, -um, [lost noun-stem, akin to **amo** + nus, cf. **amicus**], adj. Of objects of sight, *picturesque, lovely, pleasant, charming.* piorum concilia.

amōmum (-on), -ī, [Gr. ἄμωμον], n., *amomum, an aromatic shrub.*

amor, -ōris, [√am + or], m., *love, desire, longing:* casūs cognoscere nostros; edendi (*appetite, craving for food*). — Transferred, *an object producing love, a love-charm.* — Concretely, *an object of love.* — Personified, *the god of love, Cupid, Love.*

āmoveō, -mōvī, -mōtum, -ere, [ab-moveo], 2. v. a., *move away, remove, take away.*

Amphīōn, -onis, [Gr. 'Αμφίων], m., *Amphion*, a king of Thebes, husband of Niobe, famous for his performances on the lyre.

Amphitryōniadēs, -ae, m., *a descendant of Amphitryo* (king of Thebes, husband of Alcmene), *son of Amphitryo* (Hercules).

Amphrȳsius, -a, -um, adj., *belonging to Amphrysus, Amphrysian, of Apollo:* **vates** (i.e. *the Sibyl*).

Amphrȳsus (-os), -ī, [Gr. 'Αμφρυσος], m., *Amphrysus* or *Amphrysos*, a small river of Phthiotis, near which Apollo fed the flocks of King Admetus.

amplē [abl. of **amplus**], adv., *amply*. — Comp., **amplius,** *more, longer, again:* non amplius unam (*only one*).

amplector, -exus, -ectī, [amb-plecto], 3. v. dep., *wind* or *twine around, surround, encompass, encircle, embrace:* limina; tumulum (of a snake); ansas acantho (*wreathe,* in carving). —In speech, *comprehend, — discuss particularly, handle, treat:* non ego cuncta meis amplecti versibus opto.

amplexus, -a, -um, p.p. of **amplector**.

amplexus, -ūs, [amb-plexus], m., *an encircling.* — Esp., *an embrace, caress.*

amplus, -a, -um, (-ior, -issimus), [?], adj., *of large extent, great, ample, spacious, roomy:* Elysium. — Fig., *magnificent, splendid, glorious, superb.* — In fame, *illustrious, noble, renowned, distinguished.*

Amsanctus, -ī, [amb-sanctus], m., a lake in Italy, fabled as an entrance to the world below (now *Lago d'Ansante*).

amurca, -ae, [Gr. ἀμόργη], f., *the scum of oil.*

Amȳclae, ārum, [Gr. 'Αμύκλαι], plur. f.: 1. A town in Latium; 2. A town of Laconia. See **Amyclaeus**.

Amȳclaeus, -a, -um, [Gr. 'Αμυκλαῖος], adj., *of Amyclæ* (in Laconia), *Amyclæan:* canis.

Amycus, -ī, [Gr. 'Αμυκος], m.: 1. A Trojan, father of Mimas; 2. The name of two followers of Æneas, killed by Turnus.

Amyntās, -ae, [Gr. 'Αμύντας], m., a shepherd.

Amythāōnius, -a, -um, [Amythaon + ius], adj., *of Amythaon* (the father of Melampus), *Amythaonian.*

an [?], conj. In disjunctive interrogations introducing the second part, *or, or rather, or on the other hand, or in fact.* — Often with the first part suppressed, *or, or indeed, or can it be that, why! tell me!* — **annon,** *or not.* — **anne** (an ne), same as **an** alone.

Anagnia, -ae, f., a town of Latium, the chief seat of the Hernici (now *Anagni*).

anceps, -itis, [amb-caput], (*with head on both sides*), adj., *with two heads, double-headed.* — Of weapons, *two-edged:* ferrum. — Fig., *double, two-fold:* formido. —*doubtful, uncertain, undecided, dubious:* fortuna pugnae; dolus (*treacherous uncer*tainty). — Of persons, *wavering, doubtful.* — Of an oracle, *ambiguous.*

Anchemolus, -ī, [?], m., son of Rhoetus, king of the Marsians. He fled to Turnus' father on account of an incestuous crime.

Anchīsēs, -ae, [Gr. 'Αγχίσης], m., a son of Capys, father of Æneas.

Anchīsēus, -a, -um, adj., *belonging to Anchises, Anchisean.*

Anchīsiadēs, -ae, m., *the son of Anchises,* i.e. Æneas.

anchora, see **ancora**.

ancīle (-ūle), -is, [†ancŏ + ilis, cf. ἀγκυλός], n., *a small oval shield.* — Esp., the shield which was said to have fallen from heaven in the reign of Numa, and on the continued preservation of which the prosperity of Rome was declared to depend. — Also the others made like it, which were carried in procession at Rome in a religious ceremony.

ancora (anch-), -ae, [Gr. ἄγκυρα], f., *an anchor.*

Ancus, -ī, [= ancus, *ben*t, said to refer to crooked arms, cf. **anculus**], m., *Ancus Martius,* fourth king of Rome.

Androgeōs (-eus), -ī, [Gr. 'Ανδρόγεως], m.: 1. A son of Minos, king of Crete, killed by the Athenians and Megarians; 2. A Greek at the sack of Troy.

Andromachē, -ēs, (-a, -ae), [Gr. 'Ανδρομάχη], f., a daughter of King Eetion, and wife of Hector.

anēthum, -ī, [Gr. ἄνηθον], n., *dill, anise, a sweet-smelling herb.*

ānfractus (am-), ūs, [amb-fractus], m., *a bending, turning, winding.*

Angitia (Anguī-), -ae, [prob. akin to **ango**], f., a sorceress, sister of Medea and Circe, worshipped by the Marsi.

angŏ, -xī, -ctum (-xum), -gere, [√ang], 3. v. a., *squeeze, compress:* **guttura.** — Of living creatures, *choke, strangle.*

anguis, -is, [√ang + is, with parasitic u], m. and f., *a snake* or *serpent.* — Esp., as constellations, *the Dragon, the Hydra, the Serpent.*

Anguitia, see **Angitia.**

angustus, -a, -um, [†angus (noun-stem akin to **angor**) + tus, cf. **barbātus**], adj., *close, narrow, strait, contracted.* — Neut. with gen.: **angusta viarum** (*narrow ways*). — Fig., *narrow, slight, scanty:* spes. — Less exactly, *narrow, trivial:* res.

anhēlitus, -ūs, [†anhelī- (weaker stem of **anhelŏ**) + tus], m., *panting, quick* or *difficult breathing.*

anhēlŏ, -āvī, -ātum, -āre, [†an (unc. prep.) -halŏ (cf. **exhālo**)], 1. v. n. and a. Neut., *breathe with difficulty, breathe heavily, gasp, pant.* — Of flame, *roar:* fornācibus ignis.

anhēlus, -a, -um, [an (?) -hālus (cf. **hālŏ**)], adj., *panting, puffing, gasping:* equi; pectus (*heaving*);

Mars (*breathless*); senes (*short-breathed*); tussis (*hacking*).

Aniēn, see **Anio.**

Aniēnus, -a, -um, [†Anien + us], adj., *pertaining to the Anio, of the Anio.*

anīlis, -e, [†anu + īlis], adj., *of an old woman, anile, an old woman's.*

anima, -ae, [†ani (treated as root?) + ma, f. of -mus; cf. **animus** and ἄνεμος, √an, *blow*], f., *a breeze, breath, blast* (in Vulcan's bellows). — As inhaled or exhaled, *breath:* **viperea.** — Fig., *breath* (as vital principle), *life:* effundere; proicere (*throw away life*); purpurea (*crimson stream of life*). — Of living persons, *soul* (cf. Eng. "souls"). — Of the departed, *shade, soul, spirit.*

animādversus, see **animadverto.**

animādvertŏ (vort-), -tī, -sum, -tere, [animum, adverto], 3. v. a., *turn the mind* or *attention to, attend to, consider, regard.* — More simply, *notice, perceive, see.*

animal, -ālis, [n. of adj. **animalis** (with loss of e)], n., *living creature* (incl. man and beast), *animal.*

animālis, -e, [†animā + lis], adj., *pertaining to life, animate, living.*

animŏ, -āvī, -ātum, -āre, [anima], 1. v. a., *animate, quicken, give life to.*

animōsus, -a, -um, [†animŏ (reduced) + osus], adj., *courageous, bold, spirited:* Eurus (*wild, violent*).

animus, -ī, [†ani- (as root) + mus; cf. **anima,** ἄνεμος, √an, *blow*], m., *breath, life, soul* (cf. Eng. *spirit*), *mind* (including all the powers; cf. **mens,** *intellec*t). — Esp. of thought or feeling, *intention, purpose, will, desire, inclination, mind, impulse:* omnibus idem animus est (cf. "have a mind"). — Also esp. in plur., *feeling, sentiment, courage, heart, spirit:* successu animisque (*the spirit of success*). — Instead of **mens,** *the mind, the intellect.* — Less exactly, *nature, character.* — Of the winds (personified), *wrath.* — In bad sense, *arrogance, pride, passion, wrath* (esp. in plur.).

Aniŏ (Aniēn), -ēnis or -ōnis, also **Aniēnus, -i**, m., a tributary stream of the Tiber, which, taking its rise in the Apennines, passes along the southern Sabine country, separating it from Latium (now *Teverone*).

Anius, -ī (-iī), m., a king and priest of Delos, who hospitably entertained Æneas.

Anna, -ae, [a Phœnician word], f., *Anna*, the sister of Dido, honored as a goddess after her death, under the name Anna Perenna.

annālis, -e, [†annŏ- (reduced) + ālis], adj., *belonging to a year, yearly, annual.* — Masc. (sc. **liber**), *a record* (by years), *a chronicle, a repor*t: laborum (*details*).

anne, see **an**.

annīsus, see **adnīsus**.

annītor, see **adnītor**.

annŏ, see **adno**.

annōsus, -a, -um, [†annŏ- (reduced) + osus], adj., *full of years, aged, old:* bracchia (*aged limbs*).

annuo, see **adnuo**.

annus, -ī, [?], m., *a year.* — Less exactly, *season:* nunc formosissimus annus. — Adv., quot annis (as many years as there are), *yearly, every year.*

annuus, -a, -um, [†annŏ + us], adj., *pertaining to a year, that lasts a year, of a year's duration.* — *that returns, recurs,* or *happens every year, yearly, annual:* sacra.

ūnsa, -ae, [?], f., *a handle:* molli circum est ansas amplexus acantho.

ānser, -eris, [cf. Gr. χήν, Eng. *goose*], m., *a goose.*

Antaeus, -ī, [Gr. Ἀνταῖος], m.: 1. A Libyan giant slain by Hercules; 2. A Rutulian.

Antandros (-us), -ī, [Gr. Ἀντανδρος], f., a maritime town of Mysia, at the foot of Ida.

ante (old form **antid**), [abl. of †anti (cf. **antes**, Gr. ἀντί)], adv. and prep. Adv., of place, *before, in front, forward.* — Of time, *before, sooner, first:* ut ante (as *hitherto*); ante . . . quam (see **antequam**). — With abl. of diff.: multo, etc. (*long before*). — As adj., like Greek: ante malorum (*of former trials*). — Prep., of place, *before, in front of:* focum. — Of estimation or rank, *before, in preference to, above:* ante alios; ante omnia (*more than all else, above all*). — Of time, *before, ere.*

anteeŏ, -īvī (-iī), no sup., -īre, [ante-eo], 4. v. n., *go before, precede.* — Of time, *anticipate, precede.* Of degree, *excel, surpass, outdo, outstrip:* candore nives; cursibus auras.

anteferŏ, -tulī, -lātum, -ferre, [ante-fero], 3. v. a., *bear* or *carry before* one, &c. — Of estimation, *place before, prefer:* quae quibus anteferam.

Antemnae, -ārum, [?], f., a town of the Sabines, perhaps so called from its situation on the river Anio, where it falls into the Tiber.

antenna (-mna), -ae, [probably borrowed from Greek], f., *a sail-yard.*

Antēnor, -oris, [Gr. Ἀντήνωρ], m., a noble Trojan who was in favor of restoring Helen and making peace with the Greeks; after the fall of Troy he went to Italy and founded Patavium (*Padua*).

Antēnoridēs, -ae, [Gr. patronymic], m., *a son* or *descendant of Antenor.*

antequam [ante, quam], rel. adv., *sooner than, before, first before, ere.*

antēs, -ium, [√an + tis, cf. ante], m., *rows* or *ranks* of vines, &c.

anteveniŏ, -vēnī, -ventum, -venīre, [ante-venio], 4. v. n. and a., *come* or *arrive before.* — *get the start of, anticipate.* — Absolutely, *come betimes, anticipate* (a danger).

antevolŏ, āre, [ante-volo], 1. v. a., *fly before.*

Antheus, -ī, (acc., **Anthea**), [Gr. 'Ανθεύς], m., a companion of Æneas.
Antigenēs, -is, [Gr. 'Αντιγενής], m., a shepherd.
Antiphatēs, -ae, [Gr. 'Αντιφάτης], m., a son of Sarpedon, slain by Turnus.
antīquus (-os), -a, -um (-om), [†anti (with unc. lengthening) + cus, cf. **postīcus**], adj., *belonging to former times, former, old, ancient*. — Not contrasted with later times, but simply of long standing, *old, ancient.* — Of persons, *aged.*
Antōnius, -ī (-iī), m., the name of a Roman gens. — Esp., M. Antonius, the distinguished triumvir, conquered by Octavius at Actium.
Antōrēs, -ae, m., a warrior of Evander, slain by Mezentius.
antrum, -ī, [Gr. ἄντρον], n., *a cave, cavern, grotto:* viride. — Less exactly, *hollow:* **exesae arboris.**
Anūbis, is and **idis,** [Gr. 'Ανουβίς, an Egyptian word], m., an Egyptian deity, with the head of a dog, the tutelary deity of the chase.
anus, -ūs, [?], f., *an old woman.*
anxius, -a, -um, [unc. stem from √ang + ius], adj., *anxious, troubled, tormented.* — Transferred to the cause, *distressing, anxious:* **timor.**
Anxur, -uris, [?], n.: 1. A town of the Volsci, later *Terracina;* 2. Masc., an Italian killed by Æneas.
Anxurus, -a, -um, [Anxur + us], adj., *of Anxur:* **Iupiter** (worshipped at Anxur).
Āones, -um, [Gr. Άονες], adj., m. plur., *Aonian,* cf. **Aonius.**
Aonius, -a (-ē Gr. form**), um,** [†Aon (cf. Aones) + ius], adj., *Aonian, Bœotian.* — Fem., the country *Aonia,* a part of Bœotia in which are the Aonian mountains, Mt. Helicon, and the fountain Aganippe.
Aornos, -ī, [Gr. Άορνος], m., *the Lake Avernus* (now *Lago d' Averno*).

Āpennīnicola, -ae, [†Apennīnŏ- †cola (cf. **incola**)], comm., a dweller in the Apennines.
Apennīnus (App-), -ī, [Gallic *pen,* "mountain-summit"], m., *the Apennines,* the lofty mountain-chain that runs diagonally across Italy **pater** (the mount personified).
aper, aprī, [?], m., *a wild boar* setosi caput apri.
aperiō, -uī, -tum, -īre, [ab (or ad) -pario (cf. reperio), but connection unc.], 4. v. a., *uncover, lay bare, open, unclose:* **antrum apertum.** — Less exactly, *discover, display, show, reveal:* his unda dehiscens terram aperit; templum. — Pass., or with reflexive, *show itself, appear:* sidus (*rise*); Apollo (*i.e.* his temple rising above the horizon). — Neut., without **se,** *appear:* montes. — Fig., *disclose, unveil, reveal, make known, unfold:* futura. — As in Eng., *open, begin:* annum. — **apertus, -a, -um,** p.p. as adj., *open, uncovered, clear* (of the sky).
apertus, -a, -um, p.p. of **aperio.**
apex, -icis, [?] m., *a tip, point, a tongue* (of flame). — From the shape, *a cap* (of peculiar form worn by several religious functionaries at Rome).
Aphidnus, -ī, [?], m., a Trojan.
apis (-ēs), -is, [?], f., *a bee.*
apium, -ī (-iī), [?], n., *parsley, celery.* The leaves of one kind were used for garlands.
Apollŏ, -inis, [Gr. 'Απόλλων], m., the son of Jupiter and Latona, and twin brother of Diana; god of the sun, of divination, of poetry and music, and president of the Muses. He was also god of archery, of pestilence, and, on the other hand, of medicine. — Also, his *temple* (identified with the god himself).
appāreŏ, see **adpareo.**
apparŏ, see **adparo.**
Appennīnus, see **Apennīnus.**
appetŏ, see **adpeto.**
applicŏ, see **adplico.**
appōnŏ, see **adpono.**

aprīcus, -a, -um, [perhaps †aperī-
(stem of **aperio**) + **cus,** cf. **Aprī-
lis**], adj., *uncovered, lying open,
exposed to the sun, sunny:* terrae.
— Transferred, *fond of sunshine,
sunloving.*
āptŏ, -āvī, -ātum, -āre, [†aptŏ-],
1. v. a., *fit, adapt, adjust, apply.* —
Fig., *accommodate, adapt.* — As
making fit, *get ready, prepare,
equip:* classem velis. — Abs.,
without means expressed: classem
(*fit out*).
āptus, -a, -um, [√ap, *grasp* (in
apiscor) + **tus,** p.p. of lost verb],
(*fitted to*), adj., *joined, fastened,
attached.* — Transferred, *endowed,
ornamented with:* caelum stellis
aptum (*studded*). — Fig., *suited,
fitted, fit, suitable, fitting.*
apud [?], prep. w. acc. Of persons, *with, by, near.* — Esp., *at
one's house,* or *in one's possession:*
apud me. — Of place, *at, near,
in.*
aqua, -ae, [?], f., *water:* dulces
(*fresh water*). — *a stream, a river.*
aquārius, -a, -um, [†aqua (reduced) + ārius], adj., *of* or *relating to water.* — Masc., *the water-
bearer,* one of the signs of the
Zodiac.
Aquicolus, -ī, [?], m., a Rutulian.
aquila, -ae, [perhaps f. of **aquilus,**
dark gray, on account of its color],
f., *the eagle.*
aquilŏ, -ōnis, [†aquilŏ- (reduced)
+ ŏ (ōn), from its darkness, cf.
aquila], m., *the North wind.* —
Less exactly, *the North.*
aquōsus, -a, -um, [aqua (reduced)
+ osus], adj., *abounding in water,
rainy, watery, moist, humid, full
of water:* hiems; Orion.
āra, -ae, (old form **asa**), [?], f., *an
elevation* or *structure* (of wood,
stone, earth, &c.): ara sepulchri
(*a funeral pile*). — Esp., *an altar:*
illius aram imbuet agnus. —
From similarity, *the Altars,* rocks
in the Mediterranean, between
Sicily and Africa.

Arabs, -abis, [Gr. Ἄραψ], m., *an
Arabian, an Arab.*
Arabus, -a, -um, [†Arab + us],
adj., *Arabian, Arab.* — Masc. plur.,
the Arabs.
Aracynthus, -ī, [Gr. Ἀράκυνθος],
m., a mountain between Bœotia
and Attica.
arānea, -ae, [f. of adj., from Gr.
ἀράχνη], f., *a spider.*
Arar (Araris), -is, [?], m., a river
of Gaul (now the *Saône*).
arātor, -ōris, [arā (stem of **aro**) +
tor], m., *one who ploughs, a plough-
man, a husbandman, farmer.*
arātrum, -ī, [arā (stem of **aro**) +
trum], n., *a plough.*
Araxēs, -is, [Gr. Ἀράξης], m., a
river of Armenia Major.
arbor, -oris, (old form **arbōs**),
[?], f., *a tree.* — Of many things
made of wood, *a mast, an oar.*
arboreus, -a, -um, [†arbor + eus],
adj., *of a tree:* fetus (*fruit*). —
Less exactly, *tree-like:* cornua
(*branching*).
arbōs, see **arbor.**
arbustus, -a, -um, [†arbos + tus],
adj., *provided with a tree* or *with
trees.* — Neut., *a plantation of trees
with vines trained on them.* —
Neut. plur., *trees, shrubs.*
arbustum, see **arbustus.**
arbuteus, -a, -um, [†arbutŏ (reduced) + eus], adj., *of* (or *pertaining to*) *the strawberry-* or *arbute
tree:* crates (*of arbute twigs*).
arbutum, -ī, [(?) n. of **arbutus**],
n., *the strawberry-* or *arbute-tree:*
iubeo frondentia capris arbuta
sufficere. — *the fruit of the straw-
berry-* or *arbute-tree, the wild
strawberry:* glandes atque arbuta.
arbutus, -ī, [cf. **arbor**], f., *the wild
strawberry-* or *arbute-tree:* dulce
satis humor, depulsis arbutus
haedis.
Arcadia, -ae, [Gr. Ἀρκαδία, f. of
adj., sc. **terra**], f., a mountainous
district in the interior of Peloponnesus, which, from its position

long retained its primitive simplicity and sylvan wildness.
Arcadius, -a, -um, [as if 'Αρκάδιος, adj. from Ἄρκας], adj., *Arcadian.*
arcānus, -a, -um, [†arcū + nus], adj., (*secreted*), *secret, private.* — Neut., *a secret.*
Arcas, -adis, [Gr. 'Αρκάς], m., son of Jupiter and Callisto, supposed ancestor of the Arcadians. — Plur., *the Arcadians.* — As adj. (acc. **Arcada**), *Arcadian:* **rex** (Evander): **eques** (of Pallanteum).
Arcens, -entis, m., a Sicilian.
arceō, -cui, †-citum, -ēre, [noun-stem akin to **arca**], 2. v. a, *shut up, enclose, keep fast.* — From another point of view, *shut off, keep off, keep at a distance:* **periclis** (*protect from*). — With inf. or abs., *hinder, prevent:* **manus** (*bind, prevent from raising*).
arcessō (**accersō**), **-sīvī, -sītum, -sere,** [ar- (= ad) -cesso?], (as causative, *cause to come*), *call, summon, bring.* — Less exactly, *draw, take in, absorb:* **tenues vitas** (*acquire etherial souls*, of creatures at birth).
Archetius, -ī, [?], m., a Rutulian.
Archippus, -ī, [Gr. Ἄρχιππος], m., an Umbrian.
Arcitenēns, -ēntis, [†arcu- (weakened) -tenens], adj., *holding a bow, bow-bearing.* — Masc., *the bow-holder* (*Apollo*).
arctos (-us), -ī (acc. sing. **arcton**], [Gr. ἄρκτος], f., *the Great and Little Bear* (Ursa major et minor), a double constellation in the vicinity of the north pole: **gelidae arcti.** — *the north pole, the north.*
Arctūrus, -ī, [Gr. ἀρκτοῦρος], m., the brightest star in Boötes, the rising and setting of which brings bad weather. — the (whole) constellation Boötes. — *the rising of Arcturus:* **sub ipsum Arcturum.**
arctus, -a, -um, see **artus.**
arcus (old form, **-quus, -os**), **-ūs,** [? akin to **arca**], m., *a bow.* — Esp., *the rainbow:* **ceu nubibus arcus mille trahit varios adverso sole colores.** — Of anything shaped like a bow, *a curve, arch, bend, arc, loop:* **portus curvatus in arcum.**
1. **ardea, -ae,** [Gr. ἐρωδιός], f., *a heron.*
2. **Ardea, -ae,** [†ardea], f., the capital of the Rutuli, six leagues south of Rome; it was burned by Æneas, and from its ashes the heron was said to have been produced.
ardeō, arsī, arsum, ardēre, [? †ardŏ- (contr. stem of **aridus**)], *be on fire, burn, blaze.* — Fig., *flash, glow, sparkle, shine:* **oculi; clipeus.** — Of color, *glisten, glitter, blaze:* **Tyrio ardebat murice laena.** — Of emotion, *burn, glow:* **Penthesilea** (*rages*); **spe** (*be fired with*); **quibus arserit armis** (*be ablaze*). — Esp. (abs. or with acc.), *love, burn, be fired:* **Alexin.** — **ardēns, -entis,** as adj., *glowing, fiery, hot, blazing, sparkling, burning:* **Tyrii** (*eager*); **equi** (*fiery*); **virtus** (*glowing*).
ardēsco, arsī, ardēscere, [†ardē (stem of **ardeo**) + sco], 3. v. n. inch.), *take fire, kindle, become inflamed.* — Fig., *gleam, glitter.* — Of the passions, *burn, be inflamed, become more intense, increase in violence:* **tuendo.** — Of other things, *become violent* or *furious, rage, increase:* **fremitusque ardescit equorum.**
ardor, -ōris, [†ard (as if root of **ardeo**) + or], m., *burning, flame, fire, heat.* — Of the passions, &c. (cf. **ardeo**), *heat, ardor, eagerness, enthusiasm, fire.*
arduus, -a, -um [?], adj., *steep.* — *high, lofty, tall:* **campo sese arduus infert** (*towering high*): **cornua; Iupiter** (*on high*).
area, -ae, [prob.†arŏ(stem of †arus, cf. **aridus**) + ea (f. of -eus), *dry courtyard*], f., *court, yard.* — Esp., *a threshing floor.*
arēna (**harē-**), **-ae,** [†arē (stem of **areo**) + na (f. of -nus)], (*dry earth?*), f., *sand.* — Less exactly,

earth: nigra (*loam, mud*).— Esp., *the seashore, seabeach, beach, strand.*
arēnōsus, -a, -um, [arena (reduced) + osus], adj., *full of sand, sandy:* litus.
ārēns, -ēntis, p. of areo.
āreŏ, -uī, no sup., -ere, [? †arŏ- (cf. **arĭdus**)], *be dry, be parched, dry up:* ager.— **ārēns, -ēntis,** p. as adj., *dry, arid, parched:* arva.
Arethūsa, -ae, [Gr. 'Αρέθουσα], f., a fountain near Syracuse.— Personified, the nymph of the fountain addressed as a muse.
argenteus, -a, -um, [†argentŏ- (reduced) + eus], adj., *of silver, silver.*— Fig., *silvery white, white:* anser.
argentum, -ī, [√arg (cf. **arguo**) + entum, orig. p., or developed from one], n., *silver* (from its brightness).— Esp. : argentum lentum, *an alloy of silver.*— Of things made of silver, *plate, silver.*— *money.*
Argī, see **Argos**.
Argīlētum, -ī, [argilla (reduced) + ētum, *clay-pits*], (wrongly supposed to be from **Argi-letum**), n., a part of Rome.
argilla, -ae, [Gr. ἄργιλλος, cf. **argentum**], f., *white clay, potter's earth, marl.*
argītis, -ĭdis, [akin to **argentum**, etc.], m., *a vine bearing white grapes.*
Argīvus, -a, -um, [Gr. (not found) 'Αργεῖϝος, from 'Αργος (Argos), cf. **Achivus**], adj., *of Argos, Argive.*— Masc. plur., *the Greeks.*
Argō, -ūs, [Gr. 'Αργώ], f., *the ship in which Jason sailed to Colchis for the golden fleece.*
Argolĭcus, -a, -um, [Gr. 'Αργολικός, fr. 'Αργολίς, Argolis], adj., *of Argos, Argolic.*— *Grecian.*
Argos (only nom. and acc.), [Gr. 'Αργος], n., more freq. plur. **Argī, -ōrum,** m., *the capital of the province Argolis in the Peloponnesus, sacred to Juno.*

argūmentum, -ī, [†argū- (as if stem of **arguo,** cf. **argūtus**) + mentum], n., *an argument, proof, a representation* or *statement* of any kind.— Of a play, poem, &c., *subject, story, argument* (of the story of Io on a shield).
arguo, -uī, -ūtum, -uere, [†argu- (√arg, cf. **argentum**), cf. †acu-, **acuo**], (*make clear* or *bright*), 3. v. a., *show, prove, make known, indicate:* degeneres animos timor arguit (*ignoble souls are known by fear*).— Esp., *accuse, charge.*— **argūtus, -a, -um,** p.p. as adj., (*made bright*), *active, lively:* caput equi (*graceful*).— Often of sound, *piercing* (cf. **clarus,** *bright* and *loud*), *sharp, shrill, rustling, noisy, whirring:* ilex (*singing,* with the wind); serra (*squeaking*); pecten (*ringing*).
Argus, -a, -um, adj., *Argive.*— Masc. plur., *the Greeks.*
Argus, -ī, [Gr. 'Αργος], m. : 1. The hundred-eyed keeper of Io after she was changed into a heifer by Jupiter; slain by Mercury at the command of Jupiter. His hundred eyes were placed by Juno in the tail of the peacock ; 2. A fabled guest of Evander, whose death was supposed to have given the name to Argiletum (but see that word).
argūtus, -a, -um, p.p. of **arguo**.
Argyrĭpa (-ippa), -ae, [Gr. 'Αργύριππα], f., a town of Apulia, founded by Diomedes of Argos (afterwards called *Arpi*).
Arīcĭa, -ae, f., *a town of Latium on the Appian way* (now *Riccio*). From this place came Virbius (a supposed son of Hippolytus), who fought in the ranks of Turnus. His mother is by some supposed to have the same name, *Aricia.*
arĭdus, -a, -um, [†arŏ- (cf. **areo**) + dus], adj., *dry, arid, parched:* ora.— Transferred, *making dry, drying up, dry:* febris.— Also, *cracking, snapping,* as when dry wood is broken: fragor.

ariēs, -ietis, [?], m., *a ram:* candidus. — From its form and use, *a battering-ram*, an engine, with a head like a ram's, for battering walls: crebro ariete (*with frequent strokes of,* &c.).

arietŏ, -āvī, -ātum, -āre, [†ariet-], I. v. a. and n., *strike violently, dash violently* (like a ram): arietat in portas.

Ariōn, -ŏnis, [Gr. Ἀρίων], m., a celebrated player on the cithara, of Methymna in Lesbos, rescued from drowning by a dolphin which was charmed by his music.

Arisba, -ae, f., *Arisba,* a town of Troas.

arista, -ae, [?], f., *the top of an ear of grain, head* or *ear of grain.* — Fig., *summer, harvest:* aliquot aristas (*many years*).

Aristaeus, -ī, [Gr. Ἀρισταῖος], m., a son of Apollo and Cyrene, who is said to have taught men the management of bees and the treatment of milk, and to have been the first who planted olive-trees. He was the husband of Autonoë and father of Actæon.

Ariūsius, -a, -um, [Gr. Ἀριούσιος], adj., *of* or *belonging to Ariusia,* a district in Chios famous for its wine: vina (*Chian*).

arma, -ōrum, [√ar (*fit*) + mum (cf. **armus**)], n. plur., *equipments* (of every kind), *arms, weapons, armor.* — Fig., *war, battle, contest, arms:* potens armis. — Also, *armed men, warriors, forces.* — Less exactly, *means of defence* or *attack:* quaerere conscius arma. — For labor, *implements, tools, instruments:* Cerealia arma; dicendum et quae sint duris agrestibus arma. — Of a ship, *equipments, tackle.* (See **moveo.**)

armātus, -a, -um, p.p. of **armo.**

Armenius, -a, -um, [Gr. Ἀρμένιος], adj., *Armenian; of Armenia,* a country of Asia (now *Kurdistan* and *Anatolia*). — **Armenia** (sc. terra), f., the country itself.

armentālis, -e, [†armentŏ- (reduced) + ūlis], adj., *pertaining to a herd, of the herd.*

armentārius, -iī, [†armento (reduced) + arius], (*belonging to the herd*], m., *a herdsman, neatherd.*

armentum, -ī, [prob. √ar + mentum], n., *cattle for ploughing.* — Less exactly, *a drove, herd,* &c., of horses, deer, or other large animals.

armiger, -era, -erum, [†armŏ-ger (√ges + us)], adj., *bearing arms, armed, warlike, an armor-bearer:* Iovis (the eagle, bearing the thunderbolt).

armipotēns, -entis, [†armŏ-potens], adj., *powerful in arms, warlike, Lord of arms.*

armisonus, -a, -um, [†armŏ-sonus, *having the sound of arms*], adj., *resounding with arms, clad in ringing arms.*

armŏ, -āvī, -ātum, -āre, [armŏ-], I. v. a., *furnish with weapons, arm:* armare in proelia fratres; agmina. — Fig., *arm, excite, rouse, stir up.* — With other equipments, *arm, fit out, equip, furnish:* bello armantur equi; ferrum veneno; classem. — **armatus, -a, -um,** p.p. as adj., *armed, equipped:* classes. — Masc. plur., *armed men, warriors.*

armus, -ī, [√ar (*fit*) + mus, cf. **arma**], m., *the shoulder, the upper arm.* — Less exactly, *the whole arm.* — Of animals, *the shoulders, flanks.*

arŏ, -āvī, -ātum, -āre, [√ar, prob. through a noun-stem], I. v. a., *plough.* — Of a ship, *plough:* aequor. — Of age, *furrow:* frontem rugis. — Less exactly, *cultivate, inhabit.*

Arpī, -orum, m., a town of Apulia, at first called *Argos Hippium,* afterwards *Argyripa* (now *Foggia*).

arr-, see **adr-**.

Arrūns, -ūntis, [Etruscan word], m., an Etruscan name (properly a title, *younger son*).

ars, artis, [√ar (cf. **arma**) + tis

(reduced)], f., (*a fitting*), *skill, art, knowledge, workmanship, practice:* **magicae** (*arts of sorcery*). — Concretely, *a work of art.* — Of character and conduct, *habit, practice.* — Transferred, *cunning, artifice, stratagem, art.* — Of plants, *habit, artificial form.*

artifex, -icis, [†arti- (ars) -fex (√fac as stem), comm., generally in the higher sense of **ars**], *one who practises an art, an artist* (cf. **opifex,** *artisan, mechanic*), *workman* (of skill). — Esp., *one who practises arts, a trickster, contriver.*

1. **artus** (arc-), **-a, -um,** [prob. √arc (**arx, arceo**) + tus, p.p. of **arceo**], adj., *confined* (cf. **arca**), *narrow, close, strait:* **compages** (*close-fitting*); **vincla.** — Fig., *straitened, scanty, small.*

2. **artus, -ūs,** [√ar (cf. **arma**) + tus], m., (*a fitting*). Concr., *a joint.* — Less exactly, *parts* (of the world). — Extended, *the body, frame.*

arundineus (har-), **-a, -um,** (†arundin (stem of **arundo**) + eus], adj., *of or pertaining to reeds, reedy, reed-:* **silva.**

arundŏ (har-), **-inis,** [?], f., *a reed, cane.* — Sing., collectively, *reeds.* — Fig., things made of reed, *a fishing-rod, an arrow shaft, an arrow, a reed pipe, syrinx* (of several reeds).

aruspex, see **haruspex.**

arvina, -ae, [?], f., *grease, fat, suet, lard:* **pinguis.**

arvum, see **arvus.**

arvus, -a, -um, [√ar (aro) + vus], adj., *ploughed.* — Neut., *land* (cultivated), *a field.* — Transferred: **arva Neptunia** (*the sea*). — *a shore, a coast.* — *the female organs of generation.*

arx, arcis, [√arc (in **arceo, arca**) as stem], f., *a castle, citadel, stronghold.* — Less exactly, *a height:* **coeli.** — Of mountains, *peak, summit.*

Asbȳtēs, -ae, [?], m., a Trojan.

Ascanius, -ii, [Gr. Ἀσκάνιος], m.:

1. A son of Æneas and Creusa, called also *Iulus;* 2. A river and lake in Bithynia.

ascendō, see **adscendo.**
ascensus, see **adscensus.**
ascisco, see **adscisco.**

Ascraeus, -a, -um, [Gr. Ἀσκραῖος], adj., *of Ascra,* a town in Bœotia; *Ascræan:* **senex** (i.e., *Hesiod*). — Less exactly, *of Hesiod:* **carmen** (i.e., rural).

asellus, -i, [†asinŏ + lus], m. dim., *a little ass, an ass's colt.*

Asia, see **Asius.**

Asīlās, -ae, [?], m., an Etruscan warrior.

asilus, i, [?], m., *a gadfly, horsefly.*

Asius, -a, -um, [Gr. Ἄσιος], adj., *of or pertaining to Asia,* a town of Lydia, *Asian:* **palus** (the marsh of the Caÿster, near that town). — Fem., *the province of Asia* (Minor). — *the whole region Asia.*

Asius, -i, m., a Lycian with Æneas.

aspectŏ, see **adspecto.**
aspectus, see **adspectus.**

asper, -era, -erum, [unc. root + rus], (-ior, -errimus), adj., *rough, uneven:* **rubus** (*prickly*); **signis pocula; sentes.** — Of taste and smell, *harsh, sour, bitter, acrid, pungent.* — Fig., *rough, harsh, hard, bitter, violent, cruel, fierce:* **non asper egenis** (*unfeeling*); **studiis asperrima belli; odia.** — Of animals, *wild, savage.* — Of circumstances, *cruel, adverse, distressing.*

aspergo, see **adspergo.**

asperŏ, -āvī, -ātum, -āre, [†asperŏ-], 1. v. a., *make rough or uneven, roughen:* **glacialis hiems aquilonibus asperat undas.**

aspersus, see **adspersus.**
aspicio, see **adspicio.**
aspīrō, see **adspiro.**

asportō (abs-), **-āvī, -ātum, -āre,** [abs-porto], 1. v. a., *carry* or *bear away, carry off, take away* (of persons or things): **comitem asportare Creusam.**

Assaracus, -ī, [Gr. Ἀσσάρακος], m., *Assaracus,* a king of Phrygia, son of Tros, brother of Ganymede and Ilus, father of Capys, and grandfather of Anchises.
assēnsus, see adsensus.
assentiō, see adsentio.
asservō, see adservo.
assideō, see adsideo.
assiduē, see adsidue.
assiduus, see adsiduus.
assimilis, see adsimilis.
assimulātus, see ads-.
assimulō, see adsimulo
assistō, see adsisto.
assuēscō, see adsuesco.
assuētus, see adsuetus.
assultus, see adsultus.
assum, see adsum.
assurgo, see adsurgo.
Assyrius, -a, -um, (Gr. Ἀσσύριος], adj., *of Assyria* (a vaguely-bounded country of Asia), *Assyrian.* — Masc. plur., *the Assyrians.* — Less exactly, of all people of that region, *Median, Phoenician,* &c.
ast, older form of **at.**
asto, see **adsto.**
astringō, see **adstringo.**
astrum, -ī, [Gr. ἄστρον], n., *a star, a constellation, a luminous celestial body.* — As divinities: **astra vocat.** — Less exactly (in plur.), *heaven, the skies, on high:* sub astra (*up to the sky*); sic itur ad astra (*to the gods*).
Astur, -uris, m., an Etruscan.
astus, -ūs, [?], m., *craft.* — In abl. (of manner), *craftily, cunningly, with craft.*
Astyanax, -actis, (acc. **Astyanacta**), [Gr. Ἀστυάναξ], m., son of Hector and Andromache; at the destruction of Troy cast down by Ulysses from a tower.
asȳlum, -ī, [Gr. ἄσυλον (*unspoiled,* i.e., *a place safe from violence*)], n., *a place of refuge, a sanctuary, asylum.* — Esp., *the asylum* (opened by Romulus on the Capitoline hill).
at (ast), [? cf. **ad**], conj., adding a contrasted but not opposite idea, *but yet, and again, on the other hand, still.* — Of mere transition, *but, now.* — Adding a contrary or opposite idea, *but, but on the other hand, on the contrary.* — After a negative idea, *but at least, but, yet still:* si genus humanum ... temnitis (= *not regard*); at sperate deos, etc.
atavus, -ī, [ād-avus], m., *a great-great-great-grandfather.* — Less exactly, *an ancestor, a forefather.*
ater, -tra, -trum, [?], (-trior), adj., *black, dark,* opp. to **albus** (*dead white*), cf. **niger** (*jet black*). — Fig., *black, dark, gloomy, dismal, sad, melancholy, foreboding:* timor; ignes (*funereal*); venenum (*deadly*); speluncae.
Athesis, -is, [?], m., a river in Upper Italy (now the *Adige* or *Etsch*).
Athōs (gen. not found; abl. **Athone;** dat. and abl. **Atho;** acc. **Atho, Athon, Athonem,** and **Athona**), [Gr. Ἄθως, later Ἄθων, -ωνος], m., *Athos,* a high mountain on the Strymonian Gulf, in Macedonia (now *Monte Santo*).
Ātīna, -ae, [Gr. Ἄτινα], f., a town of Latium.
Ātīnas, -ātis, m., a Latin.
Ātius (Att-), -ī, [?], m., a Roman gentile name: Atii genus.
Atlās, -antis, [Gr. Ἄτλας], m., king of Mauritania, son of Iapetus and Clymene, a lover of astronomy; changed by Perseus, with the aid of Medusa's head, into Mount Atlas, because he refused him a hospitable reception. — The mountain itself in Northern Africa.
Atlantis, -idis, [Gr. patronymic], f., *a female descendant of Atlas, daughter of Atlas.* — Plur., *the Pleiades,* his daughters (as a constellation).
atque, āc, [ad-que], conj., adding with emphasis, stronger than **et,** *and also, and besides, and even, and in fact, and.* — Adding some-

thing unexpected or particularly important, *and lo, and then.* — In comparisons (= **quam**), *than, as:* haud secus ac (*just as*); haud minus ac (*not less than*).

atquī [at-qui], conj., adversative, (*but in some way*), *and yet, but now, yet still.*

Atrīdēs, -ae, [Gr. patronymic], m., *son of Atreus.* — Plur., *the sons of Atreus* (Agamemnon and Menelaus, the leaders of the Greeks at Troy).

atrium, -ī, (-iī), [perhaps †atrŏ + ium, from the blackening of the household smoke], n., *the main court, the hall,* of a Roman house. — Plur., *halls, rooms* (generally).

atrōx, -ōcis, [†atrŏ- (with lengthened o, cf. **aegrōtus**) + cus (reduced), cf. verbals in **ax**], (*terrible, dire*), adj., *savage, fierce, wild, cruel, harsh.*

attāctus (adt-), -ūs, [ad-tactus], m., *a touching, touch, contact* (only in abl. sing.).

atterŏ (adt-), -trīvī, -trītum, -terere, [ad-tero], 3. v. a., *rub against, rub:* vomer sulco (*polish*). — From the effect, *rub off, wear away.* — Fig., *destroy, injure.*

attingŏ (ad-), -tigī, -tactum, -tingere, [ad-tango], 3. v. a. and n., *touch against, come in contact with, touch:* ore; dextras (*reach*). — Of local relations, *come to a place, approach, reach, arrive at,* or *attain to* a place: proram (*gain*); te Aurora (*overtake, find*).

attollō (adt-), no perf., no sup., **-ere**, [ad-tollo], 3. v. a., *lift up, raise up.* — Pass. or with reflexive, *lift one's self up, rise up, rise, appear:* se in femur. — Of building, *erect, construct, raise:* immensam molem. — Fig., *raise, rouse, lift up:* iras (of a snake). — Pass. or with reflexive, *rise, grow:* Punica se gloria.

attondeō (adt-), -tondī, -tōnsum, -tondēre, [ad-tondeo], 2. v. a., *shave, trim, clip:* vitem. — With the teeth, *crop, gnaw, browse, graze on:* virgulta capellae.

attonitus (adt-), -a, -um, p.p. of **attono**.

attonŏ (ad-), -uī, -itum, -āre, [ad-tono], (*thunder at*), 1. v. a. Fig., *seize* with divine furor, *render frantic, infuriate, frenzy.* — **attonitus, -a, -um**, p.p. as adj., *frenzied, frantic, amazed, confounded:* matres.

attorqueo (adt-), no perf., no sup., **-ēre**, [ad-torqueo], 2. v. a., *hurl* (to or towards): iaculum.

attractus, -a, -um, p.p. of **attraho**.

attrahō (ad-), -xī, -ctum, -ere, [ad-traho], 3. v. a., *draw to or towards* one's self. — Fig., *draw, attract, allure.*

attrectŏ (adt-), -āvī, -ātum, -āre, [ad-tracto], 1. v. a., *handle, touch.*

attrītus (adt-), -a, -um, p.p. of **attero**.

Atys, -yos, [Gr. Ἄτυς], m., a young Trojan.

auctor, -ōris, [√aug + tor], m., (*agent of growth*), *father, founder* (of a family), *progenitor, sire* (of animals). — Of buildings, *founder, builder, artist.* — Fig., *promoter, adviser, contriver:* fatis auctoribus (*by order of*). — Of cause, *originator, source, author:* teli. — Of information, *author, informant, narrator, authority.* — Of responsibility, *security, voucher, surety, guarantee, authority:* certior (*more trustworthy authority*): si Iupiter auctor spondeat (*as a voucher*).

audāx, -ācis, [lost or supposed verb-stem (cf. **audeo**) + cus (reduced)], adj., *daring* (in good and bad sense), *bold, courageous, fearless, undaunted:* populus. — More commonly in bad sense, *bold, audacious, rash, presumptuous, foolhardy, reckless:* coepta; audax viribus (*presuming on*).

audēns, -entis, p. of **audeo**.

audeō, ausus sum, -ēre, (subj. perf. **ausim**), [noun-stem in ŏ, perhaps †avido-, cf. **ardeo**], 2. semi-dep., *venture, dare:* **talia; sperare.** — **audēns, -entis,** p. as adj., *daring, bold, intrepid, fearless.*

audiō, -īvī (-iī), -ītum, -īre, [akin to **auris, ausculto**], 4. v. a., *hear, hear of, listen, learn.* — Esp., *hear* (as a judge), *examine into, inquire into:* **dolos.** — *obey, heed:* **neque audit currus habenas.**

audītus, -a, -um, p.p. of **audio**.

auferō, abstulī, ablātum, auferre, [ab (abs)-fero], v. a. irreg., *take* or *bear away, carry off, remove, shut out* (of the sky, cf. **eripio**). — With reflexive, *remove, withdraw, retire, depart*. — With idea of violence or stealth, *snatch away, rob, steal, wrest from:* **animam** (*rob of life*). — Esp., *sweep off* or *away, kill, slay.*

Aufidus, ī, [?], m., a river of Apulia (now *Ofanto*).

augeō, -xī, -ctum, -gēre, [√aug, causative or fr. noun-stem], 2. v. a., (*cause to grow*), *produce, increase, augment, add to, enlarge:* **numerum** (by joining); **Italos** (through one's self, and one's descendants): **si qua dona ipse auxi** (*add more*). — Esp., *load* or *pile up* with something, *heap* upon.

augur, -uris, [†avi + unknown root], comm., *an augur, diviner, soothsayer* (who foretold the future by observing the notes or flight of birds, the feeding of the sacred fowls, certain appearances of quadrupeds, and other unusual occurrences). — Less exactly, *one who foretells futurity by any means, a soothsayer, diviner, seer; prophetic* (in app. as adj.).

augurium, -ī (-iī), [augur + ium (n. of -ius)], n., *the observance and interpretation of omens, augury.* — Less exactly, *divination, prophecy, soothsaying, interpretation.* — *a presentiment, foreboding* (of the future): **triste per augurium.** — *a sign, omen, token.* — *augury* (as an art).

augurō, -āvī, -ātum, -āre, [augur], 1. v. a., *act as an augur, take auguries.* — Fig., *surmise, conjecture, forebode, presage:* **si quid vera mens augurat.**

augustus, -a, -um, [†augus- (cf. **angor, angustus**) + tus], adj., *magnified* (cf. **adoleo** and **augeo, honor**), *sacred, honorable, august.* — Fig., *venerable, magnificent, noble.* — Masc., **Augustus,** title (used as name) of Octavius Cæsar as emperor.

Augustus, -ī, m.; see **augustus**.

aula, -ae, (gen. **aulāī**), [Gr. αὐλή], f., *a court, yard, court-yard, court* (of a house), *hall.* — Less exactly, *a palace, royal court.* — Poetically, of the queen bee, *royal cell.*

aulaeum, -ī, [Gr. αὐλαία], n., *a splendidly wrought* or *embroidered stuff, tapestry, arras, a covering, curtain, canopy, hangings.* — Esp., *the curtain of a theatre* (which, with the ancients, was fastened below; hence, at the beginning of a piece or an act, it was let down; at the end drawn up. — Also, *a covering* for beds and sofas, *tapestry.*

Aulestēs, -ae, m., an Etruscan. (Others read **Auletes**).

Aulētēs, see **Aulestes.**

Aulis, -idis, [Gr. Αὐλίς], f., a seaport of Bœotia, from which the Greek fleet set sail for Troy.

Aunus, -ī, m., a Ligurian.

aura, -ae, (gen. sing., **aurāī**), [√va + ra], f., *air* (in motion), *a breeze, a breath of air.* — In more violent motion, *wind, a breeze, a blast.* — Fig., *breath, breeze:* **famae.** — More gen., *the air, the atmosphere:* **simplex** (*ether =* **aether**). — As inhaled, *air, vital air.* — Opposed to the earth or to the world below, *the heavens, the upper air, the upper world:* **ad**

auras (*to the open air* out of concealment or retirement); **sub auras** (*to light*). — By an unc. connection of ideas, *a gleam, glittering:* **auri**. — From association, *an odor, exhalation.*

aurātus, -a, -um, [as if p.p. of **auro** (which was perhaps in use, cf. **inauro**)], adj., (*set with gold*), *overlaid, ornamented,* or *plated with gold, gilt, gilded:* **trabes**; **tempora** (*adorned with gold,*' i.e., with a helmet).

aureus, -a, -um, [†**aurŏ** (reduced) + **eus**], adj., *golden, of gold:* **corona**. — Like **auratus,** *adorned, set,* or *wrought with gold, gilded:* **tecta**; **cingula**. — Fig., of color or appearance, *gleaming, glittering, golden, yellow:* **sidera**; **mala**; **caesaries**. — Less exactly, *beautiful, magnificent, superb:* **Venus**; **gens**; **saecula** (*the golden age*).

auricomus, -a, -um, [†**aurŏ-cŏma** (declined as adj.)], adj., *with golden hair.* — Fig., *with golden leaves* or *foliage.*

auriga, -ae, [possibly akin to **auris** and **ago,** cf. **aurea,** *headstall*], comm., *driver, charioteer.* — Less exactly, *groom.*

auris, -is, [†**ausi-** (cf. οὖς, ὠτός)], f., *the ear:* **vellere** (as an admonition, the ear being the seat of memory). — Fig., the *ear* of the plough, the *mould-* or *earth-board* by which the furrow is widened and the earth turned back.

aurītus, -a, -um, [as if p.p. of †**taurio,** from **auri(s),** cf. **aurātus**], adj., *having large ears, long-eared:* **lepores**.

aurōra, -ae, [√us (see **uro**), for **ausosa**], f., *the morning, dawn, daybreak:* **rubescebat Aurora**; **nona**. — Personified, *Aurora,* the goddess of the morning, daughter of Hyperion, wife of Tithonus, and mother of Memnon. — The eastern country, *the East.*

aurum, -ī, [√us (cf. **aurora, uro**) + **um** (n. of **-us**)], (*the shining metal*), n., *gold.* — Of things of gold, *a goblet, a bit, a hair-band, gold coin, money.*

Auruncus, -a, -um, adj., *of* or *pertaining to Aurunca* (an old town in Campania), *Auruncan:* **senes**. — **Aurunci, -ōrum,** masc. plur. *the Aurunci.*

ausim, see **audeo.**

Ausones, -um, [Gr. Αὔσονες], m., a very ancient name of the people of Southern Italy.

Ausonidae, -ārum, [Greek patronymic of Auson, supposed progenitor of the Ausones, see **Ausones**], m., *the Italians.*

Ausonius, -a, -um, [**Auson + ius**], adj., *Ausonian, Italian, Latin.* — **Ausonia,** f. (sc. **terra**), *Italy.* — Masc. plur., *the Italians.*

auspex, -ĭcis, [†**avi-†spex,** √spec as stem], comm., *an augur, diviner, soothsayer.*—Fig., *director* (see **auspicium**), *guide, leader, protector:* **dis auspicibus** (*under the guidance of the gods*).

auspicium, -ī (-iī), [†**auspic-** + **ium** (n. of **-ius**)], n., *augury* (from birds), *auspices.* — Less exactly, *sign, omen, divine premonition:* **melioribus auspiciis**. — Because only a commander could take the auspices, *command, guidance, authority, right, power, inclination, will:* **meis auspiciis**; **infaustum Turni auspicium** (*ill-omened rule.*)

auster, -trī, [√us + ter (†-tro, cf. -trum)], m., *a south wind* (dry and hot).—As an agreeable wind: **sibilus iuvat**. — As disagreeable: **floribus immisi**. — For winds in general: **furentes**.

austrinus, -a, -um, [†**austrŏ** (reduced) + **īnus**], adj., *pertaining to the south, southern.*

ausum, -ī, [n. of **ausus,** p.p. of **audeo** in pass. sense], n., *an attempt, enterprise, daring deed.*

ausus, -a, -um, p.p. of **audeo.**

aut [unc., but cf. **autem** and Gr. αὖ], conj., introducing an alternative,

— Regularly exclusive, *or, or else:* quae nemora aut qui saltus; haedos depone aut si ... veremur licet eamus (*or in case*, &c.); quid furis, aut quonam nostri tibi cura recessit? (*or if you are sane*). — Repeated, *either ... or:* aut Turnus aut Rhodope puerum edunt. — After negatives (expressed or implied); not exclusive, but distributing the negation: quis aut Eurysthea aut nescit Busiridis iras; quid labor aut benefacta iuvant. — nec ... aut, *neither ... nor;* nec Austros aut imbrem. — Without exclusion or negation: Anthea siquem videat aut Capyn; aut Ararim Parthus bibet aut Germania Tygrim.

autem [cf. aut], conj. Introducing a more or less strong antithesis, or even a mere transition, but always with some contrast, *but, on the contrary, on the other hand.* — *also, too, again, now, but then, however, furthermore, then again.*

Automedōn, -ontis, [Gr. Αὐτομέδων], m., a son of Diores and charioteer of Achilles.

autor, -ōris, etc., see auctor.

autumnus(auct-), -ī, [for auctominus, †auctŏ (cf. augeo) + minus, cf. Gr. p. -μενος], m., *autumn* (the season of increase).

auxilium, -ī, [akin to augeo, lost noun-stem + ium], n. Abstr., *help, aid, support, assistance, succor.* viae auxilio (*aid for their journey*). — Concrete, usually plural, *instruments, means,* or *sources of aid, means of assistance, resources.* — Esp., *military auxiliaries, forces, allies.* — Also, fig., *remedy, help, relief.*

avārus, -a, -um, [lost noun-stem (cf. aveo and avidus) + rus], adj., *eager, eagerly desirous:* agricola. — Esp., *avaricious, covetous, greedy* of money, &c. — Of persons or things: litus.

āvectus, p.p. of aveho.

āvehŏ, -xī, -ctum, -ere,[ab-veho], 3. v. a., *bear, carry, convey away:* socios. — Pass., *be carried away, ride* or *sail away:* avecti (*having sailed away*).

āvellŏ, -vellī or -vulsī, -vulsum, -vellere, [ab-vello], 3. v. a., *tear* or *pull away* or *off, pluck out, separate from* an object *by pulling, part* or *remove forcibly:* Palladium.

avena, -ae, [?], f., *oats:* steriles avenae. — Fig., *a stem* or *stalk, a straw, reed.* — Poet., *an oaten pipe, pastoral* or *shepherd's pipe.*

1. Aventīnus, -ī, m.; -um, -ī, n. (prop. adj.), [?], *the Aventine*, one of the seven hills of Rome, extending from the Palatine to the Cœlian Hill; until the reign of Ancus Martius, without the city proper.

2. Aventīnus, -ī, m., a supposed son of Hercules.

Avernus, -a, -um, adj., *of* or *belonging to lake Avernus*, in the neighborhood of Cumæ, Puteoli, and Baiæ, almost entirely enclosed by steep and wooded hills (now *Lago d'Averno*). Its deadly exhalations killed the birds flying over it; hence in fable it was placed near the entrance to the lower world. — Neut. plur., Averna, -orum, *the neighborhood of Avernus, places near* or *about Avernus, the lower world.*

āversus, -a, -um, p.p. of averto.

āvertŏ (avor-, abv-), -tī, -sum, -tere, [ab-verto], 3. v. a., *turn away, avert, turn off, turn aside, keep off* (by turning aside): regem Italia. — Pass. or with reflexive (sometimes without), *turn away, depart, retire, withdraw.* — From driving away booty, *carry off, steal.* — Fig., *turn away, divert, keep off.* — *avert, ward off:* omen; casum; pestem (*remove*); curas (*end*). — āversus, -a, -um, p.p. as adj., *turned* or *turning away, withdrawn, retiring, looking as-*

kance. — Fig., *averse, unfriendly, hostile, estranged.*

aviārius, -a, -um, [†avi + ārius], adj., *pertaining to birds, of birds, bird-:* rete (*bird-net*). — Neut., *a place where birds are kept, a poultry-yard, an aviary.* — Less exactly, *the resort of wild birds in a forest.*

avidus, -a, -um, [†avŏ- (whence aveo) + dus], adj., *longing, desirous, eager:* medullae (*burning with passion*).

avis, -is, [?], f., *a bird.*

avītus, -a, -um, [noun-stem akin to avus + tus, cf. **aurītus**], adj., *of* or *belonging to a grandfather, derived from a grandfather.* — Less exactly, *of* or *belonging to an ancestor, ancestral:* solium.

āvius, -a, -um, [ab-via (inflected as adj.)], adj., *that is at a distance from the way, that goes out of* or *is remote from the way:* hence, also, *untrodden, unfrequented:* virgulta. — Neut., *a pathless* or *out-of-the-way place.* — Transferred, of persons, *wandering, straying:* in montes sese avius abdidit altos.

āvolŏ, -āvī, -ātum, -āre, [ab-volo], 1. v. n., *fly away.*

avunculus, -ī, [lost stem †avōn + culus, cf. **avus**], m. dim., *a mother's brother, maternal uncle* (cf. **patruus,** *paternal uncle*).

avus, -ī, [?], m., *a grandfather, an ancestor, a grandsire.*

axis, -is, [perhaps akin to ago], m., *an axle-tree:* faginus axis. — Fig., *the axis of the heavens* (supposed to turn as spheres); *the pole, the north pole.* — Less exactly, *the heavens:* atlas axem umero torquet; aetheris axis (*the ethereal heaven*).

B.

bāca (bācc-), -ae, [?], f., *a berry* (either edible or not), *small fruit* (cf. **pomum,** *larger fruit*). — Esp., of the olive.

bācātus (bācc-), -a, -um, [bacā + tus (cf. **barbātus**)], adj., *set* or *adorned with pearls.* — In later poets **baca** is used for pearls: monile (*pearl necklace*).

bacca, see **baca.**

baccar (-char), -aris, [Gr. βάκχαρις], n., *the baccar, bacchar,* or *baccharis;* a plant with a fragrant root, which yielded a kind of oil, acc. to some, *purple foxglove.* It was supposed to possess magic powers.

bacchātus, -a, -um, p.p. of **bacchor.**

Bacchicus (-ius, -eus, -ēius), -a, -um, [Gr. adjs. βακχικὸs, etc.], adj., *of* or *pertaining to Bacchus, Bacchic.*

bacchor, -ātus sum, -āri, [†Bacchŏ-], 1. v. dep., *celebrate the festival of Bacchus.* — Less exactly, *revel, rave, rage,* or *rant* in any way; *go* or *run about in a wanton, wild, raving,* or *furious manner:* per urbem. — Fig., *fly* or *run wildly:* fama. — **bacchātus, -a, -um,** p.p. in pass. sense, *sought in revels* (of a place where the orgies were celebrated): virginibus bacchata Lacaenis Taygeta (*where the maidens revel*).

Bacchus, -ī, [Gr. Βάκχος], m., *Bacchus,* a son of Jupiter and of Semele, the god of wine and of poets. — Fig., *the vine:* Bacchus amat colles. — *wine:* hilarans convivia Baccho.

Bactra, -ōrum, [Gr. Βάκτρα], n., *Bactra,* the chief city of Bactria or Bactriana (now *Balkh*).

Bāiae, -ārum, [Gr. Βαία], f., a small town in Campania, on the coast between Cumæ and Puteoli, a favorite resort of the Romans on account of its warm baths and pleasant situation.

bālātus, -ūs, [†balā (stem of **balo**) + tus], m., *a bleating:* agni balatum exercent.

Baleāris, -e, [cf. Gr. Βαλιαρεῖς], adj., *Balearic, of the Baleares,* or *Balearic Islands,* Majorca and Minorca, in the Mediterranean Sea. Their inhabitants were famed for the use of the sling. — As subst., **Baleārēs, -ium,** (sc. **incolae**), m., *the inhabitants of the Balearic Islands.*

bālŏ, -āvī, -ātum, -āre, [prob. fr. the sound], 1. v. n., *bleat.*

balsamum, -ī, [Gr. βάλσαμον], n., *a fragrant gum of the balsam-tree, balsam.*

balteus, -ī, (plur. **baltea**), [?], m., *a baldric* or *shoulder-belt* for carrying a sword, *a belt* or *band* for carrying a quiver.

barathrum, -ī, [Gr. βάραθρον], n., *an abyss, chasm, gulf, deep pit.*

barba, -ae, [?], f., *the beard,* of men or animals: barba cadebat.

barbaricus, -a, -um, [Gr. βαρβαρικός, adj. from βάρβαρος], adj., *of* or *pertaining to a barbarian, foreign, strange, barbaric, barbarous.*

barbarus, -a, -um, [Gr. βάρβαρος], adj., *foreign, strange, barbarous :* barbara tegmina crurum.

Barcaeī, -ōrum, [masc. plur. of **Barcaeus,** Gr. Βαρκαῖος], m., *Barcæans, inhabitants of Barce,* a town in Libya.

Barcē, -ēs, [Gr. Βάρκη], f., the nurse of Sichæus.

Batulum, -ī, n., a town built by the Samnites in Campania.

Bavius, -ī (-iī), m., *Bavius,* a bad poet, contemporary with Virgil and Horace, and obnoxious to both.

beātus, -a, -um, p.p. of **beo** as adj., *happy, prosperous, blessed, fortunate :* Eurotas ; sedes (Elysium).

Bebrycius, -a, -um, adj., *of* or *belonging to Bebrycia* (a province of Asia Minor, afterwards called *Bithynia,* the country of Amycus, a famous boxer), *Bebrycian.*

Belgicus, -a, -um, [†Belga- (or Belgŏ-) + cus], adj., *Belgic, of the Belgæ* or *Belgians,* a warlike people of German and Celtic origin dwelling in the north of Gaul.

Bēlīdēs, -ae, [Gr. patronymic], m., *a descendant of Belus* (see **Belus**).

bellātor, -ōris, [†bellā- (stem of bello) + tor], m., *a warrior, soldier, fighting-man.* — As adj., *that wages* or *carries on war, warlike, war-, ready to fight, martial, valorous :* deus (*the warrior-god,* Mars); equus (*war-horse*).

bellātrix, -īcis, [†bellā (stem of bello) + trix], fem. adj., *that wages* or *carries on war, warlike; warrior* (female).

bellipotēns, -entis, [†bellŏ-potēns], adj., *powerful* or *valiant in war.* — Masc., *the god powerful in war,* i.e., Mars.

bellŏ, -āvī, -ātum, āre, [†bellŏ-], 1. v. n.; and **bellor,** perhaps no perf., **-ārī,** 1. v. dep., *wage* or *carry on war, to war :* pictis bellantur Amazones armis.

Bellōna, -ae, [unc. form (cf. **patronus**) from stem of **bellum**], f., the goddess of war, and sister of Mars.

bēllua, see **belua.**

bellum, -ī, [unc. form akin to **duo** and perhaps **dis-**], n., *war, warfare.* — Personified, *War.*

bēlua (bell-), -ae, [?], f., *a beast* (large or ferocious), *a monster* (as an elephant, lion, wild boar, whale, dolphin); Lernae (the Hydra).

Bēlus, -ī, [Gr. Βῆλος, same word as *Bel* or *Baal*], m., *a mythic name* of several Eastern kings, among others, of several ancestors of Dido.

Bēnācus, -ī, m., a deep and rough lake in Gallia Transpadana, near Verona, through which the Mincius (*Mincio*) flows (now *Lago di Garda*).

bene [abl. of **bonus**], (**melius, optimē**), adv. Of every kind of excellence, *well, beautifully, ably, rightly, honorably, favorably, prosperously, fully, completely :* olentes (*sweet*).

benefactum, -ī, [p.p. neut. of

benefacio], n., (*a thing well done,* absolu*t*ely), *a good, honorable, praiseworthy act; good, honorable action; heroic deed.* — (*a thing well done* to or for some one), *a benefit, kindness, service.*

benignus, -a, -um, [†bonŏ-genus (√gen + us), *of good birth*], adj., *Of persons as to feelings or behavior, good, kind, friendly, pleasing, favorable, mild, benignant, kindly.* — Transferred, *kindly, friendly:* mens.

Berecyntius, -a, -um, (**-cynthius**), [Gr. Βερεκύντιος], adj., *of or pertaining to Berecyntus,* a moun*t*ain in Phrygia, sacred to Cybele, on the river Sangarius, *Berecyntian.* — Fem., *the Berecyntian goddess* or *mother* (Cybele).

Beroe, -ēs, [Gr. Βερόη], f.: 1. One of the Oceanidæ, or ocean nymphs; 2. The wife of Doryclus of Epirus, in the Trojan company.

Biānor, -oris, [Gr. βία, ἀνήρ], m., an ancie*nt* hero, the founder of Man*t*ua.

bibŏ, bibī, bibitum(?), **bibere,** [redup. √pa (in **potus**)], 3. v. a., *drink:* Ararim Parthus bibat (*drink of*); ut gemma bibat. — Of *t*hings, *imbibe, drink, drink in:* sat prata biberunt; bibit ingens arcus (*draw water,* of the rainbow). — Fig.: longum amorem (*drink in long draughts of love,* of Dido). — Transferred, *bring forth* or *draw forth, drink* (cf. **haurio**): hasta bibit cruorem.

bibulus, -a, -um, [lost s*t*em †bibŏ + lus], adj., *drinking readily* or *freely.* — Fig., of *t*hings, *that draws, sucks in,* or *absorbs moisture, bibulous, absorbent, thirsty:* arena.

bicolor, -ōris, [bi (for **dvi,** cf. **bis**) -color], adj., *of two colors, two-colored:* equus (*dappled*).

bicornis, -e, [bi (for **dvi,** cf. **bis**) -cornu (weakened)], adj., *with two horns, two-horned.* — Fig., *with two points, two-horned, two-pronged:* furcae.

bidēns, -entis, [bi (for **dvi,** cf. **bis**) -dēns], adj., *with two teeth.* — Fem., *an animal for sacrifice, victim.* — Fig., *with two points, two-pronged:* forfex. — Masc., *a hoe* wi*t*h two iron *t*eeth.

bifer, -fera, -ferum, [bi (for **dvi,** cf. **bis**) -fer (√fer + us)], adj., *bearing twice a year, twice-bearing:* biferi rosaria Paesti.

biforis, -e, [bi (for **dvi,** cf. **bis**) -foris], adj., *with two doors:* bifores valvae (*double doors*). — Fig., *two-fold, double:* biforem dat tibia cantum (because two pipes were used, giving a double opening).

biformis, -e, [bi (for **dvi,** cf. **bis**) -forma (weakened)], adj., *two-formed, two-shaped:* Minotaurus (par*t* man and par*t* bull).

bifrōns, -ontis, [bi (for **dvi,** cf. **bis**) -frons], adj., *with two foreheads;* or, in a wider sense, *with two faces, double-faced* (an epi*t*het of Janus).

bīgae, -ārum; also **-a, -ae,** [bi (for **dvi,** cf. **bis**) -†agus (los*t* adj., ǝkin to **ago,** cf. **agilis, auriga**)], f., *a pair* of horses, *a span, double team.* — Fig., *a car* or *chariot drawn by two horses.*

biiugis, -e, [bi (for **dvi,** cf. **bis**) -iugum (weakened)], adj., *yoked two together:* equi (*pair of horses*).

biiugus, -a, -um, [cf. preceding], adj., *yoked two together.* leones (*yoked in pairs*); certamen (*the contest with the* bigæ, *two-horse race*). — Masc. plur. (sc. **equi**), *two horses yoked abreast, a pair, span.*

bilinguis, -e, [bi (for **dvi,** cf. **bis**) -lingua (weakened, cf. **bilinguus**)], adj., *with two tongues.* — Fig., *double-tongued, false, treacherous:* Tyrii.

bilix, -icis, [bi (for **dvi,** cf. **bis**) + s*t*em akin to **licium**], adj., *with a double thread, two-threaded, two-ply, double:* loricam.

bimembris, -e, [bi (for **dvi,** cf.

bis)-membrum(weakened)], adj., *having double members.* — Masc. plur., *two-formed monsters* (the Cen*t*aurs).

bimus, -a, -um, [bi (for dvi, cf. bis)- †himus (lost s*t*em akin to hiems), *of two winters*], adj., *two years old, of two years, continuing two years, two-year-old.*

bīnī, -ae, -a, [bi (for dvi, cf. bis) + nus], distrib. adj., *two (distributively), two apiece* or *for each.* — Less exac*t*ly, *two*, wi*t*h subs*t*an*t*ives plural only. — Of *t*hings *t*ha*t* are in pairs or double: scyphos (*a pair of goblets*); bina hastilia.

bipatēns, -entis, [bi (for dvi, cf. bis) -patens], adj., *opening in two ways, open in two directions, swinging:* portae.

bipennis, -e, [bi (for dvi, cf. bis) -penna (weakened)], adj., *having two edges, two-edged:* ferrum. — Fem. (sc. securis), *an axe with two edges, double-axe, battle-axe.*

bipēs, -edis, [bi (for dvi, cf. bis) + pes], adj., *two-footed:* equi (*sea-horses*); mensa.

birēmis, -e, [bi (for dvi, cf. bis) -remus (weakened)], adj., *two-oared, having two oars.*—As subs*t*., birēmis, -is, (sc. navis), f., *a small vessel with two oars, a vessel with two rows of benches* or *two banks of oars, ships* (generally).

bis [for dvis, case-form of duo as adv. (cf. cis, uls)], adv. num., *twice, in two ways, in a two-fold manner:* bis in hora (*twice an hour*). — Wi*t*h numerals, *twice* a cer*t*ain number: bis senos. — bis tanto or tantum (*twice as great* or *as much*).

Bīsaltaē, -ārum, m., a Thracia*n* people on the S*t*rymon.

bissēnī, see bis and sēnī.

bissextus, see bis and sextus.

Bītiās, -ae, m.: 1. A Troja*n*, son of Alcanor; 2. A Car*t*haginian nobleman.

bitūmen, -inis, [?], n., *bitumen.*

bivius, -a, -um, [bi (for dvi, cf. bis) -via, declined as adj.], adj., *having two ways* or *passages:* fauces (*double*). — Neu*t*., *a place where two roads meet, cross roads, corner.*

blandus, -a, -um, [perhaps for mlandus, akin to mollis], adj., *of smooth tongue, flattering, fondling, caressing:* canes (*affectionate*). — Fig., *flattering, friendly, kind, pleasant, agreeable, enticing, alluring, charming:* laudes; flores; gaudia (*alluring*).

blatta, -ae, [?], f., *the blatta,* a night insec*t*, *moth, bee moth.*

Bōla, -ae, (-ae, -ārum), f., a very ancient *t*own of the Æqui, in La*t*ium.

bonus, -a, -um, (melior, optimus), adj. Of every kind of excellence: physical, *good, beautiful, pleasant, fit, suitable, fair.* — Neu*t*. plur., *gifts of fortune, wealth, riches, property, goods, fortune.* — Men*t*al and moral, *good, fit, able, excellent, skilful, noble, virtuous, upright, honest,* &c. (wi*t*h inf., *skilful*). — *favorable, propitious:* bonum sit (*a good omen*); bona bello cornus (*well fitted*).— Neu*t*. sing. and plur., *advantage, weal:* bonis communibus obsto.

Boōtēs, -ae, [Gr. Βοώτης, *plough-man*], m., *the constellation Boötes.*

Boreas, -ae, [Gr. Βορέας], m., *Boreas, the mountain* or *north wind* (pure Lat. aquilo): Boreae penetrabile frigus. — Personified, *Boreas,* the son of the river-god S*t*rymon, and fa*t*her of Calais and Zetes by Ori*t*hyia, daugh*t*er of Erech*t*heus, king of At*t*ica.

bōs, bovis, (gen. plur., boum), [cf. Gr. βοῦς], comm. gen., *one of the ox tribe, an ox, a cow:* pascite boves (*cattle*).

bracchium (brāch-), -ī, [?], n., *an arm; the whole arm, from the shoulder to the fingers.* — From similari*t*y, *a branch.* — Plur., *the sail-yards.* — *a* (natural *or arti*ficial*) outwork; an arm for con-*

necting two points in fortifications or *preparations for besieging.* — *a side-work, mole, dike, in the fortification of a harbor.*
bractea, see brattea.
brattea (bract-), -ae, [?], f., *a thin plate, leaf* (of metal).
brevis, -e, [for †bregvis, √bragh + us, with accidental i as in levis, gravis, cf. βραχύς], adj. In distance, extent, *little, small, short, narrow:* brevis est via. — In depth, *small, little, shallow:* vada. — Neut. plur., brevia, -ium, *shallows, shoals.*
breviter [brevi + ter (probably neuter of -terus reduced)], adv. Of space, *shortly, in a small space, at a short distance.* — In expression, *briefly, in brief, with few words, concisely, summarily.* — Of time, *shortly, in no long time.*
Briareus, -ei, [Gr. Βριαρεύς], m., a hundred-armed giant (also called *Ægæon*).
Britannus, -a, -um, [?], adj., *of Britain, British.* — Masc. plur., *Britons.* — Also their country, *Britain.*
Brontēs, -ae, [Gr. Βρόντης (Thunderer)], m., a Cyclops in the workshop of Vulcan.
brūma, -ae, [for brevima (old superlative of brevis, cf. infimus), sc. dies], f., *the shortest day* in the year, *the winter solstice.* — Less exactly, *the winter time, winter.*
brūmālis, -e, [†bruma (reduced) + ālis], adj., *of* or *pertaining to the winter solstice.* — *wintry, of winter:* frigus.
Brūtus, -i, [brutus, *heavy, dull*], m., a Roman family name. — Esp., *L. Junius Brutus,* who expelled Tarquinius Superbus. He was saved by his feigned stupidity (hence the name).
būbō, -ōnis, m. (f. only once), *an owl, the horned owl,* the cry of which was considered as ill-boding.
bubulcus, -i, [†bubulŏ + cus], m.,

an ox-driver or *wagoner, one who ploughs with oxen, a ploughman.*
buccina, -ae; see bucina.
būcina (bucc-), -ae, [?], f., *a shepherd's horn.* — *a trumpet:* bello dat signum rauca cruentum bucina.
būcolicus, -a, -um, [Gr. βουκολικός], adj., *relating to herdsmen.* — Only neut. plur., bucolica, name of the Eclogues, as the songs of herdsmen.
būcula, -ae, [†bov- (bos) + cula], f. dim., *a heifer.*
būfŏ, -ōnis, [?], m., *a toad.*
bulla, -ae, [cf. bullŏ, bulliŏ], f., *a water-bubble, bubble.* — Fig., *a boss, stud.*
būmastus, -i, [Gr. βούμαστος], f., *the bumastus,* a species of grape with large clusters.
būris, -is, [?], m., *hinder part of a plough, plough-tail.*
Būsīris, -idis, [Gr. Βούσιρις], m., *Busiris,* a king of Egypt, who sacrificed strangers, and was himself slain by Hercules.
bustum, -i, [n. p.p. of unc. verb, but cf. comburo], n., *the burned pyre, pyre* (after burning), *funeral pile:* semusta. — *the hillock raised over the ashes of a burned corpse, a tomb.* — Plur., same meaning.
Būtēs, -ae, [Gr. Βούτης], m.: 1. Son of Amycus, king of the Bebrycians, slain by Dares at the tomb of Hector; 2. An armor-bearer of Anchises and guardian of Ascanius; 3. A Trojan, perhaps the same as 2.
Būthrōtum, -i, [Gr. Βουθρωτόν], n., a maritime town of Epirus (now *Butrinto*).
buxus, -i, (sometimes -um, -i, n.), [Gr. πύξος], f., *the box-tree, boxwood.* — Of things made of boxwood, *a pipe* or *flute.*
Byrsa, -ae, [prob. a Phœnician word (= *Bosra*), confounded with βύρσα (a hide)], f., the citadel of Carthage.

C.

cacūmen, -inis, [unc. s/em (cf. Sk. *kakud,* moun/ain) + **men**], n., *the extreme end, extremity,* or *point* of a /hing; *the peak, top, utmost point* (whether horizon/al or perpendicular).

Cācus, -i, [?, cf. **Caca**], m., a mythical mons/er of I/aly who robbed Hercules of Geryon's ca/tle, and was on tha/ account slain by him.

cadāver, -eris, [akin to **cado**], n., *a dead body, a corpse.* — Of beasts, *a carcass.*

cadēns, p. of **cado.**

cado̅, cecĭdī, cāsum, cadere, [√cad], 3. v. n., *fall down, be precipitated, sink down, fall:* **barba** (under the shears); **vela** (*are lowered*); **de montibus umbrae** (*are thrown by*); **imbres** (*drop*). — Of stars, &c., *decline, set:* **sidera.** — In dea/h, *fall, perish, be slain.* — Fig., *happen, come to pass, befall one, occur to one:* **cadit in quenquam tantum scelus** (*be conceived*); **quocunque res cadent.** — *decrease, diminish, perish, decay, cease, subside, abate:* **fragor; animi** (*sink*). — p.p. as adj.: **patria cadens** (*failing, going to ruin*).

cadūcus, -a, -um, [lost s/em in u (from √cad in **cado**) + **cus**], adj., *that falls* or *has fallen, falling:* **frondes volitare caducas.** — Esp., of /hose who fall in ba//le, &c., *falling* or *having fallen dead:* **bello caduci Dardanidae.** — Less exactly, *devoted to death, destined to die:* **iuvenis.**

cadus, -i, [Gr. κάδος], m., *a large earthen vessel for containing liquids* (esp. wine), *a bottle, flask, jar.* — *a funeral urn:* **aenus.**

Caea, see **Cēa.**

Caeculus, -i, [dim. of **caecus,** †caeco + lus], m., a son of Vulcan, founder of Praenes/e.

caecus, -a, -um, [?], adj., *blind.* — Transferred, *dark, invisible, concealed, secret, hidden:* **caligo; fores; Mars** (*blind warfare*). — Fig., *uncertain, dubious, blind:* **fata; undae** (*unknown*); **parietes** (*deceptive*); **ignes** (*meaningless, acting blindly*); **murmur** (*undistinguishable*). — *blind, heedless, reckless:* **auri amor.**

caedēs, -is, [√cad + -es (-is), two s/ems], f., *a cutting* or *lopping off.* — Of persons, *a cutting down, slaughter, murder.* — Concre/ely, *a person slain* or *murdered; the slain.* — *blood shed* in slaugh/er, *gore.*

Caedicus, -i, [?, cf. **caedes**], m., a Rutulian warrior, perh. two.

caedo̅, cecĭdī, caesum, caedere, [√cad (increased, as causative)], 3. v. a., (*cause to fall*), *cut, fell, lop, cut down, hew, throw down, cut off, cut to pieces.* — Fig., *slaughter, slay, sacrifice.* — Transferred, *shed* (of blood).

caelātus, -a, -um, p.p. of **caelo.**

caelestis, -e (some/imes gen. plur., **caelestum**), [†caelit- (s/em of **caeles,** *heavenly*) + tis(cf. **agrestis** and adjs. in -ticus)], adj., (*of* or *pertaining to the heavenly*), *of heaven, heavenly, celestial:* **animi** (*souls of the gods*). — Plur., comm. gen., *the inhabitants of heaven, the gods.*

caelicola, -ae, [√caeli-†cola (cf. **incola**)], comm. gen., *inhabitant of heaven, deity, god.*

caelicolum, gen. plur.; see **caelicola.**

caelifer, -fera, -ferum, [†caelifer (√fer + us)], adj., *supporting the heavens, heaven-supporting:* **Atlas.**

caelo̅, -āvī, -ātum, -āre, [†caelo̅-], 1. v. a., *emboss, carve in relief, engrave, carve:* **bipennis; Mavors caelatus ferro** (*embossed on steel*).

caelum, -i, [?], n., *the sky* (cf. **caelō**), *the heavens, Heaven:* ruina caeli (*deluge of the sky,* the whole heavens falling); quarta caeli hora (*fourth hour,* as indicated by the sky); de caelo tactae quercus (*struck by lightning*). — *the air, atmosphere, temperature, weather:* mores caeli (*course of the weather*). — Poetically, *day.*

Caeneus, -eī, [Gr. Καινεύς], m., *Cæneus:* 1. A girl originally named Cænis, daughter of Elatus, changed by Neptune into a boy. Acc. to Virgil, he again became a female; 2. A Trojan warrior.

caenum, -ī, [?], n., *dirt, filth, mud, mire* (always with the access. idea of loathsomeness).

Caere, n. indecl., (gen. **Caeritis,** abl. **Caerēte,** f.), *Cære,* a very ancient city of Etruria, previously called *Agylla* (now *Cervetere*).

caeruleus, -a, -um, [?], adj., *dark blue, cerulean, sea-green, green:* angues; colla; glacies. — Neut. plur., *the sea.* — From similarity, of things connected with water, *blue:* Thybris. — Opposed to bright colors, *dark, gloomy, black:* vittae.

Caesar, -aris, [?], m., a family name in the gens Julia. — Esp.: 1. C. *Julius Cæsar,* the conqueror of Gaul, and the opponent of Pompey in the civil war, assassinated by Brutus and Cassius; 2. C. *Octavius Cæsar,* called Augustus, the Roman emperor, the friend and patron of Virgil.

caesariēs, ēī-, [?], f., *the hair of the head, the locks.*

caespes (cēs-), -pitis, [?], m., *turf, sod, the turf* (grassy plain): congestum caespite culmen.

caestus (ces-), -ūs, [perh. √caed + tus], m., *a cestus* (a kind of glove for boxing, made of a thong loaded with lead and worn round the hand).

caesus, -a, -um, p.p. of caedo.

caeterus, -a, -um, caetra, -ae; incorrect for **ceterus.**

caetra (cē-), -ae, [borrowed word from native Spanish], f., *a cetra* (a short Spanish buckler), *a buckler!*

Caīcus (Caȳ-), -ī, [Gr. Κάϊκος], m.: 1. A river of Greater Mysia, which takes its rise on Mount Teuthras, passes near Pergamus, and falls into the sea at Lesbos (now the *Mandragora*); 2. One of the companions of Æneas.

Cāiēta, -ae (-ē, -ēs), f.: 1. The nurse of Æneas; 2. A town and harbor in Latium (now *Gaëta*), supposed to have been named for her.

Calaber, -bra, -um, [perhaps akin to caleo], adj., *of Calabria,* the country in Lower Italy from Tarentum to the promontory Iapygium (now *Terra d' Otranto*), *Calabrian.*

Calabria, -ae, f., *Calabria.*

calamus, -ī, [Gr. κάλαμος], m., *a reed, cane.* — Fig., of things made of reeds, *a reed-pipe, an arrow.* — Less exactly, *a straw of grain, a stalk, stem, blade.*

calathus, -ī, [Gr. κάλαθος], m., *a wicker-basket, a hand-basket* (widening towards the top). — From similarity, *a milk-bowl, milk-pail; a wine-cup.*

calcar, -āris, [for **calcare,** neut. of **calcaris** (†calc + āris)], n., (*a thing belonging to the heel*), *a spur.*

Calchās, -antis, (acc. Gr. **Calchanta**), [Gr. Κάλχας], m., a son of Thestor, the most distinguished seer among the Greeks at Troy.

calcō, -āvī, -ātum, -āre, [†calc- (*heel*)], 1. v. a., *tread something* or *upon something, tread under foot:* mixtaque cruor calcatur arena (*is trampled in the sand*). — From the result, *trample in, tread down, press, crowd, press together close* or *firm, press in:* huc ager ille malus dulcesque a fontibus undae ad plenum calcentur (*into this let this poor soil and fresh water be trodden down*).

calculus, -ī, [†calc- (*stone*) + ulus, as if calcŏ + lus], m. dim., *a small stone, a pebble.* — Collec*t*ively, in sing., *gravel.*

calefaciō (calf-), -fēcī, -factum, -facere, 3. v. a.; pass., **calefīō (calfīō), -factus sum, -fierī,** [unc. form (aki*n* to caleo) -facio], *make warm* or *hot, warm, heat.* — Fig., *rouse* or *excite, fire, heat:* calefactaque corda tumultu. — *flush, cause to glow* (of blushing) : ora calefacta (*blushed*).

calefactus (calf-), -a, -um, p.p. of **calefacio.**

calefīō, -ierī; see **calefacio**

caleō, -uī, *no* sup., **-ēre,** [lost s*t*em †calŏ- (cf. **calidus**),] 2. v. n., *be warm* or *hot, glow:* ture (of an al*t*ar). — Pres. p. as adj., *warm:* membra (*still unchilled,* in dea*t*h).

Calēs, -ium, f., *Cales,* a *t*own in sou*t*hern Campania, celebra*t*ed for its wine (now *Calvi*).

calidus (caldus), -a, -um, [los*t* s*t*em †calŏ- (cf. **caleo**) + dus], adj., *warm, hot.* — Fig., *fiery, spirited, fierce.*

1. **cālīgō, -inis,** [lost s*t*em calīgŏ + o(n), root in cla*m*, celo], f., *a thick atmosphere, a mist, vapor, fog, darkness.*

2. **cālīgō,** *no* perf., no sup., **-āre,** [lost s*t*em caligŏ (whence **caligo, -inis**), same root as **clam, celo**], 1. v. *n.* and a. Neu*t.*, *be involved in darkness, be dark, gloomy:* caligans lucus. — Act., *veil in darkness, darken, obscure:* mortales visus.

Calliopē, -ēs, (-ēa, -ae), [Gr. Καλλιόπη, Καλλιόπεια (*having a beautiful voice*)], f., the chief of the Muses, goddess of epic poe*t*ry, and, in the poe*t*s, sometimes of every o*t*her kind of poetry; the mo*t*her of Orpheus and of the Sirens.

Calliopēa, see **Calliope.**

callis, -is, [?], m., *a stony, uneven, narrow foot-way; a foot-path, a mountain-path,* &c.; *a path* (of cat*t*le),

calor, -ōris, [√cal (in **caleo**) + or], m., *warmth, heat, glow* (of any kind, as in Eng.).

calta (caltha), -ae, f., a s*t*rong-smelling flower of a yellow color, perhaps *marigold.*

caltha, see **calta.**

calx, calcis, [?], f., *the heel.* Less exac*t*ly, *the foot:* calcemque terit iam calce.

Calybē, -ēs, f., pries*t*ess of Juno among the Ru*t*uli.

Calydōn, -ōnis, (Gr. acc. **Calydona**), [Gr. Καλυδών], f., *Calydon,* a very ancien*t t*own of Ætolia, o*n* the river Evenus. I*t* was the abode of Œneus, fa*t*her of Meleager and Deianira, and grandfather of Diomedes.

Camaena, see **Camena.**

Camarina, see **Camerina.**

Camēna (-aena, -oena), -ae, [†casmen (la*t*er **carmen**) + a, same roo*t* as **cano**], f., (*goddess of song,* cf. **Pomōna**), *a muse* (the proper La*t*in name, cf. **musa** borrowed from Greek).

Camerina (Camar-), -ae, [Gr. Καμάρινα], f., a *t*own of Sicily, by a marsh of the same na*m*e.

Camers, -ertis, [lost s*t*em †camer (whence also **Camerinus**) + tis (reduced)], adj., *of Camerinum* (a town in Umbria, now *Camerino*). — Name of an I*t*alian warrior.

Camilla, -ae, [cf. nex*t* word], f., a Volscia*n* heroine, killed in the war be*t*ween Æneas and Turnus.

Camillus, -i, [**camillus,** *a young religious servant,* probably akin to **cano, carmen, Camēna**], m., a name of several persons of the gens Furia, the mos*t* dis*t*inguished of whom was *M. Furius Camillus,* who conquered Veii, and delivered Rome from the Gauls.

caminus, -i, [Gr. κάμινος], m., *a smelting furnace, a forge* or *smithy.* — Plur., *chimneys,* the cra*t*er of Ætna, where were supposed *t*o be the forges of the Cyclops.

Campānus, -a, -um, [†campo (reduced) + ānus], adj., *Campanian, of Campania* (a district of southern Italy) : **urbs** (Capua).

campus, -ī, [?], m., *an even, flat place; a plain, field:* **Mavortis** (the *Campus Martius,* a plain at Rome outside the walls, once belonging to the Tarquins. Afterwards it was dedicated to Mars, and became the meeting-place of the Roman people. In it was the tomb of Augustus and his family). — Coll., *land.* — *a level surface* (of the sea or a rock) : **campi salis; immota attollitur unda campus.** — Fig., *a free, open space:* **liquentes** (*the fields of air*).

camurus (-erus), -a, -um, [akin to **camera**], adj., *crooked, turned inwards:* **camuris sub cornibus aures.**

canālis, -is, [?], m., *a channel, canal; a pipe, a trough, a conduit:* **ilignis potare canalibus undam.**

cancer, -crī, [?], m., *a crab, sea-crab.* — *the Crab* (the sign of the Zodiac).

candēns, -ntis, p. of **candeo.**

candeō, -uī, no sup., **-ēre,** [lost stem †cando- (√can in **cānus, caneo**), cf. **candor, candidus**], 2. v. n., *be of brilliant* or *glittering whiteness, shine, glitter, glisten.* — Fig., *glow* (with a glistening color), *be glowing hot:* **favilla.** — **candēns, -ntis,** p., *glistening, shining, white:* **vacca.**

candidus, -a, -um, [†candō (noun-stem, whence **candeo**) + dus], adj., *glistening, dazzling white, pure white, white, clear, bright:* **candida luna; Dido** (*fair*); **barba.** — Of the face of a divinity, *divinely fair.* — **populus** (*the white* or *silver poplar*).

candor, -ōris, [stem of **candeo,** treated as root, + or], m., *a dazzling, glossy whiteness; a clear lustre, clearness, radiance, brightness, brilliancy, splendor.*

cānēns, -ntis, p. of **caneo.**

cāneō, -uī, no sup., **-ēre,** [†canŏ-],
2. v. n., *be white, gray,* or *hoary.* — **canens, -ntis,** p., *white.* — *aged:* **lumina.**

canis, -is, [?], comm. gen., *a dog.* — *the Dog* (the constellation): **major** or **Icarius,** whose brightest star is the Dog-star (**canicula**); and **minor, minusculus,** or **Erigoneius** (commonly called **antecanis**). — *the sea-dog;* plur., and mythically, of the dogs of Scylla.

canistra, -ōrum, [Gr. κάναστρα], n. plur., *baskets woven from reeds, bread-, fruit-, flower-,* &c., *baskets* (esp. for religious use in sacrifices).

cānitiēs, -em, -ē, [**canus,** through some intermediate stem], f., *a gray* or *grayish-white color, hoariness.* — Fig., *gray hair.*

canō, cecinī, no sup., **canere,** [√can, orig. cas], 3. v. a. and n. Neut., of voice or instrument, *sing, sound, play:* **frondator ad auras.** — With cog. acc., *sing, recite, compose:* **carmina; signum** (*sound*). — Of subject of song, *sing of, celebrate:* **reges et proelia; bella exhausta** (*tell of*). — Of any religious or inspired utterance, *repeat, recite, prophesy, foretell, interpret:* **vota Iunoni.** — Of things, *forebode.*

Canopus, -ī, [Gr. Κάνωβος, Κάνωπος], m., *an island-town in Lower Egypt, on the western mouth of the Nile.*

canor, -ōris, [√can + or], m., *melody, tone, sound, song.*

canorus, -a, -um, [perhaps **canor** + us, but cf. **decorus**], adj., *of* or *pertaining to melody, melodious, harmonious, sounding:* **aves** (*tuneful*); **Threicia fretus cithara fidibusque canoris.**

cantharus, -ī, [Gr. κάνθαρος], m., *a cantharus* (a large, wide-bellied drinking-vessel with handles), *a tankard, pot* (esp., used by Bacchus and his followers).

cantō, -tāvī, -tātum, -tāre, [†canto], 1. v. n. and a. intens., *produce* (with energy) *melodious sounds, sound, sing, play.* — Neut.: **Arca-**

Vocabulary. 43

des ambo, et cantare pares, etc. — Act. wi/h cog. acc., *sing, play, recite.* — With acc. of the subjec/ of song, *sing, celebrate* or *praise in song, sing of:* dignus cantari. — Esp., *use enchantments; utter spells, charms,* or *incantations:* frigidus in pratis cantando rumpitur anguis *(by spells).*

cantus, -ūs, [√can + tus], m., *tone, sound, melody, singing, song.* — Of ins/ruments, *blast.*

cānus, -a, -um, [?], adj., *gray, ash-colored, hoary, white:* fluctus; fides *(clothed in white)*; mala *(downy,* quinces).

capella, -ae, [†capro- (cf. ager) + la], f. dim., *a she-goat.*

Capēnus, -a, -um, adj., *of Capena* (a Tuscan town founded by the Veientes).

caper, -prī, [?], m., *a he-goat, a goat.*

capessō (-isso), -essīvī or -essiī, -essītum, -essere, [akin to capio through a noun-s/em], 3. v. a. desider., *seize, take,* or *catch at eagerly; lay hold of.* — Of place, *strive after, make for, betake* one's *self to, endeavor to arrive at, go to, repair* or *resort to:* tuta *(seek);* Italas oras. — Fig., *take hold of any thing with zeal, take upon* one's *self, take charge of, undertake, enter upon, engage in:* iussa; arma *(take up);* regna *(take the throne).*

Caphāreus, -eī, [Gr. Καφαρεύς], m., a rocky promon/ory on the sou/hern coast of Eubæa (now *Capo del Oro).*

capiŏ, cēpī, captum, capere, [√cap], 3. v. a. In the wides/ sense, *take, lay hold of, seize:* saxa manū. — Of a posi/ion, *take possession of, seize, hold, occupy:* tumulum. — Wi/h ante, *anticipate.* — Also, *receive, hold, contain.* — Fig., *comprise, contain, include, have space for:* ūnda se capit *(keep within its bounds).* — Fig., *take, lay hold of, seize, resort to:* orgia *(begin).* — Of physical powers (so only pass.), *be injured, impaired, weakened:* oculis captus *(blinded).* — Of the mind, *win* or *gain by fair or foul means, captivate, ensnare, enchain; mislead, seduce, delude, deceive:* imagine *(deceive);* capta, of Dido *(betrayed).* — With the passions, &c., as subjec/s, *seize, lay hold of, affect:* captus amore; te dementia cepit. — captus, -a, -um, p.p. as adj., *captured, captive, captivated.* — Masc., *a prisoner, captive.*

capistrum, -ī, [†capid- (akin to capio) + trum], n., *(a means of holding), a halter, head-stall* for animals. — Esp., *a nose-piece* or *muzzle,* wi/h spikes to prevent young animals from sucking af/er /hey have been weaned.

Capitōlium, -ī, [developed from †capit-], n., *the Capitol* at Rome. — Also plural.

capra, -ae, [f. of same s/em as caper], f., *a she-goat* (ei/her /ame or wild).

caprea, -ae, [†caprŏ (reduced) + ea], f., *a species of wild goat, a roe, roebuck.*

Capreae, -ārum, [†capro- (reduced) + ea, cf. caprea], f., an island in the Tuscan Sea, off the Bay of Naples (now *Capri).*

capreolus, -ī, [†capreŏ- (cf. caprea) + lus], m., *a species of wild goat, chamois, roebuck.*

caprigenus, -a, -um, [†caprŏgenus (√gen + us)], adj., *goatbegotten, goat-born, of the goat kind:* pecus.

captīvus, -a, -um, [s/em akin /o captus + vus], adj., *taken prisoner, captive.* — Masc., *a prisoner, captive.* — Fem., a female *prisoner* or *captive.* — Of animals, *caught* or *taken.* — Of /hings, *captured, plundered, taken as booty, spoiled, taken by force:* vestis. — Less exac/ly, *that pertains* or *belongs to captives, captives':* sanguis.

captŏ, -āvī, -ātum, -āre, [†captŏ-], 1. v. a. in/ens., *strive to seize, lay hold of a thing with zeal,* &c.; *catch* or *snatch at.* — Fig., *strive after, desire earnestly, seek, explore, search:* frigus; auribus aera (*listen to catch*).

captus, -a, -um, p.p. of **capio.**

Capua, -ae, f., the chief city of Campania (now the village of *Sta. Maria*).

capulus, -ī, [†capŏ- (√cap, cf. **capistrum**) + lus], m., (*holder*), *the hilt* of a sword, *the handle* of any *t*hing.

caput, -itis, [akin to Eng. *head*], n., *the head* (in all senses). — Of animals (cf. **corpus**), *head, creature:* triginta capitum fetus; huic capiti (*to me*). — *chief, principal, ruler, head, author, cause:* urbibus (of Rome). — Of *t*hings, *head, top, summit, end.* — Of rivers, *source.* — Of a city personified: alias inter caput extulit urbes (of Rome).

Capys, -yos, [Gr. Κάπυς], m.: 1. A companion of Æneas, said to have founded Capua; 2. The eighth king of Alba in Latium.

Cār, -āris, (acc. plur. Gr. Caras), m., *a Carian* (of Caria, in Asia Minor).

carbaseus (-inus), -a, -um, [†carbasŏ- (reduced) + eus], adj., *of* or *made of flax* or *linen:* sinus (*of the sails*).

carbasus, -ī, (plur. **-a, -ōrum,** n.), [Gr. κάρπασυς], f., *Spanish flax.* — *a linen garment.* — *a sail.*

carcer, -eris, [Gr. κάρκαρον], m., *a prison, jail.* — From similarity, of a race-course, *the barrier* or *starting-place.*

carchēsium, -ī (-iī), [Gr. καρχήσιον], n., *a cup* (tha*t* is contracte*d* in the middle), *g*o*blet.*

cardō, -inis, [?], m., *the pivot and socket* (by which the doors of the ancien*t*s were fixed, and made to open and shu*t*), *hinge* (but not of the same kind as ours). — Fig., *that about which everything else revolves* or *on which it depends, turning point, crisis:* rerum.

carduus, -ī, [?], m., *thistle.*

cārectum, -ī, [†carec- (later -ic) + tum (n. of tus, cf. **robustus**)], n., *a place covered with sedge.*

careŏ, -uī, -itum, -ēre, [?], 2. v. n., *be without, be free from, not have:* dolis. — *deprive one's self of, do without, resign:* Latio. — *be deprived of:* matre (of a s*t*aff cut from its tree). — **carēns, -ntis,** p. as adj., *deprived of, without:* luce (of the dead).

cārex, -icis, [?], f., *reed-grass, sedge.*

carīna, -ae, [?], f., *the bottom of a ship, the keel.* — Fig., *a vessel, boat, ship.* — Plur., *the Keels,* a place in Rome between the Cælian and Esquiline hills.

carmen (old form **casmen**), **-inis,** [√cas (in **cano**) + men], n., *a poem, poetry, song, lay, verses, lines.* — *a response of an oracle; a prophecy, predic*t*ion,* as being usually given in verse. — *a magic formula, an incantation.* — Less exactly, *a tune, song, air, strain* (vocal, ins*t*rumen*t*al, or of birds).

Carmentālis, -e, [†Carmenti- (reduced) + ālis, or Carmentā + lis], adj., *of* or *pertaining to Carmentis:* porta (a ga*t*e of Rome, named from Carmen*t*is).

Carmentis, -is, (elsewhere **Carmenta**), [†carmen + tis (or ta), cf. **sementis, agrestis**], f., (*the prophetic* or *predicting one,* cf. **carmen**), the mo*t*her of Evander, who went wi*t*h him from Arcadia to Latium, and u*t*tered oracles on the Capi*t*oline Hill; af*t*erwards honored as a goddess.

Carpathius (Carphatius), -a, -um, [†Carpathŏ- (reduced) + ius], adj., *Carpathian, of Carpathus* (an island in the Ægean, now *Scarpanto*).

carpō, -sī, -tum, -ere, [akin to Gr. καρπός, Eng. *harvest*], 3. v. a., *pick, pluck, pluck off, crop, gather, cull* (plan*t*s, flowers, frui*t*s, &c.): primus vere rosam atque au-

Vocabulary. 45

tumno carpere poma. — Also of animals, *crop, pluck off, graze on, eat* (plan*t*s, &c.) : videbat carpere gramen equos. — Fig., wi*th* the idea of plucking, *t*aking, and enjoying ex*t*ended in various ways : pensa (*spin*) ; somnos (*enjoy*) ; vitales auras (*breathe*) ; viam, etc. (*tread, pursue, cleave,* cf. "pick one's way"). — Of the effec*t* of plucking, *wear away, consume, waste :* regina caeco carpitur igni (*is wasted*).

Carthāgŏ (Kar-), -inis, [prob. borrowed from Gr. Καρχηδών, but orig. Phœnician, meaning *New Town*], f., *Carthage,* the famous ci*t*y in Nor*th* Africa (near modern Tunis), once the rival of Rome.

cārus, -a, -um, [perhaps akin to careo], adj., *dear, precious, valued, esteemed, loved.*

casa, -ae, [?], f., *a simple* or *poorly built house, a hut, cottage, cabin, shed,* &c. : humiles habitare casas.

cāseus, -ī, [?], m., *cheese.*

casia, -ae, [Gr. κασία], f. : 1. A tree with an aroma*t*ic bark, like cinnamon, prob. *the wild cinnamon;* 2. A fragran*t* shrub-like plan*t*, *mezereon.*

Casīnum, -ī, [?], n., a Roman colony in La*t*ium (now *Monte Casino*).

Casmilla, -ae, [cf. Camillus], f., the mother of Camilla.

Casperia, -ae, [?], f., a *t*own of the Sabines.

Caspius, -a, -um, adj., *of* or *belonging to the Caspii* (a na*t*ion of Media) ; *Caspian :* regna.

Cassandra, -ae, [Gr. Κασσάνδρα], f., a daugh*t*er of Priam and Hecuba, pries*t*ess of Apollo. Endowed by him wi*th* prophe*t*ic powers, she con*t*inually proclaimed the destruction of Troy, but, according *t*o the *t*erms of the gift, was believed by no one.

cassēs, -ium, [?], m. plur., *hunting-net, snare.* — From similari*t*y, *a spider's web.*

cassida, -ae; see cassis.

cassis, -idis, (-ida, -ae), [?], f., *a helmet.*

cassus, -a, -um, [p.p. of quatio?], adj., *empty, void, hollow.* — Fig., *wanting, devoid of, deprived of, without :* (with abl.) lumine cassus. — *vain, empty, useless, futile, fruitless.* — Neu*t*. acc., in cassum, incassum, *in vain, vainly, idly :* studio incassum gestiri (*with an idle desire,* &c.).

Castalia, -ae, [Gr. Κασταλία], f., a foun*t*ain of Parnassus, sacred *t*o Apollo and the Muses.

castanea, -ae, [Gr. καστανέα, f. adj. from κάστανον], f., *chestnut-tree.* — Also, *a chestnut :* nuces (in adj. sense).

castellum, -ī, [†castrŏ + lum, cf. ager, from †agro], n. dim., *a castle, fort, citadel, fortress, stronghold.*— Fig., *shelter, defence, refuge.* — *a residence situated on an eminence.*

castīgō, -āvī, -ātum, -āre, [lost noun-s*t*em †castīgŏ (†castŏ-agŏ-, cf. prodigus)], 1. v. a., (*purify*), *set right, correct, chastise, punish ; reprove, chide, censure, find fault with :* moras (*chide the stragglers*); castigat auditque dolos (of a preliminary examina*t*ion of criminals).

Castor, -oris, [Gr. Κάστωρ], m., a companion of Æneas.

castorea, -orum, [castor + eus], n. plur., *the glands of the beaver, castor, musk.*

castrum, -ī, [unc. root + trum], n. Sing., *a castle, fort, fortress* Castrum Inui (a ci*t*y of La*t*ium) — Plur., (several works *t*ogether), *a fortified military camp, an encampment :* castra movere (*break up, decamp*). — Of bees : cerea (*hive*).

castus, -a, -um, [p.p. of unc. root], adj., *morally pure, unpolluted, spotless, guiltless* (of persons or *t*hings) : nulli fas casto sceleratum insistere limen.—Esp., *pure, chaste, continent :* matres.—*pious, religious, holy, sacred* (of persons or *t*hings) : hac casti maneant in religione nepotes.

cāsus, -ūs, [√cad + tus], m., *a falling down, a fall,* &c. — Esp., *a fall, overthrow.* — Fig., of *t*ime, *the end:* hiemis. — Generally, (*what befalls*), *an occurrence, event, accident, chance:* sub hoc casu (*at this crisis*); casus (*fate,* collectively); marini (*dangers of the sea*). — Esp., *an adverse event, a bad condition, a misfortune, mishap, calamity.*

catēia, -ae, [a. Celtic word], f., *a kind of missile weapon.*

catēna, -ae, [?], f., *a chain, a fetter.*

caterva, -ae, [?, cf. catena], f., *a crowd, troop, band* of men. — Esp., *a body of soldiers, a troop, company, band.* — Of animals, *a flock:* avium.

catervātim [†catervā + tis, acc.], adv., *in companies, in troops, in* or *by flocks:* catervatim dat stragem.

Catilīna, -ae, [†Catilŏ (reduced) + inus, f. of adj.], m., *L. Sergius Catiline,* the conspira*t*or driven from Rome by Cicero.

Cātillus (-ilus), -ī, m., a bro*t*her of Tiburtus and Coras, wi*t*h whom he buil*t* Tibur.

Catō, -ōnis, [†catŏ- + o], m., (*the Shrewd*), a family *n*ame in several Roman gen*t*es. — Esp., *M. Porcius Cato,* the Censor, a rigid moralis*t* and puri*t*an. — Also, *Uticensis,* who killed himself at Utica.

catulus, -ī, [los*t* s*t*em †catŏ- + lus], m. dim., *a young dog, a whelp, puppy:* sic canibus catulos similes . . . noram. — Less exactly, *a cub, the young* of animals in general (of the lion, of the serpen*t*).

Caucasius, -a, -um, [†Caucasŏ + ius], adj., *pertaining to Caucasus, Caucasian, of Caucasus.*

Caucasus, -ī, [Gr. Καύκασος], m., a chain of rough mountains, inhabited by wild *t*ribes, in Asia, between the Black and Caspian Seas.

cauda (cōd-), -ae, [?], f., *the tail* of animals: delphinum.

caudex (cōd-), -icis, [?], m., *the trunk* of a *t*ree, *stock, stem:* caudicibus sectis.

caulae, -ārum, [†cavŏ + la, dim.], f., *openings, holes, passages.* — Fig., *sheepfolds, sheepcotes:* fremit lupus ad caulas.

caulis (cōl-), -is, [Gr. καυλός], m., *a stalk, stem,* or *shoot* of a plan*t*, &c.

Caulōnia, -ae, f.; -ōn, -ōnis, [Gr. Καυλωνία], m., a *t*own founded by the Achæans o*n* the eas*t* coast of Bruttium (in the vicini*t*y of the present *Castel Vetere*).

Caurus (Cōr-), -ī, m., *the northwest wind* (violent and dry).

causa(-ssa), -ae, [akin to caveo?], f., *a cause, reason, efficient cause, motive, inducement, an occasion, opportunity:* Romam causa videndi; malorum; ad culpam. — Also, *a feigned cause, a pretext, pretence, excuse:* morandi.

causor, -ātus sum, -ārī, [†causa], 1. v. dep., *assign* or *give as a reason* (whe*t*her real or feigned), *plead as an excuse, pretend, allege,* &c.: causando nostros in longum ducis amores (*making excuses*).

cautēs, see cōtes.

cautus, -a, -um, p.p. of caveo.

cavātus, -a, -um, p.p. of cavo.

cavea, -ae, (gen. caveāī), [†cavŏ (reduced) + ea, cf. caulae], f., *a hollow place, a cavity.* — Of bees, *a hive.* — Of a *t*hea*t*re, *the theatre* (the circular par*t* in which the specta*t*ors sat), *spectators' seats* or *benches:* consessu caveae.

caveŏ, cāvī, cautum, cavēre, [?], 2. v. n. and a., *be on one's guard, take care, take heed, beware, guard against, avoid.* — Wi*t*h inf., *take care not to, beware of:* occursare capro. — cautus, -a, -um, p.p. as adj., *careful, wary.*

caverna, -ae, [los*t* s*t*em †cavus (-eris) + na (cf. caves)], f., *a hollow, cavity, cave, cavern, grotto, hole:* cavernae curvae.

cavō, -āvī, -ātum, -are, [†cavŏ-], 1. v. a., *make hollow, hollow out, excavate.* — cavātus, -a, -um, p.p. as adj., *hollow.*

cavus, -a, -um, [?], adj.,(prob. *swollen*), *concave, excavated, hollowed out, hollow, cavernous :* concha; flumina (*deep*). — Of a vision, *without substance, empty, hollow.*

Caystros(-us), [Gr. Κάϋστρος], m., a river of Ionia, celebrated for its swans (now *Little Meander*).

Cea, -ae, [Gr. Κέως], f., an island of the Ægean, birthplace of Simonides, famous for its female garments and the fertility of its soil.

Cecropidēs, -ae, [Gr. patronymic], m., *a male descendant of Cecrops.* — Masc. plur., *the Athenians*, as descendants of their ancient king.

Cecropius, -a, -um, [Gr. Κεκρόπιος], adj., *of Cecrops, Cecropian.* — Less exactly, *of Athens* or *Attica, Athenian, Attic.*

Cecrops, -opis, [Gr. Κέκροψ], m., the most ancient king of Attica, who went thither from the Egyptian Sais, and founded the citadel of Athens: acc. to the fable, half man and half serpent (or half man and half woman).

cēdō, cēssī, cēssum, cēdere, [√cēd, simplest known form], 3. v. n., *go, be in motion, move, make way* (cf. compounds). — With dat. or in, *come to, fall to, accrue :* victoria Turno. — Esp., *retire, make way, depart, withdraw :* litora cedentia retro (*receding in the distance*); ab ordine. — In military sense, *withdraw, leave one's position.* — ne fama cedat loco (fig., *lose its prestige*). — Fig., *pass, pass away, vanish, depart, forsake one ; yield, give place, submit* (of a ship in a race); salix olivae (*be inferior*); nec cedit honore (*be behind*). — *yield, comply.— prosper, succeed :* res Latio (*success is granted*).

cedrus, -ī, [Gr. κέδρος], f., *the cedar, juniper-tree.*

Celaenō, -ūs, [Gr. Κελαινώ], f., one of the Harpies.

celebrātus, p.p. of celebro.

celebrō, -āvī, -ātum, -āre, [†celebrŏ-, orig. stem of celeber], 1. v. a., *resort* or *go to in great numbers* or *often, frequent :* coetum; litora ludis. — *go in great numbers to a celebration, celebrate, solemnize, keep a festival sacred*, &c.: honorem. — *honor, praise, celebrate* a person or thing, *celebrate* in song, *render famous, signalize :* talia carminibus.

Celenna (Celem-), ae, f., *a town* of Campania.

celer, -eris, -e, [√cel + rus (reduced)], adj., (*urged on*), *swift, quick, fleet, speedy :* sagittae; iaculo celer (*throwing swiftly*).

celerō, -āvī, -ātum, -are, [†celerŏ-, orig. stem of celer], 1. v. a. and n., *quicken, hasten, hasten on.*

Celeus, -eī, [Gr. †Κελεύς], m., a king of Eleusis, father of Triptolemus. Cf. Gr. κελεύω.

cella, -ae, [?], f., *a storehouse.* — Transferred, *a cell* (of bees).

cēlō, -āvī, -ātum, -are, [akin to clam], 1. v. a., *hide, conceal, keep secret* something *from* one, *cover.*

celsus, -a, -um, [p.p. of cello as adj.], adj., *raised high, extending upwards, high, lofty :* naves.

centaurēum(-ion), -ī, [Gr. κενταύρειον and κενταύριον], n., *centaury,* a kind of gentian, a plant with a fragrant root.

Centaurus, -ī, [Gr. Κένταυρος],˙m., *a Centaur.* The Centaurs were wild people in the mountains of Thessaly, who fought on horseback; acc. to fable, monsters of a double form (the upper parts human, the lower those of a horse), sons of Ixion and of a cloud in the form of Juno. — Also, the name of a ship (hence fem.), *the Centaur :* magna.

centēnī, -ae, -a, (poet., -us, -a, -um), [stem of centum (lengthened) + nus], distrib. num. adj.,

a hundred each, a hundred. — Collec/ively : **centena arbore.**
centum, [?], indecl. num. adj., *a hundred,* indef., as Eng.
centumgeminus, -a, -um, [centum-geminus], adj., *a hundredfold:* **Briareus** (having a hundred arms).
cera, -ae, [akin to κηρός, perhaps borrowed], f., *wax.*
cerasus, -ī, [Gr. κέρασος], f., *the cherry-tree* (brought from Cerasus, in Pon/us).
ceraunius, -a, -um, [Gr. κεραύνιος], adj., *of thunder and lightning.* — Esp. masc. plur., **Ceraunii montes,** *the Ceraunian mountains* in Epirus (now *Monti della Chimæra*). — Neu/. plur., *the Ceraunian mountains.*
Cerberus, -ī, [Gr. Κέρβερος], m., *the three-headed dog tha/ guarded the entrance to the Lower World.*
Cereālis, -e, [s/em akin to Ceres + ālis], adj., *of Ceres, wheaten :* **solum** (of a cake used as a pla/e or trencher). — More generally, *pertaining to grain, agricultural :* **arma** (*tools of the husbandman*).
cerebrum, -ī, [unc. s/em (cf. cernuus) + brum], n., *the brain.*
Cerēs, -eris, [√cer (root of cresco) + ēs, cf. **pubēs**]. f., *the goddess of grain, daugh/er of Sa/urn and mo/her of Proserpine.* — In prob. earlier meaning, *grain, flour, bread.*
cereus, -a, -um, [cēra (reduced) + eus], adj., *of wax, waxen, waxy :* **castra** (of bees, *waxy fortress*). — Of color and appearance : **pruna.**
cērintha, -ae, [Gr. κηρίνθη], f., *a plant furnishing food for bees.*
cernō, crēvī, crētum, cernere, [√cer (crē), suffix †na], 3. v. a., *sif/, separate* (cf. **cribrum,** *sieve*). — Fig. (wi/h obj. or wi/hou/), *distinguish, see, discern :* **ut cernis.** — *Decide by con/es/, contend, fight :* **ferro.** — **certus, -a, -um,** p.p., *decided, fixed, certain, prescribed :* **foedus.** — Esp. : **certum est,** *it is determined, one is resolved.* — Personally, *determined, resolved to :* **eundi; mori.** — From another point of view, *fixed, established, undisturbed, sure :* **domus ; requies ; certissima proles** (*undoubted*). — So also of persons, *certain, sure, unswerving, steady, trustworthy, unerring, faithful.* — Of a mental s/ate, *certain, sure :* **certum (certiorem) facere** (*inform, make known to one*).
cernuus, -a, -um, [akin to cerebrum], adj., *head-downwards :* **incumbit cernuus.**
certāmen, -inis, [certā- (s/em of certo) + men], n., (*act or means of contending*), *contest* (either hos/ile or friendly), *struggle, battle, fight ; match, rivalry.*
certātim [†certā +tis, acc., cf. **partim**], adv., *earnestly, eagerly, in eager rivalry* (often trans/ated by a verb, *vie with each other in,* &c.).
certē [abl. of certus], adv. In affirmation, *certainly, surely, assuredly.* — Opposed to a concession, *yet surely, at least, at any rate, still at any rate.*
certō, āvī, -ātum, -āre, [†certŏ-], 1. v. n. and a. intens., (*decide by contest,* cf. **cerno**), *contend* (with hos/ility or otherwise), *fight, strive, struggle, emulate, vie with, rival :* **remi ; muneribus ; solus tibi certat Amyntas.** — Wi/h infin., *strive, endeavor :* **Phoebum superare canendo.**
certus, -a, -um, p.p. of **cerno.**
cerva, -ae, [?, akin to **cornu** and **cerebrum**], f., *a hind.*
cervix, -īcis, [akin to **cerebrum**], f., *the neck, the back of the neck* (for carrying burdens), *back* or *shoulders.*
cervus, -ī, [root of **cornu** + **vus**], m., *a stag, a deer :* **lěvis.**
cēspes, -itis, see **caespes.**
cēssō, -āvī, -ātum, -āre, [†cessŏ- (p.p. of cedo)], 1. v. a. intens., (*give way,* cf. **cedo**), *hang back,*

delay, cease, stop, abate, hesitate, go by a roundabout way, loiter: **genus telorum.** — Esp., *be idle, idle:* **siquid cessare potes; quidquid cessatum est** (*whatever idleness has been indulged*). — Also of things, *lie idle, be inactive:* **novales; furor** (*abate*).

cestus (caes-), -ūs, [Gr. κεστός], m., *a cestus,* a *thong wound round the hand loaded with lead or iron, a weapon of pugilists.*

cētē, see **cētus.**

†**cēterus** (not found, cf. **alter**, etc.], **-a, -um,** [†ce (cf. **hic**) + terus, comp. of **ce**], adj., *the other* (implying only two, cf. **alter**), *the rest, the remaining, the rest of:* **rura.** — Neut. plur. as adv., *in other respects, for the rest, for the future, otherwise.*

Cethēgus, -ī, m., a Trojan.

cētra, see **caetra.**

cētus, -ī, [plur. n. **cētē,** as if fr. κῆτος], m., *a sea-monster, whale, shark,* &c.

ceu [†ce (cf. **hic**) -ve (cf. **neu**), or *thus*], adv. *With single words, as, like, as if.* — With clauses, *as if, as when, just as.*

Chalcidicus, -a, -um, [Gr. Χαλκιδικός], adj., *of Chalcis* (the chief city of Euboea), *Chalcidian:* **versus** (of Euphorion, a native of Chalcis). — Less exactly, *of Cumæ* (a colony of Chalcis), *Cumæan:* **arx** (*heights of Cumæ*).

Chalybē, see **Calybe.**

Chalybes, -um, [Gr. Χάλυβες], m., *the Chalybes,* a people of Pontus, noted for their preparation of steel.

chalybs, -ybis, [Gr. χάλυψ], m., *steel:* **vulnificus.**

Chāōn, -onis, m., a Trojan, the brother of Helenus, and eponymous hero of the Chaonian nation.

Chāonius, -a, -um, [†Chaon + ius], adj. *of Chaonia* (a region of Epirus), *Chaonian.* — **Chaonia,** f., (sc. **terra**), the country. — Less exactly, *of Dodona* (a city of Epirus, which whole country was formerly occupied by the Chaonians), *Dodonian.*

Chaos, abl. **Chaō,** [Gr. χάος], n., (*a yawning gulf*), the boundless, empty space, as the kingdom of darkness; *the Lower World.* — Personified, *Chaos* (or *Infinite Space and Darkness*).

Charōn, -ōntis, [Gr. Χάρων], m., the ferryman of the Styx, a personage probably borrowed from Egypt.

Charybdis, -is, [Gr. Χάρυβδις], f., a dangerous whirlpool in the Strait of Messina, between Sicily and Italy.

Chēlae, -ārum, [Gr. χηλαί], f., (*the arms* of Scorpio). — Less exactly, *the constellation Libra* (into which the arms extended).

chelydrus, -ī, [Gr. χέλυδρος], m., *a water-snake.*

Chimaera, -ae, [Gr. Χίμαιρα (*a goat*)], f.: 1. A fabulous monster in Lycia, which vomited forth fire (in front a lion, in the hinder part a dragon, and in the middle a goat), slain by Bellerophon; 2. The name of one of the ships of Æneas.

Chirōn, -ōnis, [Gr. Χείρων (*the one with a large hand*)], m., *Chiron,* a Centaur distinguished by his knowledge of plants, medicine, and divination; son of Saturn and Phillyra; the tutor of Æsculapius, Hercules, and Achilles; placed among the constellations.

chlamys, -ydis, [Gr. χλαμύς], f., *a broad, woollen upper garment* (worn in Greece), sometimes purple and inwrought with gold (worn esp. by distinguished military men); *a Greek military cloak, a state mantle.*

Chlōreus, -eī, m., a Phrygian.

chorĕa, -ae, [Gr. χορεία (*pertaining to a χορός*], f., *a dance in a ring, a dance.*

chorus, -ī, [Gr. χορός], m., *a choral dance, a dance.* — Of the performers, *a chorus, dancing band, choir.* — Less exactly, *a multitude, band, troop.*

Chromis, -is, [Gr. Χρόμις], m.: A young satyr; 2. A Trojan.

cibus, -ī, [?], m., *food* (of man or beast).

cicāda, -ae, f., *the cicada* or *tree-cricket*.

cicātrīx, -īcis, [?], f., *a scar.* — Less exactly, of a plant, *mark, scar, wound*.

Cicones, -um, [Gr. Κίκονες], m., a Thracian people, whose women were fabled to have torn Orpheus in pieces.

cicūta, -ae, [?], f., *the poison hemlock; cicuta virosa.* — Less exactly, *a hemlock stalk*, or *stem* of some other similar herb used for pipes.

cieō, cīvī, citum, ciēre, (rarely **ciō, cīre,** cf. compounds), [√ci, of unc. meaning], 2. v. a. (causative), *set in motion, move, stir, agitate*: aequora; equos (*urge on*); tonitru caelum (*disturb*); aere viros (*rouse, stimulate*). — Less exactly, *produce, call forth, cause*: lacrimas; gemitus; simulacra pugnae (*counterfeit*); stragem (*make havoc*). — Fig., *call upon*: animam (cf. vocare); nocturnos manes (*invoke*).—**citus, -a, -um,** p.p. as adj., *hurried, swift, quick*.

Ciminus, -ī, m., a lake of Etruria, near Sutrium (now *Lago di Ronciglione*), with a mountain-forest near it.

1. **cinctus, -a, -um,** p.p. of cingo.
2. **cinctus, -ūs,** [√cing + tus], m., *a girding.* — Esp., **cinctus Gabīnus,** *the Gabine girding*, a manner of girding up the toga; its corner, being thrown over the left shoulder, was brought under the right arm round to the breast. (This manner was customarily employed in religious festivals.)

cingō, -xī, -ctum, -gere, [as if √cing, perhaps n inserted], 3. v. a., *surround* (in all senses). — Of persons, *gird on, gird with, gird, gird up*: inutile ferrum cingitur. — Of parts of the body, *surround, bind on, bind, encircle.* — Of things, *surround, encircle, enclose, invest*: oppida muris; urbem obsidione (*beset*); flammā (*encompass*).

cingulum, -ī, [lost noun-stem †cingo- (√cing + us) + lum], n., *a girdle, belt, sword-belt*.

cinis, -eris, [cf. Gr. κόνις], m., *ashes.* — Esp. of the dead, *ashes.* — Fig., *death, the spirit* or *shade* (of the departed).

Cinna, -ae, [cf. **cicinnus, Cincinnatus**], m., *C. Helvius Cinna,* a Roman poet, friend of Catullus.

cinnamum (-amōmum), -ī, [Gr. κίνναμον, κιννάμωμον], n., *cinnamon*.

Cīnyphius, -a, -um, [†Cinyph + ius], adj., *of the Cinyps* (a river of Libya), *Cinyphian.* — Less exactly, *Libyan, African*.

Cinyrās, -ae, [Gr. Κινύρας], m., a hero of the Ligurians. Others read **Cinyre** as from **Cinyrus**.

Cinyre, see Cinyras.

circā [abl. fem. or instr. (cf. **eā, quā**), same stem as **circum,** cf. **circulus**], adv. and prep., *around, about.* — With acc.: lucos. — Of number, *about, not far from*.

Circaeus, -a, -um, [as if from Gr. Κιρκαῖος, which was perhaps used], adj., *of Circe*.

Circē, -ēs (-ae), [Gr. Κίρκη], f., a daughter of the sun, said to have fled from Colchis to Circeii in Italy. She was famous for her sorceries, by which she changed her guests into beasts.

Circēī (-iī), -iōrum, [Gr. Κιρκεῖον], m., a town (and promontory) in Latium, famous for its oysters, the supposed abode of Circe.

Circēnsis, -e, [†circŏ (reduced) + ensis], adj., *of the Circus.* — Masc. plur. (sc. **ludī**), *the great games of the Circus*: magnis Circensibus.

circlus, see circulus.

circueō, -īre; see circumeo.

circuitus, -ūs, [circum-itus], m., *a going around, a circuit, revolution*.

Vocabulary. 51

circulus (circlus), -ī, [†circŏ+lus], m., *a circle, a ring, band* (round the neck, hair or the like), *chain :* flexilis.

circum [acc. of circus], adv. and prep. Adv., *around, round, about.* — Prep. with acc., *around, about, near by.*

circumamplector, see **amplector.**

circumdatus, -a, -um, p.p. of **circumdo.**

circumdŏ, -dedī, -datum, -dare, [circum-do, *put*], 1. v. a., *put around, place around :* loricam umeris (*buckle on*); licia tibi (*twine around*). — From another point of view, *surround with, gird, encircle, enclose :* muros igni; lapis circumdatur auro (*is overlaid*); armis circumdatus (*arrayed, begirt*); turbine corpus (*envelop*).

circumeŏ (circu-), -īvī (-iī), -itum, -īre, [circum-eo], irr. v. n. and a., *go around.* — Act., *encircle, go round, run about :* circuit Camillam (*circles around*).

circumferŏ, -tulī, -lātum, -ferre, [circum-fero], 3. v. a. irr., *bear around, carry round :* secum silvam; acies (*turn the eyes*). — From another point of view (cf. **circumdo**), *encircle :* socios pura unda (*lustrate*).

circumflectŏ, -xī, -xum, -ctere, [circum-flecto], 3. v. a., *bend or turn about, wind around :* longos circumflectere cursus.

circumfluŏ, -xī, no sup., **-ere,** [circum-fluo], 3. v. n. and a., *flow round, flow about, surround* (by flowing).

circumfundŏ, -fūdī, -fūsum, -fundere, (also separate), [circum-fundo], 3. v. a., *pour around :* nubes circumfusa (*enveloping*). — Fig. in passive, rarely active, *gather, crowd around, flock together :* circumfuso milite (*thronging*); iuventus circum fusa. — From different point of view (cf.

circumdo), *surround* (by pouring) : gradientes circum dea fudit amictu (*envelope*).

circumfūsus, -a, -um, p.p. of **circumfundo.**

circumligŏ, -āvī, -ātum, -āre, [circum-ligo], 1. v. a., *bind around, bind to* (by binding around).

circumsistŏ, -stetī, no sup., **-sistere,** [circum-sisto], 3. v. a. and n., act., *crowd around, surround.*

circumsono, no perf., no sup., **-āre,** [circum-sono], 1. v. a. and n., act., *cause to echo, make echo, fill with sound.*

circumspiciŏ, -exī, -ectum, -icere, [circum-specio], 3. v. n. and a. Neut. absolutely, *look about, look around.* — Act., *look around at :* agmina ; — *look around, survey, espy, descry :* saxum.

circumstŏ, -stetī, no sup., **-stāre,** [circum-sto], 1. v. n. and a. Neut., *stand around, be about, crowd around.* — Fig.: odia. — Act., *surround.* — Fig., *surround, encompass, beset :* horror.

circumtextus, -a, -um, p.p. of **circumtexo,** *woven round.*

circumvectŏ, no perf., no sup., **-āre,** [circum-vecto], 1. v. a., *carry around.* — Pass. as deponent (cf. **vehor**), *ride around.* — Fig., *go over* (in discourse) : singula.

circumveniŏ, -vēnī, -ventum, -venīre, [circum-venio], 4. v. a., *encompass, encircle, surround :* Cocytus. (Others read **circumfluit**).

circumvolitŏ, -āvī, -ātum, -are, [circum-volito], 1 v. n., *fly about, flit around :* lacūs hirundo.

circumvolŏ, -āvī, -ātum, -āre, [circum-volo], 1. v. a., *fly around :* praedam. — Fig., *hover around, hover over :* nox.

circumvolvŏ, perhaps no perf., **-volūtum, -volvere,** [circumvolvo], 3. v. a., *roll or turn round :* sol circumvolvitur annum (*revolves around the circle of the year*).

circus, -ī, [cf. Gr. κίρκος, prob. for

†cicrus], m., *a circle.* — From similarity, *a circus, race-course.* — Poetic, of a body of men gathered for sports, *the conclave.*
Cissēis, -ĭdos, [Gr. patronymic], f., *daughter of Cisseus* (Hecuba).
Cisseus, eī, [Gr. Κισσεύς], m., (*ivy-crowned*): 1. A king of Thrace, father of Hecuba; 2. A Latin warrior.
citātus, -a, -um, p.p. of **cito.**
Cithaerōn, -ōnis, [Gr. Κιθαιρων], a mountain in Bœotia, a favorite haunt of Bacchus.
cithara, -ae, [Gr. κιθάρα], f., *a lyre, a cithara.*
citō [abl. of **citus**], adv., *quickly:* **citius dicto** (*quicker than a word*).
cĭtŏ, -āvī, -ātum, -are, [†citŏ-], 1. v. intens., *arouse, excite.* — **citātus, -a, -um,** p.p. as adj., *hurried, swift, quick:* **equi** (*at full speed, in full career*).
citus, -a, -um, p.p. of **cieo.**
civĭcus, -a, -um, [†civi- + cus], adj., *of a citizen, pertaining to a citizen* (more literal than **cīvīlis**): **quercus** (*the civic garland,* made of oak leaves, and given to any soldier who saved the life of a fellow-citizen in war).
cīvīlis, -e, [lengthened stem from †civi + lis, cf. **Aprilis**], adj., (cf. **cīvĭcus,** which is less general), *of a citizen, citizens,* or *the citizens, civil, civic:* **quercus** (the garland of oak leaves bestowed on a soldier who saved a fellow-citizen in war, cf. **corona civica,** the usual phrase).
cīvis, -is, [√ci (in **quies,** cf. κεῖμαι) + **vis** (weakened from **-vus**)], comm., *a citizen, a fellow-citizen, fellow-countryman* (*-woman*).
clādēs, -is, [?], f., *disaster, mischief, loss, calamity.* — Esp. in war, *defeat, disaster, havoc.* (N.B. Avoid *slaughter.*) — Poetic, of persons, *scourge, destroyer.*
clam [unc. form (but see **palam,** acc. f.?), akin to **celo**], adv. and prep., *secretly, in secret, by surprise* (= *unawares*).
clāmō, -āvī, -ātum, -āre, [†clāmŏ- (√clā + mus, cf. **nomenclātor**)], 1. v. a. and n. Neut., *cry out, shout, cry, clamor, exclaim.* — With acc., *call, invoke* (with loud cry): **Hylan.** — With direct or indirect discourse, *shout, cry, exclaim:* **se causam.**
clāmor, -ōris, [†clām (as if root of **clāmō**) + or], m., *a loud cry, shriek, outcry, yell, shout, battle-cry, clamor.* — Poetic, of animals and things, *noise, din, roar, hum, bellowing:* **saxa dedere.**
clangor, -ōris, [√clang (root of **clango**) + or], m., *a sound, clang, clangor, blare, noise:* **tubarum.**
Clanius, -ī (-iī); Glanis, -is, [?], m., a river of Campania, frequently overflowing the country around, where was the town of Acerræ (now *il Lagno*).
clārēscō, -uī, no sup., **-ēscere,** [†clare + sco, cf. **clāreo, clarus**], 3. v. n., *grow loud, grow bright:* **sonitūs armorum** (*increase*).
Clarius, -a, -um, [†Clarŏ- (cf. Gr. Κλάρος) + ius], adj., *of Claros* (a town of Ionia, celebrated for a temple and oracle of Apollo), *Clarian.* —Masc., *the Clarian god* (Apollo).
clarus, -a, -um, [√clā (cf. **nomenclātor**) + rus], adj., *loud, clear, distinct.* — From similarity, *distinct, bright, brilliant, clear:* **lux; Olympo; Aquilo** (*clear, bringing clear weather*). — Fig., *clear, distinct, manifest, evident, plain:* **signum.**—Also, *renowned, famous, glorious, celebrated:* **Mycenae.**
Clārus, -ī, m., a Trojan.
classĭcum, -ī, [†classi- + cum (n. of -cus)], n., (*belonging to the army,* see **classis**), *a signal for battle* given with the trumpet. — Less exactly, *a trumpet.*
classis, -is, [√clā (cf. **clāmo**) + tis (cf. κλῆσις)], f., *a summoning,*

a levy), *the levy, the army, forces, an army, a force.* — Esp., of sea-forces, *a fleet*.
Claudius, -a, -um, [†claudŏ- (stem of **claudus** reduced) + ius], adj., *of Claudus* (*the Lame*). — Masc., **Claudius,** a Roman gentile name. — **Claudia gens,** the gens or clan of that name to which the Marcelli and other great Romans belonged.
claudŏ, -sī, -sum, -dere, [akin to **clavis**], 3. v. a., *shut, close:* lumina. — Less exactly, *stop, stay, block up:* claudite iam rivos (*shut the gates* of irrigating canals). — Of the things enclosed, *shut up, confine, hem in, enclose, house, pen up, surround, encompass, beset, besiege, shu*t *off, cut off:* agnos; claudunt convallibus umbrae; maris nos obice pontus. — **clausus, -a, -um,** p.p. as adj., *enclosed, confined, close shut, pen*t *up:* lacus; carcer. — Neut., *an enclosure.*
claudus, -a, -um, [?], adj., *limping, halting, lame, crippled* (of a wounded snake).
claustrum, -ī, [√claud (as if root of **claudo**) + trum], n., *fastening, lock, bol*t, *bar.* — Less exactly, of anything that serves the same purpose, *door, gate, barrier:* Lucrino addita (*dykes, levees*); Pelori (of the sides of a strait).
clausum, see **claudo.**
Clausus, -ī, [prob. akin to **Claudius**], m., a Sabine, the supposed founder of the house of Claudius.
clausus, -a, -um, p.p. of **claudo.**
clava, -ae, [?], f., *a stick, a staff, cudgel, club.*
clāvus, -ī, [akin to **clavis, claudo**], m., *a nail, a peg.* — From similarity, *a tiller.* — Less exactly, *a rudder, helm.*
cliēns, -entis, [p. of **cluo,** *hear, obey*], comm., *a dependan*t, *a clien*t.
Clīō, -ūs, [Gr. Κλείω], f.: 1. The muse of history; 2. A daughter of Oceanus.

clipeātus, -a, -um, see **clipeo.**
clipeō (clup-), no perf., **-ātum, -are,** [†clipeŏ], 1. v.'a., *arm with a shield.* — **clipeātus, -a, -um,** p.p. as adj., *armed with shield:* agmina.
clipeus, m., (-um, n.), -ī, [?], *a shield* (round, of the Greek pattern).
Clitius (Cly-), -ī (-iī), [akin to **inclutus**], m., a Trojan hero, perhaps more than one of the same name, cf. **Clytius.**
Clītumnus, -ī, m., a river of Umbria.
clīvosus, -a, -um, [†clivŏ- (reduced) + osus], adj., *hilly.* — Fig., *steep, difficult.*
clīvus, -ī, [√clī (as root of **clīno**) + vus], m., *a slope, a hill, an incline.*
Cloanthus, -ī, [Gr. akin to **Cluentius**], m., a Trojan leader.
Cloelia, -ae, [f. of **Cluilius,** prob. for †Clovilius, and akin to **clueo**], f., a Roman maiden who escaped from Porsenna, and swam the Tiber.
Clonius, -ī (-iī), [?], a Trojan, perhaps several of the same name.
Clonus, -ī, [?], m., a sculptor or engraver.
Clōthō (nom. and acc.), [Gr. Κλωθώ (*the spinner* or *spinster*)], one of the three Parcæ, or Fates, see **Parcae.**
cluēns, -entis, see **cliens.**
Cluentius, -a, -um, [†cluent-(stem of **cliens**) + ius], a Roman gentile name, used collectively for the clan.
clupeus, see **clipeus.**
Clūsīnus, -a, -um, [†Clusiŏ- (reduced) + īnus], adj., *of Clusium.*
Clūsium, -ī (-iī), [?, perhaps akin to **claudo**], n., an Etrurian town, formerly called *Camers.*
Clymenē, -ēs, [Gr. Κλυμένη], f., a daughter of Oceanus.
clypeus, etc.; see **clipeus.**
Clytius, -ī (-iī), [prob. akin to **cluo**], m., a name of several warriors, cf. **Clitius.**
coāctus, -a, -um, p.p. of **cogo.**

Cocles, -ĭtis, [cocles, *one-eyed*], m., the surname of Q. Horatius, who, in the war with Porsenna, alone defended the bridge across the Tiber.

coctus, -a, -um, p.p. of **coquo.**

Cōcȳtĭus, -a, -um, [†Cocyto- [reduced) + ius], adj., *of Cocytus, infernal:* virgo (*Alecto*, one of the Furies).

Cōcȳtus, -i, [Gr. Κωκυτός, *river of lamentation*], m., a fabled river of the world below.

Codrus, -ī, [Gr. Κόδρος], m., a shepherd, perhaps representing under a disguised name some contemporary poet, an enemy of Virgil.

coelum and kindred words, see **caelum,** etc.

coenum, see **caenum.**

coeō, -īvī, -ĭtum, -īre, [con-eo], irr. v. n., *come together, unite, assemble, meet, gather.* — With implied intent, either hostile or friendly (cf. **congredior**), *join, join in alliance, unite, meet, encounter, join battle:* in foedera dextrae(*be joined in*); gener atque socer (*be united*). — Fig., *curdle, congeal* (cf. **cogo**): sanguis formidine.

coepĭŏ, -ī, -tum, -ere and -isse, (rare except in perf., &c.), [co-apio, cf. **apiscor**], v. act., (*take hold*), *begin, begin to speak.* — Pass., only in p.p. and compound tenses, usual with pass. infin. — **coeptus,** -a, -um, p.p. as adj., n., *an undertaking, attempt.*

coeptus, -a, -um, p.p. of **coepio.**

coerceō, -uī, -ĭtum, -ēre, [con-arceo], 2. v. a., *shut in together, surround, restrain, confine, hold in check, restrain.* — Of troops: postrema Tyrrhidae iuvenes (*bring up the rear*, cf. cogere agmen).

coerulus, etc., see **caeruleus.**

coetus (coi-), -ūs, [con-itus, cf. **coeo**], m., *an assembling.* — Concretely, *an assemblage, an assembly, a crowd, throng, company* (at a feast), *flock* (of birds).

Coeus, -ī, [Gr. Κοῖος], m., a Titan, the father of Latona.

cōgĭtō, -āvī, -ātum, -āre, [con-agito], 1. v. a., *weigh thoroughly in the mind, weigh, reflect upon, think* (cf. **agito**). — Esp. of purpose, *have in mind, intend, meditate upon, think upon, design, plan, purpose:* quid Auster?

cognātus,-a,-um,[con-(g)natus], adj., *akin, kindred, related* (by blood). — Poetic: urbes (*whose citizens are akin*).

cognĭtus, -a, -um, p.p. of **cognosco.**

cognōmen, -ĭnis,[con-(g)nomen], n., *family-name.* — Less exactly, *name.*

cognōmĭnis, -e, [con-†(g)nomen, infl. as adj.], adj., *of like name:* terra (*bearing one's name*).

cognōscō,-gnōvī,-gnĭtum,-gnōscere, [con-(g)nosco], 3. v. a., *examine, learn, inquire into, trace out, listen to, hear, find* (*learn to know*, with two accs.): haec cognoscite; carmina; casūs. — In perf., &c., *have learned, know.* — Less exactly, *recognize, understand:* matrem; quae sit virtus. — **cognĭtus,** -a, -um, p.p. as adj., *well-known.*

cōgō, coēgī, coāctum, cōgere, [con-ago], 3. v. a., *drive together, collect, gather* (of fruits, &c.), *assemble* (of men, forces, &c.): pecus; agmina (*keep in line*, of the rear guard, or officers). — Of consistency, *condense, congeal:* aer in nubem coactus; mella.— Fig., *force, compel, oblige* (with acc. and infin.): quid (cog. acc.) non mortalia pectora cogis? — **coāctus,** -a, -um, p.p. as adj., *forced:* lacrimae.

cohĭbeō, -uī, -ĭtum, -ēre, [con-habeo], 2. v. a., *hold together, contain, confine:* spelunca Scyllam. — Fig., *restrain, check, repress:* iras.

cohors, -ortis, [?], f., *an enclosure.* — Fig., *a company* (of soldiery),

troop, squadron. — Less exactly, of other things, *band, multitude, crowd:* cuncta cohors (*line*, of ships).
coitus, see coetus.
collapsus, see conlapsus.
Collātīnus, -a, -um, [Collatia (reduced) + īnus], adj., *of Collatia* (a Sabine town): arces.
collātus, see conlatus.
collectus, see conlectus, p.p. of conligo.
colligŏ, see conligo.
collis, -is, [?], m., *a hill*.
collocŏ, see conloco.
colloquium, see conloquium.
collūceŏ, see conluceo.
collūdŏ, see conludo.
collum, -i, [?], n., *the neck*. — Poetic, of a poppy, *neck*.
collustrŏ, see conlustro.
colŏ, coluī, cultum, colere, [? √col], 3. v. a. and n., *cultivate, till, tend, take care of*. — Less exactly, *inhabit, dwell in:* Pallas arces. — Fig., *cherish, care for, regard, attend to, love, foster:* telorum amorem; reliquias meorum; vitam (*lead*); morem (*observe*). — Esp. of pious regard, *worship, revere, honor:* templum. —cultus, -a, -um, p.p. as adj., *cultivated*, tilled, *well kept*.
colocāsia, -ae, (-ium, -ī (-iī), n.), [Gr. κολοκασία or κολοκάσιον], f., a plant of the lily kind.
colōnus, -ī, [unc. stem fr. √col + nus, cf. patronus], m., *a farmer, husbandman:* veteres (*former tillers*). — From the nature of ancient colonies, *a colonist*. — Less exactly, *an inhabitant* (cf. colo).
color, -ōris, [unc. root + ōr (os)], m., *color, a color, complexion, hue*. — Esp., *fair complexion, beauty*.
colōrātus, -a, -um, p.p. of colōro.
colōrŏ, -āvī, -ātum, -are,[†color-], 1. v. a., *color, dye*. — coloratus, -a, -um, as adj., *colored*. — Esp. as opposed to light or fair, *dusky, swarthy:* Indi.

coluber, -ubrī, [?], m., *a serpent, snake*.
cōlum, -ī, [?], n., *a strainer, colander*.
columba, -ae, [? f. of columbus], f., *a dove, pigeon*.
columna, -ae, [unc. root + mna, cf. autumnus], f., *a pillar, a support, a column*.
colurnus, -a, -um, [unc.stem (akin to corulus) + nus, possibly corrupted from corulnus], adj., *of hazel* (cf. corulus), *hazel:* hastilia.
colus, -ī (ūs), [?], f., *a distaff*.
coma, -ae, [cf. Gr. κόμη], f., *the hair* (of the head), *the mane* (of animals). — From similarity, *leaves, foliage*, and even *flowers* (cf. comans). — Also plur. in all senses.
comāns, -āntis, [p. of †como, -āre, from coma], p. as adj., *hairy, shaggy, leafy* (cf. coma), *flowering:* dictamnus flore purpureo; galea (*crested*).
comes, -itis, [verb-stem (cf. commeo) + tis (reduced)], comm., *a companion, associate, follower* (as subordinate): senioris Acestae; docta comes (*guide*, of the Sibyl); comes Ascanio (*attendant, guardian*).
comētēs, -ae, [Gr. κομήτης, cf. coma], m., *a comet, shooting-star*.
cōminus, see comminus.
comitātus, -a, -um, p.p. of comito and comitor.
comitātus, -ūs, [†comitā + tus], m., (*an accompanying*), *an escort, a company, a retinue*.
comitŏ, -āvī, -ātum, -āre,[comes, cf. comitor], 1. v. a., *accompany, follow, attend*. — comitātus, -a, -um, p.p. as adj., *accompanied, attended*.
comitor, -ātus, -ārī, [pass. of comito], 1. v. dep., *accompany, follow, escort, attend*. — Esp. of funerals, *escort, attend*. — p.p., *accompanying:* filius classe catervas.
commaculŏ, -āvī, -ātum, -āre,

[con-maculo], 1. v. a., *stain, pollute, imbrue:* manus sanguine.

commemoro, -avī, -ātum, -āre, [con-memoro], 1. v. a., *recall to mind* (of one's self). — In reference to another, *remind, mention, recount, relate* (in song), *proclaim, celebrate.*

commendō, -āvī, -ātum, -āre, [con-mando], 1. v. a., *commit, entrust.* — Less exactly, *commend, recommend.*

commercium, -ī (-iī), [con-†merc (stem of merx)+ium, (n. of ius), cf. commercor], n., *traffic.* — Poetic: ista commercia belli (*such bargains of war*, ransom of prisoners).

comminus (cō-), [con-manus, petrified as adv., cf. eminus], adv., *in close combat, hand to hand* (opposed to a contest with missile weapons). — Less exactly, without actual contest, *close by, standing by, at close range:* cervos obtruncant ferro. — Poetic: arva insequitur (*hotly engages*).

commisceō, -miscuī, -mixtum or -mistum, -miscēre, [con-misceo], 2. v. a., *mix together, intermingle:* frusta mero cruento.

commissum, -ī, [n. p.p. of committo as noun], n., *offence, fault, crime.*

commissus, -a, -um, p.p. of committo; see also commissum.

commistus, -a, -um, p.p. of commisceo.

committō, -mīsī, -missum, -mittere, [con-mitto], 3. v. a., (*let go together*), *combine, join, unite:* delphinum caudas utero delphinum. — Esp. of hostility, *join* (battle), *begin* (the fight, cf. conserere): manum; proelium; funera pugnae (*begin the havoc of battle*). — With idea of a trust, *entrust, commit to, trust, consign:* sulcis semina. — Transferred, *allow to happen, allow one's self to do, allow, commit, practise, perpetrate, commit an offence.*

commixtus, -a, -um, p.p. of commisceo.

commodus, -a, -um, [con-modus], adj., (*agreeing with the measure*). — Fig., *fitting, fit, suitable, proper, favorable, adapted:* Baccho (suited to the vine).

commōtus, -a, -um, p.p. of commoveo.

commoveo, -mōvī, -mōtum, -movēre, [con-moveo], 2. v. a., *move violently, agitate:* alas; commotis sacris (*brandishing the sacred thyrsus*). — Less exactly, *stir up, rouse:* cervum. — Fig., *rouse, stir, excite, disturb, agitate, alarm, enrage, move* (with any emotion).

commūnis (old form cōmoenis), -e, [con-†munis, cf. immunis and munia], adj., (*serving together*), *belonging to two or more together, common:* periclum (*shared alike by both*); Erinys (*of both sides*); bona (*the public interests*).

cōmō, cōmpsī, cōmptum, cōmere, [? con-emo, *take*], 3. v. a., (*?gather together*), *comb, arrange, braid.* — Less exactly, *deck, adorn, array:* vitta ramos. — comptus, -a, -um, p.p. as adj.: comae (*plaited*); felici comptus olivā (*wreathed*).

compactus, -a, -um, p.p. of compingo.

compāgēs, -is (gen. plur. compagum), [com; pa(n)g-o], f., *a joining together, a connection, joint, structure.*

1. compellō, -pulī, -pulsum, -pellere, [con-pello], 3. v. a., *drive together* or *in a body:* greges in unum. — With weaker meaning of prep., *drive, force:* gregem hibisco; noto eodem compulsus.

2. compellō, -āvī, -ātum, -āre, [prob. from lost noun-stem akin to pello, cf. adpello], 1. v. a., *accost, address:* aliquem voce.

compescō, -scuī, -scitum (?), -scere, [unc. verb with con], *restrain, curb, check:* ramos fluentes (by pruning).

Vocabulary.

compingŏ, -pegi, -pactum, -pingere, [con-pango], 3. v. a., *join together, fasten together, fasten.* — **compactus, -a, -um,** p.p. as adj., *joined, fitted:* trabes (*jointed*).

compĭtum, -ī, [com-†pitum (√pet + um)], n., *meeting of roads, cross roads, corners.*

complector, -plexus, -plectī, [con-plecto], 3. v. dep., *clasp around, encircle, enfold, embrace; hold, grasp:* corpus; terra gremio ossa; Cacum complexus in nodum. — Less exactly, *surround, embrace:* Penates umbra (of a tree). — Fig., *seize, come upon, enfold:* sopor artus.

compleō, -ēvī, -ētum, -ēre, [con-pleo], 2. v. a., *fill up, fill full, fill:* loca milites; naves (*man*); litora (*crowd, throng*). — Less exactly, *fill, complete:* tempora debita; orbis completur.

1. **complexus, -a, -um,** p.p. of **complector.**
2. **complexus, -us,** [con-plexus], m., *a surrounding, encompassing, encircling, embracing, embrace* (esp. of love).

compōnŏ, -posuī, -positum, -pōnere, [com-pono], 3. v. a., *put together, bring together, lay up, collect:* opes (*hoard*); aggerem tumuli (*raise*). — With idea of union or arrangement, *found, build, dispose, array, set in order, arrange, settle, adjust:* compositi in turmas (of soldiers, *arrayed in squadrons*); urbem; genus indocile ac dispersum (*settle in law and order*); foedus; lites (*settle by deciding*): pacem. — With idea of rest, *dispose, lay, place:* defessa membra (*lay down to rest*); thalamis se composuere (of bees, *become quiet in their cells*); se (*recline*); diem (*close*); fluctus (*calm*); placida pace compōstus (*settled in peaceful repose*, by some thought to refer to death); curas. — Of putting together for comparison, *compare:* parvis magna.

— **compositus (pōstus), -a, -um,** p.p. as adj., *fixed, orderly, regular, quiet:* gradus; leges. Neut. abl. as adv., **composito,** *by arrangement, in concert.*

compositus (compōstus), -a, -um, p.p. of **compono.**

comprehendō (-prendō), -ndī, -nsum, -ndere, [com-prehendo], 3. v. a., *take hold of, grasp:* imago. — Less exactly, *seize, apprehend.* — Esp. of fire or of thing fired, *catch.* — Fig., *embrace, comprise, enumerate, include:* formas scelerum.

comprensus, -a, -um, see **comprehendo.**

compressus, -a, -um, p.p. of **comprimo.**

comprimō, -pressī, -pressum, -primere, [con-premo], 3. v. a., *press together.* — With idea of restraint, *hold in, hold back, hold, restrain, repress, check:* gressum. — Fig., *curb, check, repress, stay:* amor compressus edendi; furores caeli marisque; impetus.

cōmptus, -a, -um, p.p. of **cōmo.**

compulsus, -a, -um, p.p. of **compello.**

1. **cōnātus, -a, -um,** p.p. of **conor.**
2. **cōnātus, -us,** [†cōnā- (stem of conor) + tus], m., *an attempt, effort, exertion.*

concavus, -a, -um, [con-cavus], adj., *hollow, concave, arched, vaulted, bent, curved:* saxa (of caves).

concēdō, -cessī, -cessum, -cēdere, [con-cedo], 3. v. n. and a., *move away* (cf. cedo and adcedo), *retire, withdraw, come* or *go off:* huc; concedite, silvae (*farewell*). — Fig., *depart, cease:* superis ab oris (by death); irae deûm. — Of superiority, *give way, yield, give place, yield the palm.* — So also (act.) of withdrawing opposition, *give up, grant, allow, permit:* in iras Calydona (*sacrifice*); concessa moveri (*allowed*). — **concessus, -a, -um,** p.p. as adj., *permitted, permissible,*

lawful: concessa veto (*things not forbid*).
concentus, -us, [con-cantus], m., *harmony, harmonious songs, tuneful melody.*
conceptus, -a, -um, p.p. of **concipio.**
concessus, -a, -um, p.p. of **concedo.**
concha, -ae, [Gr. κόγχη], f., *a shell, conch shell.* — Also as an instrument, *shell, conch, horn.*
concĭdō, -cĭdī, no sup., **-cĭdere,** [con-cado], 3. v. n., *fall* (in a heap), *fall to the ground.* — Esp., of death or fainting, *fall, sink.* — Less exactly and fig., *fall, be ruined, perish.*
concīdō, -cīdī, -cīsum, -cīdere, [con-caedo], 3. v. a., *cut up, cut to pieces, cut down:* scrobibus montes (*furrow*).
conciĕō, -īvī, -ĭtum, -iēre, [concieo], 2. (also 4.) v. a., (*move together*), *assemble.* — With intensive meaning of **con,** *shake, agitate, move violently, urge on:* concita tormento saxa (*hurled violently*). — Fig., *rouse, excite, agitate, stir up, provoke:* immani concitus ira (*fired with mighty wrath*). — **concitus, -a, -um,** p.p. as adj. (cf. **citus**), *in headlong motion, headlong, violent, careering:* multa vi (*with mighty effort*); processu (*with headlong rush*).
concĭliō, -āvī, -ātum, -āre, [†conciliō-], 1. v. a., (*assemble*), *unite, join.* — Fig., *gain over, win, conciliate, gain, secure, obtain:* sceptra Iovemque (*secure the sceptre and Jove's favor*); sibi arma (*ally*).
concilium, -ī (-iī), [perhaps con-, stem fr. √cal (cf. **classis**)], n., *an assembly* (generally, cf. **consilium,** *a deliberative body*), *gathering:* piorum. — Also in sense of **consilium,** *a council:* silentum (as a jury).
concĭpĭō, -cēpī, -ceptum, -cĭpere, [con-capio], 3. v. a. and n., *take in, take, receive:* **pabula terrae** (*draw nutriment*). — Esp. of females, *conceive.* — With abstract objects, *receive, admit, harbor, take on, give way to:* ducis curam (*enter on*); furias (*be possessed by*); pectore robur (*possess*). — Of ideas in words, *comprise, express, formulate.* — Of the mind as subject, *take in, conceive, imagine:* mente furores. — **conceptus, -a, -um,** p.p. as adj. in either meaning of the verb: foedus (*drawn up, established*).
concĭtō, -āvī, -ātum, -āre, [†concitŏ- (cf. **concitus**), or perhaps con-cito], 1. v. a., *set in motion, rouse, excite, incite:* equum (*spur on*); Allecto se in Teucros (*fly fiercely at*).
1. **concĭtus, -a, -um,** p.p. of **concio.**
2. **concītus, -a, -um,** p.p. of **concieo.**
conclāmō, -āvī, -ātum, -āre, [conclamo], 1. v. a., *cry aloud, shout, cry aloud upon, call for aloud, summon with a shout.* — With direct or indirect discourse: Italiam (*cries out, Italy!*).
conclūdō, -sī, -sum, -dere, [conclaudo], 3. v. a., *shut up, enclose.* — Less exactly, *surround, include:* locum sulco (*mark out*).
concolor, -ōris, [con-†color, declined as adj.], adj., *of the same color.*
concors, -rdis, [con-†cord-, declined as adj.], adj., *united in feeling, friendly, harmonious:* frena (*peaceful*).
concrēdō, -dĭdī, -dĭtum, -dere, [con-credo], 3. v. a., *entrust, consign, commit.*
concrēscō, -crēvī, -crētum, -crēscere, [con-cresco], 3. v. n., (*grow together*), *harden, curdle, congeal, condense, freeze.* — As growing into something else, *grow into, become attached.* — **concrētus, -a, -um,** p.p. in passive force (cf. **cretus**) as adj., *condensed, hardened, congealed, curdled, clotted:* crines sanguine (*matted*).

concrētus, -ūs, [con-cretus], m., *a growing together, an adhering* (a doubtful reading).

concubitus, -ūs, [con-cubitus], m., *a lying together, coition.*

concurrō, -currī (-cucurrī), -cursum, -currere, [con-curro], 3. v. n., *run with* or *together, flock together, assemble.* — Less exactly, *rush* (to a place), *rally, hasten* (to one). — Of hostile meeting, *meet, fight, contend:* viris virgo ; montes (*dash together*)

concursus, -ūs, [con-cursus], m., *a rushing together.* — Concretely, *a crowd, an assembly, a concourse.*

concussus, -a, -um, p.p. of **concutio.**

concutiō, -cussī, -cussum, -cutere, [con-quatio], 3. v. a., *shake violently, agitate, thrust* (cf. **excutio**), *force, throw, dash:* frena; lora ; silicem dexter in adversum nitens. — Of shaking out the loose garments of the ancients, *shake out* (for examination), *search:* fecundum pectus. — Fig., of emotion, &c., *agitate, alarm, trouble:* casu acerbo (*overwhelmed*); urbs (*panic-stricken*); animum concussus. — Also, *excite, rouse, urge:* equos (*spur on*).

condēnsus, -a, -um, [con-densus], adj., *very dense, close, crowded:* columbae condensae ... sedebant.

condiciō (not **-tio**), **-ōnis,** [condicio], f., (*statement of terms*), *a stipulation, condition, terms, a compact.* — mortis (*destiny,* law of human life).

conditiō, see **condicio,** the proper form.

conditor, -ōris, [con-dator, as if condi + tor, cf. **condo**], m., *builder, founder.*

conditus, -a, -um, p.p. of **condo.**

condō, -didī, -ditum, -dere, [condo, *put*], 3. v. a., (*put together*). — With reference to the result, *build, found, make, erect:* arces. — Fig., in same sense, *found, es-* *tablish, settle:* Romanam gentem; aurea secula (*bring in*); fata (*ordain*). — So also of composition, *write, compose, describe, celebrate:* tristia bella. — With idea of preservation, *put up* (cf. **condio**), *store, lay away, hoard:* opes; signa mente (*treasure up*). — So also of concealment, *hide, secrete, conceal, suppress, withdraw* (one's self): caput inter nubila ; conditur in tenebras altum caligine caelum ; in mare Ufens (*be lost*); Nilus se alveo (*confine itself*); lumina (*close*); optato Thybridis alveo (by others referred to the first meaning). — Esp. of the dead, *bury, lay to rest:* ossa terra ; animam sepulchro; longos soles cantando (*sing the sun to rest*). — Of stars, *set:* Orion.

condūcō, -dūxī, -dūctum, -ducere, [con-duco], 3. v. a. and n., *lead together, assemble, collect, hire.* — **condūctus, -a, -um,** p.p. as adj., *rented, hired.*

condūctus, -a, -um, p.p. of **conduco.**

cōnectō (conn-), **-xuī, -xum, -ctere,** [con-necto], 3. v. a., *bind together, fasten, connect, entwine.*

cōnexus, -a, -um, p.p. of **conecto.**

cōnfectus, -a, -um, p.p. of **conficio.**

cōnferciō, -fersī, -fertum, -fercīre, [con-farcio], 4. v. a., *crowd together.* — **confertus, -a, -um,** p.p. as adj., *close, dense, serried, in close array, close packed.*

cōnferō, -tulī, -lātum (coll-), **-ferre,** [con-fero], *bring together, bear together:* gradum (*step together*). — Esp. of hostility, *join, engage:* manum (*join hand to hand*); certamina belli (*engage in strife of battle*); se viro vir.

cōnfertus, -a, -um, p.p. of **confercio.**

cōnfessus, -a, -um, p.p. of **confiteor.**

cōnfestim [con-†festim, √fed (in fendo) + tis, cf. **manifestus**], adv., (*on the stroke* (?), *in the grasp*, cf. Fr. *maintenant*), *instantly, forthwith, at once*.

cōnfĭcĭŏ, -fēcī, -fectum, -fĭcere, (also cōnfĭĕrī as pass.), [con-facio], 3. v. a., (*do up*), *finish, complete, accomplish:* immensum aequor.—In special sense (cf. Eng. *done up*), *exhaust, waste, use up, destroy:* me volnus (*exhausts my life*).—Less exactly, *bring to pass, cause.*—cōnfectus, -a, -um, p.p. as adj., *wasted, worn out, exhausted, emaciated:* macie ; curis ; aetate (*burdened with years*).

cōnfīdēns, -entis, p. of confido.

confīdō, -fīsus, -dere, [con-fido], 3. v. a. and n., *trust in, rely on, trust to, trust:* rebus ; huic monstro. — cōnfīdēns, -entis, p. as adj., *bold, undaunted, confident, shameless, unblushing.*

cōnfīgō, -fīxī, -fīxum, -fīgere, 3. v. a., *pierce through, transfix, strike down* (with a missile weapon).— cōnfīxus, -a, -um, p.p. as adj., *transfixed, struck down.*

cōnfīō, -fĭĕrī, pass. of confĭcĭo.

cōnfīsus, -a, -um, p.p. of confido.

cōnfĭteor, -fessus sum, -fĭtērī, [con-fateor], 2. v. dep., *fully or entirely acknowledge* (cf. Eng. *own up*), *confess, own, avow.* — Less exactly, *disclose a thing, reveal, manifest, show:* confessa deam (*revealed a goddess*, confessing herself).

cōnfīxus, -a, -um, p.p. of cōnfīgo.

cōnflīgō, -flīxī, -flīctum, -flīgere, [con-fligo], 3. v. a. and n. Act., *strike against* or *on, strike* or *bring together.* — Neut., *dash against* (each other), *be in conflict, contend, fight, combat:* venti (*war with each other*).

cōnflō, -āvī, -ātum, -āre, [con-flo], 1. v. a. Of fire, *blow together, blow up, stir up, kindle.* — From the use of the bellows in the forge, also of metals, &c., *smelt, fuse, melt down:* falces in ensem.

cōnflŭŏ, -fluxī, no sup., -flŭere, [con-fluo], 3. v. n. Of fluids, *flow* or *run together.* — Less exactly, of a great multitude, *flow, flock*, or *crowd together; come together in multitudes.*

cōnfŏdĭŏ, -fōdī, -fossum, -fŏdere, [con-fodio], 3. v. a., *dig thoroughly, pierce through, transfix:* super exanimem sese proiecit amicum confossus.

confossus, -a, -um, p.p. of confodio.

confŭgĭō, -fūgī, no sup., -fŭgere, [con-fugio], 3. v. n., *flee for refuge* or *succor, take refuge* (with any one).

cōnfundŏ, -fūdī, -fūsum, -fundere, [con-fundo], 3. v. a. Of liquids, *pour together.* — Less exactly, with reflexive or in pass., *mix itself, mix, mingle, blend.* — Fig., *confound, confuse, disturb, throw into disorder, disconcert:* foedus (*destroy*). — cōnfūsus, -a, -um, p.p. as adj., *confounded, perplexed, panic-stricken:* urbs ; animus.

cōnfūsus, -a, -um, p.p. of confundo.

congĕmĭnō, -āvī, -ātum, -āre, [con-gemino], 1. v. a. and n., *double, redouble, repeat again and again:* crebros ensibus ictus congeminant. — Poetically, of the instrument, *ply repeatedly:* securim.

congĕmō, -gĕmŭī, no sup., -gĕmĕre, [con-gemo], 3. v. n. and a., *sigh* or *groan deeply, heave a deep sigh.* — Fig., of a tree: congemuit supremum (*groaned its last*).

congĕrō, -gessī, -gestum, -gĕrere, [con-gero], 3. v. a., *bear, bring*, or *carry together; heap up* (cf. adgero and agger), *gather.* — With reference to the result, *build, construct, erect:* manu oppida ; aram. — Poetically, of birds, *build nests, nest.* — Less exactly, in pass., *be full, swarm, teem:* cubilia blattis. — congestus, -a, -um, p.p. as adj., *gathered, heaped:* turea dona ; culmen (*sodded*).

congestus, -a, -um, p.p. of **congero.**

congredior,-gressus, -gredī, [con-gradior], 3. v. dep., (*step together*), *go, come,* or *meet together* or *with one.* — Esp., in a hostile sense, *fight, contend, engage.*

congressus, -a, -um, p.p. of **congredior.**

congressus, -ūs, [con-gressus], m., *a meeting* (either friendly or hostile), *encounter, interview.*

cōnicio (conii-), -iēcī, -iectum, -icere, [con-iacio], 3. v. a., *throw together* or *at, hurl, cast, fling, shoot:* **coniecta sagitta ; coniecta cuspide ; saxa ; velamina.** — With reflexive, *throw one's self, rush, speed, hasten:* **sese in latebras** (*plunge*); **Iris inter medias sese** (*dashes*). — Less exactly, of direction merely, *cast, turn:* **oculos.**

cōniectus, -a, -um, p.p. of **conicio.**

cōnifer, -era, -erum, [†cono-fer (√fer + us)], adj., *cone-bearing, coniferous.*

cōnīsus, -a, -um, p.p. of **conitor.**

cōnitor (conn-), -nīsus and **-nīxus, -nītī,** [con-nitor], 3. v. dep., *lean against, strain, struggle, put forth an effort, strive:* **conixus** (*with mighty effort*). — Esp. of labor (cf. **enitor**), *be in labor, yean, bring forth young.*

cōniugium, -ī (-iī), [†coniug-+ ium, as if con-†iugium], n., *a joining, union.* — Esp. (perhaps originally, cf. **coniunx**), *marriage:* **Veneris** (*union with*). — Less exactly, of animals, *coition.* — Concretely (cf. **amor,** *beloved object*), *husband, wife.*

coniunctus, -a, -um, p.p. of **coniungo.**

coniungō, -iunxī, -iunctum, -iungere, [con-iungo], 3. v. a., *join together, unite, attach, ally.* — Esp. in marriage, *unite:* **digno coniuncta viro ; ratis coniuncta crepidine saxi** (*moored*).

cōniunx (-iux), -iugis, [con-√iug, as stem], comm., (*uniting together*), *a husband, a wife, a consort.* — Less exactly, *a betrothed.*

coniūrātus, -a, -um, p.p. of **coniuro.**

coniūrŏ, -āvī, -ātum, -āre, [coniuro], 1. v. n. and a., *swear together, conspire.* — **coniūrātus, -a, -um,** p.p. in act. sense, *having sworn, banded together, conspiring:* **rescindere caelum.**

conixus, -a, -um, p.p. of **conitor.**

conlābor (coll-), -lapsus, -lābī, [con-lābor], 3. v. dep., *fall together, fall in ruins, collapse, fall.* — Esp., in a swoon or in death, *fall, sink, drop, faint:* **membra collapsa** (*fainting*); **ferro conlapsa** (*swooning from a wound*). — Fig., *waste away:* **ossa morbo.** — **conlāpsus, -a, -um,** p.p. as adj., *fainting, swooning, sinking, lifeless.*

conlāpsus (coll-), -a, -um, p.p. of **conlabor.**

conlātus (coll-), -a, -um, p.p. of **confero.**

conligŏ (coll-), -lēgī, -lectum, -ligere, [con-lego], 3. v. a., *collect together, bring together, assemble, gather, collect:* **ex alto nubes ; nox pluviam** (*bring on*); **quarta hora sitim ; conlecta ex longo rabies edendi** (*ravening hunger grown by long privation*). — Pass., or with reflexive, *come together, gather, mass forces:* **omnibus conlectis.** — Also of strength, presence of mind, or courage, *collect, gain, regain:* **robur.** — Less exactly, *contract, shrink* (pass.) : **se in arma** (*draw behind his shield*); **alitis in figuram** (*shrunken*).

conlocŏ (coll-), -āvī, -ātum, -āre, [con-loco], 1. v. a., *put, place, set, arrange, station.*

conloquium (coll-), -ī (-iī), [con-†loquium, cf. **eloquium**], n., *discourse, conversation, talk,* con-

ference, converse, intercourse: de-orum.
conlūceŏ (coll-), no perf., no sup., -lūcēre, [con-luceo], 2. v. n., *shine brightly, blaze, gleam, glare,* ignes; moenia flammis; veste atque armis (*glitter*).
conlūdŏ (coll-), -lūsī, -lūsum, -lūdere, [con-ludo], 3. v. n., *play with, play together, sport, play.* — Poetically, of things: plumae.
conlustrŏ (coll-), -āvī, -ātum, -āre, [con-lustro], 1. v. a., *light up.* — Perhaps from an entirely different original meaning (cf. lustro), *examine, survey:* omnia.
connectŏ, see conecto.
connexus, see conexus.
connīsus, see conisus.
connīxus, see conixus.
connūbium, see conubium.
Conōn, -ōnis, [Gr. Κόνων], m., a mathematician and astronomer in the time of Ptolemy Philadelphus.
cōnor, -ātus sum, -ārī, [?, perhaps akin to onus, cf. molior], 1. v. dep., *undertake, attempt, try, venture.*
conr-, see corr-.
cōnsanguineus, -a, -um, [†con-sanguin (lost stem, con-sanguis, cf. cognominis) + eus], adj., *of kindred blood, akin, related.* — Masc., *a kinsman:* Leti (*brother*).
cōnsanguinitās, -tātis, [†consan-guin (as if consanguini-, cf. con-sanguineus) + tas], f., *kindred, relationship* (by blood), *consan-guinity.*
conscendŏ, -dī, -sum, -dere, [con-scando], 3. v. a. and n., *mount, ascend:* rogos. — Esp., *go on board a ship, embark, take ship:* aequor (*put to sea*).
cōnscius, -a, -um, [con-†scius, √sci + us (cf. inscius)], adj., *conscious, privy to, aware of:* agmina (*allied*); fati (*witness*); aether conubiis. — Transferred, *conscious* (with one's self), *conscious of guilt, self-conscious:* virtus; fama; mens conscia recti.
consequor, -secūtus, -sequī, [con-

sequor], 3. v. dep., *attend, follow.* — Esp. in hostile sense, *pursue.* — With different sense of con, *follow up, overtake, reach.*
1. cōnserŏ, -sēvī, -situm or -sa-tum, -serere, [con-sero], 3. v. a., *sow* or *plant with* something: arva. — Fig., *cover* or *strew over with* something: freta consita terris (*dotted*).
2. cōnserŏ, -seruī, -sertum, -serere, [con-sero], 3. v. a., *connect, entwine, tie, join, fit, unite, bind into a whole:* lorica conserta hamis (*woven*); tegumen spinis. — Esp. of hostilities, *join* (in fight), *engage in:* dextram; proelia.
cōnsertus, -a, -um, p.p. of 2. con-sero.
cōnsessus, -ūs, [con-sessus], m., (*a sitting together, a session*). — Concretely, *an assembly:* caveae (*spectators in the theatre*).
cōnsīdŏ, -sēdī (-sīdī), -sessum, -sīdere, [con-sido], 3. v. n., *sit down, settle, seat one's self, light* (of birds): molli in herba; Ausonio portu (*anchor*). — Esp., *halt, settle down* (to dwell), *take up one's abode.* — Of inanimate subjects, *settle, sink down, sink in, give way, subside:* in ignes; totam urbem luctu (*be plunged*).
cōnsilium, -ī (-iī), [consul + ium, cf. consulo], n., *consultation, counsel.* — Of the result, *wise counsel, resolution, plan, purpose, course of conduct* (as resolved upon), *course:* consiliis non futilis auctor. — Of advice given to another, *counsel, advice.* — Concretely (cf. concilium), *a* (formal) *council, assembly.* — Adv., cōnsiliō, *advisedly, intentionally, purposely, with design.*
cōnsistŏ, -stitī, -stitum, -sistere, [con-sisto], 3. v. a. and n., *place one's self, take one's stand, stand still, remain:* terra (*set foot on*). — Esp., *take a stand, make a halt, keep a position, stand, halt, settle.* — Fig., *rest:* mens.

cōnsĭtus, -a, -um, p.p. of 1.consero.
cōnsŏnō, -ŭī, no sup., -āre, [con-sono], 1. v. n., *sound together or at the same time, resound.*
cōnsors, -sortis, [con-†sorti-(fuller s*t*em of sors)], adj., *of equal share, partaking with:* me consortem nati concede sepulchro (*in common with*). — Also, *of equal lot, of the same condition, common, in com*mon.
1. cōnspectus, -a, -um, p.p. of conspicio as adj., *conspicuous.*
2. cōnspectus, -ūs, [con-spectus], m., *sight, view, presence:* e conspectu (*out of sight*); in conspectu; ire ad conspectum genitoris (*to meet*).
cōnspĭcĭō, -spexī, -spectum, -spĭcere, [con-specio], 3. v. a., *gaze upon, behold.* — Also, *get a sight of, espy, descry, find.* See conspectus.
cōnspīrō, -āvī, -ātum, -āre, [cōnspiro], 1. v. n., *blow together, sound together:* aereaque assensu conspirant cornua rauco.
cōnsternō, -strāvī, -strātum, -sternere, [con-sterno], 3. v. a., *strew over, bestrew, cover:* terram tergo; terram frondes.
cōnstĭtŭō, -ŭī, -ūtum, -uere, [con-statuo], 3. v. a., *set up, place, put:* taurum ante aras. — aras (*erect*); moenia (*build*); metam (*set*). — Fig., of *t*hings not ma*t*erial, *establish.* — Of purpose, *determine, resolve:* quaerere.
cōnstō, -stĭtī, -stātum, -stāre, [con-sto], 1. v. n., *stand with, stand together, stand:* cyparissi. — Fig., *agree* or *accord with, be consistent with, correspond to, fit.* — Also, *stand firm* or *immovable, be firm, remain immovable, unchanging, steadfast, be settled, last, persevere, endure:* cuncta caelo sereno (*be steady, as a sign of se*tt*led wea*t*her*); animo sententia (*is fixed*).
cōnstructus, -a, -um, p.p. of construo.
cōnstrŭō, -ūxī, -uctum, -uere, [con-struo], 3. v. a., *heap* or *pile together, heap up.* — Of the resul*t, build, erect, construct, make.* —
constructus, -a, -um, p.p. as adj., *heaped, gathered, stored, built.*
cōnsuēscō, -ēvī, -ētum, -ēscere, [con-suesco], 3. v. a. and n. inch., *accustom, habituate.* — So in pass. part., *accustomed, inured, habituated:* membra (*trained*). — Neut., *accustom one's self:* adeo in teneris consuescere multum est (*such force has habit*). — cōnsuētus, -a, -um, p.p. as adj., *accustomed, usual, ordinary.*
cōnsul, -ŭlis, [prob. con-√sal as stem (cf. praesul, exsul) wi*t*h some lost connec*t*ion of ideas, founded on religious observance, cf. Salii], m., *a consul,* one of the two chief magis*t*ra*t*es of Rome.
cōnsŭlō, -ŭī, -tum, -ere, [prob. consulo, akin to salio, cf. praesul, exsul], 3. v. n. and a., *consider, reflect, deliberate, take counsel, consult:* consulite in medium (*for the common advantage*). — Particular phrase: consulere alicui or alicui rei, *take counsel for some one* or *some thing, care for, take care of, look to, have regard for, consult for:* custodi et consule longe ne, etc. (*keep a look-out*). — Act., *consult* a person or *t*hing, *ask the opinion* or *advice of, ask counsel of:* vates consultus. — Esp., *consult* a deity, an oracle, omens: exta; lucos. — Transferred, *advise, counsel:* rem nulli obscuram (cog. acc.).
cōnsultum, -ī, [n. p.p. of consulo], n., (*a thing deliberated* or *advised*), usually plur., *resolutions, plans, oracles, advice.*
cōnsūmō, -sumpsī, -sumptum, -sūmere, [con-sumo], 3. v. a. Of food, *consume, devour:* mensas; consumptus aliis. — Less exac*t*ly, of o*t*her things, *consume, devour, waste, squander, annihilate, destroy, bring to nought, use up, use, waste away:* vaccae in

dulces ubera natos (*waste upon*); consumerer aevo; nocte consumpta (*spent*); sagitta consumpta (*by fire*).

cōnsumptus, -a, -um, p.p. of consumo.

cōnsurgŏ, -rexī, -rectum, -gere, [con-surgo], 3. v. n., *rise up, rise* (in various senses, as in Eng.). — From bed, from table: relictis mensis; in ensem (*rise with*, &c.); socii tonsis (*rise on the oars*). — Less exactly, of order or position: remi ordine (*in ranks*); mundus ad Scythiam (of the higher North); mare ad aethera (*mount to the skies*). — Of hostility: in arma (*in arms*). — Fig.: bellum (*arise*); venti.

contactus, -a, -um, p.p. of contingo.

contactus, -ūs, [con-tactus], m., *a touching, contact, touch*.

contāgium, -ī (-iī), [con-†tagium, √tag + ium], n., *contact*. — Esp. of the result, *contagion, infection*: vicini pecoris contagia.

contegŏ, -texī, -tectum, -tegere, [con-tego], 3. v. a., *cover up*.

contemnŏ (-pno), -psī, -ptum, -nere, [con-temno], 3. v. a., *set a small value on, value little, hold in contempt, despise, disdain, scorn*: ventos (*defy*); opes; favos (of bees).

contemplor, -ātus, -ārī, [†contemplŏ (con-templŏ-)], 1. v. dep., *survey* (cf. templum), *observe, notice carefully*.

contemptor, -ōris, [con-†temptor (√tem + tor), as if contem + tor, cf. contemno], m., *a scorner, despiser*.

contendŏ, -dī, -tum, -dere, [contendo], 3. v. a. and n., *stretch, strain, draw* (forcibly), *tighten*: vincla; tela ... et arcum (*draw the arrow on the bow*); nervo equino telum (cf. telum in auras). — From the result (cf. last example), *hurl, throw, cast, fling, shoot*: telum in auras. — Fig., of straining the powers of mind or body, *strive, exert one's self, struggle*. — With idea of opposition, *struggle, contend, strive for mastery*: bello; versibus; cursu; ludo; contra Paridem (in boxing). — Fig., of things in rivalry, *vie with, compare with*. — Of aim or direction (cf. trado), *direct, aim, hold* (a course); cursum (*steer*). — contentus, -a, -um, p.p. as adj., *stretched, straining*: cervix (of oxen).

1. contentus, -a, -um, p.p. of contendo.

2. contentus, -a, -um, p.p. of contineo.

conterreŏ, -uī, -itum, -ēre, [conterreo], 2. v. a., *terrify greatly, frighten, alarm*: conterrita tellus (*terror-stricken*).

conterritus, -a, -um, p.p. of conterreo.

contexŏ, -xuī, -xtum, -xere, [con-texo], 3. v. a., *weave* or *twine together*. — Less exactly, *prepare by joining together, compose, make, build, construct, form, put together*; equum trabibus acernis.

conticēscŏ, -ticuī, no sup., -ticēscere, [con-ticesco], 3. v. n. inch., *become still, grow dumb, hold one's peace*: conticuere omnes (*were hushed*).

contiguus (-uos), -a, -um, [con-†taguus, cf. nocuus (√tag+uus)], adj. Act., (*touching*), *adjoining, near*. — Pass. (cf. perspicuus), (*to be touched*), *within reach, within range*: missae hastae.

contineŏ, -tinuī, -tentum, -tinēre, [con-teneo], 2. v. a. and n., *hold in, keep together, confine*. — Less exactly (cf. cohibeo), *hold back, stay, detain, restrain, check*: imber agricolam (*detain at home*); gradum (*halt*). — Fig., of passions and the like, *restrain, curb, subdue, control*. — contentus, -a, -um, p.p. as adj. (*self-contained*), *content, satisfied:* mens contenta quiete.

contingŏ, -tigī, -tactum, -tingere, [con-tango], 3. v. a. and n., *touch, take hold of:* funem manu; avem ferro (*hit*). — Less exac*t*ly, *reach, arrive at, attain, gain, touch;* Italiam. — Of the effec*t* of *t*ouch, in p.p., *taint, affect with contagion* (cf. **contagium**). — Fig. (wi*t*h subjec*t*), *fall to, fall to the lot of* (impersonal), *happen, be one's lot, befall, be one's fate:* Turno coniunx; ire ad conspectum contingat (*may I be allowed*).

continuō[abl. of **continuus**], adv., *immediately, forthwith, without delay.*

contorqueŏ, -torsī, tortum, -torquēre, [con-torqueo], 2. v. a., *twist, turn, whirl:* proram. — From the whirling of missiles (cf. **amentum**), *hurl* · contorta phalarica venit (*came hurtling through the air*).

contortus, -a, -um, p.p. of contorqueo.

contrā [abl. of †contrŏ- (con + tero-, cf. **inter**)], adv. and prep. Adv., *opposite, on the other side, on the opposite side.* — Fig., *on the other hand, on the contrary, in return, in reply, in opposition.* — Prep., *over against, opposite:* Italiam contra. — Less exac*t*ly and fig., *against, in reply to, in opposition to:* contra quem (*answering him*); it contra dicta (*proceeds in reply to*); contendere contra Paridem.

contractus, -a, -um, p.p. of contraho.

contrahŏ, -traxī, -tractum, -trahere, [con-traho], 3. v. a., *draw together, gather, collect, assemble, draw in:* Scorpio bracchia. — Less exac*t*ly or fig., *draw on, bring on:* frigus (cf. "ca*t*ch"). — contractus, -a, -um, p.p. as adj., *contracted, narrow, confined:* locus.

contrārius, -a, -um, [†contrŏ- (reduced)+ārius, cf. **extrarius**], adj., *opposite, lying over against.* — Fig., *opposed, contrary, opposite:* fata. — Wi*t*h idea of hos*t*ili*t*y, *adverse, unfavorable, opposed:* furtis; litora litoribus (of e*t*ernal enmi*t*y).

contremiscŏ, -uī, no sup., **-iscere,** [con-tremisco], 3. v. n. inch., *tremble all over, shake, shudder, quake:* omne contremuit nemus.

contristō, -āvī, -ātum, -āre, [con-†tristo (cf. **tristor**)], 1. v. a., *sadden, cast a gloom over:* caelum.

contundŏ, -tudī, -tūsum, -tundere, [con-tundo], 3. v. a., *beat, bruise, crush, pound, bray:* herbas. — Fig., *crush, quell.* feroces populos. — **contūsus, -a, -um,** p.p. as adj., *broken, crushed, afflicted:* animi.

contus, -ī, [Gr. κοντός], m., *a punt-pole* (wi*t*h poin*t*ed iron), *setting-pole.* — Less exac*t*ly, of weapons, *a pike.*

contūsus, -a, -um, p.p. of contundo.

cōnūbium (conn-), -ī (-iī), [con-†nubium, s*t*em akin to nubo (cf. **pronuba**) + ium], n., *marriage* as an ins*t*i*t*u*t*ion (cf. **nubo**), *wedlock:* nostra conubia poscunt.

cōnus, -ī, [Gr. κῶνος, cf. **cuneus**], m., *a cone.* — From its shape (cf. the modern spiked helme*t*), *the peak* (of a helme*t*), *a crest* (to which the flowing crest was fas*t*ened).

convallis, -is, [con-vallis], f., *a valley* (enclosed).

couvectŏ, no perf., no sup., **-āre,** [con-vecto], 1. v. a., *bring together:* praedam.

convellŏ, -vellī, -vulsum, -vellere, [con-vello], 3. v. a., (*wrench*), *tear away, pluck up:* viridem silvam ab humo; funem a terra (*cast off*). — Less exac*t*ly, *tear apart, rend asunder.*

conveniŏ, -vēnī, -ventum, -venīre, [con-venio], 4. v. n. and a., *come together, assemble, gather round.* —

Fig., of things or impersonally, *be agreed upon, be determined.* — Also, *be fitting, be suitable, be right.*

conventus, -us, [con-†ventus, cf. adventus], m., *a coming together.* — Concretely, *an assembly, conclave.*

conversus, -a, -um, p.p. of converto.

converto (-vorto), -tī, -sum, -tere, [con-verto], 3. v. a., *turn around, turn, invert, reverse, turn backward:* in me ferrum; omen in ipsum (*bring the disaster*). — In pass. or with reflexive, *turn, wheel, face about.* — Fig., *alter, change, transform:* animi conversī; classem in Nymphas; viās. — **conversus, -a, -um,** as adj., *inverted, reversed, transformed:* agmina (*flying*); numina (*adverse*); conversis frontibus (*opposing,* of bulls fighting).

convexus, -a, -um, [p.p. of conveho], adj., (*brought together*), *vaulted, arched, rounded, bending, winding:* trames (*circuitous*). — Neut., *a vault, arch, concavity, recess:* caeli supera convexa (*the canopy of heaven*); convexa (*the rounded mass,* of mountains); convexo pondere (*the mass of the spheres*).

convīvium, -ī (-iī), [conviva (reduced) + ium (n. of ius)], n., *a meal in company* (cf. **conviva**), *a feast, banquet.*

convolsus, -a, -um, p.p. of convello.

convolvō, -volvī, -volūtum, -volvere, [con-volvo], 3. v. a., *roll together, roll up.* — Pass. or with reflexive, *roll together, roll up, roll, writhe, coil.*

convulsus, -a, -um, p.p. of convello.

coorior, -ortus, -orīrī, [con-orior], 3. and 4. v. dep., *arise, rise up.* — Fig., of things, *break out, arise:* seditio.

coortus, -a, -um, p.p. of coorior.

cōpia, -ae, [cōpi- (con-ops) + ia (f. of ius), cf. **inops, inopia**], f., *plenty, multitude, abundance, a supply.*—Transferred, *ability, power, means, resources, opportunity, chance* (to do anything): fandī; pugnae; adfarī (*leave*). — Concretely, in plur., *troops, forces.*

coquō, coxī, coctum, coquere, [√coc, cf. Gr. πέπω], 3. v. a., *cook.* — Less exactly of other things than food, *fire, roast, mellow* (of soil), *harden* (of wood). — Of the effect of the sun, *ripen, mellow:* coquitur vindemia. — Fig. (cf. uro), *vex, worry, harass.* — **coctus, -a, -um,** p.p. as adj., *hardened.*

cor, cordis, [unc. root, cf. Gr. κῆρ, Eng. *heart*], n., *the heart.* — Fig., *heart, soul* (of both moral and intellectual powers). — Of persons, as in English, *soul, heart:* iuvenes fortissima corda. — Phrase: cordī esse (cf. "go to one's heart"), *be dear, please, be desired.*

Cora, -ae, [Gr. Κόρα], f., *a town of Latium* (now *Core*).

cōram [con-os (or stem akin), unc. case, cf. **perperam**], adv. and prep. Adv., *in presence, before the eyes, in person:* coram adest (*is here before you*). — Prep., *in the presence of, before.*

Corās, -ae, [?], m., one of the founders of Tibur.

Corinthus, -ī, [Gr. Κόρινθος], f., a celebrated city of the Peloponnesus, famous for its bronze-foundries and artistic skill. It was conquered by L. Mummius.

corium, -ī (-iī), [Gr. χόριον], n., *skin, hide, leather.*

1. **corneus, -a, -um,** [†cornu- (reduced) + eus], adj., *of horn, horny, horn.*

2. **corneus, -a, -um,** [†cornŏ- (reduced) + eus], adj., *of the cornel tree, of cornel wood.*

corniger, -era, -erum, [†cornu- (weakened) -ger (√ger + us)], adj., *bearing horns, horned.*

cornipēs, -edis, [†cornu- (weakened) -pes], adj., *horn-footed, horny-hoofed.*

cornix, -icis, [dim., akin to Gr. κορώνη], f., *a crow.*

cornū, -ū, [unc. root (akin to κέρας) + nu], n., *a horn, horn.* — Less exactly, *a hoof.* — From similarity, *horn* (of the moon), *tip, yardarm, end, branch* (of a river), *peak* (of a helmet, cf. **conus**), *a bow* (with horn ends), *a trumpet.*

cornum, -ī, [perh. akin to **cornu**, from the hardness of its wood], n., *the cornel cherry.* — Also, *cornel.*

cornus, -ī, [see **cornum**], f., *a cornel.* — Less exactly, *cornel wood, a javelin* (made of the wood).

Coroebus, -ī, [Gr. Κόροιβος], m., a Phrygian, an ally of Priam.

corōna, -ae, [Gr. κορώνη], f., *a garland, a diadem, a wreath, a crown* (of royalty). — In astronomy, *The Crown.* — From similarity, *a circle of men, a ring, a crowd, a ring of defenders.*

corōnō, -āvī, -ātum, -āre, [corona], 1. v. a., *furnish with a garland* or *crown, to crown:* vina (*wreathe the bowl*). — Less exactly, *surround, encompass, enclose, wreathe, beset:* omnem aditum custode.

corporeus, -a, -um, [†corpos + eus], adj., *corporeal, of the body:* pestes.

corpus, -oris, [unc. root + us], n., *a body* (alive), *a lifeless body, corpse.* — *the frame, the form, the person.* — As in English, *a person, an animal* (cf. "head"), *creature:* corpora virorum (*forms of heroes*). — More abstractly, *person, form, figure:* praestanti corpore Nymphae. — Also of things, *bulk, mass, body, trunk* (of a tree): toto certatum est corpore regni (*united power*). — From association with burial, *the ghost, shade, spirit.* — Phrases: corpore exire, *elude, dodge;* toto corpore, *with all one's might.*

correptus (conr-), -a, -um, p.p. of **corripio.**

corripiō(conr-), -ripuī, -reptum, -ripere, [con-ripio], 3. v. a., *seize, snatch up, catch, lay violent hands on, grasp quickly:* bastem; caesariem; scuta correpta sub undis (*borne away*); montes unda; Marte secundo omnia (*gain*). — With **corpus** or a reflexive, *rise quickly, start up, tear one's self away, hurry off:* e stratis(*spring*); e somno. — Fig., of intangible subjects, *seize upon, catch, attack, carry away* (with any passion) : flamma tabulas; cinis altaria flammis (*break out in flames* on); mediis silvis correptis; Camilla correpta tali militia (*carried away by*); hunc plausus (*captivate*). — Of sudden motion, *occupy, hurry over:* campum (*scour*); viam (*speed on*); spatia; spatium medium.

corrumpō, -rūpī, -ruptum, -rumpere, [con-rumpo], 3. v. a., (*break up*), *spoil, destroy, ruin, damage, adulterate.* — Less exactly, *infect, poison, taint.* — **corruptus, -a, -um,** p.p. as adj., *tainted, infectious, pestilent, infected:* tractus caeli.

corruō (con-), -uī, no sup., **-ere,** [con-ruo], 3. v. n. and a., *fall together, fall down, fall, sink to the ground.*

corruptus, -a, -um, p.p. of **corrumpo.**

cortex, -icis, [?], m. and f., *bark.*

cortina, -ae, [?, perh. akin to Gr. χόρτος], f., *a kettle, a caldron.* — From the use of the utensil at Delphi, *the tripod* (at Delphi), *the oracle* (delivered from it).

corulus, -ī, see **corylus.**

Cōrus (Cau-), -ī, [?, prob. Greek], m., the North-west wind.

coruscō, no perf., no sup., **-āre,** [†coruscō-], 1. v. a. and n., *agitate, move to and fro, shake, brandish, wave:* gaesa manu. — Neut., *quiver, wave, shake:* apes pennis (*agitate their wings*). — From sim-

ilarity, of light, &c., *quiver, shimmer, flash, glitter, sparkle.*
coruscus, -a, -um, [unc. stem (akin to κορύσσω) + cus], adj., *waving, quivering, tremulous:* silvae. — From similarity (cf. **corusco**), *flashing, gleaming, coruscating:* fulmina; sol (*blazing*); iuvenes auro.
corvus, -ī, [?], m., *a raven.*
Corybantius, -a, -um, [Gr. Κορυβάντειος], adj., *of the Corybantes* (priests of Cybele who celebrated her worship with clanging cymbals), Corybantian.
Cōrycius, -a, -um, [Gr. Κωρύκαιος], adj., *of Corycus* (a place in Cilicia famous for its saffron), *Corycian.*
Corydōn, -ōnis, [Gr. Κορύδων], m., *a shepherd.*
corylus (-ulus), -ī, [Gr. κόρυλος], f., *a hazel-tree, a hazel.*
corymbus, -ī, [Gr. κόρυμβος], m., *a cluster* (of fruit, &c.), *a bunch.*
Corynaeus, -ī, [?], m.: 1. A priest of the Trojans; 2. A Rutulian.
Corythus, -ī, [?], m.: 1. A town of Etruria, *Cortona;* 2. Its mythical founder.
cōs, cōtis, [√co (cf. *sharpen*, **conus**)+**tis**], f., *a hone, a whetstone.* — Less exactly, *flint, stone* (cf. **cautes**).
Cosa, -ae, (-ae, -ārum), f., *a town of Etruria* (now *Ansedonia*).
Cossus, -ī, [?], m., a Roman family name in the Cornelian gens. — Esp., *A. Cornelius Cossus*, consul B.C. 428.
costa, -ae, [?], f., *a rib.* — Less exactly, *a side.*
cōtes (cau-), -is, [?], f., *a rough pointed rock, a crag.*
cothurnus (cotu-), -ī, [Gr. κόθορνος], m., *a hunting-boot* (covering the foot and lower part of the leg, and laced in front), *a buskin.* — From its use by tragic actors, of a lofty tragic style in poetry, *the buskin, tragedy.*
crābrŏ, -ōnis, [?], m., *a hornet.*
crās [cf. Sk. çvas], adv., *to-morrow.*
crassus, -a, -um, [?, p.p. of lost verb, perh. √cart (cf. Sk. krit, *twist, spin*) + **tus**], adj., *thickened up, thick, coarse:* cruor (*clotted*); paludes (*miry*); terga (*rough ridges*); farrago; ignis caligine (*dark with thick smoke*).
crāstinus, -a, -um, [cras + tinus, cf. **diutinus**], adj., *of the morrow, to-morrow's:* ortus (*next, next day's*).
cratēra, -ae, f.; -er, -ēris, m., (acc. Gr. sing. **cratēra**, plur. **cratēras**), [Gr. κρατήρ], *a mixing vessel, a bowl, a jar,* of large size in which the whole store of wine was mixed for the company. — Also the same vessel used for other purposes, *oil-jar:* fuso crateres olivo.
crātēs, see **cratis**.
crātis, -is, [perh. akin to **crassus**] f., *wicker-work, a hurdle* (used for many farming purposes by the ancients). — Esp., *a drag* (for harrowing). — From similarity of texture, *a net-work, a cell* (of a hive), *the breast:* pectoris (*framework*).
creātrix, -īcis, [creā(stem of creo) + trix], f., *a producer* (female), *a mother.*
creātus, -a, -um, p.p. of **creo**.
crēber, -bra, -brum, (-brior, -berrimus), [?, unc. root + rus], adj., *thick, close:* Africus creber procellis. — Of closeness in time, *repeated, frequent, numerous, constant:* sonitus pedum (*of many feet*); crebro ariete (*with frequent strokes of*); anhelitus (*quick, hurried*); turbo (*quick*); heros creber (as adv., *again and again*); tela (*showers of*); Auster (*full and strong, with incessant blasts*). — Neut. plur. as adv., *frequently, repeatedly.*
crēbrēscŏ (-bēscŏ), -bruī (-buī), no sup., -brēscere (-bēscere), [†crebrē (stem of lost **crebreo** fr. crebro-)], 3. v. n. inch., *become frequent, increase, freshen* (of winds, cf. **creber**), *become rife* (of rumors): aurae.

Vocabulary.

crēditus, -a, -um, p.p. of **credo.**
crēdō, -dĭdī, -dĭtum, -dere, [lost stem †cred (cf. Sk. *çrat*) -do, *put*], 3. v. n. and a., *put faith in, trust to, confide in, trust:* colori; Austris; auditis quicquam (*believe at all*). — Act., *entrust, confide to, commit:* anni spem terrae (of sowing); tibi sensus; custodia credita. — In same sense with reflexive, *trust one's self to, venture on, hazard·* se pugnae. — With thing as object, *credit, believe, suppose, imagine:* credas innare Cycladas; res credita; vim adfore verbo. — Irregularly with person as object, *trust, believe:* Cassandra credita.
crēdulus, -a, -um, [†crēdŏ (lost noun-stem, cf. **crēdō**) + lus], adj., *believing, trustful, confiding, credulous:* non ego credulus illis.
cremō, -āvī, -ātum, -āre, [perh. akin to **carbo**], 1. v. a., *burn, consume.*
Cremōna, -ae, [?], f., a town of Gallia Cisalpina, on the Po. Its lands were confiscated by Augustus.
creō, -āvī, -ātum, āre, [†cerō- (√cer + us, see **cerus, cresco, Ceres**)], 1. v. a., *produce, bring forth, beget.* — Less exactly, *breed* (of animals).
crepĭdō, -ĭnis, [akin to κρηπίς], f., *a base, foundation.* — Less exactly, *a quay, bank.*
crepĭtō, -āvī, -ātum, -āre, [†crepĭtō-, p.p. of **crepo**], 1. v. n., *crackle, rattle, rustle, clatter:* flamma; malae (with blows); Auster; brattea vento; undae (*murmur*).
crepĭtus, -ūs, [†crepĭ- (stem of **crepo**, as root) + tus], m., *a rattling, creaking, clattering, rustling; rattle* (of thunder).
crepō, -uī, -ĭtum, -āre, [?], 1. v. n., *crack, rattle, rustle, crash.* — From effect to cause, *break with a crash* (perhaps the original meaning).
crēscō, crēvī, crētum, crescere,
[stem akin to **creo** (perhaps same, as if crē) + sco), 3. v. n., *grow up, be born, arise.* — Less exactly, *grow, increase, swell;* Thybris (*rise*); corpus (*fatten*); umbrae (*lengthen*); aestus (*rise, flow*). — Fig., *thrive, prosper.* — **crētus, -a, -um,** p.p., *sprung from, descended from.*
Crēs, -ētis, [?], adj., *Cretan.* — Masc. plur., **Crētes, -um,** *the inhabitants of Crete, Cretans.*
Crēssius, -a, -um, [Gr. Κρήσιος], adj., *of Crete, Cretan.*
Cressus, -a, -um, [cf. Gr. Κρῆσσα], adj., *of Crete, Cretan.*
Crēta, -ae, [Gr. Κρήτη], f. of adj., *Crete* (the island in the Mediterranean, now *Candia*). — From a common export, *chalk, Cretan earth, white clay.*
Crētaeus, -a, -um, [adj. of Gr. form], adj., *of Crete, Cretan.*
Crēteus, see **Cretheus.**
Crētheus, -eos, [?], m., a Greek in the Trojan army.
crētus, -a, -um, p.p. of **cresco.**
Creūsa, -ae, [Gr. Κρέουσα (fem. p., *princess*)], f., a daughter of Priam, and wife of Æneas.
crīmen, -ĭnis, [lengthened root of **cerno + men**], n. (*a decision of a case,* cf. **cerno**), *a charge, accusation.* — Less exactly, *a reproach, a crime, a fault* (more serious than **culpa**). — Poetically : crimina belli (*charges to lead to war*); se clamat crimen (*the guilty one*).
Crīmīsus (-issus), -ī, [Gr. Κριμισός (Κριμισσός)], m., a river on the south-west coast of Sicily. — Also, the river-god.
crīnālis, -e, [†crini- (reduced) + alis], adj., *of the hair:* aurum (*golden hair-band*).
crinis, -is, [?], m., *the hair.* — From similarity, *tail* (of a comet, or shooting-star), *a trail, a train.*
crīnītus, -a, -um, [†crini (lengthened, as if stem of †crinio) + tus, cf. **armatus**], adj., *having long hair, long-haired, crested.*

crispo, no perf., -ātum, -āre, [†crispŏ], 1. v. a., *wave, brandish* (cf. **crispus**).

crista, -ae, [?], f., *a crest* (of a helmet). — Less exac*t*ly, *a helmet.*

cristātus, -a, -um, [†crista + tus, cf. **armatus**], adj., *crested* (having a crest as a famous warrior).

croceus, -a, -um, [†crocŏ- (reduced) + eus], adj., *of saffron, saffron.*

crocus, -ī, m., -um, -ī, n., [Gr. κρόκος], *saffron.* — Less exac*t*ly, *saffron-color.*

crūdēlis, -e, [†crūdē- (*s*tem of †crudeo, fr. **crudus** implied in **crudesco**) + lis, cf. **Aprilis**], adj., *harsh, severe, cruel, unrelenting, ruthless.* — Transferred, *cruel, bloody, destructive, frightful :* fu-nus; fata; arae; umbrae (of the lower world). — Also, *bitter, violent :* luctus; odium.

crūdēliter [†crudeli + ter (?, neu*t.* of terus, reduced)], adv., *cruelly, barbarously.*

crudēscō, -uī, no sup., -escere, [†crudē- (cf. **crudelis**) + sco], 3. v. n. inch., *grow hard, become aggravated, grow worse, grow fierce, wax hot :* pugnae.

crūdus, -a, -um, [*s*tem akin to **cruor** + dus], adj., *bloody, raw.* — From similari*t*y, *hard, rough.* — Less exac*t*ly, *undressed, raw :* pero. — Fig., *rough, rude, sturdy :* senectus. — Also, *cruel, harsh :* ensis.

cruentō, -āvī, -ātum, -āre, [†cru-entŏ-], 1. v. a., *make bloody, spot or stain with blood.*

cruentus, -a, -um, [√cru, in **cruor**, p. or p. developed, cf. **argentum**], adj., *bloody, gory.* — From similari*t*y, *blood-red, crimson, red :* myrta; bello signum.

cruor, -ōris, [√cru (in **cruentus,** etc.) + or], m., *blood, gore* (blood shed). — Also, *life-blood.*

crūs, -ūris, [?], n., *the leg.*

crusta, -ae, [?, but cf. **crustum** and κρύσταλλος], f., *the skin, rind,* shell, crust, bark. — Less exactly, *ice.*

crustum, -ī, [cf. **crusta**], n., *bread* (*t*hin and perhaps hard baked, as used for *t*renchers).

Crustumerī, -ōrum, [?], m., *the people of Crustumerium,* a town of the Sabines, the town i*t*self.

Crustumius, -a, -um, adj., *of Crustumium* or *Crustumerium, Crustumian.*

cubīle, -is, [n. adj. fr. lost *n*oun-s*t*em (aki*n* to **cubo**) + ilis], n., *a bed, couch.* — Less exac*t*ly, *a nest, a beehive, a stall, a burrow.*

cubitum, -ī, [†cubi- (s*t*em of **cubo,** as roo*t*) + tum (n. of tus)], n., *the elbow.*

cucumis, -eris, [?, reduplicated root + is (aki*n* *t*o -us and -or)], m., *a cucumber.*

cūius (quoi-), -a, -um, [†quŏ- (s*t*em of **qui**) + ius), pron. adj., *whose ?*

culmen, -inis, [unc. root (perhaps √col) + men, cf. **columna**], n., *top, summit, roof.*

culmus, -ī, [cf. "halm"], m., *a stalk, stem* (esp. of grain), *straw-thatch.*

culpa, -ae, [?], f., *fault, crime, defect, guilt.* — Less exactly, *infection, disease* (cf. **vitium**).

culpātus, -a, -um, p.p. of **culpo.**

culpō, -āvī, -ātum, -āre, [†culpa], 1. v. a., *blame, reproach, censure, reprove, disapprove, condemn.* — **culpātus,** -a, -um, p.p., *blameable, to be blamed.*

culter, -trī, [?], m., *a knife, sacrificial knife.*

cultor, -ōris, [√col (in **colo**) + tor], m., *cultivator, husbandman, tiller of the soil.* — Less exac*t*ly, *inhabitant.* — Also, *worshipper, priest.* — Also (cf. **colo**), *lover :* nemorum Pan (*loving to inhabit*).

cultrīx, -icis, [√col (roo*t* of **colo**) + trix], f., *a female inhabitant.* — Also, *protectress, patroness, mistress.*

cultūra, -ae, [†cultu- (leng*t*hened, perh. as if verb-stem, cf. **tribus,**

tribunus, tribuo) + ra (f. of rus, cf. maturus, also figura)], f., *cultivation, care*.
1. cultus, -a, -um, p.p. of colo.
2. cultus, -ūs, [√col (in colo) + tus], m., *cultivation, tillage* (of land). — Of o*t*her *t*hings, *care*. — Fig., *mode of life, manners, dress, care of the p*er*son, plight*.
1. cum [prob. iden*t*ical wi*t*h con], prep. with abl., *with* (in all English senses excep*t* ins*t*rumen*t*, and some*t*imes almos*t* approaching *t*hat if accompaniment is the main idea). —Appended to personal pronouns: mecum, tecum. — Phrase: cum prīmīs, *chiefly, especially*.
2. cum (earlier form quom, cf. cuius fr. qui), incorrect spelling, quum, [unc. case-form of quis, qui, cf. tum, num, dum], adv. Temporal, *when, since, while*. — Causal, *since, although, while*.
Cūmae, -arum, [Gr. Κύμη], f., an ancient colony of the Chalcidians in Campania, the residence of the Sibyl.
Cumaeus, -a, -um, [Gr. Κυμαῖος], adj., *of Cumae, Cumæan*.
cumba, see cymba.
cumque, [2. cum-que, cf. quisque], adv., usually appended to rela*t*ives, (*always*), *so ever*.
cumulātus, -a, -um, p.p. of cumulo.
cumulō, -āvī, -ātum, -āre, [†cumulŏ], 1. v. a., *heap up, pile up*. — By a change of poin*t* of view, *heap up with, load, pile with:* Acesten muneribus; altaria donis. — Poe*t*ic use: veniam cumulatam morte remittam (*increased by my death*, repaid in ample measure).
cumulus, -ī, [los*t* s*t*em †cumŏ- (cf. κυμο- in composi*t*ion, *wave*, same roo*t* as κύω) + lus], m., *a mass, a heap, a pile*.
cūnābula, -ōrum, [†cunā- (as if of lost verb, cf. cunae) + bulum], n. plur., *a cradle*. — Less exac*t*ly, *a nest, a cell* (res*t*ing-place of bees). — Fig., of a bir*t*hplace, *cradle, first home:* gentis nostrae.
cunctor, -ātus, -ārī, [†cunctŏ, p.p. of los*t* verb of unc. roo*t*, but cf. Sk. çaṅk, *waver*], 1. v. dep., *linger, loiter, hesitate, delay:* cunctando (*by dilatory measures*); cunctanti (of Palinurus, *resisting*, not yielding to sleep).
cūnctus, -a, -um, [con-iunctus, p.p. as adj.], adj., usually plur., *all* (*t*oge*t*her), *the whole*.
cuneus, -ī, [?, but cf. conus, cos], m., *a wedge*. — From the form, *a column* (of at*t*ack, in the form of a wedge). — Also, *the rows of a theatre, benches of spectators*.
cunque, see cumque.
Cupāvŏ, -ōnis, [?], m., son of Cycnus, a prince of northern I*t*aly.
Cupencus, -ī, [?], m., a Rutulian.
cupīdō, -inis, [†cupi- (ei*t*her s*t*em of cupio or lost noun-s*t*em akin) + do, perhaps *t*hrough cupēs], f., rarely m., *desire, longing, eagerness*. — Personified, *Love, Cupid*.
cupidus, -a, -um, [†cupŏ- or †cupi- (los*t* s*t*em akin to cupio) + dus], adj., *longing, eager, desirous*.
cupiō, -īvī (-iī), -ītum, -ere, [√cup, but perhaps *t*hrough nouns*t*em], 3. v. a. and n., *long for* (s*t*ronger *t*han volo), *desire, be eager, covet, wish, be anxious, long, burn to*.
cupressus, -ī, [Gr. κυπάρισσος], f., *the cypress* (a *t*all evergreen sacred to Pluto, and a sign of dea*t*h and mourning).
cūr (quor), [prob. quā-re], in*t*errog. adv., *why? wherefore? for what purpose?*
cūra, -ae, [akin to κοίρανος], f., *care, trouble, anxiety, concern, solicitude:* curae ingeminant. — Esp. of love, *distress* (of love), *love:* regina gravi saucia curā. — Concre*t*ely, the objec*t* of love, *love, flame, darling:* tua cura Lycoris. — Wi*t*h reference to an objec*t*, *solicitude, care, attention, pains, concern:* cura peculi;

grandaevis oppida curae (i.e., *are their care*); amantes curae numen habet (*has in his care*); tantae est victoria curae (*such eager desire for victory*); terrarum cura (*charge*); arva non ulli obnoxia curae (*subject to no labor of man*); omni cura vires exercet (*diligence*); curas extendit in annum. — In a weaker sense, *regard for, thought of, memory:* Corydonis (*regard for*); amissae parentis; ea cura ... rumpere, etc. (*the thought*). — Concretely, object of care, *care, business, province:* ducis concipe curam (*task,* but compare grandaevis, etc., above); quibus cura penum struere (*office*); obsidere cura datur Messapo; tenues curae (*trivial affairs*). — Personified, in first sense, *Cares:* ultrices (pangs of conscience).

curculiŏ (gurgulio), -ōnis, [?], m., *a corn-worm, weevil.*

Curēs, -ium, m. and f., the ancient chief town of the Sabines.

Cūrētes, -um, [Gr. Κουρῆτες], m., the most ancient inhabitants of the island of Crete, priests of Cybele (the same as the Corybantes).

cūria, -ae, [?], f., *the senate-house.*

cūrŏ [old form, coerŏ], -āvī, -ātum, -āre, [†cura], 1. v. a., *care for, take* or *have care of, be solicitous for, look* or *attend to, trouble one's self about, tend, cultivate, look out for* (secure): corpora (*refresh*); vites (*dress*); carmina; id venti curant; frigora (*mind*). — With inf., *care to, desire to, take the trouble to.*

curriculum, -ī, [†curru- (weakened) + culum, dim.], n., *course.* — Fig., *space, course* (of time), *career.*

currŏ, cucurrī, cursum, currere, [?], 3. v. n., *run, move quickly, hasten,* &c. — Less exactly and fig. of everything conceived as moving, *sail, flow, pass, skim, fly, run, shoot, glide* (of a shooting-star): stella; tremor; purpura; classis iter tutum (*speed*); aequor (*skim*).

currus, -ūs, [√curr (as if root of curro) + us], m., *a chariot, car.* — Less exactly, *a team, horses:* nec audit currus habenas. — *a plough* (with wheels).

cursus, -ūs, [√curr (as if root of curro) + tus], m., *a running, course, march, passage, voyage, journey, pursuit, flight, race:* hunc modum cursūs (*manœuvres*); transmittere cursum(*cross the ferry*). — Less exactly, *gait, walk, mode of running* or *going:* trepido cursu(*trembling haste*). — Transferred, *direction, way, course* (of a river), *course* (of ships, &c.): torquet medios cursus nox (*rolls in the middle of her course*).

curvātus, -a, -um, p.p. of curvo.

curvo, -āvī, -ātum, -āre, [†curvŏ-], 1. v. a., *bend, bow, bend down, curve, crook.* — curvātus, -a, -um, p.p. as adj., *bent, arched, bowed, curved.*

curvus, -a, -um, [same root as Gr. κυρτός + va], adj., *crooked, bent, curved:* aratrum; arator (*stooping*); falces (*hooked*); flumina (*winding*).

cuspis, -idis, [?], f., *a point:* acuta. — Less exactly, *a trident, a spear, javelin, lance.*

custōdia, -ae, [stem of †custōd + ia (f. of -ius)], f., *watch, guard, care, charge.*—Concretely, *a guard* or *guardian.*—Plur., *guards, guard* or *watch.*

custōdiŏ, -īvī or -iī, -ītum, -īre, [†custodi-(as if stem of custos)], 4. v. a., *watch over, protect, defend, guard.* — Esp., with the notion of hindering free motion, *hold back, preserve, keep, guard, shut up, hold in custody, hold captive.* — With clause with ne, *guard, watch.*

custōditus, -a, -um, p.p. of custodio.

custōs, -ōdis, [?], comm., *a guard, watch, preserver, keeper, overseer,*

Vocabulary. 73

protector. — Less exactly, *herdsman, porter, pilot, overseer, shepherd, watchdog, watchman, spy, priest, attendant* (of a boy).
Cybēbē (-elē), -ēs, [Gr. Κυβήβη], f., *Cybele*, a Phrygian goddess worshipped as mother of the gods. Her worship was wild and orgiastic, accompanied by drums and cymbals. Her effigies were crowned with towers, and her car drawn by lions.
Cybela, -ae, [Gr. Κυβέλη], f., a mountain in Phrygia.
Cybelē, -es; see **Cybēbe.**
Cybelus, -i, sometimes read for **Cybela, -ae.**
Cyclades, -um, [Gr. Κυκλάδες, fr. κύκλος, *circle*], f. plur., a group of islands around Delos in the Ægean.
Cyclōpeus, -a, -um, [Gr. Κυκλώπειος], adj., *of the Cyclopes :* **saxa.**
Cyclōps, -ōpis, [Gr. Κύκλωψ], m., a *Cyclops*, fabled giants with one eye in the middle of the forehead. They served as the workmen of Vulcan.
cycnus, -i, [Gr. κύκνος], m., *a swan.*
Cycnus, -i, [same word as preced.], m., a king of the Ligurians, changed to a swan.
Cydippē, -es, [Gr. Κυδίππη], f., a nereid.
Cydōn, -ōnis, m., a Latin.
Cydōn, -ōnis, [Gr. Κυδών], adj. m., a *Cydonian*, a native of Cydonia, a town of Crete, put generally for *Cretan.*
Cydōnius, -a, -um, [Gr. Κυδώνιος], adj., *a Cydonian ;* see **Cydon.**
Cygnus, -i; see **Cycnus.**
cylindrus, -i, [Gr. κύλινδρος], m., *a roller, a stone* (for rolling).
Cyllarus, -i, [Gr. Κύλλαρος], m., the horse of Pollux.
Cyllēnē, -ēs (-ae), [Gr. Κυλλήνη], f., a mountain of Arcadia, the birthplace of Mercury.
Cyllēnius, -a, -um, [Gr. Κυλλήνιος], adj., *of Cyllene.* — Masc., *Mercury.* — Less exactly, *of Mercury :* **ignis** (the planet Mercury).
cymba, -ae, [Gr. κύμβη], f., *a boat, a skiff, a bark.*
cymbalum, -ī, [Gr. κύμβαλον], n., *a cymbal.*
cymbium, -ī (-iī), [Gr. κύμβιον], n., *a cup, a bowl* (in form of a boat, cf. **cymba**).
Cȳmodocē, -ēs, [Gr. Κυμοδόκη], f., a sea-nymph.
Cȳmodocēa, -ae, [adj. fr. the preced.], f., a sea-nymph.
Cȳmothoē, -ēs, [Gr. Κυμοθόη], f., a sea-nymph.
Cȳniphius, -a, -um; see **Ciniphius.**
Cynthius, -a, -um, [Gr. Κύνθιος], adj., *of Cynthus.* — Masc., *Apollo, Lord of Cynthus.*
Cynthus, -i, [Gr. Κύνθος], m., a mountain in Delos, the birthplace and favorite haunt of Apollo.
cyparissus, -i, [Gr. κυπάρισσος], f., *the cypress* (an evergreen tree used at funerals, and planted by tombs).
Cyprus, -i, [Gr. Κύπρος], f., an island in the Mediterranean.
Cȳrēnē, -ēs, [Gr. Κυρήνη], f., the mother of Aristaeus.
Cyrneus (-naeus), -a, -um, [Gr. †Κυρνεῖος], adj., *of Corsica* (anciently called *Cyrnus*), *Corsican.*
Cythēra, -ōrum, [Gr. Κύθηρα], n. plur., the island south of Laconia (now *Cerigo*), where Venus was fabled to have landed from the sea.
Cythereūs, -a, -um, [Gr. †Κυθηρεῖος], adj., *of Cythera.* — Fem., *the goddess of Cythera, Venus.*
cytisus, -i, [Gr. κύτισος], comm., *clover* (of a special kind, perhaps *medicago arborea*).
Cytōrus, -i, [Gr. Κύτωρος], m., a mountain in Paphlagonia, famous for its boxwood.

D.

Dacus, -a, -um, [Gr. Δακός), adj., *Dacian, of the Daci* (a warlike people on the northern bank of the Danube). — Masc. plur., *the Dacians* (the people themselves).

Daedalus, -ī, [Gr. Δαίδαλος], m., a famous artisan of Athens who built the labyrinth, and escaping from Crete on artificial wings, landed at Cumae (see next word).

daedalus, -a, -um, [Gr. δαίδαλος], adj., *skilful, cunning.* — Transferred, *cunningly wrought, artistic:* tecta.

Dahae, -ārum, [Gr. Δάαι], m. plur., a Scythian tribe east of the Caspian Sea, on the Oxus, in the modern Daghestan.

dāma, see **damma.**

damma, -ae, [perhaps akin to δάμαλος], f. (rarely m.), *a deer.*

damnātus, -a, -um, p.p. of damno.

damnŏ, -āvī, -ātum, -āre, [†damnŏ-], 1. v. a., (*fine*), *sentence, judge, condemn.* — Less exactly, *bind, oblige:* votis (*bind by vows, by granting prayers*); quem damnet labor (*whom the toil of war shall condemn to death*).

Damoetās, -ae, m., a shepherd.

Dāmōn, -ōnis, [Gr. Δάμων], m., a goatherd.

Danaē, -ēs, [Gr. Δανάη], f., a daughter of Acrisius, king of Argos, beloved by Jupiter and sent adrift in a boat. Virgil interprets the story differently (see Æn. vii. 410).

Danaus, -a, -um, [Gr. Δάναος], adj., *of Danaus,* a mythic king of Egypt who settled in Argos, father of the Danaidæ, and king of Argos. — Less exactly, *Grecian.* — Masc. plur., *the Greeks.*

Daphnis, -idis, [Gr. Δάφνις], m., a mythical Sicilian shepherd, the inventor of bucolic poetry.

†daps, dapis, [akin to δαπάνη], f., *a feast, a banquet.*

Dardanidēs, -ae, [Gr. Δαρδανίδης, patronymic of **Dardanus**], m., *son of Dardanus.* — Esp., *Æneas,* descended from him. — Plur., *the Trojans.*

Dardanis, -idis, [Gr. Δαρδανίς, cf. preceding], f., *daughter of Dardanus.* — Esp., *the Trojan women.*

Dardanius, -a, -um, [Gr. Δαρδάνιος], adj., (*of Dardanus*), *of Troy, Trojan.* — Fem., *the Trojan land, Troy.*

Dardanus, -ī, [Gr. Δάρδανος], m., son of Jupiter and Electra, founder of the house of Priam and Æneas.

Dardanus, -a, -um, [Gr. Δάρδανος], adj., *of Dardanus,* son of Jupiter and Electra, father of Tros, and founder of the race of Priam and Æneas, *Dardanian.* — Less exactly, *Trojan.* — Masc. plur., *the Trojans.*

Darēs, ētis, [Gr. Δάρης], m.: 1. A Trojan boxer; 2. A Trojan warrior.

dator, -ōris, [√da + tor], m., *a giver.*

datus, -a, -um, p.p. of do.

Daucius, -a, -um, [?], adj., *of Daucus,* a noble of the Rutuli, *Rutulian.*

Daunius, -a, -um, [†Daunŏ- (reduced) + ius], adj., *of Daunus, Daunian.*

Daunus, -ī, [?], m., a mythical king of Apulia.

dē [unc. case from pron. √da, cf. **deterior, demum**], prep. with abl., (*down,* cf. compounds), *from, away from, down from, out of:* pendere de rupe. — Of part from a whole, *from, of, out of.* — Of cause, origin, and material, *from, of:* suo de nomine (*after*); de te suscepta (*begot by*). — Fig. (cf. Eng. *of-, off*), *of, in regard to, about, concerning, respecting,* as *to:* de vita certant (*for life*); de te merui (*of you*); cui tantum

de te licuit (*upon*, of an ou*t*rage). Of quasi origin, *in accordance with, by :* de more.

dea, -ae, [cf. **deus**], f., *a goddess.*

dēbellātor, -ōris, [de-bellator, cf. debello], m., *a conqueror, a subduer.*

dēbellō, -āvī, -ātum, -are, [de-bello], 1. v. a., *subdue, vanquish, crush, quell.*

dēbeō, -buī, -bitum, -bēre, [de-habeo], 2. v. a., (*keep away*), *owe.* — Pass., *be due, be destined, be appointed.* — **dēbitus, -a, -um,** p.p. as adj., *due, destined, appointed.*

dēbilis, -e, [de-habilis], adj., (*unhandy*), *weak, maimed, powerless, crippled.*

dēbilitō, -āvī, -ātum, -are, [†debilitŏ-, fr. **debilis**], 1.v.a. *weaken, enfeeble.*

dēbitus, -a, -um, p.p. of debeo.

dēcēdō, -cēssī, -cēssum, -cēdere, [de-cedo], 3. v. n., *withdraw, retire, give way to, set* (of heavenly bodies); nocti (*retire before*). — **dēcēdēns, -entis,** p. as adj., *declining, setting :* die decedenti (*declining*).

decem [cf. δέκα, petrified case-form], indecl. num. adj., *ten.*

dēceptus, -a, -um, p.p. of **decipio.**

dēcernō, -crēvī, -crētum, -cernere, [de-cerno], 3. v. a. and n., *decide* (cf. **cerno**), *determine.* — Wi*t*h inf., *resolve, determine.* — Esp. in a con*t*est, *contend, fight.*

dēcerpō, -cerpsī, -cerptum, -cerpere, [de-carpo], 3. v. a., *pluck off.*

decet, decuit, no sup., **decēre,** [√dec, akin to **dignus, doceo,** δείκνυμι], 2. v. a. and n., *only t*hird person, *befit, behoove, be fitting, be proper.* — Past *t*enses, *ought.*

dēcīdō, -cīdī, no sup., **-cidere,** [de-cado], 3. v. n., *fall down, fall.*

dēcīdō, -cīdī, -cīsum, -cīdere, [de-caedo], 3. v. a., *cut off, lop.*

dēcipiō, -cēpī, -ceptum, -cipere, [de-capio], 3. v. a., *deceive, betray.*

dēcīsus, -a, -um, p.p. of **decīdo.**

Decius, -ī (-iī), [prop. adj. ?], m., a Roman gen*t*ile name. — Esp., two dis*t*inguished Romans, P. Decius Mus, who devo*t*ed *t*hemselves to dea*t*h in ba*tt*le for *t*heir coun*t*ry, one at Veseris, the o*t*her at Sentinum.

dēclārō, -āvī, -ātum, -āre, [declaro], 1.v.a., *make plain, manifest.* — Esp. by word of mou*t*h, *pronounce, proclaim, announce, declare :* Cloanthum victorem.

dēclīnō, -āvī, -ātum, -āre, [declino], 1. v. a. and n., *bend down, turn off.* — Esp. of the eyelids, *lower, close :* lumina somno.

dēcolor, -ōris, [de-color, as adj.], adj., (*with its color off*), *discolored, dimmed :* aetas (*less lustrous,* changed from *golden* to *bronze*).

dēcoquō, -coxī, -coctum, -coquere, [de-coquo], 3. v. a., *boil down, boil away.*

decor, -ōris, [√dec (cf. **decet**) + or], m., *beauty, comeliness, grace.*

decorō, -āvī, -ātum, -āre, [†decŏrŏ-], 1. v. a., *make beautiful, adorn, embellish.* — Fig., *honor :* me sepulcro.

decorus, -a, -um, [perh. †decōr + us, more likely lost s*t*em †decŏ (cf. **decet**) + rus, cf. **avārus, severus, matūrus,** and **colōnus, aegrōtus, velox, custos, -ōdis**], adj., *decorated, adorned, beautiful, comely, lovely, brilliant.*

decumus (deci-), -a, -um, [decem (reduced or perhaps orig. s*t*em) + mus, cf. **infimus**], adj., *tenth.*

dēcurrō, -currī (-cucurrī), -cursum, -ere, [de-curro], 3.v.n., *run down.* — Less exac*t*ly, of any rapid mo*t*ion, *sail, fly, rush, march down* or *over, speed along :* circum rogos (*dance around,* of an armed dance). — Fig., *run over, pass through, finish :* laborem inceptum.

dēcursus, -ūs, [de-cursus], m., *a running down, course, descent.*

decus, -oris, [√dec + us], n.,

beauty, comeliness, grace. — Concretely, *ornament, adornment.* — Fig., *honor, glory, fame.* — Of persons concretely, *glory, pride:* decus i nostrum.

dēcutiō, -cussī, -cussum, -cutere, [de-quatio], 3. v. a., *shake off, knock off:* mella foliis.

dēdecus, -oris, [de-decus], n., *disgrace, dishonor, shame.*

dēdignor, -ātus, -ārī, [de-dignor], 1. v. dep., *disdain, scorn.*

dēdō, -didī, -ditum, -dere, [de-do], 3. v. a., (*give off* or *away*), *give up, resign, yield up.*

dēdūcō, -dūxī, -ductum, -dūcere, [de-duco], 3. v. a., *lead down, draw down, drag away, draw off, drain.* — Less exactly, *lead, conduct,* (of a triumph, *lead in triumph*), (esp. of a colony, *plant*). — Esp. of ships, *launch.* —

dēductus, -a, -um, p.p. as adj., (*drawn out*), *slender, fine spun:* carmen (cf. tenuis).

dēductus, -a, -um, p.p. of deduco.

deerro, -āvī, -ātum, -āre, [de-erro], 1. v. n., *wander away.*

dēfectus, -ūs, [de-factus, as if defic + tus], m., (*failure*), *eclipse.*

dēfendō, -dī, -sum, -dere, [de-†fendo, *strike*], 3. v. a., (*strike down*), *ward off, keep off, avert:* hunc furorem (*defend me from*). — With change of point of view, *defend from, guard, protect:* aprum palus (*harbor*).

dēfēnsor, -ōris, [de-†fensor, cf. defendo], m., *a defender, a protector, a champion.*

dēfēnsus, -a, -um, p.p. of defendo.

dēferō, -tulī, -lātum, -ferre, [de-fero], irr. v. a., *carry down, bring down.* — Esp. from sea to land, *bear, drive, land in, convey.* — Less exactly, *deliver, bear to, report, announce.* — In pass., *throw one's self down.*

dēfessus, -a, -um, [de-fessus], adj., *tired out, worn out, fatigued.*

dēficiō, -fēcī, -fectum, -ficere, (pass. defit), [de-facio], irr. v. a. and n. (*make off*, cf. **proficiscor**), *give out, fail, be wanting to, cease:* lac mihi defit (*fail me*); glandes sylvae (*the woods lack acorns*); navis (*sink*, in the sea); quā deficit ignis (*what the fire spares*); ultimus ignis (*is dying out*). — Esp. of persons, *faint, fail, sink, be exhausted:* luctu Latinus; dubiis ne defice rebus. — With acc., deficit noctes umor (*the night lacks moisture*).

dēfīgō, -fīxī, -fīxum, -fīgere, [de-figo], 3. v. a., *fasten down, plant in:* hastae defixae (*stuck in the ground*); defixa aratra (*standing in the furrow*). — Fig., *fix, fasten, cast down:* defixus lumina (*with eyes fixed*, &c.); defixi ora tenebant (*held their eyes cast down*).

dēfīō, see deficio.

dēfīxus, -a, -um, p.p. of defigo.

dēflectō, -flexī, -flexum, -flectere, [de-flecto], 3. v. a., *turn aside.*

dēfleō, -ēvī, -ētum, -ēre, [de-fleo], 2. v. a., *weep for, mourn for:* membra; haec (*mourn thus*).

dēflētus, -a, -um, p.p. of defleo.

dēfluō, -flūxī, -fluxum, -fluere, [de-fluo], 3. v. n., *flow down, float down, sail down.* — Less exactly, of things not liquid, *glide down, fall, drop, slide:* cohors ad terram equis relictis; vestis ad imos pedes.

dēfodiō, -fōdī, -fossum, -fodere, [de-fodio], 3. v. a., *dig down, dig.* — Of effect, *bury, conceal.*

dēformis, -e, [de-forma (weakened) decl. as adj.], adj., *deformed* (cf. dēcolor), *unsightly.*

dēformō, -āvī, -ātum, -āre, [†deformi-, as if †deformō-], 1. v. a., *disfigure, deform:* domum (*spoil, by killing a member*).

dēfossus, -a, -um, p.p. of defodio.

dēfringō, -frēgī, -fractum, -fringere, [de-frango], 3. v. a., *break off.*

dēfrutum, -ī, [?], n., *must* (boiled down).
dēfunctus, -a, -um, p.p. of dēfungor.
dēfungor, -functus, -fungī, [de-fungor], 3. v. dep., (*perform to the end*), *finish, complete, have done with, pass through:* vita; periclis.
dēgener, -eris, [de-genus (r for s), cf. decolor], adj., *degenerate.*— Less exac*t*ly, *of low birth, ignoble.*
dēgenerō, -āvī, -ātum, -āre, [dēgener], 1. v. n., *degenerate, deteriorate.*
dēgō, dēgī, no sup., dēgere, [de-ago], 3. v. a., *spend, lead, pass:* vitam.
dēgustō (perh. ū), -āvī, -ātum, -āre, [de-gusto], 1. v. a., (*take off to taste*), *taste.*— Fig., *of a weapon, graze.*
dehinc [de-hinc, cf. deinde], adv., *from hence* (of place or *t*ime), *hence.*— Less exac*t*ly, cf. deinde, *next, hereupon, then.*
dehīscō, -hīvī, no sup., -hīscere, [de-hisco], 3. v. n., *yawn, gape:* terrae (*crack*).
dēiciō (deii-), -iēcī, -iectum, -icere, [de-iacio], 3. v. a., *throw down, cast down, hurl down, drive down.*— Esp. of dea*t*h, *lay low, strike down, bring down, kill, slay.*— Technically, of forces, *dislodge, drive away* (also of a serpen*t*).— Fig., *cast down:* voltum.— dēiectus, -a, -um, p.p., *dejected, dismayed.*— Also, *deprived of, stricken off:* deiecto voltu (*with eyes downcast*); sors (*thrown into a helme*t).
dēiectus, -a, -um, p.p. of deicio.
dēiicio, see be*tt*er spelling deicio.
dein, see deinde.
deinde, dein, [de-inde, cf. dehinc], adv., *from thence, from here, thence, hence.*—Of time, *from this* or *that time on, thereafter, hereafter.*— Less exac*t*ly, *then, thereupon, next in succession:* nunc deinde (*now after this*); nunquam deinde (*never hereafter*).

Dēiopēia, -ae, [Gr. †Δηιοπηία], f.: 1. A nymph of Ju*n*o; 2. A nymph of Cyrene.
Dēiphobē, -ēs, [Gr. Δηιφόβη], f., a priestess of Apollo, daugh*t*er of Glaucus.
Dēiphobus, -ī, [Gr. Δηίφοβος], m., a son of Priam.
dēlābor, -lāpsus, -lābī, [de-labor], 3. v. dep., *glide down, fall down.*— Less exac*t*ly, *fall into* or *upon:* medios in hostes.
dēlāpsus, -a, -um, p.p. of delabor.
dēlātus, -a, -um, p.p. of defero
dēlectus, -ūs, [de-lectus], m., *a choice, a selection.*
dēlectus, -a, -um, p.p. of deligo.
dēleō, -ēvī, -ētum, -ēre, [de-†lec, akin *t*o letum and perhaps lino], 2. v. a., *blot out, obliterate.*— Fig., or more ex*t*ended meaning, *destroy, annihilate.*
dēlētus, -a, -um, p.p. of dēleo.
Dēlia, see Delius.
dēlibō, -āvī, -ātum, -āre, [de-libo], 1. v. a., *taste:* oscula (*kiss the lips*).
dēliciae, -ārum, [de-†licius, akin to lacio and perhaps līcium, sublica], f. plur., *delight, pleasure.*—Concretely (cf. amor), *delight, pet.*
dēligō, -lēgī, -lectum, -ligere, [de-lego], 3. v. a., *pick out, choose, select:* delecta iuventus.
dēlitēscō, -lituī, no sup., -lītēscere, [de-latesco], 3. v. inch., *hide away, lie hid, lurk, skulk.*
Dēlius, -a, -um, [Gr. Δήλιος, adj. of Δῆλος], adj., *of Delos, Delian:* Apollo (so called from his bir*t*hplace).— Fem., a name of Diana, *Diana.*
Dēlos, -ī, [Gr. Δῆλος], f., an island in the Ægean, famed as the bir*t*hplace of Apollo and Diana.
delphīn, -īnis, (delphīnus, -ī), [Gr. δελφίν], m., *a dolphin.*
dēlūbrum, -ī, [de-†lubrum (cf. luo), as if †delū+brum], n.,

(*place of cleansing*), *a temple, a shrine*.
dēlūdō, -lūsī, -lūsum, -lūdere, [de-ludo], 3. v. a., *mock, deceive, delude, cheat:* somnia sensus; animum Apollo.
dēmēns, -entis, [de-mens], adj., (*with the mind away*, cf. amens), *mad, insane, crazy* (less violen*t* than amens), *wild.* — Less exac*t*ly, *foolish, infatuated*.
dēmentia, -ae, [†dement + ia], f., *madness, insanity, frenzy.* — Less exactly, *folly, infatuation*.
dēmergō, -rsī, -rsum, -rgere, [de-mergo], 3. v. a., *sink, plunge.* — dēmersus, -a, -um, p.p., *sunken, submerged:* rostra.
demersus, -a, -um, p.p. of demergo.
demessus, -a, -um, p.p. of demeto.
dēmetō, -messuī, -messum, -metere, [de-meto], 3. v. a., *mow down.* — Less exac*t*ly, *pluck off, pluck*.
dēmissus, -a, -um, p.p. of demitto.
dēmittō, -mīsī, -missum, -mittere, [de-mitto], 3. v. a., *send down, let down, let fall:* multos Orco (*despatch*); morti corpora (*consign*); imbrem caelo (*drop*); funem. — Less exac*t*ly, *lower, throw out, cause to flow, sink, cast down, hang down, suspend, let fall, droop:* ubera vaccae (*bear hanging*); bracchia scopuli; iugulis cruorem (*drain*); demittitur caelo nova progenies (*descend*); puteum in solido; mentes (*lose courage*); demissa ex umeris laena (*hanging*); iugum clivo (*descend in a slope*); uvam ramis; demissa pectoribus monilia; demissa voltum (*with downcast face*); dicta in aures (*receive*); demissae aures (*laid back*). — demissus, -a, -um, p.p. as adj., *downcast, low, subdued, drooping:* vox; lumen; nomen Iulo(*drawn fro*m); ab Iove gens (*sprung*).
dēmō, dēmpsī, dēmptum, dēmere, [de-emo], 3. v. a., *take away* (cf. emo), *take off.* — Fig., *remove, dispel:* curas.
Dēmodocus, -ī, [Gr. Δημοδόκος], m., a Trojan.
Dēmoleus, -ī, [Gr. Δημόλεος], m., a Greek.
Dēmophoōn, -ontis, [Gr. Δημο φόων], m., a Trojan.
dēmoror, -ātus, -ārī, [de-moror], 1. v. dep., *delay, detain, linger out;* — *await, expect*.
dēmum [de + mum (n. of -mus), superl. of de (cf. iimus, sumus)], adv., (*lowest*), *at last, at length, finally.* — Esp. wi*t*h implied nega*t*ion, *at last* (and not before), *not till, only:* illa seges demum respondet; tum demum (*not till then*).
dēnī, -ae, -a, [decem (reduced) + nus, cf. nonus], dis*t*r. num. adj., *ten each, ten* (apiece). — Less exactly (regular with *n*umeral adverbs), *ten:* bis deni.
dēnique [†dēnŏ (dē + nus, cf. demum) + que (case-form of quis)], adv., (*lowest*, cf. demum), *finally, at length, at last.* — Like demum, *not till, only*.
dēns, dentis, [?, cf. Gr. ὀδούς], m., *a tooth.* — Of *t*hings of similar shape, as in English, *a sickle, a fluke* (of an anchor), *prong* (of a hoe), *point* (of a ploughshare): curvo Saturni dente; dente unco (recluditur terra).
dēnseo, no perf., -ētum, -ere; see denso.
dēnsō, -āvī, -ātum, -āre, [†densŏ-], 1. v. a. (also 2.), *thicken, make close* or *frequent:* agmina (*close up the ranks*); bastilia (*redouble, hurl thick and fast*). — Pass., *close up, stand thick, crowd together, thicken, close in:* agmina; tenebrae.
dēnsus, -a, -um, [?, p.p. of los*t* verb], adj., *thick, dense, close, crowded:* fagi; iuba; testudo (*serried*); caligo; grando; tecta ferarum; imber (*heavy*). — Less exac*t*ly, of mere numbers, or

repetition in time, *numerous, repeated, frequent, numberless :* suboles ; Austri fremitus (*incessant*); ictūs.

dentāle, -is, [†dent + ālis, n. of adj.], n. (reg. plur.), *a share beam* (part of a plough).

dēnuncio, see denuntio.

dēnuntiō, -āvī, -ātum, -āre, [denuntio], 1. v. a., *announce* (officially, cf. defero), *declare, threaten :* iras; pluviam (*portend*).

dēpascō, -pāvī, -pastum, -pascere, (also pass. dep.), [de-pasco], 3. v. a., *feed down, crop, graze, feed upon :* summa Lycaei. — Also of the shepherd : luxuriem segetum (by *t*urning in ca*tt*le). — Less exactly, of o*t*her *t*hings than ca*tt*le, *feed on, consume, tear, devour, waste :* artūs morsu (of a serpent); depasta altaria (*with the offering consumed*); saepes depasta florem apibus; artūs febris.

dēpastus, -a, -um, p.p. of depasco.

dēpectō, no perf., -pexum, -pectere, [de-pecto], 3. v. a., *comb off, comb down :* vellera foliis.

dēpellō, -pulī, -pulsum, -pellere, [de-pello], 3. v. a., *drive off, drive down, drive away :* fetus ovium (to the *t*own for sale). — Wi*t*h or wi*t*hout a de*t*ermining word, *wean :* agni a lacte depulsi ; ab ubere matris ; depulsi haedi. — Fig., *repel, save from* (changing the point of view) ; ratibus taedas ; pestem (*avert*).

dēpendeō, no perf., *no* sup., -pendēre, [de-pendeo], 2. v. n., *hang down, hang from, hang on :* lychni laqueāribus ; ex umeris amictus.

dēpōnō, -posuī, -positum, -pōnere, [de-pono], 3. v. a., *put down, lay aside, lay down :* arma umeris ; corpora sub ramis ; plantas sulcis (*plant*) ; hic haedos. — Esp. of a wager, *put down, put up, stake* (cf. " lay a wager ") ; hanc vitulam. — Of the dead, *lay out :* depositus parens (*doomed to die*). — Wi*t*h idea of abandonmen*t* or relief, *lay aside, get rid of, put off, abandon :* curam ; deposita formido ; animos ; populum (*leave behind*, of a colony).

dēpositus, -a, -um, p.p. of depono.

dēprecor, -ātus, -ārī, [de-precor], 1. v. dep., *pray off* (cf. " beg off") merui nec deprecor (*pray not to escape my fate*).

dēprehendō (-prendo), -prehendī, -prehēnsum (-prēnsum), -prehendere, [de-prehendo], 3. v. a., *overtake, catch, seize :* flamina deprensa silvis. — Fig., of danger or time : deprensi nautae (by a s*t*orm) ; deprensus mari (by a re*t*urning anniversary).

dēprēnsus, -a, -um, p.p. of deprehendo.

dēpressus, -a, -um, p.p. of deprimo.

dēprimō, -pressī, -pressum, -primere, [de-primo], 3. v. a., *press down*. —dēpressus, -a, -um, p.p. as adj., *sunken, low, deep-set :* convalles ; aratrum.

dēpromo, -prompsī, -promptum, -prōmere, [de-promo], 3. v. a., *serve out* (cf. promo), *draw out* (for use) : tela pharetris.

dēpulsus, -a, -um, p.p. of depello.

Dercennus, -ī, [?], m., an ancient La*t*in king.

dērigēscō, -riguī, no sup., -rigēscere, [de-rigesco], 3. v. n., *become stiff, become set :* oculi (*be fixed* in a frigh*t*ened s*t*are) ; sanguis (*freeze*).

dēripiō, -ripuī, -reptum, -ripere, [de-rapio], 3. v. a., *snatch off, snatch down, tear away, tear off :* cola tectis (*fetch quickly*) ; funem ; derepti cothurni.

dēsaeviō, -iī, no sup., -īre, [desaevio], 4. v. n., *rage off* or *away, spend one's rage :* pelago hiems.

dēscendō, -scendī, -scēnsum, -scendere, [de-scando], 3. v. n., *climb down, come down, go down, descend, fall:* orni; Iupiter imbri. — Less exac*tly, sink in, penetrate:* toto corpore pestis. — Esp., *lower one's self, descend to, give way to:* preces in omnes.

dēscensus, -ūs, [as if de-†scansus, cf. descendo], m., *a going down, a descent.*

dēscrībō, -scrīpsī, -scriptum, -scrībere, [de-scribo], 3. v. a., *mark off, write off, write down, draw, map out, portray:* in cortice carmina (*carve*); orbem radio.

dēsecō, -secuī, -sectum, -secāre, [de-seco], 1. v. a., *cut off, sever:* collum.

dēsectus, -a, -um, p.p. of deseco.

dēserō, -seruī, -sertum, -serere, [de-sero], 3. v. a., (as if "unjoin," cf. detego, *uncover*), *forsake, leave, abandon, quit, depart from:* ne umor deserat arenam (*the sand lose its moisture*); thalamos pactos; Hesperus Oetam (*leaves below*); ardentem ensis (*fails him*); litora naves. —dēsertus, -a, -um, p.p. as adj., *abandoned, deserted, desolate, lonely, desert:* culmina; terrae. — Neu*t.* plur., *solitudes, wilderness, desert.*

dēsertor, -ōris, [as if de-sertor, cf. desero], m., *deserter, renegade.*

dēsidia, -ae, [†desid + ia], f., *inactivity, idleness, sloth.*

dēsīdō, -sēdī, 3. v. n., *sink down.*

dēsignō, -āvī, -ātum, -āre, [designo], 1. v. a., *mark off, mark out:* urbem aratro.

dēsiliō, -siluī, -sultum, -silīre, [de-salio], 4. v. n., *leap down, jump down:* ab equo (*spring*).

dēsinō, -sīvī (-siī), -situm, -sinere, [de-sino], 3. v. a. and n. Act.,*leave off, cease, forbear:* plura (*forbear to say more*). — Neu*t., stop, close, end, cease:* aetas; alvus in Pristin (*end in*).

dēsistō, -stitī, -stitum, -sistere, [de-sisto], 3. v. n., (*stand off*), *leave off, cease, forbear, desist:* incepto; manum committere.

dēsōlātus, -a, -um, p.p. of desolo.

dēsōlō, -āvī, -ātum, -āre, [desolo], 1. v. a., *forsake, abandon, desert:* desolati manipli. — In a differen*t* sense of the primi*t*ive, *lay waste, ravage:* agros.

dēspectō, no perf., no sup., -āre, [de-specto], 1. v. a., *look down upon.*—Fig.,*command*(of a view).

dēspectus, -a, -um, p.p. of despicio.

dēspiciō, -spexī, -spectum, spicere, [de-†specio], 3. v. a., *look down on:* terras Iupiter. — Fig., as in English, *despise, slight, disregard, scorn.*

dēspūmō, -āvī, -ātum, -āre, [de-spuma, perh. *t*hrough an adj.-s*t*em], 1. v. a., *skim off.*

dēstillō, -āvī, -ātum, -āre, [de-stillo], 1. v. n., *drip down, trickle, ooze.*

dēstinō, -āvī, -ātum, -āre, [de-stano, cf. dano], 1. v. a., *set fast.* — Fig., *establish, design, destine:* me arae.

dēstituō, -uī, -ūtum, -uere, [de-statuo], 3. v. a., (*set off*), *leave, forsake, abandon.*

dēstruō, -uxī, -uctum, -uere, [de-struo], 3. v. a.,(as if *unbuild*), *tear down, demolish, destroy:* moenia.

dēsuēscō, -suēvī, -suētum, -suēscere,[de-suesco], 3.v.a.and n., *disuse, lose a custom.* — dēsuētus, -a, -um, p.p. as adj., *disused, unused.* — Less exac*t*ly, *unused* (of some*t*hing never *t*ried), *unaccustomed.* — Ac*t*ively, *unaccustomed* (to any*t*hing) : corda.

dēsuētus, -a, -um, p.p. of desuesco.

dēsum, -fuī, -futūrus, -esse, [desum], irr. v. n., *be away, be absent, be wanting, fail.*

dēsuper [de-super], adv., *from above.*

dētectus, -a, -um, p.p. of detego.

dētegō, -texī, -tectum, -tegere, [de-tego], 3. v. a., *uncover, disclose.*

dēterior, -us, [†deterŏ- (comp. of de, cf. demum and inferior) + ior, comp. of †deterus], sup. deterrimus, adj., *worse, inferior, degenerate, weaker, vanquished.*

dētexō, -texui, -textum, -texere, [de-texo], 3. v. a., *weave off, weave up* (out of the way).

dētineō, -tinui, -tentum, -tinēre, [de-teneo], 2. v. a., *hold, detain, cling to.*

dētonō, -tonui, no sup., -tonāre, [de-tono], 1. v. n., *thunder down.* — Fig., *rage out, spend its rage.*

dētorqueō, -torsi, -tortum (-torsum), -torquēre, [de-torqueo], 2. v. a., *turn off, turn aside, turn:* cornua. — Fig., *turn, divert:* cursum.

dētrahō, -traxi, -tractum, -trahere, [de-traho], 3. v. a., *drag off, drag away, draw off.* — Less exactly, *take away, steal.*

dētrectō, -āvī, -ātum, -āre, [detracto], 1. v. a:, (*keep hands off*), *refuse, decline, spurn:* iuga bos.

dētrūdō, -trūsī, -trūsum, -trūdere, [de-trudo], 3. v. a., *thrust off, thrust away, thrust down, force off, shove off:* naves scopulo; hostem e muro (*dislodge*). — Less exactly and fig., *thrust down, force down, drive:* finibus hostem; sub Tartara hoc caput; Iovem regnis (*drive out*).

dēturbō, -āvī, -ātum, -āre, [deturbo], 1. v. a., *hurl off, hurl down, drive off, drive out:* praecipitem a puppi; caput orantis (*strike off*).

Deucaliōn, -ōnis, [Gr. Δευκαλίων], m., *a son of Prometheus, king of Thessaly, the survivor with Pyrrha of the flood.*

deus, -i, [akin to Iovis, divus, and dies], m., *a god, a deity.* — Sing., collectively, *the divinity, the Deity.* — Without distinction of sex, *a deity* (female), *a goddess.* — For Bacchus, i.e. *wine.*

dēvectus, -a, -um, p.p. of deveho.

dēvehō, -vexī, -vectum, -vehere, [de-veho], 3. v. a., *bear down, carry away, bear off:* devecta sarmenta; sylvam.

dēveniō, -vēnī, -ventum, -venīre, [de-venio], 4. v. n., *come down, descend.* — Esp. (from the rising of the sea towards the horizon, *arrive at, come to, land at.*

dēvertō, see diverto.

devexus, -a, -um, p.p. of dēvehō as adj., (cf. vehor as dep.), *descending, sloping, inclined, declining, setting.*

dēvictus, -a, -um, p.p. of devinco.

dēvinciō, -vinxī, -vinctum, -vincīre, [de-vincio], 4. v. a., *bind down, bind fast.* — Fig., *fetter, hold bound:* pater devinctus amore.

dēvincō, -vīcī, -victum, -vincere, [de-vinco], 3. v. a., *subdue, conquer.* — With cognate acc., *win.* bella (*fight victoriously*).

dēvinctus, -a, -um, p.p. of devincio.

dēvolō, -āvī, -ātum, -āre, [devolo], 1. v. n., *fly down.*

dēvolvō, -volvī, -volūtum, -volvere, [de-volvo], 3. v. a., *roll down, roll off, unroll:* trabes; fusis pensa (*spin off*).

dēvōtus, -a, -um, p.p. of devoveo.

dēvoveō, -vōvī, -vōtum, -vovēre, [de-voveo], 2. v. a., (*vow away*), *devote, doom.*

dexter, -tera, -terum, (-tra, -trum), [unc. stem (in δεξιος) + terus (comp. cf. δεξιτερός)], adj., *the right* (opp. to laevus, *left*), *the right hand, on the right side.* — From the superior readiness of the right hand: *skilful, dexterous.* — From the custom of omens, *propitious, favorable.* — Fem. as subst. (sc. manus), *the right hand:* data (given as a pledge). — Phrase: ab dextera (dextra), dextra, *on the right, auspicious.*

Diāna, -ae, [perh. akin to Ianus], f., *the goddess of the moon, sister of Apollo, identified with Hecate.*

dicātus, -a, -um, p.p. of dico.

diciō (dit-), -ōnis, [†dicŏ(reduced)

+io], f., *command, sway, power, control, dominion.*
dĭcŏ, -āvī, -ātum, -āre, [los*t* noun-s*t*em †dĭcō- (cf. **maledicus**)], 1. v. a., *devote, assign, dedicate.*
dĭcŏ, dīxī, dictum, dīcere, [√dic (s*t*reng*t*hened), cf. δείκνυμι, zeigen, token)], 3. v. a., *speak, say, tell, command, sing, celebrate* (in song or s*t*ory), *name, call.* — Used of any form of u*tt*erance. — **dictus, -a, -um,** p.p. as adj.; see **dictum.**
Dictaeus, -a, -um, [Gr. Δικταῖος], adj., *of Dicte* (a moun*t*ain in Crete). — Less exac*t*ly, *Cretan, of Crete.*
dictamnus, -ī, [Gr. δίκταμνος], f., *di**tt**any* (a plant growing on Mt. Dic*t*e).
dictum, -ī, [n. p.p. of dīco as subst.], n., *a word, a saying, speech, command* (cf. **dico**): dicto parere; citius dicto.
dictus, -a, -um, p.p. of dīco.
dĭdŏ, dĭdidī, dĭditum, dĭdere, [dis-do, *put*], 3. v. a., *distribute, spread abroad, disseminate.*
Dīdō, -ūs (-ōnis), [a Car*t*haginian word], f., *the founder of Carthage, the heroine of the Æneid,* called also *Elissa.*
dīdūcŏ, -dūxī, -ductum, -dūcere, [dis-duco], 3. v. a., *draw apart, separate, divide, distract:* terram ad capita (*stir*, in cul*t*iva*t*ion); urbes litore diductae (*separated by a sho*re).
dīductus, -a, -um, p.p. of dīduco.
Dīdymāōn, -onis, [Gr. Διδυμαίων], m., *a famous ar**t**ist in me**t**al.*
dĭēs, -ēī, [same root as **deus, Iovis**, cf. Sk. *div, divas*], comm., *a day, daylight, daytime.* — Less exac*t*ly, *time, lapse of time, proper time, fitting time, allotted time.*
diffĕrŏ, distulī, dīlātum, differre, [dis-fero], irr. v. a., *bear apart, scatter:* in diversa quadri-gae (*tear asunder,* of Mettius); in versum ulmos (*transplant*). — Also, *put off, protract, defer, delay:* piacula in mortem.
difficilis, -e, [dis-facilis], adj., *not easy, difficult, hard:* terrae (*stubborn*); obitus (*painful, reluctant,* from s*t*ubborn resis*t*ance to death); scopuli (*dangerous*).
diffīdŏ, -fīsus, -fīdere, [dis-fido], 3. v. n., *distrust, have no confidence in:* armis.
diffindŏ, -fidī, -fissum, -findere, [dis-findo], 3. v. a., *cleave, split asunder.*
diffŭgĭŏ, -fūgī, no sup., -fugere, [dis-fugio], 3. v. n., *fly apart, scatter, disperse, flee* (in differen*t* direc*t*ions).
diffundŏ, -fūdī, -fūsum, -fundere, [dis-fundo], 3. v. a., *pour away, scatter abroad.* — Less exactly, of *t*hings not liquid, *spread abroad, scatter:* dederat comam diffundere ventis (*had unbound her hair the sport of the winds*); equites; haec in ora virum.
diffūsus, -a, -um, p.p. of diffundo.
dīgĕrŏ, -gessī, -gestum, -gerere, [dis-gero], 3. v. a., *carry apart, separate, distribute, arrange, dispose.* — Less exac*t*ly, *interpret, explain:* omina.
digestus, -a, -um, p.p. of digero.
digitus, -ī, [?], m., *a finger.* — Also of the fee*t*, *a toe.*
dignātus, -a, -um, p.p. of dignor.
dignor, -ātus, -ārī, [†dĭgnŏ-], 1. v. dep., *deem worthy:* me honore; Teucros dominos (*not disdain*). — Wi*t*h an ac*t*ion as obj., *deign, think fit:* sternere. — **dignatus, -a, -um,** p.p. in pass. sense, *deemed worthy:* coniugio Veneris.
dignus, -a, -um, [prob. √dic + nus], adj., (*conspicuous?*), *worthy, deserving, suitable, fitting, fit, due:* tu vitula; cantari (a poe*t*ic cons*t*ruction, cf. nex*t* example): cui pater haud Mezentius esset; digna relatu; dignum credere (*deserving of belief*); laudes (*fitting*); grates (*sufficient*).
dīgrĕdior, -gressus, -gredī, [dis-gradior], 3. v. dep., *step aside, come away, depart:* e bello.

dīgressus, -ūs, [as if dis-gressus, cf. dīgredior], m., *a departure, a parting.*

dīgressus, -a, -um, p.p. of dīgredior.

dīlābor, -lāpsus, -lābī, [dislabor], 3. v. dep., *glide away:* calor (*leave the body*). — Less exactly, *dissolve away:* cadavera tabo.

dīlāpsus, -a, -um, p.p. of dīlabor.

dīlectus, -a, -um, p.p. of dīligo.

dīligō, -lexī, -lectum, -ligere, [dis-lego], 3. v. a., (*choose out,* cf. deligo), *love, esteem.* — **dīlectus, -a, -um,** p.p. as adj., *loved, beloved, dear.*

dīluō, -luī, -lūtum, -luere, [disluo], 3. v. a., *wash away, dissolve:* labores boum pluviā; favos lacte (*dilute*).

dīluvium, -ī (-iī), [as if dis-†fluvium, cf. diluo and eluvies], n., *a deluge.* — Less exactly, *a destruction, a devastation.*

dīmēnsus, -a, -um, p.p. of dīmētior.

dīmētior, -mensus, -metīrī, [dismetior], 4. v. dep., *measure out, measure off.*

dīmittō, -mīsī, -missum, -mittere, [dis-mitto], 3. v. a., *send away, let go, send forth, send off.* — Less exactly and fig., *dismiss, give up, cease, abandon:* fugam (*stay*).

dīmoveō, -mōvī, -mōtum, -movere, [dis-moveo], 2. v. a., *move aside, separate, cleave:* polo umbram (*disperse*); terram (*stir*).

Dindyma, -orum, [Gr. Δίνδυμα], n., *a mountain in Mysia sacred to Cybele.*

dīnumerō, -āvī, -ātum, -āre, [disnumero], 1. v. a., *calculate, reckon, count up.*

Diomēdēs, -ae, [Gr. Διομήδης], m., *son of Tydeus, a famous Greek warrior at Troy.* He afterwards founded Argyrippa.

Diōnaeus, -a, -um, [adj. fr. **Dione**], adj., *of Dione* (the mother of Venus), *Dionaean:* mater (i.e. Venus).

Diōrēs, -is, [?], m., a Trojan of the race of Priam.

Dioxippus, -ī, [?], m., a Trojan.

Dirae, see dirus.

Dircaeus, -a, -um, [Gr. Διρκαῖος], adj., *of Dirce* (a fountain near Thebes). — Less exactly, *Theban.*

dīrectus (de-), -a, -um, p.p. of dīrigo.

dīreptus, -a, -um, p.p. of dīripio.

dīrigēscō, see dērigēsco.

dīrigō (dē-), -rexī, -rectum, -rigere, [dis-(de-?)-rego], 3. v. a., *dispose in line, arrange.* — Esp. of troops, &c., *array, form:* acies. — Less exactly, *aim, turn, direct:* tela; volnera; cursum.

dīrimō, -ēmī, -emptum, -imere, [dis-emo, *take*], 3. v. a., *take apart, separate, divide:* plaga (*separating others by being between*). — Esp. of strife or combatants, *separate, decide, end:* proelia; bellum.

dīripiō, -ripuī, -reptum, -ripere, [dis-rapio], 3. v. a., *tear away, tear asunder, snatch apart:* dextram ense (*strike off*). — Esp. of booty, *plunder, rifle, ravage, spoil:* dapes (of the Harpies); focos.

dīruō, -ruī, -rutum, -ruere, [disruo], 3. v. a., *overthrow.*

dīrus, -a, -um, [√di (cf. δείδω, *fear*) + rus (cf. δεινός)], adj., *dread, awful, horrible, frightful, ill-omened, ominous.* — Fem., esp. plur., *a Fury, the Furies.*

dīrutus, -a, -um, p.p. of diruo.

Dīs, Dītis, [akin to dives], m., *the god of the lower world, Pluto.*

dis- [akin to **duo**], insep. adv. expressing *separation, distribution, opposition* and *negation*, cf. discedo, diligo, diripio, digero, dispono, disiungo, diffido, difficilis.

discēdō, -cēssī, -cessum, -cēdere, [dis-cedo], 3. v. n., *go apart, go away, withdraw:* bello (*abandon*); caelum (*be rent asunder*); scena (*open*).

discerno, -crevi, -crētum, -cernere, [dis-cerno], 3. v. a., *separate, divide.* — Fig., *decide, determine, distinguish, descry, perceive:* litem (*settle*).

discerpo, -cerpsī, -cerptum, -cerpere, [dis-carpo], 3. v. a., *pluck apart, tear away, tear off, rend asunder.* — Less exactly, *scatter, disperse.*

discerptus, -a, -um, p.p. of discerpo.

discessus, -ūs, [as if dis-†cēssus, cf. discedo], m., *a departure, a parting.*

discinctus, -a, -um, p.p. of discingo.

discindō, -scidī, -scissum, -scindere, [dis-scindo], 3. v. a., *tear apart, rend asunder.* — discissus, -a, -um, p.p. as adj., *torn, mangled.*

discingō, -cinxī, -cinctum, -cingere, [dis-cingo], 3. v. a., *ungird* (cf. disiungo). — discinctus, -a, -um, p.p. as adj., *loosely clad, unbelted.*

discissus, -a, -um, p.p. of discindo.

disclūdō, -clūsī, -clūsum, -clūdere, [dis-claudo], 3. v. a., *unclose* (cf. disiungo), *open.* — In another sense of dis, *shut apart* (cf. dido), *confine.*

discō, didicī, no sup., discere, [√dic + sco], 3. v. a., *learn, find out, come to know.* — With inf., *learn how:* currere.

discolor, -ōris, [dis-color, decl. as adj.], adj., *of different color or colors, variegated:* aura auri (*of different color from the rest*.)

discordia, -ae, [†discord + ia], f., *disagreement, discordance, discord.* — Personified, *Discord.*

discors, -cordis, [dis-†cord, decl. as adj.], adj., (*with mind apart, inharmonious, discordant, contending, hostile:* arma; animi; venti (*warring*). — Less exactly, *differing, varying, discordant:* ora sono.

discrepo, -puī, no sup., -crepāre, [dis-crepo], 1. v. n., *sound out of tune, jar.* — Less exactly, *differ:* aetas.

discrīmen, -inis, [as if dis-crimen, cf. discerno], n., *a separation, a distinction:* nullo (*with no distinction*); quo; nullo discrimine habebo (*treat as of no account*). — More concretely, *a separation, a division, an interval:* dedit vobis Pallas (*make a distinction or difference*); una anima dabit tanta (*make so much difference, be of so much importance*); vocum septem (*notes of the scale*); aequo (*interval*); parvo (tenui) leti (*slight separation, narrow escape from death*); qua spina dedit costis (*intervals between*). —Also, (cf. discerno), *a decision, a turning-point, a crisis, peril, hazard:* rerum (*crises of fate*); tanto (tali) (*such a crisis*).

discrīminō, -āvī, -ātum, -āre, [†discrimin-], 1. v. a., *distinguish, divide:* via agros (*mark out with torches*).

discumbō, -cubuī, -cubitum, -cumbere, [dis-cumbo], 3. v. n., (*lie apart*), *recline* (in place, cf. dispono); super ostro (*take their places*).

discurrō, -cucurrī (-currī), -cursum, -currere, [dis-curro], 3. v. n., *run apart, rush apart, separate, divide.* — As in dispono, *rush to one's place, hasten to* (severally); discurritur in muros.

discussus, -a, -um, p.p. of discutio.

discutiō, -cussī, -cussum, -cutere, [dis-quatio], 3. v. a., (*strike apart*), *strike off.* — Fig., *dispel, dissipate:* umbras.

disiciō, (disiī-), -iēcī, -iectum, -icere, [dis-iacio], 3. v. a., (*throw apart or aside*), *scatter, disperse, strew far and wide, overthrow* (by scattering the pieces), *demolish, shatter, cleave:* montes; rates; pacem (*destroy*). — disiectus,

Vocabulary.

-a, -um, p.p. as adj., *scattered, disordered, broken, routed*.
disiectus, -a, -um, p.p. of **disicio**.
disiicio, see **disicio**.
disiungō, -iunxī, -iunctum, -iungere, [dis-iungo], 3. v. a., *disjoin* (cf. **discludo**), *separate:* Italis oris (*drive from*).
dispar, -aris, [dis-par], adj., *unlike* (cf. **difficilis**), *unequal*.
dispellō, -pulī, -pulsum, -pellere, [dis-pello], 3. v. a., *drive apart, force asunder.* — Fig., *dissipate, dispel, scatter:* umbras Somnos (*cleave* by passing *t*hrough).
dispendium, -ī (-iī), [dis-†pendium, cf. **compendium**], n., (*a paying out*, cf. **pendo**), *expense, loss*.
disperdō, -didī, -ditum, -dere, [dis-perdo], 3. v. a., *utterly destroy:* carmen (*murder, mangle*).
dispergō, -spersī, -spersum, -spergere, [dis-spargo], 3. v. a., *scatter, spread abroad, disperse:* vitam in auras (*breathe forth*).
dispersus, -a, -um, p.p. of **dispergo**.
dispiciō, -spexī, -spectum, -spicere, [dis-†specio], 3. v. a., *see through*.
displiceō, -plicuī, -plicitum, -plicēre, [dis-placeo], 2. v. n., *displease* (cf. **diffido**): mihi equus (*I disapprove the horse*).
dispōnō, -posuī, -positum, -pōnere, [dis-pono], 3. v. a., (*set apart*), *arrange* (cf. **digero**), *set in order*.
dissēnsus, -ūs, [as if dis-sensus, cf. **dissentio**], m., *dissent, dissension, variance*.
dissideō, -sēdī, -sessum, -sidēre, [dis-sedeo], 2 v. n., (*sit apart*), *be apart:* nostris sceptris terra (*not be ruled by*).
dissiliō, -siluī, no sup., **-silīre,** [dis-salio], 4. v. n., *spring apart, burst asunder, split in pieces*.
dissimilis, -e, [dis-similis], adj., *unlike* (cf. **difficilis**), *inferior to*.
dissimulō, -āvī, -ātum, -āre, [†dissimili- (cf. **simulo** and **simul**)], 1. v. a., *pretend not, dissemble, conceal, remain hid*.
dissultō, no perf., *no* sup., **-are,** [as if dis-salto, cf. **dissilio**], 1. v. n., *spring apart, spring aside, burst forth:* fulmine crepitus.
distendō, -tendī, -tentum (-tensum), -tendere, [dis-tendo], 3. v. a., *stretch apart, distend.* — Less exactly, *swell, fatten*.
distentō, -avī, -ātum, -are, [distento], 1. v. a., *stretch out, distend, extend*.
distentus, -a, -um, p.p. of **distendo**.
distillō, see **destillo**.
distineō, -tinuī, -tentum, -tinēre, [dis-teneo], 2. v. a., *hold off, keep off*.
distō, *no* perf., no sup., **distāre,** [dis-sto], 1. v. n., *stand off.* — Less exactly, *be distant, be far away*.
distractus, -a, -um, p.p. of **distraho**.
distrahō, -traxī, -tractum, [distraho], 3. v. a., *pull apart, rend asunder*.
districtus, -a, -um, p.p. of **distringo**.
distringō, -strinxī, -strictum, stringere, [dis-stringo], 3. v. a., *bind apart, stretch and bind*.
ditiō, -ōnis; see **dicio**, the proper spelling.
ditissimus, -a, -um; see **dives**.
diū [abl. of s*t*em akin *t*o **dies,** cf. **noctu**], adv., *long, a long time*.
diurnus, -a, -um, [†dius- (akin to **dies**) + nus], adj., *of the day, daily*.
dius, -a, -um, [akin *t*o **divus** (perh. same word) and **deus**], adj., *divine, godlike.* — Neu*t.*, *the sky, the open air* (cf. sub Iove).
dīvellō, -vellī, -volsum (-vulsum), -vellere, [dis-vello], 3. v. a., *tear asunder, tear apart, tear away*.
diverberō, -āvī, -ātum, -are, [dis-verbero], 1. v. a., (*strike apart*), *cleave, cut asunder*.

dīversus (-vorsus), -a, -um, p.p. of **dīverto.**

dīvertō (-vorto), -vertī, -versum (-vorsum), -vertere, [dis-verto], 3. v. a. and n., *turn aside.* — Pass., *turn aside* (intr.). — **dīversus, -a, -um,** p.p. as adj., *in different direction* or *directions, apart, separate, away.* — Less exactly, *remote, far off, different, various, other:* **ramus** (*peculiar*); **luctus** (*different forms of*). — Phrase: **ex dīversō,** *from different directions.* — Neut., *different parts, distant places, different directions.*

dīves, dīvĭtis, [?], adj., *rich, abounding in, wealthy.* — Poetically, *fertile:* **ager.** — Collateral form, **dīs, dītis (dītior, dītissimus).**

dīvĭdō, -vīsī, -vīsum, -vĭdere, [dis-†vido(*separate*, cf. **vīduus**)], 3. v. a., *part, separate, divide, cut through:* **animum** (*turn in different directions*); **muros** (*make a breach in*).

dīvīnĭtus [†dīvĭnŏ + tus], adv., *from heaven, providentially, divinely.*

dīvīnus, -a, -um, [†dīvŏ- (reduced) + īnus), adj., *of a god, heavenly.* — Less exactly, *prophetic, sacred, holy, religious, godlike, superhuman, divine:* **mens; Alcimedon; res; lacus; poeta; os.**

dīvīsus, -a, -um, p.p. of **dīvido.**

dīvĭtĭae, -ārum, [†dīvit + ia], f. plur., *riches, wealth.*

dīvortĭum, -ī (-iī), [as if dis-vortium (†vortŏ + ium, n. of ius), but cf. **dīverto**], n., *a turning aside.* — Concretely, *a parting way, cross-roads, corners.*

dīvus, -a, -um, [√div (strengthened) + us], adj., *divine, godlike, heavenly.* — Masc., *a god.* — Fem., *a goddess.*

dō, dĕdī, dătum, dāre, [√da, *give*, and √dha, *place*, confounded, cf. δίδωμι and τίθημι], 1. v. a., *give* (in all senses, mixed with idea of putting forth), *offer, present, bestow, grant, concede, permit, allow, afford, yield, supply:* **aprum dari optat; fortuna dabatur; terga** (*turn*); **sceptra** (*give away*); **animam** (*give up*); **finis dabitur; manibus dant fontes germanae; sacra deosque**(*appoint*); **fata cursum** (*ordain*); **millia leto** (*consign*); **ulmos igni** (*commit*). — Esp. of utterance, *say, tell, utter* (cf. **accipe,** *hear*): **da Tityre nobis; dicta; ululatus** (cf. **sonitum,** below). — With reflexive, or **corpora,** or the like, *throw one's self, consign one's self, spring:* **saltu sese in fluvium; sese in acies; corpora ignibus.** — In special phrases: **poenas,** *suffer*, cf. **solvo, pendo** (punishment being regarded by the ancients as a penalty paid); **iura** (**leges**), *administer* (cf. τίθημι). — Esp. of marriage, *marry* (a woman to a man), *give* (*in marriage*). — Perhaps more closely connected with √dha, *appoint, ordain:* **dies; natura modos.** — Less exactly (perhaps from influence of √dha, cf. **edo**), *cause, give forth, display, make, form, produce, bring forth,* oftener with nouns as periphrasis for verb): **placata venti maria; prolem** (*give birth to*); **tabulata iuncturas** (*offer, afford*); **funera** (*spread havoc*); **sonitum; nidorem** (*give out*); **cuneum** (*form*); **discrimina costis** (*leave*); **discrimina vobis; spatium** (*leave*); **stragis acervos** (*pile*); **colores** (*display*); **multa melius se** (*succeed, prosper*); **amplexus** (*embrace*); **cantum** (*sing*). — With participle or adj. as periphrasis for a verb (cf. **reddo, facio**), *cause to be, make:* **haec vasta** (*lay waste*); **te defensum** (*secure your defence*).

dŏcĕō, dŏcuī, doctum, dŏcēre, [akin to διδάσκω and perh. **dīco**], 2. v. a., *show, teach, tell, explain,*

inform, recount. — **doctus, -a, -um**, p.p. as adj., *skilled, skilful, experienced.*
doctissimus, -a, -um, superl. of **doctus**.
doctus, -a, -um, p.p. of **doceo**.
Dōdōna, -ae, [Gr. Δωδώνη], f., *a city of Epirus, famous for its oracle of Jupiter in an oak grove.* — *Less exactly, the grove.*
Dōdōnaeus, -a, -um, [Gr. Δωδωναῖος], adj., *of Dodona.*
doleō, -luī, -litum, -lēre, [?, perh. akin to **dolus** and **dolō**], 2. v. n. and a., *feel pain, suffer.* — Esp. in mind, *grieve, grieve for, be sorry, sorrow, be pained.*
Dolichāōn, -onis, [Gr. Δολιχάων], m., *a Trojan, father of Hebrus.*
dolō, -ōnis, [Gr. δόλων], m., *a pike.*
Dolōn, -ōnis, [Gr. Δόλων], m., *a spy of the Trojans at the siege of Troy.*
Dolopes, -um, [Gr. Δόλοπες], m. plur., *a people of Thessaly.*
dolor, -ōris, [√dol (as root of **doleo**) + **or**], m., *a pain, a pang, suffering, sorrow, grief, resentment, indignation.* — Concretely, *a grief, a cause of woe.*
dolus, -ī, [?, perh. akin to **doleo**, *a sharp stroke* (?)], m., *a stratagem, a wile, deception, deceit, treachery* (esp. in plur.).
domina, -ae, [f. of **dominus**], f., *a mistress, a lady, a queen.*
dominātus, -a, -um, p.p. of **dominor**.
dominor, -ātus, -ārī, [†dominŏ-], 1. v. dep., *lord it over, rule, govern, gain the mastery.*
dominus, -ī, [†domŏ- (cf. -δαμος and domŏ) + **nus**], m., *a lord, a ruler, a master.* — In accordance with ancient marriage relations, *a husband.*
domitō, no perf., no sup., **-āre**, [†domitŏ-], 1. v. a., *tame, break in.*
domitor, -ōris, [†domi- (weaker stem of **domo**) + **tor**], m., *a tamer, a subduer:* maris(*queller*).
domitrix, -īcis, [as if †domi- (cf. **domitor**) + **trix**], f., *a tamer* (female).
domitus, -a, -um, p.p. of **domo**.
domō, -uī, -itum, -āre, [†domŏ (cf. -δαμος and **dominus** (√dom, *tame*)], 1. v. a., *tame, quell, subdue, vanquish, conquer, master:* Centauros leto; fera corda. — Less exactly, of wild nature, *subdue, master:* terram rastris; ulmus domatur (*the stubborn elm is bent*); arbores(*domesticate*). — Fig., *overpower, overcome, crush, break the spirit, oppress:* illum cura.
domus, -us or **-ī**, [√dom (cf. δέμω) + **us** (u) or **us** (o)], f., *a building* (usually for habitation), *a house, a dwelling, a home, a habitation, home.* — Less exactly, *a palace, a workshop,* any building or structure: Vulcani (i.e. Ætna). — Fig., as in English, *a house, a family, a race, a lineage.* — **domi** (old loc.), *at home;* **domo**, *from home;* **domum**, *home.*
dōnārium, -ī (-iī), [†donŏ- (reduced) + **arium** (n. of **arius**)], n.,(*a depository for gifts*), *a temple.*
dōnātus, -a, -um, p.p. of **dono**.
dōnec [mutilated case-form of †donicus, perh. akin to **denique**, pron. √da], adv., *until, till, so long as, while.*
dŏno, -āvī, -ātum, -āre, [†donŏ-], 1. v. a., *give, present* (with acc. and dat., something to somebody). — From another point of view, *present, endow, reward* (with acc. and abl., somebody with something): te cicutā; donati omnes; donatus (*honored with a present*).
dŏnum, -ī, [√da + **num** (n. of **nus**)], n., *a gift, a present, a reward:* noctis (*cover*).
Donusa, -ae, [Gr. Δονύση], f., *a small island in the Ægean, famous for its green marble.*
Dōricus, -a, -um, [Gr. Δωρικός, adj. fr. Δῶρος], adj., *of the Dorians* (a division of the Greeks). — Less exactly, *of the Greeks, Grecian.*

Dōris, -ĭdis, [Gr. Δωρίς], f., a daughter of Oceanus, a sea-nymph, wife of Nereus. — Also, *the sea* (cf. **Bacchus,** *wine*).

dormĭŏ, -īvī(-iī), -ītum, -īre, [?], 4. v. n., *sleep.*

dorsum, -ī, [?], n., *a back* (of men or animals). — Less exactly, *a ridge, a reef, the top* (of a wave), *the side* (of a plough), *the roof* (of a cave).

Dorȳclus, -ī, [Gr. Δόρυκλος], m., the husband of Beroe, once in the Trojan expedition.

dōs, dōtis, [√da + tis (reduced)], f., (*a giving* or *gift*), *a marriage-portion, a dowry.*

dōtālis, -e, [†dōti- (reduced) + ālis], adj., *of a marriage-portion:* Tyrii (*as a dowry*).

dōtō, -āvī, -ātum, -āre, [†doti- (as if doto-)], I. v. a., *endow, portion, dower.*

Dōtō, -ūs, [Gr. Δωτώ], f., a Nereid or sea-nymph.

dracō, -ōnis, [Gr. δράκων], m., *a serpent, a dragon, the Dragon.*

Drancēs, -is, (voc. **Drance**), m., a Latin, hostile to Turnus.

Drepanum, -ī, [Gr. δρέπανον, from its shape], n., *a town on the west coast* of Sicily (now *Trapani*).

Drusus, -ī, [perh. a Gallic word], m., a family name in the gens Livia and gens Claudia. — Esp., *Marcus Livius Drusus*, tribune 91 B.C., and *Tiberius Drusus Nero,* a stepson of Augustus.

Dryas, -adis, [Gr. Δρυάς], f., *a wood-nymph, a dryad.*

Drymō, -ūs, [Gr. Δρυμώ], f., a sea-nymph.

Dryopē, -ēs, [Gr. Δρυόπη], f., a nymph, mother of Tarquitus.

Dryopes, -ae, [Gr.], m., a Trojan.

dubĭtō, -āvī, -ātum, -āre, [†dubito (stem of p.p. of lost verb †dubo (?), cf. **dubius**)], I. v. n. and a., *doubt, waver, question.* — With or without inf., *hesitate:* poscere; quid dubitas? — **dubitandus, -a, -um,** ger. participle as adj., *to be doubted, questionable, doubtful.*

dubius, -a, -um, [†dubŏ- (reduced) + ius], adj., *doubtful, wavering, in doubt, uncertain.* — Both of persons *in doubt* and things *not clear:* res (*critical*); caelum (*uncertain weather*).

dūcō, dūxī, dūctum, dūcere, [√duc (strengthened, cf. **redux**)], 3. v. a. Of living things, *guide, lead, conduct, escort, draw, entice:* te in secreta; equas amor trans Gargara; equum (*bring*); ductus cornu hircus; ducente Deo (*under the guidance of*). — Esp. of command or precedence, *lead, command, conduct, escort:* aciem; turmas; sacra; orgia; funera; triumphos; captam Iarbas (*lead captive*); examina reges. — Of marriage: tibi ducitur uxor; ducenda datur Lavinia (*in marriage*). — Fig., of a path, *lead, conduct:* quo via ducit. — Of stars, *bring in, usher in, lead on:* astra noctem; Lucifer diem; annum. — Of things, *draw* (lit. and fig.): crimen sidera; facem stella; diversa bracchia; ducantur rotae; ducto mucrone; gemitus; pectora per augurium (*lead*); muros (*extend*); iuga (*bear.*) — Esp. of lots, *draw, select* (by lot): ductis sortibus; ductus sorte sacerdos, exsortem honorem (*take*). — Of artistic work, *bring forth, draw, fashion:* ocreas argento; effigiem; vivos vultus. — Of race or line of descent, &c., *derive, draw:* genus; progeniem; ducta series (*descending, coming down*); nomen (*take*). — Of time and condition, *lead, pass:* vitam (*drag out*); somnos (*enjoy*); bellum (*carry on*). — Also, *prolong, delay, draw out:* noctem; amores; voces. — From mercantile use, *reckon, consider, think, deem:* ducebam sic animo; me crimine dignum.

dūctor, -oris, [√dūc (as if root of dūco) + tor], m., *a leader, a guide, a commander, a captain.*

dūctus, -a, -um, p.p. of duco.

dūdum [diu-dum], adv., *a while ago, just now, a long time ago, long ago.*

dulcēdŏ, -inis, [†dulcē- (cf. dulcēsco)+ do(cf. dulcis)], f., *sweetness.*—Fig., *pleasure, delight* (properly, *pleasantness, cause of pleasure*) : nescio quā laeti.

dulcis, -e, [?], adj. Of tas*t*e and smell, *sweet, fragrant.* — Of water (as opposed to **amarus,** *bitter*), *fresh.* — Transferred, *sweet, pleasant, grateful, delightful, charming, dear, much prized, much loved.* — Neut., *a boon, a blessing, a joy.*

Dūlichium, -ī (-iī), [Gr. Δουλίχιον], n., *an island near Ithaca, and of*t*en confounded wi*t*h it.*

Dūlichius, -a, -um, [prop. adj. of wh. **Dulichium** is n., but used as adj. from it], adj. (*of Dulichium*). — Less exactly, *of Ulysses.*

dum [pron. √da, prob. acc., cf. **tum, num, cum**], conj., (prop., *that time*), *while, so long as, until:* dum imitatur (*as he was,* &c.). — In a logical sense, wi*t*h or wi*t*hout **modo** (cf. "so long as"), *provided.* — Wi*t*h nega*t*ives, *yet:* nondum ; necdum.

dūmētum, -ī, [†dumŏ + etum, as if †dume (s*t*em of †dumeo from dumus) + tum (n. of tus)], n., *a brake, a bramble thicket.*

dumosus, -a, -um, [†dumo (reduced) + osus], adj., *brushy, brambly, bush-covered, briery.*

dūmus, -i, [√dus (?) + mus], m., *a bush, a briar, a bramble bush.*

duŏ, duae, duŏ, [cf. Gr. δυώ, Sk. *dva,* Eng. "two "], num. adj., *two.*

duodēnī, -ae, -a, [duo-deni], dis*t*r. num., *twelve each.* — Less exac*t*ly, *twelve.*

duplex, -icis, [duo-†plex, (√plic as stem)], adj., *twofold, double:* palmae (*both*); parentes (*two*);

amictus (cf. the Gr. διπλοίδιον, *a long robe doubled down at the top*).

duplicātus, -a, -um, p.p. of **duplico.**

duplicō, -āvī, -ātum, -āre, [†duplic-], 1. v. a., *double up, double:* duplicato poplite (*bent*); hasta virum (*bend double*). — Also, *redouble* (cf. **gemino**); sol umbras (*add another length to*); vota.

duresco, -uī, no sup., -**escere,** [†durē (s*t*em of †dureo, from durus) + sco], 2. v. n. incep., *grow hard, harden.*

dūrō, -āvī, -ātum, -āre, [†durŏ-], 1. v. a. and n. Act., *harden, toughen:* natos gelu ; umeros ad vulnera. — Neut., *harden:* solum.—Also, (*harden one's self*), *endure, persevere, hold out:* durando saecula vincit (*in endurance*). — Wi*t*h a kind of cog. acc., *endure, sustain:* quemvis laborem.

dūrus, -a, -um, [unc. root + rus (?)], adj., *hard (*t*o the* t*ouch), unyielding, stiff, rigid, stubborn, tough, rough:* cestus ; dura quies et ferreus somnus. — Of o*t*her senses, *harsh, rough:* saporem Bacchi ; hiems. — Of persons, *hardened, hardy:* agrestes.—To the feelings, *harsh, hard, grievous, severe, cruel, difficult, toilsome:* casus ; vada saxis (cf. first division); mors; labor; curae ; dolores (*bitter*); iter; volnus. — Also, fig., of persons, and things belonging to persons, *harsh, cruel, fierce, savage, unfeeling:* Scipiades ; Mars (*cruel war*); praelia (cf. preceding division); amor; regna; certamen; vis; aures. — Neu*t*. plur., *hardships.*

dux, ducis, [√duc as s*t*em], comm., *a guide, a leader, a conductor, a driver* (of a chario*t*). — Esp. of command (cf. **duco**), *a chief, a leader, a pilot, a king, a master.*

Dymas, -antis, [Gr. Δύμας], m 1. *The fa*t*her of Hecuba;* 2. *A Trojan warrior.*

E.

ē, see **ex.**
ebenus, -ī, f., (**-um,** n.), [Gr. ἔβενος], *the ebony tree, ebony.*
ebulum, -ī, [?], n., *dwarf elder* (*Sambucus ebulus*).
ebur, -oris, [?], n., *ivory.* — Less exac*tly, a pipe* (made of ivory).
eburnus, -a, -um, [ebor + nus], adj., *of ivory, ivory.* — Less exactly, *ivory-hilted:* ensis.
Ebusus, -ī, [?], m., an Etrusca*n.*
ecce [en-ce, cf. en and hic], i*n*terj., *lo, see, behold.* — Often of an unexpected occurrence, *lo, suddenly.*
ecfātus, ecfor, ecfero, etc.; see **eff-.**
Echīonius, -a, -um, [Gr. †Ἐχιόνιος], adj., *of Echion* (who assis*t*ed Amphion in building Thebes). — Less exac*t*ly, *Theban.*
ecloga, -ae, [Gr. ἐκλογή], f., (*a* selec*tion*), *an Eclogue* (name given to Virgil's Bucolic poe*t*ry).
ecquis(**-qui**), **-qua, -quid**(**-quod**), [en-quis], pron. indef. in*t*errog., (*whether*) *any? does* (*is*) *any?* &c. — Usually implying some emotion, as eagerness, impa*t*ience, surprise, or despair: **ecquis erit modus** (*will there ever be an end?*); **ecqua puero est cura** (*has the boy, tell me, any thought?*); **ecquid in virtutem excitat Hector** (*pray, does Hector excite him at all?*).
edax, -ācis [√ed + ax, as if †edā + cus (reduced)], adj., *voracious.* — Fig., *devouring, gnawing, consuming, wasting:* ignis; curae.
edīcō, -dīxī, -dīctum, -dīcere, [ex-dico], 3. v. a., (*say publicly, publish*), properly of official announcement, *order, ordain, proclaim, charge, command, bid:* oves carpere; sociis arma capessant.
ediscō, -dīdicī, no sup., **-dīscere,** [ex-disco], 3. v. a., *learn off, learn by heart, commit to memory.*
ēdisserō, -seruī, -sertum, -serere, [ex-dissero], 3. v. a., *set forth in discourse, declare, explain, relate.*
ēditus, -a, -um, p.p. of **ēdo.**
edō, ēdī, ēsum, edere (**esse**), [√ed], 3. v. a., *eat.* — Fig., *consume, devour, waste:* edendi penuria (*want of food*); flamma medullas; vapor carinas; te dolor.
ēdō, ēdidī, ēditum, ēdere, [exdo, *give* and *put*], 3. v. a., *put forth, give forth.* — Esp. of speech, *utter, set forth, speak.* — Also of genera*t*ion, *beget, bring forth.* — Fig., *produce, cause, make:* funera (*make havoc*). — **ēditus, -a, -um,** p.p. as adj., *raised, elevated, high:* editus Austro (*exposed to*).
ēdoceō, -docuī, -doctum, -docēre, [ex-doceo], 2. v. a., *show forth, declare, inform* (one) *of* (a thing, acc.).
Ēdōnus, -a, -um, [Gr. Ἠδωνός], adj., *of the Edoni* (a people of Thrace). — Less exac*t*ly, *Thracian:* Boreae (as coming from the north).
ēducō, -āvī, -ātum, -āre, [prob. †ēdŭcō- or †ēdŭc- (cf. **redux**)], 1. v. a., *bring up, rear, nurture.*
ēdūcō, -dūxī, -dūctum, -dūcere, [ex-duco], 3. v. a., *lead forth, draw forth:* adultos fetus (apes). — Less exac*t*ly, *raise up, build high:* turrim eductam. — Of a mother, *bring forth, bear.* — Also, *nurture, rear, bring up.* — Of ductile me*t*als (cf. **duco**), *forge, work:* moenia educta caminis.
ēdūctus, -a, -um, p.p. of **educo.**
ēdūrus, -a, -um, [ex-durus], adj., *very hard, very tough.*
effātus (**ecf-**), **-a, -um,** p.p. of **effor.**
effectus, -a, -um, p.p. of **efficio.**
efferō, extulī, ēlātum, efferre, [ex-fero], irr. v. a., *bring forth, carry out, bear away:* quos ex ignibus (*rescue*); ensem (*draw*);

Vocabulary.

pedem (*go forth*). — Wi*th* reflexive, *come forth* (*go forth*). — Of heigh*t* (cf. **edo, escendo**), *raise, lift up, lift:* **caput; brachia ad auras; oculos ad sidera; tellus elata mari; elatis naribus** (*tossed high*) ; **mollibus undis** (*bear up,* of the Tiber). — Wi*th* reflexive, *arise* (cf. nex*t* division). — Less exac*t*ly, *put forth, show forth, display:* **puppis flammas; aurora diem; ortūs Titan; ab arce signum.** — Wi*th* reflexive or in passive, *be puffed up, be proud:* **elate** (*proud boaster!*).

efferus, -a, -um, [ex-ferus], adj., *wild, savage, barbarous.*

effervŏ, *no* perf., *no* sup., **-fervere,** [ex-fervo], 3. v. n., *boil over.* — Fig., of *t*hings not liquid, *rush forth, swarm forth, burst forth.*

effētus, -a, -um, [ex-fetus, p.p. of feo], adj., *worn out* (by bearing), *barren, exhausted:* **senectus veri** (*incapable of*).

efficiŏ, -fēcī, -fectum, -ficere, [ex-facio], 3. v. a., *make out, form, make, produce, accomplish, achieve:* **maxima res effecta; ne lacessas** (*stop you from challenging*).

effigiēs, -ēī, [ex-†figies (√fig + ies, cf. **series** and **illuvies**)], f., *an image, a likeness, a resemblance, a copy.*

effingŏ, -finxī, -fictum, -fingere, [ex-fingo], 3. v. a., *form, mould, fashion.* — More generally, *represent, imitate.*

efflāgitŏ, -āvī, -ātum, -āre, [ex-flagito], 1. v. a., *demand urgently, call violently.*

efflŏ, -āvī, -ātum, -āre, [ex-flo], 1. v. n., *blow forth, breathe out, breathe* (out).

effodiŏ, -fōdī, -fossum, -fodere, [ex-fodio], 3. v. a., *dig out, dig up:* **signum.** — From the resul*t* (as in English), *make* (by digging), *dig:* **sepulchra.** — Less exac*t*ly, *tear out, dig out:* **lumen** (*bored out,* of the Cyclops' eye).

effoetus, see **effetus.**

†**effor, -ātus, -ārī,** [ex-†for], 1. v. dep., *speak out, say, tell, relate, disclose, divulge:* **O virgo effare** (*say*); **tantum effatus.**

effossus, -a, -um, p.p. of **effodio.**

effractus, -a, -um, p.p. of **effringo.**

effrēnus, -a, -um, [ex-†frenŏ, (infl. as adj.)], adj., (*without a bridle*), *unbridled, unbroken, untamed, savage.*

effringŏ, -frēgī, -fractum, -fringere, [ex-frango], 3. v. a., *break out, dash out.*

effugiŏ, -fūgī, *no* sup., **-fugere,** [ex-fugio], 3. v. n. and a., *flee away, escape, get off, fly from, speed away.*

effugium, -ī (-**iī**), [ex-†fugium (cf. **confugium** and **effugio**)], n., *an escape, a flight.*

†**effulciŏ, effultus,** only in p.p.; see **effultus.**

effulgeō, -fulsī, *no* sup., **-fulgēre,** [ex-fulgeo], 2. v. n., *shine forth, gleam, glitter.* (Also, -ere, 3.)

effultus, -a, -um, [ex-fultus], p.p. of effulcio, *propped up, resting on, lying on.*

effundŏ, -fūdī, -fūsum, -fundere, [ex-fundo], 3. v. a. and n., *pour out, pour forth, shed, breathe out:* **halitus; fletus; voces; vitam** (*breathe out,* prop. *shed life-blood*); **animam** (*sacrifice*); **nos lacrimis** (*dissolve in tears*); **effusi imbres** (*drenching rain*); **effusae lacrymae** (*floods of tears*). — Less exac*t*ly, *scatter, overthrow, fling:* **habenas** (*let loose*); **crines** (*dishevel*); **inbam** (*toss*); **omne genus telorum** (*let fly, discharge*); **effusus eques** (*thrown off*); **effusus labor** (*wasted*); **vires** (*waste*) ; **effunde** (Aenean) **sub altis portis** (*overwhelm*). — Wi*th* reflexive (some*t*imes without) or in pass., *rush headlong, pour forth, rush out:* **se quadrigae; matres effusae.**

effūsus, -a, -um, p.p. of **effundo.**

egelidus, -a, -um, [ex-gelidus], adj., *very cold* (?), *chill.* — Also, *somewhat cool* (a doubtful word, occurring once only in Virgil, sometimes read *ec gelido*).
egenus, -a, -um, [egē- (stem of egeo) + nus], adj., *needy, destitute:* res (*humbled, straitened*).
egeo, egui, no sup., **egēre,** [?], 2. v. n., *be in need, want, be destitute.* — Less exactly, *require, feel the need of:* laudis; radicis. — **egēns, -entis,** p. as adj., *poor, needy, destitute; caring for.*
Egeria, -ae, [?], f., a nymph of Latium who became the wife and instructress of Numa.
egestās, -tātis, [perh. †egent + tas, but more prob. fr. a stem like milit- (miles)], f., *poverty, want, need.* — Personified, *Want.*
egī, perf. of ago.
egō, meī, [cf. Gr. ἐγών, Sk. *aham*, Eng. *I*], pron., *I, me, myself.*
egomet [ego-met (intens. form fr. pron. √ma)], pron., *I myself.*
egredior, -gressus, -gredī, [ex-gradior], 3. v. dep., *walk forth, come forth.* — Esp., *land, disembark.*
egregius, -a, -um, [e-greg(e) + ius], adj., (*out of the herd*), *remarkable, excellent, famous, renowned, illustrious, noble.*
egressus, -a, -um, p.p. of egredior.
eheu [?], interj., *alas! ah!*
ei (hei), [?], interj. of sorrow, *ah, alas.* — With dative: mihi (*ah me!*).
eia [?] interj., *come on! come! away! on! ho!*
eiciō (eii-), ēiēcī, ēiectum, eicere (eiic-), [ex-iacio], 3. v. a., *throw out, cast out.* — Esp., *cast up* (on shore from shipwreck). — **eiectus, -a, -um,** p.p. as adj., *thrown on shore, shipwrecked.* — In a special sense: eiecto armo (*with his leg thrown forward*, of a horse falling in fight).
eiectus, -a, -um, p.p. of eicio.
ēlābor, -lāpsus, -lābī, [ex-labor], 3. v. dep., *glide out, dart forth, slip away.* — Poetically, *glide on* (of the constellation of the serpent), *unfold its length.* — Fig., *escape.* — Also (cf. **ex**), *shoot up* (of fire).

ēlapsus, -a, -um, p.p. of elabor.
ēlātus, -a, -um, p.p. of effero.
Ēlectra, -ae, [Gr. Ἠλέκτρα], f., a daughter of Atlas and mother of Dardanus.
ēlectrum, -ī, [Gr. ἤλεκτρον], n., *amber.* — *electrum* (a metal of mixed gold and silver).
elephantus, -ī, [Gr. ἐλέφας], m., *an elephant.* — Less exactly, *ivory.*
Ēlēus, -a, -um, [Gr. Ἠλεῖος], adj., *of Elis, Elean.* — Less exactly, *of Olympia, Olympian.*
Eleusīnus, -a, -um, [Gr. Ἐλευσῖνος], adj., *of Eleusis* (the famous seat of the mystic worship of Ceres), *Eleusinian.*
Ēlias, -adis, [Gr. Ἠλιάς], f. adj., *of Elis.* — *Olympian* (cf. Eleus).
ēliciō, -licuī (-lexī), -licitum, -licere, [ex-lacio], 3. v. a., *entice out.* — Less exactly, *draw out, draw, draw down.*
ēlīdō, -līsī, -līsum, -līdere, [ex-laedo], 3. v. a., *dash out, squeeze out, force out, crush.* — **ēlīsus, -a, -um,** p.p. as adj., *dashed up, dashing* (of spray).
ēligō, -lēgī, -lectum, -ligere, [ex-lego], 3. v. a., *choose out, select, choose.*
Ēlis, -idis, [Gr. Ἦλις], f., a district of Greece in the western part of Peloponnesus, famous on account of its chief city Olympia, where was a famous worship of Jupiter, and where the Olympic games were held.
Elīsa (Eliss-), -ae, [a Phœnician word], f., a name of Dido.
ēlīsus, -a, -um, p.p. of elido.
elleborus (hel-), -ī, [Gr. ἐλλέβορος], m., *hellebore*, a medicinal plant used by the ancients as a specific for insanity.
ēloquium, -ī (-iī), [ex-†loquium, cf. conloquium], n., *eloquence.*

ēloquor, -locūtus, -loqui, [ex-loquor], 3. v. dep., *speak out, relate, tell, speak.*
ēlūceō, -luxī, no sup., **-lūcere,** [ex-luceo], 2. v. n., *shine forth.*
ēluctor, -tātus, -tārī, [ex-luctor], 1. v. dep., *struggle out, force a way out, press out.*
ēlūdō, -lūsī, -lūsum, -lūdere, [ex-ludo], 3. v. a., (*avoid a blow by dodging*), *foil, deceive, frustrate, mock, disappoint.*
ēluō, -luī, -lūtum, -luere, [ex-luo], 3. v. a., *wash out, wash off.* — Fig., *wash away* (*atone* for).
Elymus (Hel), -ī, [?], m., a Trojan, companion of Æneas.
Elysium, -ī (-iī), [Gr. Ἠλύσιον], n., *Elysium* (the abode of the blessed dead).
Elysius, -a, -um, [prop. same word as preceding, but used as adj. from it], adj., *Elysian.*
Ēmathia, -ae, [Gr. Ἠμαθία], f., a district of Macedonia.
Ēmathīōn, -ōnis, [?], m., a Rutulian.
ēmensus, -a, -um, p.p. of emetior.
ēmētior, -mēnsus, -metīrī, [ex-metior], 4. v. dep., *measure out, measure off, measure :* spatium oculis; iter (*travel*); saxa sideraque (*passed by*). — **ēmēnsus, -a, -um,** p.p. in pass. sense, *traversed, passed over.*
ēmicō, -cuī, -cātum, -cāre, [ex-mico], 1. v. n., *spring out, leap out, leap up, spring up, spring forth, bound forward :* in currum (*spring*); equus (*prance*).
ēmineō, -nuī, no sup., **-nēre,** [ex-mineo], 2. v. n., *stand out, project :* dorso (*rise with the back above the waves*).
ēminus [e-manus, petrified as adv., cf. comminus], adv., *at a distance, at long range, from afar.*
ēmissus, -a, -um, p.p. of emitto.
emittō, -mīsī, -missum, -mittere, [ex-mitto], 3. v. a., *send forth, let go forth, let loose, hurl, throw, shoot.* — Pass., *escape, go forth.*

emo, ēmī, emptum, emere, [√em, *take*, cf. compounds], 3. v. a., (*take*), *buy :* bene emi honorem vitā (*honor not too dearly bought with life*).
ēmōtus, -a, -um, p.p. of emoveo.
ēmoveō, -mōvī, -mōtum, -movēre, [ex-moveo], 2. v. a., *displace, remove :* cardine postes (*force*); emotae curae (*dispelled*); emota fundamenta (*upturned*).
ēmūniō, -mūniī, -mūnītum, -mūnīre, [ex-munio], 4. v. a., *fortify, protect, secure.*
ēn [?], interj., *lo! behold!* — With acc.: en quatuor aras. — In question or exclamation with feeling of surprise, impatience, eagerness, or despair [cf. ecquis], *ah! pray!*
ēnārrābilis, -e, [ex-narrabilis, as if †narrā+bilis], adj., *describable.*
Enceladus, -ī, [Gr. Ἐγκέλαδος], m., one of the giants, son of Tartarus and the Earth. He was killed with the thunderbolt by Jupiter and buried under Etna.
enim [?, perh. e (cf. en) -nam], conj., *namely, for* (explaining a preceding assertion), *precisely.* — The assertion is often only implied: sed enim audierat (*but she was alarmed for her plan for she had heard*); mene iubes confidere? quid enim (*do you bid me*, &c.? I can*not, for why*, &c.). — Irregularly (used perhaps on account of the metre), *therefore :* semper enim refice.
Enīpeus, -ī (-eos), [Gr. Ἐνιπεύς], m., a river of Thessaly.
ēnīsus, -a, -um, p.p. of enitor.
ēniteō, -tuī, no sup., **-tēre,** [ex-niteo], 2. v. n., *shine forth, beam.* — Less exactly, *thrive, be bright* (opp. to squaleo): campus.
ēnītor, -nīsus (-nīxus), -nītī, [ex-nitor], 3. v. dep., (*come or force out by struggling*), *climb up.* — Esp. of travail, *bring forth, yean, farrow.*
ēnīxus, -a, -um, p.p. of enitor.

eno, -āvī, -ātum, -are, [ex-no], 1. v. n., *swim out.* — Less exac/ly, of movemen/ in the air, *float away.*
enōdis, -e, [ex-nodŏ (weakened) decl. as adj.], adj., *without knots, smooth.*
ēnsis, -is, [?], m., *a sword.*
Entellus, -ī, [?], m., a Sicilian boxer.
enumerō, -āvī, -ātum, -are, [ex-numero], 1. v. a., *count out, recount, enumerate, rehearse.*
eō, īvī (iī), itum, īre, [√i (s/rengthened)], 4. v. n., *go* (in all senses), see various synonyms in English.
eōdem [eo (dat. adv. fr. is) + dem (cf. idem)], adv., *to the same place, there* (also).
Eous, -a, -um, [Gr. 'Hῷos, adj. fr. 'Hώs. *the dawn*], adj., *of the dawn, of the morning, Eastern:* Atlantides (*the morning stars*); fluctus; acies. — Masc. sing., *the dawn, the morning, the morning star:* primo Eoo (*at earliest dawn*). — Masc. plur., *the men of the East.*
Epeus, -ī, [Gr. 'Επειόs], m., the inven/or of the Trojan horse.
Ephyrē, -ēs, (-a, -ae), [Gr. 'Εφύρη], f.: 1. Corin/h; 2. A nymph.
Ephyrēius, -a, -um, [Gr. 'Εφυρήιοs], adj., *of Corinth, Corinthian.*
Epidaurus, -ī, [Gr. 'Επίδαυροs], f., a ci/y of Argolis, famous for the worship of Æsculapius.
Ēpīrus, -ī, [Gr. "Ηπειροs], f., a distric/ of Greece, on the nor/h-east, bordering on the Adria/ic.
epulae, -ārum (-um, -ī), [?], f. plur., *a banquet, a feast, a festive entertainment.* — Less exac/ly, *food, viands.*
epulātus, -a, -um, p.p. of epulor.
Epulō, -ōnis, [epulo, *a feaster*], m., a La/in.
epulor, -ātus, -ārī, [†epulā- (or -ŏ)], 1. v. dep., *feast, banquet:* dapibus (*feast on*). — Less exac/ly, *eat:* epulandum apponere mensis (*serve up as a feast,* of Ascanius).
Ēpytidēs, -ae, [Gr. pa/ronymic fr. Epytus], m., *son of Epytus.*
Ēpytus, -ī, [?], m., a Trojan.
equa, -ae, [f. of equus], f., *a mare.*
eques, -itis, [†equŏ + tus (reduced)], m., *a rider, a horseman, a trooper, cavalry* (collec/ively). — Plur., *cavalry, horsemen, horse.*
equestris, -e, [†equit + tris, cf. sylvestris], adj., *of horsemen, equestrian:* cursus.
Equicolus, -ī, [†], m., a Rutulian.
equidem [†e- (cf. enim) -quidem], adv. of asseveration or concession, *surely, truly, by all means, no doubt, I am sure:* hoc equidem (*this at least*); certe equidem (*but I'm sure*); haud equidem dignor (*I do not, to be sure*); atque eqidem (*and in fact I do*).
equīnus, -a, -um, [†equo- (reduced) + īnus], adj., *of a horse, of horses:* pecus. — Less exac/ly, *of horse hair, horsehair.*
equitātus, -tūs, [†equitā (as if s/em of equito) + tus], m., *cavalry.*
equitō, -āvī, -ātum, -āre, [†equit- (as if equitŏ)], 1. v. n., *ride.*
equus (ccus, equos), -ī, [√ak + vas, cf. Gr. ἵππος (ἵκκος), Sk. açvas], m., *a horse.*
Eratō, -tūs, [Gr. 'Ερατώ], f., one of the Muses. — Less exac/ly, *muse* (in general).
Erebus, -ī, [Gr. "Ερεβος], m., *the god of darkness.* — Less exac/ly, *the lower world, Erebus, Hades.*
ērectus, -a, -um, p.p. of erigo.
ēreptus, -a, -um, p.p. of eripio.
Erētum, -ī, [Gr. "Ηρητον], n., an ancient city of the Sabines on the Tiber (now Cretona).
ergō [?, old case-form of unc. s/em], adv. (and noun?). Wi/h geni/ive preceding, *for the sake of,* on account of: illius ergo (*on his account*). — Wi/hout noun as illa/ive par/icle (more logical /han itaque or igitur), *therefore, then, consequently.*
Ericētēs, see Erichaetes.
Erichaetēs, -ae, [Gr.], m., a Trojan warrior.

Erichthonius, -i (-ii), [Gr. Ἐριχθόνιος], m., a son of Dardanus and father of Tros, said to have invented the harnessing of the four-horse chariot.

Eridanus, -i, [Gr. Ἠριδανός], m., the Greek name for the *Po*.

ērigŏ, -rexi, -rectum, -rigere, [ex-rego], 3. v. a., *set up straight, raise, erect, set up, rear:* malum; fluctūs; scopulos (*throw up*). — In pass., *rise:* fumus; insula. — Esp., *build:* pyram.

Erigonē, -ēs, [Gr. Ἠριγόνη], f., the daughter of Icarius, who became the constellation Virgo. — *Virgo* (the constellation itself).

erīlis (her-), -e, [†erŏ- (stem of **erus, herus**) + lis], adj., *of a master (mistress).*

Erīnys, -yos, [Gr. Ἐρινύς], f., *a Fury.* — Less exactly, *a fury, evil genius, curse.*

Eriphȳlē, -ēs, [Gr. Ἐριφύλη], f., the wife of Amphiaraus, who betrayed her husband for a golden necklace.

ēripiŏ, -ripuī, -reptum, -ripere, [ex-rapio], 3. v. a., *snatch away, wrest, catch up, tear away, take away, steal, seize, rob one of* (a thing): nubes (*shut out*). — Esp. from danger, &c., *rescue, snatch:* me leto; fugam (*save one's self by flight*); eripite socii (*save yourselves*). — Pass., *save one's self, escape.*

errābundus, -a, -um, [†terrā (stem of erro) + bundus], adj., *wandering, roving, straying.*

errātus, -a, -um, p.p. of **erro**.

errŏ, -āvī, -ātum, -āre, [?], 1. v. n., *wander, rove, stray, roam:* Mars errat (*battle hovers*). — Less exactly, of any irregular motion, *float, creep* (of a vine): halitus (*linger*); manus (*fly*, of blows). — *waver, miss, wander* (of the eyes); dexter (*shooting at random*). — **errātus, -a, -um,** p.p. in pass. sense, *wandered over.*

error, -ōris, [√err (as if root of erro) + or], m., *a wandering, turning.*

— Fig. of the mind; *a mistake, an error, madness, deceit* (prop. a mistake caused purposely).

ērubēscō, -buī, no sup., -bēscere, [ex-rubesco], 3. v. n. and a., *redden, blush, be ashamed.* — Act. (from the signs of shame), *respect, reverence.*

ēructŏ, -āvī, -ātum, -are, [ex-ructo], 1. v. n. and a., *belch forth.*

ērudiŏ, -īvī (-iī), -itum, -īre, [†erudi- (stem of †erudis)], 4. v. a., *train, teach, instruct.*

Erulus, -i, [?], m., a king of Praeneste.

ērumpŏ, -rupī, -ruptum, -rumpere, [ex-rumpo], 3. v. n., a., and caus., (cf. **rumpo**), *cause to break out, vent.* — With reflexive, *burst forth, break out, sally forth.* — As active without reflexive, *break out from, burst out from, break through:* nubem.

ēruŏ, -ruī, -rutum, -ruere, [ex-ruo], 3. v. a., *dig out, tear out, tear up, undermine, overturn* (of walls and the like).

erus, better spelling of **herus**.

ervum, -i, [perh. akin to ὄροβος], n., *a vetch* (a kind of pulse).

Erycīnus, -a, -um, [†Eryc + inus], adj., *of Eryx.*

Erymāns, -anthos, [?], m., a Trojan killed by Turnus.

Erymanthus, -i, [Gr. Ἐρύμανθος], m., *a mountain in Arcadia,* where Hercules killed the Erymanthian boar.

Eryx, -ycis, [Gr. Ἔρυξ], m.: 1. A mountain of Western Sicily, with a town of the same name (now *San Giuliano*); 2. A son of Venus, killed by Hercules in a boxing-match.

esca, -ae, [?], f., *food, bait.*

essedum, -i, [a Gallic word], n., *a war chariot* (of the Gauls).

et [akin to ἔτι], conj., *and* (stronger than **-que** and weaker than **atque**). — With correlative conj., et ... et, *both ... and, and at the same time* (omitting the first); et ... que,

both ... and; neque ... et, *not
and, not ... but, not ... and
yet;* et ... neque, *and at the same
time not* (omitting the first), *and
not.* — With emphasis, *and that too,
and also, even, and lo! and then.*
etiam [et-iam], conj., *even now,
still, yet.* — (*and now,* in addition
to what has been stated before),
even, also, likewise.
etiamnum [etiam-num, cf. etiam
nunc], conj., *even now, still.* —
Of past time, *even then, still, till
then.*
Etruria (He-), -ae, [borrowed
stem †Etrus- (?) + ia (f. of ius)],
f., *the country of Central Italy,
north of the Tiber, and west of the
Apennines.*
Etruscus (He-), -a, -um, [†Etrus-
or †Etruso- (whence Etruria, for
†Etrusia) + cus], adj., *Etruscan,
Etrurian.* — Masc. pl., *the Etruscans.*
etsi, [et-si], conj., *even if, although,
though.*
euāns, -antis, [as if p. of †euo,
fr. Euan], p., crying *Euan!* (a
name of Bacchus) or *Euoë!* —
orgia (*shouting the cry of Bacchus
in his orgies*).
Euanthēs (Evantēs), -ae, [?],
m., *a Phrygian in the Trojan
ranks.*
Euboicus, -a, -um, [Gr. Εὐβοικός],
adj., *of Euboea* (the island east of
the coast of Boeotia and Attica),
Euboean.
euhans, see euans.
Euhoë, see Euoë.
Eumēdēs, -ae, [Gr. Εὐμήδης], m.,
a Trojan herald, son of Dolon.
Eumēlus, -i, [Gr.], m., *a Trojan.*
Eumenides, -um, [Gr. Εὐμενίδες],
f. plur., *well-wishers, the Furies*
(so called to propitiate them, or to
avoid the omen of their name).
Eumenius, another reading for
Euneus, Æn. xi. 666.
Eunaeus, -i, [Gr. Εὔνηος], m., a
Trojan.
Euoë [Gr. Εὐοῖ], interj., *Evoë!* (a

shout of joy at the festivals of
Bacchus).
Euphrātēs, -is, [Gr. Εὐφράτης],
m., *a celebrated river of Asia,* rising in Armenia and uniting with
the Tigris near Babylon. — Less
exactly, for the nations dwelling
by it.
Europa, -ae, [Gr. Εὐρώπη], f.,
Europe, the continent.
Eurōtās, -ae, [Gr. Εὐρώτας], m.,
*a river of Lacedaemon, on which
Sparta stood* (now *Basilipotamo*).
Eurōus, -a, -um, [Gr. †Εὐρῶος],
adj., *of the east wind* (Eurus). —
Less exactly, *Eastern.*
Eurus, -i, [Gr. Εὖρος], m., *the south-
east wind.* — Less exactly, *wind.*
Euryalus, -i, [Gr. Εὐρύαλος], m.,
*a Trojan, the friend of Nisus, killed
in an excursion through the Rutulian camp.*
Eurydicē, -ēs, [Gr. Εὐρυδίκη], f.,
*the wife of Orpheus, for whom he
descended into the world below.*
Eurypylus, -i, [Gr. Εὐρύπυλος], m.,
a leader of the Greeks before Troy.
Eurystheus, -ei (acc. -ea, abl. -eo),
[Gr. Εὐρυσθεύς], m., *a king of Mycenae, the enemy of Hercules.* It
was he who imposed upon Hercules, by order of Juno, his twelve
labors.
Eurytidēs, -ae [†Euryto + des],
m., *son of Eurytus* (Clonus, a famous artist).
Eurytiōn, -ōnis, [Gr. Εὐρυτίων],
m., *a companion of Æneas, son of
Lycaon.*
Ēvadnē, -ēs, [Gr. Εὐάδνη], f., *the
wife of Capaneus* (one of the seven
against Thebes), *who burned herself on the funeral-pile of her husband.*
ēvādo, -vāsi, -vāsum, -vādere,
[ex-vado], 3. v. n. and a., *go out,
pass out, come out:* ex obscura
silva. — Esp., *get away, get away
from, escape:* casus; urbes; flammam; hostes. — With acc. (cognate), *pass over, pass through:*
viam; spatium. — Less exactly

Vocabulary. 97

(cf. **effero**), *go up, mount up, ascend:* ad superas auras.

ēvalēscō, -luī, *no* sup., **-lēscere,** [ex-valesco], 3. v. n. incept., *get one's strength, grow strong.* — Less exact*ly, be able, have the power.*

Ēvander (-drus), -drī, [Gr. Εὔανδρος], m., the king of Pallanteum, on the Tiber, who hospi*t*ably received Æneas.

Evandrius, -a, -um, [†Evandrŏ- (reduced)+ius], adj., *of Evander.* — Less exact*ly, of Pallas* (Evander's son).

Ēvandrus, see **Evander.**

ēvānēscō, -nuī, *no* sup., **-nescere,** [ex-vanesco], 3. v. n. incep., *vanish away, vanish.*

ēvāns, -antis; see **euans.**

Evās, see **Euanthes.**

ēvehō, -vexī, -vectum, -vehere, [ex-veho], 3. v. a., *carry out, bear away.* — Also (cf. **effero**), *bear up, bear aloft.*

eveniō, -vēnī, -ventum, -venīre, [ex-venio], 4. v. n., *come out.* — Fig., *turn out, happen.*

eventus, -ūs, [ex-†ventus (cf. adventus), as if †even- (cf. **evenio**) +tus], m., *a result, an occurrence, an issue.* — More generally, *fate, fortune, lot.*

ēverberō, -āvī, -ātum, -āre, [ex-verbero], 1. v. a., *beat, flap.*

ēversor, -ōris, [ex-versor, as if †evert- (cf. **everto**) + tor], m., *an overthrower, a destroyer.*

eversus, -a, -um, p.p. of **ēverto.**

evertō, -vertī, -versum, -vertere, [ex-verto], 3. v. a., *turn upside down, overturn, overthrow, ruin:* nemora (*prostrate*); aequora ventis (*upturn*); eversum saeculum (*debauched*).

ēvictus, -a, -um, p.p. of **evinco.**

evinciō, -vinxī, -vinctum, -vincīre, [ex-vincio], 4. v. a., *bind up, bind around.*

ēvincō, -vīcī, -victum, -vincere, [ex-vinco], 3. v. a., *vanquish, overcome.*

evinctus, -a, -um, p.p. of **evincio.**

ēviscerō, *no* perf., **-ātum, -āre,** [as if †eviscerŏ- (ex-viscus) or †evisceri-], 1. v. a., *disembowel.*

ēvoco, -āvī, -ātum, -āre, [ex-voco], 1. v. a., *call forth, call out, summon:* animas Orco (*conjure up*).

Ēvoē, see more approved spelling **euoē.**

ēvolō, -āvī, -ātum, -āre, [ex-volo], 1. v. n., *fly forth, fly out, fly away.* — Less exact*ly, spring out* or *forth.*

ēvolvō, -volvī, -volūtum, -volvere, [ex-volvo]; 3. v. a., *roll out, roll forth, unroll.* — With reflexive, or in pass., *roll, roll down.* — Of a scroll, *unroll,* — hence, *narrate, set forth.*

ēvomō, -muī, -mitum, -mere, [ex-vomo], 3. v. a., *vomit forth, cast up:* fumum.

ex (ec-, -e), [cf. ἐκ, ἐξ], prep. (wi*t*h abl.). Of space, *out of* (cf. **ab,** *away from*), *from:* ex arbore lecta mala; patria ex Ithaca (*of*). — Of *t*ime, *from, after, since, ever since:* ex imbri. — Fig., *from, of:* ex me disce; ex ira resi dunt corda. — Parti*t*ively (cf. **ab, de,** and part. gen.), *out of, from, of:* nihil ex tanta urbe. — Of ma*t*erial, *from, of, made of:* pug nam ex auro faciam; pharetra ex auro. — Of cause, *from, out of, on account of.* — Of place where (cf. **ab**), *at, in, on:* ex alia parte. — Also, (cf. **de**), *according to, in accordance with:* ex more; ex ordine (*in order*). — In adverbial expressions: ex longo collecta (*in a long time*). — In composi*t*ion (besides its li*t*eral meanings), *fully, entirely, very much* (cf. **evinco, edisco, exoro, edurus**).

exāctus, -a, -um, p.p. of **exigo.**

exacuo, -cuī, -cūtum, -cuere, [ex-acuo], 3. v. a., *sharpen.*

exaestuō, -āvī, -ātum, -āre, [ex-aestuo], 1. v. n., *boil up, foam up.* — Fig., *boil, glow, burn:* mens irā.

1. exāmen, -inis, [ex-agmen], n., *a swarm.*
2. examen, -inis, [as if †exag- (cf. exigo) + men], n., *the tongue of a balance.*
exanguis, see exsanguis.
exanimātus, -a, -um, p.p. of exanimo.
exanimis, -e (-us, -a, -um), [ex-†anima- (weakened), decl. as adj.], adj., (*out of breath*), *lifeless, dead.*—Also, *breathless* (with fear), *half dead with fear, terrified.*
exanimŏ, -āvī, -ātum, āre, [†exanimŏ (cf. exanimis, -us)], 1. v. a., *kill, frighten, terrify.*
exardēscō, -arsī, -arsum, -ardēscere, [ex-ardesco], 3. v. n. incep., *blaze up.*—Fig., of persons and feelings, *blaze forth, burst forth, be fired, be inflamed:* ignis animo; dolor; Allecto in iras.
exaudiŏ, -dīvī (-iī), -dītum, -dīre, [ex-audio], 4. v. a., *hear* (*distinctly or from afar*) : voces.— With implied favor, *hear and heed, listen to, regard.*
exaudītus, -a, -um, p.p. of exaudio.
excēdō, -cēssī, -cēssum, -cēdere, [ex-cedo], 3. v. n. (later a.), *go out, depart, withdraw:* regione viarum (*leave*); palmā (*give up*); pestes (*disappear*).
excellēns, -entis, [p. of excello as adj.], p., *eminent, noble:* cygnum.
excelsus, -a, -um, [ex-celsus, cf. excello], adj., *high, lofty.*
exceptŏ, -āvī, -ātum, -āre, [excapto], 1. v. a., *catch* (up); *take in, snuff up.*
exceptus, -a, -um, p.p. of excipio.
excerno, -crevī, -crētum, -cernere, [ex-cerno], 3. v. a., (*sift out*), *separate, keep apart.*
excidium, see exscidium.
excidō, -cidī, no sup., -cidere, [ex-cado], 3. v. n., *fall out, fall off, fall down:* Palinurus puppi; vox per auras (*descend*); ore nefas (*fall*).—Esp., *slip away, escape:* pastoribus ignis (*get away from unnoticed*); dolores animo (by forgetfulness).
excīdō, -cīdī, -cīsum, -cīdere, [ex-caedo], 3. v. a., *cut out, cut off, cut down, hew out.*—Less exactly, *raze, lay waste* (cf. exscindo).
excindo, see exscindo.
exciŏ (-cieŏ), -īvī (-iī), -cītum and -citum, -cīre, [ex-cio (cieo)], 4. v. a., *call forth, summon.*—Less exactly, *call forth, produce:* in undis molem (*cause an uproar*). — Fig., *arouse, stir, excite:* bello reges (*rouse to war*): pulsu pedum tremit excita tellus (of the Earth half personified).
excipiŏ, -cepī, -ceptum, -cipere, [ex-capio], 3. v. a., *take out, take up, take from* or *after:* clipeum sorti.— Esp., *take next, succeed* (to something), *follow, receive next:* Romulus gentem; quis te casus (*meets you*). — As a hunting term (transferred to war), *catch, cut off, overtake, engage with:* caprum; Phalarim (*cut down*); Sucronem in latus (*assail*); incautum (*catch unawares*); equitem collatis signis (*meet in conflict*); fig. in same sense: ipsas angusti terminus aevi (*overtake*); motus futuros (*catch a hint of, learn*). — Of persons, *receive, greet, welcome, treat* (in any manner) : reduces gaza agresti (*entertain*); plausu pavidos; clamore socii (*hail*, of Turnus, as he came unexpectedly) ; caeli indulgentia terras (*Heaven treat with indulgence*).—Of conversation, *take up the word, answer, reply:* sic regia Juno.
excīsus, -a, -um, p.p. of excido.
excitŏ, -āvī, -ātum, -āre, [excito], 1. v. a., *call out, call forth.* — Fig., *arouse, awaken, stimulate, excite, alarm:* iras (*call forth*). — In different sense of primitive, *raise, build, erect.*

Vocabulary.

excĭtus, -a, -um, p.p. of excĭeo.
excītus, -a, -um, p.p. of excĭo.
exclāmo, -āvī, -ātum, -āre, [ex-clamo], 1. v. a. and n., *cry out*.
exclūdŏ, -clūsī, -clūsum, -clūdere, [ex-claudo], 3. v. a., *shut out, hinder*.
exclūsus, -a, -um, p.p. of excludo.
excŏlŏ, -coluī, -cultum, -colere, [ex-colo], 3. v. a., *cultivate, improve* (by *tillage*). — Fig., *cultivate, ameliorate, civilize, improve:* vitam per artes (*adorn and improve*).
excŏquo, -coxī, -coctum, -coquere, [ex-coquo], 3. v. a., (*remove by cooking*), *boil away, roast away:* per ignem vitium (*burn away*). — With in*ten*sive force of ex, *cook thoroughly:* terram (*mellow in the sun*).
excrētus, -a, -um, p.p. of excerno, (by some assigned to excresco).
excubiae, -ārum, [ex-†cubia (cf. concubia)], f. plur., (*a lying out at night*), *a watch, guards:* vigilum (*post, outpost*). — Fig., *of a fire, sentinel, watchfire*.
excŭbō, -buī, -bitum, -bāre, [ex-cubo], 1. v. n., *keep watch, keep guard* (cf. excubiae).
excūdŏ, -cūdī, -cūsum, -cūdere, [ex-cudo]; 3. v. a., *strike out*. — Of the effect, *forge:* spirantia aera. — Less exac*t*ly, *fashion, make, build*.
excursus, -ūs, [ex-cursus, cf. excurro], m., *an excursion, an expedition*.
excussus, -a, -um, p.p. of excutio.
excŭtiŏ, -cussī, -cussum, -cutere, [ex-quatio], 3. v. a., *shake off, shake out, dash off, drive off, dislodge, dash from, drive out:* toros (*toss*, of the lion's neck and mane); excussus Aconteus (*thrown headlong*); excussus curru (*thrown from*); excutior somno (*rouse myself*); Teucros vallo; excussi manibus radii (*fell from her hands*); conceptum foedus (*break*). — With change

of point of view: navis excussa magistro (*robbed of*).
execror, see exsecror.
exedō, -ēdī, -esum, -edere, [ex-edo], 3. v. a., *eat out*. — Less exactly, *hollow out, dig out, scoop out, wear away*. — Fig., *destroy*. —
exesus, -a, -um, p.p. as adj., *hollow*.
exemplum, -ī, [?, ex-†emlum (†emŏ-, reduced, + lum, cf. templum), cf. eximo], n., *a sample, a specimen*. — More generally, *an example, a pattern, a model*.
exemptus, -a, -um, p.p. of eximo.
exeō, -īvī (-iī), -itum, -īre, [ex-eo], irr. v. n. and a., *go out, come forth, come, go:* victima saeptis; servitio (*be freed*); amnis (*arise, overflow, empty*). — Also (cf. ex), *arise, rise, mount:* sterilis stirpibus ab imis (*spring*, of suckers); arbos ad caelum. — Act., with acc., *escape from, escape, avoid:* vim viribus; tela corpore.
exequiae, see exsequiae.
exequor, see exsequor.
exerceo, -cuī, -citum, -cere, [ex-arceo], 2. v. a., (*confine* or *control*), *keep busy, busy, drive* (to labor), *exercise:* femina famulas penso; Diana choros (*lead the dance*); exercentur agris (reflex., *labor*); equos; labor apes; (agricolam) cura salicti. — Of things, *employ, drive, work, manage:* humum (*till*); turbo quem pueri exercent (*ply with blows*); flumina exercita cursu (*hurried on their course*); membra (*train*). — Of persons, *worry, drive, pursue, vex, harass, torment:* stirpem odiis; exercite fatis; exercent te irae; exercita curis Venus. — With employmen*t*s as objec*t*s, *pursue, practise, occupy one's self with, ply:* palaestras; imperia (*hold sway*); balatum (*utter*); pacem et hymenaeos (*live in*); ferrum Cyclopes; iras (*vent*); vices (*perform parts*).

exercitus, -a, -um, p.p. of **exerceo.**
exercitus, -us, [ex + arcitus, as if †exerci + tus (cf. **exerceo**)], m., (*a training*). — Concre*t*ely, *an army*. — Less exac*t*ly, *a band, a flock:* Phorci (of sea-mons*t*ers): corvorum.
exertus, see **exsertus.**
exesus, -a, -um, p.p. of **exedo.**
exhālō, -āvī, -ātum, -are, [exhalo], 1. v. a., *breathe out, exhale.*
exhauriō, -hausī, -haustum, haurīre, [ex-haurio], 4. v. a., *drain out, drain, waste, wear out, exhaust.* — Fig., of *t*rials and the like, *undergo, suffer:* bella; pericula; satis poenarum. — **exhaustus, -a, -um,** p.p. as adj., *drained, exhausted, worn out.* — Neu*t*. plur., *trials, sufferings.*
exhaustus, -a, -um, p.p. of **exhaurio.**
exhorrēscō, -horruī, no sup., **-horrēscere,** [ex-horresco], 1. v. n. incep., *shudder at, dread.*
exhortātus, -a, -um, p.p. of **exhortor.**
exhortor, -tātus, -tārī, [ex-hortor], 1. v. dep., *encourage, spur on, incite, urge.*
exigō, -ēgī, -āctum, -igere, [exago], 3. v. a., *drive out, drive, thrust;* exegit caecos rabies; ensem per costas. — Also (cf. **ago**), *pass* (comple*t*ely), *finish, end, fulfil:* aevum; exactis mensibus; annos. — Wi*t*h differen*t* meaning of **ago** (cf. 2. **examen**), *weigh, ponder.* — **exāctus, -a, -um,** p.p. as adj., *discovered, found out.* — Neu*t*. pl., *discoveries* (*t*hings found out).
exiguus, -a, -um, [ex-†aguus, as if †exig + uus, (cf. **exigo**)], adj., *weighed, exact,* (cf. **exigo**), *scanty, small, narrow, slight, little:* nox (*short*); vires (*feeble*); exigui numero (*few, scanty*); ceres (*thin cakes*).
exiliō, see **exsilio.**
exilium, see **exsilium.**
eximius, -a, -um, [ex-†emius (√em, *take*, + ius, cf. **eximo**)], adj., (*to be taken out*), *exceptional, extraordinary, select, remarkable, special:* laus.
eximō, -ēmī, -emptum, -imere, [ex-emo, *take*], 3. v. a., *take away, remove:* labem (*efface*). — Fig., *destroy:* nulla dies vos (*obliterate your memory*); fames exempta (*satisfied*).
exin [ex-im (unc. case-form of **is**, cf. **interim**), cf. **dein, dehinc**], adv., = **exinde**, which see.
exinde [exin + de, cf. **inde**], adv., (*from thence*, cf. **hinc**), *then, after that, afterwards.* — In a narra*t*ion (cf. **inde**), *then, next.*
exitiālis, -e, [†exitiō- (reduced) + alis], adj., *destructive, fatal, deadly, ruinous.*
exitium, -ī (-iī), [ex-†itium (†itŏ + ium), cf. **exeo**], n., *death.* — Less exac*t*ly, *ruin, destruction, bane.* — Still weaker, *peril, mischief, misery.*
exitus, -ūs, [ex-itus, cf. **exeo**], m., *a going out, a departure, an egress, an exit.* — Esp., *death, decease, end* (of life). — Generally, *issue* (cf. **exeo**), *event, result.*
exōdī, -ōdisse (-ōsus), [ex-odi], v. a., *abhor, detest.* — **exosus, -a, -um,** p.p. in act. sense, *hating, abhorring.*
exoptātus, -a, -um, p.p. of **exopto.**
exoptō, -avī, -atum, -āre, [ex-opto], 1. v. a., *long for, desire* (earnes*t*ly).
exordior, -orsus, -ordīrī, [ex-ordior], 4. v. dep., *begin, undertake.* — **exorsus, -a, -um,** p.p. in pass. sense, *begun, undertaken.* — Neu*t*., *an enterprise, an undertaking, a beginning, prelude, preamble.*
exordium, -ī (-iī), [ex-ordium, cf. **exordior**], n., *a beginning, an element,* (*principle of things*), *first germ.*
exorior, -ortus, -orīrī, [ex-orior], 3. and 4. v. dep., *arise, rise.*

exōrŏ, -āvī, -ātum, -āre, [exoro], 1. v. a., *implore* (earnestly or successfully), *beseech*.

exors, see **exsors**.

exorsus, -a, -um, p.p. of **exordior**.

exortus, -a, -um, p.p. of **exorior**.

exōsus, p.p. of **exodi**.

expectŏ, see **exspecto**.

expediŏ, -īvī (-iī), -ītum, -īre, [†exped- (as if expedi-)], 4. v. a. and n., *disentangle* (cf. **impedio**), *get ready, prepare, get out, bring forth, extricate*. — Pass., *make one's way* (*t*hrough difficul*t*ies) : manus (*array*). — Also, *bring to an end, accomplish*. — Fig., *unfold, describe, explain, set forth*.

expellŏ, -pulī, pulsum, -pellere, [ex-pello], 3. v. a., *drive out, drive away, dislodge, beat back, banish:* expulsa seges (*uprooted*); somnum (*banish*).

expendŏ, -pendī, -pensum, -pendere, [ex-pendo], 3. v. a., *weigh out, weigh*. — Fig., *weigh, ponder:* omnes casus. — Esp.(cf. **pendo**), *pay* (acc. of penal*t*y), *pay for* (acc. of crime), *suffer the penalty of, suffer* (as a penal*t*y).

experientia, -ae, [†experient- + ia], f., *experience*. — From the resul*t*, *skill, knowledge, sagacity*.

experior, -pertus, -perīrī, [ex-†perior, cf. **comperio**, **-pario**], 4. v. dep., *try, attempt, make trial of:* laborem (*essay*); saxa Cyclopea; procos priores; quid virtus possit; avertere sensus. — Also, *experience, find* (by experience), *come to know;* in pas*t* tenses, *know:* experto credite (*one who knows*); expertus (*having tried it*); haud ita me (*not such have you found me*). — expertus, -a, -um, p.p. as adj., *skilled, experienced, skilful*.—Also in pass. sense, *tried, proved:* expertos belli iuvenes.

expers, -ertis, [ex-pars, decl. as adj.], adj., *without a share, free from* (in good and bad sense), *destitute*.

expertus, -a, -um, p.p. of **experior**.

expiro, see **exspiro**.

expleŏ, -plēvī, -plētum, -plere, [ex-pleo], 2. v. a., *fill up, fill:* oras floribus. — Of *t*ime and number, *fill out, complete:* quinque orbes cursu; numerum; imperio triginta orbes. — Of the appe*t*ite, *fill, satiate, glut, satisfy* ingluviem ranis; expletus da pibus (*gorged*); animum flammae ultricis; mentem; sanguine poenas(*fill the full measure of punishment*, &c.).

explētus, -a, -um, p.p. of **expleo**.

explicŏ, -āvī(-uī),-ātum (-itum), -āre, [ex-plico], 1. v. a., *unfold, deploy:* cohortes; frondes (*put forth, unclose*). — Also (cf. **expedio**), *unfold, describe, express*.

explōrātor, -ōris,[†explora-(stem of exploro) + tor], m., *a scout*.

explōrŏ, -āvī, -ātum, -āre, [explōro (*cry aloud* ?)], 1.v. a., *search out, explore, reconnoitre:* urbem; portas; lupus insidias (*meditate*). — Less exactly, *observe, try:* ventos. — Poe*t*ically: robora fumus (*test*). — Fig., *ponder, consider, meditate:* quid optes.

expōnŏ, -posuī, -positum, -ponere, [ex-pono], 3. v. a., *put forth, put out, expose:* expositis scalis. — Esp. out of a ship, *unload, disembark, land, unlade:* pontibus socios; viros in undis (*plunge*, of an accidental breaking up of a ship).

exportŏ, -āvī, -ātum, -āre, [ex-porto], 1. v. a., *carry out, bear forth, convey, bring out*.

exposcŏ, -poposcī, no sup., -poscere, [ex-posco], 3. v. a., *beg earnestly*.

expositus, -a, -um, p.p. of **expono**.

expostus, -a, -um, con*t*r. p.p. of **expono**.

expromo,-prompsī,-promptum, -promere, [ex-promo], 3. v. a., *bring forth* (out of the storehouse). — Fig., *speak out, utter:* voces.

expugno, -avi, -atum, -are, [expugno], 1. v. a., *take by storm, sack:* Spartam (*ravage*).

expulsus, -a, -um, p.p. of expello.

exquiro, -quisivi, -quisitum, -quirere, [ex-quaero], 3. v. a., *search out, seek out, seek, choose out* (with pains). — Less exactly, *pray earnestly for:* pacem per aras. — With different meaning of primitive, *investigate, inquire into.*

exsanguis (exan-), -e, [ex-sanguis], adj., *bloodless, lifeless.* — Less exactly, *pallid with fear.*

exsaturābilis, -e, [ex-saturabilis, cf. exsaturo], adj., *satiable, to be satiated.*

exsaturō, -āvī, -ātum, -āre, [exsaturo], 1. v. a., *satiate* (fully), *glut.*

exscidium (exc-), -ī (-iī), [exscindō], n., *overthrow, destruction.*

exscindō (exc-), -scidī, -scissum, -scindere, [ex-scindo], 3. v. a., *cut down, tear down, overthrow, destroy, raze to the ground.*

exsecō, -secuī, -sectum, -secare, [ex-seco], 1. v. a., *cut out.*

exsecror (exec-), -ātus, -ārī, [pass. (mid.) of ex-sacro], 1. v. dep., *curse.*

exsectus, -a, -um, p.p. of exseco.

exsequiae (exe-), -ārum, [ex-†sequia (†sequŏ + ia), cf. exsequor], f. plur., *funeral rites.*

exsequor(exe-),-secūtus,-sequī, [ex-sequor], 3. v. dep., *follow out* (cf. exsequiae). — Fig., *follow out* (commands), *perform, execute.* — Also, *follow out* (in detail), *recount, dilate on:* mellis dona.

exserō (exe-), -seruī, -sertum, -serere, [ex-sero], 3. v. a., (*disjoin?*), *thrust out.* — **exsertus, -a, -um,** p.p. as adj., *bared, bare, projecting:* mamma.

exsertō, no perf., *no* sup., **-āre,** [†exsertŏ- (cf. exsero)], 1. v. a., *stretch out, thrust out* (cf. insero).

exsertus, -a, -um, p.p. of exsero.

exsiliō (exil-), -īvī (-iī), -sultum, -silīre, [ex-salio], 4. v. n., *spring forth, leap forth.*

exsilium (exil-), -ī (-iī), [†exsul + ium, cf. exsilio], n., *exile.*

exsolvō, -solvī, -solūtum, [exsolvo], 3. v. a., *unbind.* — Fig., *set free, release:* se (of a serpent, *untwine*).

exsomnis, -e, [ex-somnŏ- (weakened)], adj., *sleepless, wakeful, watchful.*

exsors, -rtis, [ex-sors, decl. as adj.], adj., *without lot* (cf. expers), *without a share in, deprived of.* — Also, *out of the lot* (i.e. order of lots), *out of course, out of order.*

exspectātus, -a, -um, p.p. of exspecto.

exspectō (exp-), -avī, -ātum, -āre, [ex-specto], 1. v. a. and n., *look out for, await, expect.* — Fig., *hope for, long for, expect.* — Less exactly, *need, require.* — Neut., *linger, delay.* — **exspectātus, -a, -um,** p.p. as adj., *expected, long-looked-for:* expectate Hector. — Neut., *expectation:* ante exspectatum.

exspīrō (exp-), -āvī, -ātum, -āre, [ex-spiro], 1. v. a., *breathe forth, breathe out.* — Esp. of the last breath or soul, *expire, die, breathe out* (the life).

exstinctus (ext-), -a, -um, p.p. of exstinguo.

exstinguō,-nxī,-nctum,-nguere, [ex-stinguo, *punch out* (?), cf. instigo, etc.], 3. v. a., *put out* (a fire), *quench, extinguish.* — Fig., *destroy, kill, slay, abolish:* exstinctus pudor (*lost*).

exstō, no perf., no sup., **-stāre,** [ex-sto], 1. v. n., *stand out, project, appear, overtop.*

exstructus (ext-), -a, -um, p.p. of exstruo.

exstruō (ext-), -struxī, -structum, -struere, [ex-struo], 3. v. a.,

Vocabulary.

build up, pile up, heap up, arrange.
— Poetically, of a person, *raise up:* tapetibus altis exstructus.
— **exstructus, -a, -um,** p.p. as adj., *high, raised, elevated.*—Neu*t.*, *a raised platform* or *mound* (on which a general appeared before his men, cf. **suggestum**).
exsūdo (exu-), -āvī, -ātum, -āre, [ex-sudo], 1. v. n., *sweat out, ooze out, exude.*
exsul (exul), -ulis, [ex-√sal, as s*t*em (cf. **praesul**), from some earlier meaning of the roo*t* or los*t* associa*t*ion of ideas], comm. gen., *an exile, a fugitive.*
exsulŏ (exul-), -āvī, -ātum, -are, [†exsul (as if exsulŏ-)], 1. v. n., *be an exile, live in exile.*
exsultŏ (exul-), -āvī, -ātum, -āre, [ex-sulto], 1. v. n., *leap up, bound, prance:* corda (*throb*). — Less exactly, *burst forth, boil up.* — Fig., *bound, exult, rejoice, triumph.* — **exsultāns, -āntis,** p. as adj., *exultant, proud, triumphant.*
exsuperābilis (exup-), -e, [ex-superabilis, as if †exsuperā + bilis, cf. **exsupero**], adj., *surmountable.*
exsuperŏ, -āvī, -ātum, āre, [ex-supero], 1. v. n. and a., *tower above, overtop, rise up, mount up.* — Fig., *excel, overcome, prevail against, gain the mastery:* moras (*conquer every obstacle*); consilium. — Also, *pass over, pass by, pass beyond:* iugum; solum.
exsurgŏ (exur-), -surrexī, -surrectum, -surgere, [ex-surgo], 3. v. n., *rise up* (cf. **evado, escendo**).
exta, -ōrum, [?, ex + tus(superl. of ex)], n. plur., *entrails* (the hear*t*, liver, &c., observed for auspices).
extemplō [ex-templo (abl. of templum, *place of observation,* cf. *sur le champ*), an augural word], adv., *forthwith, at once, on the spot, immediately.*
extendŏ, -tendī, -tēnsum (-tentum), -tendere, [ex-tendo], 3. v. a., *stretch out, spread out, extend:* extenditur antro (*is stretched at length*); moribundum arena (*lay*).
— Fig., *continue, prolong, lengthen:* famam factis; cursus. — **extentus, -a, -um,** p.p. as adj., *long, wide, extended, extensive.*
extentus, -a, -um, p.p. of **extendo**.
externus, -a, -um, [†extrŏ- (in exterus, extra) + nus], adj., *external, from abroad.* — Esp. of coun*t*ry, *foreign, alien.* — Masc., *an alien, a foreigner.*
exterreŏ, -terruī, -territum, -terrēre, [ex-terreo], 2. v. a., *affright, alarm, frighten, amaze, confound:* aestu exterritus serpens (*driven wild*).
exterritus, -a, -um, p.p. of **exterreo**.
†exterus, -a, -um, [ex + terus, comp. of ex], adj., *external.* — Esp., *foreign, from abroad.* — Comp. **exterior**.—Superl. **extrēmus** [†exterŏ + mus, or extrā + mus], *farthest, uttermost, outmost, most remote, extreme:* tellus (*farthest parts of*); finis (*the very end*); extrema in morte (*in the extremity of death*). — Of *t*ime, *last, final:* anno (*end of the year*). — Of degree, *uttermost, extreme, lowest, meanest:* fata (*final destiny,* implying a forlorn hope). — Neu*t.* plur., *extremities, last measures, dangers, sufferings:* extrema secutus (*take extreme measures, seek the last resort*); pelagi (*perils*). — Neu*t.* sing. and plur., as adv., *the last time.*
extimēscŏ, -timuī, no sup., **-timescere,** [ex-timesco], 3. v. n and a. incep*t.*, *fear greatly, dread, be in alarm, be alarmed.*
extinctus, see **exstinctus**.
extollŏ, no perf., *no* sup., **-tollere,** [ex-tollo], 3. v. a., *raise up, raise.* — Fig., *extol, laud, praise* (cf. **premere,** *depreciate*).
extorqueŏ, -torsī, -tortum, [ex-torqueo], 2. v. a., *wrench away, wrest from.*

extorris, -is, [ex-terra (weakened), decl. as adj.], comm., *an exile.*

extrā [case form, prob. abl. of †**exterus**], adv. and prep., *outside, without, beyond.*

extulī, etc., see **effero.**

extundō, -tudī, -tūsum, -tundere, [ex-tundo], 3. v. a., *strike out, beat out, emboss* (cf. *repousser*). — Fig., *invent, contrive.*

exūberō, -āvī, -ātum, -āre, [ex-ubero], 1. v. n., *overflow, abound.*

exul, see **exsul.**

exultō, see **exsulto.**

exuō, -uī, -ūtum, -uere, [?, cf. **induo**], 3. v. a., *put off, strip off, take off:* ensem umero (*take*); cestus. — Fig., *put off, put away:* alas; faciem; mentem. — With change of point of view, *strip off, free from* lacertos (*bare*); exuta unum pedem (*with one foot bare*).

exūrō, -ūssī, -ūstum, -ūrere, [ex-uro], 3. v. a., *burn up, consume, burn away:* scelus (*purge away*). — Less exactly, *scorch, dry up, parch:* exustus ager.

exūstus, -a, -um, p.p. of **exuro.**

exūtus, -a, -um, p.p. of **exuo.**

exuviae, -ārum, [?, akin to **exuo,** cf. **reduviae**], f. plur., *spoils, clothes* (stripped off), *booty.* — Less exactly, *remains, relics.* — Also, *a skin* (stripped off), *a skin, slough* (of a snake).

F.

faba, -ae, [?, perh. remotely akin to **fagus**], f., *a bean* (of no particular, perhaps several, species).

Fabaris, -is, [?], m., a river flowing into the Tiber (now *Farfaro*).

Fabius, -ī, (-iī), [†**faba** (reduced) + **ius,** prop. adj.], m., a Roman gentile name borne by a long line of distinguished citizens. — Esp., *Q. Fabius Maximus,* conqueror of Hannibal. — Plural, the various worthies of that name.

fabricātor, -tōris, [†**fabricā** (stem of **fabricor**) + **tor**], m., *a framer, a contriver.*

fabricātus, -a, -um, p.p. of **fabricor.**

Fabricius, -ī, (-iī), [†**fabricŏ-** (cf. **fabricor**) + **ius,** prop. adj.], m., a Roman gentile name. — Esp., *C. Fabricius Luscinus,* the conqueror of Pyrrhus.

fabricor, -ātus, -arī, [†**fabricŏ** (†**fabrŏ** + **cus,** cf. **fabrica**)], 1. v. dep., *fashion.* — Also as pass., *be framed, be fashioned.*

fabrīlis, -e, [†**fabrŏ-** (as if fabrī-) + **lis**], adj., *of an artisan, mechanical:* opera (*of the forge*).

facessō, -cessī, -cessītum, -cessere, [akin to **facio,** of unc. form], 3. v. a. and n. intens., *do* (eagerly), *perform, execute.*

faciēs, -ēī, [†**facŏ** (reduced, cf. **beneficus**) + **ies**], f., *make, form, shape, fashion.* — Less exactly, *appearance, aspect, kind* (cf. **species**); hostilis. — Concretely, *form, person:* faciem circumdata nimbo. — Esp., *face.* — Also (cf. **forma**), *beauty:* insignis facie. — Also, *a shape, an apparition, a spectre.*

facilis, -e, [†**facŏ-** (cf. **beneficus**) + **lis**], adj., *easy* (both actively and passively), *ready, handy, active:* tornus; oculis (*glancing eyes, quick glances*). — Of mental qualities, *good-natured, ready, willing:* nymphae; napaeas (*kindly*); facilis te sequetur (*willingly*). — Also, *easily wrought, flexible, pliable, easily moved:* fiscina; animi iuvenum (*impressionable*). — Of things, passively, *easy* (to do in any manner): cursus; victus; trames; labor; descensus; Averni; iactura sepulchri (*easily borne*); fortuna (*prosperous*); exitus; visu facilis (*of gentle* *aspect*); quarentibus herba (*easily found*); fuga (*ready*); pecori terra (*favorable*, cf. **nymphae**, etc., above). — Neu/., as adv., *easily, readily, with ease*.

facĭō, fēcī, factum, facere, [√fac akin *to* √dha], 3. v. a., *do* (abs. or with defining obj.), *make, cause, execute, perform :* quid facerem (*what could I do?*); id facere possis (*accomplish*); quid non faciebat **Amyntas**? ; et faciet (*will do it*); laetas segetes (*produce*); carmina (*compose*); ex auro pugnam (*carve*); vota (*offer*); iudicium (*give*); iussa (*ira telum* (*supply*); factura umbram (*afford*); facta silentia (*secure, enforce*). — Wi/h double acc., or equivalen/ construc/ion, *make :* te parentem; uno ore Latinos; unam utramque Troiam; facta potens promissi. — Wi/h clause, *cause, see to it, take care :* facito sis memor ; ut incipias (*grant*); me cernere (*force*); haud faxo putent (*I warrant they*, &c.). — As sacrificial word, *sacrifice* (wi/h abl.), *offer* (with acc.): **vitula** (*offer a heifer*); **facimus** (abs. *sacrifice*); factus **honos** (*perform*). — Phrases : fac, *suppose ;* facio certum (certiorem), *inform ;* facio vela, *make sail ;* facio pedem, *lack* (see **pes**). — factus, -a, -um, p.p. as adj., *made, wrought, formed.* — Neu/., *a deed, an exploit, an act, a fact*.

factum, -ī, [n. of p.p. of **facio**], see **facio**.

factus, -a, -um, p.p. of **facio**.

facultās, -tātis, [†facili (reduced, cf. **simultas, simul**) + tas], f., *facility, opportunity, occasion*.

Fādus, -ī, [?], m., *a Rutulian*.

fāginus, -a, -um, [†fagŏ + nus], adj., *beechen, of beech*.

fāgus, -ī (-ūs), [borrowed, cf. Gr. φηγός], f., *a beech, a beech tree*.

falarica, see **phalarica**.

falcātus, -a, -um, [†falc + atus, as if **falcā** + tus, cf. **auratus**], adj., *armed with scythes*. — Less exac/ly, *scythe-shaped, hooked, curved*.

Falernus, -a, -um, [unc. s/em (Falis ?, cf. **Faliscus, Falerius**) + nus], adj., *of Falernus* (prop. /erri/ory in I/aly, famous for wine), *Falernian*.

Faliscus, -a, -um, [Falis (?) (cf. **Falernus**) + cus], adj., *Faliscan* (of Falini, a city of E/ruria). — Plur., the people, *Faliscans :* Aequi Falisci (*the Aequi Falisci*, or *Falisci of the plains* (?).

fallācia, -ae, [†fallac + ia], f., *deceit, a trick, an artifice*.

fallāx, -ācis, [√fall (as if roo/ of fallo) + ax, cf. **edax**], adj., *deceitful, treacherous, false, deceptive, disappointing*.

fallit, see **fallo**.

fallō, -fefellī, -falsum, -fallere, [√fal (for sphal), akin *to* σφαλλω ?], 3. v. a. (rarely abs. wi/hout obj.), (*trip up*), ·*deceive, beguile, cheat, delude, ensnare :* feras visco ; te Phoebi cortina ; si nunquam fallit imago ; falle dolo ; si fallere possit amorem ; numen (*swear by and break the oath*); te sententia ; dextras (*break a pledge*). — Less exac/ly, *disappoint :* spem ; primus amor me morte. — In pass., *be deceived, be mistaken, mistake :* nisi fallor. — Also, *miss, fail :* longe fallente sagitta (*miss the mark*). — Wi/h cog. acc., *assume, counterfeit*. — Esp., *escape notice of, be unknown, be hid :* me fallit (*be hid from, be unknown to*).

falsus, -a, -um, p.p. as adj., *false, treacherous, deceitful, deceptive, groundless, delusive, counterfeit, imaginary, unreal :* sol (*mock*).

falsus, -a, -um, p.p. of **fallo**.

falx, falcis [perh. akin to **flecto**], f., *a hooked knife, a sickle, a scythe, a bill-hook, a pruning-knife*.

fāma, -ae, [√fa (cf. **for**) + ma], f., *report, tidings, fame, tradition :* inanis (*belief*). — Esp. (in a good

sense), *fame, reputation, glory.* — Less commonly, *ill repute* (cf. **famosus**), *infamy.*
fames, -is, [?, cf. **faba**], f., *hunger, famine, starvation.* — Fig., *hunger, greed:* auri (*thirst*). — Personified, *Famine:* male suada.
famula, -ae, [f. of **famulus**], f., *a maid-servant.*
famulus, -ī, [famŏ- (cf. Oscan, faama, *house*) + lus, cf. -lis], m., *a house-servant, attendant, manservant.* — Less exactly, *an attendant* (on a deified person).
fandus, -a, -um ; see **for.**
far, farris, [?, cf. **faba**], n., *grain* (prob. a coarse species), *spelt* (?). —Less exactly, *meal* (of the coarser kind, used as an offering, mixed with salt) : ˙pium.
farrāgŏ, -inis, [**far,** through an intermediate stem], f., *provender* (mixed), *a mash.*
fās, indecl., [√fa + as (= us), cf. **fatum**], n., (*command*), *right,* (divine) *law:* fas omne abrumpit (*violate all right*); fas immortale (*privilege of divinity*). — With **sum** (expressed or implied), *allowed, permitted, just, lawful, fitting, right.*
fascēs, see **fascis.**
fascinō, -āvī, -ātum, -are, [†fascinŏ- (stem of **fascinum,** †fasci + num,** n. of nus), cf. **fascia, fascis**; the connection of ideas is lost, but prob. through *binding*], 1. v. a., *bewitch.*
fascis, -is, [?, cf. **fascia, fascinum**], m., *a bundle* (tied up), *pack.* — Less exactly, *a burden.* — Esp., plur., *the fasces* (the bundle of rods with an axe, the emblem of authority of a Roman magistrate). — Fig., *magistracy, military power:* populi (*ensigns of power* conferred by the people, *popular honors*).
faselus, see **phaselus.**
fastīdiō,-īvī,-ītum,-īre,[†fastīdi- (adj. akin to **fastus,** *pride*), cf. **fastidium**], 4. v. n. and a., *feel disdain, disdain, scorn.* (Prob. derived from turning up the nose, cf. **fastigium**).
fastīdium, -ī (-iī), [akin to **fastus,** cf. **fastidio**], n., *disgust, loathing, disdain.* — Less exactly, *nausea, a qualm.*
fastīgium, -ī (-iī), †fastīgŏ- (cf. **fastīgō**) + ium], n., *the top* (of any thing), *a summit, a roof, a peak, battlements* (of a wall), *gable* (of a roof). — Less exactly, *slope* or *depth* (of a ditch). — Fig., *a point* (of a narrative) : summa sequar (*touch the principal points*).
fastus, -tūs, [unc. root + tus, cf. **fastidium** and **fastigium**], m., *pride, arrogance.*
fātālis, -e, [†fatŏ (reduced) + alis], adj., (*belonging to fate*), *fated,* (*fraught with fate*), *destined, appointed.* — *fatal, ruinous, destructive.*
fateor, fassus, fatērī, [lost stem, perh. akin to **fatiscor,** †fatis, **fatigo**], 2. v. dep., *confess, own, acknowledge, admit:* dicto parere (*submit*).
fātidicus, -a, -um, [†fatŏ-dicus], adj., *soothsaying, prophetic.*
fātifer, -era, -erum, [†fatŏ-fer (√fer + us)], adj., (*fate-bringing*); *fatal, deadly.*
fatīgō, -āvī, -ātum, -āre, [†fatīgŏ- (†fati-agus, cf. **prodigus**), cf. **castīgō**], 1. v. a., *tire out, weary:* equos. — Less exactly, of acts tending to weariness, *worry, ply, vex, harass, pursue:* terga iuvencum hasta ; equos sole (*worry in the heat*); Martem (*incite to war*); diem noctemque remigio (*disturb*); silvas (*scour*); metu terras (*vex*); socios (*chide*); cervos cursu (*pursue in chase*); os (*ply,* of a horse); fluctūs (of a ship, *beat*).
fatiscō, no perf., no sup., **-ere,** [?], 3. v. n., *yawn, gape, crack.*
fātum, -ī, [n. p.p. of **for**], n., *an oracle, a response, decree* (of fate),

fate, destiny. — Esp., *death* (as fa*t*ed).

fātus, -a, -um, p.p. of **for.**

faucēs, see **faux.**

†faux, †faucis, [?], f. (only abl. sing. and plur.), *the throat, the jaws:* vox faucibus haesit. — — Less exac*t*ly, *a narrow pass, a defile, the channel of a river* (probably wi*t*h a kind of personification).

Faunus, -ī, [√fav (in **faveo**) + nus], m., *a sylvan deity, patron of shepherds,* iden*t*ified wi*t*h Pan. He was supposed *t*o be an I*t*alian, son of Picus and grandson of Sa*t*urn. — Less exac*t*ly, in plur., *fauns, deities partly identified with the Greek satyrs, but with less animal characteristics than they.*

faveō, fāvī, fautum, favēre, [√fav, perh. akin to √fa, but prob. *t*hrough a noun-s*t*em, cf. **favilla**], 2. v. n., *be favorable, favor, be propitious:* terra frumentis (*be good for*); adsis faveus (*kindly aid*). — As religious expression wi*t*h (or wi*t*hou*t*) ore, *refrain from ill-omened expressions, keep religious silence:* celebrate faventes (*attend with pious lips and celebrate*); favete ore omnes. — **favēns, -ēntis,** p. as adj., *propitious* (see preceding). — Plur., *favorers, partisans:* clamor faventum.

favilla, -ae, [akin *t*o **faveo**], f., *glowing ashes, embers, cinders, sparks.*

favor, -ōris, [√fav (cf. **faveo**) + or], m., *favor, partiality.*

favus, -ī, [?], m., *a honey-comb* (usually in plur.); favos relinquunt (*leave their cells*); favorum cratis (*the net-work of the comb*). — Less exac*t*ly, *honey:* favos dilue Baccho.

fax, facis, [√fac as s*t*em, remotely akin to √fa and √fau], f., *a torch, a brand, a fire-brand:* incide (of the wood for *t*orches); inspicat (of wood to serve as ma*t*ches or torches); face ferroque (*with sword and brand*); face vim ferre (*assail with flames*); faces et saxa volant; funereae, plur. (*the funeral-torch,* from its use at funerals; also fig., as a symbol of dea*t*h); mater armata facibus (of Cly*t*emnes*t*ra in the guise of a Fury). — Less exac*t*ly, of a shoo*t*ing-s*t*ar, *a trail* (of fire).

faxo, see **facio.**

febris, -is, [akin *t*o **ferveo**], f., *a fever, fever.*

fēcundō (foe-), **-āvī, -ātum, -āre,** [†fecundō-], 1. v. a, *fertilize.*

fēcundus, (foe-), **-a, -um,** [†fē (s*t*em or root of †feo) + cundus], adj., *productive, fruitful, fertile, prolific.* — Fig., *fertile, ingenious:* pectus. — Ac*t*ively, *fertilizing:* imbres.

fel, fellis, [akin *t*o Gr. χόλος], n., *gall.* — Less exac*t*ly, of bi*t*ter *t*hings: veneni (*bitter essence*). — Fig., *anger* (supposed to be connec*t*ed wi*t*h a s*t*a*t*e of the bile, cf. "melancholy"), *fury, bitter hatred.*

fēlix, -īcis, [akin *t*o **feo, fecundus**], adj., *fruitful, productive, rich, prolific:* limus; sylvae; oliva; Massica Baccho. — Less exac*t*ly, *auspicious, favorable:* auspicia; sis felix; Zephyri (*favoring*); dies; hostia. — Passively, *blest, happy, fortunate, lucky:* arma (*successful*); animae; vivite felices; morte tua.

fēmina (also **foemina**), [†fe (s*t*em or root of †feo) + mina, cf. **alumnus, columna**], f., *a woman.* — Of animals, *a female, a mare.*

fēmineus, (foe-), **-a, -um,** [†fēmina (reduced) + ens], adj., *of a woman, female, feminine, womanly:* manus; nubes feminea tegat (*like a woman,* as a cowardly means of defence).

femur, -oris, [?], n., *the thigh.*

fenestra, -ae, [?], f., *a window*

(opening for ligh*t*).—Less exac*t*ly, *an aperture, a breach* (in a wall).

fēnīlia, (foe-), -ium, [†fenŏ- (reduced) + ilis, plu. of adj.], n., *a hay-loft.*

fērālis, -e, [?], adj., *funereal:* cupressi. — Less exactly, *mournful, dismal, ill-omened:* carmen.

ferāx,-ācis, [√fer+ax, cf. edax], adj., *productive, fruitful.*

ferĕ, [?], adv., *almost, nearly, about.* — *generally, for the most part, usually.*

feretrum, -ī, [†fere- (stem of **fero,** or *noun-s*tem akin) + trum, but perh. borrowed, cf. Gr. φέρετρον], n., *a bier.*

ferīna, see **ferīnus.**

ferīnus, -a, -um, [†ferŏ- (reduced) + inus], adj., *of beasts, of a beast* (wild). — **ferīna** (sc. **caro**), f., *game, venison,* &c.

feriō, no perf., no sup., **ferīre,** [?], 4. v. a., *strike, beat, lash:* terram pede equus (*paw*); velum procella; ora saxo. — Esp. of the effec*t, wound, pierce, kill:* venam (*o*pen); retinaculo ferro (*cut, sever*). — Fig.: aethera clamor. — Phrase: ferio foedus, *make a treaty* (prob. from killing a victim).

feritās, -tātis, [†ferŏ + tas], f., *wildness, fierceness.*

fermentum, -ī, [√ferv (in **ferveo**)+mentum], n., *yeast, leaven.*

ferŏ, tulī, lātum, ferre, [√fer, cf. Gr. φέρω, Eng. *bear,* perf. √tol (in **tollo**), p.p. √tla (colla*t*eral with √tol), cf. τλῆμι], irr. v. a. and n., *bear.*

1. Simply, *bear, carry, support, wear:* vix illam famuli (of a weigh*t*y cuirass); flammas (*t*orches); vestes; parmam hastamque; esseda collo (of a horse). — Fig.: nostrae secum omina mortis; genus incertum de patre (*claim*); hanc spem tui (*cherish*); adversum pectus in hostem (*wear a stout heart*). — Esp. of the body and its par*t*s, *hold, turn, carry:* se talem Dido (*appear such*); sic oculos (*such are the eyes*); magna se mole (*rear enormous bulk*); caput iuvencus (*hold its head*). — With idea of eleva*t*ion, *bear, raise, rear, lift:* caelo capita alta (of the Cyclops); sublimem ad sidera Aenean. — Fig., *raise, extol, laud:* factis ad aethera Troiam; insigni laude Teucros; carmine facta. — Also, cf. **tollo,** *raise* (a cry).

2. Of endurance (as in Eng.), *bear, endure, tolerate, suffer, submit to, brook, put up with:* laborem; frena (of a horse); non tulit (*could not brook*).

3. With idea of mo*t*ion, *bear, carry, convey, bring:* cineres foras; stabulis ignem (*set*); manum ad volnus (*put to, place on*); seges feratur (*transplant*); equo ferri (*ride*); equis auriga (*drive*); fertur equis (*drag*). — Less exac*t*ly, *throw, aim:* tela; saxum; plagam. — Fig., *bear, bring, carry, render, afford:* praemia digna (*bestow*); auxilium Priamo; fama salutem; sonitum venti ad litora; vox fertur ad aures; carmina per orbem (*spread*); vim tela (*offer*); letum; gloria laudem; sidera caelo dextra (*set*); viam vento facilem (*grant*); fidem vetustas; omnia sub auras (*disclose*); sitim morbosque (*bring, cause,* cf. 4). — Esp. of religious offerings and ac*t*s, *bear, offer, render, perform, utter:* sacra; absenti inferias; Iunoni preces. — Esp. also of words, messages, &c.: responsa regi; iussa; haec Ascanio; fama victorem Pallanta (*report that*); quae signa (*show,* of prophe*t*ic doves); casum portenta (*forbode*); quae ferimus (*what we propose*); quidve ferat (*what is his purpose*). — From the last use, absolu*t*ely, *report, say, tell:* ita senes; ferebatur sacrasse; ferunt (*they say*); fer-

tur (*it is said*); se de gente Amyci (*boast, claim*). — Also of des*t*iny, *ordain, order, assign :* sic fata; quid fortuna populi; casus apibus.

4. Of na*t*ural grow*t*h, *bear, generate, produce, yield, give birth to:* mala quercus; monstra pontus; me Troia. — Fig. (but cf. 3), *cause, give, afford:* taeda lumen; scabiem glacies.

5. Less exac*t*ly, of any enforced motion, *drive, bear on, turn, lead, urge on:* flamina classem; ferte rates (of rowers); ferimur procella; illam impetus (*send*); caede ferri (*be carried away*); quos dolor in hostem (*incite*); in bella urbes (*rouse*); feror incensa furiis(*be driven madly on*); veri vana feror (*be led on*); fatis incerta (*be urged on*); metum ad moenia (*spread alarm*); turbo fertur (*whirl on*); prona aqua fertur (*float down*); iter (*speed a course*); gressum (*hold, turn*); via fert; signa ad speluncam (*point*); huc ora et illuc (*turn*, cf. 3); caelo animum (in hope); pedem domum (*turn the steps*). — So in special phrases: manum, *join* (cf. "bear a hand"); pedem, *ply the foot*(in the dance); signa, *charge, join battle, move forward;* obvius(obviam), *meet;* obvia arma (*meet the foe*). — Esp. wi*t*h reflexive, or in pass. wi*t*h middle sense, *be borne on, be driven, proceed, rush, go, advance:* me extra tecta (*come forth*); furiata mente ferebar; sese obvia oculis (*offer, show*); sese halitus (*rise*); solus ego in Pallanta (*assail*); se ad auras (*soar*); saltu (*leap, spring*); quo feror; quo se ferret; ferimur (*wander*, cf. firs*t* examples under 5).

6. Of mo*t*ion from a place, *bear away, carry off* (both in bad and good sense): unda te mersum; te fata (*take off, destroy*); exstinctum Daphnim (*remove by death*); secum maria (of the winds); venti gaudia; hiems culmum; pedum Antigenes (*get*); praemia ferunt (*receive*); talentum ferre (*have*); aetas omnia (*obliterates*). — Esp.: rapio et fero, *pillage and plunder.* — Less common uses, prob. conn. wi*t*h 3, *suggest, prompt:* ita corde voluntas. — Orig. as a mercantile *t*erm, *account, deem, hold:* feretur fama levis; horrendum. — Of con*t*inuance, *prolong, perpetuate:* vivus per ora feretur (*immortalize*); ludum in lucem; fama nomen per annos. — ferens, -entis, p. as adj., *favorable* (cf. 5): ventus.

Fērōnia, -ae, [?], f., a goddess honored wi*t*h a grove and fountain near Terracina.

ferōx, -ōcis, [s*t*em akin to ferus, in ō (cf. aegrotus) + cus (reduced, cf. edax, felix)], adj., *wild, fierce, savage, spirited* (of a horse), *angry* (of a snake). Also, in an indifferent or good sense, *warlike, courageous, exultant, proud.*

ferrātus, -a, -um, [†ferrŏ- (reduced) + atus (cf. auratus)], adj.,*iron-shod, iron-bound, ironed:* calx (*spur-bound*); capistra (*spiked muzzles*); orbes (*iron-bound wheels*).

ferreus, -a, -um, [†ferrŏ (reduced) + eus], adj., *of iron, iron:* seges (of spears); gens (*the iron age*); vox (*brazen voice*); progenies (of the iron age). — Fig., *iron-hearted, inexorable:* iura (*harsh*). — Poe*t*ically, somnus (*iron, wi*t*h no awakening*); imber (*iron hail*).

ferrūgineus, -a, -um, [†ferrugin + eus], adj., (*rusty*), *dark blue, dusky.* (Apparen*t*ly a dark gray or purple, *t*hough named from the color of iron rus*t*): hyacinthi; cymba (of Charon's boa*t*).

ferrūgō, -inis, [s*t*em akin to ferrum + unc. *t*erm., cf. caligo], f., *iron rust.* — Also (cf. **ferrugineus**), *a dark purple, dark gray?, dark blue?, a murky hue* (of the sun in an eclipse): ferrugine clarus Ibera (*the color of burnished iron, purple?*).

ferrum, -ī, [?], n., *iron, steel.* — Less exactly, as in English, of tools or weapons of iron, *a sword, a ploughshare, an arrow, a knife, an axe, the steel* (as in English), *the iron* (of a spear or arrow): cedite ferro (*the sword*); ferrum lacessere; absistere ferro (*abstain from war*); amor ferri (*love of arms*).

fertilis, -e, [†fertŏ- (lost p.p. of fero) + lis (cf. **fero**)], adj., *fertile, fruitful, productive:* seges iuvencis; Ausonia.

ferula, -ae, [?], f., *fennel.*

ferus, -a, -um, [?], adj., *wild* (untamed, undomesticated), *uncultivated:* capri; fructus; montes. — Fig., *wild, rude, savage, fierce, cruel.* — Also, in a good sense (cf. **saevus**), *fierce, warlike, impetuous.* — Masc. and fem., *a wild beast, game* (deer, &c.), *a horse.*

ferveō, -buī, no sup., **-vēre,** (also **-ĕre,** as if **fervo**), [†fervŏ- (cf. **fervidus**)], 2. v. n., *be hot:* ferventes rotae (*heated*), — *boil, seethe* (as waves, &c.): aequor; omnia vento nimbisque (*seethe and eddy*). — Fig., *be alive* (of busy action), *be in a turmoil:* Marte Leucatem (*in the turmoil of war*); litora flammis (*in seething flame*); opus (*be all alive*); opere semita (*teem with busy work*); hostem caede (*be on fire*).

fervidus, -a, -um, [†fervŏ- (cf. **ferveo**) + dus], adj., *hot, glowing, seething.* — Fig., *glowing, furious, ardent, fiery:* ira.

fervō, see **ferveo.**

fervor, -ōris, [√ferv (cf. **ferveo**)], m., *heat.* — Fig., *fury.* — Plur., *summer, summer heats.*

Fescennīnus, -a, -um, [†Fescennŏ- (reduced, cf. **Porsenna**) + inus], adj., *of Fescennia* (a town of Etruria), *Fescennine.*

fessus, -a, -um, [?, akin to **fatis**], adj., *weary, tired, worn out, spent, exhausted.* — Poetically: naves (as if personified); res (*shattered fortunes*).

festīnō, -āvī, -ātum, -āre, [†festinŏ-], 1. v. n., *make haste, hasten,* — With cog. acc.: fugam; iussa.

festīnus, -a, -um, [†festi-, in confestim (with lengthened i, cf. **Portūnus**) + nus], adj., *hasty, in haste, speedy.*

festus, -a, -um, [p.p. of unc. root], adj., *festal, festive, sacred, holy:* frons; dies (*festival*).

fētūra (foe-), -ae, [†fētu (with lengthened u, cf. **Portūnus**) + ra (f. of rus)], f., *breeding, bearing.* — Concretely, *offspring, increase.*

fētus (foe-), -tūs, [√fe (in †feo) + tus], m., *bearing, breeding.* — Concretely, *offspring, brood, litter, young.* — Less exactly, *fruit, crop, produce.*

fētus (foe-), -a, -um, [p.p. of †feo], as adj., *pregnant, breeding, delivered:* vaccae (*after calving*); lupa (*with young*). — Fig., *teeming.* — Fem., *pregnant sheep or goats, yeaning animals* (just delivered).

fibra, -ae, [?, perh. akin *to* **filum**], f., *a fibre, a filament.* — Esp., in plur., of the liver, *parts* (of the liver), *the liver.* — Less exactly, *the entrails, the inwards.*

fībula, -ae, [√fig + bula (f. of bulus), but cf. **filum** (?)], f., *a buckle, a clasp, a brooch.*

fictor, -ōris, [√fig (in **fingo**) + tor], m., *a fashioner, a contriver, a deviser:* fandi (*trickster in speech*).

fictus, -a, -um, p.p. of **fingo.**

fidēlis, -e, [fidē + lis], adj. Of persons, *faithful, trusty.* — Of things, *trusty, trustworthy.*

Fīdēna, -ae, (also plur.), [?], f., a

town of Latium, five miles north of Rome (now *Castel Giubileo*).
fīdens, p. of **fīdo.**
fidēs, -ei, [√fid (akin to πείθω) + es], f., *faith, good faith, loyalty, faithfulness, honor, honesty:* **fide expertus; intemerata; si qua fides; cineri promissa.** — Also, *credibility, trustworthiness, truth:* **manifesta; nusquam tuta.** — Less exactly, the sign of faith, *a pledge, a promise, promised word:* **en dextra fidesque; accipe daque; fidem servare.** — Transferred, *confidence, trust, reliance, belief, assurance, hopes:* **fides pelago; prisca fides facto; nec vana fides.** — Personified, *Good Faith.*
fidēs, -is, [?, cf. Gr. σφίδη], f., *a string* (of the lyre). — In plur., *a lyre.*
fīdō, fīsus, fīdere, [√fid, cf. **fides, fidus**], 3. v. n., *trust, confide in, have confidence:* **terrae** (of landing); **committere pugnam** (*venture*). — **fīdēns, -entis,** p. as adj., *trustful, confident, bold.*
fīdūcia, -ae, [†fīducō (reduced, cf. **caducus**) + ia (cf. **fīdo**)], f., *confidence, courage, trust, reliance, presumption:* **generis** (*confidence in lineage*); **quae** (*on what his reliance*); **quae sit rebus** (*what reliance is to be placed*); **rerum** (*confidence in*).
fīdus, -a, -um, [√fid (cf. **fides, fido**) + us], adj., *faithful, trusty.* — Of things, *trustworthy:* **statio; litora; responsa.**
figō, fīxī, fīxum, fīgere, [√fig, perh. akin to σφίγγω], 3. v. a., *fasten, fix* (esp. by piercing), *hang up:* **humo plantas** (*set*); **arma thalamo** (*hang up*); **leges** (hang up tablets, *make laws*). — Less exactly and fig., *fix, attach, fasten, plant, set firmly:* **fixos tenebat oculos; in virgine voltus** (*fix*); **vestigia** (*plant*); **oscula** (*imprint*); **dicta animis** (*let sink deeply*); **fixa dolore** (*transfixed*);

sub pectore taedas (*plant*); **fixum animo** (*a deep-set purpose*). — Of the process, *pierce, transfix, shoot* (with spear or arrow), *hit, bring down, kill:* **verubus viscera** (*stick on*); **arundine malum.** — **fīxus, -a, -um,** p.p. as adj., *firm, resolute, unmoved.*
figūra, -ae, [†figu- (√fig + u, u lengthened as in **Portūnus**) + ra (f. of **rus**), cf. **fingo**], f., *form, figure.* — Concretely, *a shape, an apparition, a phantom.*
fīlia, -ae, [f. of **filius**], f., *a daughter.*
fīlius, -ī (-iī), [?, pern. akin to †**feo**], m., *a son.*
filix, -icis, [?], f., *fern.*
fīlum, -ī, [?, perh. akin to **fibra**], n., *a thread.* — Esp., the thread of the Parcae (of life or fate).
fimus, -ī (-um, -ī), [?], m. (n.), *filth, ordure, mud, dung.*
findō, fidī, fissum, findere, [?], 3. v. a., *split, cleave:* **finditur via cuneis** (*a way is cloven*); **arva** (*crack,* of the heat). — Fig., *divide, separate:* **se via in ambas partes.**
fingō, finxī, fictum, fingere, [√fig, cf. θιγγάνω, Eng. *dough*], 3. v. a., *fashion* (orig. of clay), *form, mould, shape:* **tecta** (of bees); **corpora lingua** (of the she-wolf, cf. "lick into shape" of the bear); **vitem** (*train*); **crinem** (*arrange*, by stroking). — Fig., *train, subdue:* **corda** (of the Sibyl). — Transferred to mental action, *frame, contrive, devise, invent, fancy, imagine; feign, pretend.*
fīniō, -īvī (-iī), -ītum, -īre, [†fini-], 4. v. a., *limit, bound, put an end to, end.*
fīnis, -is, [?], comm., *an end, a limit, a bound.* — Esp. in plur., *borders, region, country.* — Poetically, of the starting-point of a race, *barriers;* and of the end, *the goal.*
fīnitimus, -a, -um, [†fini + timus,

cf. maritimus, intimus], adj., *bordering upon, neighboring.* — Masc., *a neighbor* (esp. in plur.).

fīō, see facio.

firmātus, -a, -um; see firmo.

firmŏ, -āvī, -ātum, -āre, [†firmŏ-], 1. v. a., *make strong, strengthen, fortify:* vires (*foster*); vestigia (*steady*); firmata aetas (as adj., *mature age*). — Fig., *confirm, ratify, reassure.*

firmus, -a, -um, [√fir (form of DHAR, *hold*) + mus], adj., *steady, firm, solid, strong, lasting:* durissima vina (*best keeping*). — Fig., *stout, strong, abiding, resolute:* pectus; foedus (*good, valid*).

fiscella, -ae, [†fisculŏ- (reduced, cf. fiscus) + lus (2d dim)], f., *a basket.*

fiscina, -ae, [†fiscŏ- (stem of fiscus) + na (f. of -nus)], f., *a basket.*

fissilis, -e, [†fissŏ + lis], adj., *cleaveable, split.*

fissus, -a, -um; see findo.

fistula, -ae, [?], f., *a pipe.* — Less exactly, *the pipe* (of several reeds joined), *a shepherd's-pipe.*

fīxus, -a, -um, p.p. of figo.

flābrum, -ī, [√fla (in flo) + brum], n., *a blast, a breeze.*

flagellum, -ī, [†flagrŏ- (reduced, cf. ager) + lum (n. of lus)], n., *a whip, a scourge, a lash.* — Less exactly, *a thong* (cf. amentum). — Poetically, *a switch, a shoot* (of a vine).

flāgĭtŏ, -āvī, -ātum, -āre, [†flagitŏ- (p.p. of †flago, cf. flagrum, flagro)], 1. v. a., (*insist hotly*), *demand.*

flagrāns, p. of flagro.

flagrŏ, -āvī, -ātum, -āre, [†flagrŏ, stem of flagrum (√flag + rum, n. of rus)], 1. v. n., *burn, blaze, glow, sparkle, shine.* — Fig. (cf. ferveo), *glow, be active, be vehement.* — flagrāns, -āntis, p. as adj., *blazing, shining, bright, ardent, glowing, raging:* genas (*burning*, with blushes); voltus (*beaming*).

flāmen, -ĭnis, [†fla + men], n., *a blast, a gale, a breeze.*

flamma, -ae, [√flag (cf. φλέγω) + ma], f., *a flame, a fire.* — Poetically, *a fiery brand, a flaming torch, a blazing pyre, a burning altar, a blaze* (in the heaven), *fire* (of vengeance), *fire* or *flame* (of flashing eyes,) *fire* (of Jove, *the lightning*). — Fig. (cf. **ardeo, flagro**), *fire* (of love, or passion), *love, passion, desire, heat, fury.*

flammāns, p. of flammo.

flammātus, -a, -um, p.p. of flammo.

flammeus, -a, -um, [†flamma- (reduced) + eus], adj., *fiery, flashing:* lumina.

flammŏ, -āvī, -ātum, -āre, [†flamma-], 1. v. a. and n., *set on fire.* — Fig., *inflame, fire.* — Neut., *be on fire, be ablaze.* — flammāns, -āntis, p. as adj., *fiery, blazing:* lumina. — flammātus, -a, -um, p.p., *inflamed, infuriated.*

flātus, -tūs, [√fla (in flo) + tus], m., (*a blowing*), *a breath, a blast:* equorum (*snorting*). — Fig., from the "breath of scorn," *pride, arrogance, scorn.*

flāvēns, -ēntis, p. of flaveo.

flaveo, no perf., no sup., -ēre, [†flavŏ-], 2. v. n., *be yellow.* — flāvēns, -ēntis, p. as adj., *yellow, golden, auburn:* prima lanugine (*blooming*).

flāvēscŏ, no perf., no sup., -escere, [†flavē- (stem of flaveo) + sco], 3. v. n., *grow yellow, whiten.*

Flāvīnius -a, -um, [†Flavinŏ- (reduced) + ius], adj., *Flavinian* (of a city or region of Etruria, otherwise unknown): arva.

flāvus, -a, -um, [?], adj., *yellow, golden, golden-haired, yellowish gray, pale green:* oliva.

flectŏ, flexī, flexum, flectere, [unc. root + to], 3. v. a., *bend, turn, plait:* crates. — Less exactly, *turn, guide:* viam velis, iuvencos (*drive*); iuga habenis; habenas. — With reflexive (sometimes without, cf. **verto**), *turn, incline.* — Fig., *bend, influence, persuade:* precando fata (*turn*); flectitur violentia (*is appeased*); illum purpura regum (*move, affect*). — **flexus, -a, -um**, p.p. as adj., *curved, twining, flexible, bent.*

fleō, flēvī, flētum, flēre, [perh. akin to **fluo**], 2. v. n. and a., *weep, shed tears.* — Less exactly, *mourn, lament.* — Wi*th* acc. (cf. **doleo**), *weep for, mourn, lament, bewail:* Anchisen; me discedere (*my departure*).

flētus, -a, -um, p.p. of **fleo**.

flētus, -tūs, (†flē- (as root) + tus, cf. **fleo**], m., *a weeping, a wail, a flood of tears.*

flexilis, -e, [†flexŏ + lis], adj., *flexible, bending.*

flexus, -a, -um, p.p. of **flecto**.

flexus, -us, [√flec + tus], m., *a winding, bending.*

flīctus, -tūs, [√flig + tus], m., *a dashing, clashing of weapons.*

flōrēns, p. of **floreo**.

flōreō, -ruī, no sup., -rere, [†flos (for floseo)], 2. v. n., *blossom, be in bloom.* — Fig., *flourish, be in prime, be prosperous.* — Also, *abound* (with the accessory notion of vigor or brilliancy): Itala terra viris (*be strong in*); studiis oti (*be busy with*). — Poetically, *shine, be bright:* aere catervae (*glitter*); limina sertis (*bloom*). — **florēns, -entis**, p. as adj., *blooming, flourishing, blossoming.*

flōreus, -a, -um, [†flos + eus], adj., *flowery, blooming.*

flōrus, -a, -um; = **floreus**, read for **flavus**. Æn. xii. 605.

flōs, flōris, [√flo + as, cf. Gr. φλύω, Eng. *bloom*], m., *a flower, a blossom.* — Fig., *the bloom, the prime, the flower* (choicest part or time): primaevo flore (*in the first bloom of youth*); flos virum. — Poetically, *the down* (of early youth, cf. preceding example).

fluctuō, -āvī, -ātum, -āre, [†fluctu-], 1. v. n., *toss, ebb and flow.* —

Fig., *ebb and flow, waver, fluctuate:* aestu curarum (*be tossed by*, changing the point of view); aere tellus (*gleams with waves of shining bronze*); ira intus (*seethe*); amor irarum aestu (*alternate with a tide*).

fluctus, -ūs, [√flu(g) (cf. **confluges**) + tus], m., *a wave, a tide.* — Less exactly, *the sea, water.* — Fig. (as in Eng.), *a wave* (of passion, &c.), *a tide, a flood:* irarum.

fluens, -entis, p. of **fluo**.

fluentum, -ī, [†fluent- (cf. **fluo**) + um (or in its original form, cf. **argentum**)], n., *a stream, a river.*

fluidus, -a, -um, [†fluŏ- (cf. **circumfluus**) + dus], adj., *flowing, liquid.*

fluitō, -āvī, -ātum, -āre, [†fluitŏ- (stem of supposed or real p.p. of **fluo**, cf. **agito**)], 1. v. n., *flow.* — Less exactly, *float, drift.*

flumen, -inis, [√flu (lengthened, cf. **numen**, perh. with stem for root, cf. **fluito**) + men], n., *a river, a stream, water* (of a river). — Less exactly, of the river-god, of tears (*flood*), of sweat, of blood.

fluŏ, fluxī, fluxum, fluere, [√flug (flu with parasitic g, cf. **fruor**)], 3. v. n., *flow, run:* auro (of gold in rivers, *flow with golden sand*). — Transferred, of the source, *flow with, drip, run with:* ora tabo; vites Baccho (*stream with*). — Less exactly, of things not fluid, *flow, float, stream, glide, pour:* olli ad regia (*flock*); vestis ad pedes. — Poetically, *fall loosely, fall lifeless, droop, fail.* — **fluens, -entis**, p. as adj., *flowing, loose, unrestrained, luxuriant:* vites; coma (*dishevelled*). — **fluxus, -a, -um**, p.p. as adj., *loose, failing:* res (*feeble power*).

fluviālis, -e, [†fluviŏ- (reduced) + alis], adj., *of a river.*

fluvius, -ī (-iī), [†fluŏ- (cf. **fluidus**) + ius], m., *a river, a stream.* — Less exactly, *water* (for irrigation).

fluxus, -a, -um, p.p. of **fluo.**
focus, -ī, [perh. akin to **foveo**], m., *a hearth, a fireplace, a chimney, a brazier* (small hearth for fire). — Fig., *the hearth* (as an emblem of home), *the fireside, the household hearth.* — Poetically, *a pyre, a funeral pile, an altar* (the brazier often being set on a tripod and used as an altar. See A. & G. Virg., Fig. 90).
fodiō, fōdī, fossum, fodere, [√fod, of unc. connection], 3. v. a., *dig, prick, pierce:* calcaribus armos; humum. — Also (as in Eng.), of the result, *dig* (make by digging): cubilia talpae; sub terra larem.
foecundo, see **fec-**.
foecundus, see **fec-**.
foedātus, -a, -um, p.p. of **foedo.**
foedē [abl. of **foedus**], adv., *foully, horribly, cruelly.* — Also (cf. **foedus**), *basely, shamefully.*
foedō, -āvī, -ātum, -are, [†foedŏ-], 1. v. a., *make hideous, befoul, disfigure, lacerate, spoil:* unguibus ora; pectora pugnis; latebras ferro (*desecrate,* prob. with reference to the sanctity of the object attacked); ferro volucres (*cut in pieces*). — Fig., *pollute, defile.*
foedus, -a, -um, [?], adj., *foul, filthy.* — Of moral qualities, *foul, horrible, dreadful, base, vile:* foedissime(*miserable coward*); tempestas; ministeria.
foedus, -eris, [√fid (in **fides,** strengthened) + **us**], n. Of nations or kings, *a treaty, a compact, an alliance, a truce.* — Less exactly, of individuals, *a bargain, an agreement, a contract, a pledge* (mutual), *a compact* (esp. of marriage). — Also, *a bond* (ordained by a superior), *a condition, terms:* tyranni (*conditions imposed by*); certo foedere (*by fixed laws*); aequo foedere amantes (*on equal terms*).
foemina, see **fem-,** the proper spelling.

foemineus, -a, -um; see **fem-,** the proper spelling.
foenile, see **fen-**.
foetūra, see **fet-**.
foetus, -tūs; see **fet-**.
foetus, -a, -um; see **fet-**.
folium, -ī (-iī), [cf. Gr. φύλλον], n., *a leaf* (of a tree or of paper), *foliage.*
follis, -is, [?], m., *a bag.* — *a pair of bellows, bellows.*
fōmes, -itis, [perh. akin to **foveo,** unc. form], m., *dry fuel.*
fōns, fontis, [unc. root + **tis** (reduced)], m., *a spring, a fountain.* — Less exactly, *water, pure water:* Avernus (*lake*); irriguus (*stream*).
†**for, fātus, fārī,** [√fa, akin to φημί], 1. v. dep., *speak, say, tell, relate, foretell, predict.* — **fandus, -a, -um,** ger. p., *to be spoken.* — Neut., *right* (opp. to **nefandum**). — **fando,** ger., *by report:* fandi doctissima (*in speech*); mollia fatu (*pleasing to say*). See **fatum.**
forās [acc. plur. of †**forā-,** akin to **foris**], adv., (*to the doors*), *out of doors, forth, out.*
forceps, -cipis, [†**for-** (stem akin to **fornax**) + **ceps** (√cap as stem, cf. **princeps**)], m. and f., *tongs, pincers.*
fore, see **sum.**
forem, see **sum.**
foris, -is, [√for (akin to θύρα, Eng. *door*) + **is**], f., *a door.* — Plur., *doors, a door* (double), *the folds* (of a door). — Less exactly, *entrance, opening, door* (of a hive, &c.).
forma, -ae, [√for (I. E. DHAR, in **firmus**?) + **ma**], f., *form, figure, shape, appearance* aratri; rerum. — Esp., *fine form* (cf. **facies**), *beauty:* formā insignis. — Concretely, *a form, figure, vision, apparition.* — Fig., *species, form, kind, nature:* scelerum.
formīca, -ae, [unc. stem in **i** + **ca** (f. of **cus**)], f., *an ant.*
formīdātus, -a, -um, p.p. of **formido.**

formīdŏ, -dĭnis, [†formīdŏ- (unc. stem, cf. formīdŏ, perh. akin to formus?) + o (cf. cupido)], f., *fear* (generally violent), *dread, terror, alarm:* nigra (*awful gloom*); formidine capti (*seized with a panic*). — Concretely, *an alarm?* (a line of feathers to frighten game).—Personified, *Terror.*

formīdŏ, -āvī, -ātum, -āre, [†formīdŏ- (cf. cupes, cupido, and formido], 1. v. a., *dread.*

formŏ, -āvī, -ātum, -āre, [†forma-], 1.v. a., *form, fashion, build:* classem. — Less exactly, of living beings, *train.*

formōsus (old, formōnsus), -a, -um, [†forma- (reduced)+osus], adj., *beautiful, lovely* (usually of human beings). — Poetically, of things: annus; pedum; pecus (*handsome*).

fornāx, -ācis, [†fornŏ- (reduced), akin to formus, + ax], f., *a furnace* (for melting metal), *a forge.* — Poetically (cf. Aetna and camina), of the supposed workshop of Vulcan in Ætna.

fornīx, -icis, [akin to fornax], m., *an arch.* — Less exactly, of a rock.

fors, †fortis, (abl. forte), [√fer + tis (reduced)], f., *chance, hazard, fortune.* — Nom. (sc. est or sit, *there is a chance*), equal to an adv., *perhaps, may be, possibly.* — Abl. forte, *by chance, as it happened:* ne forte (*lest one should happen to*); si forte (*if by any chance*); quae forte paratae (*happened to be*, &c.): forte fuit (*there chanced to be*); forte sua (*by pure chance*, with perhaps a reminiscence of the etymological meaning, cf. fero).

forsan [fors an, *a chance whether,* cf. fors and forsitan], adv., *perhaps, it may be.*

forsitan [fors sit an, *it may be a chance whether,* cf. fors], adv., *perhaps, possibly, mayhap.*

fortasse [?, forte in unc. combination, perh. sis (sivis)?], adv., *perhaps, possibly, it may be.*

forte, see fors.

fortis, -e, [for forctis, √forc (root akin to √for in forma) + tis], adj., *strong, sturdy, hardy, vigorous, stalwart.* — Of mental qualities, *valiant, brave, steadfast, undaunted:* Achates (a standing epithet, weakened almost to *worthy*); corda; pectus. — Of things, in both senses above, *stout, sturdy, brave, valiant:* facta; rami; humeri; fortia surgunt (*hardy, sturdy*).

fortūna, -ae, [lost stem †fortu- (cf. fors) + na (cf. Vacuna, Portunus)], f., *fortune, chance, hazard, destiny, fate:* siqua super fortuna laborum est (*necessity of toil*). — Esp. in good sense, *good fortune, success, opportunity, chance:* si modo sequatur; fortuna fuit (*glory*); populi (*interest*); sortitus fortunam oculis; quae dabatur (*chance of success*); quaecumque...fidesque (*fortune and hope*). — In bad sense, *fortune, fate, ill luck:* mea me victam docere dolere. — Half personified, *fortune:* aspirat labori; fidem novavit. — Fully personified, *Fortune.*

fortūnātus, -a, -um, p.p. of fortuno.

fortūnŏ, -āvī, -ātum, -āre, [†fortunā-], 1. v. a., *make fortunate, bless.* — fortūnātus, -a, -um, p.p. as adj., *fortunate, blest, favored* (by fortune), *happy.*

Forulī, -ōrum, [prob. dim. of forus], m. plur., a Sabine town of Samnium.

forum, -ī, [akin to forus, foris], n., (*an open passage?*), *a market-place.* — Esp., *the Forum* (orig. market-place at Rome, place of assembly for the people, and of all public business).—Fig., *an assembly* (of the people), *the people* (as a political body).

forus, -ī, [akin to forum, foris].

m., *a gangway* (in a ship, not apparently from one deck to another, as with us, but open spaces in the ship not occupied by the rowers, cf. **forum**): laxat foros (*hold*, "*standing-room* "?); implesse flammis (*decks*). — Poetically, *cells* (of a beehive).

fossa, -ae, [√fod + ta, f. of p.p. of **fodio,** perh. with omitted noun], f., *a ditch* (for defence or farming), *a dyke, a trench.*

fossor, -oris, [√fod + tor], m., *a ditcher.*

fōtus, -a, -um, p.p. of **foveo.**

fovea, -ae, [akin to **foveo** (?), perh. orig. a cellar to keep things from cold, cf. the treatment of potatoes], f., *a pit.*

foveō, fōvī, fōtum, fovēre, [†fovŏ- (akin to **favus, favilla**)], 2. v. a., *keep warm, brood:* progeniem. — Transferred (perh. derived from brooding of fowls), *embrace, fondle, caress, nurse:* colla (*support*); germanam amplexa sinu; hiemem inter se (*spend in dalliance*). — Fig., *cherish, foster, promote:* Romanos; bella; hoc regnum gentibus esse (*cherish the purpose*, helping it *on*); famam. — Also, *cling to, love:* humum; castra (cf. "hug the fire"). — As medical term, *foment* (cf. **fomentum**), *bathe, treat* (medically), *apply* (anything to): ora (*rinse*); fovens circum; volnus lymphā.

fractus, -a, -um, p.p. of **frango.**

fraenum, see **frenum,** the better spelling.

fraenī, see **frenum.**

fraenō, see **freno.**

fragilis, -e, [†fragŏ- (cf. **navifragus**) + lis], adj., *brittle, fragile, frail, delicate.* — Also (cf. **fragor**), *crackling* (of a sound like breaking).

fragmen, -inis, [√frag + men], n., *a fragment, a broken piece.*

fragmentum, -ī, [√frag + mentum], n., *a fragment, a broken piece.*

fragor, -ōris, [√frag + or], m., *a breaking.* — Of a sound like breaking, *a crash, a dashing, a rattling, an uproar, a din, a sound of mourning* (fr. the beating of the breast, cf. **plango**), *applause* (by clapping of hands), *a cracking, a report.*

fragōsus, -a, -um, [†fragŏ- (reduced, cf. **navifragus**) + osus], adj., *crashing* (cf. **fragor**), *roaring, noisy.*

frāgrāns, p. of **frāgrō.**

frāgrō, -āvī, no sup., **-āre,** [†fragrŏ- (unc. root + rus), cf. **fragum**)], 1. v. n., *smell sweet.* — **frāgrāns, -antis,** p. as adj., *fragrant, sweet smelling.*

frāgum, -ī, [unc. root (cf. **fragro**) + um], n., *a strawberry.*

frangō, frēgī, fractum, frangere, [√frag], 3. v. a., *break, break up, break off, shatter, crush, pulverize, crunch.* — Esp. of ships, *wreck.* — Fig., *break down, crush, wear out, baffle.* — **fractus, -a, -um,** p.p. as adj., *broken, shattered, shivered, crushed:* cacumina; vires; opes; unda (*breaking*); res; voces.

frāter, -tris, [cf. φράτηρ, *clansman,* Eng. *brother,* √fra (akin to **fer**?) + ter (cf. **pater**), m., *a brother.*

frāternus, -a, -um, [†frater- (not syncopated) + nus], adj., *of a brother, a brother's, fraternal.* — Less exactly, *of a mate:* fraterna morte (of a bullock).

fraudō, -āvī, -ātum, -āre, [†fraud-], 1. v. a., *defraud, deprive of.*

fraus, fraudis, [akin to **frustum, frustra**], f., *loss, discomfiture, mischief, damage:* quis deus in fraudem egit (*ruin*). — Also, *deceit, wiles, a stratagem, deception, a trick, treachery, wickedness:* innexa clienti; caeli sereni; fraudi accomoda vallis (*ambush*); loci et noctis (*treacherous advantage*).

fraxineus, -a, -um, [†fraxinŏ- (reduced) + eus], adj., *ashen, of ash.*
fraxinus, -ī, [?], f., *an ash* (cf. **ornus,** *the mountain-ash*).
fremitus, -us, [†fremi- (stem of **fremo**) + tus], m., *a roaring, a roar, a murmur.* — Of many similar noises, *a buzzing, a neighing, the noise of battle.*
fremŏ, -uī, -itum, -ere, [√frem (cf. βρέμω)], 3. v. n. and a., *murmur, roar, shout, cry, howl* (of winds), *neigh* (of horses); **arma** (*cry for*); **Euoe Bacche, fremens.** — Transferred, of the place where noise is produced, *resound, re-echo:* **ululatu tecta; ripae undis** (*murmur*); **via plausu.** — Esp., *murmur assent* or *approval.* — Fig., (*howl with rage*), *rage, rave, be wild, exult.* — **fremēns, -entis,** p. as adj., *fierce, wild, spirited* (of a horse), *neighing.*
fremor, -ōris, [frem + or (cf. **fremo**)], m., *a murmur, a roar.*
frendŏ, no perf., **frēsum** (**fressum**), **frendere,** [?], 3. v. n., *gnash the teeth.*
frēnātus, -a, -um, p.p. of **freno.**
frēnŏ, -āvī, -ātum, -āre, [†frenŏ-], 1. v. a., *curb, restrain, bridle.* — Also fig. (as in English). — Poetically, of water, *check, stay:* **cursus aquarum.** — **frēnātus, -a, -um,** p.p. (or formed from †frenŏ- like **auratus**), *bridled, furnished with bridles.*
frenum (frae-), -ī, (pl. also **-ī, -orum**), n. and m., *a bridle, a bit, reins:* **frenis immissis** (*at full speed*, cf. **habenae**). — Fig.: **frenum accipere** (*submit to the rein,* of a nation); **ea frena furenti concutit** (*with such a powerful bit does he curb,* &c.).
frequēns, -entis, [orig. p. of lost verb, cf. **farcio,** φράσσω], adj., *crowded, in great numbers, plenty of, plenteous, very many, very much, numerous:* **socii; telis** (*a shower of*). — Of time, *frequent, repeated, constant, incessant:* **cul-**

tu (*constant*). — Fig., *abounding in, crowded with, full of:* **herbis campus.**
frequentŏ, -āvī, -ātum, -āre, [†frequent-], 1. v. a., *crowd, people, inhabit.*
fretum, -ī, [?], n., *a strait.* — Less exactly, *the sea, a river.*
frētus, -a, -um, [√for (cf. **forma, firmus**) + tus, p.p.], adj., (*supported by*), *relying on, trusting to, confiding in, by means of.*
fricŏ, fricuī, fricātum (**frictum**), **fricāre,** [?], 1. v. a., *rub:* **arbore costas** (*rub the sides against a tree*).
frīgēns, -entis, p. of **frīgeo.**
frīgeŏ, frīxī, no sup., **frīgēre,** [†frigŏ- (cf. **frigidus**)], 2. v. n., *be cold, be chilled:* **vires.** — **frīgēns, -entis,** p. as adj., *cold, stiff, lifeless.*
frīgidus, -a, -um, [†frigŏ- (cf. **frigeo**) + dus], adj., *cold, chill, cool, icy.* — Esp. of death, *fixed in death, in the chill of death:* **ille frigidus** (*that lifeless body*). — Less exactly, *growing chill* (*dying*), *benumbed, inactive, slow:* **dextera.**
frīgus, -oris, [√frig + us, cf. **frigeo**], n., *cold, chill, frost, winter, coolness, cool shade.* — In plur., without distinction of meaning, *frosts, cold blasts.*
frondātor, -tōris, [†frond + ator, as if †frondā- (stem of supposed †frondŏ) + tor, cf. **viator**], m., *a vine-dresser, a leaf-gatherer.*
frondēns, -entis, p. of **frondeo.**
frondeŏ, no perf., no sup., **frondēre,** [†frond- (as if frondŏ-)], 2. v. n., *put forth leaves, be in leaf:* **silvae** (*be in full foliage*). — **frondēns, -entis,** p. as adj., *leafy, green, springing, luxuriant:* **hospitia** (*leafy retreats, hospitable shade*).
frondēscŏ, fronduī, no sup., **frondēscere,** [†frondē- (stem of **frondeo**) + sco], 3. v. n., *put forth leaves, leave out:* **virga metallo** (*spring*).

frondeus, -a, -um, [†frond + eus], adj., *leafy.*

frondōsus, -a, -um, [†frond + osus], adj., *leafy.*

frōns, frondis, [?], f., *a leaf, leaves* (collectively), *foliage.* — Pl., *leaves, foliage* (often including the branches).

frōns, frontis, [cf. Gr. ὀφρύς, Eng. *brow*], f., *the forehead, the brow, the face.* — Esp. as showing the feelings: spem fronte serenat (*smoothes his brow with feigned hope*); haud laeta fronte (*with no cheerful countenance*).—Transferred (as in Eng.), *face, side:* sub adversa fronte. — Less exactly, *the horns, the head, the prow* (of a ship).

fructus, -ūs, [√frug (in fruor) + tus], m., (perh. orig. *eating*), *the enjoying* (of anything). — Concretely, (*food*), *fruit* (more esp. in later Eng. sense, cf. **fruges,** *grain*).

frūges, see **frux.**

frūmentum, -ī, [√fru(g) (cf. **fruor** and **fructus**) + mentum], n., *grain.* — Plur., *ears of grain.*

fruor, fructus (fruitus), fruī, [√frug (cf. **frux**)], 3. v. dep., (orig. *eat*?), *consume* (with notion of cheer and comfort): parto agricolae. — Fig., *enjoy:* luce; sermone.

frustrā [case-form (abl.?) of †frustrŏ- (cf. **frustro**)], adv., *in vain, to no purpose, uselessly, vainly.*

frustrātus, -a, -um, p.p. of **frustror.**

frustror, -ātus, -ārī, [†frustrŏ- (*with loss*? or *obstacle*?, cf. **fraus**)], 1. v. dep., *disappoint, deceive:* meos vocatus (*slight*); hiantes clamor (*fail*).

frustum, -ī, [√frud (in **fraus**) + tum (n. p.p. of lost verb, *cut off*?)], n., *a piece, a bit, a morsel.*

frutex, -icis, [?], m., *a shrub, a bush.*

†frūx, frūgis, frūge, and plur., [√frug (strengthened), as stem, cf. **fruor**], f., (orig. *food*), *fruit* (usually of the earth, cf. **fructus**), *grain.*—Esp., *meal* (ground coarse for sacrificing): salsae. — Also, *a cake* (baked): medicatae (of the cake given to Cerberus).

fūcātus, -a, -um, p.p. of **fuco.**

Fūcinus, -ī, [†1. fucŏ- (cf. **fucus,** *lichen*) + nus], m., *a lake among the Apennines* (now *Lago di Celano*).

fūcŏ, -āvī, -ātum, -āre, [†1. fucŏ-], 1. v. a., *paint, dye, color.*

1. **fūcus, -ī,** [?], m., *a lichen* (of a red color, used for a cosmetic and dye). — Also, *bee-glue.*

2. **fūcus, -ī,** [Gr. φῦκος], m., *a drone.*

fuga, -ae, [√fug (cf. Gr. φυγή, Eng. *bow*) + a], f., *a flight, an escape.* — Esp. of slaves, *running away.* — Also, *a running, speed, a course.* — Personified, *Exile.*

fugātus, -a, -um, p.p. of **fugo.**

fugāx, -ācis, [as if fug + ax, prob. †fugā + cus (reduced)], adj., *flying* (inclined or able to flee), *fleet, swift, rapid.* — Less exactly, *flying* (in act of flight), *in flight.*

fugiō, fūgī, fugitum, fugere, [√fug, cf. Gr. φεύγω], 3. v. a. and n., *fly, escape, depart, recede.*— Esp. in battle, *flee, fly.* — Less exactly, of mere motion, *fly, speed, rush.* — Esp., *escape, fail* (one). — Fig., *pass away, speed on.* — Act., *flee from, fly from, escape, fly, avoid, refuse.*

fugŏ, -āvī, -ātum, -āre, [†fuga-], 1. v. a., *put to flight, drive away, drive.*—Fig., *chase, disperse, dispel.*

fulciō, fulsī, fultum, fulcire, [?, √fulc], 4. v. a., *prop up, support, sustain, secure.* — **fultus, -a, -um,** p.p., *supported, lying, resting, secured.*

fulcrum, -ī, [√fulc + crum], n., *a support, a prop, a post, a pillar.* — Esp., *a post, a leg* (of a couch).

fulgeō, fulsī, no sup., **fulgēre** (-ere as fr. **fulgo**), [akin to Gr. φλέγω, √fulg, cf. √flag (another

form of same root)], 2. v. n., *gleam, flash, shine, blaze, glare.* —
fulgēns, -entis, p. as adj., *bright, gleaming, glittering.*
fulgō, see fulgeo.
fulgor, -ōris, [√fulg (cf. **fulgeo**) + or], m., *a blaze, a flash, a glitter.* — Less exactly, *brightness, splendor.*
fulgur, -uris, [√fulg, prob. †fulgŏ + rus (reduced)], n., *a thunderbolt, lightning.*
fulica, -ae, [?], f., *a coot* (a sea-bird).
fūligŏ, -inis, [?, unc. stem + go, cf. **caligo**], f., *soot.*
fulmen, -inis, [√fulg + men], n., *a thunderbolt* (conceived by the ancients as a missile weapon), *lightning, a flash of lightning.* — Poetically, of persons, *thunderbolt* (destroying agency in war).
fulmineus, -a, -um, [†fulmin + eus], adj., *like lightning, flashing:* Mnestheus (cf. **fulmen**).
fulminō, -āvī, -ātum, -āre, [†fulmin-], 1. v. n., *lighten, flash.* — Poetically (cf. **fulmen**), *flash and thunder:* armis Aeneas.
fultus, -a, -um, p.p. of **fulcio**.
fulvus, -a, -um, [?], adj., *tawny, yellow, dark, yellow-haired, orange, golden, auburn-haired.*
fūmeus, -a, -um, [†fuma- (reduced) + eus], adj., *smoky.*
fūmidus, -a, -um, [†fumŏ + dus], adj., *smoky.* — Less exactly, *steaming.*
fūmifer, -era, -erum, [†fumŏ + fer (√fer + us)], adj., *smoke-producing, smoky.*
fūmō, -āvī, -ātum, -āre, [†fumŏ-], 1. v. n., *smoke.* — Less exactly, *steam, reek:* sulphure (*emit a sulphurous vapor*); pulvere campi (*be in a cloud of dust*). — **fumāns, -antis,** p. as adj., *smoking, smoky, steaming, reeking.*
fumus, -ī, [√fū (cf. Gr. θύω) + mus (cf. Gr. θυμός)], m., *smoke, steam, haze.*
fūnālis, -e, [†funi- (reduced) + alis], adj., *of a rope.* — Neut., *a torch* (made on a cord).
funda, -ae, [akin to **fundo,** perh. Gr. σφενδόνη], f., *a sling.* — From the shape, *a net* (thrown by the hand).
fundāmen, -inis, [†fundā- (stem of 1. **fundo**) + men], n., *a foundation.*
fundāmentum, -ī, [†fundā- (stem of 1. **fundo**) + mentum], n., *a foundation.*
fundātor, -ōris, [†fundā- (stem of 1. **fundo**) + tor], m., *a founder.*
fundātus, -a, -um, p.p. of 1. **fundo**.
funditus [†fundŏ + tus, cf. **divinitus**], adv., *from the bottom* (cf. **fundus**), *from the foundation, utterly, entirely.*
fundō, -āvī, -ātum, -āre, [†fundo-], 1. v. a., (*set on the bottom*), *secure, make fast.* — Also, *found, build, establish:* legibus urbem (*institute*).
fundō, fūdī, fūsum, fundere, [√fud, cf. Gr. χεύω], 3. v. a., *pour, pour out, shed:* vina; lacrimas. — Of things more or less like liquids, *pour, shed, pour forth:* lumen; loquelas; flores (*lavish*); munuscula (*yield*); tela; equus armatos (*send forth*); vitam cum sanguine. — With reflexive, or in pass., *spread, extend, be spread, be shed, be scattered, scatter, press around, pour in, pour out, rush, flow.* — Also esp., *rout, put to flight.* — Poetically, *bring forth* (of a woman). — *waste.* — From the effect of pouring, *throw to the ground, lay low, prostrate, slay.* —
fūsus, -a, -um, p.p. as adj., *scattered, spread, dishevelled* (of the hair), *hanging loosely* (of the beard).
fundus, -ī, [?], m., *the bottom, the foundation:* imo fundo (*the lowest depths*); fundo vertere (cf. **funditus**). — Also, perh. by a mercantile or political connection of ideas, *a farm, an estate.*
fūnereus, -a, -um, [†funer- (for

**fūnes) + eus], adj., *of death, funereal, funeral:* faces (cf. fax, flamma); frons (*dark,* in sign of mourning).

fūnestus, -a, -um, [†funes- (cf. funus)+ tus, cf. funereus], adj., *of death, deadly, fatal.*

fungor, functus, fungī, [√fung, of unc. kindred], 3. v. dep., *perform, discharge.*

fungus, -ī, [Gr. σφόγγος], m., *a mushroom.* — Also, *an excrescence* (in a candle).

fūnis, -is, [?], m., *a rope, a cord.*

fūnus, -eris, [?, perh. root akin to φόνος (cf. φοινός) + us], n., *murder, killing, slaughter, havoc.* — Also, *death.* — Concretely, *a corpse, a funeral, funeral rites, a funeral pile, a funeral train.*

fuō, see **sum.**

fūr, fūris, [√fur (strengthened) as stem, cf. φώρ], comm., *a thief.*

fūrātus, -a, -um, p.p. of **furor.**

fūrca, -ae, [?, poss. fūr + ca (f. of cus], f., *a fork-shaped pole, a "crotch," a prop* (for vines). (Elsewhere *a V-shaped yoke,* used for the punishment of slaves, which may be the orig. meaning.)

furens, p. of **furo.**

furia, -ae, [√fur (cf. **furo**) + ia (f. of ius), perh. through an intermediate stem], f., usually plur., *rage, madness, fury, frenzy, wrath:* iustae; furiis agitatus amor; furiis incensa (accensas). — Less exactly, of the winds, *fury.* — Personified, *a Fury* (goddesses of divine vengeance). — Also of the Harpies. — Poetically (half personified), *remorse:* scelerum.

furiālis, -e, [†furiā + lis], adj., *of a fury.* — Less exactly, *maddening, exciting to frenzy.*

furiātus, -a, -um, p.p. of **furio.**

furibundus, -a, -um, [†furi- (stem of **furo**) + bundus], adj., *mad, furious, frenzied.*

furiō, -āvī, -ātum, -āre, [†furiā-], 1. v. a., *drive mad, madden, infuriate.* — **furiātus, -a, -um,** p.p. as adj., *frenzied, frantic, infuriated.*

furo, -ui, no sup., **-ere,** [√fur, of unc. kindred], 3. v. n., *rage, rave, be crazed:* turba; equus ictu; furorem (*spend rage*). — Fig., *rage, seethe, do anything wildly* (according to context): aestus ad auras (*rise wildly*); vis aquae; febris. — **furēns, -entis,** p. as adj., *distracted, passion-stricken, inspired, raging, furious, raving.*

furor, -ātus, -ārī, [†fūr-], 1. v. dep., *steal, get by stealth.* — Fig., *steal:* fessos oculos labori.

furor, -ōris, [√fur + or], m., *fury, madness, rage, raving.* — Esp. of love, *frenzy, fury, passion, craze.* — Concretely (cf. **amor**), *passion* (an object of), *an act of madness.* — Personified, *Rage.*

fūrtim [†fur + tim, as if √fur + tis in acc.], adv., *by stealth, secretly, stealthily.*

fūrtīvus, -a, -um, [†furti- (cf. **furtim**) + vus, perh. immediately fr. †fūr], adj., *stealthy.* — Less exactly, *secret, hidden:* quem furtivum edidit (*secretly*).

fūrtum, -ī, [†fūr- (as root) + tum (n. of tus)], n., *theft, stealth.* — Less exactly, and fig., *deceit, stealth, craft, concealment, a trick, a stratagem, an artifice:* belli (*ambush*). — Poetically, *clandestine love:* furto fervidus instat (*unseen slaughter*).

fuscus, -a, -um, [?], adj., *dusky, dark.*

1. **fūsus, -a, -um,** p.p. of **fundo.**
2. **fūsus, -ī,** [?, perh. same as 1. fusus], m., *a spindle.*

fūtilis (futt-), -e, [†futo- (cf. **futio**), √fud in **fundo**], adj., (*leaky*), *brittle:* glacies. — Fig., *weak, foolish.*

futūrus, -a, -um, f.p. of **sum.**

G.

Gabiī, -ōrum, [?], m. plur., a town of Latium, once populous and important, but early destroyed, between Rome and Præneste, famous for the worship of Juno.

Gabīnus, -a, -um, [†Gabio- (or simpler form) + inus], adj., *of Gabii:* cinctus (*the Gabine costume,* a peculiar arrangement of the toga used in some rites. The right end of the toga, instead of being thrown over the left shoulder as usual, was brought round the body and thrown forward over the right so as to hang in front).

gaesum, -i, [prob. Gallic], n., *a javelin* (long and heavy, used by the Gauls).

Gaetūlus, -a, -um, [?], adj., *Gætulian, of the Gætuli* (a nation of Africa, now *Morocco*). — Masc. plur., *the Gætuli* (the people of the nation). — Less exactly, *African.*

Galaesus (Galē-), -ī, [?], m.: 1. A river of Calabria, famous for its sheep; 2. An Italian.

Galatēa, -ae, [Gr. Γαλάτεια], f.: 1. A sea-nymph, beloved by Polyphemus; 2. A rustic maid.

galbaneus, -a, -um, [†galbanŏ- (reduced) + eus], adj., *of galbanum.*

galbanum, -ī, [Gr. χαλβανη], n., *galbanum* (a resinous gum from the East).

galea, -ae, [?, prob. borrowed], f., *a helmet* (of leather), *a helmet.*

galērus, -ī, [akin to galea], m., *a cap* (of skin with the hair on).

Galēsus, see **Galaesus.**

galla, -ae, [prob. f. of **Gallus**], f., *an oak gall.*

Gallus, -a, -um, [a Gallic word ?], adj., *of Gaul, Gallic.* — Masc. and fem. as subst., *a Gaul* (man or woman). — Plur., *the Gauls.*

Gallus, -ī, [?, gallus, *a cock*], m., a Roman family name. — Esp. of C. *Cornelius Gallus,* a friend and patron of Virgil. He was reckoned a poet by his friends.

Gangaridae, -ārum (-um, the shorter form), [Gr. Γαγγαρίδαι], m. plur., a people of India, on the Ganges, from which their name is derived.

Gangēs, -is, [Gr. Γάγγης], m., the famous river of India.

Ganymēdēs, -is (-ī), [Gr. Γανυμήδης], m., a beautiful youth, son of Laomedon, carried away by an eagle to be the cupbearer of Jove.

Garamantes, -um, [Gr. Γαράμαντες], m. plur., a nation in the interior of Africa.

Garamantis, -idis, [Gr. Γαραμαντίς], adj., *of the Garamantes.*

Gargānus, -ī, [?], m., a mountain-range in Apulia projecting into the Adriatic (now including *Monte Gargano* and some other peaks). — Also, as adj., *of Garganus, Garganian.*

Gargara, -ōrum, [Gr. Γάργαρα], n. plur., a part of Mt. Ida with a town near by of the same name.

garrulus, -a, -um, [†garrŏ- (cf. garrio) + lus], adj., *chattering, noisy, cawing.*

gaudeō, gāvīsus, gaudēre, [prob. †gavidŏ- (†gavi + dus), cf. gaudium with gaudimonium], 2. v. n., *feel joy, be delighted, rejoice* (internally, cf. **laetor**), *delight in, take pleasure in.* — Also, *feel proud of, boast.* — Less exactly and poetically, of things, *delight in* (*love*), *abound in* (cf. **laetus**). — **gaudēns, -ēntis,** p. as adj., *delighted, well pleased.*

gaudium, -ī (-iī), [†gavidŏ- (reduced) + ium (n. of ius), cf. gaudeo], n., *joy, delight, pleasure.* — Concretely, *a delight.* — Personified: mala (*Criminal Delights*).

gāza, -ae, [Gr. γάζα], f., *treasure, riches, wealth.*

Gela, -ae, [Gr. Γέλα], f., a city of Sicily, on the south coast, by a river of the same name (now *Terra Nuova*). From this city came several tyrants of Sicily.

gelĭdus, -a, -um, [†gelu- [weakened) + dus], adj., *icy, cold, cool, chilled, chilly.* — Less exactly, *chill, clammy, shivering:* tremor; sudor.

Gelōnus, -a, -um, [Gr. Γέλωνος], adj., *of the Geloni* (a people of Scythia). — Masc., collectively, *the Gelonian* (for the nation). — Plur., *the Geloni* (the nation).

Gelōus, -a, -um, [Gr. Γελῷος], adj., *of Gela, Geloan.*

gelū, -ūs, [?], n., *ice, icy coldness, cold, frost.* — Fig., *the chill of death, a chill* (of old age).

gemellus, -ī, [†geminŏ- (reduced) + lus], m., *twins.*

gemĭnātus, -a, -um, p.p. of geminō.

geminō, -āvī, -ātum, -āre, [†geminŏ-], 1. v. a., *repeat, redouble.*

geminus, -a, -um, [?], adj., *twin-born, twin.* — Less exactly, *double, a pair of, both, two, similar, corresponding.* — Plur., as subst., *brothers, twins.*

gemitus, -us, [†gemi- (stem of gemo) as root + tus], m., *a groaning, a groan, a roar, a hollow roar, a sigh, wailing, lamentation:* extremi (*its last groan,* of a dying bull); leonum.

gemma, -ae, [?, perh. √gen + ma], f., *a bud, an eye* (of a plant). — From similarity, *a gem, a jewel, a stone* (precious). — From the material, *a precious goblet* or *cup.*

gemō, gemuī, gemitum, gemere, [perh. akin to Gr. γέμω], 3. v. n., *groan, sigh, wail, creak, mourn* (of the plaintive song of the dove): repleti amnes.

genae, -ārum (rarely sing.), [akin to γένυ, Eng. *chin*), f., *cheeks.*

gener, generī, [?, cf. γαμβρός], m., *a son-in-law.* — Less exactly, *a proposed son-in-law, a daughter's suitor.*

generātim [acc. of supposed or real stem †generati- (cf. **certatim**), see **genus, genero**], adv., *by kinds, by races:* cultus disce (*of each after its kind*).

generātor, -ōris, [†generā- (cf. genero) + tor], m., *a breeder.*

generātus, -a, -um, p.p. of genero.

generō, -āvī, -ātum, -āre, [†genes- (of genus)], 1. v. a., *beget, become the father of.* — Less exactly, *produce, breed, raise.*

generōsus, -a, -um, [†genes- (cf. genus) + osus], adj., *(full of race), well born, nobly born, of a noble stock, of fine blood* (of animals). — Fig., *noble, famous:* metallis insula (*rich*).

genesta (genist-), -ae, [?], f., *broom* (a small fragrant shrub with bright yellow flowers), *Spartium iunceum.*

genetrix (geni-), -īcis, [†gene- (of gigno) as root + trix], f., *a mother.*

geniālis, -e, [†geniŏ + alis], adj., *(of the Genius,* or relating to his worship), *cheerful, festival* (as the rites were of a jovial nature), *devoted to joy:* tori; hiems.

genista, see **genesta.**

genitālis, -e, [†genitŏ- (reduced) + alis], adj., *of reproduction, reproductive.*

genitor, -ōris, [†geni- (of gigno) as root + tor], m., *a father, a sire.*

genitrix, see **genetrix.**

genitus, -a, -um, p.p. of gigno.

genius, -ī (-iī), [ ], m., *a tutelary divinity, a special divinity, a genius* (a semi-divine personage attached to a person or place).

gēns, gentis, [√gen (of gigno) + tis (reduced)], f., *an offspring, a race, a nation, a tribe, a breed* (of animals). — Plur., *all nations* (of the world). — Poetically, *age:* aurea, etc.

genū, -ūs, [akin to Gr. γόνυ], n., *the knee:* genua trahens (*limbs*).

genus, -eris, [√gen (in gigno) + us], n., *race, descent, family, lineage, birth.* — Of animals, *breed,*

tribe, kind.—Concretely, *offspring, progeny.* — Less exactly, *a kind, a sort, a species.*
Geōrgica, -ōrum, [Gr. γεωργικά], n. plur., *the Georgics* of Virgil.
Germānia, -ae, [†Germano̅- (reduced) + ia], f., *Germany* (loosely of the whole region now included under that name).
germanus, -a, -um, [?, akin to **germen**], adj., *akin, of the same stock.* — Masc., *a brother.* — Fem., *a sister.*
germen, -inis, [?], n., *a bud, a shoot.*
gero̅, gessī, gestum, gerere, [√ges (with r for s)], 3. v. a., *bear, carry, wield, wear.* — Also, poetically of abstract ideas: bella letumque (of a Fury); pacem; vocem et corpus; tempora umbrata quercu; pharetram; tela; os habitumque; volnera (*display*); animum (*show*); nomen decus (*possess*); curam (*exercise*).—Also (cf. **fero**), *bear, produce :* India lucos; platani malos. — Fig., of any action (esp. of war), *carry on, wage, manage :* bellum; talia (*perform such exploits*); laeti rebus bene gestis (*exultant at success*, and often with **res**).
Gēryōn, -ōnis (abl. **Gēryŏne** or **Gēryōne**), [Gr. Γηρυών], m., a famous monster of Spain whose oxen were carried off by Hercules.
gestāmen, -inis, [†gestā + men], n., *a thing borne, arms, an ornament, insignia.*
gestiō, -īvī (-iī), -ītum, -īre, [†gestā-(√ges + ti, cf. 2. gestus)], 4. v. n., *exult with joy, show a passionate desire.*
gestō, -āvī, -ātum, -are, [†gestŏ-], 1. v. a., *bear, carry, wear :* pectora (*possess*).
gestus, -a, -um, p.p. of **gero.**
Getae, -ārum, [Gr. Γέται], m. plur., *the Getes* (Dacians), a Thracian tribe on the Danube.
Geticus, -a, -um, [Gr. Γετικός], adj., *of the Getæ* or *Goths :* deserta (the modern *Bessarabia*, and *Moldavia*).
Gētūlus, etc.; see **Gaetulus.**
gigno̅, genuī, genitum, gignere, [√gen redupl., cf. γίγνομαι], 3. v. a., *beget, bring forth, bear, be a father* or *mother.* — **genitus, -a, -um,** p.p. as adj., *sprung, descended, son of.*
gilvus, -a, -um, [?], adj., *dun* or *chestnut :* equus.
glaciālis, -e, [†glaciē + lis], adj., *icy, cold, frozen, frosty.*
glaciēs, -ēī, [?], f., *ice, frost, cold.*
gladius, -ī (-iī), [?], m., *a sword.*
glans, glandis, [?], f., *an acorn, a nut.* —' Collectively, in sing., *acorns.* — From the shape, *a ball, a bullet.*
glārea, -ae, [?], f., *gravel.*
glaucus, -a, -um, [Gr. γλαυκός], adj., *blue, bluish gray, bluish green, sea green :* glauca cruentia fronde salicta; salices; ulva; arundo; equus (*gray ?*); lumen (of the sea-deity Proteus); amictus (of a river-god, and of a naiad).
Glaucus, -ī, [Gr. Γλαυκός], m.: 1. A son of Sisyphus and father of Bellerophon, torn in pieces by his own horses; 2. A fisherman of Anthedon, in Bœotia, who was changed into a sea-deity; 3. The father of Deiphobe, the priestess of Apollo at Cumæ, known as the Cumæan Sibyl; 4. A grandson of Bellerophon, leader of the Lycians in the Trojan war.
glēba, -ae, [?], f., *a clod, a lump of earth.* — Less exactly, *soil, land.*
gliscō, no perf., no sup., **gliscere,** [?], 3. v. n., *increase, grow.*
globus, -ī, [?, but akin to **glomus**], m., *a ball, a sphere :* flammarum; Lunae (*orb*). — Less exactly, *a band, a crowd, a cloud* (of dust): militum.
glomerātus, -a, -um, p.p. of **glomero.**
glomero̅, -āvī, -ātum, -āre, [†glomes- (r for s), cf. **glomus**],

1. v. a., *roll into a ball, roll up, gather, collect, mass, roll on.* — In pass., or with reflexive, *gather, assemble.* — Poetically: **gressus** (of a horse, *bring together his feet*, in making a caracole); **saxa sub auras** (*throw forth balls of melted lava*).

glōria, -ae, [supposed to be fr. †clovus- (√clu + us) + ia], f., *glory, fame, renown.* — Less exactly, *ambition, vainglory, pride.* — Concretely (as in Eng.), *the glory, the pride:* **Procas Troianae gentis.**

glūten, -inis, [†glutŏ- (of glutus) + nus (reduced)], n., *glue.* — Less exactly, *gum, resin.*

gnātus, -a, -um, p.p. of (g)nascor.

gnascor, see nascor.

Gnōsius (Gnōss-), -a, -um, [†Gnosŏ- (reduced) + ius, or perh. borrowed directly, cf. Γνωσσός], adj., *of Gnosus* (the city of Minos, in Crete), *Gnosian.* — Less exactly, *Cretan.*

Gorgō, -onis, [Gr. Γοργώ], f., *a Gorgon* (one of three mythical women of Libya, having some resemblance to the Furies). — Esp., *Medusa*, the chief of these sisters, slain by Perseus. Her head with serpent hair was placed in the shield or ægis of Jove and Pallas. — Plur., the three sisters, *Gorgons.* — Also, the head in the shield of Jove or Pallas.

Gorgoneus, -a, -um, [†Gorgon + eus], adj., *of the Gorgons:* **venena** (so called from the serpents in Medusa's hair).

Gortȳna, -ae, [Gr. Γορτύνη], f., *a city of Crete.*

Gortȳnius, -a, -um, [†Gortyna- (reduced) + ius], adj., *of Gortyna.* — Less exactly, *Cretan.*

gōrȳtus (cōry-), -ī, [Gr. γωρυτός], m., *a quiver.*

Gracchus, -ī, [?], m., a Roman family name in the Sempronian gens. — Esp., the two great reformers, *Tiberius* and *Caius* (Lat. *Gaius*).

gracilis, -e, [?], adj., *slender.*

gradior, gressus, gradī, [√grad, cf. gradus], 3. v. dep., *walk, go, move, proceed, advance.*

Gradīvus, -ī, [†gradi- (cf. gradior and aggredirī) + vus], m., (*the strider*), name of Mars.

gradus, -ūs, [√grad + us], m., *a step:* **conferre** (i.e. *move together*, of bullocks); **continere**; **revocare**; **celerare** (*pace*). — Also (as in Eng.), *a step* (of a funeral pile).

Graecia, -ae, [†Graecŏ- (reduced) + ia (f. of ius, prop. adj.)], f., *Greece.*

Grāiugena, -ae, [†Graiŏ-gena (√gen + a)], m., *a Grecian born, a Greek.*

Grāius, -a, -um, [Gr. †Γραῖος], adj., *Greek* (originally only the name of a tribe, but used by the Latins as the general name). — Masc., *a Greek.* — Plur., *the Greeks.*

grāmen, -inis, [akin to germen], n., *grass, an herb.* — Less exactly, *a grassy plain.*

grāmineus, -a, -um, [†gramin + eus], adj., *grassy.*

grandaevus, -a, -um, [†grandi-aevŏ- (decl. as adj.)], adj., *aged, old.*

grandis, -e, [?], adj., *large, great, huge.*

grandō, -dinis, [akin to χάλαζα], f., *hail.*

grātēs (abl. **-ibus**), [stem grati- (√gra + ti), cf. **gratus**], f., *thanks:* **dicere** (*render*); **referre** (*make a return*); **persolvere** (*pay a debt of gratitude*).

grātia, -ae, [†gratŏ- (reduced) + ia], f., *regard, pleasure in, fondness for.* — Also, *gratitude, thankfulness.*

grātus, -a, -um, [√gra (cf. grates) + tus, p.p.], adj., *dear, pleasing, acceptable, beloved.* — Also, *pleased, thankful, grateful.*

grātor, -ātus, -ārī, [†gratŏ-], 1. v. dep., *congratulate.*

gravātus, -a, -um, p.p. of gravo.

graveolēns (also separate), see oleo.

gravēscō, no perf., no sup., **-ēscere,**

[**†gravē-** (cf. **gravēdo**) + **sco**], 3. v. n. incept., *be burdened, be weighed down:* nemus fetu (*bend under the weigh*t, &c.).

gravĭdus, -a, -um, [**†gravi** + **dus**], adj., *heavy.* — Also, *full, laden, plentiful, prolific, heavy* (of crops), *luxuriant:* ager (*in full fruit*); uber(*distended*); aristae.— Esp., *pregna*nt, *big, impregnated.* — Also, poetically: imperiis Italiam; bellis urbem.

gravis, -e, [root akin to βαρύς + u (with added i, cf. **brevis**)], adj., *heavy, firm, solid.* — Esp. (cf. **gravidus**), *pregnant.*— Fig., *burdensome, grievous, noxious, noisome, heavy* (of sleep, of sound), *hard, toilsome, burdened* (with years), *sickly, severe* (of wounds), *serious, violen*t*:* exitus (*cruel*); nuntius (*unwelcome*); ira (*in cruel . wrath*). — Of persons, *of weigh*t (opposed to **levis**), *fierce:* victor; Osiris. — Neut. as subst., in plur., *serious events, results,* &c. —Neut. as adv., *ili, noisome:* grave olens.

Graviscae, -ārum, [?], f. pl., a town of Etruria, famous for its bad air.

graviter [**†gravi** + **ter**], adv., *heavily* (lit. and fig., cf. **gravis**), *violently, deeply, loudly:* pendens (*fiercely*); spirans (*heavy-scented,* also *poison-breathing*).

gravŏ, -āvī, -ātum, -āre, [**†gravi-** (as if **gravŏ-**)], 1. v. a., *weigh down, make heavy.* — Fig., *trouble, annoy, burden.* — Pass. as dep., *be relucta*nt, *refuse.*

gravor, see **gravo.**

gremium, -ī (-iī), [?], n., *the lap, the bosom, the breas*t*:* in vestris pono gremiis (*lay at one's feet*); fotus gremio. — Fig. (of a country, &c.), *bosom, lap, embrace:* telluris; coniugis (*lap of earth,* of Jupiter as spouse of the earth); caeruleus (of the Nile).

gressus, -a, -um, p.p. of **gradior.**

gressus, -ūs, [√**grad** + **tus**], m., *a step, a pace, a gait* (or *bearing*), *a way, course:* efferre (*proceed forth*); comprimere (*stay one's steps*); ante ferre (*go on before*); canes comitantur (*footsteps*); recipere (*retrace*); glomerare (*feet*).

grex, gregis, [?], m. (rarely f.), (of domestic animals), *a herd, a flock, a litter* (of pigs).

grūs, gruis, [?, perh. akin to Gr. γέρανος], f., *a crane.*

Grȳnaeus, -a, -um, [Gr. Γρυναῖος], adj., *of Grynia* (a town in Æolis where Apollo was worshipped), *Grynæan.*

grȳps, gryphis, [Gr. γρύψ], m.; *a griffin* (a monster with a lion's body and a bird's head and wings).

gubernāculum (-clum), -ī, [**†gubernā-** (in **guberno**) + **culum**], n., *a tiller, a helm.*

gubernātor, -ōris, [**†gubernā** + **tor**], m., *a helmsman, pilot.*

gurges, -ĭtis, [?, prob. akin to **gula, gurgulio,** and **glutio**], m., *a vortex, a whirlpool, an abyss, a gulf:* alternus (*flux and reflux, of a whirlpool*).—Less exactly, *a wave, a tide, waters, a stream, the sea, the ocean, a flood.*

gustŏ, -āvī, -ātum, -āre, [**†gustŏ-** (p.p. of √**gus,** cf. **gustus**)], 1. v. a., *taste.*

gutta, -ae, [?], f., *a drop.* — From similarity, *a spot, a blotch.*

guttur, -uris, [?, perh. akin to **gutta**], n., *the thro*at. — Less exactly, *the mouth, jaws.* — Poetically: ovantes gutture corvi (*croaking throat*).

Gyaros (-us), -ī, [Gr. Γύαρος], f., an island of the Egean (now *Calairo*).

Gyās, -ae, [Gr. Γύης], m.: 1. A companion of Æneas; 2. A Latin.

Gȳgēs, -is, [Gr. Γύγης], m., a companion of Æneas.

Gylippus, -ī, [Gr. Γύλιππος], m., an Arcadian.

gȳrus, -ī, [Gr. γῦρος], m., *a circular course, a ring, a circle, a circuit.* — Less exactly, *a coil, a fold* (of a serpent).

H.

habēna, -ae, [habē- (stem of habeo) + na (f. of nus)], f., *a rein, a thong, a lash, a bridle:* dare (immittere, effundere) habenas (*give loose rein,* lit. and fig.): immissis (datis, laxis) habenis (*at full speed, without restraint*); pressis (adductis) habenis (*with close rein*); convertere (*course*). — Fig., *reins, control:* rerum.

habēns, see **habeo.**

habeō, habuī, habitum, habēre, [?, †habŏ- (cf. habilis, habena)], 2. v. a., *hold, have, possess, keep, occupy, inhabit, wear:* arces; hostes muros; redimicula; pecus (*tend, raise*). — Fig., in same senses. — Esp. of marriage, *possess, have.* — Also of the place where one is: te pontus (*cover*); turba hunc (*surround*); vos saltus (*detain*); me thalamus (*be in,* changing point of view). — Of a council, &c., *hold.* — Of passions and the like, *possess, inspire:* omnes ardor. — Also, *hold, consider, regard:* domos suspectas; nullo discrimine(*treat*).—Peculiar uses: habendi, *of having, of wealth;* habenti, *a possessor, the rich;* hoc habet, *he is smitten.*

habilis, -e, [†habŏ- (cf. habeo) + lis], adj., *handy, convenient, fit, suited, active:* arcus; vigor; circumligat hastae natam (*lightly, deftly*).

habitātus, -a, -um, p.p. of **habito.**

habitō, -āvī, -ātum, -āre, [†habitŏ-], 1. v. a. and n., *occupy, inhabit, dwell in, dwell, live.*

habitus, -a, -um, p.p. of **habeo.**

habitus, -ūs, [†habi- (weaker stem of habeo) + tus], m., *bearing, condition, plight.* — Also, *dress, garb.* — Fig., of things, *position, nature:* locorum.

hāc [prob. abl. of **hic** (cf. eā)], adv., *this way:* hac iter est. — Often repeated, *this way ... that way.* — Less exactly, *here, there.*

hāctenus (often separated), [hac-tenus], adv., *hitherto, to this point, thus far.* — Less exactly, of time (as in English).

Hadriacus (Adr-), -a, -um, [Gr. Ἀδριακός], adj., *of Hadria* (a town on the Po, which gave its name to the Adriatic Sea). — Less exactly, *of the Adriatic:* undae.

haedus (hoe-, -ē, ae-), -ī, [?], m., *a kid.* — Plur., *the Kids* (two stars in Auriga, the rising of which was attended by storms).

Haemōn (Ae-), -onis, [Gr. Αἵμων], m., *a Rutulian.*

Haemonidēs, -ae, [Gr. patronymic of Haemon], m., *a Rutulian.*

Haemus, -ī, [Gr. Αἷμός], m., *a range of mountains in Thrace* (now *Great Balkan*).

haereō, haesī, haesum, haerēre, [†haesŏ- (unc. root)], 2. v. n., *stick, cleave, adhere, cling, stick fast, hang, hold fast, be fastened, hang to, be caught, take root* (of plants). — Less exactly, and fig., *be fastened* (of words, &c.), *stick, stand motionless, be rooted to the spot, remain, stand fast, hesitate, pause, linger, hang upon* (of the gaze, or of pursuit): hic terminus (*be fixed*); victoria Graium (*be delayed*); vox faucibus; aspectu conterritus.

haerēs, see better spelling **heres.**

Halaesus (-ēsus), -ī, [Gr. Ἁλαισος], m.: 1. A son of Agamemnon who came to Italy; 2. A Rutulian.

halcyōn, see **alcyon.**

Halēsus, see **Halaesus.**

hālitus, -ūs, [†hali- (weaker stem of halo) + tus], m., *breath, an exhalation, a vapor.*

Halius, -ī (-iī), [?], m., *a Trojan.*

hālō, -āvī, -ātum, -āre,[?], 1. v. n., *exhale, be fragrant.*

Halys,-yos,[Gr.Ἅλυς],m.,a Trojan.

Hamādryas, -ados, [Gr. Ἁμαδρυάς], f., *a Hamadryad* (a nymph whose life was bound up with a

particular tree), *a nymph*.
Hammōn, see **Ammon**.
hāmus, -ī, [cf. Gr. χαμός?, perh. borrowed], m., *a hook, a link* (hook-like, of which chain mail was made).
harēna, see **arena**.
Harpalycē, -ēs, [Gr. Ἁρπαλύκη], f., a female warrior of Thrace.
Harpalycus, -ī, [Gr. Ἁρπαλύκος], m., a Trojan.
Harpȳia, -ae, [Gr. Ἅρπυια], f., (mostly plur.), *a Harpy* (doubtless orig. a personified whirlwind), a monster with the body of a bird and a human face and voice.
harundŏ, etc.; see **arundo**.
haruspex (ar-), -icis, [stem akin to **hira, hillae** + **spex** (√spec as stem)], m., *a soothsayer* (by inspection of entrails, cf. **auspex**), *a diviner*.
hasta, -ae, [prob. akin to Gr. χανδάνω, *grasp*], f., *a spear-shaft, a spear, a wand* (sometimes without a head, **hasta pura**): **pampinea** (the thyrsus).
hastīle, -is, [†hasta- (reduced) + ilis, or †hasti- (akin to **hasta**) + lis, prop. n. of adj.], n., *a spear-shaft, a spear, a shoot, a sapling, a pole*.
haud (hau, haut), [?], neg. adv., (commonly negativing some particular word, cf. **non**, etc., general negative), *not, by no means:* haud mora (*there is no delay*); haud secius (*no less*); haud quaquam (*by no means*); haud quicquam (*nothing, not at all*).
haudquāquam, see **haud**.
hauriō, hausī, haustum, haurīre, [√haus, but prob. from a noun-stem in i], 4. v. a., *drink, drain, exhaust.* — Less exactly, *drink in, take in, draw in, receive:* caelum (*inhale*); lucem pecudes; vocem auribus; haec animo; oculis monumenta (*feast the eyes upon*).—Poetically: corda pavor (*absorb, possess*); supplicia scopulis (*suffer death by drowning*, &c.); latus gladio (*drain, as a vessel*); sol orbem (*pass, as if devour*); ensis inimicus (of persons, *drink their blood*).
haustus, -ūs, [√haus (as root) + tus, cf. **haurio**], m., *a draught, a mouthful:* aetherius (*a draught of celestial air*, of *inspired* instinct in bees).
hebeō, no perf., no sup., **hebēre**, [†hebŏ- (cf. **hebes**)], 2. v. n., *be dull:* sanguis (*be chilled*).
hebetō, -āvī, -ātum, -āre,[†hebet- (of **hebes**)], 1. v. a., *blunt, dull.* — Fig., *dull, dim, impair*.
Hebrus (Ebr-), -ī, [Gr. Ἕβρος], m.: 1. A river of Thrace, now *Maritza;* 2. A Trojan.
Hecatē, ēs, [Gr. Ἑκάτη], f., a mysterious goddess particularly associated with the lower world. Her nature and attributes were very variable, and she was especially identified as a three-formed goddess with the moon (in heaven), Diana (on earth), and Proserpine (in the world below).
Hector, -oris, [Gr. Ἕκτωρ], m., the eldest son of Priam and the most famous warrior of the Trojans, finally slain by Achilles and dragged around the walls of Troy.
Hectoreus, -a, -um,[Gr.Ἑκτόρεος], adj., *of Hector.* — Less exactly, *of Troy, Trojan*.
Hecuba, -ae, [Gr. Ἑκάβη], f., the wife of Priam.
hedera (ed-), -ae, [?], f., *ivy* (of apparently two species, *Hedera helix*, and another called *alba*).
hei, see **ei**.
hēia (ēia), [Gr. εἷα], interj. (of surprise, admiration, or encouragement), *ho! what ho! come on! come! on!*
Helena, -ae, [Gr. Ἑλένη], f., *Helen*, the famous daughter of Jupiter and Leda, carried off by Paris.
Helēnor, -oris, [Gr. Ἑλένωρ], m., a Trojan.
Helenus, -ī, [Gr. Ἕλενος], m., a son of Priam.

Helicōn, -ōnis, [Gr. 'Ελικών], m., the famous mountain in Bœotia, the abode of the Muses and favorite haunt of Apollo.

helleborus (elleborus, the spelling in vogue), -ī, [Gr. ἑλλέβορος or ἑλλ-], m., *hellebore* (cf. **veratrum,** the proper Latin word). The root of the plant was a specific for insanity.

Hellēspontiacus, -a, -um, [borrowed from Greek], adj., *of the Hellespont,* the strait, now *Dardanelles,* between Asia and Europe, running into the Ægean Sea. On its shore in Asia was Lampsacus, whence came the worship of Priapus).

Helōrus (-um), -ī, [Gr. "Ελωρος], m. and n., a city on the east coast of Sicily. A wide, slow river of the same name flowed over the flat land in the vicinity.

Helymus, see **Elymus.**

herba, -ae, [?], f. (both collectively and in plural), *an herb, grass, herbage, a weed, a plant, dried grass* (hay), *vegetation, a blade* (of grass or growing crops), *sward:* mollis; veneni; viridis (*pasture*); tenera; immemor herbae (*grazing*); olens; maiores (*stalk and leaves*); Sardoa (perh. *crowfoot*).

Herbēsus, -ī, [?], m., a Rutulian.

herbōsus, -a, -um, [†herba- (reduced) + osus], adj., *grassy, rich in vege*tation*:* flumen.

Hērculēs, -is, [Gr. Ἡρακλῆς, through a shorter form], m., the famous demigod, renowned for his strength and services to mankind, represented with a club and lion's skin. The poplar was sacred to him.

Hērculeus, -a, -um, [imitated fr. Ἡράκλειος], adj., *of Hercules:* umbra (of the poplar); corona (of poplar); sacrum; Tarentum (*Herculean,* founded by Hercules); amictus (the lion's skin).

hērēs, -ēdis, [akin to **herus**?], m. (or f.), *an heir.*

herīlis, see **erilis.**

Herilus, see **Erulus,** the approved spelling.

Hermīnius, -ī (-iī), [?], m., a Trojan warrior.

Hermionē, -ēs, [Gr. Ἑρμιόνη], f., the daughter of Menelaus and Helen, the wife of Orestes.

Hermus, -ī, [Gr. Ἕρμος], m., a river in Lydia, famous for its golden sands and the fertility of the surrounding country.

Hernicus, -a, -um, [†hernŏ- (said to mean *rock*) + cus], adj., *of the Hernici* (nom. plur. of same word), a people of Latium, said to be of Sabine origin.

hērōs, -ōis (-ōos), [Gr. ἥρως], m., *a demigod, a hero.*

herus (erus, more approved spelling), -ī, [?], m., *a master, a lord.*

Hēsionē, -ēs, [Gr. Ἡσιόνη], f., a daughter of Laomedon, sister of Priam, and wife of Telamon.

Hesperia, see **Hesperius.**

Hesperis, -idis, [Gr. ἑσπερίς, adj. of ἕσπερος], f. adj., (*Western*), *Hesperian, Italian.* — Plur., *the Hesperides, daughters of Hesperus,* keepers of a garden of golden apples in the far West.

Hesperius, -a, -um, [Gr. Ἑσπέριος, adj. of Ἕσπερος], adj., (*Western*). — Fem. (sc. **terra**), *the Western land, Italy* (as viewed from Greece), *Hesperia.* — Hence, *Italian, Hesperian.*

Hesperus, -ī, [Gr. Ἕσπερος = Lat. *Vesper*], m., *evening, the evening star.*

hesternus, -a, -um, [†hesi- (see **heri**) + ternus (cf. **externus, sempiternus**)], adj., *of yesterday, yesterday's:* Lar (*newly adopted*).

heu [?, cf. **eheu, heus**], interj. (of grief or pain), *alas! ah! oh! ah me!*

heus [cf. **heu**], interj. (of calling), *ho! hallo! ho there!*

hiātus, -ūs, [†hiā- (of **hio**) + tus], m., *a gaping, an opening, a yawning mouth, a mouth:* oris (*jaws*).

hibernus, -a, -um, [†hiem- (stem

of **hiemps**, contracted) + **ernus** (cf. **caverna**)], adj., *of winter, wintry, winter's, stormy.* — Neut. plur., *winters.*
Hibērus, -a, -um, adj., *Spanish.*
hibiscus, -ī, [Gr. ἰβίσκος], m., *the marsh-mallow, a mallow twig* or *twigs, a switch* (of mallow).
hīc, haec, hŏc, [pron. √hŏ + i + ce, cf. **ecce, cetera**], dem. pron. (as subst. or adj., of something near in time, place, or thought, cf. **ille**), *this, he, she, it, such.* — Of indefinite persons, *this man, one.* — Often repeated, or correlative with another pron., *this ... that, he ... he, one, another, the former, the latter.* — Also, *the following, as follows.* — In abl. with comparative, *so much, the more.* — Phrases: **hoc erat quod?** etc., *was it for this that?;* **hoc habet,** *he is smitten, he is hit, he is sped* (a gladiatorial word).
hīc [†hī (locative of †ho) + ce], adv., *here, there.* — Also, of time or circumstance, *here, hereupon.*
Hicetāonius, -ī, [†Hicetaon + ius, prop. adj.], m., *son of Hicetaon.*
hiemps, hiemis, [unc. root (found in χιών) + mus (reduced, cf. χειμέριος, *Himalaya*), with parasitic p], *winter, storm, tempest.* — Personified, *the Storm.*
Hiēra (Iaera), -ae, [Gr. Ἱερά], f., a priestess of Jove on Mt. Ida, mother of Pandarus and Bitias.
hilarŏ, -āvī, -ātum, -āre, [†hilarŏ-], 1. v. a., *cheer, enliven.*
Himella, -ae, [?], f., a river in Italy flowing into the Tiber.
hinc [him (case-form of †hŏ, cf. **interim**) + ce (cf. **hīc**)], adv., *from here, hence, from there, from this* (cf. **unde**), *from these.* — Of time, *then, thereupon, next, hereupon.* — Also (cf. **a parte dextera**), *here, on this side.* — Often, repeated or opposed to another pron.: **hinc atque hinc (illinc)**, *on this side ... on that, here ... there, on every side, around.* — Of

logical relations (cf. *hence, since*), *hence.*
hinnītus, -ūs, [†hinni- (of **hinnio**) + tus], m., *a neighing.*
hiŏ, -āvī, -ātum, -āre, [†hiŏ- (cf. **hiulcus, hisco**)], 1. v. n., *gape, yawn.* — **hiāns, -antis,** p., *opening the mouth, gaping, open, open-mouthed, eager:* **immane** (*opening his enormous jaws,* of a lion).
Hippocoōn, -ontis, [Gr. Ἱπποκόων, -οντις], m., a companion of Æneas.
Hippodamē, -ēs, [Gr. Ἱπποδάμη], f., *Hippodamia,* daughter of Œnomaus, won by Pelops in a chariot-race. Her story was a favorite theme for epic poetry.
Hippolytē, -ēs, [Gr. Ἱππολύτη], f., an Amazon, wife of Theseus. She fought against the Amazons on the side of Athens.
Hippolytus, -ī, [Gr. Ἱππόλυτος], m., the son of Theseus and Hippolyte, killed through the wiles of Phædra, his step-mother, but afterwards restored to life by Diana.
hippomanes (not declined in Latin), [Gr. ἱππομανές], n., an excretion of the mare used as a philter.
Hippotadēs, -ae, [Gr. Ἱπποτάδης], m., *son of Hippotas.*
Hircānus, -a, -um; see **Hyrcānus.**
hircus, -ī, [?], m., *a he-goat.*
hirsūtus, -a, -um, [†thirsu- (stem akin to **hirtus**) + tus (cf. **cornutus**)], adj., *bristly, prickly, rough:* **vepres; frondes; cristā equinā** (*bristling,* of a hero in a crested helmet); **supercilium** (*bushy*).
hirtus, -a, -um, [unc. root (cf. **horreo**) + tus, p.p. of lost verb], adj., *rough, hairy, shaggy, bristly;* **capellae** (*coarse-haired*).
hirundŏ, -inis, [?], f., *a swallow.*
Hisbō, -ōnis, [?], m., a Rutulian.
hiscŏ, no perf., no sup., **hiscere,** [√hi (perhaps †hī-) + sco, cf. **hio, hiulcus**], 3. v. n., *gape, open the mouth.*
hispidus, -a, -um, [akin to **hirtus,**

hirsutus, ?], adj., *shaggy, hairy:* frons (*bushy*).

hiulcus, -a, -um, [?, †hiulŏ- (†hiŏ + lus) + cus], adj., *gaping, cracking, furrowed* (of land cracked by the sun).

hōc, abl.; see **hic.**

hōc, adv.; see **huc.**

hodiē [†hŏ- (stem) or hō (abl.) of pron. √hŏ (cf. **hic**) -die (abl. of dies)], adv., *to-day.* — Weakened, with negatives, *now, surely:* nunquam hodie effugies (emphasizing the negative).

holus (ol-), -eris, [?], n., *vegetables.*

homo, -inis, [√hom (I.-E. GHAM, cf. Sk. *guma,* Eng. *groom*) + o (cf. **gero**), akin to **humus**], m., *a man* (or woman), *a mortal, human kind, the human race.* — Often, *the human form, human, mortal:* malis hominem (*human woes*); vox hominum sonat.

Homolē, -ēs, [Gr. Ὁμόλη], f., a mountain of Thessaly.

honestus, -a, -um, [†honŏs- (n. of honor?) + tus, cf. **arbustus, funestus**], adj., *beautiful* (cf. **honor**), *noble, fine.*

honor (-ōs), -ōris, [unc. root + or (-os)], m., *beauty, grace, dignity.* — Of moral qualities, *glory, dignity, fame, honor.* — Of beauty conferred, *adornment, decoration.* — Of glory conferred, *honor, honors* (marks of honor), *respect, regard, reward, recompense, tribute, meed of praise.* — Esp. of religious honor, *worship, sacrifice, an offering, honors, reverence, praise, festive rites.* — Technically, *honors* (of the people), *an office, a magistracy.*

honōrŏ, -āvī, -ātum, -āre, [honor], 1. v. a., *honor, respect, observe with honor.*

hora, -ae, [Gr. ὥρα, *season*], f., *an hour.* — Less exactly, *time, moment, hour:* suprema; crastina (*the morrow*).—Phrase: in horas, from hour to hour. — Personified, *the Hours* (attendants of the Sun, Moon, &c.).

hordeum, -ī, (also plur.), n., *barley.* — Plur., *grains* (of barley).

horrendus, -a, -um, ger. p. of **horreo.**

horrēns, -entis, p. of **horreo.**

horreō (horrui, assigned to **horresco**), no sup., **horrēre,** [†horrŏ- (√hors), cf. **horrificus**], 2. v. n. and a., *stand erect, bristle, be rough:* colla colubris; regia culmo; carduus. — From the tingling sensation of fear (cf. "hair standing on end." The same root in Sk. expresses the similar tingling of intense pleasure), *shudder, shudder at, dread.*
— **horrēns, -entis,** p. as adj., *bristling, rough, prickly, shaggy.*
— **horrendus, -a, -um,** ger. p. as adj., *horrible, dreadful, awful* (in bad or good sense), *frightful, dread.* — Neut. as adv., *dreadfully.* — Neut. plur., *horrors, prodigies.*

horrēscō, horrui, no sup., **horrescere,** [†horrē- (stem of horreo) + sco], 3. v. n. and a., *bristle:* seges hastis. — Also (cf. **horreo**), *shiver, tremble, shudder, dread:* campi (of the grain waving in the wind); visu; morsus mensarum (*shudder at*).

horreum, -ī, [?], n., *a granary, a storehouse, a barn.*

horribilis, -e, [†horrŏ- (cf. **horreo**) + bilis], adj., *horrible, frightful, dreadful.*

horridus, -a, -um, [†horrŏ- (cf. **horreo**) + dus], adj., *rough, shaggy, bristling:* bruma gelu; grando (*icy,* cf. last example); hastilibus myrtus. — Also, perh. from domestic animals, *rough* (in bad condition, cf. **nitidus,** *sleek*), *disordered, unseemly, uncouth, unkept, ill-kempt:* alter (of a queen-bee, opposed to **clarus**); macies (*hideous*); horridior rusco (of a man). — Transferred, and fig., *dreadful, dread, horrid, frightful, awful.*

horrificō, -āvī, -ātum, -āre, [†horrificō (stem of **horrificus**)], 1. v. a., *terrify, affright.*

horrificus, -a, -um, [†horrŏ- (cf. horreo)+ficus (√fac+us)], adj., *terrible, frightful.*

horrisonus, -a, -um, [†horrŏ- (cf. horrificus) + sŏnus], adj., *dread sounding, of awful sound.*

horror, -ōris, [√horr(cf. horreo) + or], m., *a bristling.* — Also, *a shudder, dread, horror.* — Poetically: armorum (*dread sound*).

hortātor, -ōris, [†hortā- (in hortor) + tor], m., *an encourager, a suggester.*

Hortīnus, -a, -um, [Horta- (reduced) + inus], adj., *of Horta* (a town of Etruria on the Tiber and Nar, now *Orta*).

hortor, -ātus, -ārī, [†horitŏ- (stem of lost p.p. of obs. †horior)], 1. v. dep., *exhort, encourage, advise, urge, address* (with words of encouragement as a leader). — Poetically, of animals, *urge, urge on, entice.*

hortus, -ī, [?, cf. **cohors,** Gr. χόρτος], m., (*an enclosure*), *a garden, an orchard.*

hospes, -ĭtis, [†hos- (I. E. GHAS, *eat*) -petis = potis, cf. πόσις (√pa + tis)], comm., *a host.* — Transferred, *a guest, a stranger.* — As an address, *stranger, friend.* — Also, *a friend* (*hereditary* or *family*, in the peculiar relation of antiquity, like Gr. ξένος.

hospitium, -ī (-iī), [†hospit + ium], n., *entertainment, hospitality, alliance, amity, friendship.* — Plur., *hospitalities.* — Concretely, *retreat, shelter.* — Also (cf. **hospes** and ξενία), *friendship* (family or hereditary). — Concretely, *a friend* (cf. **servitium,** *a slave*): antiquum (*long in friendly relations with*).

†hospitus, -a, -um, (only in fem. and neut. plur.), [irregular formation fr. **hospes** (cf. **sospes, sospita**), as if fr. **hospitus**], adj., *strange, foreign.* — Also, *hospitable, friendly:* unda plaustris (*passable*).

hostia, -ae, [prob. †hosti- (stem of **hostis,** reduced) + ia (f. of ius), going back to the time of human sacrifice(?), cf. Æn. x. 519], f., *a victim* (for sacrifice).

hostīlis, -e, [†hosti- (lengthened, cf. **civīlis**) + lis], adj., *of an (the) enemy, the enemy's, hostile:* facies (*to disturb a sacrifice*).

hostis, -is, [?, poss. †hos- (cf. **hospes**) + tis, orig. *a guest,* then *stranger,* then *foe*], comm., *a stranger.* — Also, *an enemy* (of the country, cf. **inimicus,** *one's own private enemy*), *a foe, the enemy.*

hūc (old **hōc**), [dat. adv. hō-ce, cf. illō], adv., *hither, here* (of motion), *into this, into that,* &c., *thither, there* (cf. **hic**), *this way:* includunt (*in this*); asperge sapores (*here,* on this place); huc atque illuc (*this way and that*).

hūmānus, -a, -um, [†humŏ- (reduced) + anus, cf. **homo**], adj., *of man, human, mortal, of mortals.*

hūmectō, see **umecto,** the spelling now in vogue.

hūmens, see **umeo.**
hūmeō, see **umeo.**
humerus, see **umerus.**
hūmēscō, see **umesco.**
hūmidus, see **umidus.**

humilis, -e, [†humŏ + lis], adj., *low* (lit. and fig.), *mean, humble:* Italia (*low-lying*); casae; fossa (*shallow,* cf. **altus,** *deep*); pavor (*dispirited*).

humō, -āvī, -ātum, -āre, [†humŏ-], 1. v. a., *bury, inter:* solamen humandi (*of burial*).

hūmor, see **umor,** the spelling in vogue.

humus, -ī, [√hom (cf. **homo**) + us, cf. χαμαί], f., *the ground, the earth, the soil:* exercebis; rastros patietur; te condet humi; me tollere humo; cadavera tegere humo. — humi, *on the ground:* humi nascentia fraga; procumbit humi bos.

hyacinthus, -i, [Gr. ὑάκινθος], m., *a hyacinth* (so called), an uncertain flower variously identified (cornflower, iris, rocket, martagon lily).

Hyades, -um, [Gr. Ὑάδες], f. plur., *the Hyades,* a group of seven stars in the head of Taurus (the Bull), the setting of which was attended by storms.

hyalus, -i, [Gr. ὕαλος], m., *glass: color* (i.e. green).

hybernus, see **hibernus.**

Hybla, -ae, [Gr. Ὕβλη], f., a mountain in Sicily famous for its bees.

Hyblaeus, -a, -um, [Gr. Ὑβλαῖος], adj., *of Hybla, Hyblæan.*

Hydaspes, -is, [Gr. Ὑδάσπης], m.: 1. A river of India.— Less exactly, for the people in its vicinity: regem observant (the same figure is admissible in Eng.); 2. A Trojan (cf. **Hebrus** and **Hypanis**).

hydra, -ae, [Gr. ὕδρα], f.: 1. *The hydra,* a water-snake killed by Hercules. It had seven heads, which multiplied as fast as they were cut off; 2. Another water-serpent (or the ghost of the same?) in the infernal regions, acting (like monsters generally) as a minister of divine vengeance.

hydrus, -i, [Gr. ὕδρος], m., *a water-snake, a snake* (in general): immanis (the dragon of Cadmus).

hyems, see **hiemps,** the better spelling.

Hylaeus, -i, [Gr. Ὑλαῖος], m., a Centaur who offered violence to Atalanta.

Hylas, -ae, [Gr. Ὕλας], m., a youth who accompanied Hercules in the Argonautic expedition, and was carried away by the nymphs of a fountain.

Hylax, -acis, [Gr. Ὕλαξ], m., the name of a dog.

Hyllus, -i, [Gr. Ὕλλος], m., a Trojan.

Hymenaeus, -i, [Gr. ὑμέναιος], m., *Hymen,* the marriage god.—Transferred, *marriage, wedlock, nuptial rites, a wedding, a nuptial song.* — Also in plur. in same senses. — Also, of animals, *mating.*

Hypanis, -is, [Gr. Ὕπανις], m..: 1. A river of Scythia (now *Boug*), a roaring and rocky river: saxosum sonans; 2. A Trojan (cf. **Hebrus**).

Hyperboreus, -a, -um, [Gr. Ὑπερβόρεος], adj., (*beyond the North*), *far Northern, Northernmost.*— The plur. is the name of the people of those regions, as usual.

Hyrcanus, -a, -um, [Gr. Ὑρκανός], adj., *of the Hyrcani* (a nation on the Caspian Sea, comprehended under the general idea of the Parthians, with whom the Romans were long at war). — Plur., *the Hyrcani* (the nation itself).

Hyrtacides, -ae, [Gr. patronymic]; m., *son of Hyrtacus* (Nisus or Hippocoon).

Hyrtacus, -i, [borrowed fr. Greek], m., the father of Nisus. Perhaps another, the father of Hippocoon.

I (vowel).

Iacchus, -i, [Gr. Ἴακχος], m., a name of Bacchus. — Also, *wine.*

Iaera, see **Hiera.**

Iapetus, -i, [Gr. Ἰαπετός], m., one of the Titans, father of Prometheus and Atlas.

Iapis, -idis, [borrowed fr. Greek], m., the physician of Æneas.

Iapys, -ydis, [Gr. Ἴαπυς], m., *of the Iapydes* (a race around the head of the Adriatic): Timavus. — Pl., the race itself, *the Iapydes.*

Iapyx, -ygis, [Gr. Ἰᾶπυξ], adj., *Iapygian, of Iapygia* (a name of Apulia).— Less exactly, *Apulian.* —Masc., *Iapyx,* the north-westerly wind (blowing from Iapygia into Greece).

Vocabulary. 133

Iarbās, -ae, [?], m., a king of the Gætulians, son of Jupiter Ammon, and a suitor of Dido.

Iasīdēs, -ae, [Gr. patronymic of Iasius], m., *descendant of Iasius*.

Iasius, -ī (-iī), [Gr. 'Ιάσιος], m., the brother of Dardanus, son of Jupiter and Electra. He became a special favorite of Ceres (Demeter). Among other myths he is said to have married a daughter of Teucer, and so to have been one of the founders of the Trojan race.

iaspis, -ĭdis, [Gr. ἴασπις], f., *jasper* (a precious stone).

Iber (Ibērus), see Hiberus.

ibī [pron. √i (cf. **is**) + bi (loc. suffix, cf. **-bus** and **tibī**)], adv., *there* (less demonstrative than **illīc,** cf. **is**): respexit, ibi omnis effusus labor (*in that look*).— Of time, *then, thereupon:* ibi memento.

ibīdem [ibi-dem, cf. **idem**], adv., *in the same place, on the same spot.* — Of time, *at the same time.*

Icarus, -ī, [Gr. 'Ίκαρος], the son of Daedalus, who fell accompanying his father's flight.

īcō, īcī, īctum, īcere, 3. v. a., *strike, hit.* — Of a treaty, *ratify, make.*

ictus, -ūs, [√ic + tus], m., *a stroke, a blow:* certus (*aim*); quo ictu furit equus (*wound*); cuspidis (*wound*); totus (*force*); ventos lacessit ictibus (*thrusts*).— Collectively, *throwing:* cursu et ictu.

Īda, -ae, [Gr. 'Ίδα], f.: 1. A mountain in the middle of Crete, the seat of a famous worship of Jupiter. Here Jupiter was supposed to have been nursed in secret ; 2. The mountain of Phrygia, near Troy, famous for many divine incidents, and especially for the worship of Cybele ; 3. The name of the mother of Nisus.

Īdaeus, -a, -um, [Gr. 'Ιδαῖος], adj., *of Ida* (the mountain in Crete), *Idæan.* — *of Ida* (cf. 2. **Ida**), *Idæan.* — Less exactly, *Trojan.* — Masc., *Idæus,* name of two Trojan companions of Æneas.

Īdalius, -a, -um, [Gr. 'Ιδάλιον], adj., *of Idalium, Idalian.* — Fem., *Idalia,* a town and grove of Cyprus. — Neut., *Idalium,* another form of the same name. Both forms are properly adj., but the adj. is used as if from the nouns.

Īdas, -ae, [Gr. 'Ίδας], m.: 1. A Trojan ; 2. A Thracian.

idcircō [id (n. acc. of **is**) circo (dat. or abl. of **circus,** cf. **circa, circum**)], adv., *for that reason, therefore, for this purpose.* — With negatives, *for all that, for that, on that account.*

īdem, eadem, idem, [is + dem (pron. √da, in acc.?, cf. **quidam, dum**)], adj. pron., *the same, the very, the like.* — Often equivalent to a mere connective, *also, likewise, as well.*

ideō [id (n. acc. of **is**) eo, strictly, *and that for this reason* or *purpose*], adv., *for this reason, therefore, on this account.* — With negatives (cf. **idcirco**), *for all that.*

Idmōn, -onis, [Gr. 'Ίδμων], m., a Rutulian.

Īdomeneus, -eī (acc. **-ea**), [Gr. 'Ιδομενεύς], m., a hero of the Trojan war, leader of the Cretans.

Idūmaeus, -a, -um, [Gr. 'Ιδυμαῖος], adj., *of Idume (Edom),* a region of Syria, famous for its palms, *Idumæan.*

iēns, euntis, p. of eo.

igitur [perh. unc. stem + tus (cf. **divinitus**)], adv., *in that case.* — Weakened as conj., *accordingly, therefore.* — Also in questions and the like (implying that what follows is the logical consequence of what precedes or has been implied), *then :* mene igitur fugis (*do you then,* &c.? as your action seems to indicate).

ignārus, -a, -um, [in-gnarus (√gna + rus)], adj., *not knowing, ignorant, unacquainted with, unaware, unsuspecting, in igno-*

rance, taken by surprise. — Rare in pass. sense, *unknown:* ignarum habet ora Mimanta (*in obscurity*).

ignāvē [abl. of ignavus], adv., *slothfully, negligently:* carpere herbas (*heedless of plucking*).

ignāvia, -ae, [†ignavŏ- (reduced) + ia], f., *slothfulness, cowardice:* animi (*cowardly spirit*).

ignāvus, -a, -um, [in-gnavus (√gna + vus)], adj., *idle, slothful, without spirit, cowardly.* — Poetically: hiems ignava colono (*an idle time*, &c.). — Also, *idle, unproductive, unfruitful:* nemora.

ignēscŏ, no perf., no sup., **-escere,** [†ignē- (of supposed or lost verb †igneo) + sco], 3. v. n. incept., *take fire.* — Fig., *be fired, be inflamed.*

igneus, -a, -um, [†igni- (reduced) + eus], adj., *fiery, blazing, burning.* — Fig., *fiery, ardent, burning, like fire* (swift), *like a flash.*

ignipotēns, -entis, [†igni-potens], m., *Lord of fire,* a name of Vulcan.

ignis, -is, [I. E. √AG (of unc. meaning) + nis], m., *fire, flame, heat, brand:* rapidus (*lightning*); Luna colligit ignes (*light,* conceiving the heavenly bodies as blazing); Cyllenius (the planet Mercury); rutilus (*redness*); aeterni (the *stars*). — Fig., of the passions, *passion, love, fury, wrath, frenzy.* — Concretely (as in English), *flame* (object of love).

ignōbilis, -e, [in-(g)nobilis], adj., *ignoble, inglorious, obscure, worthless, unhonored.*

ignōminia, -ae, [†ignomini- (reduced, cf. cognominis) + ia], f., *want of fame, ignominy, disgrace, shame.*

ignōrŏ, -āvī, -ātum, -āre, [†ignarŏ-], 1. v. a., *not know, be unaware of, be ignorant of.* — Poetically, of *transplanting:* semina matrem (*become unacquainted with*).

ignōscŏ, -nōvī, -nōtum, -nōscere, [in-(g)nosco, formed perh. in imitation of cognosco, *investigate*], 3. v. n., *pardon, forgive.* — **ignoscendus, -a, -um,** ger. p., *pardonable.*

ignōtus, -a, -um, [in-(g)notus], adj., *unknown, obscure, strange, unobserved.*

īlex, -icis, [?], f., *an oak* (of a particular species, the holm-oak), *a holm-oak.*

īlia, -ium, [perh. akin to εἴλω, *roll* (cf. εἴλεος)], n. plur. (sing. rare), *the groin, the flanks, the side* (between the ribs and hips): rumpere (*burst the sides,* with envy and the like).

Īlia, -ae, [†Ilŏ + ia], f., a name for Rhea Silvia (the mother of Romulus and Remus).

Īliacus, -a, -um, [Gr. Ἰλιακός], adj., *of Ilium* (another name for Troy), *Trojan.*

Īlias, -adis, [Gr. Ἰλιάς], f. adj., *a Trojan woman.*

īlicet [i (imper. of eo) licet, *go, you may*], adv., (orig. formula of dismissal for an assembled people, *it is over, you may depart*). — Transferred, *immediately, forthwith, at once.*

īlignus, -a, -um, [†ilic- (of ilex) + nus], adj., *of holm-oak, oaken.*

Īlionē, -ēs, [Gr. Ἰλιόνη], f., the oldest daughter of Priam, married to Polymestor, king of Thrace.

Īlioneus, -eī (acc. **-ea**), [Gr. Ἰλιονεύς], m., an aged Trojan, companion of Æneas.

Īlium, ī (**-iī**), [Gr. Ἴλιον], prop. n. of adj., see Ilius], n., a name of Troy, city of Ilus.

Īlius, -a, -um, [cf. Ἴλιον], adj. (of wh. Ilium is neut., but it is treated as adj. from Ilium), *Ilian, Trojan.*

illābor, see **inlabor.**

illacrimo, see **inlacrimo.**

illaetābilis, see **inlaetabilis.**

illaudātus, see **inlaudatus.**

ille (ollus), illa, illud, [unc. pron. stem + lus (cf. **ullus**)], dem. pron.

(conceived as more remote than **hic**), *that, these.* — Without noun, *he, she, that, it.* — Contrary to Eng. usage, of what follows, *this, these, these things.* — Often repeated or opposed to another pron., *the other, that one, that, the former* (cf. **hic**). — Of a conspicuous person or object (as if pointed at), *the great, that.* — In comparisons (to make the comparison more vivid, as if it were actually in sight), *some, a.* — In imitation of Homeric ὅγε, redundant, merely continuing the subject of discourse. — **ex illo,** *from that time.*

illecebrae,-arum; see **inlecebrae.**

illīc [illi (loc. adv. fr. **ille**) -ce (cf. **hic**)], adv., *there, in that place, with them* (cf. **hic, hinc**), *on this.* — hic ... illic, *here ... there, in this place ... in that.*

illīdō, see **inlido**.

illinc [illim (case-form of **ille**, cf. **interim**) -ce (cf. **hic**)], adv., *thence, from there.* — Also (cf. **hinc**), *on that side, that side:* hinc atque illinc (*on this side and that*).

illīsus, see **inlisus.**

illōtus, see **inlotus.**

illūc [illo (dat. adv. fr. **ille**, cf. **eo**) -ce (cf. **hic**)], adv., *thither, that way:* huc illuc volvens oculos; huc caput atque illuc pependit (*on his side and that*)

illūcēscō, see **inlucesco.**

illūdō, see **inludo.**

illustris, see **inlustris.**

illūsus, see **inlusus.**

illuviēs, see **inluvies.**

Illyricus, -a, -um, [†Illyri- (stem of **Illyris**) + cus], adj., *of Illyria*, (or Illyris, an indefinite region east of the Adriatic, to the north of Greece proper): aequor (the Adriatic).

Īlus, -ī, [Gr. Ἶλος], m.: 1. The mythical founder of Ilium, grandfather of Priam; 2. A son of Dardanus, and great-uncle of No. 1; 3. A name of Iulus; 4. A Rutulian.

Ilva, -ae, [prob. borrowed], f., *Elba,* the island off the coast of Etruria, famous for its rich iron-mines.

imāgō, -inis, [†imā- (stem of †imŏ, simple verb, whence **imitor**, cf. **dictito, dicto**) + go (cf. **vorago**)], f., *a representation, an imitation, a copy:* genitoris (*a resemblance*); formae (*empty form*); Lunae (*reflection*); Aeneae (*appearance*, in a comparison). — Concretely, *a statue, a representation* (in art): Iani; maris; rerum. — Esp., *a phantom, a shade, an apparition, a form:* magna mei (*I, a renowned shade*); pallentis Adrasti. — Of the mind, *a picture, a conception, an image, an idea:* confusa rerum; pietatis; pugnae; maior Martis (*more vivid picture*); plurima mortis (*form*). — Fig., echo.

Imāōn, -onis, m., a Rutulian.

imbellis, -e, [in-bellŏ- (reduced, and decl. as adj., cf. **exanimis**)], adj., *unwarlike, peaceful, effeminate:* telum (*ineffective*); Indi.

imber, -bris, [√imb + rus (weakened), akin to ὄμβρος, Sk. *abhras*], m., *rain* (violent and sudden, cf. **pluvia**), *rain-storm, storm, rain-cloud:* frigidus; hibernus; aestivus effusus imbribus; verberat humum; ater; extremus brumae. — Also, as a genial agency, *showers, rain:* largus; amicus; laetus; fecundi. — Less exactly, *water* (of the sea): inimicus. — Poetically, as in Eng.: ferreus (*hail*, of weapons).

Imbrasidēs, -ae, [Gr. patronymic fr. Imbrasus], m., *son of Imbrasus.*

Imbrasus, -ī, [?], m., a Lycian, father of Glaucus and Lades.

imbrex, -icis, [†imbri + cus (reduced)], f. (or m.), *a tile* (hollow, of the Italian form, for covering roofs). — Collectively, in sing., *tiles, tiling.*

imbrifer, -era, -erum, [†imbrifer (√fer + us)], adj., *bringing rain, rainy.*

imbuŏ, -buī, -būtum, -buere,
[?, perh. akin to **imber,** fr. †imber- (√imb + u, cf. **acuo,** cf. also Sk. ambhas, *water*)], 3. v. a., *soak, wet* (either used of the liquid or with the liquid). — Less exactly, *stain:* agnus aram (by sacrifice); sanguis arma; sanguine bellum.

imitābilis, -e, [†imitā- (stem of **imitor**) + bilis], adj., *imitable:* non imitabile fulmen (*inimitable*).

imitātus, -a, -um, p.p. of **imitor.**

imitor, -ātus, -ārī, [†imitŏ- (stem of **imitus,** p.p. of †imŏ, cf. **imago, aemulus**)], 1. v. dep., *imitate, counterfeit, represent, copy:* Pana canendo (*rival*); Satyros; imitata vox sonitus tubarum (*resembling, ringing like*).

immānis (in-), -e, [in- stem akin to **manus,** perh. **manus** itself], adj., (either *savage* or *monstrous,* both which meanings are common and run into each other), *huge, monstrous, enormous:* membra; dorsum; antrum; armenta (*of monsters*). — In fig. sense, *monstrous, inhuman, wild, fierce, savage, cruel:* nefas; gens. — Neut. as adv., *enormously, wildly:* immane sonat (*roars wildly*); spirans (*fiercely,* in wrath).

immātūrus (in-), -a, -um, [in-maturus], adj., *unripe, immature.* — Fig., *premature, untimely.*

immedicābilis (in-), -e, [in-medicabilis], adj., *incurable:* telum (because poisoned).

immemor (in-), -oris, [in-memor], adj., *unmindful, forgetful, regardless, thoughtless, heedless, unheeding.* — Poetically, *free from memory* (of the souls of the dead drinking the waters of Lethe).

immensus (in-), -a, -um, [in-mensus], adj., *unmeasured, immeasurable, immense, huge, unbounded, enormous, boundless, vast.* — Fig., *tremendous, prodigious:* clamor; agmen; aquarum.

immergo, -mersī, -mersum, -mergere, [in-mergo], 3. v. a., *plunge, drown, overwhelm:* me ponto; unda virum.

immeritus (in-), -a, -um, [in-meritus], adj., *undeserving.* — Esp., undeserving of evil, *unoffending:* Priami gens.

immineō (in-), no perf., no sup., **-ēre,** [in-mineo], 2. v. n., *overhang, project over.* — Less exactly and fig., *threaten, menace, be close at hand:* globus (of the enemy); hostis muris.

inmisceō (in-), -miscuī, -mistum (-mixtum), -miscēre, [in-misceo], 2. v. a., *mix in, mingle:* maculae igni. — Less exactly and fig.: admonet immiscetque preces (*mingles prayers with his warning*); manus manibus (*mingle fist with fist,* poetically of boxers); immixti Danais (*mingled with*); crabro se imparibus armis (*join in unequal combat*); se armis (*plunge*); nocte (nubi) se (*vanish, be lost*).

inmissus (in-), -a, -um, p.p. of **immitto.**

inmitis (in-), -e, [in-mitis], adj., *cruel, ruthless, ferocious:* nidi (poetically of birds that feed on bees).

immittō (in-), -mīsī, -missum, -mittere, [in-mitto], 3. v. a., *let go in, send in, let in, send to:* apros fontibus; socios portis (*admit*); vadis ratem (*drive, force*); immittuntur plantae (*set in, graft in*); Alpes apertas (*bring down,* of Hannibal bringing the Gauls against Rome). — Esp. in p.p.: lumen immissum (*shining in*); hostes (*bursting in*); immissae ferae silvis et sidera caelo (*let loose,* see next division, ... *sent abroad*); superis Allecto (*sent down,* with accessory notion of *let loose*); ignes (*let loose*). — Less exactly (cf. last examples. above), *let loose, let fly, let go:* hastile; immissa barba;

(*flowing*). — With reflexive, or in pass., *throw one's self, rush :* **aestus** (*flow*). — Esp. of driving, *let loose, let go, spur on :* habenas; iuga; — so also: funes; velis rudentes; palmes immissus(*unchecked*). — Fig., *inspire, inflict :* curas.

immixtus (in-), p.p. of immisceo.

immō [abl. of **īmus** (in-mus, superl. of **in**)], adv., (*in the lowest degree*), more or less contradicting what precedes, often to assert something stronger, *no, nay, nay rather, nay but.*

immōbilis (in-), -e, [in-mobilis], adj., *immovable, unmoved* (lit. and fig.) : Ausonia (*unshaken*).

immolō (in-), -āvī, -ātum, -are, [†immolō- (in-mola, decl. as adj.), from sprinkling the meal on the head of the victim], 1. v. a., *immolate, sacrifice, offer.* — Less exactly, *kill* (cf. **macto**), *slay.*

immortālis (in-), -e, [in-mortalis], adj., *immortal, undying, eternal :* fas (of immortality).

immōtus (in-), -a, -um, [in-motus, p.p. of moveo], adj., *unmoved, undisturbed, immovable, unshaken, secure, fixed :* unda (*tranquil*). — Also, fig. in same senses : mens ; fata lumina (*fixed*); immotum sederet animo (*immovably fixed*).

immūgiō (in-), -īvī (-iī), -ītum, -īre, [in-mugio], 4. v. n., *roar within, bellow within.* — Fig., *resound within :* regia luctu.

immulgeō (in-), no perf., no sup., **-mulgēre,** [in-mulgeo], 2. v. a., *milk into :* ubera labris.

immundus (in-), -a, -um, [in-mundus], adj., *unclean, foul, filthy :* cinis (*unsightly*).

immūnis (in-), -e, [in-munis, *without a share*, cf. **communis**], adj., *free from, secure from :* belli. — Also (contributing nothing), *idle, inert.*

immurmurō (in-), -āvī, -ātum, **-āre,** [in-murmuro], 1. v. n., *murmur in.*

impācātus (in-), -a, -um, [in-pacatus], adj., *unpacified, unconquered.*

impar (in-), -paris, [in-par], adj., *unequal, uneven, ill-matched, odd* (of number); puer congressus Achilli (*on unequal terms*) ; fata (as between two combatants).

impāstus (in-), -a, -um, [in-pastus], adj., *unfed, hungry.*

impatiēns (in-), -ēntis, [in-patiēns], adj., *impatient :* vulneris (*frenzied by*).

impavidus (in-), -a, -um, [in-pavidus], adj., *unterrified, undaunted, without fear.*

impediō (in-), -īvī (-iī), -ītum, -īre, [†imped- (cf. **expedio, compes**) as if †impedi-], 4. v. a., *entangle, entwine :* loricam hasta (*pin fast*). — Less exactly, *hinder, impede, hamper.* — Fig., *hinder, prevent, delay :* mora ignaros.

impellō (in-), -pulī, -pulsum, -pellere, [in-pello], 3. v. a., *strike upon, strike, lash :* luctus aures; marmor remis. — Also, of the result, *push over, overthrow, overturn.* — Esp., *urge on, urge, drive, force on :* puppim; impulsa sagitta; impulsus furiis Cassandrae; impulsus vomer (*driving the plough*); undas Zephyri. — Fig., *urge, impel, induce, force, compel;* also (see second division above), *shake :* animum. — Poetically : arma (*excite war*, as by the clash of weapons).

impendeō (in-), no perf., no sup., **-pendēre,** [in-pendeo], 2. v. n., *overhang.* — Fig., *threaten, impend :* ventus.

impendō (in-), -pendī, -pēnsum, -pendere, [in-pendo], 3. v. a., *expend on.* — Fig., *expend, devote, bestow, apply :* laborem; curam. —

impēnsus, -a, -um, p.p. as adj., *spent, expended.* — Neut. plur., *expenses, cost.*

impēnsē [abl. of **impensus**], adv.,

expensively. — Less exactly, *earnestly, seriously, vehemently.*
impēnsus, -a, -um, p.p. of **impendo.**
imperditus (in-), -a, -um, [in-perditus], adj., *undestroyed:* corpora Graiis (*not slaughtered*).
imperfectus (in-), -a, -um, [in-perfectus], adj., *unaccomplished, unfinished.*
imperitŏ (in-), āvī, -ātum, -āre, [as if †imperitŏ- (stem of supposed p.p. of **imperŏ**)], 1. v. n., *command, be lord of:* pecori (of a bull).
imperium (in-), [†imperŏ-, *arranging*, cf. **opiparus** (reduced) + ium (n. of -ius), cf. **imperŏ**], n., *requisition* (prob. orig. meaning), *command, control, authority, sway, rule.* — Concretely, *a command, an order, an empire, a power.*
impero (in-), -āvī, -ātum, -āre, [†imperŏ- (cf. **imperium**), but cf. **paro**], 1. v. a. and n., *demand* (of a requisition, prob. the original meaning). — *command* (esp. of military authority), *rule, order:* tolli corpus; arvis.
imperterritus (in-), -a, -um, [in-perterritus], adj., *unterrified, undaunted, undismayed.*
impetus (in-), -ūs, [in-†petus (√pet+us, cf. **petulcus, perpetuus**)], m., *an inpinging, a violent rush, an impetus, an impulse, force, violence* (of attack), *vehemence, momentum.*
impexus (in-), -a, -um, [in-pexus], adj., *uncombed, unkempt.*
impiger (in-), -gra, -grum, [in-piger], adj., *active, energetic:* hausit pateram (*nothing loth*).
impingō (in-), -pēgī, -pactum, -pingere, [in-pango], 3. v. a., *dash against:* agmina muris (*force to*).
impius (in-), -a, -um, [in-pius], adj., *impious, sacrilegious, godless.*
— Less exactly, *accursed* (of anything without divine qualities of mercy and justice): **Mars; Furor; Fama.** — Poetically: fata (of impiety); **Tartara** (*impious*, the abode of the impious). — Masc., *impious wretch.*
implācābilis (in-), -e, [in-placabilis], adj., *inexorable, unappeasable, implacable.*
implācātus (in-), -a, -um, [in-placatus], adj., *inexorable, insatiable.*
impleō (in-), -plēvī, -plētum, -plēre, [in-†pleo, cf. **compleo**], 2. v. a., *fill in, fill up, fill:* mulctralia vaccae; implentur fossae; sinus (*swell*); manum pinu (*seize with full hand*). — Less exactly, of sounds, &c., *fill with, inspire:* nemus querelis; animum veris; Rutulos animis; nuntius Turnum (*fill the ears of*); sinum sanguis (*overflow*). — Fig., *satisfy, satiate:* implentur Bacchi veteris (*drink their fill*); amorem genitoris.
implicō (in-), -plicāvī (-plicuī), -plicātum (-plicitum), -plicāre, [in-plico], 1. v. a., *entwine, interweave, enfold, entangle:* comam laeva (*grasp*); se dextrae (*clasp*); pedes (of an eagle seizing a serpent, *grasp with*); tempora ramo (*encircle*); ossibus ignem (*kindle*); equitem (of a falling horse, *pin down*); natam telo (*bind*); totas acies (*mingle in confusion*). — Fig., *entangle, involve:* vos fortuna bello.
implōrō (in-), -āvī, -ātum, -āre, [in-ploro], 1. v. a. and n., *call upon* (cf. **exploro**), *beseech, implore, beg for.*
implūmis (in-), -e, [in-†pluma (*weakened*, decl. as adj.)], adj., *impeded.*
impōnō (in-), -posuī, -positum, -pōnere, [in-pono], 3. v. a., *place upon, place, lay, pour* (of a libation), *serve up.* — Fig., *impose, lay upon, fix, put, enjoin:* finem pugnae; pacis morem (*ordain*); dominum patriae.

importūnus (in-), -a, -um, [in-portunus, cf. **Portunus**], adj., (doubtless a sea-term, cf. **opportunus**), *untimely, unsuitable, inconvenient.* — Also, *troublesome, dangerous.* — Of moral qualities, *cruel, unreasonable.* — Transferred to augury, *ill-boding, ill-omened.*

impositus, -a, -um, p.p. of **impono.**

imprecor (in-), -ātus, -ārī, [in-precor], 1. v. dep., *pray* (for something against some one): litora litoribus contraria.

imprimŏ, -pressī, -pressum, -ere, [in-premo], 3. v. a., *impress.*

imprīmīs, see **in.**

improbus (in-), -a, um, [in-probus], adj., *wicked, bad, villainous, malicious, mischievous, fierce, cruel, shameless, ravenous, unprincipled:* fortuna (*malicious goddess*); mons (*destructive*); rabies ventris (*ravening*); labor ("*rascal,*" as if the enemy of man). — Rarely in a good sense, *cunning, shrewd.*

improperātus (in-), -a, -um, [in-properatus], adj., *lingering.*

imprōvidus (in-), -a, -um, [in-providus], adj., *unforeseeing:* pectora turbat (*startled*).

imprōvīsus (in-), -a, -um, [in-provisus], adj., *unforeseen, unexpected, sudden.* — **imprōvīsō,** abl., *on a sudden, unexpectedly.*

imprūdēns (in-), -entis, [in-prudens], adj., *not anticipating, surprised, incautious, ignorant:* frons laborum (*unused to*); evaserat hostes (*without knowing it*).

impūbes (in-), -is (also **-eris**), [in-pubes, decl. as adj.], adj., *beardless, youthful.*

impulsus (in-), -a, -um, p.p. of **impello.**

impulsus (in-), -ūs, [in-pulsus, cf. **impello**], m., *a shock.*

impūnis (in-), -e, [in-†poenā (weakened, decl. as adj., cf. **examinis**)], adj., *unpunished.* —

impūne, neut. acc. as adv., *with impunity.* — Less exactly, *without danger, safely, without harm.*

īmus, -a, -um, superl. of **inferus.**

in [I. E. pron. √AN, cf. Gr. ἀνά, ἐν], prep. With abl., *in, within, on, upon, among.* — In all Eng. senses. — Special phrases: in manibus, *close at hand:* bis in hora, *twice an hour;* in primis (imprimis), *among the first, especially.* — Often, *in the matter of, in case of, in regard to:* in hoste; in Daphnide (*for*); in hoste Priamo. — With acc., *into, upon, among, to, towards, against, at, for:* nos in sceptra reponis (*restore to power,* &c.); in solidum finditur via; adspirant aurae in noctem (*blow on into,* &c.); in te committere (*upon*); quietum in Teucros animum (*towards*); compositi in turmas; cura in vitulos traducitur (*to*); se condit in undas (*in*); in agros (*over*). — Esp. of distribution, *among:* in naves; spargere in volgum; in versum distulit ulmos (*in*). — Also of purpose, tendency, &c., *for:* usum in castrorum; audere in praelia; in lumina; in medium (*for the common advantage,* but also, *into the middle*). — Often, on account of different English conception, *in, on:* considere in ignes; in numerum (*in time, to the measure*); in spem; in puppim ferit. — Special phrases: in plumam (*in the manner of,* so as to make); in obliquum (*transversely*); in dies (*from day to day*); in vicem, invicem (*in turn*); in octo pedes (*up to*); in noctem (*towards*). — Of apparel, &c., *in, with:* ignota in veste.

inaccessus, -a, -um, [in-accessus], adj., (*unapproached*), *inaccessible* (cf. **acceptus,** *acceptable*)

Īnachius, -a, -um, [†Inachŏ- (reduced) + ius], adj., *of Inachus, Inachian.* — Less exactly, *of Argos, Argive, Grecian.*

Inachus, -ī, [Gr. Ἴναχος], m., son of Oceanus and Tethys, the mythic founder of Argos, and father of Io.
inamābilis, -e, [in-amabilis], adj., *unlovely, hateful.*
inānis, -e, [?], adj., *empty, void, substanceless :* rotae (*unloaded*); regna (of the shades). — Fig., *empty, idle, useless, purposeless, meaningless :* verba (*counterfeit*).
inarātus, -a, -um, [in-aratus], adj., *unploughed, untilled.*
inardēsco, -arsī, no sup., **-ardēscere,** [in-ardesco], 3. v. n. incept., *take fire.* — Less exactly, *blaze, glow, redden.*
Īnarimē, -ēs, [Gr. εἰν Ἀρίμοις, the place where Typhoeus was supposed to lie], f., an island in the Tuscan Sea, also called Ænaria (now *Ischia*).
inausus, -a, -um, [in-ausus], adj., *undared, unattempted.*
incandēscō, -canduī, no sup., **-candēscere,** [in-candesco], 3. v. n. incept., *glow.*
incānēscō, -canuī, no sup., **-cānescere,** [in-canesco], 3. v. n. incept., *whiten, become gray.*
incanus, -a, -um, [in-canus], adj., *covered with gray, gray, hoary.*
incassum (also separate), see **cassus.**
incautus, -a, -um, [in-cautus], adj., *incautious, careless, off one's guard, in one's ignorance.*
incēdō, -cēssī, -cessum, -cēdere, [in-cedo], 3. v. n., *move on, proceed, move, advance.*
incendium, -ī (-iī), [in-†candium, or †incendŏ- (in-candŏ-, cf. candificus) + ium], n., *a burning, a fire, fire, a conflagration.*
incendō, -cendī, -cēnsum, -cendere, [in-cando, cf. accendo], 3. v. a., *set on fire, kindle, burn :* aras votis (*light*); squamam fulgor (*light up*). — **incēnsus, -a, -um,** p.p., *burning, on fire, fired.* — Fig., *fire, excite, set on fire :* caelum clamor (*fill*).

incēnsus, -a, -um, p.p. of **incendo.**
inceptus, -a, -um, p.p. of **incipio.**
incertus, -a, -um, [in-certus], adj., *uncertain, doubtful, wavering, unsteady, irregular, vague.*
incēssō, -īvī, 3. v. a., *assault, attack.*
incessus, -ūs, [in-†cessus], m., *a walk, a gait, an advance.*
incestō, -āvī, -ātum, -āre, [†incestŏ-], 1. v. a., *defile, pollute.*
inchoō, see **incoho,** the more approved spelling.
incidō, -cidī, -cāsum, -cidere, [in-cado], 3. v. n., *fall upon, happen upon, meet :* animo deus (*enter*).
incīdō, -cīdī, -cīsum, -cīdere, [in-caedo], 3. v. a., *cut into, cut off, cut, hack.* — Of the effect, *cut* (make by *cut*ting). — So also : amores arboribus (*cut on*). — Fig., *cut off, sever, decide, settle :* lites.
incinctus, -a, -um, p.p. of **incingo.**
incingō, -cinxī, -cinctum, -cingere, [in-cingo], 3. v. a., *gird* (upon one's self or another). — From the fashion of ancient garments, *clothe.*
incipiō, -cēpī, -ceptum, -cipere, [in-capio], 3. v. a. and n., *begin, undertake.* — **inceptus, -a, -um,** p.p. as adj., *begun, inceptive, incipient, partially accomplished, attempted.* — Neut., *an undertaking, an attempt, a purpose* (partially accomplished). — Also (as in English), *begin* (to speak, &c.).
incitō, -āvī, -ātum, -āre, [†incitŏ-], 1. v. a., *set in motion, agitate, urge on.* — Fig., *arouse, excite, spur on.*
incitus, -a, -um, [p.p. of †incieo, in-citus], adj., (*set in motion*), *rapid, swift, active.*
inclēmentia, -ae, [†inclement + ia], f., *cruelty, rigor, harshness.* — Also, of things, *cruel fate, harsh condition, bitterness :* mortis.
inclīnātus, -a, -um, p.p. of **inclino.**
inclīnō, -āvī, -ātum, -āre, [in-clino], 1. v. a. and n., *bend*

(*t*owards), *incline.* — Esp., *bend downwards.* — **inclīnātus, -a, -um**, p.p. as adj., *bent downwards, falling, failing:* domus.

inclūdō, -clūsī, -clūsum, -clūdere, [in-claudo], 3. v. a., *shut up, shut in, enclose, surround:* vitam sanguine (*choke*). — **inclūsus, -a, -um**, p.p. as adj., *shut up; in confinement, enclosed, confined:* in flumine cervus (*caught*).

inclūsus, -a, -um, p.p. of **includo**.

inclutus (incly-), -a, -um, [†clutus, p.p. of clueo, wi*t*h in], adj., *famous, renowned, famed.*

inclytus, -a, -um; see **inclutus**.

incoctus, -a, -um, p.p. of **incoquo**.

incoguitus, -a, -um, [in-cognitus], adj., *unknown, uncertain.*

incohō (inchoo), -āvī, -ātum, -āre, [?], 1. v. a., *begin, undertake.*

incolō, -coluī, no sup., **-colere**, [in-colo], 3. v. a., *dwell in, inhabit.*

incolumis, -e, [?], adj., *safe, unharmed, uninjured.*

incomitātus, -a, -um, [in-comitatus], adj., *unattended, unaccompanied.*

incommodus, -a, -um, [in-commodus], adj., *inconvenient, unpleasant.* — Neu*t*., *an inconvenience, a trouble, a misfortune.*

incompositus, -a, -um, [in-compositus], adj., *not arranged, irregular, rude.*

incomptus, -a, -um, [in-comptus], adj., *unadorned, rude, unpolished.*

inconcessus, -a, -um, [in-concessus], adj., *unallowed, forbidden, unlawful.*

inconditus, -a, -um, [in-conditus], adj., *not arranged, rude, unpolished.*

inconsultus, -a, -um, [in-consultus], adj., *unadvised, without advice.*

incoquo, -coxī, -coctum, -coquere, [in-coquo], 3. v. a., *boil in, cook in.* — From the process, *dye, color:* vellera Tyrios incocta rubores (Gr. acc., *dyed with*, &c.).

increbrescō (-bēsco), -bruī, no sup., **-brēscere**, [in-crebresco], 3. v. n., *thicken, increase, grow louder* (cf. creber): nomen (*be spread abroad*).

incrēdibilis, -e, [in-credibilis], adj., *incredible.*

incrēmentum, -ī, [as if †incrē- (cf. incresco) + mentum], n., *increase.* — Less exac*t*ly, *progeny, offspring.*

increpitō, -āvī, -ātum, -āre, [in-crepito], 1. v. a., (*rattle*), *chide* (cf. increpo), *rebuke, taunt, find fault with.*

increpō, -āvī(-uī), -ātum(-ītum), -āre, [in-crepo], 1. v. a. and n., *rattle, clatter, sound:* malis (*gnash*); sonitum (*blare*). — Of a continued cry, *chide, rebuke, taunt, upbraid.*

increscō, -crēvī, -crētum, -crescere, [in-cresco], 3. v. n., *grow in, grow up.* — Fig., *arise, swell.*

incubō, -āvī(-uī), -ātum(-ītum), -āre, [in-cubo], 1. v. n., *lie down upon, lie upon.* — Fig., *fall upon* (of a s*t*orm), *brood upon, strike* (of winds, &c.), *burst, bend one's energies, strive, exert* one's *self*. — Esp., *lie upon* (*t*o watch), *guard* (in secre*t*), *hoard.*

incultus, -a, -um, [in-cultus], adj., *uncultivated, untilled, wild.* — Fig. (cf. colo), *unkempt, uncared for.* — Neu*t*. plur., *wild regions, deserts.*

incumbō, -cubuī, -cubitum, -cumbere, [in-†cumbo], 3. v. n., *lie upon, lean upon, lean over:* laurūs arae (*overhang*). — Fig., *brood upon, settle on, bend to* (of oars, &c.), *strive, threaten, aim at.* — In proverbial expressions: fato urgenti, *lend one's weight to, urge on, hasten.*

incurrō, -currī (-cucurrī), -cursum, -currere, [in-curro], 3. v. n., *rush on, rush in, rush.*

incursus, -ūs, [in-cursus, cf. in-

curro], m., *a rush, an attack, an inroad.*
incurvo, -āvī, -ātum, -āre, [incurvo], 1. v. a., *bend.*
incurvus, -a, -um, [in-curvus], adj., *bent, crooked.*
incūs, -ūdis, [in-√cud (as stem)], f., *an anvil.*
incūsŏ, -āvī, -ātum, -āre, [in-†causo, cf. causor], 1. v. n., *accuse, blame, find fault with.*
incusus, -a, -um, p.p. of incūdŏ (unused), *hammered out, wrought.*
incutiŏ, -cussī, -cussum,-cutere, [in-quatio], 3. v. a., *strike into.* — Fig., *dash, lend, inspire.*
indāgŏ, -inis, [†indagŏ- (induagus, cf. prodigus) + o], f., *toils, nets.*
inde [im (case of is, cf. hinc) -de (cf. dehinc)], adv., *from there, from this, from that place, thence.* — Less exactly, *then, next, afterwards.* — Phrases: iam inde a teneris, *even from infancy;* iam inde ut, *immediately when.*
indēbitus, -a, -um, [in-debitus], adj., *not due, unpromised.*
indecor (indecoris), -oris, [indecus, decl. as adj.], adj., *without honor, inglorious, unhonored:* indecores non erimus regno (*no disgrace*).
indēfessus, -a, -um, [in-defessus], adj., *unwearied, untiring, unfailing.*
indēprehēnsus (-prēnsus), -a, -um, [in-deprehensus], adj., *unobserved, undiscovered, unperceived.*
India, -ae, [f. of adj. fr. Indus], f., *the country beyond the Indus,* embracing loosely much more than the modern region of that name.
indicium, -ī (-iī), [†indic- (index) + ium], n., *an information, a disclosure, a charge, testimony.* — Less exactly, *a sign, indication, a mark* (to give information).
indīcŏ, -dīxī, -dictum, -dīcere, [in-dico], 3. v. a., *declare, make known, publish, proclaim.* — Esp.

of authoritative utterance, *order, appoint, enjoin:* primis iuvenum iter (*command to make*); choros tibia Bacchi (*summon*).
indictus, -a, -um, [in-dictus], adj., *unsaid, unsung* (cf. dico): nec te abibis nostris carminibus (*unhonored*).
indigena, -ae, [indu-†gena (cf. Graiugena)], m. or f. (used as adj.), *native born, native, of the country* (opp. to *foreign*).
indigeō, -iguī, no sup., -igēre, [indigŏ-], 2. v. n., *need, want, require.*
indiges, -etis, [indu-†ges (√ga, shorter form of √gen + tis, reduced)], m., *native.* — Esp., a native god or hero raised to the rank of a local divinity, *home-born.*
indignātus, -a, -um, p.p. of indignor.
indignor, -ātus, -ārī, [indignŏ-], 1. v. dep., *deem unworthy, be indignant at, disdain, scorn, chafe at, be indignant, be angry.*
indignus, -a, -um, [in-dignus], adj., *unworthy, undeserving, shameful, unbecoming, undeserved, unjust:* digna atque indigna relatu (*just and unjust taunts*); digna indigna pati (*both just and undeserved woes*).
indigus, -a, -um, [indu-†tegus? (cf. egeo), but cf. also prodigus], adj., *in need, needing:* nostrae opis (*requiring*).
indiscrētus, -a, -um, [in-discretus], adj., *undistinguishable* (cf. acceptus, *acceptable*).
indocilis, -e, [in-docilis], adj., *unteachable, untamed, untamable.*
indoctus, -a, -um, [in-doctus], adj., *untaught, unlearned, ignorant, unskilled.*
indolēs, -is, [indu-†toles (lost stem fr. √ol, cf. olesco)], f., *character* (inborn), *native worth, nature, spirit* (as natural disposition).
indomitus, -a, -um, [in-domitus], adj., *untamed, untrained, unbroken, wild, savage, rude.* — Less ex-

Vocabulary. 143

actly, *untamable, indomitable.* — Fig., *fierce, untamed, invincible.*
indormiō, -īvī, -ītum, -īre, [in-dormio], 4. v. n., *sleep on.*
indu [in-do (case-form of pron. √da)], old form of in in comp.
indubitō, -āvī, -ātum, -āre, [in-dubito], 1. v. n., *doubt, distrust :* viribus.
indūcō, -dūxī, -dūctum, -dūcere, [in-duco], 3. v. a., *lead on, lead, bring in :* fluvium (*let in*); onus Aurora. — Less exac*t*ly, *draw on, draw over :* caestus manibus. — So by change of poin*t* of view: inducitur artus tunica, *clothes his frame with* &c.; fontes umbra, *cover with.* — Fig., *induce :* inductus pretio (*bribe*).
indūctus, -a, -um, p.p. of induco.
indulgentia, -ae, [†indulgent + ia], f., *favor, indulgence.*
indulgeō, -ulsī, -ultum, -ulgēre, [?, prob. fr. noun-s*t*em, perh. akin to volgus, cf. firs*t* example], 2.v.n., *give room to :* ordinibus. — Also, wi*t*h unc. connec*t*ion of ideas, *favor, be complaisant, indulge, be indulgent.* — Esp., *indulge in, give way to :* vino; choreis.
induō, -uī, -ūtum, -uere, [?, cf. exuo], 3. v. a., *put on, assume, take on.* — Wi*t*h change of point of view, *clothe* (*one's self* or *another*), *deck with, adorn :* quos ex facie hominum in voltus ferarum (*change from* &c., *clothing in* &c.); se nux in florem (*clothe itself in bloom*). — Esp. in pass., *put on, clothe one's self with :* loricam; indutus exuvias (*clad in*); vestes indutae (*on the body*).
indūrēscō, -dūruī, no sup., dūrēscere, [in-duresco], 3. v. n. incep*t*., *grow hard, harden, congeal.*
Indus, -a, -um, [Gr. Ἰνδός], adj., *of India, Indian.* — Plur., *the Indians, people of India.*
industria, -ae, [†industri- (?, indu +unc. s*t*em) + ia, cf. industrius], *diligence, industry.*
indūtus, -a, -um, p.p. of induo.

inēluctābilis, -e, [in-eluctabilis], adj., *inevitable.*
inemptus (-emtus), -a, -um, [in-emptus], adj., *unbought, of no cost :* dapes.
inermis, -e (-us, -a, -um), [in-†armō- (weakened and decl. as adj.)], adj., *unarmed, defenceless.*
ineō, -īvī (-iī), -itum, -īre, [in-eo], irr. v. a. and n., *go in, come in, enter, enter upon, go into.* — Less exac*t*ly and fig., *enter upon, fall into, take up, take part in :* proscenia ludi (*come upon*).
iners, -ertis, [in-ars, decl. as adj.], adj., (*without skill*), *helpless, inactive, idle, sluggish, cowardly, spiritless :* oculi (*heavy*); voces (*useless*); corpora (*lifeless, dead*); umor (*stagnant*).
inexcitus, -a, -um, [in-excitus], adj., *unmoved, undisturbed.*
inexhaustus, -a, -um, [in-exhaustus], adj., *unexhausted, inexhaustible.*
inexōrābilis, -e, [in-exorabilis], adj., *inexorable :* fatum.
inexpertus, -a, -um, [in-expertus], adj., *untried, unattempted.*
inexplētus, -a, -um, [in-expletus], adj., *unsatisfied, insatiable.* — Neu*t*. as adv., *insatiably :* lacrimans (*not to be sated with weeping*).
inexsaturābilis, -e, [in-exsaturabilis], adj., *insatiate.*
inextrīcābilis, -e, [in-extricabilis], adj., *inextricable.*
īnfabricātus, -a, -um, [in-fabricatus], adj., *unwrought, unformed.*
īnfandus, -a, -um, [in-fandus], adj., *unspeakable.* — Less exac*t*ly, *horrible, dreadful, accursed.* — Neu*t*., in apposi*t*ion with the sentence, O horror ! — As adv., *horribly.*
īnfāns, -āntis, [in-fans, p. of for], adj., *speechless.* — As subs*t*., *an infant, a child.*
īnfaustus, -a, -um, [in-faustus], adj., *ill-omened, ill-fated :* omen (*evil, ill-boding*).

infectus, -a, -um, p.p. of **inficio.**
infectus, -a, -um, [in-factus], adj., *not made, not done, undone, incomplete, unfinished :* **aurum** (*unwrought*); **foedus** (*invalid*).
infēcundus (foe-), -a, -um, [infecundus], adj., *sterile, unfruitful.*
infēlīx, -īcis, [in-felix], adj., *unfruitful* (cf. **felix**), *sterile.*—Also, *unlucky, unfortunate, ill-omened, wretched, ill-fated :* **equus infelix studiorum** (*disappointed in his favorite pursuit*).
infēnsus, -a, -um, [p.p. of †**infendo,** cf. **defendo**], adj., (*dashed against ?*), *hostile, deadly, dangerous, inimical.* — Esp. of weapons, *levelled, at charge :* **tela; spicula vertunt** (*level*).
inferiae, -ārum, [†**inferŏ-** (reduced) + **ia** (prob. a noun omitted, **victimae?**)], f. plur., *a sacrifice* (to the gods below in honor of the dead), *funeral rites.*
infernus, -a, -um, [†**inferŏ-** (reduced) + **nus**], adj., *of the lower world, of the gods below, of Hades.*
inferŏ, intulī, inlātum, īnferre, [in-fero], irr. v. a., *bring in, bring to, bear on, bring, introduce :* **bellum** (*make,* of offensive war); **deos** (*introduce*); **acies** (*lead*); **gressus** (*turn*); **ignes** (*hurl*); **rates** (*urge on*). — Esp. of offerings, *offer, sacrifice :* **honores.** — With reflexive or in pass., *rush, advance, proceed.*
inferus, -a, -um, [unc. stem+**rus**], adj., (**inferior, infimus, imus**), *low, below, beneath.* — Comp., *inferior, less :* **inferiora secutus** (*a lower destiny*) : **numero** (*weaker in numbers*). — Superl., *lowest, deepest, nethermost, the bottom of, the depths of, innermost :* **ad pedes** (*even to the very feet*); **manes** (*the lowest depths*).—Phrases: **ab imo, ex imo,** *from the bottom, utterly, from the foundations.*
infestus, -a, -um, [p.p. of †**infendo,** cf. **infensus**], adj., *hostile,*

destructive, fatal : **hasta** (*levelled*); **volnus** (*deadly thrust*).
inficiŏ, -fēcī, -fectum, -ficere, [in-facio], irr. v. a., (*work in ?*), *dye, stain.* — Also, *mix, poison, taint, infect, impregnate.* — **Infectus, -a, -um,** p.p. as adj., *stained, impregnated.* — Also, poetically : **venenis Allecto,** *overflowing ;* **scelus,** *ingrown,* of the earthly *taint* of crime.
infīdus, -a, -um, [in-fidus], adj., *faithless, treacherous.*
infīgŏ, -fīxī, -fīxum, -fīgere, [in-figo], 3. v. a., *fix in, fasten in :* **cornua** (*interlock*).
infindŏ, -fidī, -fissum, -findere, [in-findo], 3. v. a., *cleave.*—Of the effect, *cleave* (make by cleaving).
infit [in-fit, of fio], defective v. n., *begin.* — Esp. (cf. **incipio**), *begin to speak,* &c.
infīxus, -a, -um, p.p. of **infigo.**
inflammātus, -a, -um, p.p. of **inflammo.**
inflammŏ, -āvī, -ātum, -āre, [inflammo], 1. v. a., *set on fire.* — Fig., *fire, excite, inflame.*
inflātus, -a, -um, p.p. of **inflo.**
inflŏ, -āvī, -ātum, -āre, [in-flo], 1. v. a., *blow into, fill* (with wind), *swell* (of sails) : **calamos** (*play*); **classica** (*sound*); **ebur** (*blow*). — Less exactly, *puff up, swell.*
inflectŏ, -flexī, -flexum, -flectere, [in-flecto], 3. v. a., *bend.* — Fig., *move, affect, touch.* — **Inflexus, -a, -um,** p.p. as adj., *curved, crooked, bent.*
inflētus, -a, -um, [in-fletus], adj., *unwept, unmourned.*
inflexus, -a, -um, p.p. of **inflecto.**
inflīctus, -a, -um, p.p. of **infligo.**
inflīgŏ, -flīxī, -flīctum, -flīgere, [in-fligo], 3. v. a., *dash upon, dash against.*
influŏ, -fluxī, -fluxum, -fluere, [in-fluo], 3. v. n., *flow in, flow into, empty* (of rivers).
infodiŏ, -fōdī, -fossum, -fodere, [in-fodio], 3. v. a., *dig in, plant.* — Esp., *bury.*

Vocabulary.

infoecundus, see **infecundus.**

informātus, -a, -um, p.p. of **informo.**

informis, -e, [in-forma (weakened and decl. as adj.)], adj., *shapeless.* — Also (cf. **forma**), *unsightly, misshapen, hideous, horrid:* letum (*shameful,* by hanging).

informŏ, -āvī, -ātum, -āre, [informo], 1. v. a., *shape, form, fashion.*

infrā [prob. abl. of †inferŏ-, cf. **supra**], adv., *below, beneath:* mare quod alluit infra (of the Tuscan Sea).

infractus, -a, -um, p.p. of **infringo.**

infraeno, see **infreno.**

infraenus, see **infrenis.**

infremŏ, -fremuī, no sup., **-fremere,** [in-fremo], 3. v. n., *growl, roar.*

infrendeŏ, no perf., no sup., **-frendēre,** [in-frendeo], 2. v. n., *gnash* (the *t*eeth).

infrēnis, -e, (-us, -a, -um), [in-†frenŏ- (decl. as adj.)], *unbridled:* Numidae (*with unbridled horses*), perhaps in a double sense.

infrēnŏ, -āre, 1. v. a., *harness.*

infringŏ, -frēgī, -fractum, -fringere, [in-frango], 3. v. a., *break off, break, crush, shiver.* — Fig., *crush, shatter, break down, vanquish.* — **infractus, -a, -um,** p.p. as adj., *shattered, broken, crushed, overborne.*

infula, -ae, [perh. akin to Gr. φάλος], f., *a fillet* (a head-band of wool used in sacred ri*t*es).

infundŏ, -fūdī, -fūsum, -fundere, [in-fundo], 3. v. a., *pour on, pour out, pour down:* latices (*administer*); sol infusus (*shedding its light*); populus (*crowded*); nix infusa (*fallen*); mens infusa per artus (*permeating, diffused*); infusus gremio (*lying languidly,* of Vulcan).

infuscŏ, -āvī, -ātum, -āre, [infusco], 1. v. a., *darken, stain.*

infūsus, -a, -um, p.p. of **infundo.**

ingemīnātus, -a, -um, p.p. of **ingemino.**

ingemīno, -āvī, -ātum, -āre, [in-gemino], 1. v. a. and n., *redouble, repeat, renew:* vulnera lateri (*strike thick and fast*); vox, ingeminata (*echoed*); ingeminans Creusam vocavi (*with repeated cries*). — Wi*t*hou*t* obj., *redouble, increase, be repeated:* ignes (*flash repeatedly*); Troes hastis (*redouble their showers of spears*); Austri (*freshen*); clamor (*is redoubled*).

ingemo, -gemuī, no sup., **-gemere,** [in-gemo], 3. v. n. and a. (cf. **doleo**), *groan, sigh, mourn, lament, moan.* — Also, of animals, *roar, low, bellow.*

ingenium, -ī (-iī), [in-†genium (√gen + ium, cf. **genius**), cf. **ingeno**], n., *nature, intelligence.* — Less exac*t*ly, of *t*hings, *nature, character:* arvorum.

ingēns, -entis, [in-gens, decl. as adj., *out of its kind*], adj., *enormous, huge, vast, immense, great:* argentum (*a vast amount of*); rura; fumus. — Less exac*t*ly, of in*t*angible objec*t*s, *great, deep, severe, intense, mighty, marvellous, loud:* pectus (*mighty heart*); umbra (*dense*); gemitus; ruina (*mighty*); pluvia (*heavy*); nox (*thick*); exitus (*great, important*); manus (*stout*); volnus. — Also, as in English, of men, *great, mighty, famous, illustrious:* genus a proavis; animis corpore armis Herminius.

ingerŏ, -gessī, -gestum, -gerere, [in-gero], 3. v. a., *heap up, hurl.*

inglōrius, -a, -um, [in-†gloria (decl. as adj.)], adj., *without honor, inglorious, unhonored.*

ingluviēs, -ēī, [in-†gluviēs (√glu + ies, cf. **glutio, gula**)], f., *the gullet, the crop, the maw.*

ingrātus, -a, -um, [in-gratus], adj., *unpleasing, disagreeable, ungrateful.* — Also, *ungrateful, unheeding, thankless:* pericula (*yielding no return*).

ingravŏ, -āvī, -ātum, -āre, [ingravo], 1. v. a., *weigh down.* — Fig., *aggravate.*
ingredior, -gressus, -gredī, [ingradior], 3. v. dep., *walk, proceed, go, enter, land* (from a vessel): altius (*step higher,* of a horse). — Fig., *enter upon, begin, undertake, enter on a way, proceed, go on.*
ingressus, -a, -um, p.p. of **ingredior.**
ingressus, -ūs, [in-gressus, cf. **ingredior**], m., *an entrance, a beginning, a rise.*
ingruŏ, -uī, no sup., -uere, [?], 3. v. n., *rush upon, assail, make an inroad upon.* — Less exactly and fig., *come on, fall upon, assail one, burst forth:* umbra vitibus (*break over*); horror armorum (*roll on*); imber.
inguen, -inis, [?], n., *the groin.* — Plur. in same sense.
inhaereō, -haesī, -haesum, -haerēre, [in-haereo], 2. v. n., *cling to.*
inhĭbeō, -uī, -itum, -ēre, [in-habeo], 2. v. a., *hold in, check, restrain, stay.*
inhiŏ, -āvī, -ātum, -āre, [in-hio], 1. v. n., *gape at, stand open-mouthed* (with sudden emotion). — Also, from the expression of the face, *gaze open-mouthed, pry into, gaze at.*
inhonestus, -a, -um, [in-honestus], adj., *inglorious, dishonorable.*
inhorreō, -uī, no sup., -ēre, [in-horreo], 2. v. n., *bristle, grow rough, roughen:* messis campis (*wave trembling*). — So also, irr. as causative: aper armos, *bristle up.*
inhospitus, -a, -um, [in-hospitus, see **hospitus**], adj., *inhospitable, dangerous.*
inhumātus, -a, -um, [in-humatus], adj., *unburied.*
iniciŏ (inii-), -iēcī, -iectum, -icere, [in-iacio], 3. v. a., *throw upon, cast upon, hurl.* — With reflexive, *throw one's self, rush.*

inimīcus, -a, -um, [in-amicus], adj., *unfriendly, hostile, of an enemy, of the foe, as an enemy.*
iniquus (-os), -a, -um, [in-aequus], adj., *unequal, uneven:* silvae (*rough*). — Also (cf. **aequus**), *unfair, unjust, hostile, unfavorable, unfortunate:* sol (*oppressive*); sors (*unhappy*); fata (*unlucky*); spatia (*insufficient*).
iniectus, -a, -um, p.p. of **inicio.**
iniiciŏ, see **inicio.**
iniūria, -ae, [in-†ius + ia, cf. **iniurius**], f., *injustice, wrong, outrage:* longa (*tale of wrong*); sceleris nostri (*guilt*).
iniussus, -a, -um, [in-iussus], adj., *unbidden, unforced.*
iniustus, -a, -um, [in-iustus], adj., *unjust, unfair, unreasonable.*
inlābor (ill-), -lāpsus, -lābī, [in-labor], 3. v. dep., *glide in, move in.* — Fig., of a divinity, *enter, fill, inspire:* nostris animis.
inlacrimŏ (ill-), -āvī, -ātum, -āre, [in-lacrimo], 1. v. n., *weep.* — Poetically, of statues, *weep, distil tears.*
inlaetābilis (ill-), -e, [in-laetabilis], adj., *joyless, mournful.*
inlaudātus (ill-), -a, -um, [in-laudatus], adj., *detested* (cf. **immitis**), *execrated.*
inlecebrae (illec-), -arum, [†inlece- (cf. **inlicio**) + bra], f., *enticements, allurements, charms.*
inlīdŏ (ill-), -līsī, -līsum, -līdere, [in-laedo], 3. v. a., *dash in* (to something), *dash upon.* — Also, *dash in* (to itself, *crush*).
inligātus (ill-), -a, -um, p.p. of **inligo.**
inligŏ (ill-), -āvī, -ātum, -āre, [in-ligo], 1. v. a., *bind on, tie up.* — Less exactly, *entangle, hamper, fetter.*
inlīsus, -a, -um, p.p. of **inlido.**
inlōtus (ill-), -a, -um, [in-lotus], adj., *unwashed, not cleansed.*
inlūcēscō (ill-), -lūxī, no sup., -lūcēscere, [in-lucesco], 3. v. n incept., *dawn, break* (of day).

inlūdō (ill-), -lūsī, -lūsum, -lūdere, [in-ludo], 3. v. n. and a., *mock at, make sport of.* — Also, *destroy* (as if in spor*t*), *waste, injure.*—Also, *play upon, sport with:* vestes illusae (*wrought with sportive designs*).
inlustris (ill-), -e, [in-†lustrō- (weakened and decl. as adj.)], adj., *famous, noble, illustrious.*
inlūsus, -a, -um, p.p. of inludo.
inluviēs (ill-), -ēī, [in-†luvies (√lu, in luo + ies)], f., *dirt, filth.*
innāscor, -nātus, -nāscī, [in-nascor], 3. v. dep., *grow in, be born in.*— innātus, -a, -um, p.p., *inborn, innate.*
innatō, -āvī, -ātum, -āre, [in-nato], 1. v. n. and a., *swim on, float on.*
innātus, -a, -um, p.p. of innascor.
innectō, -nexuī, -nexum, -nectere, [in-necto], 3. v. a., *entwine, bind, enwrap.* — Fig., *weave, entwine, devise, invent, plan:* fraus innexa clienti ; morandi causas.
innexus, -a, -um, p.p. of innecto.
innītor, -nisus (-nixus), -nītī, [in-nitor], 3. v. dep., *lean upon, rest on, be supported by.*
innixus, -a, -um, p.p. of innitor.
innō, -nāvī, -nātum, -nāre, [in-no], 1. v. n. and a., *swim in* or *into, float, swim, sail.*
innocuus, -a, um, [in-nocuus], adj., *harmless, innocent, unoffending:* litus (*that will do no harm*). — Also, actively, *unharmed.*
innoxius, -a, -um, [in-noxius], adj., *harmless, innocent.*
innumerus, -a, -um, [in-numerus, decl. as adj.], adj., *without number, numberless, unnumbered.*
†innūptus, -a, †-um; [in-nuptus], adj., *unmarried* (of a woman), *maiden.* — As subs*t.*, *a maid.*
inoffēnsus, -a, -um, [in-offensus], adj., *unbroken, unimpeded, unhindered.*
inolēscō, -lēvī, -litum, -lēscere, [in-olesco, cf. adulesco], 3. v. n., *grow in* (*into*), *become implanted.*

inopīnus, -a, -um, [in-†opinus, cf. opinor], adj., *unexpected.*
inops, -opis, [in-ops, decl. as adj.], adj., *without resources, helpless, poor, destitute:* senecta ; inops animi (*bereft of sense, frenzied*); res (*scanty fortune*).
Inōus, -a, -um, [Gr. Ἰνῶος], adj., *of Ino* (the daugh*t*er of Cadmus and wife of A*t*hamas of Thebes. Flying from her husband, she *t*hrew herself in*t*o the sea and became a divini*t*y), *son of Ino.*
inquam (-iō), [?], v. def., *say.*
inremeābilis (irr-), -e, [in-remeabilis], adj., *irretraceable.*
inreparābilis (irr-), -e, [in-re parabilis], adj., *irrecoverable, irreparable.*
in rīdeō (irr-), -rīsī, -rīsum, -rīdēre, [in-rideo], 2. v. a., *laugh at, scorn, ridicule.* — inrīsus, -a, -um, p.p., *mocked, scorned, insulted, with ridicule.*
i nrigō (irr-), -āvī, -ātum, -āre, [in-rigo], 1. v. a., *drop upon, pour down upon, shed.* — With change of poin*t* of view, *bedew with, moisten, bathe, water.* — Also fig. in bo*t*h senses.
inriguus (irr-), -a, -um, [†in-riguus], adj., *moistening, watering.*
in rītātus, -a, -um, p.p. of inrito.
in rītō (irr-), -āvī, -ātum, -are, [†in-ritō- (cf. inrio, *snarl*, of dogs)], 1. v. a., *excite, anger, incense.*
inritus (irr-), -a, -um, [in-ratus], adj., *invalid, annulled.* — Less exac*t*ly, *useless, ineffective, idle, in vain, empty:* sceleris vestigia (*harmless*).
iu rōrō (irr-), -āvī, -ātum, -āre, [in-roro], 1. v. a., *bedew, sprinkle, shed moisture.*—Less exac*t*ly, *flood* (of ligh*t*) : terras sole.
in rumpō (irr-), -rūpī, -ruptum, -rumpere, [in-rumpo], 3. v. a. and n., *break in, burst in, break through, force.*
i nruō (irr-), -ruī, no sup., -ru-

ere, [in-ruo], 3. v. n. and a., *rush in, rush on, fall down.*

insalūtātus, -a, -um, (separa*te*, inque salutātus), [in-salutatus], adj., *not saluted:* hanc insalutatam relinquo (*without saying farewell*).

insānia, -ae, [†insano- (reduced) +ia], f., *madness, insanity, frenzy, rage:* scelerata belli.

insāniō, -īvī (-iī), -ītum, [†insanō- (as if insani-)], 4. v. n., *be insane, rave, play the fool.*

insanus, -a, -um, [in-sanus], adj., *unsound* (of mind), *mad, wild, insane, frantic, crazy.* — Less exactly, *inspired.* — Fig., *wild, violent, mad, crazy, insane:* cupido; fluctus; amor; forum (*turbulent*).

inscius, -a, -um, [in-†scius, cf. nescius], adj., *unconscious, ignorant, untaught, unaware, bewildered* (not unders*t*anding): haud inscius (*with full knowledge*).

inscrībō, -scrīpsī, -scrīptum, -scrībere, [in-scribo], 3. v. a., *write upon, inscribe, mark* (of the tracing of a spear): pulvis hasta.

inscriptus, -a, -um, p.p. of inscribo.

insector, -ātus, -ārī, [in-sector, cf. insequor], 1. v. dep., *pursue.* — Fig., *harass, worry, persecute, pursue:* rastris terram (*ply*).

insequor, -secūtus, -sequī, [insequor], 3. v. a. and n., *follow up, pursue:* illum Pyrrhus; cominus arva (in a s*t*rong poe*t*ical figure). — Fig., *pursue, follow up, harass, be close upon:* quid te casus. — Neu*t., follow, come next, ensue.* — With inf., *continue, proceed.*

inserō, -ruī, -rtum, -rere, [insero], 3. v. a., *put in, insert.*

insero, -sevi, -situm, -serere, [in-sero], 3. v. a., *implant, plant, set out, engraft, graft* (both of the s*t*ock and the graf*t*): insere piros; arbutus ex fetu nucis.

insertō, -āvī, -ātum, -āre, [inserto, cf. insero], 1. v. a., *put in, thrust in, insert.*

insertus, -a, -um, p.p. of insero.

insideō, -sēdī, -sessum, -sīdēre, [in-sedeo], 2. v. n. and a., *sit upon, sit down on.* — Esp., *settle on, settle, occupy.* — Also, *lie in wait* (cf. insidiae), *plot.* (In perf. *t*enses undis*t*inguishable from insido.)

insidiae, -ārum, [†insid- (or insidŏ- reduced) +ia (cf. deses, desidia)], f. plur., *an ambush, an ambuscade, a lying in wait.* — Less exac*t*ly, *treachery, a stratagem, wiles, a trick, secret mischief.* — Personified, *Craft, Treachery.* — Poetically, *secret flight* (of Nisus and Euryalus *t*hrough the enemy's camp).

insidiātus, -a, -um, p.p. of insidior.

insidior, -atus, -ārī, [†insidiā-], 1. v. dep., *lie in wait:* ovili lupus (*prowl around*).

insīdō, -sēdī, -sessum, -sīdere, [in-sido], 3. v. a. and n., *settle on, sit on, alight upon.*

insigniō, -īvī (-iī), -ītum, -īre, [†insigni-], 4. v. a., *mark, adorn, deck.*

insignis, -e, [†in-signŏ- (weakened, decl. as adj.)], adj., *marked, conspicuous, adorned, splendid, decked, brilliant.* — Fig., *conspicuous, famous, renowned, glorious, noble, remarkable, distinguished, extraordinary.* — Neut. sing. and plur. as subs*t*., insigne (insignia), *a device, an ornament, a decoration, an ensign, trappings, insignia.*

insincērus, -a, -um, [in-sincerus], adj., *impure, co*r*rupt, tainted, putrid.*

insinuō, -āvī, -ātum, -āre, [insinuo], 1. v. a. and n., *work in* (by winding or bending). — Wi*t*h reflexive (or wi*t*hout), *work one's way in, steal in.* — Fig.: pavor per pectora (*steal over*).

insistō, -stitī, no sup., -sistere, [in-sisto], 3. v. a. and n., *stand upon, set foot upon, tread, enter*

Vocabulary. 149

upon, begin.—Actively, *plant, set:* vestigia.
īnsĭtus, -a, -um, p.p. of **īnsero.**
īnsŏlĭtus, -a, -um, [in-solitus], adj., *unwonted, unaccustomed to.*— Also, *unusual, strange, unwonted:* phocae fugiunt (*against their wont*).
īnsomnis, -e, [in-†somnŏ- (weakened and decl. as adj.)], adj., *sleepless, unsleeping.*
īnsomnĭum, -ī (-iī), [†insomni-? (reduced) + ium], n., *a dream, a vision.*
īnsŏnō, -sŏnŭī, no sup., **-sŏnāre,** [in-sono], 1. v. n., *sound, resound, roar:* flagello (*crack*); illa demissa per auras (*come with a clang*); verbera (cog. acc., *rattle blows, crack the lash*).
īnsons, -sontis, [in-sons], adj., *innocent, unoffending, guiltless.*
īnspērātus, -a, -um, [in-speratus], adj., *unhoped for, unlooked for.*
īnspĭcĭō, -spexī, -spectum, -spĭcere, [in-spicio], 3. v. a., *look in upon, overlook, spy out.*
īnspīcō, -āvī, -ātum, -āre, [in-†spico], 1. v. a., *sharpen, point.*
īnspīrō, -āvī, -ātum, -āre, [in-spiro], 1. v. a., *breathe in, breathe upon.*— Fig., *inspire, infuse:* ignem (*enkindle*).
īnspŏlĭātus, -a, -um, [in-spoliatus], adj., *undespoiled, unspoiled.*
īnstăbĭlis, -e, [in-stabilis], adj., *unsteady, unstable.*— Fig., *fickle, wavering, vacillating.*
īnstar [akin *to* in-sto], n. indecl., *an image, a likeness, a resemblance.*— In appos., as adj., *like, equal:* montis equus (*huge as*); agminis Clausus (*the equal*).
īnstaurātus, -a, -um, p.p. of **īnstauro.**
īnstaurō, -āvī, -ātum, -āre, [in-†stauro (†staurŏ-, cf. Gr. σταυρός), cf. **restauro**], 1. v. a., (*set up*), *renew, repeat, begin anew, rally:* acies; diem donis (*repeat another day*); talia Grais (*repeat, requite*); instaurati animi (*courage restored*).
īnsternō, -strāvī, -strātum, -sternere, [in-sterno], 3. v. a., *spread over:* pontes (*throw out*).— With change of point of view, *cover, spread:* instratum cubile (*strewn with*); instrati ostro alipedes (*housed*).
īnstīgō, -āvī, -ātum, -āre, [in †stigŏ, cf. **instinguo,** Gr. στίζω], 1. v. a., *goad on.*— Fig., *stimulate, encourage, incite, urge* on.
īnstĭtŭō, -tŭī, -tūtum, -tŭere, [in-statuo], 3. v. a., *set up, build, found.*— Less exactly, *establish, ordain, introduce a custom, teach* (a custom): vestigia nuda (*have by long established custom*); dapes (*prepare*).
īnstō, -stĭtī, -stātum, -stāre, [in-sto], 1. v. n. and a., *stand on, stand over.*— Less exactly (of military action), *press on, pursue, assail, attack, threaten:* iugis (*threaten, make a demonstration*).— Also in other connections, *be busy, urge on, be troublesome, threaten, impend, be urgent, be at hand, be ready, press on, ply, be eager, strive, be bent* on: currum (cog. acc., *busily prepare*); aristis (*be devoted to*); operi; tumultus (*be imminent*); aquae (*overhang,* of a figurehead).
īnstrātus, -a, -um, p.p. of **īnsterno.**
īnstrĕpō, -ŭī, -ĭtum, -ere, [in-strepo], 3. v. n., *rattle, creak.*
īnstructus, -a, -um, p.p. of **īnstruo.**
īnstrŭō, -struxī, -structum, -struere, [in-struo], 3. v. a., (*pile up on*), *pile up:* mensas (*spread*).— Less exactly, *arrange, draw up, array, prepare, set in order, furnish.*— With change of point of view, *provide* (with), *furnish, arm:* armis socios; instructus Eois adversis (*in array with*); instructus dolis (*armed with*).
īnsŭētus, -a, -um, [in-suetus],

adj., *unaccustomed to, unused, not wont.* — Passively, *unaccustomed, unusual, unwonted, unfamiliar.* — Neu*t*. plur. as adv., *in unwonted wise, unusually, beyond one's wont.*

īnsula, -ae, [in-s*t*em akin to sal], f., *an island.*

īnsultō, -āvī, -ātum, -āre, [in-salto, cf. **īnsiliō**], 1. v. a. and n., *bound upon, leap upon, dance on, prance* (on): solo; floribus haedi; aequore sonipes. — Fig., *exult over, insult.* — Also, *bound into, rush into.*

īnsum, īnfuī, īnesse, [in-sum], irr. v. n., *be in, be on, be there.*

īnsuō, -suī, -sūtum, -suere, [in-suo], 3. v. a., *sew in, stitch in.*

īnsuper [in-super], adv., *above, over, over all.* — Less exac*t*ly, *moreover, besides, in addition to.*

īnsuperābilis, -e, [in-superabilis], adj., *unconquerable, invincible.*

īnsurgō, -surrēxī, -surrēctum, -surgere, [in-surgo], 3. v. n., *rise upon.* — Less exac*t*ly, *rise, arise:* campis tenebrae (*overspread*).

īnsūtus, -a, -um, p.p. of **īnsuō**.

intāctus, -a, -um, [in-tactus], adj., *untouched, unhurt, unharmed:* seges (*without touching*); silvas (*unvisited*, an untried *t*heme). — Esp. of domes*t*ic animals, *unbroken, ignorant of the yoke.* — Also of women, *maiden, chaste, pure.*

integer, -gra, -grum, [in-†tagrŏ- (√tag + rus), cf. **intāctus**], adj., (*untouched*), *unbroken, entire, whole.* — Fig., *fresh, vigorous, unimpaired.* — ab integro, as adv., *anew, afresh.*

integrō, -āvī, -ātum, -āre, [†integrō-], 1. v. a., *renew* (cf. **ab integrō**), *repeat, begin anew.*

intemerātus, -a, -um, [in-temeratus], adj., *unpolluted, untainted, pure, chaste:* vinum (*unmixed*). — Fig., *inviolate, pure:* Camilla (*a maid*).

intempestus, -a, -um, [in-††tempestus (cf. **honestus**), cf. **tempestīvus**], adj., *untimely, unseasonable:* nox (a *t*echnical exp., *the dead of night*). — Also, nox (with reference to the orig. meaning, *gloomy, unpropitious*). — Also (cf. **temperies**), *unwholesome, unhealthy.*

intemptātus (inten-), -a, -um, [in-temptatus], adj., *untried.*

intendō, -tendī, -tentum (-tēnsum), [in-tendo], 3. v. a., *stretch upon, stretch to, stretch, strain:* arcum (*bend*, from s*t*re*t*ching the s*t*ring); vela (*spread*); sagittam (*aim*, cf. **arcum** above); vincula (*strain*); vela Zephyri (*swell*). — Wi*t*h change of point of view, *stretch with, hang with, cover with:* bracchia tergo; bracchia velis; locum sertis.—Poetically: vocem cornu(*strain with*); numeros nervis (*strain the strings with notes*). — intentus, -a, -um, p.p. as adj., *strained, stretched.* — Fig., *on the stretch, strained, straining, intent, eager.*

intentātus, -a, -um; see **intemptatus**.

intentō, -āvī, -ātum, -āre, [†intentō- (but cf. **tento**)], 1. v. a., *stretch out:* angues (*hold threateningly, brandish*). — Fig., *threaten, menace.*

intentus, -a, -um, p.p. of **intendo**.

intepeō, -tepuī, no sup., -tepēre, [in-tepeo], 2. v. n., *become warm, be warmed:* mucro (*taste blood*).

inter [in + ter (reduced from -tero, cf. **subter, interior**), comp. of **in**], prep. and adv. Prep., *between, among, amid, in among, into the midst of.* — Some*t*imes from a different concep*t*ion in La*t*in, *in, through, on:* inter valles (of the two sides); arva inter opima. — Esp.: inter manus, *in the hands, in the power.* — With gerund, *while:* inter bibendum. — Wi*t*h reflexive (as reciprocal), *with each other, on, from, by, to,* &c., **in** all reciprocal relations: **inter vos** (*with each other*); **inter sese** (*alternately*). — Adv. in composition, *between, off, away, among, together*, cf. **intercipio, intercludo, intereo, intermisceo, internecto.**

intercipiō, -cēpī, -ceptum, -cipere, [inter-capio], 3. v. a., *intercept.*

intercludō, -clūsī, -clūsum, -cludere, [inter-cludo], 3. v. a., *shut off, cut off, detain.*

interdum [inter-dum, cf. **interim**], adv., *sometimes.*

intereā [inter-ea (prob. abl. of **is**, cf. **supra**)], adv., *meanwhile, meantime.* — Less exactly, *in these circumstances, at that time.*

intereō, -īvī (-iī), -itum, -īre, [inter-eo], irr. v. n., *perish, die, be slain, fall* (in battle).

interfātus, -a, -um, p.p. of **interfor.**

interficiō, -fēcī, -fectum, -ficere, [inter-facio, cf. **intereo**], 3. v. a., *kill.* — Less exactly, *destroy, kill* (of harvests), *lay waste.*

interfor, -fātus, -fārī, [inter-for], 1. v. dep., *interrupt.*

interfundō, -fūdī, -fūsum, -fundere, [inter-fundo], 3. v. a., *pour between.* — Pass., *flow between.* — With change of point of view, *overflow, suffuse, stain, fleck.*

interfūsus, -a, -um, p.p. of **interfundo.**

interimō, -ēmī, -emptum, -imere, [inter-emo, *take* (cf. **interficio**)], 3. v. a., *kill, slay, strike down.*

interior, -ius, [†interŏ- (reduced, cf. **inter**)+ior], comp. adj., *inner, inside:* **domus** (*the interior of*, &c.). — Neut. as adv., *more deeply.* — Superl., **intimus, -a, -um,** [in + timus, cf. **finitimus**], *inmost, farthest.*

interitus, -ūs, [inter-itus, cf. **intereo**], m., *death.*

interlegō, -lēgī, -lectum, -legere, (also separated), [inter-lego], 3. v. a., *cull here and there, pluck here and there.*

interlūceō, -lūxī, no sup., **-lūcēre,** [inter-luceo], 2.v. n., *shine through.* —Less exactly, *show light through.*

interluō, no perf., no sup., **-luere,** [inter-luo], 3. v. a., *flow between, wash* (of rivers).

intermisceō, -miscuī, -mixtum (mistum), -miscēre, [intermisceo], 2. v. a., *mix in, intermingle.*

internectō, no perf., no sup., **-nectere,** [inter-necto], 3. v. a., *bind together, bind up, knot up.*

interpres, -etis, [?], comm., *an agent, a messenger, an interpreter:* **divum** (*a prophet*); **harum curarum** (*author,* of Juno as agent in the marriage relation).

interritus, -a, -um, [in-territus], adj., *undaunted, unterrified, fearless, undismayed, without fear* (of danger).

interrumpō, -rūpī, -ruptum, -rumpere, [inter-rumpo], 3.v.a., *break off, discontinue:* **ignes** (*die out*).

interruptus, -a, -um, p.p. of **interrumpo.**

interstrepō, no perf., no sup., **-strepere,** [inter-strepo], 3. v. a., *make a noise among, drown* (of noise): **anser** (*cackle among,* drowning the notes of others).

intersum, -fuī, no sup., **-esse,** [inter-sum], irr. v. n., *be engaged in, join, share.*

intertexō, -texuī, -textum, -texere, [inter-texo], 3. v. a., *interweave.*

intertextus, -a, -um, p.p. of **intertexo.**

intervallum, -ī, [inter-vallum], n., (*space between pales or stakes of the rampart*), *distance* (between), *interval.*

intexō, -texuī, -textum, -texere, [in-texo], 3. v. a., *weave in, interweave, entwine, interlace.* — With change of point of view, *surround, entwine* (with something): **vitibus ulmos.** — Of the effect, *weave, weave in:* **intextum opus:**

intexti Britanni (in a work of art).
intextus, -a, -um, p.p. of **intexo**.
intimus, see **interior**.
intŏnŏ, -uī, -ātum, -āre, [in-tono], 1. v. n., *thunder*.
intōnsus, -a, -um, [in-tonsus], adj., *unshorn, unshaven.*—Less exactly, of mountains, *unshorn, rough*.
intorqueŏ, -torsī, -tortum, -torquēre, [in-torqueo], 2. v. a., *turn, roll.* — Also, *brandish, hurl*.
intortus, -a, -um, p.p. of **intorqueo**.
intrā [†interŏ- (syncopated), prob. abl. case, cf. **infra**], prep., *within* (of position or motion), *inside*.
intractābilis, -e, [in-tractabilis], adj., *unmanageable, fierce, violent*.
intractātus, -a, -um, [in-tractatus], adj., *untried* (by others read **intemptatus**).
intremŏ, -uī, no sup., **-ere,** [intremo], 3. v. n., *tremble, quake, quiver*.
intrŏ, -āvī, -ātum, -āre, [†interŏ- (syncopated), cf. **intra**], 1. v. a., *enter:* **ripas** (*sail within*). — Fig., *enter, penetrate, pervade:* **calor medullas**.
intrōgredior, -gressus, -gredī, [intro-gradior], 3. v. dep., *enter, come in*.
intrōgressus, -a, -um, p.p. of **introgredior**.
intubus (-um), -ī, [Gr. ἔντυβον], m., f., n., *endive, succory*.
intulī, see **infero**.
intus [in+tus, cf. **divinitus**], adv., *within* (cf. **a dextra parte**), *inside, in doors, in the house*.
intybus, see **intubus**.
inultus, -a, -um, [in-ultus], adj., *unavenged*.
inumbrŏ, -āvī, -ātum, -āre, [inumbro], 1. v. a., *overshadow, shade, canopy*.
inundŏ, -āvī, -ātum, -āre, [inundo], 1. v. n. and a., *overflow, flow.* — Less exactly, *swarm*.
inūrŏ, -ūssī, -ūstum, -ūrere, [inuro], 3. v. a., *burn in, brand*.

inūtilis, -e, [in-utilis], adj., *useless, unavailing, impotent.* — Less exactly, *injurious*.
Inuus, -ī, [akin to **ineo**], m., a god identified with Pan as guardian of cattle. — **Castrum Inui,** a town of Latium.
invādō, -vāsī, -vāsum, -vādere, [in-vado], 3. v. n. and a., *go into, go against, proceed, go on, begin.* —Also, *attack, invade, storm, rush into, rush in, force:* **thalamum** (*violate*). — Fig., *enter upon, undertake*.
invalidus, -a, -um, [in-validus], adj., *infirm, feeble, weak, powerless*.
invectus, -a, -um, p.p. of **inveho**.
invehŏ, -vexī, -vectum, -vehere, [in-veho], 3. v. a., *bear on, bear against.* — Pass., *ride, sail, be borne*.
inveniŏ, -vēnī, -ventum, -venīre, [in-venio], 4. v. a., *come upon, hit upon, find* (esp. by accident, cf. **reperio**, *find by search*), *discover, find* (learn). — **inventus, -a, -um,** p.p. — Neut., *a discovery, an invention*.
inventor, -ōris, [in-†ventor, cf. **invenio**], m., *a finder, a discoverer, a deviser, a contriver*.
inventrix, -īcis, [in-†ventrix, cf. **inventor** and **invenio**], f., *a finder, an inventor* (female), *a discoverer, an originator*.
inventus, -a, -um, p.p. of **invenio**.
invergo, no perf., no sup., **-vergere,** [in-vergo], 3. v. a., *turn downward, empty.* — Less exactly, *pour down upon* (a sacrificial word), *pour* (by inversion of a vessel).
invertō, -vertī, -versum, -vertere, [in-verto], 3. v. a., *upturn, overturn.* — Esp. with the plough, *turn in furrows.* — Less exactly, *change:* **caelum nox** (*change the aspect of*).
invictus, -a, -um, [in-victus], adj., *unconquered, unconquerable, invincible*.

Vocabulary.

invĭdĕō, -vīdī, -vīsum, -vĭdēre, [in-video], 2. v. n. and a., (*look askance at*), *envy, be jealous of, grudge, deny* (as if from jealousy). — **invīsus, -a, -um,** p.p. as adj., *hateful, hostile, troublesome.* — Passively, *an object of hatred, hated, detested, odious:* haud invisus caelestibus (*not unfriended by*).

invidia, -ae, [†invĭdŏ- (reduced) + ia], f., *envy, hatred, malice, grudging, jealousy:* quae est? (*why grudge?*).

invĭgĭlō, -āvī, -ātum, -āre, [invigilo], 1. v. n., *be awake, be diligent, be attentive to.*

inviolābĭlis, -e, [in-violabilis], adj., *inviolable, sacred.*

invīsō, -vīsī, -vīsum, -vīsere, [inviso], 3. v. a., *look upon, view.* — Also, *visit, go to see* (cf. **viso**).

invīsus, -a, -um, p.p. of **invideo.**

invīsus, -a, -um, [in-visus], adj., *unseen.*

invītō, -āvī, -ātum, -āre, [?], 1. v. a., *invite, allure, persuade.* — Esp., *entertain:* Aenean solio acerno (*seat hospitably*).

invītus, -a, -um, [?], adj., *unwilling, with reluctance, reluctant, against one's will.* — Often equal to an adverb.

invius, -a, -um, [in-†via (decl. as adj.)], adj., *pathless, inaccessible, difficult of access, difficult* (of passage), *dangerous.*

invŏcō, -āvī, -ātum, -āre, [invoco], 1. v. a., *call upon, worship, adore, invoke.*

involvō, -volvī, -volūtum, -volvere, [in-volvo], 3. v. a., *roll upon, roll over, roll in, roll along.* — With change of point of view, *enwrap, involve, surround, cover, shut in, engulf.* — Often of fire, water, and the like.

Iō [Gr. ἰώ], interj., *ho!* (a cry of wild excitement, either of joy or grief).

Iō, -ūs, [Gr. Ἰώ], f., daughter of Inachus, beloved by Jupiter, and changed by Juno, from jealousy, into a cow.

Iollās, -ae, [Gr. Ἰόλλας], m.: 1. A shepherd; 2. A Trojan.

Iōnius, -a, -um, [†Ion + ius], adj., (*of Ion*), *Ionian* (of the sea so called): fluctus; mare. — Neut., *the Ionian Sea.*

Iōpās, -ae, [?], m., a Carthaginian bard.

Īphĭtus, -ī, [Gr. Ἴφιτος], m., a Trojan.

ipse, -a, -um, -īus, [is-pse (cf. -pte, perh. = potis)], pron. intens., *self, very, even.* — Without other pronoun or noun, *himself, yourself,* &c. — In special phrases: ipsi venient, *of themselves, voluntarily;* ipse, *the chief, the leader* (as opposed to the men); ipsi, *the men* (as opposed to the ships).

ira, -ae, [?], f., *anger, wrath, rage, fury.* — Also plur. — Personified, *Passion* (of wrath).

īrāscor, īrātus, īrāscī, [†irā- (of lost †iro) + sco], 1. v. dep., *be angry, become enraged.* — Less exactly, *vent one's rage, angrily attack.* — **īrātus, -a, -um,** p.p. as adj., *angry, enraged, furious.*

īrātus, -a, -um, p.p. of **irascor.**

Īris, -ĭdis (also -is), f., the messenger of the gods, the personified rainbow.

irreměābĭlis, see **inremeabilis.**

irr-, compounds of **in,** see **inr-,** the more approved spelling.

is, ea, id, ēius, [pron. √i], pron. dem., *he, she, it, they, this, that, these, those, such, a* (with a correlative), *so great.*

Ismara, -orum, [cf. **Ismarus**], n., a town in Thrace near Mt. Ismarus.

Ismarius, -a, -um, [†Ismaro + ius], adj., *of Mt. Ismarus.* (Others read **Imarius.**)

Ismarus, -ī, [Gr. Ἴσμαρος], m.: 1. A mountain of Thrace; 2. A Lydian in the Trojan ranks.

iste, ista, istud, istīus, [is-tus (pron. √ta, cf. **tum, tam, tantus**)], pron. dem., *that* (esp. referring in some way to the person addressed), *he, she, they, these,* *those.* — Esp. of one's opponent or one against whom one has a grudge, *such as you, that, those, such, that sort of.*

Ister, -rī, [Gr. Ἴστρος], (**Hister,** the spelling now in vogue], m., *the Danube.* — Less exactly, of the nations around it.

istīc [isti-ce, cf. **hīc**], adv., *there* (where you are, or the like, cf. **iste**).

istinc [istim-ce, cf. **hinc**], adv., *from there* (where you are, cf. **iste**), *where you are.*

ita [pron. √i-ta (unc. case of pron. √ta, cf. **tam**, etc.)], adv., *so, in that way, just so, thus, such a:* ita ... ut (*just as*); haud ita me experti (*not like that*). — In asseverations (cf. the form of oath in English), *so* (and only so as what I say is true).

Ītalia, -ae, [†Italŏ- (reduced) + ia, f. of -ius], f., *Italy.* — Less exactly, the people (as in Eng.).

Ītalis, -idis, [Gr. patronymic from Italus], f. adj., *an Italian* (woman), *of Italy.*

Ītalus, -a, -um, [prob. Gr. Ἰταλός, *bull*, cf. **vitulus**], *Italian.*

item [pron. √i + tem (pron. √ta, cf. **ita**)], adv., *likewise, also, as well.*

iter, itineris, [unc. formation of √i], n., *a way, a course, a journey, a passage.*

iterum [neut. of †iterŏ- (pron. √i + terus, cf. **alter**)], adv., *a second time, again, repeatedly, once more.*

Ithacus, -a, -um, [Gr. Ἰθάκη], adj. (used as adj. of Ithaca, which is properly its fem.), *Ithacan, of Ithaca* (the home of Ulysses in the Ionian Sea). — Fem., the island itself, *Ithaca.*

Ityraeus, -a, -um, [Gr. Ἰτυραῖα], adj., *of Ituraea* (a region of Syria, famous for its bowmen).

Itys, -yos, [Gr. Ἴτυς], m., a Trojan.

Iūlus, -ī, [Gr. Ἴουλος], m., a name of Ascanius, son of Æneas.

Ixīōn, -onis, [Gr. Ἰξίων], m., a king of the Lapithæ, who was bound to a wheel in the world below as a punishment for his crimes.

Ixionius, -a, -um, [†Ixion + ius], adj., *of Ixion.*

I (consonant).

iaceō, iacuī, iacitum, iacere, [prob. adj. stem akin to **iacio**], 2. v. n., *lie, lie down.* — Esp., *lie dead, lie low.* — Also, *lie, be situated.* — Also, *lie (remain).* — Fig., *lie prostrate, succumb, be exhausted, be overcome.* — **iacēns, -ntis,** p. as adj., *prostrate, low-lying, fallow.*

iaciō, iēcī, iactum, iacere, [√iac (of unc. kindred)], 3. v. a., *throw, cast, hurl, fling.* — Esp. of foundations, &c., *lay, throw, throw up:* muros. — Fig., in similar sense, *found, rest:* spem. — Of sowing and the like, *cast, sow, scatter:* flores; iacto semine.

iactātus, -a, -um, p.p. of **iacto**.

iactō, -āvī, -ātum, -āre, [†iactŏ-], 1. v. a., *throw, cast, hurl, scatter, strew.* — Also, *toss, agitate, throw* (to and fro): bidentes (*ply*); iactata tellus (*stir*). — Fig., *toss, drive, pursue.* — Also, *throw out, emit, send forth, utter, pour forth:* voces; odorem; iurgia (*bandy*); volnera (*inflict*). — Also, *revolve:* pectore curas. — With reflexive, *boast, plume one's self, glory, vaunt one's self, show one's pride, pride one's self.* — Phrase: prae se iacto, *boast, assert boastfully, vaunt.* —

iactāns, -antis, p. as adj., *boastful, arrogant.*

iactūra, -ae, [†iactu- (lengthened, cf. **figura**) + ra (f. of -rus)], f., *a throwing away.* — Fig., *loss.*

iactus, -a, -um, p.p. of **iacio.**

iactus, -ūs, [√iac + tus], m., *a throwing, a throw, a cast, a leap, a spring, a shot* (of an arrow).

iaculātus, -a, -um, p.p. of **iaculor.**

iaculor, -atus, -ārī, [†iaculŏ-], 1. v. dep., *hurl a javelin.* — Less exactly, *throw, cast, fling, dart.*
iaculum, -ī, [†iacŏ- (√iac + us, cf. **iaceo, iacio**)], n., *a javelin, a dart, a missile weapon.*
iam [?], adv., *now* (implying a continuance, cf. **nunc**, an immediate now), *already, now (as soon as), at last, now at length, from this time on, presently.* — Often with pres. and imperf., *begin to* (do anything). — Phrases: nec iam, *and now no more;* iam inde, *immediately;* iam tum, *even then;* iam dudum, *long ago, long since, already;* iam pridem, *long since;* iam iam, *at every moment, even now;* iam nunc, *even now.* — In logical sense, *now, again, moreover.* — With comparatives, *still, even, now.*
iamdūdum, see **iam.**
iampridem, see **iam.**
Iāniculum, -ī, [†Ianŏ+culum], n., *the Janiculine* (the hill at Rome).
Iānitor, -ōris [Ianŏ (cf. **ianua**) + tor (cf. **viator**)], m., *a doorkeeper, guardian* (of an entrance).
Iānua, -ae, [akin to **Ianus**], f., *a door, an entrance.* — Less exactly, *an avenue, a means of access, a way.*
Iānus, -ī, [akin to **dies, Jupiter,** and **Diana**], m., *an Italian divinity,* represented with two faces, presiding over doorways and beginnings of things.
iecur, iecoris (iecinoris), [two stems from unc. root, cf. **iter**], n., *the liver.*
iēiūnium, -ī (-iī), [†ieiunŏ- (reduced) + ium], n., *a fast, fasting.* — From the effect, *leanness.*
iēiūnus, -a, -um, [unc. root redupl. + nus], adj., *fasting.* — Less exactly and fig., *barren, scanty, meagre.*
Iovis, see **Iupiter.**
iuba, -ae, [?], f., *the mane.*—Transferred, *the crest* (of a helmet, made of hair).

iubar, -aris, [akin to **iuba**], n., *rays of light, brightness.* — Less exactly, *the dawn, the morning.*
iubeō, iussī, iussum, iubēre, [?, ius habeo, cf. **veto**], 2. v. a., *bid* (in all shades of meaning), *order, command, ordain.* — **iussus, -a, -um,** p.p. as adj., *bidden, presented, ordered, directed.* — Neut., *a command, an order, a mandate.*
iūcūndus, -a, -um, [perh. akin to **iuvo**], adj., *pleasant, agreeable, grateful.*
iūdex, -icis, [†ius-dex (√dic as stem)], comm., *a judge, an arbitrator:* iudice te (*with you to decide*).
iūdicium, -ī (-iī), [†iudic + ium], n., *a decision, a judgment.*
iugālis, -e, [†iugŏ- (reduced) + alis], adj., *of the yoke.*— As subst., *horses.* — Fig., *of the marriage bond, conjugal, of marriage.* — *nuptial.*
iūgerum, -ī, [akin to **iugum**], n., *an acre* (loosely; properly a little more than one-half an acre).
iugō, -āvī, -ātum, -āre, [†iugŏ-], 1. v. a., *unite* (in marriage).
iugulō, -āvī, -ātum, -āre, [†iugulŏ], 1. v. a., *cut the throat.* — Less exactly, *kill, slay, slaughter, sacrifice.*
iugulum, -ī, [†iugŏ + lum], n., *the collar bone* (forming a kind of yoke). — Less exactly, *the throat, the neck.*
iugum, -ī, [√iug + um], n., *a yoke, a team, a pair of horses.* — From similarity, *a ridge, a thwart.* — Esp., *the yoke* (under which conquered soldiers were sent, and also used generally to signify conquest).
Iūlius, -a, -um, [†Iulŏ- (reduced) + ius], adj., *Julian* (the name of the gens at Rome to which Caesar belonged). — Esp., *Julian* (of Julius Caesar). — Masc., **Iulius,** the name of Caius Caesar, and his adopted son Augustus.
iunctūra, -ae, [†iunctu- (length-

ened) + ra], f., *a joint, a fastening*.

iunctus, -a, -um, p.p. of **iungo.**

iuncus, -ī, [?], m., *a rush, a bulrush.*

iungŏ, iunxī, iunctum, iungere, [√ing], 3. v. a., *join, unite, fasten, yoke, harness, attach.* — Esp. of the hand, *clasp, join.* — Of treaties, *join, unite, make, celebrate.* — Of marriage, *unite.* — Of the effect, *make* (by joining): **pontes** (*throw out*).

iūniperus, -ī, [?], f., *the juniper.*

Iūnŏ, -ōnis, [prob. for Iovino, akin to Iupiter], f., *the queen of the gods, wife of Jupiter, patroness of the Greeks against the Trojans, identified with Astarte, the deity of the Phœnicians.* — Less exactly, of Proserpine, *queen.*

Iūnōnius, -a, -um, [†Iunon+ius], adj., *of Juno.*

Iūppiter (Iūpi-), Iovis, [†Iovi- (perh. nom. Iovis) -pater, akin to Ζεύς], m., *Jupiter, Jove, the supreme divinity of the Romans, identified also with the Greek Zeus, being originally the same divinity, though later with somewhat different attributes.* — Also, as a personification of the atmosphere, *the sky, the air, the weather, the rain.* — Less exactly of Pluto, *the king of the lower world.*

iūrgium, -ī, (-iī), [†iurgŏ- (iusagus, cf. **prodigus**) reduced, + ium], n., *quarrelling, a quarrel, strife, upbraiding, reproof, reviling, altercation, abuse, a complaint.*

iūrŏ, -āvī, -ātum, -āre, [†ius- (or †iurŏ, cf. **periurus**)], 1. v. n. and a., *swear, swear by.*

iūs, iūris, [√iu (simpler form akin to √iug)+us], n., *right, justice, law* (unwritten, cf. **lex**, *statute*). — Concretely, *a right, a privilege, a claim.* — Also, *a tie* (of right that one holds over another), *a claim, a right.* — Abl. **iure,** as adv., *with justice, justly, deservedly, rightly.*

iussum, -ī; see **iubeo.**

iussus, -a, -um, p.p. of **iubeo.**

iussus, -ūs, [root of **iubeo** + tus], m., *a command, a mandate.*

iustitia, -ae, [†iustŏ+tia (as if †iustitŏ+ia, cf. **amicitia**)], f., *justice, right, uprightness.* — Personified, *Justice.*

iustus, -a, -um, [†ius+tus, cf. **robustus**], adj., *just, fitting, right, regular.* — Of persons, *just, upright.* — Less exactly, *fair, proportional, equal.* — Abl. **iusto,** with comparatives, *than is right, than is just.*

Iūturna, -ae, [?], f., *the sister of Turnus.*

iuvenca, -ae, [f. of **iuvencus**], f., *a heifer.*

iuvencus, -ī, [†iuven- (earlier form of †iuveni) + cus], m., *a bullock, a steer, a bull.*

iuvenīlis (-ālis), -e, [†iuveni-+ ilis (-alis)], adj., *of youth, of a youth, youthful.*

iuvenis, -e, [?, stem orig. without the i, cf. gen. plur. **iuvenum** and **iuvencus**], adj., *young, youthful.* — As subst., *a young man* (in the prime of life, up to forty-five years). — Also, of animals, *young cattle.*

iuventa, -ae, [†iuven+ta (f. of tus?)], f., *youth.*

iuventūs, -ūtis, [†iuven+tus (as if †iuventu+tis, cf. **senectus** and **Carmentis**)], f., *youth.* — Concretely, as in Eng., *the youth, young men.* — Also, *the young* (of cattle).

iuvŏ, iūvī, iūtum, iuvāre, [prob. akin to **iuvenis, iocus,** and **iucundus**], 1. v. a. and n., *help, aid, assist, profit, avail, be of use.* — Also, *please, give pleasure, delight.* — Often impers. with an inf., *it delights, one is pleased, one rejoices, one is glad.*

iuxtā [case-form of †iuxtŏ- (superl. of †iugŏ-, cf. Gr. -ιστος)], adv. and prep., *near by, near, closely, next to, next, by one's side.*

L.

labans, -antis; see labo.
labefaciŏ, -fēcī, -factum, -facere, [†labe- (unc. form, cf. labes) facio], 3. v. a., *make to totter.* — Esp., *crumble* (of the soil, by digging). — Fig., *weaken, cause to waver.* — **labefactus, -a, -um,** p.p. as adj., *shaken, agitated, overcome, shattered, crumbled.*
labefactus, -a, -um, p.p. of labefacio.
labellum, -ī, [†labrŏ- (cf. ager) + lum], n., *a lip* (dim. of affection).
lābēs, -is, [√lab (cf. lābor) + es], f., *a fall, a slide, a giving away:* prima mali (*first stroke of misfortune*).
lābēs, -is, [?, perh. same word as preceding], f., *a taint, a spot, a stain, a plague spot.*
Labīcī, -ōrum, [?], m. plur., name of a people of La*t*ium, of the *t*own of Labicum.
labŏ, -āvī, -ātum, -are, [√lab (prob. through no*u*n-s*t*em)], 1. v.n., *totter, stagger.* — Fig., *waver, vacillate.* — **labāns, -āntis,** p., *tottering, wavering, vacillating, yielding.*
lābor, lāpsus, lābī, [√lab, cf. labo, labes], 3. v. dep., *slide, glide, fall, slip, float, descend, sink, swoop* (of birds), *penetrate.* — Fig., *glide on, glide away, slip away, pass away, fall, fail, decline.* — **lābēns, -entis,** p. as adj. wi*t*h par*t*icipial meanings; also, *slippery:* oleum.
labor, -ōris, [√lab + or (os)], m., *toil, labor, exer*t*ion, strength.* — Also, less exac*t*ly, *sorrow, pangs, trial, trouble, misfortune.* — Also, of the effec*t*, *fatigue, training;* also, *fruit of toil.* — Esp. of travail, *pangs, throes, labor.* — Also, *task, care, business.* — Of the sun and moon, *struggle, eclipse.* — Personified, *Toil.*
labōrātus, -a, -um, p.p. of laboro.

labōrō, -āvī, -ātum, -āre, [†labor-], 1. v. a. and n., *elaborate, work out, work, labor, take pains.* — **labōrātus, -a, -um,** p.p., *wrought, worked, wrought out.* — **labōrāns, -āntis,** p. as subs*t*., *one struggling.*
1. **labrum, -ī,** [?], n., *a lip.* — Less exac*t*ly, *an edge.*
2. **labrum, -ī,** [?], n., *a vat, a tub, a vessel, a vase.*
labrusca, -ae (-um, -ī), [?], f. and n., *a wild vine.*
labyrinthus, -ī, [Gr. λαβύρινθος], m., *a labyrinth.* — Esp., *the labyrinth* at Cre*t*e.
lac, lactis, [perh. akin to γάλα], n., *milk.* — Less exac*t*ly, *milky juice.* — Phrase: pressum lac, *cheese.*
Lacaenus, -a, -um, [Gr. Λάκαινος], adj., *Lacedæmonian, Laconian.* — Esp. in fem., *the Spartan dame, Helen.*
Lacedaemon, -onis, [Gr. Λακεδαίμων], f., *Lacedæmon,* or *Sparta.*
Lacedaemonius, -a, -um, [Gr. Λακεδαιμόνιος], adj., *Spartan, Lacedæmonian.*
lacer, -era, -erum, [√lac (dac?, cf. lacrima) + rus], adj., *torn, mangled, maimed, bruised, disfigured.*
lacerŏ, -āvī, -ātum, -are, [†lacerŏ-], 1. v. a., *tear, rend, tear in pieces, mangle.*
lacerta, -ae (-us, -ī), [?], f. and m., *a lizard.*
lacertus, -ī, [?], m., *the forearm, the arm.* — Less exac*t*ly, *a claw, a leg* (of any creature).
lacessītus, -a, -um, p.p. of lacesso.
lacessŏ, -sīvī, -sītum, -sere, [√lac (in lacio?) + esso (prob. *t*hrough no*u*n-stem)], 3. v. a., *provoke, challenge, irritate, excite, rouse, encourage.* — Also (perh. in original meaning), *assail, attack, invade, beat, strike, smite:* ventos ictibus; manibus pectora (*pat*): lacessita sole aera. — Poe*t*ically:

bellum (*stir up*); ferrum (*bare*); pugnam (*provoke*, by sparring, of boxers).

Lacīnius, -a, -um, [Gr. Λακίνιον], adj., *of Lacinium* (a promontory of Southern Italy, on which was a temple of Juno, a land-mark for sailors). The name of the promontory is the neut. of the adj.

lacrima, -ae, [perh. stem akin to Gr. δάκρυ + ma (f: of mus)], f., *a tear, weeping.* — Poetically: *narcissi, nectar* (of flowers).

lacrimābilis, -e, [†lacrimā- (cf. lacrimo) + bilis], adj., *tearful, mournful, melancholy:* bellum; gemitus.

lacrimŏ, -āvī, -ātum, -āre, [†lacrimā-], 1. v. n. and a., *weep, shed tears, mourn, weep for, lament.*

lacrimōsus, -a, -um, [†lacrimā- (reduced) + osus], adj., *tearful, mournful.* — Less exactly, *plaintive:* voces.

lacteŏ, no perf., no sup., **-ere,** [†lact- (as if lactŏ)], 2. v. n., *suck.* — Also, *be in milk:* frumenta.

lacteus, -a, -um, [†lact + eus], adj., *milky, rich in milk.* — Less exactly, *milk white.*

lacuar, see **laquear.**

lacūna, -ae, [†lacu- (lengthened) + na, cf. **Fortuna**], f., *a pond, a pool, a cavity, a hollow.*

lacus, -ūs, [perh. akin to Gr. λάκκος], m., *a lake, a pond, a pool, a reservoir.* — Less exactly, *a river, a stream.* — Also, *a pool* (in a stream).

Ladēs, -is, [?], m., *a Trojan.*

Lādōn, -ōnis, [Gr. Λάδων], m., *a Trojan.*

laedŏ, laesī, laesum, laedere, [?], 3. v. a., *strike, dash* (cf. compounds). — Also, *hurt, pain, mar, wound, damage.* — Less exactly, *injure, trouble, hurt, offend, thwart, break* (of a treaty), *violate.*

laena, -ae, [Gr. χλαῖνα], f., (a coarse outer garment), *a cloak, a mantle.*

Laertius, -a, -um, [Gr. Λαέρτιος], adj., *of Laertes* (the father of Ulysses).

laesus, -a, -um, p.p. of **laedo.**

laetātus, -a, -um, p.p. of **laetor.**

laetitia, -ae, [†laetŏ + tia, cf. **amicitia**], f., *joy, gladness, cheerfulness, enjoyment.*

laetor, -ātus, -ārī, [†laetŏ-], 1. v. dep., *rejoice, be glad, sport.*

laetus, -a, -um, [prob. for **hlaetus**, akin to Eng. *glad*], adj., *glad, joyous, cheerful, merry, joyful, happy, delighting in, proud of, exultant with.* — Also of things (as in Eng.): spes; carmina; saecula (*happy*); tempora (*bright*); columba; laeti auxilio (*cheered by*); fortuna (*smiling, propitious*); res (*fortunate*). — Also (perh. in orig. meaning), of productiveness, *rich, fertile, productive, prolific, luxuriant, copious;* — *rich in, abounding in.* — So of animals, *fat, sleek, in good condition, fine.* — Also (cf. Eng. *glad*), *pleasing, grateful, agreeable:* aestas; imber.

laevŏ, see **levo.**

laevus, -a, -um, [?, akin to λαιός], adj., *left, on the left hand.* — Also, from inferior readiness of the left hand, *foolish, silly, awkward.* — From science of auspices, *ominous, boding, unpropitious.* — But also (fr. the Roman usage), *fortunate, propitious.* — Fem. (sc. **manus**), *the left hand.* — Neut. sing. and plur., *the left hand, places on the left.* — Neut. as adv., *on the left.*

lageos, -ī, [Gr. λάγειος], f., *a vine* (of a special kind), *lageos.*

Lagus, -ī, [Gr. Λάγος], m., *a Latin.*

lambŏ, lambī, lambitum, lambere, [√lab, cf. **labrum**], 3. v. a., *lick.* — Less exactly, of fire and the like, *play around, lick.*

lāmentābilis, -e, [†lamentā- (cf. **lamentum**) + bilis], adj., *lamentable, pitiable.*

lāmentum, -ī, [unc. root + mentum], n., *a shriek, a groan, a cry, a lamentation, a wailing.*

lāmina, -ae, [unc. root + mina

(cf. **columna**)], f., *a plate* (of metal), *a blade.*
lampas, -adis, [Gr. λαμπάς], f., *a light, a lamp, a torch* (both for light and as a weapon of war), *a burning brand.* — Poetically, of the celestial bodies.
Lamus, -ī, [Gr. Λάμος], m., a warrior of Turnus.
Lamyrus, -ī, [Gr. Λαμυρός], m., a warrior of Turnus.
lāna, -ae, [?], f., *wool, fleece.* — Less exactly (cf. "cotton wool"), *cotton, down.* — Also fig., of the clouds.
lancea, -ae, [prob. Gr. λόγχη], f., *a lance, a spear.*
lāneus, -a, -um, [†lana- (reduced) + eus], adj., *woollen, woolly, of wool.*
langueō, -uī, no sup., **-uēre,** [√lang, through adj. stem, cf. **languidus**], 2. v. n., *grow faint, languish, fail.* — **languēns, -entis,** p., *tired, feeble, fading, languid:* pelagus (*subsiding*); hyacynthus (*drooping*).
languēscō, -languī, no sup., **-escere,** [†languē- (cf. **langueo**) + sco], 3. v. n., *languish, faint, droop.*
languidus, -a, -um, [†languŏ- (cf. **langueo**) + dus], adj., *languid, fainting.* — Transferred, *relaxed, inactive, restful:* quies.
laniātus, -a, -um, p.p. of **lanio.**
lānicium (-itium), -ī (-iī), [†lana + cium, prob. through intermediate stem, perh. **lanicŏ-**], n. (of adj.), *wool.*
lāniger, -era, -erum, [†lana- (weakened) -ger (√ges + us, cf. **gero**)], adj., *wool-bearing, fleecy, tufted* (with wool).
laniō, -āvī, -ātum, -āre, [†laniŏ-], 1. v. a., *tear, rend, mangle, mutilate, disfigure* (by tearing).
lānūgō, -inis, [†lanu- (akin to **lana**) + go], f., *woolliness, down.*
lanx, lancis, [perh. akin to πλάξ], f., *a dish* (flat and broad), *a platter, a charger.* — Plur., *pans* (of a balance), *scales.*

Lāocoōn, -ontis, [Gr. Λαοκόων], m., a priest of Apollo, killed by two serpents on the day of the destruction of Troy for his supposed sacrilege in violating the wooden horse.
Lāodamīa, -ae, [Gr. Λαοδάμεια], f., wife of Protesilaus, who killed herself for love of him.
Lāomedontiadēs, -ae, [Gr. patronymic of Laomedon], m., *son (descendant) of Laomedon.* — Plur., *the Trojans* (descendants of him as founder of the race).
Lāomedontius, -a, -um, [†Laomedont + ius], adj., *of Laomedon, descended from Laomedon.* — Less exactly, *Trojan.*
lapidōsus, -a, -um, [†lapid + osus], adj., *stony, gritty.* — Less exactly, *hard as stone, stony:* corna.
lapillus, -ī, [†lapid + lus], m., *a small stone, gravel, a pebble.*
lapis, -idis, [?], m., *a stone, stone, a rock:* Parius (*marble*). — Less exactly, *a statue:* Parii lapides (*marbles of Paros*). — Esp.: incusus (of a millstone).
Lapithae, -ārum, [Gr. Λαπίθαι], m., *a tribe of Thessaly, famous for their battle with the Centaurs.*
lappa, -ae, [?], f., *a bur.*
lapso, -āvī, -ātum, -āre, [†lapsŏ-], 1. v. a., *slip.*
lapsus, -a, -um, p.p. of **labor.**
lapsus, -ūs, [√lab + tus], m., *a falling, a fall, a slip, a gliding motion, a swoop* (of birds), *course* (of stars): rotarum (*rolling wheels*).
laquear (-āre), (also **lacuar**), **-āris,** [†lacu + are (n. of aris)], n., (*a lakelike place*), *a hollow* (in a ceiling made by the crossing of beams), *a ceiling:* tecti (*fretted ceiling*).
laqueus, -ī, [perh. †lacu + eus], m., (*pitfall?*), *a springe, a trap, a noose, a gin, a snare.*
Lār, Laris, [?, orig. **las**], m., *a household god, a tutelary divinity.*

— Usually in the plur., the special pro*tec*/ors of the household, the spiri*t*s of deceased ances*t*ors, or some deified persons, represen*t*ed as you*t*hs in a short tunic, generally pouring a libation, and worshipped wi*t*h flowers, frui*t*, wine, incense, and fine grain or cakes. — Less exac*t*ly, *hearth* (as in Eng. for *home*), *home, house, habitation.*

largior, -ītus, -īrī, [†largŏ- (as if largi-)], 4. v. dep., *bestow freely, freely accord* (a boon).

largus, -a, -um, [perh. akin *t*o **longus,** Gr. δολιχός], adj., *wide, spacious:* largior aether (*freer, less confined,* as opposed *t*o the ear*t*hy a*t*mosphere). — Less exactly, *copious, plenteous, abundant:* fletus (*flood of tears*); sanguis (*a stream of blood*); fetus (*prolific*); copia fandi (*a ready flow*). — Also, of persons, *rich, lavish, generous.*

Lārĭdēs, -ae, [?], m., a Rutulian.

Larīna, -ae, [?], f., a companion of Camilla.

Lārissaeus, -a, -um, [Gr. Λαρισσαῖος], adj., *of Larissa* (a town of Thessaly, the supposed abode of Achilles), *Larissæan.*

Larius, -ī (-iī), [?], m., a lake of Cisalpine Gaul, *Lake Como.*

lascīvus, -a, -um, [?], adj., *frisky, frolicsome, sportive, wanton:* capellae; puella.

lassus, -a, -um, [prob. p.p. (unc. root + tus)], adj., *weary, worn, tired, fatigued.* — Of things: res (*broken fortune*); collum (*drooping,* of a poppy).

Latagus, -ī, [Gr.], m., a Trojan.

lātē [abl. of lātus], adv., *broadly, widely, far and wide, afar, in all directions, far and near:* discedere late (*leave a wide passage*).

latĕbra, -ae, [†late- (of lateo) + bra], f., *hiding-place, lurking-place, covert, cavern, retreat, place of ambush.* — Plur. in same sense.

latĕbrōsus, -a, -um, [†latebra- (reduced) + osus], adj., *full of hiding-places, apt for concealment, cavernous.*

lateō, -uī, no sup., -ēre, [√lat, akin *t*o Gr. λανθάνω], 2. v. n. and a., *lie concealed, be hidden, skulk, hide, be covered, be unseen, lurk, hide one's self, take (find) shelter.* — Fig., *be hidden, be unknown, be unknown to, lie hid.* — **latēns, -ēntis,** p. as adj., *hidden, secret, unknown.*

latex, -icis, [?], m., *a fluid, a liquid.* — Esp., *water* or *wine.*

Latīnus, -a, -um, [†latu- (or -o), akin to πλατύs (reduced) + inus, cf. **Latium**], adj., *of Latium* (the plain be*t*ween the Tiber, the Apennines, and the sea), *Latin.* — As subs*t*., masc. sing., *Latinus* (king of the region). — Masc. or fem. plur., *the Latins* (men or women).

Latium, -ī (-iī), [†latu- (or o), akin to πλατύs, + ium (n. of ius), cf. **Latinus**], n., the plain of I*t*aly sou*t*h of the Tiber.

Lātōna, -ae, [Gr. Λητώ + na, cf. **Diana, Neptunus**], f., the mo*t*her of Apollo and Diana.

Lātōnius, -a, -um, [†Latona- (reduced) + ius], adj., *of Latona, son (daughter) of Latona, Latonian* (connec*t*ed wi*t*h La*t*ona). — As subs*t*., fem., *daughter of Latona* (Diana).

lātrātor, -ōris, [†latrā- (of latro) + tor], m., *a barker.* — In appos. as adj., *the barking:* Anubis (wi*t*h a dog's head).

lātrātus, -ūs, [†latrā- (of latro) + tus], m., *a barking, a yelping, a cry* (of hounds).

lātrō, -āvī, -ātum, -āre, [?], 1. v. n. (and a.), *bark, yelp, roar.*

latrō, -ōnis, m., *a robber, a hunter.*

lātus, -a, -ūm, p.p. of fero.

lātus, -a, -um, [for stlatus, akin to sterno], adj., (*spread out*), *broad, wide:* agri; umeri; lancea (*broad-pointed*).

latus, -eris, [akin to Gr. πλατύs, cf. **Latium**], n., (orig. *width*), *the* *side, the flank.* — Less exact*l*y (as in Eng.), *the side* (of any*t*hing).

laudŏ, -āvī, -ātum, -āre, [†laud-], I. v. a., *praise, commend, approve, speak well of, extol.*

Laurēns, -entis, [perh. akin to **laurus**], adj., *of Laurentum, Laurentian.* — Masc. plur., *the Laurentians.*

Laurentum, -ī, [longer form of **Laurens**, cf. **argentum**], n., a town of La*t*ium, occupied by Turnus as the chief sea*t* of the war wi*t*h Æneas.

laureus, -a, -um, [†laurŏ- (reduced) + eus], adj., *of laurel.* — Fem., **laurea,** *the laurel tree, the laurel.*

laurus, -ūs and **-ī,** [?], f., *the laurel, the bay.* — Also, *a laurel crown, laurel* (used *t*o decorate the vic*t*or in any con*t*es*t*).

laus, laudis, [?], f., *praise* (bo*t*h as given and enjoyed), *glory, fame, renown, credit.* — Concre*t*ely, *virtue* (as deserving praise), *merit, a noble action.*

Lausus, -ī, [?], m., the son of Mezentius.

lautus, -a, -um, p.p. of **lavo.**

Lāvīnia, see **Lavinius.**

Lāvīnius, -ā, -um, [†Lavinŏ- (reduced) + ius], adj., *of Lavinium* (the *t*own buil*t* by Æneas in Latium and named in honor of Lavinia his wife), *Lavinian.* — Fem., *Lavinia,* daughter of King La*t*inus, married to Æneas. — Neu*t*., *Lavinium,* the *t*own itself.

Lāvīnus, -a, -um, [?], adj., *of Lavinium, Lavinian.* Many editors read only **Lavinius.**

lavŏ, lavāvī (lāvī), lavātum (lautum, lōtum), lavāre (lavere), [akin to **luo** and Gr. λούω], I. and 3. v. a., *wash, bathe, wash off.* — Also, *wet, moisten, bedew, bathe, soak.* — **lautus, -a, -um,** p.p. as adj., *clean, elegant, rich, costly, magnificent.* — **lavandi,** gerund, *of bathing* (one's self, absolutely).

laxātus, -a, -um, p.p. of **laxo.**

laxŏ, -āvī, -ātum, -are, [†laxŏ-], I. v. a., *loosen, relax, unbind, open :* rudentes (*let go*); foros (*clear*); laxata est via voci (*set free*); arva sinus (*open her bosom,* of the ear*t*h as spouse of Jove). — Fig., *relax, relieve, refresh :* somno curas; membra quiete.

laxus, -a, -um, [p.p. perh. √lag (cf. λαγγάζω) + tus], adj., *loose, slack, wide* (as not drawn *t*igh*t*), *unstrung:* casses (*fine spun, thin,* as if not *t*igh*t*ly woven, the fineness of the thread producing the same effect).

leaena, -ae, [Gr. λέαινα], f., *a lioness.*

lebēs, -ētis, [Gr. λέβης], m., *a kettle, a caldron.*

lector, -ōris, [√leg + tor], m., *a reader.*

lectus, -a, -um, p.p. of **lego.**

lectus, -ī, [?], m., *a bed, a couch.*

Lēda, -ae, [Gr. Λήδη], f., the mo*t*her of Helen and Cas*t*or and Pollux.

Lēdaeus, -a, -um, [Gr. Ληδαῖος], adj., *of Leda, descendant of Leda* (child or grandchild).

lēgātus, -ī, [p.p. of **lēgŏ**], m., *an embassador, a messenger, an envoy.*

lēgifer, -era, -erum, [†lēg- (as if legi-) + fer (√fer + us)], adj., *lawgiving, lawgiver.*

legiŏ, -ōnis, [√leg + io, as if †legŏ- (weakened) + o], f., (*a levy,* cf. **lego**), *a legion* (the regular uni*t* of force of the Roman army). — Less exac*t*ly, *a company, a band, an army.*

legŏ, lēgī, lectum, legere, [√leg, cf. Gr. λέγω], 3. v. a., *gather, collect, pick, pluck, pick up, choose, elect, select :* vela (*take in*). — Less exac*t*ly, *review, contemplate, pick out, scan ;* — hence *read,* and *coast along, skim, pass over, pass by, trace.* — Esp. (cf. **sacrilegus**), *steal :* socios (*deceive*). — **lectus, -a, -um,** p.p. as adj., *chosen, gathered, choice, picked, select, eminent.*

legūmen, -inis, [†legu- (akin to †lego?) + men], n., *pulse, beans.*
Leleges, -um, [Gr. Λέλεγες], m. pl., a *t*ribe or s*t*ock occupying the coas*t*s of Greece and Asia Minor before the his*t*oric inhabi*t*an*t*s of those countries.
lembus, -ī, [Gr. λέμβος], m., *a skiff, a boat.*
Lēmnius, -a, -um, [Gr. Λήμνιος], adj., *of Lemnos* (the island upon which Vulcan fell from heaven), *Lemnian.*—As subs*t*., *the Lemnian god* (Vulcan).
Lēnaeus, -a, -um, [Gr. Ληναῖος], adj., *(of the wine-press), of (to) Bacchus, Lenæan.* — Masc., *Lenæus,* a name of Bacchus.
lēniŏ, -īvī (-iī), -ītum, -īre, [†leni-], 4. v. a., *mitigate, relieve, assuage, soothe, moderate.*
lēnis, -e, [?], adj., *moderate, gentle.*
lēns, lentis, [?], f., *a lentil* (a kind of pulse).
lentēscō, no perf., no sup., **-escere,** [†lentē- (s*t*em of lost **lenteo**) + sco], 3. v. n., *stick, adhere.*
lentŏ, -āvī, -ātum, -āre, [†lentŏ-], 1. v. a., *bend.*
lentus, -a, -um, [perh. akin to **lenis**], adj., *tenacious, adhesive, sticky, viscid, clinging, tough, malleable, ductile, flexible, pliant, bending, twining.*—Also, *sluggish, slow, tranquil, idle, at ease.*
leō, -ōnis, [akin to Gr. λέων], m., *a lion.*
lepus, -oris, [?], m., *a hare.*
Lerna, -ae, [Gr. Λέρνη], f., a lake and marsh near Argos, where Hercules slew the famous hydra.
Lernaeus, -a, -um, [Gr. Λερναῖος], adj., *of Lerna, Lernæan.*
Lesbos, -ī, [Gr. Λέσβος], f., an island in the Ægean famous for its wine.
lētālis, -e, [†letŏ- (reduced) + alis], adj., *deadly, mortal, fatal, of death.*
Lēthaeus, -a, -um, [Gr. Ληθαῖος], adj., *of Lethe* (the river of forgetfulness in the world below), *Le-*

thaean. — Less exac*t*ly, *soporific.* **somnus** (*lethargic*).
lētifer, -era, -erum, [†letŏ-fer (√fer + us)], adj., *mortal, deadly, fatal.*
lētum, -ī, [√le or †lē + tum (n. of tus), cf. **deleo**], n., *death.*— Less exac*t*ly, *destruction, ruin.*
Leucaspis, -is, [Gr. Λεύκασπις], m., a Trojan.
Leucātē, -ēs (-ēs, -ae), [Gr. Λευκάτη], f., a promon*t*ory at the sou*t*h ex*t*remi*t*y of Leucadia, off the western coas*t* of Acarnania.
levāmen, -inis, [†leva- (of levŏ) + men], n., *means of relief, solace, comfort, relief.*
lēvātus, -a, -um, p.p. *polished.*
levis, -e, [†leg + u (with added i), cf. ἐλαχύς], adj., *light, slight, swift, agile, rapid.* — Fig., *slight, trivial, of little weight, unimportant.* — Also, *gentle, mild.*
lēvis, -e, [unc. root + vis (cf. Gr. λεῖος)], adj., *smooth, polished.*
levŏ, -āvī, -ātum, -āre, [†levi- (as if levŏ-)], 1. v. a., *lighten, lift up, lift, raise.* — Less exac*t*ly and fig., *lighten, relieve, alleviate.* — Wi*t*h change of poin*t* of view, *relieve of, assist, free, rescue, disburden :* **terras invisum numen** (*relieve of its presence*).
lēx, lēgis, [prob. √leg (of legŏ) as s*t*em, cf. **legunt iura magistratusque**], f., *a law* (written, cf. **ius,** *prescriptive right*), *a statute, a decree, an ordinance.*— Less exac*t*ly, *a term, a condition, terms of peace, a bond, an institution :* **leges et foedera** (*conditions of a treaty*).
lībāmen, -inis, [†libā- (cf. **libo**) + men], n., *a libation, a first sacrifice, an offering.*
lībātus, -a, -um, p.p. of **libo.**
libēns, see **libeo.**
libeō (lub-), libuī (libitum est), libitum, libēre, [√lib (lub), cf. English *love*], 2. v. n., *be pleasing, please.* — Esp. impers., *it pleases, is one's pleasure.*—**libēns, -entis,**

Vocabulary.

p. as adj., *willing, ready, with a free will, gladly.*
liber, -brī, [?], m., *bark.*
1. **liber, -era, -erum,** [prob. √lub (through stem) + rus], adj., *free, unrestrained, in one's power, untamed.*
2. **Līber, -erī,** [?], m., an Italian divinity identified with Bacchus.
līberē [abl. of **liber**], adv., *freely, generously, of one's own accord.*
lībertās, -ātis, [†liberō- (reduced) + tas], f., *liberty, freedom, permission.*
libet, see **libeo.**
Lībēthris, -idis, [Gr. Λειβηθρίς], f. adj., *of Libethra* (a fountain in Macedonia, a favorite haunt of the Muses).
lībō, -āvī, -ātum, -āre, [†libŏ- (cf. λοιβή, **libum,** and also λείβω)], 1. v. a., *pour* (a libation), *make a libation.* — As the libation was the beginning of drinking, *drink, quaff.* — Also, *sip, taste:* **oscula** (*gently kiss*). — With change of point of view: **pateris altaria** (*sprinkle with a libation*). — Less exactly, *offer, sacrifice.*
libra, -ae, [?], f., *a balance.* — Esp., *Libra* (the constellation).
lībrō, -āvī, -ātum, -āre, [†librā-], 1. v. a., *balance, poise.* — Also, *swing, brandish;* — hence, *hurl, cast, throw, fling.*
libum, -ī, [√lib (cf. **libo,** Gr. λείβω)], n., *a cake* (of a peculiar kind used in sacrifice).
Liburnus, -a, -um, [?], adj., *of the Liburni* (a nation of Illyria, on the eastern side of the Adriatic), *Liburnian.* — Plur., *the Liburni* (the people themselves).
Libya, -ae, [Gr. Λιβύη], f., *a region of Africa.*
Libycus, -a, -um, [†Libya- (reduced) + cus], adj., *Libyan, of Libya.* — Less exactly, *African.*
Libystis, -idis, [Gr. Λιβυστίς], f. adj., *Libyan, of Libya.* — Less exactly, *African.*
licenter [†licent- (p. of **liceo**) + ter (n. of **terus,** reduced)], adv., *freely, with freedom.*
liceō, licuī (licitum est), licitum, licēre, [√lic (akin to **linquo?**) through adj. stem, cf. **reliquus** and Eng. "*leave*"], 2. v. n., *be allowed, be permitted.* — Esp. impers., *it is allowed, it is permitted, it is granted, it is lawful, it is possible, one may.* — **licet,** *although* (cf. Eng. "*may*"), *though.*
— **licitus, -a, -um,** p.p., *conceded, lawful, permitted, allowable.*
Lichas, -ae, [Gr. Λίχας], m., a Latin.
licitus, -a, -um, p.p. of **liceo**
licium, -ī (-iī), [cf. **bilix**], n., *a leash* (a string attached to each thread of the warp to draw it back and forth, making what is called "the harness"). — *a thread.*
Licymnia, -ae, [?], f., a slave.
Lĭgēa, -ae, [Gr. Λιγεία], f., a wood-nymph.
Liger, †-eris, [?], m., a Rutulian.
lignum, -ī, [?], n., *wood, timber.* — Less exactly, *a trunk* (of a tree), *a stock, a stump.* [*fasten.*
ligō, -āvī, -ātum, -āre, 1. v. a., *bind,*
Ligur (-us), -uris, [?], adj., *Ligurian.* — Sing., *a Ligurian.* — Pl., *the Ligurians* (a people of Cisalpine Gaul, about modern Genoa and the neighborhood).
ligustrum, -ī, [?], n., *privet.*
lilium, -ī (-iī), [Gr. λείριον], n., *a lily.*
Lilybaeus, -a, -um, [Gr. Λιλύβαιον], adj., *of Lilybæum* (a promontory on the southern coast of Sicily).
limbus, -ī, [poss. akin to **libo,** from the resemblance to drops?], m., *a fringe, a border.*
limen, -inis, [unc. root (in **limus** and **limes**) + men], n., (*the crosspiece?*), *a lintel, a threshold.* — More generally, *a house, a palace, a temple, a chamber, a home, a habitation, an abode.* — Less exactly, *an entrance, a passage-way, a door, a gate.* — Fig., *the border* (of a

country), *the starting-post* (of a race), *the beginning, threshold:* in limine (*close at hand*).

līmes, -itis, [prob. akin to **līmus** and **līnen**], m., *a cross-path, a boundary* (in form of a path), *a limit*. — Less exactly, *a path, a by-way, a passage, a road*. — Fig., *a track* (of a meteor, &c.), *a path:* limitem agit ferro (*hews a path*).

līmōsus, -a, -um, [†līmō- (reduced) +osus], adj., *muddy, miry, swampy*.

līmus, -ī, [√li + mus], m., *mud, slime, clay, soil*.

līmus, -ī, [?], m., *a girdle* (of thread, a peculiar sort worn by priests). Others read **līnum**.

lingua, -ae, [√ling (cf. Gr. λείχω) + a], f., *a tongue* (of men and animals). — Fig., *language, tongue, note, voice*.

linō, lēvī, litum, linere, [√li], 3. v. a., *besmear, anoint, daub*. — Less exactly, *spatter, spot*.

linquō, līquī, lictum, linquere, [√lic (-qu), cf. Gr. λείπω], 3. v. a., *leave, abandon, forsake, quit:* animas (*lose*); habenas (*let go*); alitibus feris (*expose*). — Fig., *cease, leave off, desist from*.

linter, -tris, [?], f., *a boat, a skiff, a canoe*.

linteum, -ī, [†linō- (through stem in -to)], n., *canvas, a sail*.

līnum, -ī, [perh. Gr. λίνον], n., *flax*. — Less exactly, *a thread, a line, a net, linen, linen cloth*.

Līnus, -ī, [Gr. Λίνος], m., a famous musician, instructor of Orpheus and Hercules.

Liparē, -ēs, [Gr. Λιπάρη], f., *Lipara*, one of the Æolian islands (now *Lipari*).

liquefaciō, -fēcī, -factum, facere, [case-form of †liquŏ- (or stem, cf. **liquidus**) -facio], 3. v. a., *melt, dissolve, liquefy*. — Esp., *putrefy*.

liquefactus, -a, -um, p.p. of **liquefacio**.

liquēns, -entis, p. of **liqueo**.

liquens, -entis, p. of **liquor**.

liqueō, liquī, no sup., **liquēre**, [†liquŏ-], 2. v. n., *flow, be clear, be limpid*. — **liquēns, -entis**, p., *clear, liquid, limpid*.

liquescō, licuī, no sup., **liquēscere**, [†liquē- (cf. **liqueo**, fr. †liquus, cf. **liquidus**) + sco], 3. v. n., *begin to melt, soften, be smelted*.

liquidus, -a, -um, [†liquŏ- (√li + cus, cf. **liqueo, liquefacio**) + dus], adj., *liquid, flowing, clear, pure, limpid*. — Less exactly, *pure, clear, serene:* nox; nubes; iter (*liquid*, as in Eng.); voces; aestas; odor; nox; electrum.

liquor, no perf., **-ī**, [†liquŏ- (cf. **liquidus**) as verb-stem], 3. v. n., *dissolve, flow, liquefy, flow with, be bathed*.

liquor, -ōris, [†liquŏ- (cf. **liquidus**, reduced) as root + or], m., *fluid, water, moisture, humor* (of the body).

Līris, -is, [?], the river dividing Latium and Campania (now *Sarigliano*).

līs, lītis, [for stlis (unc. root + tis,) cf. Eng. *strife*], f., *strife, a dispute, a contest, rivalry*.

litātus, -a, -um, p.p. of **lito**.

litō, -āvī, -ātum, -āre, [?], 1. v. a. and n., *sacrifice* (with favorable omens), *appease an offended divinity* (by sacrifice). — Act., *offer successfully, perform acceptably*.

litoreus (litt-), -a, -um, [†litor + eus], adj., *of the shore, of the beach*.

littus, etc.; see **lītus**, etc.

litus, -a, -um, p.p. of **lino**.

lītus (litt-), -oris, [unc. root + us], n., *the shore, a beach, the strand, the coast, a bank* (of a river).

lituus, -ī, [?], m., *a staff* (curved at the end, used in augury). — From the shape, *a trumpet, a horn*.

līveō, no perf., no sup., **-ēre**, [†līvo- (cf. **līvidus**)], 2. v. n., *be blue* or *lead color*. — **līvēns, -entis**, p. as adj., *blue, black and blue, lead-colored*.

līvidus, -a, -um, [†līvŏ- (cf. lī-

veo) + dus], adj., *dark blue, livid, dusky, leaden* (lead-colored).

locŏ, -āvī, -ātum, -are, [†locŏ-], 1. v. a., *place, put, set, set up, build, fix, station, settle, dispose:* in partem caeli (*give a share in, give a place in*).

Locrī, -ōrum, [Gr. Λόκροι], m. plur., a race of Greece who settled in Southern Italy.

locus, -ī, [orig. stlocus, remotely akin to √sta], m. (also n. in plur.), *a place, space, room, a region, a site, a situation, a position, a spot* (of ground), *a tract.* — Fig., *condition, situation, state.* — Esp.: dare locum (*give way, make way*); loco cedere (*give way, decline*); loco movere (*dislodge*); hic tibi Fortunaeque locus (*chance, opportunity*).

locūtus, -a, -um, p.p. of loquor.

lolium, -ī (-iī), [?], n., *darnel, cockle, tares* (or some similar weed infesting grain).

longaevus, -a, -um, [†longŏ-aevŏ- (declined as adj.)], adj., *of great age, aged, in one's old age.*

longē [abl. of longus], adv., *afar, far off, at a distance, far away.* — Also, *from afar, from a distance.* — Of degree, *by far, far.* — Of time, *long, at great length.*

longinquus, -a, -um, [stem akin to longus + cus, cf. propinquus], adj., *distant, remote, far off.* — Of time, *ancient, long-continued.* — Neut., *a distant land, a distant region.*

longus, -a, -um, [akin to largus and Gr. δολιχός], adj., *long, spacious, wide, extensive, extended, extending, prolonged, distant.* — Of time, *long, continued, long-continued, lingering.* — Neut. as adv., *far, long, a long time.*

loquāx, -ācis, [√loqu + ax, as if †loquā + cus (reduced)], adj., *talkative, loquacious, garrulous.* — Less exactly, *noisy, chattering, croaking.*

loquēla (-ella), -ae, [√loqu +ela, as if †loquē + la (f. of -lus)], f., *speech, discourse, words* (in plur.).

loquor, locūtus, loquī, [√loqu, of unc. kindred], 3. v. dep., *speak* (in any form of utterance).

lōrīca, -ae, [†lorŏ- (reduced, or a kindred stem in i) + īca (f. of icus)], f., (perh. orig. a cuirass of leather straps), *a coat of mail, a cuirass.*

lōrum, -ī, [?], n., *a thong, a strap, a rein, a bridle.*

lōtus (-os), -ī, [Gr. λωτός], f.: 1. Name of a fruit-tree; 2. Name of a kind of water-lily.

lūbricus, -a, -um, [?, stem akin to luo + cus], adj., *slippery, slimy.* — Fig., *deceitful, tricky, false.* — Neut. plur. lubrica, *slippery ground.*

Lūcagus, -ī, [?], m., a Rutulian.

lūceō, lūxī, no sup., **lūcēre,** [†lucŏ- (cf. noctiluca)], 2. v. n., *shine, gleam, be bright.* — Less exactly, *be resplendent, be splendid.* — Fig., *appear, show itself.* — **lūcēns, -entis,** p. as adj., *bright, splendid, brilliant.*

lūcesco, no perf., no sup., **-escere,** [†lūcē- (of luceo) + sco], 3. v. n., *clear up, shine out, shine.*

Lūcetius, -ī (-iī), [akin to luceo], m., a Rutulian.

lūcidus, -a, -um, [†lucŏ- (cf. luceo) + dus], adj., *bright, shining, brilliant, glittering, radiant.*

Lūcifer, -era, -erum, [†luc- (as if luci) -fer (√fer+us)], adj., *light-bringing.* — Masc. as subst., *the morning star.*

lūcifugus, -a, -um, [†luc- (as if luci) -fugus (√fug + us)], adj., *light-shunning, avoiding the light.*

Lucīna, -ae, [†luc + inus (as if †luci + na, f. of nus)], f., a name of Diana, applied also to Juno, as protectress of child-bearing women. — Also, *bearing* (as Ceres, *grain*), *breeding.*

Lucrīnus, -a, -um, [Gr. Λοκρῖνος], adj., *Lucrine.* — Masc. (sc. lacus), *the Lucrine Lake* (the north-west

end of the Gulf of Pozzuoli, anciently cut off by a dam and made a kind of inland sea).
luctāmen, -inis, [†luctā- (stem of luctor) + men], n., *struggling, wrestling, toil.*
lūctificus, -a, -um, [†luctu- (weakened) -ficus ($\sqrt{}$fac + us)], adj., *grief-bringing, bringer of grief.*
luctor, -ātus, -ārī, [lost noun-stem], 1. v. dep., *struggle, wrestle, strive.*
lūctus, -ūs, [$\sqrt{}$lug+tus, cf. lugeo], m., *grief, sorrow, mourning, distress; wailing, mournful complaint.* — Personified, *Grief.*
lūcus, -ī, [prob. $\sqrt{}$luc (cf. luceo) + us (orig. opposed to thick, dark woods)], m., *a sacred grove.* — Less exactly, *a wood, a thicket.*
lūdibrium, -ī (-iī), [†ludibri- (reduced, cf. **lugubris, Mulciber**) + ium], n., *sport.* — Concretely (of things), *the sport* (as, of the winds).
lūdicer, -cra, -crum, [as if (perh. really) †ludico- (reduced) + rus, cf. **volucris, sepulcrum**], adj., *sportive, in sport, trifling:* praemia (of sportive games).
lūdō, lūsī, lūsum, lūdere, [$\sqrt{}$lud, unc. kindred], 3. v. a. and n., *play, sport, frolic, do in sport:* carmina (*sing in sport*); coloni versibus; in sicco fulicae; iubae per colla; Aeneas parvulus in aula; calamo. — Also, *mock, deceive, delude, cheat, trick:* vana spem amantem.
lūdus, -ī, [$\sqrt{}$lud + us], m., *sport, play, a game, a pastime.* — Esp., *a play* (on the stage), *a festival game.* — Plur., *games* (a set festival), *sports.*
luēs, -is, [?], f., *a plague, a pestilence, a blight.* — Also, *a pest, a bane.*
lūgeō, lūxī, lūctum, lūgēre, [?, cf. Gr. λυγρός, ὀλολύζω], 2. v. n. and a., *mourn, lament.* — Esp.: Lugentes Campi, *the Fields of Mourning.*
lūgubris, -e, [†luge- (or kindred stem) + bris (cf. **ludibrium**)], adj., *mournful.* — Less exactly, *ominously* (boding grief)
lumbus, -ī, [?], m., *the loin.*
lūmen, -inis, [$\sqrt{}$luc + men], n., *light, a glare.* — Esp., *the light of life.* — Also, *a lamp.* — Transferred, *the eye.* — Phrases: lumina ducum, *bright stars;* caeli spirabile lumen, *light and air.*
lūna, -ae, [$\sqrt{}$luc + na (f. of nus)], f., *the moon,* — *moonlight.* — Personified, *Luna, Diana.* — Also, *a lunation, a moon.*
lūnātus, -a, -um, [p.p. of luno], adj., *half-moon shaped, crescent-shaped.*
1. **luō, -uī, -uitum (-ūtum), -uere,** [akin to lavo], 3. v. a., *wash.* — Fig., *wash out, atone for, expiate.*
2. **luō, -uī, -uitum (-ūtum), -uere,** [cf. λύω, solvo], 3. v. a., *pay, pay for.* — Also, *undergo.*
lupa, -ae, [f. of **lupus**], f., *a she-wolf.*
lupātus, -a, -um, [†lupā + tus, cf. auratus], adj., *set with wolf's teeth.* — Neut. plur. (sc. **frena**), *a curb bit, a curb.*
Lupercal, -ālis, [†Lupercŏ- (reduced) + alis], n. of adj., *Lupercālis, a grotto sacred to Lupercus.*
Lupercus, -ī, [†lupŏ-arcus (cf. arceo)], m., usually plur., *priests of Pan, the Luperci.*
lupīnus (-um), -ī, [?], m., *a lupine* (a kind of pulse).
lupus, -ī, [?, cf. Gr. λύκος], m., *a wolf.*
lūstrālis, -e, [†lustrŏ- (reduced) + alis, cf. also **lustrō**], adj., *expiatory.*
lūstrō, -āvī, -ātum, -āre, [†lustrŏ-], 1. v. a., *purify* (by lustration), *sprinkle* (with holy water). — Pass., *purify one's self, sacrifice for expiation.* — From the process of lustration, *traverse, pass over, pass around, encircle, rove over, pass through, sail over.* — Also, *examine, search, reconnoitre, track, trace, observe, survey, review.* — Of the sun, &c., *encompass, encircle, illuminate.*

lūstrum, -ī, [stem from √lu, *wash,* + trum], n.: 1. *A purification.* — From the periodic purification at Rome, *a lustre* (period of five years). — Less exactly (in plur.), *years, time;* 2. Prob. a different word, *a bog, a den, a forest.*
lūteolus, -a, -um, [†luteŏ+lus], adj., *yellowish, yellow.*
lūteus, -a, -um, [†lutŏ- (reduced) +eus], adj., *saffron-colored, yellow.*
lūtum, -ī, [?], n., *weld* (a yellow plant used in dyeing).
lūx, lūcis, [√luc (increased) as stem], f., *light, splendor, daylight, sunlight, dawn, morning, daybreak*—Also, *a day;*—*the light of life, life;*—*light* (solace, stay). — Also, *the upper light, the upper world.*
luxuria (-iēs), -ae (-ēī), [†luxurŏ or i (†luxu + rus or ris], f., *rankness, luxuriance* (of growth).
luxuriŏ, -āvī, -ātum, -āre, [†luxuria-], 1. v. n., *frisk, wanton, prance.* — Also, *be rank, luxuriate, swell, be full.*
luxus, -ūs, [poss. akin to Gr. λοξός], m., *luxury, debauchery, dalliance, wantonness.*—Also, *splendor, pomp, magnificence.*
Lyaeus, -ī, [Gr. Λυαῖος], m., a name of Bacchus.
Lyaeus, -a, -um, [same word as last], adj., *of Bacchus.*
Lycaeus, -a, -um, [Gr. Λυκαῖος], adj., *Lycæan, of Mt. Lycæus* (in Arcadia, a favorite resort of Pan). — Masc., *Lycæus* (the mountain).
Lycāōn, -onis, [Gr. Λυκάων], m., a Cretan worker in metals.
Lycāonius, -a, -um, [Gr. Λυκαόνιος], adj., *son of Lycaon* (or else *Lycaonian*), *of Lycaonia:* Ericetes.
lychnus, -ī, [Gr. λυχνός], m., *a lamp.*
Lycidās, -ae, [Gr. Λυκίδας], m., a shepherd.

Lycimnia, -ae, [?], f., a Phrygian slave. See **Licymnia.**
Lycisca, -ae, [Gr. λυκισκή], f., the name of a dog.
Lycius, -a, -um, [Gr. Λύκιος], adj., *Lycian, of Lycia.* — Fem., *Lycia,* a division of Asia Minor famous for its bowmen, and in alliance with Troy. — Plur., *the Lycians* (the people).
Lycōrias, -adis, [Gr. Λυκωριάς], f., a sea-nymph.
Lycōris, -idis, [Gr. Λυκωρίς], f., a girl loved by Cornelius Gallus.
Lyctius, -a, -um, [Gr. Λύκτιος], adj., *of Lyctos* (a city of Crete), *Lyctian.* — Less exactly, *Cretan.*
Lycurgus, -ī, [Gr. Λυκοῦργος], m., a Thracian king who persecuted the worshippers of Bacchus.
Lycus, -ī, [Gr. Λύκος], m.: 1. A river of Colchis; 2. A companion of Æneas.
Lȳdius, -a, -um, [Gr. Λύδιος], adj., *Lydian, of Lydia.* — Fem., *Lydia,* the country. — Less exactly (from supposed kindred), *Tuscan, Etrurian.*
Lȳdus, -a, -um, [Gr. Λῦδος], adj., *of Lydia* (a province of Asia Minor), *Lydian.* — Pl., *the Lydians.*
lympha, -ae, [?, but cf. **limpidus**], f., (perhaps confounded with Gr. νύμφη), *water.*
lymphātus, -a, -um, p.p. of **lympho.**
lymphŏ, -āvī, -ātum, -āre, [†lymphā-, but the connection of ideas is not clear, cf. Gr. νύμφη], 1. v. a., *distract, craze, madden.*
Lynceus, -eī, [Gr. Λυγκεύς], m., a Trojan.
lynx, -ncis, [Gr. λύγξ], comm., *a lynx.*
Lyrnēsius (-essius), -a, -um, [Gr. Λυρνήσιος], adj., *of Lyrnesus, Lyrnesian.*
Lyrnēsus (-ēssus), -ī, [Gr. Λυρνησός], f., a town of Troas.

M.

macer, -cra, -crum, [√mac+rus, cf. **maceo**. The roots MAC, MAG, and MAGH are exceedingly confused, and have probably been confounded with each other in their developed forms; see **magnus, macto**], adj., *lean, thin, meagre.*

Machāōn, -onis, [Gr. Μαχάων], m., a famous surgeon and warrior of the Trojan war.

māchina, -ae, [Gr. μηχανή], f., *a machine, a derrick, an engine.*

maciēs, -ēī, [√mac (cf. **macer**) + ies], f., *leanness, emaciation, a pinched appearance.*

mactātus, -a, -um, p.p. of **macto.**

mactē [abl. of **mactus** (whence **macto**)], adv. (only with **esto** expr. or supplied), *increased, advanced:* **macte nova virtute, puer** (*a blessing on* &c., *success attend*).

mactŏ,-āvī,-ātum,-āre,[†mactŏ- (√mag + tus, cf. **magnus**), but perh. confused with √MAG and √MAGH, cf. **macer, macellum**], 1. v. a., (*magnify*). — Transferred (of the victim sacrificed, cf. **macellum**), *sacrifice, offer.* — Less exactly, *slay, kill, slaughter.*

macula, -ae, [lost stem †macŏ+ la], f., *a spot, a stain.*

maculŏ, -āvī, -ātum, -āre, [†maculā-], 1. v. a., *spot, stain, defile, sully.*

maculōsus, -a, -um, [†macula- (reduced) + osus], adj., *spotted, marked with spots.*

madefaciō, -fēcī, -factum, -facere, [†made- (cf. **madeo, madidus**)], 3. v. a., *wet, soak, stain* (of blood).

madeō, -uī, no sup., **-ēre,** [†madŏ- (cf. **madidus**), √mad, cf. μαδάω], 2. v. n., *be wet, flow, drip, be soaked.* — **madēns, -entis,** p. as adj., *wet, soaked, drenched, besmeared.*

madēscŏ, maduī, no sup., **madēscere,** [†madē- (of **madeo**) + sco], 3. v. n., *become moist, moisten.*

madidus, -a, -um, [†madŏ- (cf. **madeo**) + dus], adj., *moist, wet, dripping, soaking.*

Maeander, -drī, [Gr. Μαίανδρος], m., a river of Lydia famous for its windings.—Fig., *a winding border.*

Maecenas, -ae,[an Etruscan word], m., *C. Cilnius Mæcenas,* the great patron of Virgil and Horace, and the friend of Augustus.

Maenalius, -a, -um, [Gr. Μαινάλιος], adj., *of Mænalus, Mænalian.* — Less exactly, *Arcadian.*

Maenalus, -ī (-a, -ōrum), [ ], m. and n., a mountain of Arcadia.

Maeon, -onis, [Gr. Μαίων], m., a Rutulian.

Maeonidēs, -ae, [Gr. Μαιονίδης], m., *of Mæonia* (a part of Lydia), *a Mæonian.* — Less exactly (cf. **Lydius**), *an Etrurian.*

Maeonius, -a, -um, [Gr. Μαιόνιος], adj., *Mæonian.* — Less exactly, *Lydian.* — Fem. (cf. Gr. Μαιονία), *Mæonia, Lydia.*

Maeōtius, -a, -um, [Gr. Μαιώτιος], adj., *of the Mæotæ* (a people of Scythia), *Mæotian.*

maereo, no perf., no sup., **-ēre,** [√mis (cf. **miser**) through adj. stem], 2. v. n., *be sad, mourn, lament.*

maestus, -a, -um, [root of **maereo** and **miser** + tus, p.p.], adj., *sad, mournful, sorrowful, anxious.* — Also, *gloomy, stern* (cf. **tristis**).— Also, *sorrowful* (causing sorrow).

Maevius, -ī (-iī), [?], m., a poetaster, an enemy of Virgil.

māgālia,-ium,[a Phœnician word], n. plur., *huts.*

mage (reduced form of **magis**), see **magis.**

magicus, -a, -um, [Gr. μαγικός], adj., *magic.*

magis (-e), [√mag (cf. **magnus**) + ius (syncopated), a comparative neut.], adv., *more, rather.*

magister, -trī, [magis (for magius) + ter (for -terus, cf. Gr. -τερος)], m., *a chief, a leader, an overseer, a herdsman, a master, a keeper, a captain, a steersman, a pilot.* — Esp., *a master, a teacher.*

magistra, -ae, [f. of **magister**], f., *a mistress.* — Of things, as adj., *of a master, masterly:* ars.

magistrātus, -ūs, [†magistrā- (as if of magistro, fr. **magister**) + tus], m., *office, a magistracy.* — Concretely, *a magistrate.*

magnanimus, -a, -um, [†magnŏanimus, declined as adj.], adj., *great-souled, generous, noble-minded.* — Of animals, *high-spirited, spirited.* — Poetically, of bees: **magnanimi duces** (*spirited leaders,* preserving the figure).

magnus, -a, -um, [√mag (cf. **macte** and Gr. μέγας) + nus (cf. **plenus**)], comp. **māior** [√mag + ior], superl. **maximus** [√mag + timus, cf. **finitimus**], adj., (*increased*), *great* (in almost all Eng. senses), *large, spacious, vast, huge, mighty, high, lofty.* — Less exact and fig. uses, of degree and the like, *great, loud, powerful, mighty, fearful, rich, immense, intense, ardent, distinguished, serious, important, portentous, long, powerful, weighty, dire.* — **magno,** *at a great price.* — **magnum,** as adv., *greatly, loudly:* magnum fluens Nilus (*mighty river*). — **māior,** *older, more ancient, ancestors* (pl.). — **māiora,** n. plur. as subst., *nobler deeds, more important matters, worse sufferings.* — **maximus,** *oldest, eldest.* — Masc., **Maximus,** a name of several Roman families, esp. *Q. Fabius Maximus,* a hero of the second Punic war.

Magus, -ī, [?], m., *a Rutulian.*

Māia, -ae, [Gr. Μαῖα], f.: 1. The mother of Mercury, daughter of Atlas; 2. The same person as one of the Pleiades.

māiestās, -ātis, [†maius (see **mag-**nus) + tas], f., *dignity, honor, grandeur.*

māior, māiores; see **magnus.**

māla, -ae, [? for **maxilla,** cf. **ala**], f., *the cheek-bone, the jaw.* — Less exactly, *the cheek.*

male [abl. of **malus**], adv., *badly, ill, not very, not well, not much:* male temperat (*little spares*); male defendet (*insufficiently*); male erratur (*it is not very safe to wander*); male fidus (*untrustworthy*); male sanus (*distracted*); male pinguis (*too solid*).

Malea (-ēa), -ae, [Gr. Μαλέα (-λεια)], f., a dangerous headland at the south-eastern extremity of Peloponnesus.

malesuādus, -a, -um, [male-suadus (cf. **suadeo**)], adj., *tempting to ill.*

mālifer, -era, -erum, [†mālŏ-fer (√fer + us)], adj., *apple-bearing.*

malignus, -a, -um, [†malŏ-†genus], adj., *spiteful, ill-disposed, malicious, envious.* — Fig. (from idea of grudging?): colles (*stubborn,* of soil); aditus (*narrow*); lux (*scanty*).

mālō, maluī, no sup., **mālle,** [mage-volo], irr. v. a., *wish more, choose rather, choose, prefer, would rather, wish rather.*

mālum, -ī, [Gr. μῆλον], n., *an apple;* — *a quince, a citron.*

malus, -a, -um, [?, akin to μέλας], comp. **peior** [?], superl. **pessimus** [cf. **pessum**], adj., *bad, evil.* — Of moral qualities, *evil, wicked, vicious, bad, spiteful:* lingua (referring to enchantment); falx (transferred from the owner). — Of things, *bad, injurious, troublesome, pernicious, fatal, noxious, poisonous.* — Masc., *a wicked person.* — Plur., *the wicked.* — Neut., *an evil, a disaster, a misfortune, mischief, a pest, a plague, a poison, venom, adversity, misery, hardship, disaster.*

1. **mālus, -ī,** [prob. same word as **mālum**], m., *a mast.*

2. **mālus, -ī,** [cf. 1. malus], f., *an apple-tree.*

mamma, -ae, [?], f., *the breast, a breast, the dugs* (of an animal).

mandātus, -a, -um, p.p. of mando.

mandō, -āvī, -ātum, -āre, [†manu- and do, but through adj. stem, †mandŏ-?], 1. v. a., *entrust, command, order, enjoin.* — Less exactly, *consign, commit:* foliis carmina; hordea sulcis; terrae corpora; humo solita (*inter*). — **mandātum, -ī,** p.p. neut., *a command, an injunction, an order, an instruction.*

mandō, mandī, mānsum, mandere, [?], 3. v. a., *chew, champ:* pecus (*devour*); humum ("*bite the dust*").

māne [prob. loc. of †mani (√ma + ni, cf. maturus, Matuta)], adv., *in the morning, early.* — As subst., *the morning, the dawn.*

maneō, mānsī, mānsum, manēre, [√man (cf. Gr. μένω), through adj. stem?, perh. akin to memini, mens], 2. v. a. and n., *remain, continue, linger, await, abide, remain unchanged.* — Also, *abide by, stand by.* — Act., *await, wait for.*

mānēs, -ium, [?, cf. obs. manus, *good*], m. plur., *the gods below* (spirits of the departed), *the blessed dead.* — Hence, *the lower world, the regions below.* — Also, *the spirits of the departed, a ghost, a shade, a spirit.* — Esp.: quisque suos patimur manes, *destiny in the world below* (considered as a state of each departed spirit).

manica, -ae, [†manu- (weakened) + ca (f. of cus)], f., *a sleeve* (coming down to the hands). — Plur., *manacles, chains.*

manifestē [abl. of manifestus], adv., *clearly, manifestly, obviously, plainly.*

manifestus, -a, -um, [†manu- (weakened) -festus (p.p. of fendo)], adj., (*struck* or *seized with the hand,* hence *caught in the act,* of crime, as opposed to circumstantial evidence). — Fig., *clear, plain, evident, obvious, made plain, clearly visible.*

maniplus (-pulus), -ī, [†manu- (weakened) -plus (akin to **pleo**)], m., *a handful.* — Esp., *a handful of straw.* — Hence, *a company* (with a handful of straw for a standard), *a troop, a band.*

Manlius, -ī (-iī), [?], m., a Roman gentile name. — Esp., *M. Manlius Capitolinus,* who saved the Capitol from the Gauls.

mānō, -āvī, -ātum, -āre, [?, but cf. madeo], 1. v. n., *flow, run, drip.*

mansuēscō, -suēvī, -suētum, -suēscere, [†manu- (reduced) suesco, *become wonted to the hand*], 3. v. n., *become tame.* — Less exactly, *be subdued* (by cultivation), *be improved.* — Fig., *soften, become gentle, become mild.*

mantēle (-ile), -is, [†mantŏ- (or other form in t, akin to manus) + lis, n. of adj.], n., *a towel, a napkin.*

Mantō, -ūs, [Gr. Μαντώ], f., an Italian nymph, supposed to have founded Mantua.

Mantua, -ae, [?], f., a city of Gallia Transpadana, near Virgil's birthplace.

manus, -ūs, [?], f., *a hand.* — Also fig. in many senses, as in English, *might, force, violence, force of arms, deeds of might, valor, bearing in arms.* — *art, skill, effort, labor.* — Corresponding to English *arms:* inter manus (*in one's grasp*); effugit imago (*grasp*); pacem orare manu (*call for peace with uplifted hands*). — Also (cf. **maniplus**), *a band, a company, a troop.* — Phrases: manus committere Teucris, *join battle* &c.; manus ferre, *enter on a work,* also, *raise the hands* (in boxing); conferre manum (manus), *join battle;* impono extremam manum, *the last hand, the finishing-*

touch; manus dare, *surrender;* in manibus, *in one's possession, in one's power, at hand;* inter manus, *in one's grasp;* medica manus, *the healing hand* (skill); larga manus, *a generous hand* (*generosity*); manus artificum, *handiwork.*

mapalia, -ium, [said to be Phœnician], n. plur., *huts, cottages.*

Marcellus, -i, [†marculo- (†marcŏ-, *hammer,* + lus) + lus, second dim. of Marcus], m., a family name in the Claudian gens. — Esp., *M. Claudius Marcellus,* who conquered the Gauls, Germans, and Insubrians, slew Viridomarus, the German king, with his own hand, gaining the technical *spolia opima,* and took Milan. He afterwards was successful against Hannibal, and captured Syracuse. — Also, *M. Marcellus,* the nephew of Augustus, who died young.

mare, -is, [?], n., *a sea, the sea, the waves.*

Mareōtis, -idis, [Gr. adj. from Μαρεία], f. adj., *of Mareotis* (or *Marea*), (a lake and city of Egypt famous for excellent wine), *Mareotic.*

Marica, -ae, [?], f., an Italian nymph, wife of Faunus, and mother of King Latinus.

marīnus, -a, -um, [†mari- (lengthened) + nus], adj., *of the sea, sea-, marine, of the deep:* casus; canes.

marītus, -ī, [stem akin to mas + tus], m., (prob. *masculine*), *a married man, a husband, a bridegroom, a lord* (of women in slavery). — Less exactly, *a suitor.* — Of animals, *a mate, a he-goat, a stallion:* pecori (*lord,* of the male of a flock).

Marius, -ī (-iī), [prob. †mas + ius], m., the name of a humble Roman family. — Esp., C. *Marius,* the conqueror of the Cimbri and Jugurtha, and opponent of Sulla in the civil war. — Plur., *Marii,* men of Marius' stamp.

marmor, -oris, [unc. root redupl.], n., *marble.* — Fig., *the sea.*

marmoreus, -a, -um, [†marmor + eus], adj., *of marble.* — Fig., *smooth, marble* (of the sea, also of a man's neck).

Marpēsius (-ēssius), -a, -um, [Gr. Μαρπήσσιος], adj., *of Marpesus* (a mountain of Paros), *Marpesian.* — Less exactly, *Parian.*

Marruvius (-bius), -a, -um, [?], adj., *of Marruvium* (a city of Latium, capital of the Marcian territory), *Marruvian.* — Neut., *Marruvium* (the city itself).

Mars, Martis, [prob. contracted fr. Mavors], m., *the Latin god of war.* — Fig., *war, battle, conflict, warfare.* — Phrases: adverso Marte, *defeat, unsuccessful conflict;* secundo Marte, *success, prosperous issue;* aequo Marte, *undecided combat;* praesenti Marte, *with threats of immediate war.*

Marsus, -a, -um, [?], adj., *of the Marsi* (a Sabellian mountain race of Italy, famed for magic rites), *Marsian.* — Plur., *the Marsi* (the nation itself).

Martius, -a, -um, [†Mart + ius], adj., *of Mars, of war, martial, warlike:* lupus (*sacred to Mars*).

mās, maris, [?], m., *a male.*

masculus, -a, -um, [†mas+culus], adj., *male:* tura (*coarse, large grains of*).

massa, -ae, [√mag + ya, cf. Gr. μάζα], f., *a mass* (orig. of dough), *a lump.*

Massicus, -a, -um, [?], adj., *of Mt. Massicus* (a mountain on the borders of Latium and Campania, famous for its wine), *Massic.* Masc. (with or without mons), *the mountain itself.* — Neut. plur., *the Massic land, the soil of Mt. Massicus.* — Also, *Massicus,* name of a king of Clusium.

Massȳlus, -a, -um, [Gr. Μασσύλιος], adj., *of the Massylii* (a nation of northern Africa), *Massylian.* — Masc. pl., the nation itself.

māter, -tris, [?, √ma + ter (cf. pater)], f., *a mother, a matron.* — Less exactly, as an appellative of gods and as a term of respect, *mother, venerable dame, lady.* — Also, *a dam, a breeding animal.* — Of plants, *the parent, the mother.* — Also of a country as the parent of her children.

māteriēs, -ēī, [†mater- (unsyncopated) + ies], f., *stuff, material.* — Esp., *timber.*

māternus, -a, -um, [†mater- (unsyncopated) + nus], adj., *of a (one's) mother, maternal.*

mātrōna, -ae, [†matro- (akin to mater, cf. aegrotus) + na, cf. patronus], f., *a matron, a dame, a woman* (married).

mātūrŏ, -āvī, -ātum, -āre, [†maturŏ-], 1. v. a., *hasten.* — Esp., *hasten to prepare.*

mātūrus, -a, -um, [†matu- (akin to mane, cf. Matuta) + rus], adj., *early.* — Also, by some uncertain connection, *ripe, mature, full-grown.* — Transferred: *soles (at their height).*

mātūtīnus, -a, -um, [†Matuta- (reduced, or stem akin) + inus], adj., *early, morning:* Aeneas (*early in the morning*).

Maurūsius, -a, -um, [Gr. Μαυρούσιος], adj., *of the Mauri* (a race of northern Africa), *Moorish.* — Less exactly, *African, of Africa.*

Māvors, -ortis, [?, cf. **Mars**], m., *Mars.* — Also, *war, conflict, fighting, deeds of arms.*

Māvortius, -a, -um, [†Mavort + ius], adj., *of Mars, martial, of war, warlike, son of Mars, sacred to Mars.*

maximus, see **magnus.**

me, see **ego.**

meātus, -ūs, [†meā- (of meo) + tus], m., *a movement, a revolution:* caeli (*courses of the heavenly bodies*).

medeor, -ērī, (only pres. stem), [†medŏ- (√med + us, cf. medicus, remedium)], 2. v. dep., *treat* (medically), *heal, cure:* medendi usus (*the healing art*); medendo aegrescere (*by treatment*).

Mēdia, -ae, [†Medŏ- (reduced) + ius, prop. adj.], f., *a country of Asia south of the Caspian, used loosely for the whole region thereabout.*

medicātus, -a, -um, p.p. of **medico.**

medicīna, -ae, [†medicŏ-(reduced) + ina, prop. adj. (sc. ars ?)], f., *medicine, the art of healing.* — Also, *remedy, cure.*

medicŏ, -āvī, -ātum, -āre, [†medicŏ-], 1. v. a., *medicate, give (medicinal) virtue to, prepare with drugs, steep* (of seeds). — Pass. as dep., *treat, cure, heal.* — **medicātus, -a, -um,** p.p. as adj., *prepared* (with drugs), *scented, medicated.*

Mēdicus, -a, -um, [Gr. Μηδικός], adj., *Median.* — Fem., (sc. **herba,** cf. μηδική), *clover, lucerne* (introduced into Greece by the Persians).

medicus, -a, -um, [†medŏ- (cf. medeor, remedium) + cus], adj., *healing:* manus.

meditātus, -a, -um, p.p. of **meditor.**

meditor, -tātus, -tārī, [†meditŏ- (p.p. of medeor?)], 1. v. dep., *practise, experiment, play* (on an instrument). — Also, *contrive, invent, intend, purpose, think of, premeditate.*

medius, -a, -um, [same root as modus + ius, cf. Gr. μέσος], adj., *middle, the middle of, the midst of, central, between, mid, midway between, in the centre, in the midst, in the middle, the thickest of, the depth of, the height of, the extreme of, in the thickest of, in the centre, just between, right among:* est via media nobis (*we are half way there*); vallum (*the inside of*); medio de cortice (*from the smooth bark,* opposed to regular knots); medio in conspectu (*right in one's sight*); medios cursus torquet nox (*midway in her course*); medium mare (*depths of the sea*); medius dies (*the South*); medium se offert (*a mediator*); in medio ictu (*just at the stroke*); medium per femur (*straight through*). — Neut., as subst.: in medio, *in the middle;* in medium, *for the common advantage.*

Medōn, -ontis, [Gr. Μέδων], m., a Trojan warrior or ally of the Trojans.

medulla, -ae, [akin to **medius,** cf. Gr. diminutives in -υλλον], f., *the marrow of the bones, the marrow, the inmost frame.*

Mēdus, -a, -um, [Gr. Μῆδος], adj., *Median, of the Medes.* — Less exactly, *Persian.* — Masc. plur., *the Medes, the Persians.*

Megaera, -ae, [Gr. Μέγαιρα], f., one of the Furies.

Megarus, -a, -um, [Gr. Μέγαρος, or kindred form], adj., *of Megara* (a city of Sicily, also called *Hybla*), *Megarian.*

mel, mellis, [cf. Gr. μέλι, English *mead*], n., *honey:* pabula melli (*for making honey*).

Mēla, see **Mella.**

Melampūs, -odis, [Gr. Μελάμπους], m., a famous physician and seer, who was fabled to understand the songs of birds.

Meliboeus, -ī, [Gr. Μελίβοιος], m., a shepherd.

Meliboeus, -a, -um, [Gr. Μελίβοιος], adj., *of Melibœa* (a town of Thessaly, whence came Philoctetes), *Melibœan.* — Fem., *Melibœa* (the town itself).

Melicerta (-ēs), -ae, [Gr.' Μελικέρτης], m., the son of Ino and Athamas. Being drowned with his mother, he was changed into a sea-god.

melior, see **bonus.**

melisphyllum, -ī, [Gr. μελισσόφυλλον], n., *balm* (?), *mint* (?), an aromatic herb, a favorite flower for bees. Lat. *apiastrum.*

Melitē, -ēs, [Gr. Μελίτη], f., a seanymph.

Mēlla (Mēla), -ae, [?], m., a river of Cisalpine Gaul flowing through Brescia.

membrum, -ī, [?], n., *a limb, a member, the frame, the body, the form, the person.*

meminī, -isse, (only perf. stem in sense of present), [√men, cf. **mens, reminiscor**], v. a., *remember, recollect, recall, call to mind:* quorum poetae (*mention*).—Less exactly, *think of, care for.* — With inf., *remember to, not forget, take care to.* — With negatives, *forget, neglect.*

Memmius, -ī (-iī), [?], m., a Roman gentile name.

Memnon, -onis, [Gr. Μέμνων], m., son of Aurora and king of the Ethiopians. His arms were fabled to have been made by Vulcan at the request of Aurora.

memor, -oris, [prob. √SMAR (reduplicated) as stem], adj., *remembering, mindful, with a good memory, thoughtful, careful, provident, caring for:* memor esto (*remember*); ira (*unrelenting, that cannot forget*); aevum (*unforgetful*); dum memor ipse mei (*so long as I retain a remembrance of myself*); ipsae redeunt in tecta (*without fail*); memores referte (*carefully*); apud memores stat gratia (*memory remains in grateful hearts*).—With negatives, *heedless, unmindful, careless, without thought of.*

memorābilis, -e, [†memorā (of memoro) + bilis], adj., *memorable, glorious.*

memorātus, -a, -um, p.p. of **memoro.**

memorŏ, -āvī, -ātum, -āre, [†memor- (as if memorŏ-)], 1. v. a., *call to mind, tell, say, narrate, relate, speak of, tell of, mention, call.* — **memorandus, -a, -um,** ger. p. as adj., *memorable, famous, deserving of mention.* — **memorātus, -a, -um,** p.p, as adj., *renowned, much talked of.*

Menalcās, -ae, [?], m., *a shepherd.*
mendāx, -ācis, [stem akin to **menda, mendum** + **ax** (cf. **audax**), cf. also **mentior,** which has however a different stem formation], adj., *false, lying, untruthful, deceitful.*
Menelāus, -ī, [Gr. Μενελαος], m., the husband of Helen of Greece, and brother of Agamemnon.
Menestheus (Mnes-), -eī (-eos), [Gr. Μενεσθεύς], m., a Trojan, companion of Æneas.
Menoetēs, -ae, [Gr. Μενοίτης], m., a Trojan, companion of Æneas.
mēns, mentis, [√men (cf. **memini**) + **tis** (reduced)], f., *the mind* (cf. **animus,** the soul and intellect together), *the intellect, the intelligence, the memory, the senses, sense, reflection* (as an act, perh. the orig. meaning), *thought.* — Less exactly, *an idea, a mind, a purpose, a resolution.* — Often not differing from **animus,** *heart, soul, feelings, desire.*
mensa, -ae, [fem. of p.p. of **metior,** sc. **tabula**?], f., *a table.* — Less exactly, *food, banquet, feast.*
mēnsis, -is, [akin to Gr. μήν, Eng. *moon, month*], m., *a month :* **caeli** (*the phases of the moon*).
mēnstruus, -a, -um, [†mensi- (of unc. termination)], adj., *monthly.*
mentior, -ītus, -īrī, [prob. †menti- (through idea of imagination)], 4. v. a. and n., *lie, pretend falsely :* **lana colores** (*assume false colors*); **mentita tela** (*counterfeit, lying*).
mentītus, -a, -um, p.p. of **mentior.**
mentum, -ī, [√men, in **mineo** + **tum** (n. of **tus**)], n., *the chin.*
mephītis, -is, [?], f., *foul air, an exhalation.*
mercātus, -a, -um, p.p. of **mercor.**
mercēs, -ēdis, [†merce- (as if of †merceo, cf. **merx, mercenarius**) + **dus** (reduced)], f., *pay, wages, hire, reward.*—With change of point of view, *cost, price, loss.*
mercor, -ātus, -ārī, [†merc-], 1. v. dep., *buy, purchase, pay a price for :* **magno mercentur Atridae** (*pay a great price for*).
Mercurius, -ī (-iī), [stem in -ro or -ri from †merc- (reduced) + **ius**], m., *Mercury,* the god of gain among the Romans. On account of some similar attributes he was identified with the Greek Hermes, and as such regarded as the son of Jupiter and Maia, grandson of Atlas, messenger of the gods, and conductor of souls to the infernal world, in which last capacity he carried the rod twined with serpents, or caduceus, identical with the herald's staff.
mereō, -uī, -itum, -ēre, [?], 2. v. a., *earn, win, gain, deserve, deserve well* (or *ill*), *merit.* — Pass. as dep., same sense. — **meritus, -a, -um,** p.p. as adj., act., *well-deserving, useful, faithful,* — but also, *ill-deserving, offending.* — Pass., *deserved, well won, due, as one deserves, just.* — Neut., *a service, a merit, desert, a favor.*
merges, -itis, [?], f., *a sheaf.*
mergo, mersī, mersum, mergere, [√merg, cf. **mergus**], 3. v. a., *plunge, drown, overwhelm, swallow up.* — Also fig.: **me malis.**
mergus, -ī, [√merg + **us**], m., *a sea-bird, gull*(?), *cormoran*t(?).
meritō [abl. of **meritus**], adv., *deservedly, as one deserves, justly, rightly.*
meritus, -a, -um, p.p. of **mereo** and **mereor.**
Meropēs, -ae, [Gr. Μερόπη], m., a Trojan.
merops, -opis, [Gr. μέροψ], f., *"a bee-eater,"* some kind of bird that attacks bees.
mersō, -āvī, -ātum, -āre, [†mersŏ-], 1. v. a., *plunge, drown, overwhelm, wash, dip.*
mersus, -a, -um, p.p. of **mergo.**
merus, -a, -um, [?], adj., *pure, unmixed, unadulterated.*—Neut. (sc. **vinum**), *unmixed wine, pure wine.*
merx, mercis, [perh. root of **mereo**

+ cus (reduced)], f., *merchandise, wares.*

Messāpus, -i, [a foreign word, †messŏ- (akin to medius) -apus (apia akin to aqua)], m., a king of Messapia (the country forming the heel of the boot of Italy, between the Adriatic and the Gulf of Otranto).

messis, -is, [√met (in meto) + tis], f., *a harvest.* — Less exactly, *a crop, standing grain, a gathering* (of other products). — Of time, *harvest, harvest-time.*

messor, -ōris, [√met (in meto) + tor], m., *a reaper, a harvester.*

messus, -a, -um, p.p. of meto.

met [pron. √ma, cf. me], insep. intens. particle used with pronouns, *self, own.*

mēta, -ae, [akin to metior], f., *a goal, a limit, a boundary, the end:* media (*middle point*).

Metabus, -i, [?], m., a Volscian, father of Camilla.

metallum, -i, [Gr. μέταλλον], n., *a mine.* — Less exactly, *metal, ore.*

Mēthymnaeus, -a, -um, [Gr. Μηθυμναῖος], adj., *of Methymna* (a city of Lesbos famous for its wine), *Methymnian.*

mētior, mēnsus, mētīrī, [akin to modus through noun-stem], 4. v. dep., *measure:* Hesperiam iacens (of a warrior slain). — Less exactly, *traverse, pass over.*

Metiscus, -i, [?], m., the charioteer of Turnus.

Metius, see Mettus.

metō, messuī, messum, metere, [√met, prob. akin to Gr. ἀμάω, Eng. *mow*], 3. v. a., *mow, reap, cut.* — Less exactly, *gather, sip* (of bees). — Fig., of slaughter, *mow down.*

mētor, -ātus, -ārī, [†metā-], 1. v. dep., *measure, lay out, survey.*

Mettus (-tius), -i, [?], m., an Alban name. — Esp., *Mettus Fuffetius,* an Alban dictator who on account of treachery was drawn asunder by horses.

metuō, metuī, metūtum, metuere, [†metu-], 3. v. a. and n., *fear, dread, be alarmed, be afraid of;* — *be in fear, be concerned for.* — metuēns, -entis, p. as adj., *fearful, dreading, apprehensive, concerned for.*

metus, -ūs, [?], m., *fear, dread, alarm, terror, consternation;* — *awe, reverence.*—Personified, *Fear.*

meus, -a, -um, [pron. √ma + ius], poss. adj., *my, mine, my own.* — Masc. sing. and plur., *my son* (*friend, follower, countryman, subject, kindred,* &c.). — Neut., *my* (*fortune, destiny, resources,* &c.).

Mezentius, -i (-ii), [?], m., an Etruscan king, famous for his cruelty, whose subjects revolted and joined Æneas.

micō, -āvī, -ātum, -āre, [?], 1. v. n., *quiver, dart, move* (rapidly to and fro). — Also, *flash, sparkle, gleam.*

Micōn, -ōnis, [Gr. Μίκων], m., a shepherd.

migrō, -āvī, -ātum, -are, [?], 1. v. n., *move* (in a body), *migrate, depart.*

mīles, -itis, [†mile- (as root, cf. mille) + tus or tis (reduced)], comm., *a soldier.* — Collectively, *soldiery, soldiers, troops.*

Milēsius, -a, -um, [Gr. Μιλήσιος], adj., *of Miletus* (a city of Asia Minor famous for its wool), *Milesian.*

mīlitia, -ae, [†milit + ia], f., *military service, warfare.*

milium, -i (-ii), [?], n., *millet.*

mille, plur. milia, -ium, [petrified formation from √mil, cf. miles], *a thousand* (either definitely, or indefinitely as a large number).

Mimās, -antis, [Gr. Μίμας], m., a Trojan.

minae, -ārum, [√min, cf. mineo], f. plur., *threats, menaces, threatening perils.* — Poetically (perh. in orig. meaning): minae murorum, *threatening walls;* tollentem minas, *raising his angry head,* of a serpent.

mināx, -ācis, [†mina- (cf. **minor**) + cus (reduced)], adj., *threatening, menacing, ill-boding:* **arma minacis** (*of his threatening enemy*).

Mincius, -ī (-iī), [?], m., *the Mincio,* a river of Cisalpine Gaul, near Mantua, a branch of the Po.

Minerva, -ae, [?, perh. akin to **mens**], f., the Roman goddess of wisdom, partially identified with the Greek Pallas Athene. She was reckoned as the daughter of Jupiter, the patroness of all arts and sciences, especially the household arts, and the inventress of the olive. — Also (cf. **Ceres,** *grain*), *spinning, weaving.*

minimē [abl. of **minimus**], adv., *least.*

Miniō, -ōnis, [?], m., a river of Etruria.

minister, -trī, [†minus + ter, cf. **magister**], m., *a servant, an attendant.* — Esp., *an attendant priest.* — In apposition (as adj.), *aiding, abetting:* **Calchante ministro** (*by the aid of*).

ministerium, -ī (-iī), [†ministro + ium], n., *a service, an office.*

ministra, -ae, [f. of **minister**], f., *an attendant* (female).

ministrō, -āvī, -ātum, -āre, [†ministrŏ-], 1. v. a. and n., *attend, serve.* — Also, *serve, supply, afford.*

minitor, -ātus, -ārī, [†minitŏ- (as if p.p. of **minor**)], 1. v. dep., *threaten, menace.*

minium, -ī (-iī), [?], n., *cinnabar, red lead.*

Minōius, -a, -um, [Gr. Μινώιος], adj., *of Minos.*

minor, -ātus, -ārī, [†minā- (minae)], 1. v. n. and a., *threaten, menace, tower* (threateningly), *bode, portend, threaten to fall:* **mortem mihi** (*me with death,* changing the construction).

minor, see **parvus.**

Minōs, -ōis, [Gr. Μίνως], m., a king of Crete, made a judge in the world below.

Minōtaurus, -ī, [Gr. Μινώταυρος], m., *the Minotaur,* a monster, half man, half bull, killed by Theseus.

minus, see **parvus.**

minūtātim [as if acc. of †minuta- (cf. **minutus**) + tis], adv., *piecemeal, bit by bit, by degrees, gradually.*

mirābilis, -e, [†mira- (of **miror**) + bilis], adj., *wonderful, marvellous, admirable.*

mirāculum, -ī, [†mira- (**miror**) + culum, as if †miracŏ- (mira + cus) + lum], n., *a marvel, a prodigy, a wonder.*

mirātus, -a, -um, p.p. of **miror.**

miror, -ātus, -ārī, [†mirŏ-], 1. v. a. and n., *wonder, marvel.* — Act., *marvel at, wonder at, admire, see with surprise, gaze at with admiration.*

mīrus, -a, -um, [√SMI + rus, cf. μειδάω], adj., *strange, marvellous, wondrous, surprising, extraordinary.*

misceō, miscuī, mixtum (mistum), miscēre, [†miscŏ- (cf. **promiscuus**), akin to Gr. μίσγω], 2. v. a., *mingle, mix, confuse, confound, unite, blend:* **operi metum; maria caelo; vina cum sanguine; lilia rosā.** — Passive, or with reflexive, *mingle, unite, be united, be joined:* **se corpore** (of the soul of the world, *permeate, be diffused*). — Of any confusion, *disturb, confound, embroil, trouble:* **tellurem diluvio** (*overwhelm*); **agmina** (*scatter*); **se maria** (*are thrown into confusion*). — Of the effect, cause (confusedly), *raise:* **proelia** (*raise wild warfare*); **incendia** (*spread*); **inter se volnera** (*exchange*); **inania murmura** (*spread confused and meaningless murmurs*); **acies** (*form a motley line*). — **mixtus, -a, -um,** p.p., *mingled,* often with change of point of view, *mingled with, with mingled,* &c.: **laetitia mixtoque metu** (*with mingled joy and fear*); **mixto pulvere fumus**

Vocabulary. 177

(*smoke mingled with dust*).—Also (cf. third division above): **mixtae glomerantur** (of bees, *swarming*); **miscentur**(*swarm*, of bees).

Misēnus, -ī, [Gr. Μισηνος], m.: 1. The trumpeter of Æneas; 2. (sc. **mons**), *Misenum*, the promontory north of the Bay of Naples (now *Miseno*).

miser, -era, -erum, [†misĕ as root (cf. **maereo**) + **rus** (reduced)], adj., *wretched, pitiable, unfortunate, ill-fated, unhappy, distressed.* — As subst., *a wretch, unhappy man, a wretched being.* — Neut., *a pity, a wretched thing.* — In a kind of apposition, *Oh misery! Oh pitiable fate!*

miserābilis, -e, [†miserā- (stem of **miseror**) + bilis], adj., *miserable, pitiable, unhappy, deplorable, wretched, shocking, lamentable.*

miserātus, -a, -um, p.p. of **miseror.**

misereŏ, -uī, -ĭtum, -ēre, [†miserŏ-], 2. v. a. and n., *feel pity, take pity on, have compassion on.* — Impersonal (with person as object, cf. "it repenteth him"), *pity, feel compassion, commiserate :* te lapsorum (*you pity the fallen*). — Pass., as dep., in same sense.

miserēscŏ, no perf., no sup., -ere, [†miserē- (of **misereo**) + sco], 3. v. n., *pity, have compassion on, take pity on.*

miseror, -ātus, -ārī, [†miserŏ-], 1. v. dep., *pity, have compassion on, take pity on.*

missilis, -e, [†misso + lis], adj., *missile, flying.* — Neut., *a missile, a weapon* (hurled).

missus, -a, -um, p.p. of **mitto.**

missus, -ūs, [√mit (**mitto**)+tus], m., *a sending, a command.*

mistus, -a, -um, p.p. of **misceo.**

mītēscŏ, no perf., no sup., -ēscere, [†mitē- (as if stem of **miteo**, cf. **mitis**) + sco], 3. v. incept., *grow mild, soften, become gentle.*

mītĭgŏ, -āvī, -ātum, -āre, [†mitigŏ- (†miti-agus, cf. **prodigus**),

cf. **navigo**], 1. v. a., *soften, appease.*

mītis, -e, [?], adj., *mellow* (of fruit or wine), *soft, ripe.* — Also, *gentle, calm, still.*

mitra, -ae, [Gr. μίτρα], f., *a cap* (of the Phrygian form, with lappets tied under the chin).

mittŏ, mīsī, missum, mittere, [?], 3. v. a., *let go* (cf. **omitto**), *dismiss, suffer to go, omit, send* (in any direction), *despatch, consign, send forth, throw, shoot, let in, admit :* funera Teucris (*spread among*); se in foedera (*submit to*); sub leges orbem (*subject to*); signa Bootes (*give, afford*); se (*throw one's self, descend*); fulgura (*emit*); alnus missa Pado (*sent down*); sub amnem (*admit within*); animas in pericula (*risk*); sub pericula (*expose to*); certamen (*dismiss.*) — Esp. of funeral offerings: sollemnia, *offer ;* quos umbris inferias, *sacrifice.*

mixtus, -a, -um, p.p. of **misceo.**

Mnāsȳlus, -ī, [Greek], m., *a young satyr.*

Mnestheus, see **Menestheus.**

mōbilis, -e, [†movi- (in **moveo**, cf. **motus**) + bilis], adj., *free to move.* — Fig., *changeable, varying, flexible, pliable.*

mōbilitās, -tātis, [†mobili + tas], f., *freedom of motion, swiftness, rapidity of motion.*

modŏ [abl. of **modus**], adv., (*in a measure* or *minute portion*, of time or degree), *just now, lately, a little while ago.* — Of degree, *only, merely :* modo non (*all but, almost*). — Esp., with hortatory subj. or similar construction, *only, provided, so long as.* — So also with **dum, tantum,** in same sense.

modulor, -ātus, -ārī, [†modulŏ- (dim. of **modus**)], 1. v. dep., *set to measure, sing, play.*

modus, -ī, [perh. akin to **metior**, √mod (cf. **modius**) + us], m., *a measure, a note* (measured interval), *a strain, a song* (in plur.), *a limit, a bound, an end.* — Hence also, *prescribed method, manner, way, mode, fashion, form, habit, law* (of nature).

moenia, -um (-ōrum), [stem moeni- (muni-), akin to **munus**, cf. **communis**, orig. *assigned parts or tasks*, cf. the mode of building country roads], n., only pl., *walls, fortifications.*—Less exactly, *a city, a citadel.*

moereo, see **maereo**, the proper spelling.

Moeris, -is, [?], m., a farm-servant.

moerus, see **murus**.

mola, -ae, [√mol + a, cf. **molo**], f., *meal* (coarse-ground, used in sacrifices).

molāris, -is, [†mola + ris], m., (adj., *of meal*, sc. **lapis**), *a millstone.*— Less exactly, *a rock* (huge as a mill-stone).

mōlēs, -is, [?, two stems in -us and -i], f., *a mass, bulk, a heap, a weight, a mass of rocks* (or other material), *size, weight, a massive structure, a massive pile, a huge frame, a burden, massy waves, mass* (array of men). — Esp., *a wall, a dyke, a mole.*—Fig., *trouble, labor, toil.*

mōlior, -ītus, -īrī, [†moli- (cf. **moles**)], 4. v. dep., *pile up, heap, build* (with toil or difficulty), *frame, construct:* **fugam** (*undertake*); **terram molitus** (*turning the massive earth*); **bipennem** (*wield*); **insidias** (*plot, contrive*); **moram** (*cause*); **talia** (*undertake*); **laborem** (*engage in*); **viam** (*force*); **iter** (*pursue*); **locum** (*fortify*); **habenas** (*handle*); **morbos** (*send*).

mōlitus, -a, -um, p.p. of **molior**.

molliŏ, -īvī, -ītum, -īre, [†molli-], 4. v. a., *soften.* — Less exactly, *improve, domesticate, mellow* (of fruits by cultivation). — Fig., *soothe, calm, appease.*

mollis, -e, [?, perh. for MARDUIS (cf. **tenuis**), √mar (cf. **molo**) + du (cf. **lacrima**)], adj., *soft,* *tender, mellow, delicate, pliant, flexible:* **aurum** (*ductile*); **pecus** (*tender, young*).—Fig., *gentle, easy, mild:* **haud mollia iussa** (*by no means easy*, cf. **immitis**); **flamma** (*pleasing*, of love); **Sabaei** (*effeminate*); **umbra** (*pleasant*); **collum** (*submissive, tractable*); **vina** (*mellow*); **haud mollia fatu** (*no easy things to say*); **pilenta** (*easy*).

molliter [†molli + ter, (prob. -terum, reduced)], adv., *softly, gently:* **excudent alii spirantia mollius aera** (*gracefully, softly-flowing*, of the lines in art).

mollītus, -a, -um, p.p. of **mollio**.

Molorchus, -ī, [Gr. Μόλορχος], m., the entertainer of Hercules when he killed the Nemean lion: **luci Molorchi** (of the haunt of the lion).

Molossus, -a, -um, [Gr. Μολοσσός], adj., *of the Molossi* (a nation of Crete), *Molossian.* — Masc. (sc. **canis**), *a Molossian dog, a mastiff.*

moneo, monuī, monitum, monēre, [√man (cf. **memini**), prob. an old causative], 2. v. a., *remind, advise, warn, admonish, teach, show, suggest, advise, direct:* **menstrua Iuna** (*forebode*).

monīle, -is, [unc. stem + ilis], n., *a necklace.* — Less exactly, *a collar.*

monimentum, see **monumentum**.

monitum, -ī, [n. p.p. of **moneo**], n., *a warning, advice, a command, a precept, an admonition, a prophecy* (divine suggestion).

monitus, -ūs, [†moni- (weaker stem of **moneo**) + tus], m., *a suggestion, a warning, advice, counsel, a command, a mandate.*

monitus, -a, -um, p.p. of **moneo**.

Monoecus, -ī, [Gr. Μόνοικος], m., a name of Hercules. — Also: **arx Monoeci**, a town in Liguria (now called *Monaco*), so called from a legend of Hercules.

mōns, montis, [√man (cf. **mineo**) + tis (reduced)], m., *a* *mountain, a hill.* — Used poetically for other things, as in Eng.

mōnstrātor, -ōris, [†monstrā- (stem of mōnstro) + tor,] m., *pointer-out:* aratri (*discoverer, inventor*).

mōnstrātus, -a, -um, p.p. of **mōnstro.**

mōnstrŏ, -āvī, -ātum, -āre, [†monstrŏ-], 1. v. a., *point out, show.* — Less exactly, *appoint, direct, impel, teach, command.*

mōnstrum, -ī, [†mon (as root) + trum (the s is of doubtful origin, cf. **lustrum**)], n., *a prodigy* (as an indication from the gods), *a marvel, a wonder, a portent, a portentous sight.* — Less exactly, *a hideous creature, a monster, a pest, a fiend, vermin.* — Also, plur., *spells* (dreadful magic arts). — Poetically, *of the sea.*

montānus, -a, -um, [†mont- (reduced stem of **mons**) + anus], adj., *of the mountain, mountain-.*

montōsus, -a, -um, [†mont- (reduced stem of **mons**) + osus], adj., *mountainous.* — Less exactly, *on a mountain, high-perched.*

monumentum (moni-), -ī, [†moni- (weaker stem of **moneo**) + mentum], n., *a memorial, a souvenir, a monument, a record, a relic, a reminder.*

Mopsus, -ī, [Gr. Μόψος], m., *a shepherd.*

mora, -ae, [prob. akin to **memor,** √SMAR + a, *hesitation?*], f., *delay, hesitation, reluctance, objection, loitering, stay, pause, respite.* — Concretely, *a hindrance, an obstacle, a defence:* pretium morae (*worth the time*); castigant moras (*punish the laggards*). — Phrases (cf. derivation): rumpere moras, *break off delay;* praecipitare moras, *speed without delay;* trahere moras, *prolong delay.*

morātus, -a, -um, p.p. of **moror.**

morbus, -ī, [√mor (cf. **morior**) + bus (cf. **superbus, turba**)], m., *sickness, illness, a disease, a malady, a disorder:* caeli (*an epidemic*). — Personified, plur., *Diseases.*

mordeŏ, momordī, morsum, mordēre, [†mordŏ- (cf. **mordosus, mordicus**)], 2. v. a., *bite.* — Fig., *clasp* (of a buckle).

moribundus, -a, -um, [as if †mori- (of **morior**) + bundus, prob. †moribon + dus, cf. **rubicundus**], adj., *dying.* — Less exactly, *doomed to die, mortal.*

Morīnī, -orum, [a Celtic word, akin to **mare**], m. plur., *a people of Gaul, in the extreme west.*

morior, mortuus (moritūrus), morī (morīrī), [√mor, cf. **mors**], 3. v. dep., *die, be slain, fall* (in battle), *perish.* — Less exactly, *wither, die* (of plants).

moriēns, -entis, p. as adj., *dying, failing.* — Masc. as subst., *a dying man, the dying.*

moror, -ātus, -ārī, [†morā-], 1. v. dep., *delay, linger, loiter, lag, be detained, be delayed, pause, wait, be hindered, be held back, stay, cling to.* — Act., *stay, retard, hold back, delay, put off.* — Also, *prolong.* — With negatives, *care for, prize, desire, care.*

mors, mortis, [√mor + tis (reduced), cf. **morior**], f., *death:* mortis honos (*honors due to death, burial*). — Plur., *kinds of death.* — Less exactly, *annihilation, death* (as destruction of matter). — Personified, *Death* (as an object of worship).

morsus, -ūs, [mord- (reduced stem of **mordeo** as root) + tus], m., *a bite.* — Often rendered in Eng. by *jaws, teeth, fangs, fluke* (of an anchor). — Less exactly, *clasp, hold* (of wood).

mortālis, -e, [†mort- (shorter stem of **mors**) + alis], adj., *mortal, liable to death, human, of man, of a mortal man, of mortals.* — Masc., *a mortal.* — Neut. plur., *mortal affairs, affairs of men.*

mortifer, -era, -erum, [†morti-†fer (√fer + us)], adj., *deadly, fatal.*
mortuus, -a, -um, [√mor+tuus], p.p. of **morior.**
mōrus, -ī, [Gr. μόρον], f., *a mulberry.*
mōs, mōris, [?], m., *a manner, a habit, a custom, a usage, a fashion, a form, a rite, an institution:* caeli (*the weather*); supra morem. — Plur., *character, habits.* — Also, *a law, a precept, a rule, restraint, limit:* sine more (*without restraint, wildly*).
mōtŏ, -āvī, -ātum, -āre, [†motŏ-], 1. v. a., *agitate, move, shake, wave.*
mōtus, p.p. of **moveo.**
mōtus, -ūs, [†movi- (weaker stem of **moveo**) + tus], m., *motion, a movement, an impulse, a shock, commotion:* pedum (*activity*). — Esp. (for motus terrae), *earthquake.* — Fig., *commotion, disturbance, tumult.* — Esp. (for motus animi), *emotion.*
moveo, mōvī, mōtum, movere, [?], 2. v. a. and n., *set in motion, move, agitate, shake, stir, brandish, disturb, break up, plough* (of the earth). — Esp.: castra, *break camp, march;* signa, *advance;* pubem portis, *set in motion.* — With reflexive or in pass., *move, proceed.* — Also, *remove, change, disturb.* — Fig., *stir up, agitate, excite, rouse, disturb, set on foot, cause, revolve* (in the mind), *meditate, intend, begin, disclose* (disturb what is quietly concealed): arma (*prepare for fight*). — Also esp., *influence, affect, attract, move:* motus tumultu (*struck by*).
mōx [?], adv., *presently, soon, hereafter, later on.*
mucro, -ōnis, [?], m., *the edge, the point* (of a sword, &c.), *a sword.*
mūgiō, 4. v. n., *bellow, roar.*
mūgītus, -us, [†mugi- (of **mugio**) + tus], m., *a bellowing, a lowing.*
mulcātus, -a, -um, p.p. of **mulco.**
mulceō, mulsī, mulsum (mulctum), **mulcēre,** [akin to **mulgeo**], 2. v. n., *stroke, soften* (by stroking), *caress.* — Fig., *soothe, allay, mollify, assuage, calm.* — Poetically: aethera cantu, *cheer, delight.*
Mulciber, -brī, [as if †mulci- (weaker stem of **mulceo**) + ber (perh. †mulcibŏ + rus)], m., a name of Vulcan (*the softener of iron*).
mulcō, -āvī, -ātum, -āre, [?, perh. fr. same stem as **mulceo**], 1. v. a., *beat, bruise, mangle.*
mulctra, -ae, [†mulg + tra], f., *a milk-pail.*
mulctrāle, -is, [†mulctrā + le (n. of -lis)], n., *a milk-pail.*
mulctrārium, -ī (-iī), [as if †mulctrā- (reduced) + arium], n., *a milk-pail.*
mulgeō, mulsī, mulsum (mulctum), **mulgēre,** [√mulg, akin to **mulceo** and Gr. ἀμέλγω], 2. v. a., *milk.* — Of the effect, *milk* (obtain by milking).
muliebris, -e, [†mulier + bris (cf. -ber, -brum), cf. **Mulciber**], adj., *womanly, a woman's, of a woman.*
mulier, -eris, [?], f., *a woman.*
multātus, -a, -um, p.p. of **multo.**
multiplex, -icis, [†multo-plex (cf. **duplex**)], adj., *many fold, manifold.*
multŏ (mulctŏ), **-āvī, -ātum, -āre,** [†multā- (*fine*)], 1. v. a., *fine, punish, visit* (with a penalty).
multus, -a, -um, [?, cf. **mille, miles**], adj., *many, many a, much.* — Translated by numerous words of quantity, size, and degree, *great, full, numerous, plentiful, copious, thick, loud, a great deal of, heavy, constant.* — Masc. plur., *many, many men.* — Fem. plur., *many, many women.* — Neut. sing. and plur., *much, many things* (often with a defining word to be supplied from the context): multum est (*it is a great thing*); — adverbially, *much, greatly, deeply, loudly.* — Abl. **multo,** as adv., *much,*

a great deal, far: **multo ante** (*long before*).—Comparative **plūs,** [†plē- (cf. **pleo**) + ius], n., (**plūres, plura,** plur.), *more, greater, more numerous.* — Also, *many, several, much.* — As adv., *more, much.* —Superlative, **plūrimus, -a, -um,** [†plus+imus], *very much, very many, very large, very great, very many a* (cf. **multus**), *in large numbers, very deep, very high, very thick,* and the like.

mundus, -ī, [translation of Gr. κόσμος, lit. *well-ordered, clean*], m., *the universe, the world, the earth.*

mūnīmen, -inis, [†muni- (of **munio**) + men], n., *a protection, a defence.*

mūniō, -īvī (-iī), -ītum, -īre, [†muni- (cf. **moenia**)], 4. v. a., *fortify, protect.*

mūnus (moen-), -eris, [√min (cf. **moenia, communis**), strengthened, + us], n., (*distributive share?*), *office, duty, function.* — Also, *an honor, a dignity.—a rite, a religious service, a sacrifice, an offering.* — Less exactly, *a gift, a favor, a boon, a prize, a present, a service:* **haec ipsa ad munera** (*for this purpose*).

mūnusculum, -ī, [†munus+culum], n., *a little gift, a modest gift.*

mūrālis, -e, [†murŏ- (reduced) + alis], adj., *of (for) walls:* **tormentum** (*battering-engine*).

mūrex, -icis, [?], m., *a shell-fish* (used for dyeing purple). — Less exactly, *a jagged rock.* — Also, *purple dye, purple.*

murmur, -uris, [unc. root redupl.], n., *a murmur, a whisper, murmuring, a humming, a muttering* (of thunder).

murmurō, -āvī, -ātum, -āre, [†murmur-], 1. v. n., *murmur.*

murra (myrrha), -ae, [Gr. μύρρα], f., *myrrh* (a gum as a perfume).

Murrānus, -ī, [?], m., *a Latin.*

mūrus (moer-), -ī, [perh. remotely akin to **moenia**], m., *a wall* (less general than **moenia**).

mūs, mūris, [akin to Gr. μῦς and Sk. mush, *steal*], comm., *a mouse.*

Musa, -ae, [Gr. μοῦσα], f., *a muse.* — Also (cf. **Ceres,** *grain*), *a song, a lay, verses.*

Musaeus, -ī, [Gr. Μουσαῖος], m., a pre-Homeric Athenian bard and musician.

muscōsus, -a, -um, [†muscŏ- (reduced) + osus], adj., *mossy.*

muscus, -ī, [?], m., *moss.*

mussō, -āvī, -ātum, -āre, [perh. akin to **mutus**], 1. v. n., *murmur, mutter* (with compressed lips), *hesitate, hum* (of bees), *low with fear* (of cattle).

mustum, -ī, [?], n., *new wine, must.*

mūtābilis, -e, [†mutā- (of **muto**) + bilis], adj., *changeful, changeable, fickle, inconstant, changing.*

mūtātus, -a, -um, p.p. of **muto.**

mūtō, -āvī, -ātum, -āre, [perh. †mutŏ- (for movito-), cf. **moveo,** and **mutuus**], 1. v. a., *change, alter, transform, exchange, remove* (change place): **vellera luto** (*dye,* change the color); **mutata flumina** (*reversed*). — Esp. of traffic. *exchange, barter, sell, buy.*

mūtus, -a, -um, [√mu (cf. **musso, muttio**)+tus], adj., *dumb, speechless, mute, silent.*

Mutusca, -ae, f., a Sabine town.

mūtuus, -a, -um, [akin to **muto,** cf. **mortuus**], adj., *exchanged, reciprocal, mutual, on both sides* (reciprocally).—Phrase: **per mutua,** *with each other, mutually.*

Mycenaeus, -a, -um, [Gr. Μυκηναῖος], adj., *of Mycene, Mycenaean*

Mycēnē, -es (-ae, -ārum; -a, -ae), [Gr. Μυκῆναι, -η], f., the city of Agamemnon in Greece. — Less exactly, *Greece.*

Mycon, see **Micon.**

Myconos (-us), -ī, [Gr. Μύκονος], f., one of the Cyclades. Also read **Myconē, -es.**

Mygdonidēs, -ae, [Gr. patronymic], m., *son of Mygdon.*

myrīca, -ae, [Gr. μυρίκη], f., *the tamarisk* (a shrub).

Myrmidones, -um, [Gr. Μυρμιδόνες], m. plur., a tribe of Thessaly, subjects of Achilles.
myrrha, see **murra,** the more correct spelling.
myrtētum (mur-), -ī, [†myrtŏ- (reduced) + etum], n., *a myrtle grove.*
myrteus, -a, -um, [†myrtŏ- (reduced) + eus], adj., *of myrtle.*
myrtum, -ī, [Gr. μύρτος], n., *a myrtle berry.*
myrtus, -ī (also, -ūs), [Gr. μύρτος], f., *a myrtle tree, a myrtle.* — Less exactly, *myrtle* (leaves), *a myrtle staff.* — Collectively, *myrtles.*
Mȳsius, -a, -um, [Gr. Μύσιος], adj., *of Mysia* (a district of Asia Minor), *Mysian.* — Fem., *Mysia* (the country).
mysticus, -a, -um, [Gr. μυστικός], adj., *mystic, mystical.*
Mȳsus, -a, -um, [Gr. Μυσός], adj., *Mysian, of Mysia.*

N.

nactus, -a, -um, p.p. of **nanciscor.**
Nāis, -idos, [Gr. Ναίς], f., *a Naiad, a water-nymph.*
nam [pron. √na, in acc. fem. (?), cf. **tam, quam**], conj., (explanatory of a preceding statement), *for.* — Also with interrogatives (usually appended as one word, but sometimes preceding or separated), making the question emphatic, *pray, now, why, tell me, indeed:* quaenam vos fortuna implicuit (*pray what?*); quis est nam ludus in undis (*what sport can there be?*); nam quis te iussit (*why, who,* &c.).
namque [nam-que, cf. **etenim**], conj., (stronger than **nam**), *for surely, for mind you, for I say, for no doubt, for in fact.* — Also, *assuredly, I'm sure.*
nanciscor, nactus (nanctus), nanciscī, [√nac], 3. v. dep., *get, find, light upon, catch:* ver (*be favored with*).
napaeus, -a, -um, [Gr. ναπαῖος], adj., *of the dell.* — Plur. fem., *the wood-nymphs.*
Nār, -āris, [?], m., *a tributary of the Tiber.*
narcissus, -ī, [Gr. νάρκισσος], m., *the narcissus.*
nārēs, -ium, [†nasi-, akin to †nasŏ-], f., *the nostrils, the nose.*
nārrō, -āvī, -ātum, -āre, [for gnarigo(old),†gnarigŏ-(†gnarŏ- †agus, cf. **prodigus**)], 1. v. a., *tell, relate, recount.*
Nārycius, -a, -um, [Gr. Ναρύκιος], adj., *of Narycium* (a city of the Locri on the Euboean Sea, the birthplace of Ajax Oileus; also another city of the same name in Bruttium), *Narycian.*
nāscor, nātus, nāscī, [√gna + sco], 3. v. n., *be born.* — Less exactly, *spring up, arise, grow.* — Fig., *begin, spring up, arise, succeed.* — **nāscēns, -entis,** p. as adj., *new-born, at birth, growing, early:* ortus (*rising dawn*). — Plur. as subst., *the young* (of animals). — **nātus, -a, -um,** p.p. as subst., *son, daughter, offspring, a young one* (according to the context).
nāta (gna-), see **nāscor.**
nātālis, -e, [†natŏ- (reduced) + alis], adj., *of birth.* — Masc., (sc. dies), *birthday.*
natō, -āvī, -ātum, -āre, [†natŏ- (p.p. of nō)], 1. v. n., *swim, float.* — Less exactly, *be submerged, swim, be flooded.* — **natāns, -antis,** p. as adj., *swimming, floating, waving* (of grain). — Neut. plur., *fish.* — So also (as in English): lumina (*swimming*).
nātū (only in abl.), [√gna + tus], m., *by birth.* — Regularly used to define **maior** and **maximus,** *older, eldest.*
nātūra, -ae, [†natu + ra (f. of

-rus), cf. **figura**], f., *birth.* — Fig., *nature, character* (innate), *disposition, quality:* **natura** loci (*position of the ground*). — Also, *the power of growth, nature* (natural phenomena).
nātus (gna-), see **nascor.**
naufragus, see **navifragus.**
nauta, -ae, [prob. borrowed fr. Gr. ναύτης], (also **navita**), [perhaps original fr. †navi-, or worked over by popular etymology], m., *a sailor, a seaman, a mariner, a boatman, a ferry-man.*
Nautēs, -is, [?], m., a Trojan, companion of Æneas.
nauticus, -a, -um, [†nauta-(weakened) + cus], adj., *of sailors:* **clamor** (*of the sailors*); **pinus** (*manned by seamen*).
nāvālis, -e, [†nav- (earlier form?) + alis], adj., *of ships, naval, nautical:* **corona** (made in form of beaks of ships, the honor of a naval engagement). — Neut. plur., (sc. **castra**), *ship-yards, docks;* also? (as subst.), *ship stores, materials, rigging.*
nāvifragus, -a, -um, [†navi-fragus (√frag + us, cf. **frango**)], adj., *wrecking ships, dangerous.* — Pass., *shipwrecked.*
nāvigium, -ī (-iī), [†navigŏ- (see **navigō**) reduced + ium], n., *a boat, a vessel, a ship.*
nāvigō, -āvī, -ātum, -āre, [†navigŏ- (†navi-agus, cf. **prodigus**)], 1. v. n., *sail, set sail, embark.* — With cognate acc., *sail* upon, *navigate, traverse.*
nāvis, -is, [√nu (strengthened) as stem, with added -i, cf. ναῦς], f., *a ship, a boat, a vessel, a fleet* (in plural).
nāvita, see **nauta.**
Naxus (-os), -ī, [Gr. Νάξος], f., one of the Cyclades.
nē (nī), [unc. case-form, pron. √na], adv. (only in special forms of speech), *no, not.* —With **quidem,** *not even, not either.* — With **dum** and **dummodo** (cf. **modo ne**), *so long as not, provided not.* — With other particles requiring the subjunctive, **ut, utinam.** — In composition, cf. **neque, nemo,** etc. —In hortatory forms of speech: **ne crede colori.**— Conj., with subjunctive (orig. the adverb with hortatory forms), *that not, that no,* &c., *lest, not to.* — With verbs of fearing (perh. hortatory in origin), *that lest.*
-ne (n') [prob. same word as **nē,** cf. -ne in sense of **nonne**], enclitic interrogative, *whether* (but usually omitted in Eng. in direct questions). — Also in double questions in second place, *or.*— Also, = **nonne,** *whether not, is not, do not,* &c.
Neaera, -ae, [Gr. Νέαιρα], f., a rustic maid.
Nealcēs, -ae, [Gr.], m., a Trojan.
nebula, -ae, [stem akin to **nubes** + la], f., *a mist, a fog, a cloud.*
nec (neque), [nē (shortened)-que], conj., *and not, neither, nor, and yet not.* — With **et,** *not . . . and, not . . . and yet, not . . . but.* — **nec non (et),** *and also, nor less, so too, then too, as well.*
necdum, see **nec** and **dum.**
necesse (-um, -us, -is), [petrified case-form of unc. origin], adj. and adv., *necessary, fated, required.* — With **est,** *it is necessary, it must be that, one cannot but.*
necō, -āvī, -ātum, -āre, [†nec- (of **nex**)], 1. v. a., *kill, put to death.*
nectar, -aris, [Gr. νέκταρ], n., *nectar* (the drink of the gods). — Less exactly, of other drinks.
nectō, nexuī, nexum, nectere, [√nec, cf. **plecto**], 3. v. a., *bind, tie, twine.* — Of the effect, *tie* (make by tying), *twine.* — Fig., *spin out, frame, weave.* — With change of point of view (cf. **circumdo**), *encircle, twine with.* — **nexus, -a, -um,** p.p. as adj., *close-twined, clinging.*
nefandus, -a, -um, [nē (short-

ened) -fandus (see for)], adj., *unspeakable* (cf. **infandus**), *horrible, accursed, impious, criminal* (cf. **nefas**), *godless:* gens; enses; odia (*unutterable*). — Neut. as subst., *crime, wrong.*

nefās [nē (shortened) -fas], n. indecl., *impiety, wrong, crime, sacrilege, an impious deed:* nefas dictu (*horrible to tell*). — With est (often omitted), *it is impious (a crime, wrong,* &c.). — Concretely, *an impious creature, a curse, a tale of crime.* — In a kind of apposition as an exclamation, *oh horror!* (cf. **infandum**).

negŏ, -āvī, -ātum, -āre, [?, perh. ne-aio, in its earlier form, through noun-stem], 1. v. n. and a., (*say no*), *say ... not, deny, say that no,* &c. — Also, *refuse, deny* (one anything), *decline.*

Nemea, -ae, [Gr. Νεμέη], f., a city of Argolis, near which Hercules killed the Nemean lion.

nēmŏ, -inis, [nē-homo (hemo)], m., *no man, no one, nobody.* Almost degenerated into a pronoun.

nemorōsus, -a, -um, [†nemor + osus], adj., *woody, well-wooded.*

nempe [nam-pe, of unc. orig., perh. dialectic form of **que**, cf. **quippe**], conj., *no doubt, surely, certainly.* — Also in answer to a question or statement, *that is to say, why! in sooth.*

nemus, -oris, [√nem (cf. **numerus,** Gr. νόμος, νέμω)], n., (*assigned grazing-ground*), *a wooded pasture.* — Less exactly, *a grove, a forest, a vineyard* (cf. **arbustum**).

neŏ, nēvī, nētum, nēre, [√ne, cf. Gr. νήθω], 2. v. a., *spin.* — Less exactly, *weave, interweave.*

Neoptolemus, -ī, [Gr. Νεοπτόλεμος], m., a name of Pyrrhus, the son of Achilles.

nepōs, -ōtis, [?], m., *a grandson, a nephew.* — Less exactly (in plur.), *descendants, progeny, offspring, posterity.*

Neptūnius, -a, -um, [†Neptunŏ- (reduced) + ius], adj., *of Neptune:* Troia (*built by Neptune*).

Neptūnus, -ī, [†neptu-, akin to Eng. *naphtha* (a Persian word) + nus, cf. **Fortuna, Portunus**], m., *the god of the sea,* brother of Jove and Pluto. — Also (cf. **Ceres,** *grain*), *the sea.*

neque, see **nec.**

nequeo, -quīvī (-iī), -quitum, -quīre, [nē-queŏ], 4. v. irr., *cannot, not be able, be unable.*

nēquicquam (-quidquam), see **nequīquam,** the spelling now in vogue.

nēquīquam (nequic-, nequid-, prob. both forms of diff. orig. were once in use), [ne-quīquam (quid quam, cf. **quisquam**)], adv., (*not in any manner*), *in vain, uselessly, to no purpose, without effect, without reason.*

nē quis, etc.; see **ne** and **quis,** etc.

Nērēis, -idis, [Gr. Νηρεΐς, f. patronymic of Nereus], f., *a daughter of Nereus, a Nereid, a sea-nymph.*

Nērēius, -a, -um, [†Nereu- (reduced) + ius], adj., *of Nereus, child of Nereus.*

Nereus, -eī, [Gr. Νηρεύς], m., a sea-god, father of the Nereids. — Less exactly, *the sea, the water.*

Nērīnē, -ēs, [Gr. Νηρίνη], f., *daughter of Nereus, a Nereid.*

Nēritos, -ī, [Gr. Νήριτος], f., a mountain of the island of Ithaca.

Nersae, -ārum, [?], f. plur., a city of the Æqui (sometimes read **Nursae,** which see).

nervus, -ī, [√SNAR + vus, cf. Gr. νεῦρον, Eng. *snare*], m., *a sinew, a tendon.* — From the original material, *a bowstring, a string.*

Nēsaeē, -ēs, [Gr. Νησαίη], f., a sea-nymph.

nescio, -īvī (-iī), -ītum, -īre, [nē-scio], 4. v. a., *not know, know not, be ignorant, be unaware, be unacquainted with:* nescit quis aras (*has not heard of*); puellae hiemem (*learn to know*). — Also, *not know how to, be unable to.* —

nescio quis, *some one or other, some one I know not who, some one, some.*
nescius, -a, -um, [ne-scius, cf. **conscius, inscius**], adj., *not knowing, ignorant, unaware, in ignorance, untaught* (cf. **nescio**), *unable to.* — With negative, *well aware, well taught, not without knowledge, not in ignorance.*
neu, see **neve**.
nēve (neu), [ne-ve], conj., *or not, and not.* — The regular connective with **ne**, and so equivalent to **neque** in clauses which require **ne**.
nex, necis, [√nec as stem (cf. **pernicies, noceo**)], f., *death, slaughter.*
nexō, nexui, no sup., **nexāre,** [†nexŏ-], 1. v. a., *twine, bind.*
nexus, -a, -um, p.p. of **necto**.
nī, see **ne**.
nī [prob. same word as **nē**, used in concessive clauses], conj., (equal to **nisi**), *if not, unless.*
nīdor, -ōris, [unc. root + or, cf. Gr. κνῖσα], m., *odor* (of burnt flesh in sacrifice). — Less exactly, *odor* (of any kind).
nīdus, -ī, [?], m., *a nest.* — Less exactly, *young* (of birds in a nest), *cells* (of bees).
niger, -gra, -grum, [?], adj., *black* (opp. to **candidus**, cf. **ater**, opp. to **albus**), *dark, dusky, swarthy, gloomy, blackened.*
nigrēscō, nigrui, no sup., **nigrēscere,** [†nigrē-(of **nigreo**)+ sco], 3. v. incept., *blacken, grow black, turn black.*
nigrō, -āvī, -ātum, -āre, [†nigrŏ-], 1. v. n., *be black.*—**nigrāns, -antis,** p. as adj., *black, dark.*
nihil (nihilum, nīl), [ne-hilum (*a spot*?, *a trifle*), cf. *not, ne pas*], n. indecl., *nothing.*— As adv., *not at all, not in the least, not a whit, not.* — With partitives, *no, none.*
nīl, see **nihil**.
Nīlus, -ī, [Gr. Νεῖλος], m., *the Nile,* the famous river of Egypt.
nimbōsus, -a, -um, [†nimbŏ- (reduced)+osus], adj., *cloudy, cloud-capped, stormy* (bringing storms).
nimbus, -ī, [perh. akin to **nubes**], m., *a storm-cloud, a cloud, a dark cloud, a storm, a tempest, rain.* — Also, *a bright cloud* (enclosing the gods). — Fig., *a cloud, a great number, a swarm.*
nimīrum [nē-mirum, *no wonder*], adv., *doubtless, no doubt, surely.*
nimis [?], adv., *too much, too, over much:* **nota** (*too well known*).
nimius, -a, -um, [akin to **nimis**], adj., *too much, excessive, too great, immoderate.* — Without idea of excess, *very, exceedingly.*— Neut. as subst., *too much.*— Neut. as adv., *too, too much, all too;* — also, *very, most indeed.*
ningō, ninxi, no sup., **ningere,** [√nig, cf. **nix**], 3. v. n., *snow.* — Usually impersonal, *it snows.*
Niphātēs, -ae, [Gr. Νιφάτης], m., *a high snowy mountain in Armenia.* — Less exactly, for the people near it.
Niphaeus, -ī, [?], m., *a Rutulian.*
Nīsa, -ae, [?], f., *a rustic maiden.*
Nīsaeē, -ēs, [?], f., *a sea-nymph* (see also **Nesaee**).
nisi [nē-si], conj., *unless, if not, except:* **nisi fata locum dedissent** (*had not,* &c.).
Nīsus, -ī, [Gr. Νῖσος], m.: 1. A king of Megaris, betrayed by his daughter Scylla, and robbed of a fatal hair upon which his life depended. He was changed into a hawk; 2. A Trojan who, with his companion Euryalus, was slain in attempting to pass the enemy's lines.
nīsus, -ūs, [√nit+tus], m., *an effort:* **rapidus** (*flight, plunge*); **idem** (*position, poise*).
niteō, (nitui, referred to **nitesco**) no sup., **nitēre,** [?], 2. v. n., *shine, glisten, sparkle.* — **nitēns, -entis,** p. as adj., *shining, bright, sparkling, sleek* (in good condition), *well-tilled* (cf. Eng. *foul*), *bright, flourishing.*

nitēscō, nituī, no sup., **nitēscere,** [†nitē- (cf. **niteo**) + sco], 3. v. n., *shine.*

nitidus, -a, -um, [adj. stem fr. wh. **niteo** + dus], adj., *bright, shining, blooming, sleek.*

nītor, nīsus (nīxus), nītī, [poss. for **gnitor,** from †genu or some stem akin], 3. v. dep., *lean against, brace against, struggle, strive, rest on, lean on, climb, climb up:* paribus alis (*be poised* on).

nitrum, -ī, [Gr. νίτρον], n., *soda* (a mineral alkali, properly carbonate of soda, used for potash by the ancients).

nivālis, -e, [†niv- (**nix**) + alis], adj., *snowy, snow-clad.* — Less exactly, *snowy-white, snowy.*

niveus, -a, -um, [†niv + eus], adj., *of snow, snowy;* — *snowy-white, pure white.*

nix, nivis, [√nig- (as stem), cf. **ningo**], f., *snow.*

nixus, -a, -um, p.p. of **nītor.**

nixus, -ūs, [some form of √nit + tus], m., *an effort, labor* (of travail).

nō, nāvī, no sup., **nāre,** [cf. Gr. νέω], 1. v. n., *swim.* — Less exactly, *float, sail, fly.*

nōbilis, -e, [√gno (cf. **nosco**) + bilis], f., *well-known, famous.*

nōbilitās, -tātis, [†nobili + tas], f., *high birth, illustrious origin.*

noceo, nocuī, nocitum, nocēre, [adj.stem in -ŏ, cf. nocuus (√nec, cf. **pernicies**)], 2. v. n., *do mischief, be hurtful, be injurious, injure, harm, do harm:* haud ignara nocendi (*of mischief*). — **nocēns, -entis,** p. as adj., *harmful, pernicious.*

noctivagus, -a, -um, [†nocti- (unreduced stem of **nox**) + vagus], adj., *night-roving.*

noctua, -ae, [†noctu + a (f. of us), *bird of night*], f., *an owl.*

nocturnus, -a, -um, [†noctu- (as if **noctus,** cf. **diurnus**) + nus], adj., *of the night, nocturnal, nightly.* — Often rendered as if an adverb, *by night, in the night.*

nōdō, -āvī, -ātum, -āre, [†nodŏ-], 1. v. a., *knot, tie up, bind in a knot.*

nōdus, -ī, [?], m., *a knot* (of a cord, &c., or of a branch), *an eye* (of a plant), *a fold* (of a serpent), *a clasp* (of the arms): pugnae nodum moramque (*the centre and bulwark*).

Noēmōn, -onis, [?], m., a Trojan.

Nomas, -adis, [Gr. Νομάς], m., *a Nomad* (one of a wandering, pastoral people). — Plur., *the Numidians.*

nōmen, -inis, [√gno (cf. **nosco**) + men], n., *a name, a word.* — As in Eng., *a hero* (cf. "*great names*"), *a family, a race.* — Fig., *renown, name, glory, distinction, reputation.*

Nōmentum, -ī, [?], n., *a Sabine city.*

nōn (old **noenum**), [ne-unum, cf. "*nought,*" "*not*"], adv., *no, not.*

nondum, see **dum.**

nonne, see **non** and **ne.**

nonnullus, -a, -um, [non-nullus], adj. (as pron.), *some, some or other.*

nōnus, -a, -um, [unc. stem (of **novem**) + nus], adj., *the ninth.*

Nōricus, -a, -um, [?], adj., *of Noricum* (a mountainous country north of the Alps, west of Pannonia, and south of the Danube), *Norican.*

nōs, plur. of **ego,** which see.

nōscō, nōvī, nōtum, nōscere, [√gno (cf. *know*) + sco], 3. v. a., *learn, recognize,* — (in perf., &c.), *know* (a thing, cf. **scio,** *know a fact*), *be acquainted with, be sensible of, experience.* — Less exactly, *know* (a fact, like **scio**). — **nōtus, -a, -um,** p.p. as adj., *well known, familiar, wonted, usual, customary, habitual;* — *famous, renowned, famed:* notum quid femina possit (*the knowledge,* &c.).

noster, -tra, -trum, [nos (as stem) + terus (reduced), cf. **uter**], adj. pron., *our, my, of us, of me, in my power.* — Also, *favorable* (*to us*), *prosperous.* — As subst. (in plur.),

Vocabulary. 187

our (*my*) *friends* (countrymen, &c.).
nota, -ae, [√gno + ta], f., *a mark, a sign.* — Less exactly, *a spot, a scar, a mark* (of wounds).
nothus, -ī, [Gr. νόθος], m., *an illegitimate son, a bastard.* — Of animals, *a mongrel, a cross-breed.*
notŏ, -āvī, -ātum, -āre, [†notā-], 1. v. a., *mark.* — Of the effect, *mark down, inscribe.* — Less exactly, *mark, observe, notice.*
Notus, -ī, [Gr. Νότος], m., *the South Wind.* — Less exactly, *the wind.*
nōtus, -a, -um, p.p. of **nosco.**
novālis, -e, [†novŏ- (reduced) + alis], adj., (*new*). — Fem., (sc. **terra**), *fallow land* (left to be renewed by lying). — Neut., *fallow land,* (less exactly) *fields* (cultivated).
novellus, -a, -um, [†novŏ- (reduced) + ellus, as if †novulŏ + lus], adj., *young, tender, new.*
novem [unc. case-form petrified, cf. Gr. ἐννέα, Eng. *nine*], indecl. adj., *nine.*
noverca, -ae, [?, akin to **novus**], f., *a stepmother.*
noviēns (-iēs), [stem of **novem,** with unc. term.], num. adv., *nine times.*
novitās, -tātis, [†novŏ- (weakened) + tas], f., *newness:* regni (*infancy*).
novŏ, -āvī, -ātum, -āre, [†novŏ-], 1. v. a., *renew, make new, repair, refit, repeat.*—Fig., *change:* fidem (*break*).
novus, -a, -um, [akin to.Gr. νέος], adj., *new, fresh, strange, young:* ver (*new, early*); sol (*new risen*); soles (*of early spring*). — **novissimus, -a, -um,** superl., *newest, latest, last, rear.*
nox, noctis, [perh. √noc (cf. noceo) + tis (reduced), cf. Gr. νύξ, Eng. *night*], f., *night, darkness, the influence of night.* — Personified, *Night.*
noxa, -ae, [√noc + ta (?)], f., (*harm*), *a fault, guilt.*

noxius, -a, -um, [†noxa-(reduced) + ius], adj., *harmful, guilty.*
nūbēs, -is, [√nub- (cf. **nubo**) + es (and -is)], f., *a cloud.*— Fig., *a cloud, a swarm:* facta nube (*gathering like a cloud,* of birds); belli (*storm-cloud*). — Also, *the region of clouds, the clouds, the heavens.*
nūbigena, -ae, [†nubi-(see **nubes**) -gena (√gen + a, cf. **Graiugena**)], m., *cloud-born, a centaur, a cloud-born monster.*
nūbila, -ōrum, [†nubi- (see **nubes**) + la (n. plur. of lus)], n., prop. adj., *the clouds, the region of clouds.*
nūbilis, -e, [†nubŏ- (cf. **pronuba, conubium**) + lis], adj., *marriageable.*
nūdātus, -a, -um, p.p. of **nudo.**
nūdŏ, -āvī, -ātum, -āre, [†nudŏ-], 1. v. a., *strip, make bare, lay bare, bare, uncover.* — **nūdātus, -a, -um,** p.p. as adj., *bared, stripped, naked, uncovered.*
nūdus, -a, -um, [prob. for †nugdus, cf. Eng. *naked*], adj., *naked, bare, uncovered, stripped, exposed, defenceless:* aetheris axis (*open*); ensis (*alone*). — Less exactly, *in a single garment* (without an outer garment), *uncloaked.*
nullus, -a, -um, [ne-ullus], adj., *no, none:* non nullis oculis (*without regard*). — Masc. and fem., *none, no one, nobody.* — **nonnullus, -a, -um,** *some, some one.*
num [pron. √na, acc., cf. **tum, cum, dum**], conj., interrog., *whether* (often not expressed in Eng., but indicated by the order, *is any, does any,* &c.). — Regularly expecting the answer "no."
Numa, -ae, [?], m., a Roman name. — Esp., *Numa Pompilius,* the second king of Rome, to whom were attributed the religious institutions of the Romans; 2. Two Rutulians.
Numanus, -ī, [†Numā + nus], m., a Rutulian, with the surname Remulus.

nūmen, -ĭnis, [√nu (lengthened, cf. **nuo**) + **men**], n., (*a nod*). — Esp., *the divine will, power* (of the gods), *authority, permission, purpose, consent, approval, decree, inspiration, presence* (of a god), *divine nature, divine interposition, oracle* (declared purpose). — Also, *divinity, divine essence, deity* (with genitive of the god used concretely): Iunonis; Fauni; vestra (of the stars). — Also concretely, *a divinity, a divine being:* numina magna Deum (*forms*); media inter numina (*images*).

numerŏ, -āvī, -ātum, -āre, [†numerŏ-], 1. v. a., *count, reckon up, recount.*

numerus, -ī, [stem akin to νόμος (cf. **numus**) + **rus**], m., *number, a number.* — Esp., *a large number, a number.* — Also, *order, proportion:* pares numeri (*equal dimensions*); compositi numero in turmas (*in equal numbers*); stellis numeros fecit (*places,* by calculation); nec numero nec honore cremant (*without distinction*). — Also, *musical measure, time, tune, the notes of the scale* (pl.). — Phrases: in numerum, *in time, in order, in turn, in measure;* sideris in numerum, *to the place of a star;* neque est numerus, *it is impossible to count, there is no numbering.*

Numīcus, -ī, [?], m., *a river of Latium,* where Æneas was said to have disappeared.

Numĭdae, -ārum, [Gr. νομάς], m. plur., *the Numidians* (a people of Northern Africa).

Numĭtor, -ōris, [?], m.: 1. The grandfather of Romulus and Remus; 2. A Rutulian.

nunc [num-ce (cf. **hic**)], adv., *now.* — Repeated, *now . . . now, sometimes . . . again.*

nuncius, etc.; see **nuntius**.

nunquam [ne-unquam], adv., *never.* — Less exactly, *not at all, by no means* (see **hodie**).

nuntia, -ae, [f. of **nuntius**], f., *a messenger* (female).

nuntĭŏ, -āvī, -ātum, -āre, [†nuntiŏ-], 1. v. a., *report, announce, bring tidings.*

nuntius, -ī (-iī), [prob. †novŏ-†ventius (†ventŏ + ius)], m., *a messenger, a reporter.* — In appos., as adj., *bringing tidings, reporting.* — Also, *news, message, tidings, report.*

nūper [prob. novum-per, cf. **parumper**], adv., *lately, just now, not long ago.*

Nursae, -ārum, [?]; see **Nersae**, the approved spelling.

Nursia (Nurt-), -ae, [?], f., *a town of the Sabines* (now *Norcia*).

nurus, -ūs, [akin to Gr. νυός (for SNUSUS)], f., *a daughter-in-law.*

nusquam [nē-usquam], adv., *nowhere.* — Also equal Eng. *never* (with a different conception).

nūtŏ, -āvī, -ātum, -āre, [†nutŏ- (cf. **abnuo**)], 1. v. n., *nod, totter, swing, wave.*

nūtrīmentum, -ī, [†nutri- (of **nutrio**) + **mentum**], n., *food, nourishment.* — Less exactly, *fuel.*

nūtrĭŏ, -īvī (-iī), -ītum, -īre, [?, cf. **nutrix**], 4. v. a., *nurse, nourish, suckle.* — Less exactly, *bring up, rear.* — Pass. as dep., *cultivate, raise.*

nūtrior, see **nutrio**.

nūtrīx, -īcis, [unknown root (cf. **nutrio**) + **trix**], f., *a nurse.*

nūtus, -ūs, [†nū- (as root) + **tus**, cf. **abnuo, numen**], m., *a nod.* — Fig., *will, an order, a command.*

nux, nucis, [?], f., *a nut* (of various kinds). — Also, *an almond-tree.*

nympha, -ae, [Gr. νύμφη], f., *a nymph* (a goddess of the sea or woods, more or less allied to the human race). — Less exactly, *a muse* (as the muses proper were of this general class).

Nȳsa, -ae, [Gr. Νῦσα], f., *a city of India,* said to have been built by Bacchus in his expedition to India.

O.

O, interj. (of all emotions), *oh! O!* — With acc., nom., or voc.

Oaxēs, -is, [Gr. Ὄαξις], m., *a river in Crete.*

ob (obs), [akin to Gr. ἐπί], prep., *towards* (archaic).—*near, around.* —Fig. (cf. the provincial "all along of"), *on account of, for, for the sake of, through.*—In comp., *to, towards, against, before, over,* &c.

obambulŏ, -āvī, -ātum, -āre, [ob-ambulo], 1. v. n., *walk about, roam about.*

obdūcŏ, -dūxī, -dūctum, -dūcere, [ob-duco], 3. v. a., *draw over, spread over.*—With change of point of view, *overspread, cover, overgrow, choke.* — **obdūctus, -a, -um,** p.p., *overspread, surrounding;* — *hidden, covered.*

obdūctus, -a, -um, p.p. of **obduco.**

obeŏ, -īvī (-iī), -itum, -īre, [ob-eo], irr. v. a., *go to, go over, go around, visit:* **pugnas** (*engage in*); **terras maria** (*wash, encompass*); **omnia visu** (*view, survey*); **mortem** (*suffer, meet*).—Also, *surround, encircle, cover.*

obēsus, -a, -um, [ob-esus], adj., *fat, swollen.*

ōbex, -icis, [ob-√iac (as stem)], m. or f., *a bar, an obstacle, a barrier.*

obfero and compounds of **ob** with **f,** see **offero.**

obiciŏ (obii-), -iēcī, -iectum, -icere, [ob-iacio], 3. v. a., *throw against, throw to, expose, throw in the way of, offer:* **clipeos ad tela** (*oppose, present*); **equites sese** (*array themselves in opposition*); **portas** (*shut against one*).—Fig., *expose, offer to the sight, throw out against, throw at* (of taunts, &c.): **rabiem canibus** (*inspire*).— **obiectus, -a, -um,** p.p. as adj., *thrown in the way, lying in the way, opposing.*

obiectŏ, -āvī, -ātum, -āre, [ob-iacto, cf. **obicio**], 1. v. a., *throw against.*—Fig., *expose, risk, sacrifice* (in war).

obiectus, -a, -um, p.p. of **obicio.**

obiectus, -ūs, [ob-iactus, cf. **obicio**], m., *a throwing in the way:* **laterum** (*opposition, obstacle,* of an island).

obitus, -a, -um, p.p. of **obeo.**

obitus, -ūs, [ob-itus (cf. **obeo**)], m., *a going down, setting, death* (cf. **obire mortem**), *dissolution.*

oblātus, -a, -um, p.p. of **offero.**

oblīmŏ, -āvī, -ātum, -are, [oblimo], 1. v. a., *clog* (orig. with mud), *stop.*

obliquŏ, -āvī, -ātum, -āre, [ob-liquŏ-], 1. v. a., *turn obliquely:* **sinus in ventum** (*brace, swing*).

oblīquus (-cus), -a, -um, [ob-†liquus (cf. **limus** and Gr. λέχριος)], adj., *sidewise, slantwise, slanting, sidelong, oblique:* in **obliquum** (*across, transversely*); **obliqua invidia** (*with eyes askance*).

oblītus, -a, -um, p.p. of **obliviscor.**

oblīviscor, oblītus, oblīviscī, [†oblivi- (of verb akin to **lividus** compounded with **ob**) + sco, *become dark to* (?)], 3. v. dep., *forget, think no more of.*— **oblītus, -a, -um,** p.p., *forgetting, forgetful, careless of, heedless of:* **sucos poma** (*losing*).— Also, *forgotten.*

oblīvium, -ī (-iī), [†oblivo- (cf. **obliviscor** and **liveo**)], n., *forgetfulness.*

obloquor, -locūtus, -loquī, [ob-loquor], 3. v. dep., *speak against.* — Also, *sing to* (with accompaniment of).

obluctor, -ātus, -ārī, [ob-luctor], 1. v. dep., *struggle against.*

obmūtēscŏ, -mūtuī, no sup., **-mutēscere,** [ob-mutesco], 3. v. n. incept., *hush, become speechless, be silent.*

obnītor, -nīsus (-nīxus), -nītī, [ob-nitor], 3. v. dep., *struggle*

against, lean against, lean on, struggle, strive.
obnīxus, -a, -um, p.p. of **obnitor.**
obnoxius, -a, -um, [ob-noxius, *guilty towards*], adj., *guilty.* — From ancient mode of administering justice, *bound to, subject to, exposed to.*
obnūbō, -nūpsī, -nūptum, -nūbere, [ob-nubo, in its orig. sense, *veil*], 3. v. a., *veil, cover.*
oborior, -ortus, -orīrī, [ob-orior], 4. v. dep., *rise against, rise over.* — **obortus, -a, -um,** p.p. as adj., *rising, flowing* (of tears), *blinding.*
obortus, -a, -um, p.p. of **oborior.**
obruō, -ruī, -rutum, -ruere, [ob-ruo], 3. v. a., *overwhelm, bury.*
obrutus, -a, -um, p.p. of **obruo.**
obscēnus, -a, -um, [prob. obs- (see ob) †caenŏ- (decl. as adj.)], adj., *filthy, foul.* — Less exactly, *unsightly, ugly, hideous, horrible.* — Esp., *ill-omened, ill-boding.*
obscūrō, -āvī, -ātum, -āre, [†obscurŏ-], 1. v. a., *darken, obscure.*
obscūrus, -a, -um, [ob-†scurus (cf. scutum), *covered over, shut in*], adj., *dark, dim, gloomy, dusky.* —Transferred, *obscured, unknown, little known, in the dark, unseen:* fama (*doubtful, dimmed*); haud obscura signa (*no uncertain signs*); obscuris vera involvens (*dark hints*); sub obscurum noctis (*under the darkness of night*).
obserō, -sēvī, -situm, -serere, [ob-sero], 3. v. a., *plant over.* — **obsitus, -a, -um,** p.p., *covered, beset, overgrown:* aevo (*heavy with, full of years*).
observātus, -a, -um, p.p. of **observo.**
observō, -āvī, -ātum, -āre, [observo], 1. v. a., *watch, mark, observe, notice, trace.* — Esp., *honor:* regem.
obsessus, -a, -um, p.p. of **obsideo.**
obsideō, -sēdī, -sessum, -sidēre, [ob-sedeo], 2. v. a., *blockade, beset, guard, besiege, occupy.* — ob-

sessus, -a, -um, p.p. as adj., *blocked up, beset, choked.*
obsidiō, -ōnis, [†obsidiŏ- (reduced) + o], f., *a blockade, a siege.*
obsīdō, no perf., no sup., **-sīdere,** [ob-sido], 3. v. a., *beset, occupy.*
obsitus, -a, -um, p.p. of **obsero.**
obstipēscō (-stupesco), -stipuī, no sup., **-stipēscere,** [ob-sti(stu)pesco], 3. v. n., *be amazed, be struck with astonishment, be stunned, be dazed, be struck dumb, stand amazed, be thunderstruck, be paralyzed.*
obstō, -stitī, -stātum, -stāre, [ob-sto], 1. v. n., *stand in the way of, hinder, withstand, stay, retard:* obstitit quibus Ilium (*be obnoxious*). — Also, *congeal* (of blood).
obstruō, -strūxī, -structum, -struere, [ob-struo], 3. v. a., *block up, choke, obstruct, seal* (of the ears).
obstupesco, see **obstipesco.**
obsum, -fuī, -esse, [ob-sum], irr. v. n., *be opposed* (cf. **prosum**), *injure, harm.*
obtectus, -a, -um, p.p. of **obtego.**
obtegō, -tēxī, -tectum, -tegere, [ob-tego], 3. v. a., *cover over, cover, obscure.*
obtendō, -tendī, -tentum, -tendere, [ob-tendo], 3. v. a., *spread before, outspread, shed:* obtenta nox (*spreading*).
obtentus, -a, -um, p.p. of **obtendo.**
obtentus, -ūs, [ob-tentus, cf. obtendo], m., *a spreading out.* — Concretely, *a canopy:* frondis.
obtestor, -ātus, -ārī, [ob-testor], 1. v. dep., *entreat* (by some sacred object called to witness), *beseech, adjure.*
obtexō, -texuī, no sup., **-texere,** [ob-texo], 3. v. a., *weave over.* — With change of point of view, *overspread.*
obtorqueō, -torsī, -tortum, -torquēre, [ob-torqueo], 2. v. a., *twist.*

obtortus, -a, -um, p.p. of obtorqueo.

obtruncō, -āvī, -ātum, -āre, [ob-trunco], 1. v. a., *cut down, butcher, slay.*

obtulī, see offero.

obtundō, -tudī, -tūsum, -tundere, [ob-tundo], 3. v. a., *dull* (orig. by beating), *blunt.* — obtūsus, -a, -um, p.p., *dulled, blunted, dull, dim, less vigorous.* — Fig., *obtuse, unfeeling.*

obtūsus, -a, -um, p.p. of obtundo.

obtūtus, -ūs, [ob-tutus, cf. obtueor], m., *a gaze, a fixed stare.*

obumbrō, -āvī, -ātum, -are, [ob-umbro], 1. v. a., *overshadow.*

obuncus, -a, -um, [ob-uncus], adj., *hooked, curved.*

obūstus, -a, -um [ob-ustus (see uro)], adj., *burnt around, hardened in the fire.*

obversus, -a, -um, p.p. of obverto.

obvertō, -vertī, -versum, -vertere, [ob-verto], 3. v. a., *turn towards, turn.* — obversus, -a, -um, p.p., *in opposition, facing, standing in front, firm* (as unflinching), *resolute:* huc obversus et huc (*turning this way and that*).

obvius, -a, -um, [ob-†via (decl. as adj.), cf. obviam], adj., *in the 'way, opposed, exposed, in front, before, to meet.*

occāsus, -ūs, [ob-casus, cf. occido], m., *a fall, ruin.* — Esp., the *setting* (of a heavenly body): solis (*sunset*). — Also (cf. last division), *sunset, the west.*

occīdō, -cīdī, -cāsum, -cidere, [ob-cado], 3. v. n., *fall, perish, be slain, disappear, be lost, be undone.* — Esp., *set.*

occīdō, -cīdī, -cīsum, -cidere, [ob-caedo], 3. v. a., *slay, kill.*

occīsus, -a, -um, p.p. of occido.

occubō, no perf., no sup., -āre, [ob-cubo], 1. v. n., *lie* (dead or buried): occubat umbris (*has fallen a prey*).

occulō, -culuī, -cultum, -culere, [?, cf. clam], 3. v. a., *bury, cover, hide, conceal.*—occultus, -a, -um, p.p. as adj., *concealed, secret, hidden:* sapor (*slight, scarcely distinguishable*).

occultē [abl. of occultus], adv., *secretly, privately.*

occultō, -āvī, -ātum, -are, [†occulto-, cf. occulo], 1. v. a., *hide, conceal.*

occultus, -a, -um, p.p. of occulo.

occumbō, -cubuī, -cubitum, -cumbere, [ob-cumbo], 3. v. n., *fall, die, be slain:* morti (*fall a prey*).

occupō, -āvī, -ātum, -āre, [†occup-, cf. †aucup- (ob-√cap as stem)], 1. v. a., *take in advance* (as against somebody else), *seize, take possession of, assail, strike, fill:* manicis (*bind*). — Fig., *overspread, fill, seize.*

occurrō, -currī, -cursum, -currere, [ob-curro], 1. v. n., *run to meet, rush to, rush in, come in the way, meet:* medius (*come in to interrupt*). — Fig., *appear, meet one's eyes.*

occursō, -āvī, -ātum, -āre, [ob-curso, cf. occurro], 1. v. n., *rush in the way, fall in the way of, meet.*

Ōceanītis, -idis, [Gr. patronymic], f., *daughter of Ocean.*

ōceanus, -ī, [Gr. Ὠκεανός], m., *the ocean.* — Personified, *Ocean*, conceived by the ancients as the universal parent.

ōcior, -us, [†ocu- (cf. Gr. ὠκύς) + ior, compar. of lost positive], adj., *swifter.* — Neut. as adv., *more swiftly, quicker.* — Also, *quickly, forthwith, at once.*

Ocnus, -ī, [Gr. Ὄκνος], m., the founder of Mantua.

ocrea, -ae, [†ocri- (cf. ocris, Ocriculum) + ea, f. of -eus], f., *a legging, a greave* (usually plur.).

octō [akin to Gr. ὀκτώ, Eng. *eight*]. indecl., num. adj., *eight.*

oculus, -ī, [†ocŏ- (akin to Gr. ὄσσε, for ὀκγε, Eng. *eye*, √ac, cf. **acies**) + lus, a dim.], m., *an eye.* — Also, from similarity (cf. Eng. "eye"), *a bud.*

odī, ōdisse, ōsus, [?, perf. of lost pres.], v. a., *hate:* diem (*curse*).

odium, -ī (-iī), [akin to **odi**], n., *hatred, hate, a grudge.* — est odio, *is hateful.*

odor, -ōris, [√od (cf. Gr. ὄζω) + or (os)], m., *an odor, a fragrance, a perfume.*

odōrātus, -a, -um, p.p. of **odoro.**

odōrifer, -era, -erum, [†odor- (as if odori-) + fer (√fer + us)], adj., *sweet-smelling, fragrant.*

odōrŏ, -āvī, -ātum, -āre, [†odōr-], 1. v. a., *perfume.* — odoratus, -a, -um, p.p., *perfumed, sweet-smelling, fragrant.*

odōrus, -a, -um, [perh. †odōr + us, but cf. **canorus**], adj., *sweet-smelling.* — Also (see etymology above), *keen-scented.*

Oeagrius, -a, -um, [Gr. Οἰάγριος], adj., *of Œagrus* (a Thracian king). — Less exactly, *Thracian.*

Oebalius, -a, -um, [Gr. Οἰβάλιος], adj., *of Œbalus* (a king of Sparta, the founder of Tarentum). — Fem., *Œbalia* (sc. **terra**), a name of Tarentum.

Oebalus, -ī, [Gr. Οἴβαλος], m.: 1. A king of Sparta (see above); 2. A king among the Campanians.

Oechalia, -ae, [Gr. Οἰχαλία], f. (prop. adj.), a city of Eubœa.

Oenōtrius, -a, -um, [†Oenotrŏ- (reduced) + ius], adj., *Œnotrian* (of the southern part of Italy). — Less exactly, *Italian.*

Oenōtrus, -a, -um, [perh. akin to Gr. οἶνος, cf. οἴνωτρος, *a vine prop*], adj., *of Œnotria* (the southern part of Italy), *Œnotrian.*

oestrus, -ī, [Gr. οἶστρος], m., *a gadfly.*

Oeta, -ae (-ē, -ēs), [Gr. Οἴτη], f., a mountain range of Thessaly running from Pindus easterly to the coast.

offa, -ae, [?], f., *a ball of dough, a cake.*

offendō, -fendī, -fēnsum, -fendere, [ob-fendo, cf. **defendo**], 3. v. a., *strike against, dash against.* — offensus, -a, -um, p.p., *striking against, striking:* exsultat imago vocis.

offēnsus, -a, -um, p.p. of **offendo.**

offerō (off-), **obtulī** (optulī), **oblātum, offerre** (obf-), [ob-fero], irr. v. a., *bring to, present, hold out.* — With reflexive or in pass., *appear, present one's self, come in one's way, expose, offer one's self.* — Less exactly and fig., *offer, show, grant.*

officiō, -fēcī, -fectum, -ficere, [ob-facio], 3. v. n., (*do something towards* or *to some one,* cf. **officium**). — Esp., *act against, hinder, thwart, injure.*

officium, -ī (-iī), [†offic- (ob-fac, as stem, cf. **artifex**) + ium], n., *a service, a kind office.* — Also, *a duty, a task.*

Oīleus, -eī (-ēī, -eos), [Gr. Ὀιλεύς], m., a king of Locris, father of Ajax. The name was added to that of Ajax either in the genitive or nominative, or as an adj., to distinguish him from Ajax son of Telamon.

olea, -ae, [akin to Gr. ἐλαία, poss. borrowed], f., *an olive* (berry or tree).

oleāginus (-neus, -nius), -a, -um, [†oleagin- (fr. **olea**, cf. **virago**) + us], adj., *of the olive.*

Olearos, -ī, [Gr. Ὀλέαρος], f., one of the Cyclades (now *Antiparos*).

oleaster, -trī, [†olea + term. akin to comparative], m., *a wild olive.*

oleō, oluī, no sup., **olēre,** [†olŏ- (cf. **olidus**), prob. √od in **odor**, ὄζω, cf. **lacrima**], 2. v. n. and a., *smell.* — olens, -entis, p. as adj., *smelling* (good, bad, or indifferent), *fragrant, odoriferous;* — *rank, ill-smelling, noisome.*

oleum, -ī, [see **olea**], n., *oil.*

ōlim [case-form of **ollus (ille)**, cf.

hinc], adv., *at that time, formerly, once, just now:* iam olim cum (*now at last, at the time when*). — Of future time, *hereafter, at some time, at any time.* — Indefinitely, *sometimes, often.*
oliva, -ae, [prob. same stem as olea, cf. Achivus], f., *the olive-tree.* — Less exactly, *an olive trunk, an olive branch, olive leaves.*
olīvifer, -era, -erum, [†oliva- (weakened) -fer (√fer + ns)], adj., *olive-bearing.*
olīvum, -ī, [see oliva], n., *oil.*
ollus, -a, -um; see ille.
olor, -ōris, [?], m., *a swan.*
olōrīnus, -a, -um, [†olor + inus], adj., *of the (a) swan.*
olus, -erts; see holus, the better spelling.
Olympiacus, -a, -um, [Gr. Ὀλυμπιακός], adj., *of Olympia* (the city of Elis, where the Olympic games were held), *Olympian.*
Olympus, -ī, [Gr. Ὄλυμπος], m., *a mountain on the northern frontier of Thessaly.* — From a notion of the ancients, *the heavens, heaven, the sky.*
ōmen, -inis, [?, but cf. oscines], n., *an omen, a portent, a prodigy:* in omen (*as an omen*); primis ominibus (*first marriage,* on account of the ancient custom of taking omens); regibus omen erat (*sacred custom,* which was an omen of prosperity, and the omission of which would be an evil omen); omina (*auspices*).
omnigenus, -a, -um, [†omni-genus (√gen + us, cf. benignus)], adj., *of all kinds, of all sorts, of every kind.*
omnīnō [abl. of †omninō- (†omni + nus)], adv., *altogether, entirely, utterly.*
omniparēns, -entis, [†omni-parens], adj., *all-producing, parent of all.*
omnipotēns, -entis, [†omni-potens], adj., *all-powerful, all-mighty, omnipotent.* — As subst., *the All-powerful* (Jupiter).

omnis, -is, [?], adj., *all, every:* cura (*the utmost*). — Often like totus, *the whole, the entire.* — Neut. plur., *everything, all, all things* (often to be rendered in Eng. by a defining word).
Omolē, see Homole.
onager, -grī, [Gr. ὄναγρος], m., *a wild ass.*
onerātus, -a, -um, p.p. of onero.
onerŏ, -āvī, -ātum, -āre, [†oner- (onus)], 1. v. a., *load, burden, fill, cover, heap, pile:* aggere ossa; sulcos proventu; epulis mensas; iaculo palmas (*seize the heavy javelin,* &c.); membra sepulcro (*cover deep*). — Fig., *burden, overwhelm:* his onerat dictis (*heap reproachful words,* &c.); me malis (*heap troubles upon*); aethera votis (*fill*). — With change of point of view, *load* (*into*), *pile, put up.* — onerātus, -a, -um, p.p. as adj., *heavy-laden.*
onerōsus, -a, -um, [†oner- (onus) + osus], adj., *burdensome, heavy, weighty.*
onus, -eris, [?], n., *a burden, a weight, a load.*
onustus, -a, -um, [†onus + tus, cf. honestus], adj., *laden, loaded.*
Onȳtēs, -is, [?], m., a Rutulian.
opācō, -āvī, -ātum, -āre, [†opacŏ-], 1. v. a., *darken, shade, overshadow, throw a shadow on.*
opācus, -a, -um, [?], adj., *dark, shaded, shady, overshadowed:* frigus (*cool shade*). — Less exactly, *overshadowing, shady.* — Neut. pl opaca locorum (*dark places*).
opera, -ae, [†oper- (of opus) + a], f., *labor, service, attention:* operam dare (*do service*).
operātus, -a, -um, p.p. of operor.
operiō, operui, opertum, operīre, [ob-pario, cf. aperio], 4. v. a., *cover, enshroud.* — opertus, -a, -um, p.p., *covered, secret, hidden:* telluris operta (*depths*).
operor, -ātus, -ārī, [†opera-], 1. v. dep., *be busied.* — Esp. p.p., *engaged in* (rites), *sacrificing.*

Opheltēs, -ae, [Gr. Ὀφέλτης], m., a Trojan, father of Euryalus.

opīmus, -a, -um, [stem akin *to* ops + mus], adj., *fruitful, rich, fertile:* arva; dapes. — Esp.: spolia (*princely,* technically of spoils taken by a commander-in-chief from a commander-in-chief in personal combat).

Ōpis, Ōpis, [Gr. Ὦπις], f.: 1. A nymph of Diana; 2. A naiad.

oportet, oportuit, no sup., **oportēre,** [?, cf. opportunus], 2. v. impersonal, *it behooves, it befits, one ought.*

opperior, -peritus (-pertus), -periri, [ob-perior, cf. **experior**], 4. v. dep., *wait for, await, expect.*

oppetō, -petīvī (-iī), -petitum, -petere, [ob-peto], 3. v. a., *fall to, fall upon, assail, meet, encounter.* — Esp. (sc. **mortem**), *fall, perish, be slain, meet death.*

oppidum, -ī, [prob. ob-pedum, *solid ground* (cf. Gr. πέδον and **oppido**)], n., (*a fastness?*), *a town* (fortified, as opposed to a mere hamlet or a large city), *a city.* — Fig., of bees, *fortress, abode.*

oppōnō, -posuī, -positum, -pōnere, [ob-pono], 3. v. a., *place towards, set against, array against.* — In pass., or with reflexive, *turn against, set one's self in the way, offer one's self, expose one's self, oppose, stand in the way, face* (something). — **oppositus, -a, -um,** p.p., *opposing, coming in the way, in opposition, facing, in front, before one, opposite, resisting.*

opportūnus, -a, -um, [ob-portunus, cf. **importunus**], adj., *opportune, fit, favorable, well suited, advantageous.*

opprimō, -pressī, -pressum, -primere, [ob-premo], 3. v. a., *press against, overwhelm, crush, subdue.*

oppugnō, -āvī, -ātum, -āre, [ob-pugno], 1. v. a. and n., *fight against, attack, assail, lay siege to.*

Ops, opis, [√op as stem, cf. **optimus, opto**], f. sing. (exc. nom.), *wealth, means, aid, help, assistance:* non opis est nostrae (*it is not in our power*). — Personified, the goddess of plenty and resources. — Plur., *means, resources, power, riches, might.*

optātō [abl. of **optatus**], adv., *opportunely, as one could wish.*

optātus, -a, -um, p.p. of **opto**.

optimus, -a, -um; see **bonus**.

optō, -āvī, -ātum, -āre, [†optŏ- (p.p. of √op, cf. **Ops, optimus**)], 1. v. a., *wish, desire, long, long for,* — *pray, hope, choose, prefer.*

opulentia, -ae, [†opulent + ia], f., *wealth, riches.*

opulentus, -a, -um, [†op- (as if opu-) + lentus], adj., *wealthy, rich.*

opus, -eris, [unc. root + us], n., *work* (in reference to its results, cf. **labor**), *labor, toil, activity.* — Concretely, *a work, a task, a labor, an undertaking, an employment, a deed* or *action.* — Of the result, *a work, a production:* operum labor (*the labor,* as a burden, *of the works,* as a production).

opus [same word as preceding, petrified as a predicate], indecl. (with esse expr. or implied), *there is need, one needs, one requires:* non mihi opus est, *I need not.*

ōra, ae, [?], f., *an edge, a border, an extremity:* loricae (*joints*). — Hence, *a coast* (the extreme edge, cf. **litus,** *the whole shore*), *a shore.* — Less exactly, from the maritime habits of the ancients, *a country, a region, a shore:* luminis orae (*the regions of light,* as opposed to the world below).

ōrāculum, -ī, [†orā- (of **oro,** *speak*) + culum], n., (*an announcement*). — Esp. of the gods, *a response, prophetic words, a prophecy, inspired words, a divine command.* — Less exactly, *an oracle* (place or source of prophetic words).

ōrātor, -ōris, [†orā (of **oro**) + tor], m., *a speaker.* — Also (cf. **oro**), *an embassador, a messenger.*

orbis, -is, [?], m., *a circle, a circuit, a course* (circular), *a ring, a disc, a wheel, a winding:* oculorum (*ball*). — Esp., *a region, the circle of the world, the world, the heavens.* — Also, *a circular cluster.* — Fig., *a cycle* (of time), *a revolution* (of the heavenly bodies).

orbita, ae, [†orbi + ta (cf. Gr. -της)], f., *a track, a path.*

orbus, -a, -um, [cf. Gr. ὀρφανός], adj., *deprived, bereft.*

orchas, -adis, [Gr. ὀρχάς], f., *an olive* (of a peculiar kind).

Orcus, -ī, [perh. akin to arceo], m., *a god of the lower world identified with Pluto, Death.* — Also, *the world below, Hades.*

ordior, orsus, ordīrī, [†ordi-, cf. ordo], 4. v. dep., *begin, commence, undertake, enter upon.* — Esp., *begin* (to speak). — **orsus, -a, -um,** p.p., *beginning.* — Neut. plur., *undertakings.* — Also (cf. **ordior**), *words, speech.*

ordō, -inis, [†ordi- (whence ordior, cf. exordium) + o], m., *a row, a rank, a series, a line.* — Abstractly, *order, array, arrangement, sequence:* uno habetis Achivos (*estimation*); fatorum (*fixed order*); vertitur (*succession of events*). — Phrases: ordine, *regularly, in detail;* ex ordine, *continuously;* in ordine, *in regular series.*

Oreades, -um, [Gr. Ὀρειάς], f. pl., *mountain-nymphs.*

Orestēs, -ae (-is), [Gr. Ὀρέστης], m., *the son of Agamemnon.* He killed his mother Clytemnestra, and was driven mad by the Furies. His career was a favorite subject for the dramatic art.

orgia, -ōrum, [Gr. ὄργια], n. plur., *the orgies* (feast of Bacchus, celebrated with wild frenzied revelry), *feast of Bacchus.*

orichalcum, -ī, [Gr. ὀρείχαλκος], n., *mountain bronze* (a peculiar mixture of copper used by the ancients).

Ōricius, -a, -um, [†Oricŏ- (reduced) + ius], adj., *of Oricum* (a town of Epirus). — Less exactly, *of Epirus.*

orīgō, -inis, [†orī- (of orior) + go, cf. imago], f., *a beginning, an origin, a source, a common cement, a first production, a birth.* — Also, *a race, a stock,* — *an ancestor, a progenitor.* — Phrase: ab origine, *from the foundation, utterly, root and branch.*

Ōriōn, -onis (-ōnis), [Gr. Ὠρίων], m., *a mythic hunter of antiquity placed in the heavens as a constellation.* — Also, *Orion* (the constellation, whose rising and setting were attended by storms).

orior, ortus, orīrī, [?, cf. Gr. ὄρνυμαι], 3. and 4. v. dep., *rise, begin, appear, originate, be born, spring.* — **oriēns, -entis,** p., *rising.* — As subst., *the rising sun, the dawn, the East, the East* (country).

Ōrīthyia, -ae, [Gr. Ὠρείθυια], f., *a daughter of King Erechtheus of Athens.*

ornātus, -ūs, [†ornā- (of orno) + tus], m., *adornment, ornament, attire, ornaments* (collectively, of a headdress).

ornātus, -a, -um, p.p. of **orno.**

ornō, -āvī, -ātum, -āre, [prob. fr. a stem in -nŏ-, of unc. root], 1. v. a., *adorn, deck, equip, furnish.*

ornus, -ī, [?], f., *an ash-tree, an ash.*

Ornytus, -ī, [?], m., an Etruscan.

ōrō, -āvī, -ātum, -āre, [†or-(os)], 1. v. a. and n., (*speak*), *plead, beg, beseech, entreat, implore, beg for, supplicate.*

Orōdēs, -is, [Gr. Ὀρώδης], m., a warrior in the army of Æneas.

Orontēs, -is (-ī), [Gr. Ὀρόντης], m.: 1. A river of Syria; 2. The commander of Æneas' Lycian allies.

Orpheus, -eī (-eos), [Gr. Ὀρφεύς], m., a mythic bard of antiquity. He rescued his wife from the world below by his skill in music, but

was afterwards torn in pieces by the Thracian women.
orsa, see **ordior**.
Orsēs, -is, [?], m., a Trojan.
Orsilochus, -ī, [Gr.], m., a Trojan.
orsus, -a, -um, p.p. of **ordior**.
ortus, -a, -um, p.p. of **orior**.
ortus, -ūs, [√or (of **orior**)+ tus], m., *a rising, the dawn*.
Ortygia, a e, [Gr. 'Ορτυγία, *Quail island*], f.: 1. A name of Delos; 2. An island in the harbor of Syracuse, forming part of the city.
Ortygius, -ī, [?], m., a Rutulian.
os, ōris, [?], n., *the mouth*. — Less exactly, *the face, the countenance, the lips, the jaws; language, words, speech :* **ante ora** (*before the eyes*); **ora discordia** (*language*); **manus inter -que ora** (*under the hands and before the face*); **ora exsertans** (*head*); **virum diffundit in ora** (*spread abroad in the mouths of men*); **ora implet** (*ears*); **formidinis ora** (*phantoms*); **tria Dianae** (*forms*); **tali ore locutus** (*words*); **uno ore** (*with one accord*); **magno ore** (*voice*). — Often it may be omitted with words of speech.— Less exactly, *an opening, mouth* (of a river), *aperture, head* (of an ulcer).
os, ossis, [cf. Gr. ὄστεον], n., *a bone*. — Plur., *the bones, the frame, the inmost frame, the remains*.
Oscī, -ōrum, [?], m. pl., the early inhabitants of Campania, *the Oscans*.
ōscillum, -ī, [†osculŏ + lum], n., *a little face, a little mask*.
osculum, -ī, [†os + culum, dim.], n., *a lip, the mouth, a kiss*.

Osīnius, -ī (-iī), [?], m., a king of Clusium.
Osiris, -idis (-is), · [Gr. Ὄσιρις], m.: 1. An Egyptian divinity; 2. A Rutulian.
Ossa, a e, [Gr. Ὄσσα], f., a mountain of Thessaly.
ostendŏ, -tendī, -tēnsum (-tentum), -tendere, [obs-tendo], 3. v. a., *stretch before, stretch out, expose, raise, show, exhibit, point out*. — With reflexive or in pass., *show one's self, appear*.
ostentŏ, -āvī, -ātum, ā re, [obstento, cf. ostendo], 1. v. a., *show, display, point out*.
ostium, -ī (-iī), [perh. akin to **os**], n., *the mouth*. — Less exactly, *a door, a gate, an entrance*. — Plur., *the mouth* (of a river), *a harbor*.
ostrifer, -era, -erum, [†ostrŏ-fer (√fer + us)], adj., *oyster-bearing, rich in oysters*.
ostrum, -ī, [prob. borrowed fr. Gr. ὄστρεον], n., (*a shell-fish*). — Less exactly, *purple* (a color made from the fish), *purple* (purple fabrics).
Othryadēs, a e, [Gr. Ὀθρυάδης], m., *son of Othrys*.
Othrys, -yos, [Gr. Ὄθρυς], m., a mountain in Thessaly.
ōtium, -ī (-iī), [?], n., *rest, ease, idleness, quiet, leisure, repose*.
ovīle, -is, [†ovi-(lengthened)+le (n. of lis), prop. adj.], n., *a sheep-fold*.
ovis, -is, [cf. Gr. ὄϊς, Eng. *ewe*], f., *a sheep*.
ovŏ, -āvī, -ātum, -āre, [?], 1. v. n., *rejoice, triumph, exult, express one's joy*. — **ovāns, -āntis**, p. as adj., *rejoicing, delighted, glad*.
ōvum, -ī, [prob. akin to **avis**, cf. Gr. ᾠόν], n., *an egg*.

P.

pābulum, -ī, [as if √pa (in **pasco**) + bulum, but cf. **cingulum** and **ferculum**], n., *food, fodder, pasturage, nourishment*.
pācātus, -a, -um, p.p. of **paco**.
Pachȳnus (-um), -ī, [Gr. Πάχυνος], m. and n. (f.), the southeastern extremity of Sicily (*Capo di Passaro*).
pācifer, -era, -erum, [†pac- (as if paci-) -fer (√fer + us)], adj., *peace-bringing:* **oliva** (*peaceful, the emblem of peace*).

Vocabulary. 197

pacisco, no perf., **pactum, paciscere**, [√pac, *bind*, cf. obs. **păco, pax, pecus**], 3. v. a., (archaic exc. p.p.), *agree, bargain, agree upon, promise*. — **pactus, -a, -um**, p.p., *stipulated, agreed upon, betrothed, promised, plighted.* — Fem., *a bride, an affianced wife, a betrothed* (wife). — Neut., *an agreement.*—Less exactly (in abl.), *a manner, means, a way, a method.* — **paciscor**, pass. as dep., *bargain, stipulate, agree, barter :* vitam pro laude ; letum pro laude (*pay the price of*).
paciscor, see **pacisco**.
păcō, -āvī, -ātum, ā re, [†pac-], 1. v. a., *reduce to peace, give peace to.* — **pācātus, -a, -um**, p.p., *brought to peace, peaceful, freed from war.*
Pactōlus, -ī, [Gr. Πακτωλός], m., a river of Lydia famous for its gold.
pactum, see **pacisco**.
pactus, -a, -um, p.p. of **pacisco**.
Padus, -ī, [?], m., *the Po*, the famous river of Northern Italy.
Padūsa, ae, [akin to **Padus**], f., an artificial mouth of the Po, or canal, running into the Adriatic near Ravenna.
Paeān, -ānis, [Gr. Παιάν, Παιών], m., the physician of the gods; also used as a name of Apollo, — Also, *a hymn to Apollo, a hymn* (to any deity), *a song of triumph, a song of thanksgiving.*
paene (pēne), [?], adv., *almost, nearly, all but.*
paenitet, -uit, no sup., **-ere**, [adj.-stem akin to **poena**], 2. v. a. impers., *it repents.* — Translated by a change of construction, *one repents, regrets, is ashamed, disdains.*
Paeonius, -a, -um, [Gr. Παιώνιος, cf. **Paean**], adj., *of Paeon* (the god of medicine) : Paeonium in morem (*in medical guise*). — Less exactly, *medicinal.*
Paestum, -ī, [Gr. Παῖστον], n., a city of Lucania, formerly called

Posidonia, famed for its roses.
Pagasus, -ī, [?], m., an Etruscan.
pāgina, -ae, [†pagi- (as root, in pango) + na (f. of -nus)], f., *a leaf* (of a book), *a page.*
pāgus, -ī, [perh. akin to **pango**], m., *a village* (unwalled, cf. **oppidum**) or *farming district, a town.*
Palaemōn, -onis, [Gr. Παλαίμων], m., a son of Athamas and Ino, changed to a sea-god. A shepherd.
palaestra, -ae, [Gr. παλαίστρα], f., *a palæstra* or *place for wrestling.* — Less exactly, *wrestling, games* (in which wrestling predominated).
palam [unc. case-form (cf. **clam, coram**), perh. akin to **palea, pālor**], adv., *openly.*
Palamēdēs, -is, [Gr. Παλαμήδης], m., a famous Grecian hero of the Trojan war.
pālāns, -tis, *wandering, straggling.*
Palātīnus, -a, -um, [†Palatio- (reduced) + inus], adj., *of the Palatine* (the famous hill at Rome).
Palātium, -ī (-iī), [†palatŏ- (reduced) + ium (n. of ius)], n., *the Palatine hill* (on which was the imperial residence of Augustus). — From association, *a palace.*
palātum (-us), -ī, [?, akin to **palea, pālor**, *the broad canopy of the mouth*?], n. and m., (*a broad canopy*, archaic). — Esp., *the roof of the mouth, the palate.*
palea, -ae, [perh. akin to **pālor, palam**], f., *chaff* (as scattered abroad?).
palear, -āris, [†palea- (or stem akin) + re (reduced, n. of ris)], n., *the dewlap* (of cattle).
Palēs, -is, [?, √pal (in **palea, pālor**) + is (-es)], f. (anciently m.), the divinity of shepherds (of the wandering flocks?).
Palĭcus, -ī, [?], m., the name of two sons of Jupiter deified in Sicily.
Palinūrus, -ī, [Gr. Παλίνουρος], m., the pilot of Æneas, murdered on the coast of Italy after swimming to land.
paliūrus, -ī, [Gr. παλίουρος], m.,

a thorn-bush (said to be the *Rhamnus paliurus*).
palla, a e, [?], f., *a robe* (for women, of somewhat uncertain nature, prob. a mantle or shawl of varying size, sometimes, when confined by a girdle, taking the place of an undergarment).
Palladius, -a, -um, [Gr. Παλλάδιος], adj., *of Pallas.* — Neut. (cf. Gr. Παλλάδιον), *a statue of Pallas.* — Esp., *the Palladium* (or statue of Pallas in Troy, stolen by Ulysses and Diomede).
Pallantēus (-ius), -a, -um, [†Pallant + eus], adj., *of Pallas* (an ancient king of Arcadia). — Less exactly, *of Pallanteum:* moenia. — Neut., *Pallanteum,* a city of Arcadia whence Evander came to Italy. — Also, the city built by him in Italy on the site of Rome.
Pallas, -adis, [Gr. Πάλλας], f., the Grecian divinity identified by the Romans with Minerva, a goddess of war and of household arts and of learning, the discoverer of the olive.
Pallās, -antis, [Gr. πάλλας, *a young man*], m., the son of Evander, killed by Turnus while fighting for Æneas; 2. An Arcadian.
Pallēnē, -ēs, [Gr. Παλλήνη], f., a peninsula of Macedonia whence came Proteus the sea-god.
palleō, palluī, no sup., **pallēre,** [†pallŏ-, cf. **pallidus**], 2. v. n., *be pale, be pallid.* — **pallēns, -entis,** p. as adj., *pale, pallid, colorless, pale green, blue, gray,* &c.
pallidus, -a, -um, [†pallŏ- (cf. **palleo**) + dus], adj., *pale, pallid, colorless, wan.*
pallor, -ōris, [pall- (as root of palleo)+or], m., *paleness, pallor.*
palma, ae, [perh. √pal (cf. **palea, palor**) + ma, but cf. Gr. παλάμη], f., *the palm* (of the hand), *the hand.* — Also, from the shape of the leaf, *the palm-tree, the palm, a palm branch.* — Fig., *victory, a prize* (of victory), *a victor.*

palmes, -itis, [perh. akin to **palma**], m., *a young shoot* or *branch* (of the vine), *a vine.*
palmōsus, -a, -um, [†palma- (reduced) + osus], adj., *abounding in palms, palm-grown, palmy.*
palmula, ae, [†palmŏ- (cf. **palma**) + la], f., *an oar-blade.*
Palmus, -ī, [?], m., an Etrurian slain by Mezentius.
palumbēs, -is, [?], m. and f., *a wood-pigeon.*
palūs, -ūdis, [?], f., *a marsh, a pool, a lake, water* (stagnant).
palūster (-tris), -tris, -tre, [†palud+tris (reduced)], adj., *marshy, of the marsh.*
pampineus, -a, -um, [†pampinŏ- (reduced) + eus], adj., *of vine leaves, vine-wreathed:* auctumnus (*crowned with vine leaves*).
pampinus, -ī, [?], m. and f., *a vine leaf, a vine shoot, a vine branch.*
Pān, -os, [Gr. Πάν], m., the god of shepherds, represented as half goat and playing on the syrinx.
panacea, -ae, [Gr. πανάκεια], f., *panacea* (an herb famed for its all-healing properties).
Panchaeus, -a, -um, [Gr. Παγχαία], adj., *of Panchæa* (an island of Arabia famous for its frankincense). — Fem. **Panchāia,** the island itself.
Pandarus, -ī, [Gr. Πάνδαρος], m.: 1. A Lycian archer who shot an arrow among the Greeks, and thus broke the treaty between them and the Trojans; 2. A companion of Æneas.
pandō, pandī, pansum (passum), pandere, [?], 3. v. a., *spread out, unfold, extend, spread, expose, open, lay open.* — In pass. or with reflexive, *extend, lie open.* — Fig., *show, disclose, unfold, lay open, expose, relate, reveal.* — **passus, -a, -um,** p.p. as adj., *spread, extended, dishevelled* (of hair), *dried* (spread in the sun). — Neut., *raisin wine* (made of grapes spread to dry in the sun).

pandus, -a, -um, [prob. **pand** (as root of **pando**) + **us**], adj., *bent, curved:* lances (*hollow*, bent inwards).

Pangaea, -orum (-us, -ī), [Gr. Πάγγαιον], n. plur., a mountain-range between Macedonia and Thrace.

pangŏ, panxi (pegi, pepigī), panctum (pactum), pangere, [√pag, cf. Gr. πήγνυμι, perh. **pax, paciscor**], 3. v. a., *fasten, fix.* — Fig., *agree upon, appoint* (by agreement), *contract* (a treaty or alliance). — Also, *put together, contrive.*

Panopēa, -ae, (Panope-, -es), [Gr. Πανόπη], f., a sea-nymph.

Panopēs, -is, [Gr. Πανόπη], m., an attendant of Acestes.

Pantagiās, -ae, [Gr. Πανταγίας], m., a river of Sicily.

panthēra, -ae, [Gr. πάνθηρ], f., a *panther*, especially sacred to Bacchus.

Panthūs, -ī, [Gr. Πάνθοος], m., a Trojan priest of Apollo, father of Euphorbus.

papaver, -eris, [?], n., *a poppy.* — Used loosely for the juice in a medical form, *poppy.*

Paphius, -a, -um, [Gr. Πάφιος], adj., *of Paphos, Paphian.* — Less exactly, *of Venus.*

Paphos (-us), -ī, [Gr. Πάφος], f., a city of Cyprus famous for an ancient temple of Venus.

papilla, -ae, [†papula + la], f., *a nipple, the breast.*

papula, -ae, [?], f., *a pimple.*

pār, paris, [?, perh. akin to **paro, pario,** as *equivalent* in barter], adj., *equal, no less, like, well-matched, corresponding, even :* aetas (*the same*); discurrere pares (*in equal numbers*); alae (*even*); leges (*impartial*).

parātus, -a, -um, p.p. of **paro.**

Parcae, -ārum, [?, prob. akin to **parco**], f. plur., *the Fates*, goddesses of birth and death (Nona, Decuma, and Morta), and so the arbiters of human destiny, identified with the Greek Μοῖραι (Clotho, Lachesis, and Atropos).

parce [abl. of **parcus**], adj., *sparingly, carefully.*

parco, peperei (parsi), parcitum (parsum), parcere, [?], 3. v. n. and a., *spare* (refrain from using), *be sparing of, save, husband, refrain from* (as if from using), *forbear, cease, restrain :* futuro (*be prudent, take thought for*); parcite Rutuli (*hold!*); flatibus Euri (*spare,* deal gently with). — Also, *spare* (refrain from destroying as if from wasting), *preserve.* — Active, *save, keep :* talenta natis.

parcus, -a, -um, [akin to **parco**], adj., *frugal, sparing, thrifty.* — Transferred, *scanty, a little.*

parens, -cutis, [aorist part. of **pario**, cf. ὁ τεκών], comm., *a parent, a father, a mother, a sire, a dam.* — Less exactly, *an ancestor, a forefather.* — Fig., of a country: magna parens frugum.

pāreō, pārui, pāritum, pārēre, [?, prob. adj.-stem akin to **pario**], 2. v. n., *appear, show one's self :* sidera (*be intelligible* or *well-known*). — Esp., *appear* (at a summons?), *obey, be subject to, submit to.* — **parēns, -entis,** p., *obedient.*

pariēs, -etis, [?], m., *a wall* (within a house, cf. **murus, moenia,** of a city).

pariō, peperī, paritum (partum), parere, [?, √par, cf. **paro, opiparus**], 3. v. a., *secure, procure, win :* sibi letum (*find a means of,* &c.). — Esp., *bring forth, bear.* — Pass., *be born.* — **partus, -a, -um,** p.p., *acquired, secured, won.* — Neut., *gain, gathered store, acquired gains.*

Paris, -idis, [Gr. Πάρις], m., the son of Priam and Hecuba. He awarded the prize of beauty to Venus over Juno (Here) and Minerva (Pallas), and thus won Helen as the most beautiful woman living. He is sometimes represented as effeminate and weak, whence his name is used as a term of reproach.

pariter [†pari- (of **par**) + **ter**, cf. **acriter**], adv., *equally, alike, in like manner, not less, as well ... as, together, at the same time:* pariter cum flamma (*no less swift than*).

Parius, -a, -um, [Gr. Πάριος], adj., *of Paros, Parian.*

parma, -ae, [?], f., *a shield* (small and round), *a buckler, a shield* (in general).

Parnāsius (-assius), -a, -um, [Gr. Παρνάσιος], adj., *of Parnassus, Parnassian.*

Parnāsus (-assus), -ī, [Gr. Παρνασός], m., *a mountain in Thessaly, the favorite haunt of the Muses.*

parŏ, -āvī, -ātum, -āre, [†parŏ- (cf. **opiparus** and **pareo**)], 1. v. a., *procure, provide, secure, prepare, prepare for, get ready.* — Fig., *prepare, begin, endeavor, attempt, aim at, be about to, intend, arrange:* parabitur imber (*be gathering*); iussa parat (*make the preparations ordered*). — **parātus, -a, -um,** p.p., *prepared, ready, arranged.*

Paros, -ī, [Gr. Πάρος], f., *one of the Cyclades islands, famous for its white marble.*

Parrhasius, -a, -um, [Gr. Παρράσιος], adj., *of Parrhasia* (a town in Arcadia). — Less exactly, *Arcadian.*

pars, partis, [√par (akin to ἔπορον) + tis (reduced)], f., *a part, a portion, a share, a place, a region, a direction, a side:* naturae (*branch*); pacis (*a pledge*). — Repeated, *one part ... another, some ... some.*

Parthenius, -ī (-iī), [Gr. Παρθένιος], m., *a Trojan.*

Parthenius, -a, -um, [Gr. Παρθένιος], adj., *of Parthenius* (a mountain in Arcadia), *Parthenian.*

Parthenopaeus, -ī, [Gr. Παρθενοπαῖος], m., *the son of Atalanta and Meleager, who fought in the Theban and Trojan wars.*

Parthenopē, -ēs, [Gr. Παρθενόπη], f., *the ancient name of Naples, or of the city for which Naples (New city) was substituted.*

Parthus, -a, -um, [Gr. Πάρθος], adj., *Parthian, of the Parthians* (a nation northeast of the Caspian, famous as archers). — Masc. plur., *the Parthians,* the nation itself.

partim [acc. of **pars**], adv., *partly, in part.* — Distributing a plur. subj. or obj., *some ... others, a part ... a part.*

partiŏ, -īvī, -ītum, -īre, [†parti- (of **pars**)], 4. v. a., (*divide*). — Pass. as dep., *divide, share:* curas (*impart*). — **partītus, -a, -um,** p.p. (in pass. sense), *divided.*

partitus, -a, -um, p.p. of **partio** and **partior.**

parturiŏ, -īvī (-iī), -ītum, -īre, [prob. †parturŏ- (old fut. p. of **pario**)], 4. v. a. desid., *be pregnant, teem, be in bloom.*

partus, -a, -um, p.p. of **pario.**

partus, -ūs, [√par (in **pario**) + tus], m., *birth, bearing, delivery, motherhood.* — Concr., *offspring.*

parum [acc. of stem akin to **parvus**], adv., *little, not much, not very:* laetus (*far from*).

parumper [parum-per (cf. **nuper, semper**)], adv., *a little while, for a moment.*

parvulus, -a, -um, [†parvŏ+lus], adj., *little, small.*

parvus, -a, -um, [√par (cf. **parcus, pars**) + vus], adj., *small, little, slender, slight, trifling, humble:* pabula (*bits of*). — Neut., *a little, humble circumstances, a small thing.* — Abl., *a small price, small cost.*

pāscŏ, pāvī, pāstum, pāscere, [√pa + sco], 3. v. a. and n., *pasture, feed, tend.* — Less exactly, *nourish, feed, foster, support, grow* (act.). — Intrans., *graze, feed, browse.* — Pass. as dep., *graze, feed,*

feed on, pluck. — Less exactly (of flame, &c.), *be fed, be supplied with food, play around.*

pascuum, -ī, [n. of adj., akin to pasco, cf. **nocuus**], n., *pasture-land, pasture.*

Pāsiphaē, -ēs, [Gr. Πασιφάη], f., the daughter of Minos king of Crete, the mother of the Minotaur.

passim [acc. of passis (√pad + tis, cf. **pando**)], adv., *far and wide, all around, everywhere, here and there, in all directions.*

passus, -a, -um, p.p. of **pando.**

passus, -a, -um, p.p. of **patior.**

passus, -us, [√pad + tus], m., *a step:* longi passus (*a long distance*).

pāstor, -ōris, [√pa (with unc. s, cf. **lustrum**) + tor (cf. pasco)], m., *a shepherd, a herdsman:* Phrygius (i.e. *Paris*).

pāstōrālis, -e, [†pastor + alis], adj., *of shepherds:* myrtus (*the shepherds'*).

pastus, -a, -um, p.p. of **pasco** and **pascor.**

pastus, -ūs, [√pa (with unc. s, cf. **pastor**) + tus], m., *feeding, pasture.* — Concretely, *a pasture.*

Patavium, -ī (-iī), [?], n., *Padua* (a city near the Adriatic, founded by Antenor).

patefaciō, -fēci, -factum, -facere, [unc. stem (akin to pateo) -facio], 3. v. a., *lay open, open.*

patefactus, -a, -um, p.p. of **patefacio.**

pateō, patui, no sup., **patēre,** [†patŏ- (cf. **patulus**), √pat, akin to πετάννυμαι], 2. v. n., *lie open, be opened, be open, open, be extended, extend, be exposed:* Tartarus (*yawn*). — Fig., *appear, be disclosed.* — **patēns, -entis,** p., *wide, open, free.*

pater, -tris, [√pa (in potis) + ter, cf. mater], m., *a father, a sire, an ancestor, a forefather, a parent.* — As a term of respect or worship, of gods, kings, ancient worthies, &c., *father, venerable sire, venerable.* — Alone of Jupiter and Vulcan, also of Æneas: Teucrum (as the father of his people); Oceanus rerum (*parent*). — Also usually in plur., *the nobles, chiefs, the senate, the elders:* pater Romanus (*the Roman senate*).

patera, -ae, [akin to pateo, cf. πατάνη, patina], f., *a bowl* (flat like a saucer, for libations), *a plate, a cup* (for drinking).

paternus, -a, -um, [†pater- (unsyncopated) + nus], adj., *of a father, paternal, hereditary, ancestral.*

patēscō, -uī, no sup., **-escere,** [†patē- (of pateo) + sco], 3. v. n., *lie open.* — Fig., *be disclosed, become manifest.*

patior, passus, pati, [√pat, prob. akin to πάσχω], 3. v. dep., *suffer, endure, bear, undergo.* — Also, *tolerate, have to bear, suffer, allow, permit.* — Absolutely, *live in suffering:* lituos (*become inured to*). — **patiēns, -cutis,** p. as adj., *capable of enduring, enduring, submissive to, patient, trained to, broken to.*

patrius, -a, -um, [†pater (syncopated) + ius], adj., *of a father, a father's, of one's ancestors, ancestral, filial* (paid to a parent). — Also used as adj. of **patria** (see below), *of one's country, national, native.* — Fem. (sc. **terra**), *one's country, a country* (of one's own), *home, native city, native country.*

Patrōn, -ōnis, [?], m., an Acarnanian in the company of Æneas.

patruus, -ī, [†pater (syncopated) + uus], m., *an uncle* (on the father's side, cf. **avunculus**, *a mother's brother*).

patulus, -a, -um, [†patŏ- (cf. pateo) lus], adj., *spreading, wide, broad, flat.*

paucus, -a, -um, [?], adj. (mostly plur.), *a few* (only), *few.* — Masc. plur., *a few, few.* — Neut. plur., *a few things, a few words.* — Abl., *briefly, in a few words.*

paulātim [†paulŏ- (reduced) + atim, cf. **catervatim**], adv., *little by little, gradually, slowly, by degrees.*

paulisper [unc. form of †paulo + per, cf. **nuper**], adv., *a little while, for a while, a while.*

paulus, -a, -um, [?, akin to **paucus**], adj., *a little.* — **paulo,** abl. as adv., *a little, somewhat.* — **paulum,** acc. as adv., *a little, a while, a moment.*

pauper, -eris, [?], adj., *poor, in humble circumstances, in poverty, humble, lowly.* — Masc., *a poor man.*

pauperiēs, -ēī, [†pauper + ies], f., *poverty, humble circumstances.*

pausia (-ea), -ae, [?], f., *an olive* (of a special kind).

pavidus, -a, -um, [†pavŏ-, of unc. kin., cf. **paveo**], adj., *timid, trembling, frightened, in alarm, awed, awe-stricken, in awe, anxious.*

pavitŏ, -āvī, -ātum, -āre, [†pavitŏ- (as p.p. of **paveo**)], 1. v. n., *tremble* (with fear).

pavor, -ōris, [√pav (cf. **paveo**) + or], m., *fear, terror, dread, anxiety:* pavor pulsans (*anxious throbbing*).

pāx, pācis, [√pac (in **paciscor**, perh. **pecus**)], f., *peace, pardon, favor.* — pace, abl., *by permission.*

peccātum, -ī, [n. p.p. of **pecco**], n., *a sin, a fault, a crime.*

peccŏ, -āvī, -ātum, -āre, [?], 1. v. n., *sin, err, do wrong.*

pecten, -inis, [pect (as root of **pecto**) + en (cf. **unguen**)], m., *a comb.* — From similarity, *a sley* or *reed* (the instrument by which the thread is beaten into place). — Perhaps from some earlier form of the instrument, *a quill* or *plectrum* (with which the strings of the lyre were struck).

pectŏ, pexī (pexuī), **pexum** (pectītum), **pectere,** [√pec (cf. **plecto**), akin to πέκω], 3. v. a., *comb.*

pectus, -oris, [perh. akin to **pecto**, cf. **pectinatus,** *sloping both ways*], n., *the breast-bone, the breast, the chest.* — Fig., for both soul and mind (cf. Eng. *heart, head*), supposed by the ancients to be situated in the chest, *the mind, wisdom, the heart, the soul, courage.*

pecuārius, -a, -um, [†pecu + arius], adj., *of cattle.* — Neut. pl., *herds.*

pecūlium, -ī (-iī), [†peculi (†pecu + lis) + ium], n., (*a slave's cattle*), *property* (of a slave).

pecus, -oris, [prob. √pac, *bind* (in **paciscor**) + us], n., *cattle, a flock, a herd, a stud, sheep.* — Less exactly, *a herd* (of wild animals), *a swarm.*

pecus, pecudis, [prob. †pecu + dus (reduced)], m. and f., *a beast* (of any kind of cattle), *a brute.* — Esp., *a sheep, a victim* (for sacrifice). — Plur., *beasts, brutes, flocks, herds.*

pedes, -itis, [†ped (as if pedi-) + tis, or -tus (reduced)], comm. or adj., *on foot, a foot-soldier.* — Collectively or in plur., *infantry, foot-soldiers, the foot.*

pedester (-tris), -tris, -tre, [†pedit + tris], adj., *of the foot* (soldiers): acies (*of the foot*); pugna (*infantry*).

pedica, -ae, [†ped (as if pedi-) + ca, cf. **manica**], f., *a fetter, a slip-noose, a springe,*

pedum, -ī, [perh. akin to **pes**], n., *a crook* (of a shepherd), *a staff* (with a hooked end).

Pēgasus, -ī, [Gr. Πήγασος], m., the winged horse of the Muses.

pēior, see **malus.**

pelagus, -ī, [Gr. πέλαγος], n., *the sea, a sea, the deep.*

Pelasgus, -a, -um, [Gr. Πελασγοί], adj., *Grecian* (from the supposed ancient inhabitants). — Masc. pl., *the Greeks.*

Pelethronii, -ōrum, [Gr. Πελεθρόνιοι], m. plur., a name of the Lapithæ from a town or tribe in Thessaly where the Lapithæ dwelt.

Peliās, -ae, [Gr. Πελίας], m., a Trojan.
Pelidēs, -ae, [Gr. Πηλείδης], m., *son (descendant) of Peleus.* — Esp., of Achilles his son, and Pyrrhus his grandson.
Pēlion, -ii, [Gr. Πήλιον], n., a mountain of Thessaly, fabled to have been used by the giants in scaling Olympus. Saturn also fled thither in the form of a horse.
Pellaeus, -a, -um, [Gr. Πελλαῖος], adj., *of Pella* (the birthplace of Alexander of Macedon). — Also, *Alexandrian* (of Alexandria in Egypt, founded by Alexander). — Less exactly, *Egyptian.*
pellāx, -ācis, [per-lax (root of lacio as stem, cf. **pellicio**], adj., *alluring, enticing, deceitful.*
pellis, -is, [akin to πέλλα, πέλας], f., *a skin, a hide.*
pellō, pepulī, pulsum, pellere, [?, akin to πάλλω], 3. v. a., *strike, thrust, beat.* — Also of the effect, *drive away, drive back, overcome, conquer, beat, chase, repel, repulse, expel, banish, reject.* — Fig., *dispel, banish, remove, drive out:* lacrimas (*dry up*); pestis pulsa (*heal*); hiemem (*put to flight*). — Also, *set in motion, move, impel, strike.*—**pulsus, -a, -um,** p.p. in all meanings. — Also, *echoing, clashing, flying, a fugitive, stricken:* quo amor nostri (*whither fled,* &c.).
Pelopēius, -a, -um, [Gr. Πελοπήιος], adj., *of Pelops:* moenia (of Argos, the chief city of the Peloponnesus).
Pelops, -opis, [Gr. Πέλοψ], m., the son of Tantalus and father of Atreus. He was served up as food for the gods by his father, restored to life by Jupiter, and furnished with an ivory shoulder in place of the one eaten at the banquet. He gained control of the Peloponnesus, which was named for him.
Pelōrus (-um), -ī, [Gr. Πέλωρος], m. and n., a promontory on the northeast coast of Sicily, now *Capo di Faro*, one of the headlands of the Straits of Messina.
pelta, -ae, [Gr. πέλτη], f., *a shield* (small and light and curved, used by barbarians, cf. **clipeus,** the round shield of the Greeks, and **scutum,** the oblong shield of the Romans).
Pēlūsiacus, -a, -um, [Gr. Πηλουσιακός], adj., *of Pelusium* (a city of Egypt). — Less exactly, *Egyptian.*
penātēs, -ium, [prob. †penu- (reduced)+ atis, *dwellers in the inner house*], m. plur., *the Penates, the household gods,* gods of the household, or of the state considered as a household. What particular divinities, if any, they represented is uncertain, as is also their relation to the Lar or Lares, with whom they have much in common. Their images, apparently of small size, were kept in the interior of the house and carried with the family in migrations. — Fig., *a home, a house, a habitation, an abode, a dwelling.*
pendeō, pependī, no sup., **pendēre,** [†pendŏ- (√pend + us, cf. pendulus)], 2. v. n., *hang, be suspended, overhang, hover, lean forward, swing, droop, be perched.* — Also, *linger, be suspended* (of work).
pendō, pependī, pēnsum, pendere, [?, cf. pendulus, pendeo, √pend], 3. v. a., (*hang, suspend*) —Esp., *weigh* (hang on steelyards) — Fig., *pay, suffer* (a penalty).
pēne, see **paene,** the proper spelling.
Pēnēius, -a, -um, [Gr. Πηνήιος], adj., *of the Peneus, Peneian.*
Pēneleus, -ei (-eos), [Gr. Πηνελεύς], m., a leader of the Boeotians in the Trojan war.
penes [prob. acc. n. of adj.-stem akin to **penitus, penetro**], prep., *in the power of:* imperium te penes (*depends on you*).
penetrābilis, -e, [†penetrā- (of penetro) + bilis], adj., *penetrable.* — Act., *piercing, penetrating.*

penetrālis, -e, [†penetrŏ- (cf. penetrŏ, reduced) + alis], adj., *of the interior, inner, interior, inmost, within.* — *Neut.* plur., *the interior, the inmost recesses, the inner shrine, a sanctuary.*

penetrŏ, -āvī, -ātum, -āre, [†penetrŏ- (†pene + trus, cf. penes, penitus, penus)], 1. v. a., *set within, put inside.* — Without immediate object, but with acc. of end of motion, *penetrate, enter, go within, make one's way into.*

Peneus, -ī, [Gr. Πηνειός], m., a river of Thessaly flowing through the vale of Tempe.

penitus [stem akin to **penes + tus,** cf. **divinitus**], adv., *from within.* — Also (cf. **hinc**), *within, far, far down, far away, deeply.* — Fig., *utterly, wholly, entirely.*

penna (pin-), -ae, [√pet (in peto, cf. πίτνημι) + na], f., *a wing, a feather, a plume.*

pennātus, -a, -um, [†penna + tus, cf. armatus], adj., *feathered, winged.*

pensum, -ī, [n. p.p. of pendo], n., *wool* (weighed out as a task for spinning), *a task.*

Penthesilēa, -ae, [Gr. Πενθεσίλεια], f., the queen of the Amazons who fought in the Trojan war.

Pentheus, -eī (-eos), [Gr. Πενθεύς], m., a king of Thebes who despised the rites of Bacchus, and was torn in pieces by his mother and sisters. He was also supposed to have been driven mad by the Furies, and this myth was often dramatically treated.

pēnūria, -ae, [?], f., *poverty, scarcity:* edendi (*want of food*).

penus, -ūs (-ī), [?, akin to penes, penitus, Penates, prob. *inner store-room*], m. and f., *provisions, store.*

peplum, -ī, [Gr. πέπλον], n., *a robe* (for women, a large and splendid outer mantle). — Esp., the state robe carried in procession at Athens and offered to Pallas Athene every five years.

per [petrified case-form, cf. **παρά**], prep., *through, by, over, throughout, along, among, across, during:* per aras (*by*); per aures (*to*); per annos (*for*); per augurium (*into*). — Fig. (cf. **ob**), *through, by means of, by, on account of.* — In adjurations, *by.* — As adv. in comp., *through, thoroughly, over,* &c., see perago, percurro, pereo, perfidus.

perāctus, -a, -um, p.p. of perago.

peragŏ, -ēgī, -āctum, -agere, [per-ago], 3. v. a.; *perform* (to the end), *finish, complete, accomplish*). — Also, *go over* (cf. **ago**), *consider.*

peragro, -āvī, -ātum, -āre, [†peragrŏ- (cf. peregre, peregrinus)], 1. v. a., *wander over, roam over, traverse, prowl around.*

percellŏ, -culī, -culsum, -cellere, [per-†cello (cf. procella, celox)], 3. v. a., *strike* (through), *strike down, fell, overwhelm.* — Fig., *lay prostrate.* — Also, *move, affect, strike.* — **perculsus, -a, -um,** p.p., *stricken, smitten, filled, inspired.*

percipiŏ, -cēpī, -ceptum, -cipere, [per-capio], 3. v. a., *take in, gather, receive.* — Fig., *hear, notice, understand, learn.*

perculsus, -a, -um, p.p. of percello.

percurro, -cucurrī (-currī), -cursum, -currere, [per-curro], 3. v. a., *run over* or *through* (lit. and fig.): nomina; pectine telas; nimbos (*pierce, traverse*).

percussus, -a, -um, p.p. of percutio.

percutiŏ, -cussī, -cussum, -cutere, [per-quatio], 3. v. a., *strike* (with violence), *beat.*—Fig., *strike, move, affect.*

perditus, -a, -um, p.p. of perdo.

perdŏ, -didī, -ditum, -dere, [perdo, cf. perco, intereo, and Gr. πέρθω], 3. v. a., *destroy, ruin.*—Also, *lose.* — **perditus, -a, -um,** p.p. as adj., *ruined, desperate, wretched.*

Vocabulary.

perdūco, -dūxī, -dūctum, -dūcere, [per-duco], 3. v. a., *lead to, bring to.*—Also, *cover over, anoint.*

peredō, -ēdī, -ēsum, -edere, [per-edo], 3. v. a., *devour, consume, waste away, gnaw.*

peregrīnus, -a, -um, [†peregrŏ- (cf. **peregre**) + inus], adj., *from far away, from abroad, foreign.*

peremptus, -a, -um, p.p. of **perimo.**

perennis (-ennius), -e, [per-†anno- (weakened and decl. as adj.)], adj., *eternal, perpetual, everlasting, undying.*

pereō, -ivī (-iī), -itum, -īre, [per-eo, cf. **perdo**], irr. v. n. (a kind of pass. of **perdo**), *go to ruin, perish, be destroyed, fall, die, be slain.* — Esp. of love, *die of love, pine away.* — Less exactly, *be undone, be ruined.*

pererrātus, -a, -um, p.p. of **pererro.**

pererrō, -āvī, -ātum, -are, [pererro], 1. v. a., *wander over, roam over.*—Less exactly and fig., *spread through, scan, examine, search, survey.*

perēsus, -a, -um, p.p. of **peredo.**

perfectus, -a, -um, p.p. of **perficio.**

perferō, -tulī, -lātum, -ferre, [per-fero], irr. v. a., *carry through, maintain* (to the end), *keep up, retain.* — Also, *bring, carry off, convey, bear, bring news:* **perfer te** (*proceed, go on*); **hasta perlata** (*forced through*).—Also, *bear* (to the end), *endure, suffer, have to bear.*

perficiō, -fēcī, -fectum, -ficere, [per-facio], 3. v. a., *perform, complete, finish, accomplish.* — Also, *make, work, fashion.*

perfidus, -a, -um, [per-fidus, cf. **periurus**], adj., *false, perfidious, treacherous.*

perflō, -āvī, -ātum, -āre, [per-flo], 1. v. a., *blow over.*

perfodiō, -fōdī, -fossum, -fodere, [per-fodio], 3. v. a., *pierce, penetrate, make a breach in, burst open.*

perforō, -āvī, -ātum, -āre, [perforo], 1. v. a., *pierce, penetrate.*

perfossus, -a, -um, p.p. of **perfodio.**

perfractus, -a, -um, p.p. of **perfringo.**

perfringō, -frēgī, -fractum, -fringere, [per-frango], 3. v. a., *break through, crush.*—Also, *force through, accomplish* (by force).

perfundō, -fūdī, -fūsum, -fundere, [per-fundo], 3. v. a., *pour over.* — With change of point of view, *drench, drown, bedew, sprinkle, bathe, plunge, moisten, wash, dip, dye.*

perfurō, no perf., no sup., **-furere,** [per-furo], 3. v. n., *rave wildly.*

Pergameus, -a, -um, [†Pergamŏ + eus], adj., *of Pergamum, of Troy, Trojan.* — Fem., *Pergamea,* the name given by Æneas to his city in Crete.

Pergamum, -ī, (-a, -ōrum), [Gr. Πέργαμον], n., the citadel of Troy.

pergo, perrexī, perrectum, pergere, [per-rego], 3. v. n., *keep on, proceed, advance, go on.*

perhibeō, -hibuī, -hibitum, -hibēre, [per-habeo], 2. v. a., *hold out, bring forward.* — Esp., *report, assert, say, declare, call.*

perīculum (-clum), -ī, [†perī- (of **perior**, cf. **experior**) + culum], n., *a trial, an attempt.* — Also, *peril, hazard, risk, danger.*

Peridīa, -ae, [Gr. Περιδία], f., the mother of Onytes.

perimō, -ēmī, -emptum, -ere, [per-emo], 3.v.a., *destroy, kill, slay.*

Periphās, -antis, [Gr. Περίφας], m., a companion of Pyrrhus at the sack of Troy.

perītus, -a, -um, [p.p. of †perior, see **experior**], adj., *experienced, skilled, skilful.*

perīūrium, -ī, [†periurŏ- (reduced) + ium], n., *perjury.*

periūrus, -a, -um, [per-†iur-, decl. as adj., cf. **perfidus**], adj., *perjured.*

perlābor, -lāpsus, -lābī, [per-labor], 3. v. dep., *glide over, glide through.* — Fig., *spread to, reach.*

perlātus, -a, -um, p.p. of **perfero.**

perlegō (pellego), -lēgī, -lectum, -legere, [per-lego], 3. v. a., *survey, scan.*

permensus, -a, -um, p.p. of **permetior.**

Permessus, -ī, [Gr. Περμησσός], m., a river of Bœotia flowing from Mt. Helicon, sacred to Apollo and a favorite haunt of the Muses.

permētior, -mensus, -mētīrī, [per-metior], 4. v. dep., *measure over, traverse.*

permisceō, -miscuī, -mixtum (-mistum), miscēre, [per-misceo], 2. v. a., *mix (t*horoughly*), mingle.* — **permixtus, -a, -um,** p.p., *mingled, mixed, mingling, united.*

permissus, -a, -um, p.p. of **permitto.**

permittō, -mīsī, -missum, -mittere, [per-mitto], 3. v. a., *let go by* or *through, give up, give over, commit, consign.* — Fig., *allow, permit, grant:* permisso nomine (*using the name by permission*).

permixtus, -a, -um, p.p. of **permisceo.**

permulceō, -mulsī, -mulsum (-ctum), -mulcēre, [per-mulceo], 2. v. a., *stroke.* — Fig., *soothe.*

permūtō, -avī, -ātum, -are, [per-muto], 1. v. a., *exchange* (something with one).

pernix, -īcis, [?], adj., *active, agile, swift.*

pernox, -noctis, [per-†nocti- (decl. as adj.)], adj., *through the night* (with force of adverb).

pērō, -ōnis, [?], m., *a boot* (rough and heavy, used by soldiers and the like).

perōdī, -ōsus, -ōdisse, [per-odi], def. v. a., *utterly hate, execrate, curse.* — **perōsus, -a, -um,** p.p. in act. sense.

perōsus, -a, -um, p.p. of **perodi.**

perpessus, -a, -um, p.p. of **perpetior.**

perpetior, -pessus, -petī, [per-patior], 3. v. dep., *suffer, endure, undergo.* — Also, *allow, permit, suffer.*

perpetuus, -a, -um, [per-†petuus (√pet, in peto + uus)], adj., *continuing, continuous, entire.* — Of time, *continual, constant, incessant.*

perplexus, -a, -um, [per-plexus (p.p. of plecto)], adj., *confused, entangled, intricate.*

perrumpō, -rūpī, -ruptum, -rumpere, [per-rumpo], 3. v. a., *break through, break across:* tellurem (*plough across*).

persentiō, -sēnsī, -sēnsum, -sentīre, [per-sentio], 4. v. a., *feel* (deeply), *perceive.*

persequor, -secūtus, -sequī, [per-sequor], 3. v. dep., *follow up, pursue.*

persīdō, -sēdī, -sessum, -sīdere, [per-sido], 3. v. n., *settle through, penetrate, sink in.*

Persis, -idis, [Gr. Περσίς], f., the original country of the Persians. — Less exactly, *Persia,* the whole region occupied by the kingdom of the Persians.

persolvō, -solvī, -solūtum, -solvere, [per-solvo], 3. v. a., *pay in full, pay, render, give in payment.*

personō, -uī, -itum, -āre, [per-sono], 1. v. n. and a., *sound through* or *over, cause to resound, sound:* citharā (*play*).

perstō, -stitī, -stātum, -stāre, [per-sto], 1. v. n., *stand firmly.* — Fig., *persist, remain unmoved, remain fixed.*

perstringō, -strinxī, -strictum, -stringere, [per-stringo], 3.v.a., *graze, touch lightly.*

persuādeō, -suāsī, -suāsum, -suādēre, [per-suadeo], 2. v. n. and a., *induce* (by persuasion), *induce to believe, persuade.*

pertaesum, see taedet.

pertemptō (-tento), -āvī, -ātum,

-āre, [per-tempto], 1. v. a., *try* (thoroughly). — Fig., *pervade, seize, fill, possess :* gaudia pectus; sensūs lues; corpora tremor.

perterreō, -terruī, -terrĭtum, terrēre, [per-terreo], 2. v. a., *terrify, alarm, frighten.* — perterrĭtus, -a, -um, p.p., *panic-stricken, in alarm.*

perterrĭtus, -a, -um, p.p. of perterreo.

perveniō, -venī, -ventum, -venīre, [per-venio], 4. v. n., *come through, arrive, come, reach :* pervenimus vivi ut, etc. (*lived to see*).

perventus, -a, -um, p.p. of pervenio.

perversus, -a, -um, p.p. of perverto.

pervertō, -vertī, -versum, -vertere, [per-verto], 3. v. a., *overturn, turn awry.* — perversus, -a, -um, p.p. as adj., *awry.* — Fig., *perverse, wrong-headed, obstinate, bad :* perverso numine (*by a fatal impulse*).

pervigilō, -āvī, -ātum, -āre, [per-vigilo], 1. v. n., *watch* (continually), *keep watch.*

pervius, -a, -um, [per-†via-, decl. as adj.], adj., *passable :* usus tectorum (*a much-used passage*, &c.).

pervolitō, -āvī, -ātum, -āre, [per-volito], 1. v. a., *flit around, fly about.*

pervolō, -āvī, -ātum, -āre, [per-volo], 1. v. a., *fly through.*

pēs, pedis, [√ped as stem, cf. ποῦς, Eng. *foot*], m., *the foot.* — Also of animals, *a foot, a hoof, a claw, a paw, a leg* (of an insect). — Often represented in Eng. by *step :* ferte pedem, *come ;* referens pedem, *retreating ;* pedem tulisset, *turn the steps ;* pedem reportat, *retrace his steps ;* aequo pede, *with equal pace ;* pede secundo, *with favoring steps ;* retrahit pedes, *withdraws ;* revocat pedem, *draws back.* — Also, *the rope at the lower corner of a sail, the sheet :* facere pedem, *make a tack* (drawing in first one and then the other).

pessimus, -a, -um; see malus.

pestifer, -era, -erum, [†pesti-fer (√fer + us)], adj., *plague-bringing, pestilent.*

pestis, -is, [?], f., *a plague, a pest, an infection, a taint.* — Less exactly, *a calamity, ruin, destruction, mischief, trouble.* — Concretely, *a pest, a plague, a curse, a nuisance, vermin.*

Petīlia (-ēlia), -ae, [Gr. Πετηλία], f., *a city on the Gulf of Tarentum,* founded by Idomeneus.

petō, petīvī (-iī), petītum, petere, [√pet, akin to πίπτω], 3. v. a., (*fall, fly,* in various modifications), *go to, assail, attack, make for, fall upon,* aim at, seek (go to), *pursue :* Troianos monstra (*be aimed at*); me fraude (*aim at*); peteretur Troia (*sail to* (*seek*) *Troy*); terram (*fall to*); exscidiis urbem (*plot destruction against*); aethera sol (*rise in*); thorax petitus (*hit*). — From the idea of aiming at, *seek, search for, look for, ask for, ask, beg, desire, want, be in search of :* quidve petat (*what his purpose*); petentur praemia (*be in question*).

petulcus, -a, -um, [†petulŏ- (reduced, cf. petulans) + cus], adj., *butting, wanton.*

Phaeāces, -um, [Gr. Φαίακες], m. plur., *the Phæacians,* the mythic inhabitants of Corcyra, famed for their luxury.

Phaedra, -ae, [Gr. Φαῖδρα], f., the wife of Theseus and daughter of Minos. She became enamored of her stepson Hippolytus.

Phaethōn, -ontis, [Gr. Φαέθων], m., a son of the Sun who drove his father's horses to prove his lineage. They became unmanageable, and he was destroyed by a thunderbolt. His sisters mourning for him were changed into poplars. — Also (perhaps in its original sense, *the bright one*), a name of the Sun.

Phaethontiades, -um, [Gr. patronymic], f. pl., *the sisters of Phaethon.*

phalanx, -angis, [Gr. φάλαγξ], f., *a phalanx* (a body of Grecian troops). — Less exactly, *an army, a force, a battalion, a funeral escort, a train, a fleet.*

phalārica (fal-), -ae, [?], f., *a falarica, a huge spear* (used by barbarian nations).

phalerae, -arum, [Gr. φάλαρα], f. plur., *an ornament* (of metal plates worn on the breast of soldiers), *a decoration.* — A similar decoration on horses, *trappings.*

Phaleris, -is, [?], m., a Trojan.

Phanaeus, -a, -um, [Gr. Φαναῖος], adj., *of Phanae* (a place in Chios famous for its wine). — Masc., *Phanaean* (Chian) *wine:* rex ipse Phanaeus (*Phanaeus king of wines*).

pharetra, -ae, [Gr. φαρέτρα], f., *a quiver.*

pharetrātus, -a, -um, [†pharetra + tus, cf. **armatus**], adj., *armed with a quiver, quiver-bearing.*

Pharus, -i, [Gr. Φάρος], m., an Italian.

phasēlus, -i, [Gr. φάσηλος], m. and f., *a bean.* — Also, *a skiff* (used by the Egyptians).

Phāsis, -idis, [Gr. Φᾶσις], m., a river of Colchis.

Phēgeus, -ei (-eos), [Gr. Φηγεύς], m.: 1. A slave of Æneas; 2. A Trojan (perhaps two of the same name).

Pheneus, -i, [Gr. Φένεος], f., a town and lake in Arcadia.

Pherēs, -ētis, [Gr. Φέρης], m., a Trojan.

Philippi, -ōrum, [Gr. Φίλιπποι], m. plur., a town of Macedonia near the foot of the range of Haemus. It was famous for the battle between Brutus and Cassius on the one side and Octavius and Antony on the other, by which the Caesarian party was established in power.

Philoctētēs, -ae, [Gr. Φιλοκτήτης], m., a celebrated archer, son of Paean king of Meliboea. He received from Hercules the famous poisoned arrows on which depended the destruction of Troy. According to a legend he came to Italy after the Trojan war and founded Petilia.

Philomēla, -ae, [Gr. Φιλομήλη], f., a daughter of Pandion king of Thebes, who with her sister Procne served up to Tereus, her sister's husband, his son Itys prepared for food. They were all changed into birds, Philomela into a nightingale, for which bird her name often stands.

Philyrides, -ae, [Gr. patronymic], m., *son of Philyra* (beloved by Saturn, by whom she became the mother of the centaur Chiron).

Phīneus, -ei (-eos), [Gr. Φινεύς], m., a king of Thrace, who was struck blind and afterwards tormented by the Harpys.

Phīnēius, -a, -um, [Gr. Φινήιος], adj., *of Phineus.*

Phlegethōn, -ontis, [Gr. Φλεγέθων], m., a river of fire in Hades.

Phlegyās, -ae, [Gr. Φλεγυάς], m., a king of Orchomenus in Boeotia, father of Ixion, who burned the temple of Apollo to avenge the seduction of his daughter by that divinity, and who was punished in the Infernal regions for this act of impiety.

phōca, -ae, [Gr. φώκη], f., *a seal, a sea-calf.*

Phoebē, -ēs, [Gr. Φοίβη], f., a name of Diana (Artemis) as goddess of the moon (cf. **Phoebus**).

Phoebēus, -a, -um, [Gr. Φοίβειος], adj., *of Phoebus* (Apollo or the Sun).

Phoebigena, -ae, [†Phoebŏ- (weakened) -†gena (cf. **nubigena**)], m., *son of Phoebus* (Æsculapius).

Phoebus, -i, [Gr. Φοῖβος], m., a name of Apollo as god of the sun (*the Bright one*). — Also, *the Sun.*

Phoenīces, -um, [Gr. Φοίνικες], m. plur., *the Phoenicians* (the inhab-

itants of Phœnicia, the coast-land east of the Mediterranean.)
Phoenissa, -ae, [Gr. Φοίνισσα, f. of Φοῖνιξ], f. adj., *Phœnician.* — As subst., *a Phœnician woman* (used of Dido).
Phoenix, -īcis, [Gr. Φοῖνιξ], m., the instructor of Achilles and his companion in the Trojan war.
Pholoē, -ēs, [Gr. Φολόη], f., a female slave.
Pholus, -ī, [Gr. Φῶλος], m.: 1. A centaur, the host of Hercules, but accidentally slain by one of his guest's arrows; 2. A Trojan.
Phorbās, -antis, [Gr. Φόρβας], m., a sailor of Æneas' fleet.
Phorcus, -ī (-ys), [Gr. Φόρκος(-υς)], m.: 1. A sea-divinity; 2. A Latin.
Phrygius, -a, -um, [Gr. Φρύγιος], adj., *Phrygian.* — Less exactly, *Trojan.* — Fem. (sc. **terra**), *Phrygia,* the country of Asia Minor of which Troy was a small district. — Fem. plur. (as subst.), *the Phrygian women, the Trojan women.*
Phryx, Phrygis, [Gr. Φρύξ], m., *a Phrygian.* — Less exactly, *a Trojan.*
Phthia, -ae, [Gr. Φθία], f., a district of Thessaly, the home of Achilles.
Phyllis, -ĭdis, [Gr. Φύλλις], f., a rustic woman.
Phyllodocē, -ēs, [Gr. Φυλλοδόκη], f., a Nereid.
piāculum, -ī, [†pia- (of pio) + culum], n., *an expiatory rite or offering, a purification:* commissa piacula (*atonement for guilt incurred*).
piceus, -a, -um, [†pic + eus], adj., *of pitch, pitchy.*—Less exactly, *dark* (like the smoke of pitch), *thick, lurid, smoky:* flumen (*thick and dark,* of sweat and dust); turbo (*pitch-black wreaths*); caligo (of burning pitch). — Fem., (sc. **arbor**), *a pine tree.*
pictūra, -ae, [†pictu + ra (f. of rus), cf. **figura**], f., *a painting, a picture.*
pictūrātus, -a, -um, [†pictura + tus, cf. **armatus**], adj., *embroidered, wrought with designs.*
pictus, -a, -um, p.p. of **pingo.**
Pīcus, -ī, [picus, *woodpecker*], m., a mythic king of Italy, son of Saturn and father of Faunus, changed into a woodpecker by Circe.
Pīerides, -um, [Gr. Πιερίδες], f. pl., the Muses, so called from their haunt Pieria in Thessaly.
pietās, -tātis, [†piŏ + tas], f., *filial affection, dutiful love, filial piety.* — Hence, *reverence* (for the gods), *piety, devotion.* — Also (reciprocally), *justice* (recognition of piety).
piger, -gra, -grum, [√pig (in piget) + rus (reduced)], adj., *slothful, slow, sluggish.*
piget, -uit, (-itum est), -ēre, [unc. adj.-stem, cf. **piger**], 2. v. impers., *it irks, one regrets, one is loth, one loathes, it is irksome.*
pignus, -oris, [prob. pang (as root of pango) + us], n., *a pledge* (deposited as security).—Less exactly, *a wager, a stake.* — Fig., *a security, a pledge, a sign* (as by giving the hand), *a token* (as a gift). — So of children, *pledges.*
pīla, -ae, [?], f., *a pier, a mole.*
pilātus, -a, -um, [†pilŏ + tus, cf. **armatus**], adj., *armed with the javelin.*
pilentum, -ī, [prob. akin to **pileus,** on account of the wool or felt covering], n., *a carriage,* with four wheels and covered, used for carrying sacred emblems; utensils, &c., and later employed by Roman women.
pīlum, -ī, [perh. akin to **pinso**], n., *a pestle.* — Also, *a javelin* (the heavy spear used by the Romans).
Pīlumnus, -ī, [†pīlŏ + mnus, cf. Gr. -μενος], m., an old Latin divinity or deified king, an ancestor of Turnus, represented with a pestle.
Pīnārius, -a, -um, [?], adj., a Roman gentile name (which are all originally adj.): domus (*the family of the Pinarii,* who with the

Potitii first assisted at the rites of Hercules).

Pindus, -ī, [Gr. Πίνδος], m., a mountain in Thessaly.

pīneus, -a, -um, [†pinŏ- (reduced) + eus], adj., *of pine, of pines.*

pingō, pinxī, pictum, pingere, [√pig], 3. v. a., *paint, dye, color, embroider* (with or without **acu**), *ornament* (with color). — **pictus, -a, -um,** p.p. as adj., *embroidered, painted, particolored, spotted, variegated, wrought* (with color), *ornamented* (with designs).

pinguescō, no perf., no sup., **-escere,** [†pingui + sco, cf. **pinguis**], 3. v. n. incept., *grow fat, grow rich, become fertile, be enriched.*

pinguis, -e, [?], adj., *fat, rich, resinous, pitchy, oily, unctuous, fertile, thick, milky* (of herbs): **oves** (*well-fed*); **ara** (*rich in victims*).

pinifer, -era, -erum, [†pinŏ-fer [√fer + us)], adj., *pine-bearing, pine-clad.*

pinna, -ae, [same word as **penna**], f., *a turret* (part of a fortification), *a battlement.* See also **penna.**

pīnus, -ī (-ūs), [akin to **pix,** πίτυς], f., *a pine tree, a pine.* — Of things made of pine, *a ship, a torch, a shaft.*

piō, -āvī, -ātum, -āre, [†piŏ-], 1. v. a., *purify.* — Also, *appease, propitiate.* — Hence, *expiate, atone for.*

Pīrithous, -ī, [Gr. Πειρίθοος], m., a son of Ixion who attempted to carry off Proserpine from the world below.

pirus, -ī, [?], f., *a pear-tree.*

Pīsa, -ae, [Gr. Πίσα], f., a city of Elis near Olympia, with which town it was sometimes identified.

Pīsae, -ārum, [?], f. plur., *Pisa,* a city of Etruria, supposed by the ancients to have been colonized from Elis.

piscis, -is, [?], m., *a fish.* — Also (usually in plur.), *Pisces,* the constellation.

piscōsus, -a, -um, [†pisci- (reduced) + osus], adj., *full of fish, fish-haunted.*

pistrix, -icis, [Gr. πίστρις], f., *a sea-monster.* — As name of a ship, *the Pistrix.*

pius, -a, -um, [?], adj., *filial, devoted* (to parents), *pious, virtuous, just.* — Also, *pure, holy, sacred:* **amor** (*devoted*); **far** (*consecrated*); **sanguis** (*innocent*); **piorum concilia** (*of the blest*); **numina** (*righteous,* cf. **pietas**); **manus** (*pure*).

pix, picis, [akin to **pīnus** and πίτυς, cf. πίσσα], f., *pitch.*

plācābilis, -e, [†placā- (of **placo**) + bilis], adj., *easy to be entreated, placable, gentle:* **ara** (*propitious,* where sacrifices easily appease the divinity).

plācātus, -a, -um, p.p. of **placo.**

placeō, placuī, placitum, placēre, [†placŏ- (cf. **placidus, placo, Viriplaca**)], 2. v. n., *please, delight, give pleasure.* — Often to be translated by a change of construction, *approve, delight in, adopt.* — Also impersonally, *it is one's will, one determines, it is determined, it is thought best.* — **placitus, -a, -um,** p.p. in act. sense, *pleasing, agreeable, determined* on, *decided:* **placida paci oliva** (*favorable*); **sic placitum** (*so it is fated*); **ultra placitum** (*more than is agreeable*).

placidē [abl. of **placidus**], adv., *quietly, gently, peacefully.*

placidus, -a, -um, [†placŏ- (cf. **placeo**) + dus], adj., *calm, quiet, peaceful, gentle, placid, kindly, propitious:* **palus** (*gently-flowing, slow*); **aequora; pax; aures; urbes; pectus; os; caput; placidum ventis mare** (*stilled*).

placitus, -a, -um, p.p. of **placeo.**

plācō, -āvī, -ātum, -āre, [†placŏ- (cf. **Viriplaca**)], 1. v. a., *appease, pacify, calm, quiet.*

1. **plaga, -ae,** [?], f., *a region, a quarter, a zone, a tract.*

2. **plāga, -ae,** [Gr. πληγή], f., *a*

blow, a stroke, a lash, a thrust, a wound.

3. **plaga, -ae,** [?], f., *a hunting-net, a snare.*

plangō, planxī, planctum, plangere, [√plag, akin to πλήσσω, cf. **plāga**], 3. v. a. and n., *beat, strike.* — From beating the breasts in mourning, *wail, cry.* — Less exactly, *roar, murmur.*

plangor, -ōris, [plang (as root of **plango**) + or], m., *a shriek, an outcry.*

plānitiēs, -ēī, [†planŏ + ties, cf. **amīcitia**], f., *a plain, a level.*

planta, -ae, [akin to **planus**], f., *the sole, the foot.* — Also, *a scion, a slip, a plant, a shoot.*

plantārium, -ī (-iī), or **-āre, -is,** [†planta + arium (n. of arius)], n., *a shoot, a scion.*

plānus, -a, -um, [akin to πλατύς (perh. √pal in **palor**)], adj., *level, flat.* — Neut. as subst., *a plain, a level, level ground.*

platanus, -ī, [Gr. πλάτανος], f., *a plane tree.*

plaudō (plō-), plausī, plausum, plaudere, [?], 3. v. a. and n., *clap, beat* (with the feet or hands), *flap* (of the wings), *pat* (of caressing): **choreas** (*dance a measure*).

plaustrum, -ī, [√plaud + trum], n., *a cart, a wagon.*

plausus, -ūs, [plaud (as root of **plaudo**) + tus], m., *clapping, flapping, applause.*

plēbs, plēbis, [akin to **plenus** (cf. **plerique**), πλῆθος], f., *the multitude, the common people, the people, the vulgar, common soldiers.*

Plēias, -adis, [Gr. Πληιάς], f., *a Pleiad,* one of the seven daughters of Atlas who were changed into the constellation of the Pleiades. — Also, one of the stars. — Plur., *the Pleiades,* the constellation.

Plēmyrium, -ī (-iī), [Gr. Πλημμύριον], n., *a promontory of Sicily, near Syracuse.*

plēnus, -a, -um, [†plē- (of **pleo**) + nus, cf. **plerique**], adj., *full, filled, well-filled:* **vox** (*loud*); **flumina** (*swelling*); **annis** (*completed, mature*); **mensa** (*laden*); **portae** (*thronged*); **ad plenum** (*full, to the top*); **campus** (*crowded,* with sheep).

plerusque(masc.notfound),**-aque, -umque,** [plerus (†ple + rus, cf. **plenus**) -que (cf. **undique, quisque**)], adj., *the greater part.* — Neut. as adv., *for the most part, usually, commonly.*

plicō, -āvī (-uī), -ātum (-itum), -āre, [√plic, akin to πλέκω], 1. v. a., *fold, roll up.*

plūma, -ae, [?], f., *feathers.*

plumbum, -ī, [?], n., *lead.*

pluō, pluī (plūvī), no sup., **pluere,** [√plu, of unc. kin.], 3. v. a. and n., *rain, rain down, shower down.* — Impersonal, *it rains.*

plūrimus, -a, -um; see **multus.**

plūs, see **multus.**

Plūtōn (-ŏ), -ōnis, [Gr. Πλούτων], m., *Pluto,* the brother of Jupiter and Neptune, the king of the lower world.

pluviālis, -e, [†pluviŏ- (reduced) + alis], adj., *rainy.* — Often in the sense of bringing rain.

pluvius, -a, -um, [√plu (in **pluo**) + ius], adj., *rainy, showery:* **pluvium frigus** (*cold rain*). — Fem. (sc. **aqua**), *rain, a shower, a fall of rain, rainy weather.*

pōculum, -ī, [√po (cf. **poto**) + culum], n., *a drinking-cup, a goblet, a bowl.* — Less exactly, *a watering-place, a water-trough.* — Often, as in Eng., for the liquid contained in the vessel.

podagra, -ae, [Gr. ποδάγρα], f., *the gout.* — A similar disease in sheep.

Podalīrius, -ī (-iī), [Gr. Ποδαλείριος], m., *a Trojan.*

poena, -ae, [√pu (in **purus,** with stem-vowel and strengthened) + na, cf. ποινή], f., *a penalty, punishment, revenge, vengeance.* Regularly regarded as a penalty by the ancients, and hence *demanded, taken, received,* &c., by the inflicter, and *paid, given, owed, satisfied*, by the sufferer.

Poenus, -a, -um, [akin to Φοινίξ, a simpler form corrupted], adj., *Carthaginian* (properly *Phœnician*). — Masc. plur., *the Carthaginians.*

poenitet, see **paenitet.**

poëta, -ae, [Gr. ποιητής], m., *a poet.*

polio, -īvī (-iī), -ītum, -īre, [?], 4. v. a., *polish.*

Polītēs, -ae, [Gr. Πολίτης], m., a Trojan, son of Priam.

politus, -a, -um, p.p. of **polio.**

pollex, -icis, [?], m., *the thumb.*

polliceor, -licitus, -licērī, [por (old prep., cf. πρός) -liceor], 2. v. dep., *offer, promise* (voluntarily, cf. **promitto,** *promise* on request), *engage.*

pollicitus, -a, -um, p.p. of **polliceor.**

Polliō (Pōl-), -ōnis, [?], m., a Roman surname. — Esp., *Caius Asinius Pollio,* a distinguished orator, statesman, and author of the time of Augustus. He was an intimate friend and a patron of Virgil.

polluō, -luī, -lūtum, -luere, [perh. por-luo], 3. v. a., *pollute, infect, defile.*—Less exactly, *violate:* **pollutus amor** (*blighted, disappointed*).

Pollūx, -ūcis, [Gr. Πολυδεύκης, corrupted], m., one of the sons of Jupiter and Leda, brother of Castor, famed as a pugilist. Virgil alludes to his skill in horsemanship, for which generally his brother is famous. Upon the death of Castor, Pollux obtained permission to relieve his brother in the world below by alternately taking his place, thus sharing with him his immortality.

polus, -ī, [Gr. πόλος], m., *the pole* (end of the earth's axis), *the North pole, the Heavens.*

Polybōtēs, see **Polyphoetes.**

Polydōrus, -ī, [Gr. Πολύδωρος], m., a son of Priam, sent to Thrace, and slain by Polymnester.

Polyphēmus, -ī, [Gr. Πολύφημος], m., the Cyclops whose eye was put out by Ulysses.

Polyphoetēs (-bōtēs), -ae, [Gr. Πολυφοίτης], m., a Trojan, priest of Ceres.

Polȳtes, see **Polites.**

Pōmetiī, -ōrum, [?], m. plur., *Suessa Pometia,* a city of the Volsci, in the region of the Pomptine Marshes.

pompa, -ae, [Gr. πομπή], f., *a sacred procession, a sacred rite, a funeral train.*

pōmum, -ī, [?], n., *a fruit* (apple, pear, plum, &c., cf. **baca,** *a small fruit*). — Less exactly, *a fruit-tree.*

pondus, -eris, [√pend + us], n., *a weight, a burden, a load, a heavy missile, a mass.*

pōne [perh. akin to **post**], adv., *behind.*

pono, posuī, positum, pōnere, [unc. stem+sino, cf. **pone**], 3. v. a., (*leave behind?*), *lay down, put down.*—With idea of loss (lit. and fig.), *lay aside, lose, abandon, drop, shed, give up, yield* (of fruits). — With some purpose, *place, put, set, found, lay, set up, put up* (a stake), *set on foot* (a contest), *serve up, plant, fix* (a limit, &c.), *assign* (a name), *lay down* (for rest), *determine, pitch* (a camp), *place* (hope), *lay* (one's fortunes in the lap of another), *lay to rest* (bury), *lay out* (a body), *lay low* (raze), *make* (a keel). — Intrans., (sc. **se**), *decline* (of winds), *go down.*

pōns, pontis, [?], m., *a bridge, a gangway, a drawbridge, a floor* (of a tower).

pontus, -ī, [Gr. πόντος], m., *the sea, a wave.* — Esp. (sc. **Euxinus**), *the Euxine,* the Black Sea.

Pontus, -ī, [Gr. Πόντος], m., the region south of the Black Sea.

poples, -itis, [?], m., *the ham* (the back of the knee): **succiso poplite** (*cutting the cords of the knee, with the hamstrings cut*); **duplicato poplite** (*with bent knees*).

populāris, -e, [†populŏ- (reduced) + aris], adj., *popular, of the people.*
populātus, -a, -um, p.p. of populo.
pōpuleus, -a, -um, [†pōpulŏ- (reduced) + eus], adj., *of the poplar, of poplar, poplar.*
populō, -āvī, -ātum, -āre, [prob. †populŏ-, but the connection is uncertain], 1. v. a., *ravage, despoil, lay waste, devastate, plunder.* — Also of animals, *prey upon.* — Pass. as dep. in same senses. — Of a river, *devastate, lay waste:* iter (*its path*). — **populātus, -a, -um,** p.p. in act. and pass. sense: tempora raptis auribus (*despoiled*).
Populōnia, -ae, [?], f., a city on the coast of Etruria.
pōpulus, -ī, [?], f., *a poplar tree, poplar* (the leaves in a crown). This *t*ree was sacred to Hercules.
populus, -ī, [redupl. root in πολύς (cf. plebes) + us], m., *a people, a state, a nation, a tribe.* — Also, *the common people, the populace, the crowd.* — Poetically, of bees, viewed as social and intelligent.
†por (port-), [cf. πρός, προτί], a prep. only found in obscure composition. Apparently, *to, towards,* cf. **porricio, polliceor, portendo.**
porca, -ae, [?], f., *a pig* (female), *a sow.*
porgo, see **porrigo.**
porrectus, -a, -um, p.p. of **porrigo.**
porriciō, -ēcī, -ectum, -icere, [prob. por-iacio, cf. **polliceor**], 3. v. a., *cast as an offering* (a sacrificial word), *scatter, offer.*
porrigō (porgō), -rexī, -rectum, -rigere, [por-rego], 3. v. a., *stretch out, extend, hold out.* — Pass. or with reflexive, *extend.*
porro [unc. form akin to **pro, por,** and πρόσω], adv., *forward, afar off, beyond.* — Of time, *hereafter, in later times, later.*
Porsena (-enna), -ae, [prob. an Etruscan word], m., a king of Etruria who attempted to restore the banished Tarquins.

porta, -ae, [√por (akin to portus, πόρος) + ta], f., *a gate, a passage, an entrance, an exit, a way* (in or out).
portendō, -tendī, -tentum, -tendere, [por-tendo], 3. v. a., (a religious word, *hold out*), *portend, forebode, foretell, threaten.*
portentum, -ī, [n. p.p. of **portendo**], n., *a prodigy, a portent, a sign, an omen.*
porticus, -ūs, [porta- (weakened) + unc. stem or termination], f., *a colonnade, a gallery, an arcade.*
portitor, -ōris, [prob. †portu- (or †porta) + tor, cf. **viator**, but cf. also **porto**], m., *a boatman, a ferryman.* — Esp. of Charon, the ferryman of the Styx.
portō, -āvī, -ātum, -āre, [†porta- (or †portŏ-, or †portu-)], 1. v. a., *convey* (perh. orig. of merchandise), *carry, bear, bring:* quem portat equus (*who is borne on,* &c.). — Poetically: te septima aestas. — Also, *carry off, bear away.* — Fig.: bellum (*make, declare*).
Portūnus, -ī, [†portu- (lengthened) + nus (cf. **Vacuna**)], m., the god of harbors.
portus, -ūs, [√por (cf. **porta,** πόρος) + tus], m., (*an entrance*), *a harbor, a haven.* — Fig., *a refuge, a haven.*
posco, poposcī, no sup., **-poscere,** [?, perh. akin to **precor**], 3. v. a., *ask, beg, demand, claim, require, call for, enquire for:* ventos (*invoke*); poscente nullo (*spontaneously*); fatis poscentibus (*at the call of the fates*); sic ventos (*require*); numina (*supplicate*).
positus, -a, -um, p.p. of **pono.**
possessor, -ōris, [por-sessor, cf. **possideo**], m., *a possessor, an occupant* (by force), *a master* (of property by occupation).
possum, potuī, posse, [potis(-e) -sum], irr. v. n., *can, be able, have power.* — Often with acc. of pron., *have power, can do.* — **potēns,**

-entis, p. as adj., *powerful, great, mighty, ruling over, master of, potent:* potentum munera (*the great*); potentes terrae (*rulers of*); potens promissi Dea (*having accomplished*); seditione potens (*skilful*).

post [abl. of †posti- (pos + ti, cf. pone), cf. postidea], adv., (*from behind*), *behind, after.* — Of time, *later, afterwards, next, hereafter, in after times.*—Prep., *behind, after.*

†posterus, -a, -um, [†posti + rus], adj., *coming after, following, next.* — posterior, -us, -ōris, comp., *later, latter.* — postrēmus (postumus), -a, -um, [posterā + imus (cf. supremus), post + timus (cf. intimus)], superl., *latest, last, lowest, least.* — Neut. plur., *the rear.* — postumus, *last, posthumous* (born after a father's death).

posthabeō, -habuī, -habitum, -habēre, [post-habeo], 2. v. a., *hold in less esteem, neglect, postpone* (in favor of something else).

posthabitus, -a, -um, p.p. of posthabeo.

posthāc [post-hac, cf. postidea], adv., *hereafter, henceforth, in future.*

posthinc [post-hinc], adv., *hereafter, then, next, thereupon.*

postis, -is, [perh. †pos (cf. post, pone, pono) + tis, cf. antae], m., *a doorpost, a pillar* (of an entrance), *a column.* — Less exactly, *a door, an entrance.*

postquam [post-quam], adv., (*later than*), *after, when, as soon as, since, now that.*

postrēmus, see posterus.

postumus, see posterus.

potēns, -entis, p. of possum.

potentia, -ae, [†potent + ia], f., *power, might, influence, force, sway, rule:* dura nostra (exercise of power); mea magna (source of power).

potestās, -tātis, [stem akin to potis + tas], f., *power, might, rule, sway,* *opportunity, chance:* **potestates** herbarum (*virtues*).

potior, -ītus, -īrī, (potītur, in 3.), [†poti-], 4. v. dep., *become master of, gain, possess, win, gain possession of, seize, occupy, secure:* auso (*succeed in*); campo equus (*gain*); tellure(*gain, arrive at*).

potior, -us, [prob. comp. of potis], adj., *preferable, better, more desirable.* — potius, neut. as adv., *rather, more.*

potis, -e, [prob. akin to pater and πόσις], adj., *powerful, able.*—Usually not declined: potis (pote) est, *be able, one can, be possible.* See also potior.

Potītius, -ī (-iī), [?], m., a Roman gentile name (prop. adj.). — Esp. of one of the family who with the head of the Pinarii assisted at the rites of Hercules.

potītus, -a, -um, p.p. of potior.

Potnias, -adis, [Gr. Ποτνιάς], adj., *of Potniae,* a town of Bœotia, the residence of Glaucus, son of Sisyphus, whose horses went mad and tore their master in pieces. There are other forms of the story.

pōtŏ, -āvī, -ātum, -āre, [†potŏ- (freq. of lost verb)] 1. v. a., *drink.* — pōtāns, -āntis, p. as subst. (plur.), *revellers, drinkers.* See also pōtus (-ūs), pōtus, -a, -um.

pōtus, -ūs, [√po (cf. poculum) + tus], m., *a drinking.*—Esp. acc. (as supine of poto), *to drink.*

pōtus, -a, -um, [p.p. of √po, cf. poculum], p.p., act. and pass., *being drunk, having drunk.*

prae [?, same stem as pro], adv. and prep., *before, in front.* — In comp., *before, in front, at the extremity, very.*

praebeō, -buī, -bitum, -bēre, [prae-habeo], 2. v. a., (*hold out*), *afford, yield, offer, furnish.*

praecēdō, -cēssī, -cēssum, -cēdere, [prae-cedo], 3. v. a. and n., *go before, precede.*

praecelsus, -a, -um, [prae-celsus], adj., *very high, lofty.*

praeceps, -cĭpĭtis, [prae-caput (reduced, and decl. as adj.)], adj., *head-foremost, headlong, in* (one's) *haste, with speed, speedy, flying, swift, hurrying, driven headlong, plunging, pell mell.*—Transferred, *straight downward, precipitous:* in praeceps (*straight downward, perpendicularly*); in praecipiti (*straight up on the very edge*).

praeceptum, -ī, [n. p.p. of **praecipio**], n., *an instruction, an injunction, a rule, an order, a charge, a precept.*

praeceptus, -a, -um, p.p. of **praecipio**.

praecīdō, -cīdī, -cīsum, -cīdere, [prae-caedo], 3. v. a., *cut off.* — **praecīsus, -a, -um,** p.p. as adj., *steep, precipitous.*

praecipĭō, -cēpī, -ceptum, -cipere, [prae-capio], 3. v. a., *take beforehand:* spe hostem (*conquer in advance*); aestus lac (*dry up, in advance*). — Also, *prescribe, enjoin, give instructions, command.*

praecipĭtō, -āvī, -ātum, -āre, [†praecipit-], 1. v. a. and n., *send headlong, hurry on, hurl headlong:* moras (*break down*). — Intrans., *go headlong, fall swiftly, hurry, hasten:* curae(*are excited*); flumina mento (*pour*).

praecĭpuē, [abl. of **pracĭpuus**], adv., *especially, particularly.*

praecĭpuus, -a, -um, [prae-cepuus (√cap + uus, cf. perspĭcuus)], adj., (*taken before*), *especial, chief, the greatest:* accipit Aenean (*with special honor*).

praecīsus, -a, -um, p.p. of **praecido**.

praeclārus, -a, -um, [prae-clarus], adj., *very bright.* — Fig., *distinguished, famous, renowned, glorious, splendid, magnificent.*

praecŏ, -ōnis, [?], m., *a crier, a herald.*

praecordia, -ōrum, [prāe-cord + ium], n. plur., *the diaphragm, the region of the heart, the vitals, the breast, the heart.*

praeda, -ae, [prob. akin to prehendo], f., *booty, a prize, plunder, spoil, prey* (of wild beasts), *game* (prey of the hunter), *a prize.*

praedīcō, -dīxī, -dictum, -dīcere, [prae-dico], 3. v. a., *foretell, give warning, prophesy, forebode.* — Also, *warn, inform.*

praedictum, -ī, [n. p.p. of **praedico**], n., *a prediction, a prophecy.*

praediscō, -didicī, no sup., **-discere,** [prae-disco], 3. v. a., *learn beforehand, forecast, recognize in advance.*

praedīves, -itis,[prae-dives], adj., *very rich, wealthy.*

praedō, -ōnis, [†praeda-(reduced) + o], m., *a robber, a pirate, a marauder.*

praedor, -ātus, -ārī, [†praeda-], 1. v. dep., *prey, prowl.*

praedulcis, -e, [prae-dulcis], adj., *very sweet, precious.*

praedūrus, -a, -um, [prae-durus], adj., *very hard, hardy, stout, sturdy.*

praeĕō, -īvī (-ĭi), -ĭtum, -īre, [prae-eo], irr. v. a. and n., *go in advance, precede, lead, be in advance.*

praefātus, -a, -um, p.p. of **praefor**.

praeferō, -tulī, -lātum, -ferre, [prae-fero], irr. v. a., *carry in front* (before one), *offer:* frons hominem (*represent*).—Also, *prefer, choose rather, choose in preference.*

praeficiō, -fēcī, -fectum, -ficere, [prae-facio], irr. v. a., *set over, put in charge.*

praefīgō, -fīxī, -fīxum, -fīgere, [prae-figo], 3. v. a., *fix in front, hang up on, fix upon:* ora praefixa (*impaled*); praefixa cuspide (*with iron head*). — With change of point of view, *fix* (something with another in front): ora capistris (*bind*). — So **praefīxus, -a, -um,** p.p., *pointed, headed.*

praefīxus, -a, -um, p.p. of **praefigo**.

praefodĭō, -fōdī, -fossum, -fo-

dere, [prae-fodio], 3. v. a., *dig in front of, ditch.*

praefor, -fātus, -fārī, [prae-for], 1. v. dep., *say before, preface, invoke first* (beforehand).

praefulgeō, -fulsī, -no sup., fulgēre, [prae-fulgeo], 2. v. n., *shine in front* or *on the edge:* pellis unguibus (*glitter with hanging claws*).

praegnāns (-ās), -antis (-ātis), [prae-gnans (prob. p. of stem fr. √gen, cf. **nascor**)], adj., *pregnant.*

praelābor, -lāpsus, -lābī, [prae-labor], 3. v. dep., *glide by, fly by.*

praelātus, -a, -um, p.p. of **praefero**.

praemetuō, -metuī, -metūtum, -metuere, [prae-metuo], 3. v. n., *fear beforehand, be anxious.*

praemissus, -a, -um, p.p. of **praemitto**.

praemittō, -mīsī, -missum, -mittere, [prae-mitto], 3. v. a., *send before, send in advance, send forward.*

praemium, -ī (-iī), [prob. akin to prae-emo], n., *a prize, a reward, a recompense* (in good or bad sense), *a prize* (in an ironical sense): Veneris (*delights*); pugnae (*prize,* taken in war); inter praemia ducet (*the prizes of battle,* to the battle-field).

praenatō, -āvī, -ātum, -āre, [prae-nato], 1. v. a., *swim by, float by, flow by* (of a river).

Praeneste, -is, [?], f. and n., a strongly fortified ancient city of Latium, famous for an oracle and a temple of Fortune (now *Palestrina*).

Praenestīnus, -a, -um, [†Praenesti + nus], adj., *of Præneste.*

praenuntia, -ae, [prae-nuntia], f., *forerunner, harbinger, bearing news* (in app. as adj.).

praepes, -etis, [prae-pes (√pet as stem, cf. **peto**)], adj., *swiftly-flying, swift.*

praepinguis, -e, [prae-pinguis], adj., *very fat, very rich, fertile, teeming.*

praereptus, -a, -um, p.p. of **praeripio**.

praeripiō, -ripuī, -reptum, -ripere, [prae-rapio], 3. v. a., *snatch away* (in advance, so as to deprive some one of a thing), *wrest away, wrest from, occupy* (against some one).

praeruptus, -a, -um, [p.p. of **praerumpo**], as adj., (*broken off in front*), *precipitous, steep, broken.*

praesaepe (-sēpe), -is, [prae-saepe (akin to **saepio**)], n., *a stall, a stable.* — Poetically, of bees, *a hive.*

praesāgus, -a, -um, [prae-sagus, cf. **sagax**], adj., *foreknowing, prescient, foreboding.* — Also, *ominous, boding.*

praesciscō, -scīvī, -scītum, -sciscere, [prae-scisco], 3. v. a., *learn beforehand, see in advance.*

praescius, -a, -um, [prae-scius, cf. **nescius**], adj., *foreknowing, divining, prescient, presaging.*

praescrībō, -scrīpsī, -scrīptum, -scrībere, [prae-scribo], 3. v. a., *write before, prefix:* pagina sibi nomen (*has written on its front,* as a dedication).

praesens, -entis, [prae-†sens, p. of **sum**], adj., *present, before one, immediate, imminent, instant:* animus (*stout heart*).— Also of divinities, *favorable, propitious, present to help.*— Also, *potent, advantageous, helpful, powerful.*

praesentia, -ae, [†praesent + ia], f., *presence.*

praesentiō, -sēnsī, -sēnsum, -sentīre, [prae-sentio], 4. v. a., *feel beforehand, foresee, divine, detect,* (something about to be done).

praesertim [acc. akin to **sero**], adv., *especially, particularly, chiefly, most of all.*

praeses, -idis, [prae-ses (√sed as stem)], comm., (*presiding over*), *a ruler, an arbiter, an arbitress.*

praesideō, -sēdī, -sessum, -si-

dēre, [prae-sideo], 2. v. n., *preside over*.

praesidium, -ī (-iī), [†praesid+ium], n., *a defence, a protection, a garrison*.

praestāns, -āntis, p. of praesto.

praestō, -stitī, -stitum, -stāre, [prae-sto], 1. v. n. and a., *stand before, excel, surpass*. — Impers., *it is better!* — praestāns, -āntis, p., *surpassing, superior, excellent, splendid, magnificent, skilful*.

praesūmō, -sūmpsī, -sūmptum, -sumere, [prae-sumo], 3. v. a., *anticipate*.

praetendō, -tendī, -tentum, -tendere, [prae-tendo], 3. v. a., *stretch before, hold out, bear before, put before :* saepem segeti (*throw around*); muros morti (*keep off death by walls*); fumos manu (*throw a veil of smoke*). — Fig., *pretend, make a pretence of*. — praetentus, -a, -um, p.p. as adj., *stretched before, lying along, opposite*.

praetentus, -a, -um, p.p. of praetendo.

praeter [prae + terum (reduced), comp. of prae, cf. inter], adv. and prep., *along by, beyond, past, beside, contrary to*. — In compos., *by, beyond*.

praештereā[praeter-eā, cf. intereā], adv., *further, besides, moreover, afterwards, again, hereafter*.

praetereō, -īvī (-iī), -itum, -īre, [praeter-eo], irr. v. a. and n., *pass beyond, pass by*. — Fig., *omit, pass over*. — Intrans., *go by, pass, pass by*. — praeteritus, -a, -um, p.p. in intrans. sense, *gone by, past, bygone*.

praeteritus, -a, -um, p.p. of praetereo.

praeterlābor, -lāpsus, -lābī, [praeter-labor], 3. v. dep., *glide by, flow by, sail by*.

praetervehor, -vectus, -vehī, [praeter-vehor as dep.], 3. v. dep., *ride by, sail by*.

praetexō, -texuī, -textum, -texere, [prae-texo], 3. v. a. (*weave in front*). — With change of point of view, *cover* (with some*th*ing), *fringe, line*. — Fig., *conceal, disguise :* funera sacris (*conceal by pretence of*, &c.).

praetōrium, -ī (-iī), [†praetor + ium (n. of -ius)], n., (prop. adj., sc. tabernaculum), *the general's tent, headquarters*. — Of bees, *the queen's abode*.

praeūrō, -ūssī, -ūstum, -ūrere, [prae-uro], 3. v. a., *burn at the point, harden in the fire*.

praeūstus, -a, -um, p.p. of praeuro.

praevalidus, -a, -um, [prae-validus], adj., *over strong, too thrifty*.

praeveniō, -vēnī, -ventum, -venīre, (also separate), [prae-venio], 4. v. n., *precede, come before*.

praevertō, -vertī, -versum, -vertere, [prae-verto], 3. v. a., *turn aside, turn off*. — Fig., *divert*. — Intrans. and pass. (as dep.), *outstrip*.

praevideō, -vīdī, -vīsum, -vidēre, [prae-video], 2. v. a., *foresee, see* (in advance).

prātum, -ī, [?], n., *a meadow*.

prāvus, -a, -um, [?], adj., *crooked*. — Fig. (cf. Eng. *wrong*), *false*. — Neu*t*. as subs*t*., *falsehood*.

precātus, -a, -um, p.p. of precor.

preciae, -ārum, [?], f., (adj., sc. vites), *early-ripe grapes*.

precor, -ātus, -ārī, [†prec-], 1. v. dep., *pray, supplicate, pray for, beg :* precando (*by prayers*); precantemdextram (*suppliant*); precans (precantes), (*suppliant, suppliants*); foedus infectum (*pray that the truce be*, &c.); cui (*offer prayers*); precanti multa (*offering many prayers*); precor (paren*th*e*t*ical, *I pray*); socios (*entreat, exhort*).

prehendō, prehendī, prehēnsum, prehendere, (prendo, etc.), [prae-hendo, akin to χανδάνω], 3. v. a., *seize, grasp, grasp at*.

prchēnsŏ, -avī, -ātum, -āre, (prēnso, etc.), [?], 1. v. a., *grasp, catch at, catch, seize.*
prēlum, -ī, [?], n., *a wine-press,* properly *the pressing-beam* or *beams.*
premo, pressī, pressum, premere, [?], 3. v. a., *press, press down :* pressum lac (*cheese*); caseum ; mella ; pressae mammae; sulcum (*dig, trace*); pressi arcus (*forced down*); pressae carinae (*laden*); hasta pressa (*forced down*); presso vomere (*deep-set*); virgulta (*sink, plant*); fronde crinem (*adorn, confine*); vestigia (*plant, set,* but see also below); mundus premitur (*descends*); partem rostro (*overlap*); solo presso (*on the ground which one presses*); fauces lingua (*stop, choke*); guttur pressum (*closed*). — Also, with idea of repression (lit. and fig.), *repress, confine, hold in check, control, keep down, rule, hold in subjection, overwhelm, coerce :* vocem (*check*); vestigia (*check,* but see above); placida aequora pontus (*calm*); pelago arva; te iussa Fauni (*restrain, hamper*); animae premuntur nocte (*are plunged, hidden*); quies oculos (*close*); quies iacentem (*overcome*); falce umbras (*prune*); corde dolorem (*suppress, conceal*); ore responsa (*keep secret*); luna lumen (*hide*); presso ore (*closed lips*); habenas (*hold in, tighten*); pressa est gloria (*obscured*); arma Latini (*depreciate*); os (*control*); Ausoniam; populos dicione; Simois vivos (*rolls under its waves*); mentem pressus formidine (*overwhelmed, weighed down*); lilia (*pluck*). — Also, *press hard, pursue, attack, assail, chase, beset, drive :* apri cursum; ad retia cervum; hostem per auras; famulos (*strike down*).
prendo, see prehendo.
prenso, see prehenso.

prensus, see prehendo.
pressō, -āvī, -ātum, -āre, [†pressō-, cf. premo], 1. v. a., *press.*
pressus, -a, -um, p.p. of premo
pretium, -ī (-iī), [?, perh. akin to πρίαμαι], n., *a price, a reward, a bribe, a prize, a ransom.*
†prex, †-cis, [?], f., *a prayer.*
Priamēius, -a, -um, [Gr. Πριαμήιος], adj., *of Priam, son (daughter) of Priam.*
Priamidēs, -ae, [Gr. Πριαμίδης], m., *son of Priam.*
Priamus, -ī, [Gr. Πρίαμος], m., the aged king of Troy, father of Hector and Paris.
Priāpus, -ī, [Gr. Πρίαπος], m., a god of horticulture and protector of gardens against thieves and birds. He was not highly venerated, and his image served as a kind of scarecrow.
prīdem [prae-dem, cf. idem], adv., *some time ago, for some time.*
prīmaevus, -a, -um, [†primo-aevŏ- (decl. as adj.)], adj., *first in age, eldest.* — Also, *of the first age, in the bloom of youth, youthful.*
prīmitiae, -ārum, [†primo + tia, cf. amicitia], f. plur., *the first fruits.* — Poetically, *first trophies, first exploits,* but cf. Eng. figure.
prīmus, see prior.
princeps, -ipis, [†primo- (reduced) + ceps (√cap as stem)], adj., *first, foremost, at the head.* — As subst., *a chief, a leader, an originator, a protector, a founder* (of a family).
principium, -ī (-iī), [†princip + ium], n., *the beginning, the origin.* — Abl. as adv., *in the beginning, in the first place, first, first of all.*
prior, -ōris, [stem akin to pro and prae + ior, comp. of pro or prae], adj., *former, first, ancient, original.* — Of degree, *superior.* — Masc. plur., *the ancients, men of former times, ancestors.* — Neut. as adv., *before, earlier, first, formerly, sooner, rather,* see also priusquam (*earlier than, before*).

—**prīmus, -a, -um,** [probably **prae** + **mus**, cf. **imus**], superl., *first, foremost, earliest, the outer, the end, the edge, the extremity, the front, front, rising* (of the sun, &c.), *most ancient:* **pes** (*fore*); **primis plantis** (*childish feet*). — Of degree, *first, highest, chief, best, most noble.* — Often equal to an adv. with subj. or obj., *first.* — As subst. in plur., *the first, the best, the chief, the noblest.* — Neut. plur., *first principles, elements, — the first place, the van.* — **primo,** abl. (of time, opp. to **mox,** etc., cf. **primum,** also of order, opp. to **tum,** etc.), *first, at first.* — **primum,** acc. (cf. **primo**), *first, in the first place, for the first time, in advance, immediately.*—**ut** (**cum**) **primum,** *when first, as soon as;* **quam primum,** *as soon as possible;* **nunc primum,** *only now;* **primum ante omnia,** *before all else;* **in primis** (**imprimis**), *especially, chiefly;* **cum primis,** *especially, chiefly;* **ad prima,** *particularly, very, exceedingly.*

prīscus, -a, -um, [†**prius**- (of **prior**) + **cus**], adj., *ancient* (often with idea of approval, or veneration, *good old*), *antique, early, venerable.*

prīstinus, -a, -um, [†**prius**- (of **prior**)+**tinus,** cf. **diutinus**], adj., *former, old, original.*

pristis, see **pistrix.**

priusquam (often separated) [**priusquam**], adv., *sooner than, rather than, before.*

Prīvernum, -ī, [?], n., a town of the Volsci, the birthplace of Camilla.

Prīvernus, -ī, [see **Prīvernum**], m., a Rutulian.

prō (**prōd**) [abl. of same stem as **prae**], prep., *before, in front of.* — Hence, *in defence of, on behalf of, on account of, for, for the sake of.* — Also, *in the place of, in return for, for, instead of:* **pro re** (*under the circumstances, for the occasion*); **pro se** (*according to one's ability*). — In compos., **pro, prōd,** *before, in front, forward, down, forth, for, in favor of.*

prō (**proh**), [?], interj., *oh!* (of surprise, grief, or indignation).

proavus, -ī, [**pro-avus**], m., *a great-grandfather.* — Less exactly, *an ancestor.*

probō, -āvī, -ātum, -āre, [†**probŏ**-], 1. v. a., (*make good by testing*), *test.* — Also, *approve, permit* (approve of an action).

Procās, -ae, [?], m., a king of Alba.

procāx, -ācis, [†**procā**- (of **proco**) + **cus** (reduced), cf. **capax**], adj., *insolent* (in demand). — Transferred, *boisterous.*

prōcēdō, -cēssī, -cēssum, -cēdere, [**pro-cedo**], 3. v. n., *go forward, advance, come forward, go on, go, come forth, proceed.* — Fig., *glide on, pass, go, roll on.*

procella, -ae, [**pro**-†**cella,** cf. **percello, excello**], f., *a storm, a blast, a squall, a tempest.* — Fig., of popular fury, as in English.

procerēs, -um, [?, cf. archaic **procus**], m. plur., *the chiefs, the leaders, the nobles.*

procerus, -a, -um, [unc. comp. with **pro**], adj., *tall, stately, lofty.*

processus, -us, [**pro-cessus,** cf. **procedo**], m., *an advance.*—Fig., *progress, a course.*

Prochyta, -ae (**-ē, -ēs**), [Gr. Προχύτη], f., an island off the coast of Campania (now *Procida*).

prōclāmō, -āvī, -ātum, -āre,[**proclamo**], 1. v. a., *cry aloud, cry out.*

Procnē, see **Progne.**

Procris, -is (**-idis**), [Gr. Πρόκρις], f., the wife of Cephalus, who was accidentally shot by her husband.

prōcubō, -cubuī, -cubitum, -cubāre, [**pro-cubo**], 1. v. n., *lie along, lie at length, fall.*

prōcūdō, -cūdī, -cūsum, -cūdere, [**pro-cudo**], 3. v. a., *hammer out, sharpen.*

procul [?], adv., *at some distance,*

at a distance, afar, far, far away, from far, from afar: procul este (*withdraw, come not near*).—Also, *near by, not far.*—Also, *high, on high.*

prōculcō, -āvī, -ātum, -āre, [pro-calco], 1. v. a., *trample down.*

prōcumbō, -cubuī, -cubitum, -cumbere, [pro-cumbo], 3. v. n., *lie prostrate, lie at length, lie down, lie, be prostrated, fall forward, fall prostrate, fall, be slain, sink to sleep.*—Perf., *have fallen, lie.*—Less exactly, *bend forwards* (cf. **incumbo**), *bend to* (of oars).—Fig., *be overthrown, fall.*

prōcūrō, -āvī, -ātum, -are, [pro-curo], 1. v. a., *take care of:* corpus (*refresh one's self*).

procurrō, -currī (-cucurrī), -cursum, -currere, [pro-curro], 3. v. n., *run forward, advance, rush against, charge.*—Fig., of a tongue of land, *run out.*

procursus, -us, [pro-cursus, cf. **procurro**], m., *a rush, an onset.*

procurvus, -a, -um, [pro-curvus], adj., *curved, bent, winding.*

procus, -ī, [?, perh. root of **precor** + us], m., *a suitor.*

prōdeō, -ivī (-iī), -itum, -īre, [prod-eo], irr. v. n., *go forward, go forth, advance.*—Fig., of a projecting point, *run out.*

prōdigium, -ī (-iī), [poss. prōdigium (√dic + ium, cf. **digitus**)], n., *a portent, a prophetic sign, a prodigy, an omen, an evil prophecy.*—Also, *a monster.*

prōdigus, -a, -um, [prod-agus (√ag+us)], adj., *wasteful, lavish.*

prōditiō, -ōnis, [as if pro-ditio, cf. **prodo**], f., *treachery.*

prōdō, -didī, -ditum, -dere, [pro-do], 3. v. a., *give forth, put forth, propagate, found* (a race).—Also, *give away, betray, treacherously destroy.*—Also, *show, declare.*

prōdūcō, -dūxī, -dūctum, -dūcere, [pro-duco], 3. v. a., *bring forward, lead forth, bring out* (from the house, of a dead body, = *lay in the grave*).—Also, *produce, bring forth.*—Also, *prolong.*

proelium, -ī (-iī), [?], n., *a battle, a combat, fighting.*—Less exactly, *a war.*

Proetides, -um, [Gr. Προιτίδες], f. plur., *the daughters of Proteus*, king of Argos, who were changed by Juno into cows.

prōfānus, -a, -um, [pro-fano, decl. as adj.], adj., *unholy, profane.*—Masc. plur. as subst., *the unholy, the uninitiated.*

profectō [pro-facto], adv., *surely, truly.*—With hortatory expressions, *pray, I beg.*

prōfectus, -a, -um, p.p. of **proficio.**

profectus, -a, -um, p.p. of **proficiscor.**

prōferō, -tulī, -lātum, -ferre, [pro-fero], irr. v. a., *carry forward, extend, prolong, put off, postpone.*

prōficiō, -fēcī, -fectum, -ficere, [pro-facio], 3. v. a. and n., *go forward* (cf. **proficiscor**), *make progress:* nil profeci (*I have gained nothing*).

proficiscor, -fectus, -ficiscī, [as if pro-†fasciscor (lost incept. of **facio**)], 3. v. dep., (*go forth*, cf. **proficio**), *set out, set out for, proceed from, come from.*—Also, of descent, *proceed from, originate with.*

prōflō, -āvī, -ātum, -āre, [pro-flo], 1. v. a., *blow forth, breathe forth.*

prōfluō, -fluxī, -fluxum, -fluere, [pro-fluo], 3. v. n., *flow forth, flow out, flow.*

†profor (not found), **-fātus, -fārī,** [pro-for], 1. v. dep., *speak out, speak.*

profugus, -a, -um, [pro-†fugus (√fug + us)], adj., *flying, in flight, fugitive, exiled.*—As subst., *a fugitive, an exile.*

prōfundō, -fūdī, -fūsum, -fundere, [pro-fundo], 3. v. a., *pour forth, shed.*

profundus, -a, -um, [pro-fundus], adj., *deep, profound, the depths of: caelum.* — Fig., of darkness, *deepest.* — Neut. as subst., *the deep.*

prōgeniēs, -eī, [†pro-†genies (√gen + ies, cf. **series**)], f., *offspring, progeny, a line, a race.* — Of individuals, *a son, offspring.* — Also of animals, *young, offspring, a brood, a swarm.*

prōgīgnō, -genuī, -genitum, -gīgnere, [pro-gigno], 3. v. a., *beget, bring forth.*

Prognē, -ēs, [Gr. Πρόκνη], f., the wife of Tereus and sister of Philomela. She was changed into a swallow. See **Philomela.** — Poetically, for the swallow itself.

prōgredior, -gressus, -gredī, [pro-gradior], 3. v. n., *proceed, go forth, advance, come forth.*

progressus, -a, -um, p.p. of **progredior.**

proh, see **prō.**

prohibeō, -hibuī, -hibitum, -hibēre, [pro-habeo], 2. v. a, *hold off, keep off, drive off, ward off, avert, debar, shut out.* — Also, *forbid, prevent, restrain, keep from* (some action).

prōiciō, -iēcī, -iectum, -icere, [pro-iacio], 3. v. a., *throw forth, throw away, cast away, cast up, throw off, expose.* — Also, *throw forward, cast, throw down, throw, put forward, let drop.* — **prōiectus, -a, -um,** p.p. as adj., *projecting, lying at length, prostrate, lying.*

prōiectus, -a, -um, p.p. of **proicio.**

proinde [pro-inde], adv., *hence, therefore.*

prōlābor, -lāpsus, -lābī, [pro-labor], 3. v. dep., *slide forward, slide down* (cf. **proicio**), *fall to ruin, fall.*

prōlāpsus, -a, -um, p.p. of **prolabor.**

prōlēs, -is, [pro-oles, cf. **suboles**], f., *progeny, offspring, a line* (of descendants), *a family, a race.* — Of individuals, *a son, a descendant:*

Cyllenia (*the son born on*, &c.); alia (*another year's offspring*). — Also, of plants, *growth, increase.*

prōlixus, -a, -um, [pro-laxus], adj., *long:* barba (*flowing*).

prōlūdō, -lūsī, -lūsum, -lūdere, [pro-ludo], 3. v. n., *fence beforehand.* — Less exactly, of animals, *prepare, practise, try its strength.*

prōluō, -luī, -lūtum, -luere, [pro-luo], 3. v. a., *wash up, throw up.* — Also, *wash away, wash out.* — Fig.: proluit se, *drains a mighty draught.*

prōluviēs, -eī, [pro-†luvies (√lu + ies, cf. **illuvies**)], f., *an overflow.* — Less exactly, *excrement.*

prōmereō, -meruī, -meritum, -merēre, [pro-mereo], 2. v. a., *deserve.* — Pass. as dep., *deserve* (well or ill of one), *serve one:* plurima te promeritam (*the very many favors I owe you*).

Promētheus, -eī (-eos), [Gr. Προμηθεύς], m., the son of Iapetus. He stole fire from heaven to animate the man he had formed of clay. For this act he was punished by a vulture on Mt. Caucasus.

prōmissum, -ī, [n. p.p. of **promitto**], n., *a promise, what one has promised, a promised prize* (*boon*, &c.).

prōmissus, -a, -um, p.p. of **promitto.**

prōmittō, -mīsī, -missum, -mittere, [pro-mitto], 3. v. a., *let go forth, let grow* (of the hair). — Fig., *give out, promise* (generally on request, cf. **polliceor**), *agree:* me promisi ultorem (*promise to be*). — **promissus, -a, -um,** p.p. as adj., *long, flowing:* barba (see also **promissum**).

prōmō, prōmpsī, prōmptum, prōmere, [pro-emo], 3. v. a., *take out.* — With reflexive, *come forth.* — Esp., *draw out* of the general stock for use (cf. **promus,** *a steward*), *bring out, put forth, employ.* — **prōmptus, -a, -um,** p.p., *drawn out, ready, at hand, easy.*

Promolus (-ulus), -i, [?], m., a Trojan.

prōmoveo, -movī, -mōtum, -movēre, [pro-moveo], 2. v. a., *move onward, impel.*

prōnubus, -a, -um, [pro-†nubus (root of nubo + us)], adj., *of marriage.* — Fem. as subst., *a witness* or *guardian* (the matron attending the bride at a marriage, cf. **auspex**). — Hence as epithet of Juno and poetically of other divinities, *Pronuba, goddess of marriage.*

prōnus, -a, -um, [stem of pro + nus], adj., *bending forward, headlong, headforemost, forward, downward, falling.* — Fig., *rapid, swift, swift-flowing:* prona aqua (*down stream*); prona maria (*unobstructed*).

prōpāgō, -inis, [as if pro-†pago (stem from √pag + o), cf. **propages, compages**], f., *a layer* (a shoot pegged down to root again, as is still practised), *layers* (collectively). — Fig., *offspring, progeny, descendants, a line* (of descendants).

prope [prob. pro-pe, cf. **quippe**], adv. and prep., *near, near by, close to.*

properātus, -a, -um, p.p. of **propero.**

properē [abl. of properus], adv., *quickly, hastily.*

propero, -āvī, -ātum, -āre, [†properŏ-], 1. v. a. and n., *hasten, make haste, hasten to do* (*to have done*), *do with haste* (what is indicated by the context): adiungi generum (*be in haste to have united,* &c.); properanda (*to be done in haste*); fulmina (*forge with speed*); properari vides (*you see men hastening*); properata (of seeds, *forced*); arma (*bring with haste*); mortem (*haste to win*).

properus, -a, -um, [pro-†parus, whence **paro**], adj., *hastening, active, busy.*

prōpexus, -a, -um, [pro-pexus, p.p. of **pecto**], adj., *combed down, hanging down.*

propinquŏ, -āvī, -ātum, -āre, [†propinquŏ-], 1. v. a. and n., *bring near.* — Intrans., *approach, be near, come near, draw near, come* (to a place expressed by the context).

propinquus, -a, -um, [stem akin to **prope** + cus], adj., *near, neighboring, near by, akin, kindred.*

propior, -us, -ōris, [**prope** (or stem akin) + ior, compar.], adj., *nearer.* — Neut. plur., *the nearer space.* — Neut. sing. as adv., *nearer, more closely.* — **proximus, -a, -um,** [?, unc. stem + timus], superl., *nearest, next, close by, most like.* — Neut. plur.: proxima quaeque, *whatever comes nearest.*

prōpōnō, -posuī, -positum, pōnere, [pro-pono], 3. v. a., *set forth, propose, offer.*

proprius, -a, -um, [?, poss. akin to **prope**], adj., *one's own, of one's own, peculiar, appropriate, one's natural.* — Hence, *lasting, continuing, perpetual:* propriam dicabo (*make one's own forever*).

propter [prope + ter, cf. **praeter**], adv. and prep., *near by, not far from.* — Also (cf. **ob**), *on account of, for the sake of.*

prōpugnāculum, -ī, [propugnā- (stem of **propugno**) + culum], n., *a bulwark, a rampart, a means of defence* (protection for defenders of walls).

prōra, -ae, [Gr. πρῷρα], f., *the prow* (of a ship). — Less exactly, *a ship.*

prōripiō, -ripuī, -reptum, -ripere, [pro-rapio], 3. v. a., *drag forth.* — With reflexive (sometimes omitted), *hasten, hurry away.*

prōrumpō, -rūpī, -ruptum, -rumpere, [pro-rumpo], 3. v. a. and n. Causative (cf. **rumpo**), *cause to break forth, belch forth.* — Pass. or with reflexive, *break forth:* proruptum mare (*a raging sea*); proruptus sudor (*bursting forth*). — Intrans., *rush forth, fling one's self forward.*

Vocabulary. 223

prōruptus, -a, -um, p.p. of prorumpo.

proscaenium (proscē-), -ī (-iī), [Gr. προσκήνιον], n., *a stage*, properly the place in front of the scene (see scaena), where the action was performed.

prōscindō,-scidī,-scissum,-scindere, [pro-scindo], 3. v. a., *tear, rend in pieces, cut.*—Esp., *plough;* particularly for the first time, *break up.*

prōscissus, -a, -um, p.p. of proscindo.

prōsequor,-secūtus, -sequī, [prosequor], 3. v. dep., *follow out, follow after, attend, speed on one's way, follow, escort.*—Also, *proceed, go on.*—Also, *follow up, treat of* (cf. "pursue a subject").—From last words at parting, *dismiss, take leave of, send on one's way* (with wishes, &c.); so, *receive, reply to.*

Prōserpina, -ae, [prob. corrupted fr. Gr. Περσεφόνη, with an idea of connection with proserpo], f., the wife of Pluto, daughter of Ceres. She was stolen by Pluto from her mother, who sought her over the world.

prōsiliō, -siluī (-ivī, -iī), no sup., -silīre, [pro-salio], 4. v. n., *leap forth, dart forth.*

prōspectō, -āvī, -ātum, -āre, [pro-specto], 1. v. a., *look out upon, gaze at.*—Also, *expect, await.*

prōspectus, -ūs, [pro-spectus, cf. prospicio], m., *an outlook, a prospect, a view, a sight.*

prosper, -era, -erum, [pro-†sperus, wh. spero], adj., *according to one's hopes, favorable, propitious.*

prōspiciō,-spexī, -spectum, -spicere, [pro-specio, cf. conspicio], 3. v. a. and n., *look out upon, behold, espy, gaze at, see, look out, gaze, look forth.*—Also, *foresee, prognosticate.*

prōsubigō, no perf., no sup., -igere, [pro-subigo], 3. v. a., *tear up.*

prōsum, prōfuī, prōdesse, [pro- (prod-) -esse], irr. v. n., *be of advantage, profit, avail, be well.*

prōtectus, -a, -um, p.p. of protego.

prōtegō, -texī, -tectum, -tegere, [pro-tego], 3. v. a., *cover, protect, defend.*

prōtendō, -tendī, -tentum (-tensum), -tendere, [pro-tendo], 3. v. a., *stretch out, stretch, strain* hastas (*poise*); protentus temo (*extending*).

prōtentus, -a, -um, p.p. of protendo.

prōtenus, see protinus.

prōterō, -trīvī, -trītum, -terere, [pro-tero], 3. v. a., *trample down.*

prōterreō, -terruī, -territum, -terrēre, [pro-terreo], 2. v. a., *frighten away, put to flight.*

Prōteus, -eī (-eos), [Gr. Πρωτεύς], m., a prophetic "old man of the sea," having a view of the entire abyss of the sea, and shepherd of the flocks of Neptune, the seacalves. His dwelling was in the east of the Mediterranean (the island Pharos or Carpathus), near the mythic stream Ægyptus: and he was otherwise associated with Egypt. He had to be caught and bound to elicit prophetic answers from him, and he had the power of changing himself into all kinds of forms to avoid capture.

prōtinus (prōtenus),[pro-tenus], adv., *forward, further on, on:* protinus una (*continuously*); ae quasset nocti ludum (*throughout*).—Also, *next, then, afterwards, in after time.*—Also, *immediately, forthwith, at once.*

prōtrahō, -traxī, -tractum, -trahere, [pro-traho], 3. v. a., *drag forth.*

prōturbō, -āvī, -ātum, -āre, [proturbo], 1. v. a., *drive away, repel, force back.*

prōvectus, -a, -um, p.p. of proveho.

prōvehō, -vexī, -vectum, -vehere, [pro-veho], 3. v. a., *carry for-*

ward, bear on. — Pass. as dep., *sail, ride, proceed.*

prōveniō,-vēnī,-ventum,-venīre, [pro-venio], 4. v. n., *come forth, spring up.* — Fig., *come to pass, happen.*

prōventus, -us, [pro-ventus, cf. provenio], m., *a growth, increase, crop.*

prōvideō, -vīdī, -vīsum, -vidēre, [pro-video], 2. v. a. and n., *take care for, take care of, provide, get ready.*

prōvīsus,-a,-um, p.p. of **provideo.**

prōvocō, -āvī, -ātum, -āre, [pro-voco], 1. v. a., *call forth.* — Esp., *challenge.* — Fig., *challenge, vie with.*

prōvolvō, -volvī, -volūtum, -volvere, [pro-volvo], 3. v. a., *roll down, roll forward, roll over.*

proximus, see **propior.**

prūdēns,-ēntis,[pro-videns], adj., *wise, far-seeing.*

prūdēntia, -ae, [†prudent + ia], f., *wisdom, skill.*

pruīna, -ae, [?], f., *hoar-frost, snow, frost.* — Poetically for winter.

pruna, -ae, [?], f., *a live coal.*

prūnum,-ī,[Gr. προῦνον], n., *a plum.*

prūnus, -ī, [Gr. προῦνος], f., *a plum-tree.*

Prytanis, -is, [Gr. Πρύτανις], m., a Trojan.

psythius, -a, -um, [Gr. Ψύθιος], adj., *psythian* (a kind of vine). — Fem., *the psythia,* the vine itself.

pūbēns, -ēntis, [p. of †pubeo †pubi-), cf. pubesco], adj., *full grown, juicy* (of herbs at maturity).

pūber, -eris, [?, cf. pubes], adj., *downy, full grown.*

pūbēs, -is, [?], f., *down* (as a sign of manhood). — Hence, *the groin.* — Fig., *youth, young men* (arrived at manhood). — Often of an army, which consisted of able-bodied males. — Hence, generally, *people.* — Less exactly, *the young,* of bullocks.

pūbēscō, pūbuī, no sup., **pūbēscere,** [†pubē- (of pubeo, cf. pubens) + sco], 3. v. n., *grow up, come to manhood.* — Less exactly, *ripen.*

pudendus, -a, -um; see **pudeo.**

pudeō, -uī (-itum est), -itum, -ere, 2. v. a. and n., *shame, be ashamed.* — Esp. impers. with acc. of person, *shame one, one is ashamed, one disdains:* Æneae segnes (*be ashamed in the sight of*). — **pudendus, -a, -um,** p. ger., *to be ashamed of, shameful.*

pudīcitia, -ae, [†pudicŏ + tia (cf. amicitia)], f., *modesty, chastity, purity* (as a quality, cf. **pudor**). — Also, *a feeling of shame.*

pudor, -ōris, [pud (as root of pudeo) + or], m., *a feeling of shame, shame, modesty, chastity, honor, decency.*

puella, -ae, [†puerŏ (cf. **puer**) + la], f., *a girl, a maid, a young bride.*

puer, -erī, [?], m., *a child, a babe, a boy, a lad, a youth.* Properly not over seventeen, but the word is naturally not used with exactness. — Also, *a slave, a "boy."*

puerīlis, -e, [†puerŏ- (reduced) + ilis], adj., *childish, of children, of boys.*

pugna, -ae, [√pug (in pugno) + na], f., *a fight, a combat, a battle, a contest.* — Less exactly, *a war.*

pugnātor, -ōris, [†pugna- (stem of pugno) + tor], m., *a fighter.* — In app. as adj., *pugnacious.*

pugnātus, -a, -um, p.p. of **pugno.**

pugnō, -āvī, -ātum, -āre, [†pugna-], 1. v. n., *fight, wage war, contend.* — Fig., *resist, fight against, struggle.* — **pugnātus, -a, -um,** p.p. in pass. sense (derived from use of cognate acc.), *fought.*

pugnus, -ī, [√pug (in pugno) + nus], m., *a fist.*

pulcher, -chra, -chrum, [?], adj., *beautiful, fair, splendid, comely.* — Fig., *glorious, noble, excellent, famous.*

pullulō, -āvī, -ātum, -āre, [†pullulŏ-], 1. v. n., *sprout, grow rank.*

pullus, -i, [?, cf. Gr. πῶλος, Eng. *foal*], m., *a young one, a foal.*

pullus, -a, -um, [?, but cf. πελλός], adj., *black, dark.*

pulmō, -ōnis, [perh. akin to Gr. πνεύμων, perh. borrowed], m., *the lungs.*

pulsātus, -a, -um, p.p. of **pulso.**

pulsō, -āvī, -ātum, -āre, [†pulsŏ-], 1. v. a. and n., *beat, strike, batter, hit, strike against, quiver, palpitate, sound* (on the lyre): ilia singultibus (*shake*); pulsante nervo (*twanging,* as it snaps and drives the arrow); pulsans pavor (*anxious throbbing*). — **pulsātus, -a, -um,** p.p. as adj., *wave-beaten, re-echoing* (struck by a sound), *insulted* (as if by a blow).

pulsus, -ūs, [√pel + tus, cf. pello], m., *a beating, a stroke, a trampling:* pulsu saxa sonant (*with an echo*).

pulsus, -a, -um, p.p. of **pello.**

pulvereus, -a, -um, [†pulver- (of pulvis) + eus], adj., *of dust.*

pulverulentus, -a, -um, [†pulver- (as if pulveru-) + lentus], adj., *dusty, in a cloud of dust.*

pulvis, -eris, [?], m. and f., *dust, dry ground* (*drouth*), *earth, mould:* in pulvere (on *the dusty field*).

pūmex, -icis, [?], m., *pumice-stone, porous rock.*

pūniceus (poen-), -a, -um, [†Punicŏ- (reduced) + eus], adj., *red* (made from Tyrian dye, cf. **Poenus**), *crimson, purple* (bordering on red).

Pūnicus (Poen-), -a, -um, [†Poenŏ + cus], adj., *Punic, Carthaginian, of Carthage.*

puppis, -is, [?], f., *the stern* (of a ship), *the poop.* — Less exactly, *a ship, a boat, a vessel.* — **a puppi,** *astern.*

purgō, -āvī, -ātum, -are, [†purgŏ- (†puro-†agus), cf. narro], 1. v. a., *clean, clear:* se nubes (*clears away*).

purpura, -ae, [Gr. πορφύρα], f., *purple, crimson, red.* — Also, *purple* (purple fabrics).

purpureus, -a, -um, [†purpura- (reduced) + eus], adj., *purple* (of various shades, with a tendency generally towards red), *red, crimson:* purpurei cristis iuvenes (*with purple crests*); purpureus pennis (*purple-crested*). — Hence, *bright, gay, brilliant.*

pūrus, -a, -um, [√pu (*clean*) + rus, cf. putus], adj., *clean, pure, clear, bright, limpid:* vestis (*fair white*). — Also, *unobstructed, open:* per purum (*through the open air*). — Fig., *unmixed, pure:* hasta (*headless*); parma (*with no device*).

putātor, -ōris, [†putā- (of puto) + tor], m., *a pruner, a vinedresser.*

puteus, -i, [poss. †puto- (of putus) + eus], m., *a well, a pit.*

putō, -āvī, -ātum, -āre, [†putŏ- (of putus, √pu, *clean*, + tus)], 1. v. a., *clean.* — Esp., *trim, prune.* — Fig., *clear up* (accounts). — Hence, *reckon, account, consider, think, suppose, revolve* (in the mind), *ponder.*

putris (-ter), -is, -e, [√put (in puteo) + ris], adj., *rotten, mellow, crumbly, loose:* fungi (*sooty*).

Pygmalion, -ōnis, [Gr. Πυγμαλίων], m., Dido's brother, who killed his sister's husband.

pyra, -ae, [Gr. πυρά], f., *a funeral pile, a pyre.*

Pyracmon, -onis, [Gr. Πυράκμων], m., a Cyclops, a blacksmith in the forge of Etna.

Pyrgī, -orum, [Gr. Πύργοι], m. plur., a town of Etruria.

Pyrgo, -ūs, [Gr. Πυργώ], f., the nurse of Priam's children. She accompanied the expedition of Æneas.

Pyrrha, -ae, [Gr. Πύρρα], f., the wife of Deucalion, who with her husband survived the deluge, and who by throwing stones behind her repeopled the earth.

Pyrrhus, -i, [Gr. Πύρρος], m., the son of Achilles (called also Neoptolemus). After fighting in the Trojan war, he founded a kingdom in Epirus. Becoming a suitor for the hand of Hermione, he was slain by Orestes.

Q.

qua, fem. sing. and neut. plur. of **quis** indef.

quā [abl. of **qui,** cf. **ea**], rel. adv., *by which way, whereby, where, by which, as.*

quā [abl. of **quis** (same word as preceding)], interr. adv., *how? in what way?*

quācunque (also separate), [**quacunque**], rel. adv., *in whatever way, whichever way, wherever.* — Also, *in any way whatever, in whatever way one can, by any means.*

quadra, -ae, [some form of **quattuor** + **a** (f. of -**us**)], f., *a square, a table.*—Also of the *square loaves* used as trenchers and eaten by the Trojans.

quadrifidus, -a, -um, [†quadrŏ- (cf. **quadra**) -**fidus** (†**fid** in **findo** + **us**)], adj., *four-cleft, four-parted.*

quadrīgae, -arum, [perh. †quadrŏ-†agus,'cf. **prodigus**], f. plur., *a four-horse team, four horses* (abreast), *horses* (for the chariot), *a four-horse chariot.*

quadriiugis, -e, = **quadriiugus,** [same stem weakened].

quadriiugus, -a, -um, [†quadrŏ-†iugo-, cf. **iugum,** decl. as adj.], adj., *with four horses, four-horse, four abreast:* equos (*double pair of*).

quadrŏ, -āvī, -ātum, -are, [†quadrā-], 1. v. a. and n., *form in a square.*—Intrans., *to fit squarely with.*

quadrupedāns, -āntis, [p. of obs. or imaginary **quadrupedo**], adj., *galloping:* sonitus (*sound of galloping feet*).— Plur., *steeds, horses.*

quadrupēs, -pedis, [†quadrŏ-pes, decl. as adj.], adj., *going on four feet.* — As subst., *a quadruped, a horse, a stag.*

quaero, quaesīvī, quaesītum, quaerere, [?, originally **quaeso,** √quaes as root], 3. v. a., *seek, seek to gain, search for, look for, seek out, go to, endeavor, desire.* — Esp., *seek for gain, seek gain, gain, win, acquire.* — Also, *ask for, ask, enquire.* — Also, *miss, look for* (and not find): te suum dextera (*finds not you its owner*). — **quaesītus, -a, -um,** p.p. as adj.: munus (*acquired*); herbae (*gathered*); artes (*applied, employed*); boves (*missing*). — Neut. plur., *gains.* — **quaerēns, -entis,** p. as subst., *a seeker.* — **quaeso,** *enquire* (rare and archaic): talia (*make such enquiries*).—Parenthetically, *I pray, I beg, pray.*

quaesītor, -ōris, [†quaesī- (stem of **quaero,** in 4. conj.) + **tor**], m., *an investigator, a judge* (in ancient sense as investigator).

quaesītus, -a, -um, p.p. of **quaero.**

quaeso, see **quaero.**

quālis, -e, [†quŏ- (of **qui** and **quis**) + **alis**], pron. adj. 1. Interr. (in questions and exclamations), *of what sort, what, what a man* (or the like), *what kind of.* — 2. Rel. (with correl. expressed or implied), (*of which kind*), *as* (the quality being implied in Eng. in a preceding *such,* or the like), *such* (implied in what precedes) . . . . *as.* — Equal to an adv., *just as, as.*

quālus (-um), -i, [?, cf. **colum**], m. and n., *a basket.* — Esp. for straining wine, *a wicker strainer.*

quam [unc. case-form of **quis** and **qui,** cf. **nam**], adv. 1. Interr., *how, how much.* — 2. Rel., *as much, as, than.*—Its force after **prius, ante,**

and **post** is in Eng. *often contained in some other word.* — *With comparatives,* (*the*) ... *the.* — *With superlatives, as much as possible, very.* — *With anteced. omitted, as many as, so ... as.* — See also **ante, prior, post,** and **tam.**

quamvīs [quam-vīs], adv., *as you wish, as you will, however much, however.* — Also, *although, though.*

quandō [prob. abl. of unc. stem (quam? + dus)], adv. and conj. 1. Interr., *at what time? when?* — 2. Indef., *at any time, ever* (affirmative, cf. **unquam** with negatives), *at some time.* — 3. Rel., *when, now that, since, as.* — Fig. (in causal sense), *since, inasmuch as, seeing that.*

quandōquidem (rarely **quandŏ-**) [quando-quidem], adv., *since, inasmuch as, seeing that.*

quanquam(**quam-**)[quam-quam, cf. **quisquis**], adv., (*however*), *although, though.* — Also (in a corrective sense, as often in Eng.), *though, still, however, but.*

quāntus, -a, -um, [pron. √quŏ + antus (with lost v), cf. Sk. -vant], pron. adj. 1. Interr., *how great? how much? what a, what.*—2. Rel., *as* (cf. **qualis**).—With omitted antecedent, *as great as, as much as, not less than.* — Acc. as adv. (both senses), *how much, how, how long, as much, as, as far as, as much as, as long as.* — Abl. as adv., *how much, how, as much, as.* — With comparatives, (*the*) ... *the.*

quārē [quā rē], adv. 1. Interr., *on what account? why?* — 2. Rel., *on which account, wherefore, therefore.*

quartus, -a, -um, [†quattuor + tus], num. adj., *fourth.*

quassātus,-a, -um, p.p. of **quasso.**

quassō,-āvī, -ātum, -āre, [†quas-sŏ- (cf. **quatio**)], 1. v. a. and n., *shake, toss, brandish.*—Of the effect, *shatter, batter.* — Intrans., *shake:* siliqua quassans (*rattling*).

quater [unc. form fr. **quattuor,** cf. **ter**], num. adv., *four times.*

quaternī, -ae, -a, [†quattuor + nus], adj. plur., *four at a time, four in each.*

quatiŏ, †quassī (only in compos.), **quassum, quatere,** [?], 3. v. a., *shake, agitate, cause to tremble, stir.* — Also, *batter, shatter, demolish, overthrow, beat, lash, drive, worry, harass:* campos (*scour,* of horsemen sent on a raid); cursu (*subdue,* of horses); fundamenta (*rend*).

quattuor (**quātuor**) [?, petrified and reduced nom., cf. τέτταρες], num. adj. indecl., *four.*

-que [unc. case-form †quŏ-, cf. τε], conj., *and* (connecting the word to which it is affixed or the clause in which that word is). — Repeated (or with **et, atque,** or **ac**), *both ... and, as well ... as, and* (omitting the first). — Equal to **cum,** *when:* vix fatus erat, subitoque intonuit. — Equal to Eng. *or* (fr. a different view in Latin): ter quaterque. — With explanatory force: segetes altae campique natantes (both meaning the same thing).

queō, quīvī (-iī), quitum, quīre, [?], 4. v. n., *can, be able.*

Quercēns, -entis, [perh. †quercu-], m., *a Rutulian.*

quercus, -ūs, [?], f., *an oak* (sacred to Jove), *oak leaves, a twig of oak:* civilis (the civic crown of oak leaves, given for saving the life of a fellow-citizen).

querēla (**-ella**), **-ae,** [as if querē-, supposed stem of **queror**'(cf. **suadela**) + la], f., *a complaint, a plaint* (of songs of birds), *a cry* (of distress).

quernus, -a, -um, [†quercu- (reduced) + nus], adj., *of oak, oaken:* glandes (*oak mast, acorns*).

queror, questus, querī, [√ques], 3. v. n. and a., *complain, bewail, complain of:* plura querens (*uttering further complaints*). — Poetically: bubo (*wail, cry*).

querulus, -a, -um, [†querŏ- (lost

o̓r assumed, akin to **queror**)+ lus], adj., *complaining:* cicadae (*melancholy*).
questus, -ūs, [√**ques** (in **queror**) + tus], m., *a complaint.* — Poetically, *complaining note, plaint.*
quī, quae, quod, [pron. √**quo** + i(?) and √**qui**], rel. pron., *who, which, that.* — Often with antecedent not expressed, *these who, those who, what, whoever, whatever.* — Where in Eng. a demonstrative is used, *and he* &c., *but he, he, this.* — Also, *as* (cf. **qualis**). — **quod,** neut., *as to which, now, but, and:* quod si (*now if*); quod ut (*and*); quod te oro (*and so I pray*). — Also, *a thing which* (so id quod in same sense): quod superest (*furthermore, it is further to be said, the only thing remaining*). — **ex quo,** *from the time when, since, after.*
quī, abl. of **qui.**
quia [case-form of †**qui**- (prob. acc. plur. neut.)], conj., *because* (a real reason, cf. **quoniam** and **quod**): quiane (*is it because*).
quianam (or separate), [quia (as interr.) -nam], adv., *why, pray?*
quiane, see **quia.**
quicquam, see **quisquam.**
quīcumque (-cunque), **quae-, quod-,** (also separate), [quīcumque (cf. **quisque**)], indef. rel. pron., *whoever, whatever, all who:* quicunque violavimus (*all of us who*); sive quicunque furor (*whatever other*). — Also, *any whatever, every possible:* quocunque modo (*in any way whatever*). — Neut. with partitive gen.: quodcunque regni (*this realm such as it is*).
quīdam, quae-, quod- (quid-), [qui-dam (pron. √**da,** cf. **nam, tam**)], indef. pron., *some one, some* (regularly a definite person, though not named), *certain, a.* — Less exactly, *some* (indef.), *one man.*
quidem [prob. **quī** (abl. of **qui**) -dem, cf. **idem**], adv., (*in which way?*), (confirmatory particle, very often unnecessary in Eng.), *truly, also, too.* — Concessive, *to be sure.* —Adversative, *but, however:* haud impune quidem; et quidem (*and yet*)..— ne ... quidem (enclosing the emphatic word), *not even, nor ... either, not ... any more.*
quiēs, -ētis, [†**quiē**- (cf. **quiesco**) + tis (reduced, cf. **sementis**)], f., *rest, repose, sleep, slumber, leisure, ease, stillness, quiet.*
quiēscō, quiēvī, quiētum, quiescere, [†**quiē**- (of lost or assumed †**quieo,** √**qui,** cf. **civis,** κεῖμαι) + sco], 3. v. n., *come to rest, go to rest, rest, repose, cease, be stilled, become silent, lie idle, die down.* — **quiētus, -a, -um,** p.p. as adj., *quiet, calm, peaceful, still, undisturbed, unruffled, gentle:* quietos cura sollicitat (*their tranquil rest*); quae vos fortuna quietos sollicitat (*your peace*).
quīn [qui (abl. of **quis**) -ne], adv. 1. Interr., (*how not?*), *why not?* (in exhortations) *come, now, nay, even, nay even, but rather, indeed.* — 2. [abl. of **qui**]ne, rel. conj., *so that not, but that, so but what, that, from* (doing anything, with verbs of hindrance), *to* (do anything, with verbs of hindrance): non possum quin (*I cannot but*).
quīn etiam, *nay even, moreover.*
quīnī, -ae, -a, [quinque (reduced) + nus], num. adj. plur., *five each, five at a time.* — Less exactly, *five.*
quingentī, -ae, -a, [quinque (or quini?) -genti (fr. **centum**)], num. adj. plur., *five hundred.*
quīnquāgintā [quinque + unc. form, cf. πεντήκοντα], num. adj. indecl., *fifty.*
quīnque [?, cf. πέντε], num. adj. indecl., *five.*
quīntus (old **quinct-**), **-a, -um,** [quinque (reduced) + tus], num. adj., *the fifth.*
quippe [quid-pe, cf. **nempe**], adv., *truly, no doubt, in fact, doubtless:* subito quippe fugit dolor (*strange*

to say). — Ironical, *forsooth, indeed*. — Also, *for* (strictly not causal but explanatory).

Quirīnālis, -e, [†Quirinŏ- (reduced) + alis], adj., *of Quirinus* (Romulus).

Quirīnus, -ī, [?, akin to **Quiris**], m., the name given to Romulus as the divinity of Rome.

Quirīs, -ītis, (usually plur.), [†Curi- (of **Cures**), (lengthened, cf. **civīlis**) + tis (cf. **Carmentis**)], m., *inhabitant (inhabitants) of Cures, the Quirites*. — Also, *Roman citizens, Quirites*. — Poetically, *citizens* (of bees).

quīs, abl. or dat. plur. of **qui**.

quis (qui), quae (qua, indef.), **quid (quod),** [pron. roots quo and qui as stems; same word as **qui**], interr. pron., *who, what, what sort of, in what condition*. — **quid,** neut., *why, what;* (interrog. and exclam.), *how is it with? what about? what of?* — As indef., *any, anyone* (sometimes equal *each one*), *anything, one, some one, something*.

quisnam (qui-), quae-, quid- (quod-), (also separate), [quisnam, cf. **nam**], interr. and indef., *who pray, what pray, who, what* (emphatic).

quisquam, quae-, quid- (quic-), [quis (as indef.) -quam], indef. pron. (universal, hence only with a negative expressed or hinted at, cf. **aliquis, quis,** with affirmatives), *anyone, any man, anything:* **minatur si quisquam adeat** (*if anyone should,* &c., implying that they will not). — With expressed neg., *no one, nothing*.

quisque, quae-, quid- (quic-), [quis-que], indef. pron., *each one* (of several, cf. **uterque**), *each, every, everyone, every man, everything, all*. — Often with a superlative: **proxima quaeque** (*everything in the way*, with idea of succession). — With two, equal to two comparatives, *the more . . . the more*.

quisquis, quidquid (quicquid), [quis doubled], indef. rel. pron., *whoever, whatever*.

1. **quō** [prob. old dat. pron. √quo], adv., *whither* (both interr. and rel.), *where* (in corrupt Eng. sense of *whither*). — Fig., *to what end, for what purpose, of what use*.

2. **quo** [abl. of pron. †quo-], conj. (adv.), (*by which*), *in order that, that*.

quōcircā (also separate), [quo (abl. or dat.) -circa], adv., *wherefore*.

quocunque (also separate), [quo cunque], rel. adv., *whithersoever, wherever, however, whichever way* (acc. to English idiom), *whatever way*.

quod [n. of **qui**, acc. or nom. (perh. both)], conj., *that, because* (a real cause, cf. **quoniam**), *in that, as to, as for* (with participle in Eng.). — **est quod,** *there is reason why*. See also **qui**.

quom, see **cum**.

quōmodo (or separate), [quo (abl.) modō], adv., *in what way, how, in which manner, as*.

quōnam [1. quo-nam], adv., *whither pray, Oh whither, whither* (emphatic), *where*.

quondam [quom (cum) -dam, cf. **quidam**], adv., (*at a certain time*), *once, formerly, before, just now*. — Of time future, *one day, hereafter, by and by*. — Indef., *some time, sometimes*.

quoniam [quom-iam], adv. (conj.), *now that*. — Also, *seeing that, since* (of an explanatory fact, cf. **quod**), *inasmuch as*.

quoque [unc. form of **qui** + que, cf. **quisque**], conj., *also, too, as well, not less, even*.

quot [prob. pron. √quŏ + ti, cf. Sk. kati], adj. indecl. (interr. and rel.), *how many, as many, as* (cf. **qualis**), *as many as* (with omitted antecedent). — **quot (quod) annis** (*as many years as there are*), *yearly, every year*.

quotannis, see **quot** and **annus**.

quotiēns (-ēs), [†quoti + ēns, cf. **quinquiens**], adv., *how many times, how often, as often, as often as, as many times as* (cf. **quot**).
quousque (also separate), [1. **quousque**], adv., *how far, how long*.

R.

rabidus, -a, -um, [noun-stem akin to **rabies** (cf. **rabula**) + **dus**], adj., *raving, raging, furious, savage.* — Transferred, *ravenous, ravening:* fames.
rabiēs, -em, -ē, [√rab (in **rabio**, etc.) + ies], f., *madness, rage, raving* (inspiration), *fury* (of storms, &c.): edendi, ventris (*ravening hunger*).
racēmus, -ī, [?], m., *a cluster* (of berries or grapes), *a bunch, grapes, berries.*
radiō, -āvī, -ātum, -āre, [†radiŏ-], 1. v. a. and n. (*furnish with rays*). — Intrans., *shine.* — **radiāns, -antis**, p. as adj., *bright, radiant, gleaming.*
radius, -ī (-iī), [perh. akin to **rādix**], m., *a staff, a rod* (esp. for measuring), *a spoke, a shuttle, an olive* (of a peculiar kind, *elongated*), *a strand* or *spike* (of a thunderbolt). — Esp., *a ray, a beam.*
rādīx, -īcis, [perh. akin to **radius**], f., *a root.* — Also, *a foundation, a fastening* (at the bottom).
rādō, rāsī, rāsum, rādere, [?], 3. v. a., *scrape, shave, peel.* — Fig., *graze, pass closely, coast along.* — With cogn. acc., *cleave, skim.*
Raeticus (Rhae-), -a, -um, [†Raetŏ + cus], adj., *of the Raeti* (a nation south of the Danube, in Tyrol, &c.), *Raetian;* Raetica (a kind of grapes).
rāmeus, -a, -um, [†ramŏ- (reduced) + eus], adj., *of branches.*
rāmōsus, -a, -um, [†ramŏ- (reduced) + osus], adj., *branching.*
rāmus, -ī, [perh. akin to **radix**], m., *a bough, a branch, a twig.* (Boughs hung with woollen fillets were borne by suppliants). — Poetically as yielding fruit.

rāna, -ae, [?], f., *a frog.*
rapāx, -ācis, [√rap + ax, cf. **capax**], adj., *snatching, greedy:* fluvii (*rapid*, carrying everything with them).
rapidus, -a, -um, [†rapŏ- (or -i) + dus, cf. **rapio**], adj., (*seizing*), *fierce, consuming, blazing, fiery* (of heat). — Also, *swift* (cf. **rapax**), *rapid, hurrying, quick, active:* ungula (*flying*); vortices (*whirling*).
rapīna, -ae, [†rapi- (as if stem of **rapio**) + na], f., *robbery, plunder.* — Concretely, *booty.*
rapiō, rapuī, raptum, rapere, [√rap, akin to ἁρπάζω], 3. v. a., *snatch, snatch away, seize, carry off, hurry away, hurry, drag, wrest away, tear from, rob of, sweep away, sweep along.* — Esp., *plunder, steal, ravish, take, capture.* — **raptum, -ī**, n. p.p. as subst., *rapine, plunder, booty, spoil.* — Intrans., *hurry on.*
Rapō, -ōnis, [rapo], m., a Rutulian.
raptātus, -a, -um, p.p. of **rapto**.
raptim [as if acc. of †raptis (√rap + tis), cf. **partim**], adv., *hastily, swiftly.*
raptō, -āvī, -ātum, -āre, [†raptŏ- (cf. **rapio**)], 1. v. a., *drag away, hurry off, drag.*
raptor, -ōris, [√rap + tor], m., *a plunderer.* — In app. as adj., *plundering, prowling.*
raptus, -a, -um, p.p. of **rapio**.
rārēscō, no perf., no sup., **-ēscere**, [as if †rarē- (of lost or supposed †rareo) + sco, cf. **rarus**], 3. v. n. incept., *grow thin:* claustra Pelori (*widen, become less close together.*)
rārus, -a, -um, [?], adj., *loose* (opposed *to* densus), *wide apart, thin, scattered, rare, straggling,*

few, here and there, scanty, rarefied: **retia** (*large-meshed, coarse*); **voces** (*broken*).
rāsilis, -e, [†rasŏ + lis], adj., *polished, worked with a chisel.*
rāstrum, -ī, (pl. **-ī, -ōrum**), [√rād + trum], n. and m., *a hoe* (*toothed and heavy for breaking the soil*).
rāsus, -a, -um, p.p. of **rado.**
ratio, -ōnis, [as if √ra (in **reor**) + tio (perh. †rati + o)], f., *a reckoning, account, a plan, a way, means.* — Also, *intelligence, counsel, devices:* **sat rationis in armis** (*any sense,* &c.).
ratis, -is, [?, but cf. **remus**?], f., *a raft.* — Poetically, *a boat, a ship, a vessel.*
ratus, -a, -um, p.p. of **reor.**
raucus, -a, -um, [†ravŏ- (or -ī, cf. **ravus, ravis**) + cus], adj., *hoarse, deep, harsh, roaring, murmuring, screaming, shrill, clanging:* **rauco assensu** (*harsh accord*). — Neut. as adv., *harshly.*
re- (**red-**), [abl. of unc. stem], prep. in comp., *back, again, un-* (reversing the action), *forth.*
rebellis, -e, [re-†bello- (weakened and decl. as adj.), cf. **exanimis**], adj., *renewing a war, insurgent, rising* (in arms, after conquest).
reboŏ, no perf., no sup., -**āre**, [re-boo], 1. v. n., *resound, re-echo.*
recaleō, no perf., no sup., **-ēre**, [re-caleo], 2. v. n., *be warmed:* **fluenta sanguine** (*run warm*).
recēdō, -cēssī, -cēssum, -cēdere, [re-cedo], 3. v. n., *move back, withdraw, retire, retreat, come off, give way, recede, draw back, go away, pass away.*
recens, -entis, [?, p. of lost verb], adj., *fresh, new* (not long in existence, opposed to **vetus**, cf. **novus**, opposed to **antiquus**), *recent, new-made, just risen:* **prata rivis** (*kept fresh*); **praedae** (*newly-won*); **recens a volnere** (*with her wound still fresh*). — Neut. as adv., *just, lately.*
recēnseō,-cēnsuī,-cēnsum(-cēn-sītum), -cēnsēre, [re-censeo], 2. v. a., *recount, enumerate, reckon up, count.*
receptō, -āvī, -ātum, -āre, [†receptŏ- (p.p. of **recipio**)], 1. v. a., *draw back.* — With reflexive, *retire, withdraw, hide.*
receptus, -a, -um, p.p. of **recipio.**
receptus, -ūs, [as if **re-captus**, cf. **recipio**], m., *a retreat, place of refuge.*
recēssus, -ūs, [**re-cessus**, cf. **recedo**], m., *a retreat, a withdrawal:* **vastus** (*depth*). — Concretely, *a recess.*
recidīvus, -a, -um, [as if †recidi + vus, cf. **recido, nocīvus**], adj., *recurring.* — Poetically, *renewed, restored.*
recīdō, -cīdī, -cīsum, -cīdere, [re-caedo], 3. v. a., *cut away, cut off, sever.*
recinctus, -a, -um, p.p. of **recingo.**
recingō, perf. not found, **-cinctum, -cingere,** [re-cingo], 3. v. a., *unbind, unloose, loosen:* **recincta veste** (*in flowing robe,* a style peculiar to some rites).
recipiō, -cēpī, -ceptum, -cipere, [re-capio], 3. v. a., *take back, withdraw, draw back, recover, rescue, receive* (of something due), *exact.* — Also, *receive* (generally), *admit:* **ad se** (*receive by one's side*). — With reflexive, *withdraw, retire.*
recīsus, -a, -um, p.p. of **recīdo.**
reclāmō, -āvī, -ātum, -āre, [re-clamo], 1. v. a., *cry out, roar.*
reclīnō, -āvī, -ātum, -āre, [re-clino], 1. v. a., *lean back:* **scuta** (*rest* against their spears).
reclūdō, -clūsī, -clūsum, -clūdere, [re-cludo], 3. v. a., *unclose, open, uncover, lay bare, disclose, unsheath, pierce, turn up* (of the earth). — Poetically: **caelum sol** (*unlock the gates of*).
reclūsus, -a, -um, p.p. of **recludo.**
recoctus, -a, -um, p.p. of **recoquo.**
recognōscō, -gnōvī, -gnitum, -gnoscere, [re-cognosco], 3. v. a., *review, examine.*

recolo, -colui, -cultum, -colere, [re-colo], 3. v. a., *retill.* — Fig., *consider, contemplate, survey.*
recondō, -condidī, -conditum, -condere, [re-condo], 3. v. a., *hide away, conceal, bury* (of a weapon), *plunge, deposit.*
recoquo, -coxī, -coctum, -coquere, [re-coquo], 3. v. a., *reforge, refine* (by melting).
recordor,-ātus,-ārī, [lost stem †record- (re-†cord-, cf. **concors**)], 1. v. dep., *recall to mind, recall.*
rector, -ōris, [√reg + tor], m., *a ruler, a director, a leader, a pilot, a steersman.*
rectus, -a, -um, p.p. of **rego.**
recubō, no perf., no sup., **-cubāre,** [re-cubo], 1. v. n., *lie on the back, recline, lie at length, lie.*
recumbō, -cubuī, -cubitum, -cumbere, [re-cumbo], 3. v. n., *lie down, lie, fall back, fall, lie low* (of clouds), *sink.*
recurrō, -currī, -cursum, -currere, [re-curro], 3. v. n., *hasten back:* sol recurrens (*revolving*).
recursō, -āvī, -ātum, -are, [re-curso, cf. **recurro**], 1. v. n., *run back.* — Fig., *recur, return, be renewed, be repeated:* curae tuo dulci ex ore.
recursus, -ūs, [re-cursus, cf. **recurro**], m., *a returning course, a reflux, the ebb* (of the waves).
recurvus, -a, -um, [re-curvus], adj., *curving backward, curved.*
recūsō, -āvī, -ātum, -āre, [re-†causō, cf. **causor**], 1. v. a. and n., *excuse one's self, make objection, be reluctant, refuse, reject, decline, disavow:* longe (*shrink back afar*).
recussus, -a, -um, p.p. of **recutio.**
recutiō, perf. not found, **-cussum, -cutere,** [re-quatio], 3. v. n., *strike back.* — **recussus, -a, -um,** p.p., *re-echoing.*
redarguō, -uī, no sup., **-uere,** [red-arguo], 3. v. a., *disprove, refute.*
redditus, -a, -um, p.p. of **reddo.**

reddō, -didī, -ditum, -dere, [reddo], 3. v. a., *give back, restore, return, repay, pay, render.*— With reflexive or in pass., *return, go back:* redditus (*returning*). — Also, *give forth, give up, yield, render up, utter, send forth.* — Passive, *appear, come forth, be heard.* — Also of *things given as due, give, consign, bestow, offer* (as a sacrifice), *impose.* — Also, *render, make, imitate, express.*
redemptus, -a, -um, p.p. of **redimo.**
redeō, -iī (-īvī), -itum, -īre, [red-eo], irr. v. n., *go back, return, come back, come again, come in* (of a race), *bend around* (of a mountain-range): anni (*revolve*).
redimīculum, -ī, [†redimi- (of redimio) + culum], n., *a band, a headband, a fillet, a headdress.*
redimiō, -iī, -ītum, -īre, [?], 4.v. a., *bind around, encircle, wreathe.*
redimītus, -a, -um, p.p. of **redimio.**
redimō, -ēmī, -emptum, -imere, [red-emo, *buy*], 3. v. a., *buy back, ransom, redeem.*
reditus, -ūs, [red-itus, cf. **redeo**], m., *a return.*
redoleō, -oluī, no sup., **-olēre,** [red-oleo], 2. v. a. and n., *smell of, emit an odor, be fragrant.*
redūcō, -dūxī, -dūctum, -dūcere, [re-duco], 3. v. a., *lead back, bring back, draw back, restore, rescue:* reducti remi (*plied with force*); reducitur aestas (*returns*). — **redūctus, -a, -um,** p.p. as adj., *retired, secluded.*
redūctus, -a, -um, p.p. of **reduco.**
redux, -ucis, [re-dux], adj. (pass. sense), *returning; returned, restored.*
refectus, -a, -um, p.p. of **reficio.**
refellō, -fellī, no sup., **-fellere,** [re-fallo], 3. v. a., *refute, disprove.*
referō, rētulī (rett-), relātum, referre, [re-fero], irr. v. a., *bring back, answer, bear back, bring again, restore, give back (echo), change:*

pedem, vestigia (*turn backward, retreat*); consilia in melius (*change*); referri omnia (*decline*); vina throw up); fert refertque fletus (*bear again and again*); vestigia in decimum annum (*delay*). — With reflexive or in pass., *return, come back, go back:* huc omnia; currus; referuntur habenis datis (*ride back*); relatam classem nuntio (*returned*). — Also, *carry* (something which is due or to the place where it belongs), *bear, offer, pay, render, consign:* hunc sedibus suis; venti ad aures divum (*bear*, whither it is sent); terrae cacumen (*plant*); hoc manibus patrum (*give this message*); numerum (*report, account for*); grates (*make return*, cf. gratias ago, gratias habeo); se pestis (*flies*); sollemnia tumulo (*perform*); in te oculos (*turn*). — Also, *repeat, represent, show signs of, betray, resemble:* nomen avi (*bear again*); nomine avum; te ore; saporem salis (*show*). — Also, *bring forth, utter, give out, report, relate, tell, mention, recite:* pectore voces; horresco referens (*to relate*); signa sol (*show, give*); valles pulsae (*echo*); gemitum ictus (*give forth*); ipse parentem te (*claim*).
rēfert, rētulit, rēferre, [unc. case of res-fert], irr. v. imp., *it is important, it is expedient.*
reficĭō, -fēcī, -fectum, -ficere, [re-facio], irr. v. a., *change, renew, repair, restore, reinforce, refresh, encourage.*
refīgō, -fīxī, -fīxum, -fīgere, [re-figo], 3. v. a., *unfix, unloosen, tear down:* fixit leges refixitque (*publish and tear down again*, as laws were hung up on tablets).
refingō, no perf., no sup., -fingere, [re-fingo], 3. v. a., *refashion, mould again.*
refīxus, -a, -um, p.p. of refigo.
reflectō, -flexī, -flexum, -flectere, [re-flecto], 3. v. a., *bend back,* *turn back, bend, change:* **animum** (*turn one's attention*). — In pass., *bend:* reflexus (*bending round*).
reflexus, -a, -um, p.p. of reflecto.
refluō, no perf., no sup., -fluere, [re-fluo], 3. v. n., *flow back, recede, subside.*
reformīdō, perf. not found, -ātum, -āre, [re-formido], 1. v. a., *dread.* — Poetically, of trees injured by pruning.
refringō, -frēgī, -fractum, -fringere, [re-frango], 3. v. a., *break off.*
refugĭō, -fūgī, no sup., -fugere, [re-fugio], 3. v. a. and n., *fly back, shrink back, flee away, recede.* — Fig., *shrink, be reluctant, refuse, shrink from:* fugit refugit (*fly this way and that*): animus meminisse (*shrinks from the recollection*); sol (*hide himself*).
refulgĕō, -fulsī, no sup., -fulgēre, [re-fulgeo], 2. v. n., *shine forth, gleam, shine, glitter.*
refundō, -fūdī, -fūsum, -fundere, [re-fundo], 3. v. a., *pour back, pour forth, throw back.* — **refūsus, -a, -um,** p.p., *thrown up, poured forth, overflowing:* refuso Oceano (*in the surrounding ocean*).
refūsus, -a, -um, p.p. of refundo.
refūtō, -āvī, -ātum, -āre, [re-†futo, cf. **futatim, futilis**], 1. v. a., (*force back*), *repel.* — Also, *refute, confute, prove false.*
rēgālis, -e, [†reg- (of **rex**)+ alis], adj., *kingly, royal, regal:* comae (*of the princess*).
rēgĭfĭcus, -a, -um, [†reg- (as if regi-) -ficus], adj., *regal.*
rēgīna, -ae, [†reg + ina, cf. gallina], f., *a queen, a princess.* — Of a divinity, *royal mistress.* — In app. as adj., *royal* (of the royal blood).
regĭō, -ōnis, [as if √reg + io (prob. through adj.-stem)], f., *a direction, a course.* — Also (cf. **fines**), *a region, a quarter.*
rēgĭus, -a, -um, [†reg + ius], adj.,

of a king, royal (cf. **regalis,** *regal*). — Also, *princely, queenly, magnificent.* — **rēgia,** fem., (sc. domus), *a royal abode, a palace, a royal city.*

regnātor, -ōris, [†regnā (of regno) + tor], m., *a ruler, a sovereign, a king.*

regnātus, -a, -um, p.p. of **regno.**

regnŏ, -āvī, -ātum, -āre, [†regnŏ], 1. v. n. and a., *reign, rule, bear sway.* — Act., *rule over.* — Impersonal: regnabitur (*the rule shall be*). — regnandam Albam acceperit (*the throne of Alba*); regnandi cupido (*of regal power*); ignis regnat per ramos (*rage uncontrolled*).

regnum, -ī, [√reg + num (n. of -nus, cf. **plenus**)], n., *a realm, a kingdom, regal power, a throne, a reign, command, authority.*

regō, rexī, rectum, regere, [√reg, akin *to* Gr. ὀρέγω, Sk. *rajan* (cf. Rajah), Eng. *right*], 3. v. a., *direct* (orig. as of a *line,* &c.?), *guide, steer:* sol orbem (*hold its course*). — Esp., *govern, rule, sway, control:* imperium Dido (*hold sovereign command*). — **rectus, -a, -um,** p.p. as adj., *straight, direct, right:* rectis vestigia pedibus (*straight-forward tracks*); recto flumine (*straight up the river*); recto litore (*straight along the shore*). — Neut. as subst., *right, virtue.*

regressus, -ūs, [re-gressus, cf. **regredior**], m., *a return, a change* (going back)

rēiciŏ (relic-, relc-), -iēcī, -lectum, -icere, [re-iacio], 3. v. a., *throw back, throw away, throw off, throw down, drive back, hurl back.* — Fig., *reject, refuse, cast* (of the eyes), *turn away.*

reiectŏ, -āvī, -ātum, -āre, [re-iacto, cf. **reicio**], 1. v. a., *throwing forth, throwing out.*

reiectus, -a, -um, p.p. of **reicio.**

relābor, -lāpsus, -lābī, [re-labor], 3. v. dep., *glide back, recede.*

relātus, -a, -um, p.p. of **refero.**

relaxō, -avī, -ātum, -āre, [re-laxo], 1. v. a., *loosen, free, open, rarefy*

relegŏ, -lēgī, -lectum, -legere, [re-lego], 3. v. a., *coast by again, sail along again.*

relēgō, -āvī, -ātum, -āre, [re-lēgo], 1. v. a., *remove, send away, banish, consign, entrust.*

relictus, -a, -um, p.p. of **relinquo.**

religātus, -a, -um, p.p. of **religo.**

rēligio (rell-), -ōnis, [prob. relegio, cf. **relego**], f., (*reverence, diligent attention to a person,* cf. **observantia**). — Esp., *reverence for the gods, piety, devotion, religion, veneration.* — Also, *a ceremony, an observance, a rite, sacred rites:* prospera (*omens*). — Also, *of things, sanctity, holiness.* — Transf., *divinity* (*thing sacred*).

rēligiōsus (rell-), -a, -um, [†religion + osus, poss. fr. some simpler stem], adj., *sacred, venerable.*

religŏ, -āvī, -ātum, -āre, [re-ligo], 1. v. a., *bind fast, fasten, tether.* — Esp. of vessels, *moor.*

relinō, -lēvī, -litum, -linere, [re-lino], 3. v. a., *unseal, open.*

relinquŏ, -līquī, -lictum, -linquere, [re-linquo], 3. v. a., *leave behind, leave, abandon, depart from, forsake, give up, relinquish, desert.*

rēliquiae (rell-), -ārum, [†reliquŏ- (reduced) + ia], f. plur., *remnants:* Danaum (*remnants left by,* &c.).

relūceō, -lūxī, no sup., **-lūcēre,** [re-luceo], 2. v. n., *shine forth, blaze up, shine, glare.*

reluctor, -ātus, -ārī, [re-luctor], 1. v. dep., *struggle.*

remēnsus, -a, -um, p.p. of **remetior.**

remeŏ, -āvī, no sup., **-āre,** [re-meo], 1. v. n., *return.*

remētior, -mēnsus, -mētīrī, [re-metior], 4. v. dep., *measure back, retrace, traverse again.*

remex, -ĭgĭs, [prob. †remŏ-agus (reduced, cf. **prodigus**)], m., *an oarsman, a rower.*— Collec*t*ively, *oarsmen.*

rēmigium, -ī, (-ĭī), [†remig + ium], n., *rowing, oars* (collec*t*ively), *oarsmen.* — Poe*t*ically: *alarum* (*machinery*).

reminiscor, *no* p.p., **reminiscī,** [re-miniscor, cf. **comminiscor,** √**man**], 3. v. dep., *remember.*

remissus, -a, -um, p.p. of **remitto.**

remittō, -mīsī, -missum, -mittere, [re-mitto], 3. v. a., *let go back, send back, return, repay.* — With reflexive, *return, come back.* — Also, *give up, yield, relax, abate.* — With reflexive, *yield, admit one's self conquered.* — Also, *send forth, yield, give out.*

remordeŏ, perf. *not* found, **-morsum, -mordēre,** [re-mordeo], 2. v. a., *gnaw, vex, trouble.*

remōtus, -a, -um, p.p. of **removeo.**

removeŏ, -mōvī, -mōtum, -movere, [re-moveo], 2. v. a., *move away, remove, conceal.*

remūgio, no perf., *no* sup., **-mūgīre,** [re-mugio], 1. v. n., *bellow forth, resound, bellow, roar, murmur.*

remulceo, -mulsī, -mulsum, -mulcēre, [re-mulceo], 2. v. a., *droop* (of an animal's *t*ail, wi*t*h allusion to the pe*tt*ing of domestic animals).

Remulus, -ī, [?], m., a Rutulian.

remurmurŏ, *no* perf., *no* sup., **-āre,** [re-murmuro], 1. v. n., *give forth a murmur, murmur, roar.*

Remus, -ī, [?], m.: 1. The brother of Romulus; 2. A Rutulian.

rēmus,´-ī, [prob. akin to ἐρετμός], m., *an oar.*

renārrŏ, -āvī, -ātum, -āre, [re-narro], 1. v. a., *relate, tell.*

renascor, -nātus, -nāscī, [re-nascor], 3. v. dep., *spring again, grow again.*

renātus, -a, -um, p.p. of **renascor.**

renideŏ(-nĭduī), *no* sup., **-nĭdēre,** [?], 2. v. n., *beam forth, gleam.*

renovŏ, -āvī, -ātum, -āre, [re-novo], 1. v. a., *renew.*

reor, ratus, rērī, [†rē- (of res), or s*t*em akin], 2. v. dep., *reckon, — think, suppose, judge, suspect.*

ratus, -a, -um, p.p. in act. sense, *thinking,* &c.; in pass. sense, *confirmed, certain, valid, settled, secured.*

repellō, rĕpulī (repp-), repulsum, repellere, [re-pello], 3.v.a., *drive back, dash back, spurn, repel, thwart, reject.*

rependō, -pendī, -pēnsum, -pendere, [re-pendo], 3. v. a., *weigh back.* — Also (cf. **pendo**), *pay back, requite:* magna (*fully requite*); fata fatis (*balance*).

repens, -entis, [?], adj., *sudden, unexpected.*

repente [abl. of **repens**], adv., *suddenly, unexpectedly.*

repercussus, -a, -um, p.p. of **repercutio.**

repercutiō, -cussī, -cussum, -cutere, [re-percutio], 3. v. a., *strike back, reflect.*

reperiŏ, rĕperī (repp-), repertum, reperīre, [re(red)-pario], 4. v. a., *find, discover, detect.*

repertor, -ōris, [as if re-partor, cf. **reperio**], m., *a discoverer, an inven*tor*, a progeni*tor (cf. pario).

repertus, -a, -um, p.p. of **reperio.**

repetītus, -a, -um, p.p. of **repeto.**

repetō, -petiī (-īvī), -petītum, -petere, [re-peto], 4. v. a., *go back for, go back to, seek again, return, bring back, demand back, trace back, begin again, repeat, remember.*

repleō, -plēvī, -plētum, -plēre, [re-†pleo, cf. **compleo**], 2. v. a., *fill up, fill, swell* (of rivers): populos sermone (*fill the ears of,* &c.).

replētus, -a, -um, p.p. of **repleo.**

repōnō, -posuī, -positum, -pōnere, [re-pono], 3. v. a., *put back, replace, restore, repair, renew.* — Also, *put aside, lay down, put down, set down, abandon:* falcem

arbusta (*need no more*). — Also, *carry away, lay away, put away, lay, serve up, confer upon, store away:* haec imis sensibus (*let sink deep*). — repositus (repostus), p.p. as adj., *far away, distant, remote.* — Also, *buried.*
reportŏ, -āvī, -ātum, -āre, [re-porto], 1. v. a., *bring back, carry back, report, announce:* pedem ab hoste (*turn back*).
reposco, no perf., no sup., -poscere, [re-posco], 3. v. a., *demand back, demand* (as due), *claim, call for.*
repostus, -a, -um, see repono.
reprimŏ, -pressī, -pressum, -primere, [re-primo], 3. v. a., *hold back, check, restrain, stop.*
repugnŏ, -āvī, -ātum, -āre, [re-pugno], 1. v. n., *resist, struggle.*
repulsus, -a, -um, p.p. of repello.
requiēs, -ētis (-ēī), [re-quies], f., *rest; repose, respite, cessation:* tu requies miserae (*rest, solace*); ea certa laborum (*rest, haven*).
requiēscŏ, -quiēvī, -quiētum, -quiēscere, [re-quiesco], 3. v. n., *rest:* flumina (*stay their course*).
requīrŏ, -quīsīvī, -quīsītum, -quīrere, [re-quaero], 3. v. a., *seek out, search for, seek, call for, miss, feel the need of, ask, enquire.*
rēs, reī, [?, cf. reor], f., *a thing, a matter, an event, an affair, an occurrence, a circumstance, an exploit, an enterprise, an undertaking, a state of things:* res Italae (*exploits, history*). — Also (plur.), *nature, the earth, the universe:* sors rerum (*part of the universe*); rerum (*in the world,* with superl.); rerum dominos (*of the world*); res tenerae (*frail creatures*); maxima rerum (*of all things*). — Also (with or without an adj., *fortune* (either good or bad), *circumstances, power, the State, empire, condition, property, estate:* summae res (*the highest interests*); tenues res (*humble fortunes*); fessi rerum (*weary of their lot*). — Also: rebus novandis (*for the new course of action*); res tuae (*your interests, party*); res incognita (*uncertain state of things*); res divinae (*religious rites*); res summa (*the main struggle, the general success*); pro re (*under the circumstances*).
rescindŏ, -scidī, -scissum, -scindere, [re-scindo], 3. v. a., *cut away, tear away, tear down, lay open, cut into.*
reseco, -secuī, -sectum, -secāre, [re-seco], 1. v. a., *cut away, cut off, trim off.*
reserŏ, -āvī, -ātum, -āre, [re-sero], 1. v. a., *unbar, unclose, open, disclose, reveal.*
reservŏ, -avī, -ātum, -are, [re-servo], 1. v. a., *keep back, reserve, hold in reserve, keep, save.*
†reses, -idis, [re-√sed as stem, cf. deses], adj., *idle, inactive, dormant, peaceful.*
residĕŏ, -sēdī, -sessum, -sidēre, [re-sedeo], 2. v. n., *sit down.*
resīdŏ, -sēdī, no sup., -sīdere, [re-sido], 3. v. n., *sit down, sink down, halt, encamp, settle, fall back.* — Fig., *subside, abate, cease, become calm* (of the heart from passion).
resignŏ, -āvī, -ātum, -āre, [re-signo], 1. v. a., *unseal, open.* — Poss. also, *seal, close* (?).
resistŏ, -stitī, no sup., -sistere, [re-sisto], 3. v. n., *stop, make a stand, stand back* (away), *stand firm, resist, oppose, withstand.*
resolūtus, -a, -um, p.p. of resolvo.
resolvŏ, -solvī, -solūtum, -solvere, [re-solvo], 3. v. a., *unloose, unbind, unseal, disentangle, open, break through, relax, scatter, dissolve:* ambages (*unravel*); iura (*violate,* break the tie); curas (*break the bonds of care*). — With reflexive or in pass., *dissolve, thaw, mellow.*
resonŏ, -āvī, no sup., -āre, [re-sono], 1. v. n., *resound, murmur.* — Active, *cause to sound, fill with* (song), *make echo.* — Also, *sound* (*with the notes of*), cf. redoleo,

(*smell of*). — With cogn. acc., *resound with, echo the name of:* Amaryllida silvae.

resorbeō, no perf., no sup., -sorbēre, [re-sorbeo], 2. v. a., *draw in again, draw in, suck in.*

respectō, -āvī, -ātum, -āre, [respecto], 1. v. a., *look back upon, regard.*

respergō, -spersī, -spersum, -spergere, [re-spergo], 3. v. a., *besprinkle, sprinkle.*

respiciō, -spexī, -spectum, -spicere, [re-spicio, cf. **conspicio**], 3. v. a. and n., *look back, look behind one, look around, look up.* — Act., *look back for, see behind one, looking round see, notice, consider, regard, have regard for.*

respirō, -āvī, -ātum, -are, [re-spiro], 1. v. n., *breathe, draw breath.*

resplendeo, no perf., no sup., -ēre, [re-splendeo], 2. v. n., *shine forth, glitter.*

respondeō, -spondī, -sponsum, -spondēre, [re-spondeo], 2. v. n., *answer, reply, correspond to, respond, match, reciprocate, answer expectations (produce, grow).* — Poetically, with cogn. acc., *echo back.*

respōnsō, no perf., no sup., -āre, [†responsŏ-], 1. v. n., *respond, re-echo.*

responsum, -ī, [n. p.p. of respondeo], n., *an answer, a reply.* — Esp., *an oracle, a prophecy, prophetic words, a response.*

restinctus, -a, -um, p.p. of **restinguō**.

restinguō, -stinxī, -stinctum, -stinguere, [re-stinguo], 3. v. a., *quench, extinguish.* — Also of thirst.

restituō, -stituī, -stitūtum, -stituere, [re-statuo], 3. v. a., *set up again, restore.*

restō, -stitī, no sup., -stāre, [re-sto], 1. v. n., *stop behind.* — Fig., *remain, be left, be in store for one.*

resultō, no perf., -ātum, -āre, [re-salto, cf. **resilio**], 1. v. n., *spring back, rebound, echo.* — Also of the object from which, *re-echo, echo back.*

resupīnus, -a, -um, [re-supinus], adj., *on the back.*

resurgo, -surrēxī, -surrectum, -surgere, [re-surgo], 3. v. n., *rise again:* amor (*return*).

retardō, -āvī, -ātum, -āre, [retardo], 1. v. a., *delay, hinder.*

rēte, -is, [?], n., *a net.*

retectus, -a, -um, p.p. of **retego**.

retegō, -texī, -tectum, -tegere, [re-tego], 3. v. a., *uncover, lay bare, disclose, expose.*

retentō, -āvī, -ātum, -āre, [retento, cf. **retineo**], 1. v. a., *hold back, detain, retard.*

retexō, -texuī, -textum, -texere, [re-texo], 3. v. a., *weave again:* totidem orbes (*interweave in the opposite direction*).

retināculum, -ī, [†retinā- (as if stem of retineo, cf. **tenax**) + culum], n., *a rope, a cable, a tether, a withe.*

retineō, -tinuī, -tentum, -tinēre, [re-teneo], 2. v. a., *hold back, detain, stop, restrain.*

retorqueō, -torsī, -tortum, -torquēre, [re-torqueo], 2. v. a., *turn back, twist around, throw back:* mentem (*changed her purpose*); retorto amictu (*thrown over the shoulder*).

retortus, -a, -um, p.p. of **retorqueo**.

retractō, -āvī, -ātum, -āre, [retracto], 1. v. a., *handle again, seize again:* ferrum digiti (*clench*). — Also (trans. and intrans.), *draw back:* dicta (*retract*).

retrahō, -traxī, -tractum, -trahere, [re-traho], 3. v. a., *draw back:* pedem (of the under*tow* of the wave). — Also, *drag again:* fata trahunt retrahunt (*drag to and fro*).

retrō [dat. of †retrŏ- (re + terus, cf. **intro**)], adv., *back, backward* (sometimes pleonastic with **re-**):

arva cedentia retro (*receding in the distance*); retro residunt (*draw back*).

retrōrsum (-rsus), [retrō-vorsus, p.p. of verto], adv., *backward, back*.

retundō, -tudi, -tūsum, -tundere, [re-tundo], 3. v. a., *beat back, blunt:* retusum ferrum (*a dull knife*).

retūsus, -a, -um, p.p. of retundo.

reus, -ī, [†re- (of res) + us (or -ius)], m., *a party* (to a suit, res). — Esp., *a defendant*. — Hence, *guilty, bound:* voti (*bound by one's vow*, having obtained his prayer).

revehō, -vexī, -vectum, -vehere, [re-veho], 3. v. a., *carry back, bring back*.

revellō, -vellī, -vulsum (vols-), **-vellere**, [re-vello], 3. v. a., *wrench away, tear away, drag from:* cineres (*dig up*).

revertor, -versus, (also act. **revertī**), reverti, [re-vertor], 3. v. dep., *turn back, return, be renewed* (grow again).

revinciō, -vinxī, -vinctum, -vincīre, [re-vincio], 4. v. a., *bind back, bind fast, wreathe:* quas serpentum spiris (*crown, arm, of the Furies*).

revinctus, -a, -um, p.p. of revincio.

revirēscō, -viruī, no sup., **-virēscere**, [re-viresco], 3. v. n., *sprout again*.

revīsō, no perf., no sup., **-vīsere**, [re-viso], 3. v. a. and n., *revisit, return to*.

revocātus, -a, -um, p.p. of revoco.

revocō, -āvī, -ātum, -āre, [re-voco], 1. v. a., *call back, restore, renew, revive, bring to life:* gradum, pedem (*retrace*); exordia pugnae (*recall, relate*). — Also, *detain, dissuade*.

revolō, -āvī, no sup., **-āre**, [re-volo], 1. v. n., *fly back*.

revolūtus, -a, -um, p.p. of revolvo.

revolvō, -volvī, -volūtum, -volvere, [re-volvo], 3. v. a., *roll back, throw back, throw over*. — Also, *go round again, repeat:* iter (*retrace*); casus (*repeat the round of*, &c.); haec ingrata (*repeat, renew*, in narration). — **revolūtus, -a, -um**, p.p. in several special senses: ter revoluta toro est (*fell back*); Caeneus in veterem figuram (*restored again*); dies (*returning*); pensa (*fell from the hands*); aequora (*turbulent*); aestu revoluta saxa (*washed down*, by the undertow); ille iacuit (*rolling over*); alter suffosso equo (*thrown backward*).

revomo, -vomuī, no sup., **-vomere**, [re-vomo], 3. v. a., *throw up*.

revulsus (-volsus), **-a, -um**, p.p. of revello.

rēx, rēgis, [√reg (increased) as stem], m., *a king, a prince, a leader*. — Also of divinities, rivers, a mountain (producing the "prince of wines"). — As adj. in app., *ruling*.

Rhadamanthus, -ī, [Gr. Ῥαδάμανθος], m., a brother of Minos, and son of Jupiter, who was driven from Crete by his brother. After his death he was made a judge in the world below.

Rhamnēs, -ētis, [?], m., a prince, and augur of Turnus.

Rhēa, -ae, [?], f., a mythic priestess, mother of Aventinus by Hercules.

Rhēnus, -ī, [?], m., *the Rhine*, the river separating Gaul and Germany.

Rhēsus, -ī, [Gr. Ῥῆσος], m., a king of Thrace whose horses were carried away before Troy by Ulysses and Diomed, before they had eaten or drunk, according to an omen or prophecy.

Rhodius, -a, -um, [Gr. Ῥόδιος], adj., *of Rhodes* (an island in the eastern Mediterranean), *Rhodian*.

Rhodopē, -ēs, [Gr. Ῥοδόπη], f., a mountain of Thrace.

Rhodopēius, -a, -um, [Gr. Ῥοδοπήιος], adj., *of Rhodope*. — Less exactly, *Thracian*.

Rhoebus, -ī, [?], m., the war-horse of Mezentius.

Rhoetēius, -a, -um, [Gr. Ῥοιτήιος],

adj., *of Rhœteum* (a promontory of the Troad).— Less exactly, *Trojan*.
Rhoeteus, -eī (-eos), [?], m., a Rutulian.
Rhoetus, -ī, [?], m.: 1. A king of the Marsi; 2. A centaur.
rīdeō, rīsī, rīsum, rīdēre, [?], 2. v. a. and n., *laugh at, smile at, smile upon, smile.*— Fig., *bloom, smile.*
rigeō (riguī, referred to **rigesco),** no sup., **rigēre,** [?, √rig, *through* adj.-stem, cf. **rigidus,** perh. akin to **frigeo**], 2. v. n., *be stiff, be stiffened.* — **rigēns, -entis,** p. as adj., *stiff, stiffened.*
rigēscō, riguī, no sup., **rigēscere,** [†rigē- (of **rigeo**) + sco], 3. v. n. incept., *grow stiff, stiffen, congeal, freeze.*
rigidus, -a, -um, [†rigŏ + dus, cf. **rigeo**], adj., *stiff, rigid, hard, unbending, solid.*— Of weapons, *irresistible* (*unbending,* as *not* yielding to any obstruction).
rigō, -āvī, -ātum, -āre, [?, cf. Gr. βρέχω, fr. adj.-stem, cf. **riguus**], 1. v. a., *water, wash, wet, bathe, stain.*
rigor, -ōris, [√rig (in **rigeo**) + or], m., *hardness :* **ferri** (*unyielding iron*).
riguus, -a, -um, [√rig (in **rigo**) + uus, cf. **nocuus**], adj., *watering, irrigating.*
rīma, -ae, [prob. root of **ringor** + ma], f., *a crack, a chink, a seam, a cleft :* **ignea** (*a fiery cleft,* of the lightning).
rīmor, -ātus, -ārī,[†rima-],1.v.a., *pry into, search, dig up, hunt for, hunt for food in, tear* (by rummaging).
rīmōsus, -a, -um, [†rima- (reduced)+osus], adj., *full of chinks :* **cubilia** (*loose-jointed*); **cymba** (*leaky*).
rīpa, -ae, [?, same root as **rivus**?], f., *a bank* (of a river, &c., cf. **litus,** and **ora,** of the sea). — Less exactly, *shore.*— Poetically, of the river itself, *shore* (as in Eng.).

Rīphaeus, -a, -um, [Gr. 'Ρίπαια], adj., *of the Riphæi* (a range of mountains in Thrace), *Riphæan.*
Rīpheus, -eī (-eos), [Gr. 'Ριφεύς], m., a Trojan warrior at the sack of Troy.
rīsus,-ūs, [√rid (in **rideo**)+tus], m., *laughter, a laugh, a smile.*
rīte [prob. abl. of stem akin to **ritus**], adv., *with due ceremony, in due form, duly.* — Less exactly, *as usual, rightly, fitly, aptly.*
rītus, -ūs, [√ri (of unc. kin.) + tus, cf. **rite**], m., *a form, a rite, a ceremony.* — Less exactly, *a custom, a usage.* — **ritu,** abl., *in the manner of, just like.*
rīvus, -ī, [?, cf. **ripa,** perh. akin to Gr. ῥέω], m., *a stream, a brook, a river, a canal, a sluice.*— Also, *a vein.* — Poetically, of sweat and the like.
rōbīgō (rūb-), -inis, [stem akin to **rubeo** + go, cf. **aerugo**], f., *rust* (of metals or of grain), *blight.*
rōbur, -oris, [?, unc. root+us], n., *hardwood, timber, wood, a beam, a log, a stout stick :* **annoso robore quercum** (*of aged trunk*). — — Esp., *an oak tree, oak.* — Fig., *strength* (of resistance), *force, vigor, courage :* **pubis** (*the flower*); **quae robora cuique** (*virtue,* of soils); **ferri** (*strong bars*).
rōbustus, -a, -um, [†robus + tus, cf. **honestus**], adj., *stout, sturdy.*
rogitō, 1. v. a., *ask, enquire.*
rogō, -āvī, -ātum, -āre, [?], 1. v.a., *ask, beg, sue for, ask for.*
rogus, -ī, [?], m., *a funeral pile, a pyre.*
Rōma, -ae, [most likely akin to Gr. ῥέω], f., *Rome.*
Rōmānus, -a, -um, [†Romā + nus], adj., *Roman, of Rome.*— Masc., *a Roman.*
Rōmuleus, -a, -um, [†Romulŏ- (reduced)+eus], adj., *of Romulus.*
Rōmulidēs, -ae, [Romulŏ + des (Gr. form of patronymic)], m. only in plur., *descendants of Romulus* (the Romans), *sons of Romulus.*

Rōmulus, -ī, [stem akin to **Roma** + **lus**], m., *the mythic founder of Rome.*

Rōmulus, -a, -um, [same word as preceding, decl. as adj.], adj., *of Romulus.*

rŏrŏ, -āvī, -ātum, -āre, [†ror- (for ros) as if †rorŏ-], 1. v. n. and a., *drop dew, drip* (as with dew).

rōs, rōris, [?, prob. an initial cons. lost], m., *dew.* — Less exactly, *water, rain, moisture, drops* (of other fluids), *spray.* — **ros marīnus** (sometimes omitted), *rosemary.*

rosa, -ae, [perh. akin to Gr. ῥόδον], f.; *a rose, roses* (collectively).

rosārius, -a, -um, [as if (or really) †rosari- (†rosā + ris) + us], adj., *of roses.* — As subst., *a rose-bed.*

rōscidus, -a, -um, [†roscŏ- (†ros + cus, cf. iuvencus) + dus], adj., *wet with dew, dewy.*

rosētum, -ī, [†rosa- (reduced) + etum, cf. dumetum], n., *a rose-bed, a rose-garden.*

roseus, -a, -um, [†rosa- (reduced) + eus], adj., *of roses.* — Less exactly, *rose-colored, rosy.*

Rōseus, -a, -um, [prob. †rosa-], adj., *of Rosea* (a district of middle Italy famous for fertility), *Rosean.*

rostrātus, -a, -um, [†rostrŏ- (reduced) + atus, cf. auratus], adj., *furnished with beaks.*

rostrum, -ī, [√rod + trum], n., *a beak, a bill, a proboscis* (of the bee). — Esp., *a beak* (of a ship).

rota, -ae, [akin to Sk. *ratha*, Germ. *Rad*], f., *a wheel* (with spokes), *a chariot, a cart.* — Poetically: **volvere rotam** (*run a course*, of years).

rotŏ, -āvī, -ātum, -āre, [†rotā-], 1. v. a. and n., *whirl about, brandish.* — Intrans., *roll.*

rubeŏ, no perf., no sup., **-ēre,** [†rubŏ- (√rub + us, cf. robus, robigo, ruber)], 2. v. n., *be red, redden, blush, shine, glow.* — **rubēns, -entis,** p. as adj., *red, ruddy, blushing, rosy.*

ruber, -bra, -brum, [√rub + rus, cf. rubeo], adj., *red, ruddy, crimson, rosy-tinted:* **litus** (*of the Red Sea*).

rubēscŏ, -rubuī, no sup., **-rubēscere,** [†rubē (of rubeo) + sco], 3. v. n., *redden, be reddened.*

rubeus, -a, -um, [†rubŏ- (reduced) + eus], adj., *of brambles:* **virga** (*a bramble-twig*).

rubicundus, -a, -um, [as if rubi- (weak stem of rubeo) + cundus (cf. verecundus), prob. really †rubicon + dus (i.e., √rub + o + co + on + dus), cf. rotundus], adj., *ruddy, blushing.*

rubor, -ōris, [√rub + or], m., *redness, a blush, a flush.*

rubus, -ī, [prob. √rub + us, cf. rubeo], m., *a bramble.*

rudēns, -entis, [?], m., *a rope* (of a ship), *a hawser, a line, a sheet, cordage.*

rudīmentum, -ī, [†rudi- (of rudis, foil, or lost verb rudio, *practise with foil*) + mentum], n., *a first attempt, a beginning.*

rudis, -e, [?], adj., *rough, rude.*

rudŏ, -īvī, -ītum, -ere, [?], 3. v. n., *roar, bellow, creak.*

Rufrae, -ārum, [same word as ruber, cf. rufus], f. plur., *a town of the Samnites or of Campania, variously located.*

rūga, -ae, [?], f., *a wrinkle.*

ruīna, -ae, [†ruŏ- (reduced) + ina, cf. ruo], f., *a fall, a crash, a convulsion:* **caeli** (*downfall*, of pouring rain); **horrificae** (*crashing*, of Ætna); **dare ruinam** (*fall with a crash*); **primi dant ruinam** (*fall on each other like an avalanche*). — Fig., *downfall, ruin, disaster, calamity, destruction:* **urbis; rerum** (*ruined fortunes*). — Concretely (perh. orig. meaning), *a falling mass, a fleeing mass* (like a falling body): **trahere ruinam** (*fall in confusion, fall in a mass, fall in a heap of ruins*); **urgente ruina** (*borne on by the rush of the crowd*).

rūmĭnō, *no* perf., *no* sup., -āre, [†rumin-], 1. v. n., *ruminate, chew, chew the cud of:* herbas. — Pass. as dep. (the usual form), in same sense.

rūmor, -ōris, [?], m., *common talk, a rumor, report:* rumore secundo (*with general words of good omen*).

rumpō, rūpī, ruptum, rumpere, [√rup], 3. v. a. and n., lit., *break, burst, break down, break through, pierce, break off, sever, tear, bruise, crush, shatter:* horrea messes (*fill to bursting*); rumpantur ilia (*may split*); postes (*burst open*); arbusta cicadae (*split*); rumpuntur pectora (*burst with rage*). — Of the effect (with cognate acc.), *break a path, force, rive* (a cleft). — Causative, *throw out, let fall.* — Hence, with reflexive or in passive, *break forth, burst forth, dart forth.*—Fig., *break off, break, break through, annul, violate, interrupt, destroy, rend asunder:* somnum (*banish*); fata (*escape*); moras (*break through*). — ruptus, -a, -um, p.p.: rupto Acherunte (*through a breach into Acheron*); ruptis fornacibus (*the broken vent of its forges*); ruptis caminis (*broken vent,* of a volcano, as having been burst through by the fire itself).

ruō, rui, rutum, ruere, [√ru, of unc. kin.], 3. v. a. and n. Act., *overthrow, throw in confusion, hurl down, destroy, break up, lay waste, prostrate; throw up, dash up, roll up:* rapiunt ruuntque (*plunder and lay waste*); confusa ossa (*throw pell-mell*); ignis nubem; omnia late; cumulos arenae (*shatter,* with a military figure). — Intrans., *fall* (with idea of violence), *fall in torrents, flow in torrents, fall in ruins, set* (of the sun, *hasten to its setting*). — Also, *run blindly, rush, rush in, rush on, come on quickly, hurry, be borne headlong, flee:* nox Oceano (*hasten up*); clamor (*burst forth*); voces (*pour forth*).—Fig., *end, approach the end, deteriorate:* in peius omnia (*grow worse and worse*).

rūpēs, -is, [√rup + es (and is)], f., *a rock* (broken or precipitous, in position, cf. saxum), *a cliff.*

ruptus, -a, -um, p.p. of rumpo.

rursum (rursus), [re-vorsus (-um)], adv., *back, again, anew.* — Sometimes pleonastic with re (cf. "*back again*").—Fig., *besides, again, once more, on the other hand, a second time then again.*

rūs, rūris, [?], n., *the country* (opposed to the city), *a farm, a field, land:* rus opacum (*shady ground*).

ruscum, -ī, [?], n., *butcher's broom,* a useless wild plant.

rūsticus, -a, -um, [†rus (orig. stem of rus) + ticus], adj., *of the country, woodland, rustic.*—Masc., *a rustic, a countryman.*

rutĭlō, -āvī, -ātum, -āre, [†rutilŏ-], 1. v. a. and n., *glow with red* or *orange, glimmer red.*

rutilus, -a, -um, [akin to ruber, perh. for †rudtilus], adj., *red, orange, red-gold.*

Rutulus, -a, -um, [?], adj., *of the Rutuli,* a small people of Latium whose chief city was Ardea. They serve as the mythic foes of Æneas, and under the lead of Turnus their king were supposed to have resisted the settlement of the Trojans in Italy. — Masc. plur., the people.

S.

Sabaeus, -a, -um, [Gr. Σαβαῖος], adj., *of Saba* (a town in Arabia famous for its myrrh, frankincense, and the wealth and luxury of its inhabitants), *Sabæan.*—Masc. pl., *the Sabæans,* the people themselves.

Sabellĭcus, -a, -um, [†Sabellŏ + cus], adj., *Sabellian, Sabine.*

Sabellus, -a, -um, [prob. †Sabinŏ

+lus], adj., *Sabellian, of the Sabelli* (an offshoot of the Sabine stock, embracing the small nations of the Marsi, Peligui, and others). — More generally, *Sabine.*

Sabīnus, -a, -um, [?], adj., *Sabine, of the Sabines,* the great people occupying the high lands of Central Italy, who overran parts of Latium and Southern Italy. — Masc. plur., *the Sabines,* the people. — Fem. plur., *the Sabine women.* — Masc. sing., *Sabinus,* the mythic ancestor of the Sabines, deified and represented with a pruning-hook.

saburra, -ae, [?], f., *sand, ballast.*

sacellum, -ī, [†sacrŏ+lum (n. of lus)], n., *a shrine, a sacred grotto.*

sacer, -cra, -crum, [√sac (in sancio) + rus], adj., *consecrated, sacred, holy, devoted, dedicated:* sacra sedes (i.e., on the steps of an altar); ignis (*St. Anthony's fire,* a disease of the skin). — Also (as devoted to sacrifice), *accursed, devoted.* — Neut. plur., *sacred utensils, holy emblems, sacred images, sacrifices, ceremonies, offerings, sacred rites, mysteries, sacred hymns, magic rites.*

sacerdōs, -dōtis, [†sacrŏ-dos(√da + tis, reduced)], comm., *a priest, a priestess.* — Less exactly, *a sacred bard.*

Saces, -ae, [Gr. Σάκαι], m., a Rutulian.

Sacranus, -a, -um, [?], adj., *of the Sacrani,* a people of Latium.

sacrārium, -ī (-iī), [†sacrŏ- (reduced) + arium, n. of adj.], n., *a sanctuary, a shrine:* Ditis (*sacred abode*).

Sacrātor, -ōris, [?], m., a Rutulian.

sacrātus, -a, -um, p.p. of sacro.

sacrilegus, -a, -um, [†sacro+legus (√leg, in lego, +us)], adj., *stealer of things sacred, sacrilegious, impious.*

sacrŏ, -āvī, -ātum, -āre, [†sacrŏ-], 1. v. a., *consecrate, dedicate, make sacred:* hunc honorem sacravit (*bestowed this sacred honor*). — Also, *devote* (as *to* death, &c.). —

sacrātus, -a, -um, p.p. as adj., *consecrated, sacred, holy:* sacrata iura (*sacred oaths*).

sacculum (saeclum, sē-), -ī, [√sa (in sero) + culum], n., (*a year's increase?*), *a generation, a race of men, men.* — Also of *time, a generation, a lifetime, an age.* — Plur., *ages, posterity, years, an age:* per saecula (*forever*).

saepe [acc. of saepis, cf. saepes], adv., *frequently, oftentimes, often.* — saepius, compar., *oftener, often, now and then.*

saepēs, -is, [unc. root (cf. saepio) + es (and -is, cf. sedes)], f., *a fence, a hedge, an enclosure, a hurdle* (for fencing), — *an orchard* (cf. saeptum).

saepiŏ (sēp-), saepsī, saeptum, saepīre, [†saepi- (of saepes)], 4. v. a., *enclose, hedge about, surround, invest, hem in.* — saepit se tectis (*shut himself up,* &c.). —

saeptus, -a, -um, p.p., *enclosed,* &c. — Neut., *an enclosure, an orchard:* inter saepta domorum (*in the precincts,* of bees).

saeptus, -a, -um, p.p. of saepio.

saeta (sēt-), -ae, [?], f., *a stiff hair, a bristle, bristling hair, shaggy hair.*

saetiger (sēt-), -era, -erum, [†saeta- (weakened) -ger (√ger, in gero, + us)], adj., *bristly.*

saetōsus (sēt-), -a, -um, [†saeta- (reduced) + osus], adj., *bristly.*

saeviŏ, -īvī (-iī), -ītum, -īre, [†saevŏ- (as if saevi-, cf. exanimus, -is], 4. v. n., *rage, rave, be angry, become furious.* — Also of animals and things.

saevus, -a, -um, [?], adj., *raging, furious, roused to fury, fierce, savage, relentless, cruel, angry.* — Transferred to things, *cruel, wild, raging, savage, deadly, bitter:* mephitis; faces; dolores; vada. — In good sense, *fierce in conflict.*

Sagaris, -is, [from a Phrygian river], m., a Trojan.

Vocabulary. 243

Sagēs, (-is?), [?], m., a Rutulian.
sagitta, -ae, [?], f., *an arrow.*
sagittifer, -era, -erum, [†sagitta- (weakened) -fer (√fer + us)], adj., *armed with arrows.*
sagulum, -ī, [†sagŏ + lum (n. of lus)], n., *a cloak* (worn by soldiers over their armor), *a mantle.*
sāl, salis, [√sal (*flow*, cf. Sk. *sarit*, river), cf. Gr. ἅλς], (m.) n., *water, salt water, the salt wave, the salt sea, the sea, the deep, a sea.* — Also (a very old and the most common meaning), *salt.* — Fig., *wit.*
Salamīs, -mīnis, [Gr. Σαλαμίς], f., the island in the Saronic Gulf, where the victory of the Athenians over the Persians took place, formerly the home of Telamon.
Sālentīnus (Sall-), -a, -um, [?], adj., *of the Salentini* (a people dwelling in Calabria), *Salentine.*
salictum, -ī, [†salic + tum (n. of -tus, cf. **honestus**)], n., *a willow thicket, a willow hedge, willows.*
salignus, -a, -um, [†salic + nus], adj., *of willow, willow :* **falx.**
Saliī, -ōrum, [√sal (in **salio**) + ius], m. plur., *the Salii,* twelve dancing priests of Mars, who went through the city annually in a solemn dance bearing the ancilia or sacred shields. The rite is dated back by Virgil to the time of Evander.
saliō, -uī (-īvī), tum, -īre, [√sal, cf. ἅλλομαι], 4. v. n., *leap, dance, spring.* — Fig., of things, *spring:* **saliens vena** (*throbbing*); **saliens rivus** (*dancing*); **grando** (*dance, rebound*).
saliunca, -ae, [?], f., *saliunca,* an odoriferous plant (perh. *valerian*).
Salius, -ī, [?], m., the name of a Trojan, perh. of more than one.
salix, -icis, [?], f., *a willow, willow* (*willow branches*).
Salmōneus, -eos, [Gr. Σαλμωνεύς], m., a son of Æolus. He ruled in Elis, and in his pride imitated the thunder and lightning of Jupiter, for which impiety he was hurled to the world below by a thunderbolt.
Salmōnia, -ae, [Gr. Σαλμωνία], f., a city of Elis, on the river Enipeus.
salsus, -a, -um, [p.p. of **salo** (fr. **sal**)], adj., *salted, salt, briny* (of the sea) : **robigo** (caused by salt water or with a briny taste?); **sudor.** — Esp. with **fruges, mola,** of the salt and meal offered as a sacrifice, apparently as the first necessaries of life.
saltem [acc. of lost word **saltis**, of unc. kin.], adv., *at least* (if nothing more or better), *at any rate.*
saltō, -āvī, -ātum, -āre, [†saltŏ- (p.p. of **salio**)], 1. v. a., *dance, leap.*
1. **saltus, -ūs**, [√sal + tus], m., *a leap, a bound, a spring.*
2. **saltus, -ūs**, [?, poss. √sal in a more primitive meaning, or perh. from *breaking out* of the woods into the opening], m., *an opening* (in the woods), *a pasture, a mountain-pass, a glade, open woods, a grove, woodland.*
salūbris, -e, [†salu- (akin to **salvus**, cf. **salus**) + bris (cf. **lugubris**)], adj., *healthful, wholesome, salutary, healing.*
salum, -ī, [†sal + um (n. of us)], n., *the sea, the deep.*
salūs, -ūtis, [†salu- (akin to **salvus**) + tis (reduced, cf. **sementis**)], f., *health, welfare, safety, well-being, salvation, preservation.* — Also, *hope of safety, remedy, means of safety, relief.*
salūtō, -āvī, -ātum, -āre, [†salut- (of **salus**)], 1. v. a., (*wish health to anyone*), *greet, salute, hail, welcome.* — **salūtāns, -antis,** p. as subst., *a visitor* (calling in the morning to salute a great man, as was the Roman custom).
salvē, see **salveo.**
salveō, no perf., no sup., **salvere**, [†salvŏ-], 2. v. n., *be well.* — **salvē** (-ēte), imperat., as an address, *hail, welcome.*
salvus, -a, -um, [√sal (cf. **salus**,

sollus) + vus (cf. ὅλος) for ὅλϝος], adj., *safe, unharmed.*

Samē, -ēs, [Gr. Σάμη], f., an island (later *Cephalonia*) in the Ionian Sea.

Samos (-us), -ī, [Gr. Σάμος], f.: 1. A large island off the coast of the Ionian part of Asia Minor, famous for its temple of Juno; 2. **Threicia,** another name for Samothracia.

Samothrācia, -ae, [Gr. Σαμοθρᾳκία], f., an island off the coast of Thrace, famous for its mystic worship of the mysterious Cabiri. Several traditions connected its settlement with Phrygia. It was also called *Samos Threicia.*

sancĭō, sanxī, sanctum, sancīre, [√sac, in sacer, perh. through adj.-stem, cf. **Sancus**], 4. v. a., *make sacred, make inviolable, ratify.* — **sanctus, -a, -um,** p.p. as adj., *sacred, holy, inviolable, sainted, reverend, venerable, venerated:* fides(*unsullied, inviolate*).—Also, *pure, saintly, chaste.*

sanctus, -a, -um, p.p. of **sancio.**

sandyx, -ўcis, [Gr. σάνδυξ], f., *scarlet* (a dye of that color).

sānē [abl. of **sanus**], adv., *very much* (cf. "soundly"). — As confirmatory particle, *truly, no doubt, to be sure* (concessive).

sanguineus, -a, -um, [†sanguin + eus], adj., *of blood, bloody, bloodstained, bloodshot, blood-red;* **Mavors** (*bloodthirsty*, prop. only covered with blood).

sanguis (sanguen), -inis, [?, two stems, -in and -ī], m., *blood* (properly in the body, cf. cruor).— Also, *blood* (shed), *gore, bloodshed.*— Also (as in Eng.), *race, blood, descent, stock, family, progeny.*— Also of blood as a sign of vital force.

saniēs, -ēī, [?], f., *matter, foul gore, froth* (of a serpent).

sānus, -a, -um, [unc. root (prob. akin to σῶς) + nus (cf. **plenus**)], adj., *sound, healthy.* — Also, *rational, sound* (in mind): **male sana** (*distracted*).

sapor, -ōris, [√sap (in sapio) + or], m., *taste, flavor:* **tunsus gallae** (*a flavoring of the pounded gall-nut*). — Less exactly, *odor:* iussi sapores (*fragrant herbs*).

sarcĭō, sarsī, sartum, sarcīre, [?], 4. v. a., *patch, mend, repair.*

Sardōus, -a, -um, [Gr. Σαρδῷος], adj., *Sardinian, of Sardinia* (famous for its bitter herbs).

sarmentum, -ī, [apparently √sarp (in sarpo, *prune*) + mentum], n., *prunings, twigs, brushwood.*

Sarnus, -ī, [?], m., a river of Campania on which Pompeii formerly stood, but by the great eruption its course was changed.

Sarpēdōn, -onis, [Gr. Σαρπηδών], m., a king of Lycia killed before Troy.

Sarrānus, -a, -um, [†Sarra+nus], adj., *of Sarra* (the ancient name of Tyre), *Tyrian.*

Sarrastēs, -um, [?], m. plur., a people of Campania, about Sorrento.

sat, see **satis.**

sata, see **sero.**

Satīculus, -a, -um, [?], adj., *of Saticula,* a city of Samnium. Masc., *a Saticulan:* **asper** (*the fierce Saticulan,* collectively).

satĭō, -ōnis, [√sa (of sero) + tio, cf. **ratio**], f., *a sowing, planting, layering.* — May be rendered in Eng., *seed-time, planting-time.*

satĭō, -āvī, -ātum, -āre, [stem of satis or stem akin, cf. **satietas**], 1. v. a., *satisfy, satiate:* **cineres meorum** (*appease, avenge*).

satis (abbreviated **sat**), [?, cf. **satias, satietas,** perh. contracted for **satius**], adv. Apparently adj. (cf. **bene esse**), *enough, sufficient.* —Adv., *sufficiently, enough.*—With negatives, *not very, not very much.* — **satius,** compar., *better, preferable.*

satius, see **satis.**

sator, -ōris, [√sa (in sero) + tor],

m., *planter.* — Also (cf. **satus**), *a progenitor, a father.*
satur, -ura, -urum, [akin to **satis**, perh. †sati + rus], adj., *full, well-fed.* — Less exactly, *well-stocked, rich, fertile, deep-dyed* (*rich,* of color).
Satura, -ae, [?], f., a lake or swamp in La/ium : **Saturae palus.**
saturātus, -a, -um, p.p of **saturo.**
Sāturnia, -ae, [cf. **Saturnius**], f., an ancient name of the settlement on the Capitoline Hill, the supposed nucleus of ancient Rome.
Sāturnius, -a, -um, [†Saturnŏ- (reduced) + ius], adj., *of Saturn, son of Saturn, daughter of Saturn,* used of Jupiter, of Neptune, and of Juno.
Sāturnus, -ī, [stem fr. √sa (in **sero**) + **turnus,** cf. **taciturnus**], m., an ancient divinity of Italy, no doubt presiding over agriculture. His supremacy was supposed to mark the golden age of primitive virtue and simplicity. In later times he was identified with the Greek Κρόνος, and to him were attached the myths of that ancient divinity. Hence, he was son of Uranus, and father of Jupiter, Juno, Neptune, and other gods.
saturŏ, -āvī, -ātum, -āre, [†saturŏ- (of **satur**)], 1. v. a., *fill, satiate, satisfy, feed full, saturate, fill full.*
satus, -a, -um, p.p. of **sero.**
Satyrus, -ī, [Gr. Σάτυρος], m., *a Satyr,* one of a subordinate class of deities of the woods, of a frolicsome and mischievous disposition, represented with goats' legs and with horns. They often appear as companions of Bacchus, whose attendant Silenus seems to have been one of them. They are hardly distinguishable from the Latin Fauns.
saucius, -a, -um, [?], adj., *wounded, smitten, mangled* (of a snake). — Fig., *stricken.*
saxeus, -a, -um, [†saxŏ- (reduced) + eus], adj., *of rocks, rocky, of stone* (fragments) : **umbra** (*of the rocks*).
saxōsus, -a, -um, [†saxŏ- (reduced) + osus], adj., *stony, rocky.* — Neut. as adv.: **saxosum sonans** (*roaring among the rocks*).
saxum, -ī, [?], n., *a rock* (detached, cf. **rupes**), *a stone.* — Less exactly, *a broken rock* (on a shore), *a rock* (unbroken).
scaber, -bra, -brum, [√scab (in **scabo**) + rus (reduced)], adj., *rough.* — Transferred, *roughening, corroding :* **robigo.**
scabiēs, -ēī, [√scab (in **scabo**) + ies, cf. **inluvies**], f., (*a scratching*), *a roughness* (of decay), *rust, corrosion, the itch, the scab* (in sheep), *the scurf.*
Scaea, -ae, (Scaeae, -ārum), [Gr. Σκαιαί], adj. fem. (with **porta**), *Scæan,* the western (left) gate of Troy, the principal and most famous entrance.
scaena (scē-), -ae, [Gr. σκηνή], f., *a scene* (the arched back of the stage, in front of which the action took place), *a canopy* (of woods like the scene), *the side scenes, the stage.*
scālae, -ārum, [√scad (in **scando**) + la], f. plur., *a scaling-ladder* or *ladders, a ladder* (of a ship).
scandō, perf. and sup. not found, **scandere,** [√scad, but with n permanent], 3. v. a. and n., *climb, scale, ascend, mount.*
scatebra, -ae, [†scate- (of **scateo**) + bra, f. of -ber, cf. **Mulciber**], f., *a bubbling stream, a spring.*
scelerātus, -a, -um, p.p. of **scelero.**
scelerō, no perf., **-ātum, -are,** [†sceler- (of **scelus**)], 1. v. a., *pollute, defile.* — **scelerātus, -a, -um,** p.p. as adj., *wicked, guilty, impious, infamous, accursed :* **frigus** (cf. Eng. colloquial language). — Transferred, *of the accursed, of guilt :* **poenae** (*inflicted on the guilty*).

scelus, -eris, [unc. root + us, but cf. σκέλος, with **pravus,** and **rectus**], n. Abs*t*rac*t*, *villany, wickedness, guilt, wrong-doing.* — Concretely, *a crime, an evil deed, a deed* (impliedly evil from the con*text*) : pro scelus (*O cursed crime*); scelus infectum (*taint of guilt*); quod scelus tantum merens (*for what crime so great deserving punishment*).—Also, *a villain, a criminal:* artificis scelus (*crafty villain*).

sceptrum, -i, [Gr. σκῆπτρον], n., *a sceptre.* — Fig., *rule, power, dominion, a kingdom, a realm, the throne.*

scilicet [sci (imper. of scio) -licet, cf. ilicet], adv., *certainly, no doubt, of course, naturally, truly.* — Ironically, *forsooth, truly, doubtless.* — As connec*t*ive, *yes for, for of course, but I may say, for we see.*

scilla, -ae, [Gr. σκίλλα], f., *a squill* (a kind of bulbous plan*t*).

scindō, scidī, scissum, scindere, [√scid, cf. σχίζω], 3. v. a., *cut* (wi*t*h a sharp tool, cf. **rumpo**), *tear, split, cleave, rive, rend:* vallum ferro; crines (*tear*); scissa veste. — Fig., *divide:* with reflexive (or in pass.), *divide, separate:* sese unda (*separate*); se genus (*branch off*); vulgus (*is rent,* into factions).—Esp., *plough, break up.* — Of the effect: viam (*cleave*).

scintilla, -ae, [?], f., *a spark:* ab ore absistunt (*fire flashes*).

scintillō, -āvī, no sup., **-are,** [†scintilla-], 1. v. n., *throw sparks:* oleum (*snap, sputter,* in a lamp).

sciō, scīvī, scītum, scīre, [prob. akin to κείω], 4. v. a., *know, know how to, learn:* scit triste sidus (*can bear witness*).

Scipiadēs, -ae, [Gr. form of pa*t*ronymic, fr. Scipio], m., *son of the Scipios.* — Plur., *the Scipios,* the famous family of leaders and statesmen at Rome.

scissus, -a, -um, p.p. of **scindo.**

scitor, -ātus, -ārī, [†scitŏ- (of scio)], 1. v. dep., *enquire, learn, search into:* oracula (*consult*).

scopulus, -ī, [Gr. σκόπελος], m., *a crag* (projecting, cf. **rupes** and **saxum**), *a cliff, a rock* (generally), *a reef.*

Scorpius, -ī, [Gr. σκορπίος], m., *Scorpio,* the constellation.

scrobis (scrobs), scrobis, [√scrib (orig. *dig*) as stem], m. and f., *a ditch, a trench, a pit, a drill* (a straight furrow for planting).

scrupeus, -a, -um, [†scrupŏ- (reduced)+eus], adj., *of sharp stones, stony, flinty:* spelunca (*of jagged rocks*).

scūtātus, -a, -um, [†scutŏ- (reduced)+ atus, cf. **armatus**], adj., *armed with shields:* scutati omnes (*all with shields*).

scūtum, -ī, [Gr. σκῦτος], n., *a shield* (of the Roman pattern, oblong and bent around the body, originally made of wood covered with leather, cf. **clipeus**).

Scylacēum, -ī, [Gr. Σκυλάκειον], n., a town of Southern Italy on the coast of Bruttium, near a promontory supposed to be dangerous for ships.

Scylla, -ae, [Gr. Σκύλλα], f.: 1. A sea-monster supposed to inhabit some rocks in the Strait of Messina, on the coast of Bruttium. Her parentage is variously represented in the myths. The rocks at present seem to be perfectly harmless; 2. Another personage, daughter of Nisus, who betrayed her father to Minos by plucking out from his head a red hair, and was changed to a bird (cf. **Nisus**). She is sometimes confounded with the one first mentioned; 3. Plur., *Scyllas,* including several monsters of the kind first mentioned.

Scylla, -ae, [see 1. **Scylla**], f., the name of a ship.

Scyllaeus, -a, -um, [Gr. Σκυλλαῖος], adj., *of Scylla.*

scyphus, -ī, [Gr. σκύφος], m., *a cup, a goblet.*

Scyrius, -a, -um, [Gr. Σκύριος], adj., *of Scyros* (the island off the coast of Euboea where Achilles was concealed, disguised as a girl), *Scyrian.*

Scythia, -ae, [Gr. Σκυθία], f. (of adj.), the country north of the Black Sea.

sē- (sĕd-), [cf. **sed**], prep. only in comp., *apart, without, away.*

se, see **sui.**

Sēbēthis, -ĭdis, [?], f., a nymph (of the river Sebethos, in Campania).

sēcernō, -crēvī, -crētum, -cernere, [se-cerno], 3. v. a., *separate, set apart.* — **sēcrētus, -a, -um,** p.p. as adj., *separate, apart, retired, remote, obscure, concealed, hidden, reticent, silent, in silence, alone.* — Neut. pl., *private abode.*

sēcessus, -ūs, [se-cessus, cf. secedo], m., *a retirement.* — Concretely, *a retreat, a recess.*

secius, see **secus.**

sēclūdō, -clūsī, -clūsum, -clūdere, [se-claudo], 3. v. a., *shut off, shut up.* — Fig., *put aside, banish.* — **sēclūsus, -a, -um,** p.p. as adj., *secluded, retired.*

sēclum, see **saeculum.**

sēclūsus, -a, -um, p.p. of **secludo.**

secō, secuī, sectum, secāre, [?], 1. v. a., *cut* (apparently *across,* cf. **scindo,** *split*), *carve, wound, hew, sever, cut out, cut off;* also, *split.* — Fig. (of mere passing through), *cleave, cut, plough* (the sea), *divide, cut through.* — With acc. of effect, *cut:* **viam** (*take one's way*); **secto limite** (*the cross path*); **sub nubibus arcum** (as cutting the heavens). — In a peculiar sense (poss. a diff. word): **secat spem** (*indulges,* takes as his share ?, cf. noun **sector**).

sēcrētus, -a, -um, p.p. of **secerno.**

sector, -ātus, -ārī, [†secto- (old p.p. of **sequor**)], 1. v. dep., *pursue, hunt, chase.*

sectus, -a, -um, p.p. of **seco.**

sēculum, see **saeculum.**

sēcum, see **sui** and **cum.**

secundo, no perf., no sup., **-āre,** [†secundŏ-], 1. v. a., *favor, prosper.*

secundum [n. acc. of **secundus**], adv. and prep., (*following*), *along, near by.*

secundus, -a, -um, [p. ger. of **sequor,** cf. **rotundus**], adj., (*following*), *second* (in time, order, or degree), *inferior:* **secundae mensae** (*second course, dessert*); **mensis et Dis accepta secundis** (*the second course, and the gods invoked to share it*). — Of water, &c. (cf. **adversus**), *favoring, favorable, fair:* **secundo amni, flumine** (*down the stream*); **secundi spirate** (*blow favoring breezes*); **venti secundi** (*favoring winds*). — Transferred, *prosperous, favorable, propitious, auspicious:* **ventis et Dis secundis** (*fair winds and favoring gods*); **curru secundo** (*flying*); **secundo Marte** (*in successful combat,* of Mars); **secundo plausu, rumore** (*auspicious, cheering,* as of good omen); **vires secundae** (*successful efforts*); **adi pede secundo** (*approach to favor*); **secundus aruspex** (*auspicious*); **secundo clamore** (*joyous, auspicious*); **sinus implere secundos** (*fill the bellying sail with favoring winds*). — Often with **res,** *prosperity, success.*

secūris, -is, [as if †secu- (√sec, in **seco,** + u) + ris, cf. **molaris**], f., *an axe, a battle-axe.*

sēcūrus, -a, -um, [se-cura- (weakened and decl. as adj.)], adj., *free from care, regardless, fearless, secure:* **pelagi** (*secure of*). — Transferred: **latices** (*that free from care*); **otia** (*untroubled*); **quies** (*secure*).

secus [√sec (in **sequor**) + unc. term. (poss. compar., like **magis**)], adv. (*following* ?, *worse* ?), *otherwise.* — With negatives, *not otherwise, not less, no more, just so, even so;* — with **atque (quam),** *just like, even as.* — Compar., **sē-**

tius (sēcius, sectius), *ill.*—With negatives, *no less, none the less, nevertheless, even thus, even then, even so.*

secūtus, -a, -um, p.p. of **sequor**.

sed [abl. of stem akin to **sine**, cf. **pone**], conj., *but, yet.*

sēdātus, -a, -um, p.p. of **sedo**.

sedeō, sēdī, sessum, sedēre, [√sed, cf. ἕζομαι, prob. through adj.-stem], 2. v. n., *sit, sit down.* — Less exactly, *lie* (of ships), *come to anchor, light* (of birds), *encamp* (of armies), *remain* (of a weapon). — Esp., *sit by* (inactive), *sit idle, linger.* — Fig., *be settled, be fixed, be determined, please* (be one's pleasure) : **certa sedet sententia** (*is surely fixed*).

sedēs, -is, [√sed (strengthened) + es and -is)], f., *a seat, a throne, a resting-place.*—Less exactly (either sing. or plur.), *a house, a habitation, a dwelling-place, a dwelling, a home, an estate, a foundation, a position, a spot, a region, a place, a temple, a city.*—Esp. of burial, *a last resting-place, a tomb :* **imae sedes** (*the lowest depths*); **sacra sedes** (*of the steps of an altar*); **sedes Pelori** (*region*); **penetralis sedes** (*the inner court*); **Tarpeia sedes** (*rock*); **locus sedesque** (*place of abode*).

sedīle, -is, [†sedi- (cf. **sedes**) + le (n. of lis)], n., *a seat, a bench, a thwart* (for rowers).

seditiō, -ōnis, [sed-itio (cf. **eo**)], f., *a civil dissension, a mutiny, an outbreak* (of the people), *a riot, an uprising* (of the people), *faction, sedition.*

sedō, -āvī, -ātum, -āre, [†seda- (√sed+a, cf. **domiseda**)], 1.v.a., *settle down.* — Fig., *calm, quiet, allay.*

sēdūcō, -dūxī, -ductum, -dūcere, [se-duco], 3. v. a., *draw apart, separate, part asunder.*

seges, -etis, [?, perh. akin to **sagmen**], f., *growing grain, a crop* (standing), *grain* (planted), *a grain field, a field, land* (as covered with growth), *the seed* (about to be planted), *a growth* (of trees), *a nursery.* — Fig. of other things, *a crop, a growth, a thicket, a field :* **virum** (*a crop of heroes*); **seges horret ferrea.**

segnis, -e, [?], adj., *slow, sluggish, idle, listless, inactive, laggard, slothful, cowardly, unproductive :* **carduus** (*sterile, unprofitable*). — Compar. **segnior, -us**, *slower*, &c., *less active, less prolific :* **haud illo segnior** (*not less vigorous*, &c.).

segniter [†segni+ter, cf. **acriter**], adv., *inactively :* **non segnius** (*not less vigorously*).

segnitiēs, -ēī, [†segni + ties, cf. **amicitia**], f., *sloth, tardiness.*

Selīnūs, -ūntis, [Gr. Σελινοῦς], f., *a town on the southern coast of Sicily, famous for its palms.*

sella, -ae, [prob. √sed + la], f., *a seat, a chair* (of state), *a throne.* — Esp., the *sella curulis* of the Romans, made of ivory, with crossed legs, and used by magistrates.

semel [n. of **similis** (or word akin) reduced], adv., *once, once for all.*

sēmen, -inis, [√sa (of **sero**) + men], n., *a seed.* — Less exactly, *a scion, a shoot, a cutting.* — Fig. (plur.), *elements, vital principles, seeds of life, germs* (*of life, of fire*). — Also, *a race, a stock, progeny, young.*

sēmentis, -is, [†semen + tis], f., *a sowing :* **sementem extende** (*prolong the seed-time*).

sēmēsus (sēmiēsus), -a, -um, [semi-esus], adj., *half eaten.*

sēmianimis, -e, [semi-animus (weakened and decl. as adj.)], adj., *half alive, half lifeless, expiring, dying.*

sēmifer, -era, -erum, [semi-ferus], adj., *half brute, monstrous.* — Also, *half savage.*

sēmihomō, -inis, [semi-homo], adj., *half man.* — Also, *half savage.*

sēminex, -necis, [semi-nex (decl.

as adj.)], adj., *half dead, half life-less, dying, wounded to death.*

sēminō, -āvī, -ātum, -āre, [†semin-], 1. v. a., *sow, plant.* — Less exactly, *produce.*

sēmiputātus, -a, -um, [semi-putatus], adj., *half pruned.*

sēmita, -ae, [se-mita(akin to meo, cf. **comes**)], f., *a by-path, a path, a way.*

sēmiūstus (semūst-), -a, -um, [semi-ustus], adj., *half burned, half consumed, charred.*

semivir, -virī, [semi-vir], adj., *half man, effeminate.*

semper [stem akin to **similis** + per, cf. **nuper**], adv., *always, forever, ever, constantly.*

senātus, -ūs, [as if †senā- (of verb seno, from †sen in **senex,** cf. **senator, senaculum**) + tus, cf. **exsulo, exsulatus**], m.,(*old age?,* cf. **iuventus**), *the elders.* — Esp., *the senate,* or body of nobles who composed the grand council of a nation, particularly the *Roman senate.*

senecta, -ae, [†senec- (of senex) + ta, cf. **matuta**], f., *age, old age.*

senectūs, -tūtis, [†senec- (of senex) + tus, cf. **iuventus**], f., *age, old age.* — Personified, *Age.*

senex, senis, [two stems, √sen (as stem); and †seni+cus (reduced), akin to ἔνος and *senes-chal*], adj., *old, aged, venerable.* — Usually as subst., *an old man* (over forty-five years), *an aged sire;*— also of gods conceived or represented as old: **Proteus ; Saturnus.** — **senior, -ōris,** compar., *older.* — Also, *old, aged, venerable, an elder, an old man.*

sēnī, -ae, -a, [sex + nus], adj. plur., *six each, six at a time:* **bis seni** (*twice six, twelve*).

sēnsus, -ūs, [√sent (of sentio) + tus], m., *taste, feeling, perception.* — Concretely, *a feeling, the intellect, the mind, intelligence, the passions, the senses, the sense:* **sanos sensus avertere** (*to charm away the sober sense, drive mad*); **sensus inflexit** (*moved the feelings*); **sopitos sensus** (*the slumbering senses,* of the effect of sleep); **imis sensibus** (*in the depths of the soul*).

sententia, -ae, [†sentent- (p. of simpler form akin to **sentio**) + ia], f., *a way of thinking, a judgment, a purpose, a resolution, a sentiment, a determination, an opinion, a view of things, counsel* (a plan of action), *an idea* (of a situation). — Esp., *an opinion expressed* (in a deliberative body).

sentiō, sēnsī, sēnsum, sentīre, [?], 4. v. a., *perceive* (by the senses), *hear, feel, see, notice, observe.* — Also by the mind, *perceive, be conscious of, become aware, know, feel, learn, learn to know, find out, understand.* — Esp., *feel, experience, come to feel, endure.* — Also, *think, suppose, judge.*

sentis, -is, [?], m., *a thorn-bush, a briar, a bramble.*

sentus, -a, -um, [akin to **sentis**], adj., *rough, overgrown.*

sepeliō, sepelīvī (-iī), sepultum, sepelīre, [?], 4. v. a., *bury, inter.* — **sepultus, -a, -um,** p.p. as adj., *buried;* — also of wine and sleep, *overcome, buried:* **parce sepulto** (*spare one in his grave*); **custode sepulto** (*laid asleep*).

sēpēs, sēpiō; see **saepes, saepio.**

septem [petrified case-form, akin to ἑπτά], indecl. num. adj., *seven.*

septemgeminus, -a, -um, [septemgeminus], adj., *sevenfold, seven-mouthed:* **Nilus.**

septemplex, -plicis, [septem-plex, cf. **duplex**], adj., *seven-fold* (of seven thicknesses).

septēnī, -ae, -a, [stem of septem + nus], num. adj. plur., *seven each, seven at a time.* — Also, *seven.*

septentriō, -ōnis, (also separate) [septem-triones], m., *Charles' Wain, the Great and Little Bear.* Cf. **trio.**

septimus, -a, -um, [stem of septem + mus, cf. **primus**], num. adj., *seventh.*

septus, -a, -um; see **saepio.**

sepulcrum, -ī, [sepel (as if root of sepelio) + crum], n., *a tomb, a burial-place.*—Less exactly, *burial.*

sepultus, -a, -um, p.p. of **sepelio.**

sequāx, -ācis, [as if sequā- (cf. sequor) + cus (reduced), cf. **capax**], adj., *following, pursuing:* caprae (*greedy,* pursuing the vine as enemies); fumi (*penetrating,* pursuing the bees); Latium (*in pursuit*); undae (as if chasing a ship to sink it).

sequester, -tra, -trum, [†sequit- (formed like **comes,** cf. **sequor**) + ter (cf. **magister**)], adj., *depositary, intermediate.*—As subst., *a mediator, mediatress:* pace sequestra (*reconciled by the truce*).

sequor, secūtus, sequī, [√seq akin to ἕπομαι], 3. v. dep., *follow* (lit. and fig.), *pursue, chase:* sequendi (*traces to follow*); quem armenta; signa sequantur (*keep the ranks*); qui me casus; iussa (*obey*); haec exempla; secutae aera (of bees). — Less exactly, *follow* (in order), *come next, ensue, follow* (in a course of action), *do the like:* frumenta (*follow*); de cortice sanguis; laetum paeana (*take up, continue*). — Also, *follow with, follow* (in company), *accompany, side with:* factum fortuna (*prosper*); me fama (*attend*); manum sagitta (*yield to, come away with*); sequetur facilis (*come away,* of plucking a branch); non sequitur vox (*does not come,* follow the effort); quam fama secuta est (*of whom the story goes*). — Also, *follow after, aim at, seek:* Italiam; pennis astra; sidera voce (*soar to heaven with a song*). — Also of the route passed over, *follow out, follow, pursue, trace, pass through, go over, undergo:* saltus; quid sequens (*following what course*); maiora (*deal with*); fastigia; sudor membra (*creep over*); fata (*accomplish*); arma (*take up*); bella (*engage in*); meliora (*a higher destiny*); extrema ferro (*seek a desperate remedy*). — Also, *overtake:* meliora miseros. — **sequēns, -entis,** p. as subst. (esp. plur.), *a pursuer, those behind, the next, one in search, a follower.*

serēnō, -āvī, -ātum, -āre, [†serenŏ], 1. v. a., *clear, calm.* — Poetically: spem fronte serenat (*smooths his brow with hope*).

serēnus, -a, -um, [?], adj., *clear, fair, cloudless, calm, placid:* nubes (*light, dry*); vultus. — Neut., *fair weather.*

Sēres, -um, [Gr. Σῆρες], m., plur., the people of Eastern Asia (including prob. the Chinese), where the cotton-tree grows.

Serestus, -ī, [?], m., a follower of Æneas.

Sergestus, -ī, [?], m., a follower of Æneas.

Sergius, -a, -um, [?], adj., a Roman gentile name: domus (*the Sergian house*).

seriēs, -ēī, [√ser (in 1. **sero**) + ies, cf. **inluvies**], f., *a row, a line, a succession, a chain, a train.*

sērius, -a, -um, [?], adj., *serious.* — Neut. plur. as subst., *serious business.*

sermō, -ōnis, [√ser (in 1. **sero**) + mo, but prob. through intermediate stem, cf. **homo**], m., *discourse, talk, speech, words* (spoken), *common talk, rumor, murmurs.*— Also, *language, tongue.*

1. **serō,** perf. not found, **sertum, serere,** [√ser, akin to ἔρω, εἴρω], 3. v. a., *join, plait, weave.* — Fig.: multa serebant (*talked much*).

2. **serō, sēvī, satum, serere,** [√sa (Eng. *sow*), reduplicated (with **r** for **s**)], 3. v. a., *sow, plant.* — Fig., *scatter, spread.* — Poetically, *be a farmer.* — Also, *beget* (in p.p.). — **serens, -entis,** p. as subst., *a sower.* — **satus, -a, -um,** p.p. as adj., *sown, planted, growing;* — also, *sprung from, born, descended from.* — Masc. and fem., *son of,*

descendant of, daughter of.—Neut. plur., *sown fields, growing crops, tilled fields.*
serpēns, -entis, [p. of serpo], m., *a serpent, a snake.*
serpō, serpsī, serptum, serpere, [√serp, akin to ἕρπω], 3. v. n., *crawl, creep.*—Fig., *glide, twine, creep on, spread.*
serpyllum, -ī, [Gr. ἕρπυλλον], n., *wild thyme.*
serra, -ae, [poss. √sec + ra], f., *a saw.*
Serrānus, -ī, [akin to sarrio], m.: 1. C. Atilius Regulus Serranus, a famous Roman whose election to the consulship was announced to him while ploughing; 2. A Rutulian.
sertum, -ī, [n. p.p. of 1. sero], n., *a garland, a wreath.*
serum, -ī, [?, akin to ὀρός], n., *whey.*
serus, -a, -um, [?], adj., *late, too late, tardy, latest:* vires (*too far gone*); mea sera voluptas (*of my age*); nepotes (*far distant*). — Neut. as adv., *late.*
serva, -ae, [f. of servus], f., *a maid-servant.*
servātus, -a, -um, p.p. of servo.
serviō, -īvī (-iī), -ītum, -īre, [†servŏ-], 4. v. n., *be a slave, serve.* — Less exactly, *obey, be subject to.*
servitium, -ī (-iī), [†servŏ+tium, cf. amicitia], n., *slavery, servitude.*—Less exactly, *subjection* (of men and animals).
servŏ, -āvī, -ātum, -āre, [†servŏ-], 1. v. a., *watch over, guard, keep* (from harm), *look out for, take care of, protect, save* (by protection), *preserve, keep alive.* — Hence, *retain, maintain, hold, keep, save, stay by, continue in, stand by, reserve, observe* (a rite or occasion): fidem (*keep one's word* or *faith,* the regular expression). — Also, *observe, watch, watch for, note, search, trace, gaze on, reach* (of the eyesight). — **servans, -antis** (superl. **servantissimus**), p. as adj., *observant.*

sescentī (sex-), -ae, -a, [sex-centum], adj., *six hundred.*
sēsē, see suī.
sēta, sētiger, setosus; see saeta, etc., the approved spelling.
seu, see sive.
severus, -a, -um, [?, poss. akin to σέβομαι, *revere*], adj., *strict, stern, severe, austere.* — Poetically, *cruel, awful:* amnis Cocyti, Eumenidum.
Severus, -ī, [see severus], m., a mountain in the Sabine territory, on the borders of Picenum.
sex [?, akin to ἕξ], indecl. num. adj., *six.*
sexcentī, see sescentī.
sī [prob. loc. of pron. √ra (or √sa), *in that case* (cf. sic)], conj., *if, in case,* in conditions. — Also, where the condition is a mere form, *if* (it is true that), *since, as, when, whenever.* — Esp.: si quidem, *if... really, since, seeing that.* — In wishes: si, O si, *if only, oh if, oh that, would that.* — With indef. pron. and adverbs: si quis, etc., *if any one,* &c., *whoever, whenever,* &c. — In a proviso, *if, in case, provided.* — Esp.: si modo, *if only, provided that.* — Also: quam si, in comparisons, *than if, than when, as if, as when.* — In apparent indirect questions, *in case, if, whether.* — Concessive, *even if, though.* — In asseverations, *if, as sure as.*
sībilō, -āvī, -ātum, -āre, [†sibilŏ-], 1. v. n., *hiss.*
sībilus, -a, -um, [?], adj., *hissing,* — Less exactly, *whispering, rustling.*—Masc., *a rustle, a murmur.*
Sibylla, -ae, [Gr. Σίβυλλα], f., *a Sibyl, a female seer.* A large number of such personages are mentioned, of which one of the most famous is the Cumæan, who was visited by Æneas, and by whom he was conducted to the world below. The idea of such persons seems to have been of foreign origin (probably Hebrew), though their functions were closely connected with

the worship of Apollo, the Greek and Latin god of divination.

sīc [si-ce, cf. **sī** and **hīc**], adv., *so, thus, in this way.* — *Of a proviso, so* (and so only), *thus* (and not otherwise).

Sīcānius, -a, -um, [†Sicanŏ- (reduced) + ius], adj., *of the Sicani, Sicanian.*—Less exactly, *Sicilian, of Sicily.* — Fem., *Sicily.*

Sīcanus, -a, -um, [†Sicŏ-(reduced, cf. **Siculus**) + anus], adj., *of the Sicani* (an ancient race of Central Italy, supposed to have colonized Sicily), *Sicanian.* — Masc. plur., *the Sicani.*—Less exactly, *Sicilian.*

siccō, -āvī, -ātum, -āre, [†siccŏ-], 1. v. a., *dry, drain:* **cruores**(*stanch*).

siccus, -a, -um, [?], adj., *dry, dried up, thirsty, parched.* — Neut., *the dry land.*

Sīcelis, -ĭdis, [Gr. Σικελίς], f. adj., *Sicilian, a Sicilian woman.*

Sīchaeus, see **Sychaeus.**

sīcubī [supposed to be si-†cubi (old form of **ubi**), but cf. **sic** and **ubi**], adv., *if anywhere, wherever, where.*

Sīculus, -a, -um, [†Sicŏ- (cf. **Sīcanus**) + lus, akin to Σικελός], adj., *Sicilian, of Sicily.*

sīcut [sic-ut], adv., *so as, just as, as.*

Sicyōnius, -a, -um,[Gr. Σικυώνιος], adj., *of Sicyon* (a city of Peloponnesus famous for its olives), *Sicyonian.*

sīdereus, -a, -um, [†sider + eus], adj., *starry, star-like:* **clipeus** (*orb-like*).

Sīdīcīnus, -a, -um, [?], adj., *of the Sidicini* (a people of Campania).

sīdō, sīdī, no sup., **sīdere,** [√sed, reduplicated], 3. v. n., *sit down.* — Less exactly, *alight.*

Sīdōn, -ōnis, [Gr. Σιδών], f., *an ancient city of Phœnicia,* from which Tyre was colonized.

Sīdōnius, -a, -um, [Gr. Σιδώνιος, -ονιος], adj., *of Sidon, Sidonian.* Less exactly, *Tyrian, Phœnician:* **urbs** (*of Tyre*).

sīdus, -eris, [poss. sid (as root of sido) + us, *position* ?, as a nautical, augural, or astrological word], n., *a constellation, a quarter of the sky.* — Less exactly, *a heavenly orb* (including the sun and moon), *a star:* **sidera emensae** (*starry regions*). — Also, mostly plur., *the heavens, Heaven, the stars of Heaven, the skies, the sky:* **ad sidera** (*to the skies, aloft*). — Poetically, *a season, a storm:* **mutato sidere** (*at the change of seasons*).

Sīgēus, -a, -um, [Gr. Σίγειον], adj., *of Sigeum,* a promontory of the Troad). — Neut., *Sigeum,* the promontory.

sīgnificō, -āvī, -ātum, -āre, [as if †signific-, cf. **artifex**], 1. v. a. and n., *make a sign, signal, beckon.*

signō, -āvī, -ātum, -āre,[†signŏ-], 1. v. a., *mark, distinguish* (by marking), *mark out.* — Of the effect, *draw, trace.* — Also, *discern, mark, notice, fix the eye on:* **se signari oculis** (*that all eyes are turned upon him*). — Also, *honor, distinguish, mark:* **nomen ossa.** — Poetically: **ora puer iuventā** (*show marks of youth in his face*).

signum, -ī, [unc. root + **num,** n. of -nus, cf. **magnus**], n., *a mark, a sign, an indication, a trace* (as a mark), *a track, a signal, a watchword.* — Esp., *an image, a figure, a representation, a carving* (poss. the orig. meaning, cf. **seco**), *a relief, embroidery,* — Also, *a constellation, a star, a sign* (of the Zodiac, plur. *the Zodiac*). — Also (in plur.), *the standards* (of an army, as a rallying-point or as a trophy of victory): **referens** (of Camillus); **reposcere Parthos** (of the standards taken by the Parthians from Crassus); **ferre** (*bear, serve in the ranks*); **sequi** (*keep the ranks*); **conferre** (*join battle, charge*); **collatis signis** (*in close combat*); **movere** (*break camp, advance*); **vellere** (*pluck up* the standards, set in the ground, *break camp, advance*).

Sīla, -ae, [?], f., *a forest in Bruttium.*

Vocabulary. 253

Silarus,-i, [Gr. Σίλαρις], m., a river between Lucania and Campania, around which were extensive pasture-grounds. It flows into the sea near Pæstum.

silentium, -i (-ii),[†silent+ium], n., *silence, stillness, quiet.* — Also, *secrecy.*

Silēnus, -i, [Gr. Σειληνός], m., an old Satyr, the chief attendant of Bacchus. He is represented as a fat old man, generally intoxicated.

sileō, -ui, no sup., -**ēre**, [?], 2. v. n., *be silent, keep silence, be mute, be dumb, be still, be noiseless.* — Poetically, act., *leave unsung.* — **silēns, -ēntis**, p. as adj., *silent, still, mute, in silence, voiceless, soundless.* — Masc. plur., *the silent shades, the voiceless ghosts.*

siler, -eris, [?], n., *a willow* (of a particular kind, perh. *Salix vitulina*), *osier.*

silēscō, no perf., no sup., -**escere**, [†sile- (of sileo) + sco], 3. v. n. incept., *be silent, be hushed.*

silex, -icis, [?], m. and f., *a flint, a pebble, flint, pebbles, a stone.* — Less exactly, *rock* (in position), *a cliff.*

siliqua, -ae, [?], f., *a pod, a husk* (of grain).

silva, -ae, [akin to ὕλη], f., *a wood, a forest, woodland:* iuga silvarum (*wooded heights*). — Also, of other thick growths, *a thicket, a thick growth, a growth.* — Poetically, of darts in a shield. — Less exactly (esp. in plur.), *trees, woods, a growth of trees, wood, fruit-trees, orchards, pastures* (wooded). — Esp., *the woods* (as opposed to cities or villages).

Silvānus, -i, [†silva + nus, cf. **Portunus**], m., an Italian woodland deity, presiding over woods, tillage, and cattle. He is represented with a garland of flowers and reeds, carrying a tree-trunk, and is often associated with Pan and the Nymphs.

silvestris, -e, [stem akin to **silva** + tris, cf. **equestris**], adj., *woodland* (adj.), *forest* (adj.), *woody, wild, of the woods:* Hiera (*dwelling in the woods*). — Fig., *rustic, woodland.*

Silvia, -ae, [f. of **Silvius**], f., a Latin maid whose pet stag was killed by Iulus.

silvicola, -ae, [†silva- (weakened) -cola, cf. **incola**], m., *dwelling in the woods, woodland* (adj.).

Silvius, -i (-ii), [†silva- (reduced) + ius], m., a name of several kings of Alba, esp. the supposed son of Æneas and founder of the line, and *Silvius Æneas*, a later offshoot of the stock.

similis, -e, [†simŏ- (cf. ὅμος, **simplex**)+ lis], adj., *like, resembling, of the same kind, similar, the same.*

Simoīs, -entos, [Gr. Σιμοείς], m., a river of the Troad.

simplex, -icis, [†simo- (reduced, cf. **similis**) -plex, cf. **duplex**], adj., *single, simple, pure, untainted:* herba (*plain*). — With negatives, *not uniform, manifold:* simplex nec modus inserere (*and the method &c. is not uniform, is manifold*).

simul [n. of **similis** (cf. **facultas**)], adv., *at the same time;* — repeated, *at once . . . and, and at the same time, no sooner . . . than.* — simul atque (ac), *as soon as.* — Without atque, in same sense. — Also, *at once, immediately, together:* arma simul iacere vina simul (*all together*).—Rarely (with abl. without prep.), *at the same time with* (*as*) *:* his dictis (*with these words*). — With a participle, *while:* simul hoc dicens.

simulācrum, -i, [†simulā- (of simulo) + crum], n., *an image, a statue, a spectre, a ghost, a phantom.* — *a mimicry, an imitation.*

simulātus, -a, -um, p.p. of **simulo**.

simulō, -āvi, -ātum, -āre, [†simili- (cf. **simul**)], 1. v. a., *make like, counterfeit, imitate.* — Also, *make a pretence, pretend, feign*ₙ *:* simulans multa (*making many pretences*). — **simulātus, -a, -um,** p.p., *made like, counterfeit, pretended, false:* simulata mente (*with deceitful purpose*); verba (*assumed*); magnis Pergama (*imitating,* &c.); simulato numine Bacchi (*pretending an inspiration,* &c.).

sīmus, -a, -um, [?, cf. σιμός], adj., *flat-nosed.*

sin [si-nē, *if not*], conj., *but if, if however, if on the other hand.*

sine [?, akin to sed, cf. pone], prep., *without.* — Wi*t*h abl. in adj. or adv. phrase: tenuem sine viribus umbram; sine fine furens; sine more furit (*ungovernably*); raptae sine more Sabinae (*lawlessly*).

singultō, *no* perf., **-ātum, -āre,** [†singultu-], I. v. n., *hiccough, sob:* singultantem sanguine truncum (*spouting jets of blood*).

singultus, -ūs, [†singulŏ- (reduced) + tus, as if fr. stem of lost verb, cf. **singultim**], m., *gasping, panting, a gasp.*

(**singulus, -a, -um,** archaic), Plur. **singulī, -ae, -a,** [akin to **simul**], adj., *one at a time, one by one, each in detail, singly* (in adv. force): nec singula corpora (*and not single creatures merely*); inter singula verba (*with every word*). — Neut. (as subst.), *each thing, every detail, everything, every point, every object.*

sinister, -tra, -trum, [unc. stem + ter, cf. **minister**], adj., *left hand, left, on the left.* — From auspices, *ill-boding, inauspicious, mischievous, hurtful* (but also, *favorable,* from a different doctrine of augury).—Fem. (sc. **manus**), *the left hand.*

sinō, sīvī, situm, sinere, [√si, of unc. kin.], 3. v. a., (*place, put*), *leave* (cf. **pono**), (rarely exc. in comp. and p.p.): sinite arma viris. — Fig. (cf. Eng. "leave"), *permit, allow, let, suffer, let be:* non perterrita sinit agmina (*suffer to be,* &c.). — Also (perh. imitation of Greek, cf. *ἐάω*), *spare, forbear, leave off, desist:* hanc animam; nunc sinite. — **situs, -a, -um,** p.p., *situated.*

Sinōn, -ōnis, [?], m., the spy who induced the Trojans to admit the wooden horse within their walls.

sīnum, -ī, [akin to **sinus**], n., *a bowl* (for drinking).

sinuŏ, -āvī, -ātum, -āre, [†sinu-], I. v. a., *bend, fold, twist* (in folds)

sinuōsus, -a, -um [†sinu + osus], adj., *in folds, winding, coiled, tortuons, sinuous.*

sinus, -ūs, [?], m., *a bend, a hollow surface, a fold* (of a garment), *a coil* (of a serpent), *a curve, a bellying* (swelling) *sail, the hollow* (of a wave): sinus extremi orbis (*the farthest curve of the circle of the world*); vasto sinu (*in its mighty embrace,* of a wave); sinum trahit fluctus (*the swell rolls on*); Cocytus sinu labens (*in its winding course*).—Esp., *the bosom* (where the folds of the garment cross), *the lap, the breast, an embrace.* — Hence, poetically, of things half personified (cf. "the lap of earth"), *bosom, lap:* laxant arva sinus (*the Earth opens her bosom,* at the coming of Spring); Nilum pandentem sinum (*opening her arms*).— Also, *a bay, a gulf, a cove; a slit.*

sīqua, sīquando, sīquis; see **sī, quis,** etc.

Sīrēn, -ēnis, [Gr. Σειρήν], f., mostly plur., *the Sirens.* Monsters with women's heads and the bodies of birds, who enticed mariners to the shore. Their abode was (according to one story), upon three islands off the bay of Naples, which were hence called *Sirenum scopuli.*

Sīrius, -ī (-iī), [Gr. Σείριος], m., *Sirius,* the Dog-star, which rose with the sun (at the period when the popular astronomy began), about the middle of July. Hence the star is associated with extreme heat. — Also in appos. as adj.: Sirius ardor (*the heat of the Dogstar*).

sistŏ, stitī (stetī), statum, sistere, [√sta reduplicated, cf. ἵστημι], 3. v. a. and n. Act. (causative), (*cause to stand*), *set, place, bring, fetch.* — Also, *stop, stay, rein in* (of horses), *cause to stand still.* — Also, *set up, reinstate, restore, be the stay of.* — With reflexive, *place one's self, stand.* — Intrans., *stand still, stop, stay, settle, strike* (of a missile) : sistere contra (*make a stand against, withstand, resist*).

sistrum, -ī, [Gr. σεῖστρον], n., *a sistrum*, a metallic musical instrument of rods playing in a frame, which produced a rattling sound when shaken. It belonged particularly to the Egyptians, and was used in the worship of Isis and apparently also in war.

Sīthonius, -a, -um, [Gr. Σιθώνιοι], adj., *of the Sithonii* (a Thracian tribe), *Sithonian, Thracian.*

sitiō, -īvī(-iī), no sup., -īre,[†siti-], 4. v. n. and a., *thirst, be thirsty, be parched, be dry.* — sitiēns, -entis, p. as adj., *thirsty, parched, greedy.*

sitīs, -is, [?], f., *thirst.* — Fig., *drought, parching heat :* ignea sitis (*burning fever*).

situs, -a, -um, p.p. of sino.

situs, -ūs, [√si (of sino) + tus], m., (*a placing, a leaving*), *neglect, lying fallow, want of care, inactivity :* victa situ senectus (*rust,* as of one's dotage).—Also, *a position.*

sīve (seu), [sī-ve], conj., *or if.* — Repeated, *if either . . . or, whether . . . or, if . . . or if, if . . . or if on the other hand, either . . . or* (where the force of si is lost in Eng.).— So in other combinations with same sense.

sobolēs, see suboles.

socer, -erī, [?, cf. ἑκυρός], m., *a father-in-law.* — Plur., *parents-in-law.*

sociātus, -a, -um, p.p. of socio.

sociŏ, -āvī, -ātum, -are, [†sociŏ-], 1. v. a., *ally, attach, unite, join, associate :* urbe domo nos (*adopt us* &c., *share with us* &c.).— Esp. by the bond of marriage.

socius, -a, -um, [√sec (in sequor) + ius], adj., *accompanying, allied, associated, friendly :* agmina (*allied, of friends*); arma (*alliance in arms*); agmen (*band of allies*); rates (*allied, of his countrymen*); Penates (*kindred*).— Masc. and fem. (as subst.), *a companion, an ally, a follower, a friend, an associate, an abettor, an assistant :* socii comitentur ovantes (*friends and neighbors*); O socii (*comrades, companions*).

sodālis, -is, [?], comm., *a comrade* (intimate friend).

sōl, sōlis, [?, cf. ἥλιος], m., *the sun,* conceived as driving in a chariot from ocean to ocean, and more or less identified with Apollo the sun-god. — Less exactly, *sunshine, the heat of the sun* (as in Eng.), *the light of the sun :* alio sub sole (*in another clime*); sol cadens (*the west, the setting sun,* also *the region of sunset*). — Plur. (each day having its own sun), *the sun, days of sunshine, days, sunshine :* soles condere (*see the sun to rest, close the day*).

sōlācium (sōlāt-), -ī (-iī), [†solac- (cf. ferocia) or solatŏ- (cf. initium) + ium], n., *solace, consolation.* — Plur.: tua (*the solace you afford*); nostri (*my solace*); luctus (*of a grief*).

sōlāmen, -inis, [†sola- (of solor) + men], n., *solace, comfort, alleviation, relief, consolation.*

sōlātium, see solacium.

sōlātus, -a, -um, p.p. of solor.

sōlemnis, see sollemnis.

soleŏ, solitus sum, solēre, [?], 2. v. n., *be wont, be accustomed, use.* — solitus, -a, -um, p.p. as adj., *wonted, customary, accustomed, usual.*

solers, see **sollers**.

olidŏ, -āvī, -ātum, -āre, [†solidŏ-], 1. v. a., *make solid, harden.*

solidus, -a, -um, [†solŏ- (of solum) + dus], adj., *solid, firm, stout, strong.* — Also (without the idea of strength), *solid, entire.* — Fig., *unimpaired, vigorous.* — Neut., *the solid ground, firm ground, solid wood.* — Fig.: in solido (*on firm ground, on a firm footing*).

solium, -ī (-iī), [poss. †solŏ- (reduced) + ium], n., *a seat, a throne.*

sollemnis, -e, [?, †sollo-annus (reduced and declined as adj.)], adj., *yearly, annual, stated, appointed.* — From association with sacred rites, *solemn, sacred, festival, customary, wonted:* imperium (*as before, time-honored*). — Neut., *a sacred rite, funeral rites* (plur.).

sollers, -ertis, [†sollŏ-ars, decl. as adj.], adj., *skilful, expert, well-skilled.*

sollicitŏ (sōl-), -āvī, -ātum, -āre, [†sollicitŏ-], 1. v. a., *stir up, stir, agitate:* telum (*work back and forth*). — Fig., *disturb, trouble, agitate, worry, harass, provoke, stimulate.*

sollicitus (sōl-), -a, -um, [†sollŏcitus], adj., *violently agitated:* mare (*troubled*). — Fig., *agitated, troubled, anxious, in anxiety, in suspense:* amores (*unhappy*).

sōlor, -ātus, -ārī, [?, poss. †sŏlŏ- (cf. in solido)], 1. v. dep. (of persons), *console, relieve, comfort, cheer, encourage.* — Of evils, &c., *alleviate, relieve, lighten:* metum (*calm*); amorem (*solace, lighten the pains of*); solando lenire (*relieve by consolation*).

sōlstitium, -ī, (-iī), [†sol-stitium, cf. iustitium], n., *the summer solstice* (cf. **bruma**, *the winter solstice*), *the summer, the summer heat.*

solum, -ī, [cf. solidus], n., *the ground, the land, the earth, the soil, earth, land, a site:* subtrahitur solum (*the surface flies beneath them*); quocunque solo exis (*spot of earth*); tremefacta solo tellus (*beneath*); urbs Etrusca solo (*in situation*); nostrum solum (*our land*); aequo crede solo (*on an equal footing*); Cereale solum (*support, receptacle*).

sōlum, see **solus**.

sōlus, -a, -um, gen. -īus, [perh. akin to sollus with different suffix], adj., *alone, single, only, the only, in solitude:* lumen quod solum (*his only one*). — Also, *lonely, solitary, deserted.*

solūtus, -a, -um, p.p. of solvo.

solvŏ, solvī, solūtum, solvere, [prob. se- 2. luo, cf. λύω], 3. v. a. Of a bond, *unbind, untie, unloose, cast off, break down:* funes; nexus solvuntur (*are relaxed*); crates; iuga tauris; vittas. — So fig., *loosen, dismiss:* corde metum (cf. **corda metu**) pudorem (*do away with*); foedus (*break*). — Also of the thing bound, *release, set free, let loose, loosen* (from its hold), *detach, let go, unloose, unfurl, break up, open out, extend, break, destroy:* equum colla (*free from the yoke*); crines (*unbind*); agmina caudae solvuntur (*are unwound*, cf. **manipli soluti**); se luctu (*throw off*); puppis solvitur (*is broken up, goes to pieces*); agmina (*break up, divide*); oculos (*close, relax*); solutae Iliades crinem (*with flowing hair*); caelum in Tartara (*confound Heaven and Hell*). — Esp., *paralyze, relax, enervate, dissolve, thaw;* membra; latera solvuntur (*become flabby*); viscera; solvitur in somnos (*sinks*). — Also, *pay* (unbind an obligation), *discharge, perform* (a due). — **solūtus**, -a, -um, p.p. as adj., *unbound, loose, relaxed, free, opened, extended, unrestrained:* ite solutae; manipli (*open, extended*); risus (*unrestrained*); somno vinoque soluti (*buried*).

somnifer, -era, -erum, [†somnŏ-

fer ($\sqrt{}$fer + us)], adj., *soporific :* **cantus** (*that lull to sleep*).

somnium, -ī (-iī), [†somnŏ- (reduced) + ium], n., *a dream.* — Personified, *a Dream.*

somnus, -ī, [$\sqrt{}$sop+nus, cf. ὕπνος], m., *sleep, slumber :* **somno iacens** (*lying asleep*). — Also, *a dream, a vision.* — Also, *night.* — Personified, *Sleep.*

sonipēs, -edis, [†sonŏ-pes], m., *the prancing steed, the horse with ringing hoof.*

sonitus, -ūs, [†soni- (weaker stem of sono) + tus], m., *a sound, a noise, a din, a rattle, a ring, a clang, a roar, a hum, a ringing, clanging, clashing,* or *crackling noise :* **pedum** (*tramp*).

sonŏ, -uī, -itum, -āre, [†sonŏ-], 1. v. n., *give forth a sound, sound, resound, sing noisily, ring, roar, echo, rattle, twang* (of a bow, &c.), *whiz, thunder:* **magno ore** (*sound the loudest tones*); **gradibus sonant** (*plant their ringing hoofs*). — With cogn. acc., *resound with, speak noisily :* **atavos** (*loudly boast*) ; **sonans acerba** (*harsh sounding*); **nec mortale sonans** (*with no mortal voice*); **classica ; nec vox hominem sonat** (*sound human*). — **sonāns, -āntis,** p. as adj., *sounding, resounding, roaring, murmuring, rattling, twanging, noisy, screaming.*

sonor, -ōris, [$\sqrt{}$son (in **sonus**) + or], m., *a sound, a noise, a roar, a ring.*

sonōrus, -a, -um, [perh. †sonor + us, but cf. **decorus**], adj., *sounding, noisy, roaring, rattling, ringing.*

sōns, sontis, [?], adj., *guilty.* — Masc. plur., *the guilty.*

sonus, -ī, [$\sqrt{}$son (cf. **sonor**) + us], m., *a sound, a ring, a murmur, a din, an uproar :* **fit sonus** (*there is a crash*).

Sophoclēus, -a, -um, [Gr. Σοφόκλειος], adj., *of Sophocles,* the great master of tragic poetry. — Also (almost reduced to), *tragic.*

sōpiŏ, -īvī (-iī), -ītum, -īre, [$\sqrt{}$sop (cf. **sopor**), perh. through adj. stem], 4. v. a., *lull to sleep.* — **sōpītus, -a, -um,** p.p. as adj., *put to sleep :* **sopitus somno** (*buried in sleep*). — So, fig.: **arae, ignes** (*half extinguished*); **sensus** (*slumbering*).

sōpītus, -a, -um, p.p. of **sopio.**

sopor, -ōris, [$\sqrt{}$sop (cf. **sopio**) + or], m., *sleep.* — Personified, *Sleep.*

sopōrātus, -a, -um, [p.p. of **soporo**], adj., *soporific, endued with sleep.*

sopōrifer, -era, -erum, [†sopor- (as if †sopori) -fer ($\sqrt{}$fer + us)], adj., *sleep-inducing, drowsy.*

soporus, -a, -um, [perh. †sopor + us, but cf. **decorus**], adj., *drowsy.*

Sōracte, -is, [?], n., a high mountain in Etruria, a few miles from Rome. On its top was a temple of Apollo, where a festival was held in his honor with peculiar rites. (*Mt. St. Oreste.*)

sorbeō, -uī, no sup., **-ēre,** [perh. akin to ῥοφέω], 2. v. a., *suck in, swallow up.*

sorbum, -ī, [?], n., *the sorbus,* a berry, prob. the service berry, *Sorbus domestica.*

sordeō, no perf., no sup., **sordēre,** [†sordi- (of **sordes**)], 2. v. n., *be foul.* — Fig., *be worthless.*

sordidus, -a, -um, [†sordi + dus], adj., *foul, filthy, squalid :* **rura** (*the humble country*).

soror, -ōris, [?, akin to Eng. *sister*], f., *a sister.* — Plur., of the Muses, *the Sisters ;* of the Nymphs, as of kin, *sister nymphs, sisters.*

sors, sortis, [unc. root (cf. **2. sero,** + tis)], f., *a lot, an assigned portion, a division, a part.* — Also, *a lot* (cast), *fate, destiny, fortune, an allotment :* **pugnae, Martis** (*fortune of war*); **ultra sortem senectae** (*beyond the common lot,* &c.) ; **sorte** (*by lot, by fate, by allotment*); **sine sorte** (*without* *lots*, by which the judges were chosen). — Also (from the Italian divination by lots), generally plur., *an oracle*, or *acles, responses, prophetic words*.

sortior, -ītus, -īrī, [†sorti-], 4. v. dep., *allot, choose by lot, take by lot, take* (what is assigned by lot), *divide by lot:* remos (*choose the oarsmen by lot*); fata (*decide*). — Less exactly, *choose, select:* sortitus fortunam oculis (*choosing his opportunity*).

sortītus, -a, -um, p.p. of sortior.

sortītus, -us, [†sorti- (of sortior) + tus], m., *an assignment, an allotment*.

sospes, -itis, [?], adj., *safe, saved, alive*.

spādīx, -īcis, [Gr. σπάδιξ], adj., *bay, brown*.

spargō, sparsī, sparsum, spargere, [√sparg, of unc. kin.], 3. v. a., *strew, scatter, sprinkle, fling around, hurl, cast, spatter:* sparsa per orbem (*dispersed*). — Fig., *spread, diffuse, scatter, fling out*. — With change of point of view, *bestrew, strew, sprinkle, cover far and near* (*here and there*), *spot:* sparsis pellibus albo (*their skins spotted with white*).

sparsus, -a, -um, p.p. of spargo.

Sparta, -ae, [Gr. Σπάρτη], f., also called *Lacedæmon*, the capital of Laconia.

Spartānus, -a, -um, [†Sparta + nus], adj., *Spartan*.

sparus, -ī, [?], m., *a bill-hook* (a rustic weapon of some kind), *a hunting-spear* (?).

spatior, -ātus, -ārī, [†spatiō-], 1. v. dep., *walk back and forth*.

spatium, -ī, (-λ- [?, cf. Æol. σπάδιον, stadium], n. (often plur.), *a space, a distance, an interval, a stretch* (of distance or extent), *room, bounds* (enclosing space), *a course, an extent:* corripiunt spatia (*fly over the course*); addunt se in spatia (*leave the course behind them*, see addo); spatia in sua (*within their bounds*); curvatis spatiis (*in circular course*, enclosing circles); spatiis propioribus (*nearer in its course*). — Fig., *time, room*.

speciēs, -ēī, [√spec (in specio) + ies], f., *an appearance, a sight:* specie movetur (*by appearances*). — Also, *a form, a shape, a phase, a kind:* species animōrum (*the moods*, of living creatures).

specimen, -inis, [†speci- (stem of specio) + men], n., *a mark, a token, an emblem, an example, an instance, a test, a proof*.

spectāculum, -ī, [†spectā- (of specto) + culum], n., *a spectacle, a sight, a display, an exhibition*.

spectātor, -ōris, [†spectā- (of specto) + tor], m., *a spectator*.

spectātus, -a, -um, p.p. of specto.

spectō, -āvī, -ātum, -āre, [†spectŏ- (cf. specio)], 1. v. a., *gaze upon, gaze at, behold, see, watch, look on* (absolutely): ad vitulam (*have an eye on*). — Fig., *view, consider, regard*. — spectātus, -a, -um, p.p., *tried, tested, proved*.

specula, -ae, [†specŏ- (√spec + us) + la, cf. speculum and σκόπελος], f., *a watch-tower, a look-out, a height*.

speculātor, -ōris, [†speculā- (of speculor) + tor], m., *a spy*.

speculātus, -a, -um, p.p. of speculor.

speculor, -ātus, -ārī, [†specula-], 1. v. dep., *watch, reconnoitre, search, examine, look on* (absolutely), *spy out, take sight at, aim at, espy, catch sight of*.

specus, -ūs, [?], m., f., and n., *a cave, a cavern, a chasm*. — Less exactly, *a cavity* (of a wound, *a gash*).

spēlaeum, -ī, [Gr. σπήλαιον], n., *a cave, a cavern, a den*.

spēlunca, -ae, [Gr. σπήλυγξ], f., *a chasm, a cavern, a cave, a cleft* (in a rock), *a grotto*.

Sperchīus (-ēus), -ī, [Gr. Σπερχεῖος], m., *a noted river of Thessaly* flowing from Mt. Pindus to the Maliac Gulf. It was celebrated in Greek poetry.

spernō, sprēvī, sprētum, spernere, [?, √sper], 3. v. a., *remove* (prob. orig. with violence), *spurn.* — Fig., *spurn, scorn, reject, despise, disdain:* spreta forma (*slighted*).

spērŏ, -āvī, -ātum, -āre, [orig. stem of spes, or kindred stem], 1. v. a. and n., *hope.* — Less commonly, *expect, look for, wait for, fear.*

spēs, speī, (old nom. plur. **speres**), [?], f., *hope, expectation.* — Also, *a hope* (i.e. an object on which hope is founded): spemque gregemque (*the flock and its future hopes*).

spīceus, -a, -um, [†spīcā- (reduced) + eus], adj., *bearded.*

pīculum, -ī, [†spīca- (weakened) + lum (n. of -lus)], n., *a dart* (a light missile weapon), *a javelin, an arrow, the sting* (of a bee).

spīna, -ae, [perh. akin to **spīca**], f., *a thorn.* — Also, *the back-bone, the spine.*

spīnētum, -ī, [†spīna- (reduced) + etum, cf. dumetum], n., *a thorn brake, a thicket of thorns.*

spīnus, -ī, [cf. **spīna**], f., *a thorn bush, a sloe tree.*

Spīō, -ūs, [Gr. Σπειώ], f., *a sea-nymph or nereid.*

spīra, -ae, [Gr. σπεῖρα], f., *a coil, a fold.*

spīrābilis, -e, [†spīrā (of spiro) + bilis], adj., *respirable:* spirabile lumen (*light and air*).

spīrāculum, -ī, [†spīrā- (of spiro) + culum, cf. miraculum], n., *breathing-place, vent-hole.*

spīrāmentum, -ī, [†spīrā- (of spiro) + mentum], n., *an air-hole, a pore, a chink:* spiramenta animae (*the air-passages, the lungs*).

spīritus, -ūs, [†spīri- (as if stem of spiro) + tus], m., *the breath, a blast, the breath of life, life, inspiration.* — Also, *high spirit, cour-*age. — Also, *a celestial soul* (the divine ether).

spīrŏ, -āvī, -ātum, -āre, [?], 1. v. n. and a., *breathe, blow, puff, exhale.* — Fig., *breathe from, be diffused from.* — With cog. acc., *breathe forth, breathe, shed.* — Also, *bubble, effervesce, boil:* freta (*seethe*). — spīrāns, -āntis, p.: spirans graviter thyma (*of heavy odor*); aera (*breathing,* alive); exta (*palpitating*).

spissus, -a, -um, [?], adj., *thick* (opposed to **rarus**), *close, crowded:* ager (*compact soil*); arena (*close-packed*).

splendeŏ, -uī, no sup., **-ēre,** [?, †splendŏ- (cf. splendidus)], 2. v. n., *shine, be bright, glisten.*

splendēscŏ, -duī, no sup., **-dēscere,** [†splendē- (of splendeo) + sco], 3. v. n., *shine.*

splendidus, -a, -um, [†splendŏ- (cf. splendeo)+dus], adj., *bright.* — Fig., *magnificent, stately.*

spoliātus, -a, -um, p.p. of spolio.

spoliŏ, -āvī, -ātum, -āre, [†spoliŏ-], 1. v. a., *strip, despoil, spoil.* — Fig., *deprive, bereave, rob.*

spolium, -ī (-iī), [√spol (?, cf. σκύλλω) + ium, perh. through intermediate stem, cf. σκῦλον], n., *spoil, spoils.* — Poetically of other advantages, cf. "conquest," as in English.

sponda, -ae, [?], f., *a bed, a couch.*

spondeŏ, spopondī, spōnsum, spondēre, [√spond, *pour* (libations), through noun-stem, cf. σπονδαί, *a truce*], 2. v. a. and n., *promise, agree, promise one's self, be assured of.* — **spōnsus, -a, -um,** p.p. as subst. Masc., *a betrothed bridegroom.* — Fem., *a betrothed bride, one's betrothed.*

spōnsa, see spondeo.

sponte [abl. of lost **spons,** of unc. kin.], f., *of one's own accord, voluntarily, by one's own wishes, by one's own will, spontaneously:* sponte sua (*spontaneously, of it-*

self, of themselves, without one's agency); sponte mea componere curas (*in my own way, by my own will*); non sponte (*not of his own will*).

sprētus, -a, -um, p.p. of sperno.

spūma, -ae, [√spu (of spuo) + ma], f., *froth, foam:* argenti (*scum of silver, litharge*).

spūmeus, -a, -um, [†spuma- (reduced) + eus], adj., *foamy, foaming, foam-wreathed, foam-covered.*

spūmŏ̄, -āvī, -ātum, -āre, [†spuma-], 1. v. n., *foam, froth, be covered with foam.*—spūmāns, -āntis, p. as adj., *foaming, foamy, frothing, frothy:* spumantes rates (*foam-tossing*); ensis cruore (*reeking*).

spūmōsus, -a, -um, [†spuma- (reduced) + osus], adj., *foamy, foaming.*

spuŏ̄, spuī, spūtum, spuere, [√spu, akin to πτύω], 3. v. a. and n., *spit, spit out.*

squāleŏ̄, -uī, no sup., -ere, [†squalŏ- (perh. of squālus, √squa + lus?, *dogfish*, cf. also squālidus)], 2. v. n., *be rough:* squalentes infode conchas (*rough*).—Of lands, *be ill tilled, be rough, lie waste.*— squālēns, -ēntis, p. as adj., *rough, rugged, scaly, unkempt, embroidered* (cf. asper), *embossed.*

squālor, -ōris, [√squal (as root of squaleo) + or], m., (*roughness*), *foulness, rustiness, filthiness.*

squāma, -ae, [perh. √squa (cf. squalus, squaleo) + ma], f., *a scale, a plate* (in armor).

squāmeus, -a, -um, [†squama- (reduced) + eus], adj., *scaly.*

quāmōsus, -a, -um, [†squama- (reduced) + osus], adj., *scaly.*

stabilis, -e, [√stā (of sto) + bilis], adj., *stable, firm.*—Fig., *lasting, unchanging.*

stabulŏ̄, no perf., no sup., -āre, [†stabulŏ-], 1. v. n. Of animals, *have a stable, be kept.*—Of the Centaurs, *live, dwell, have their stalls.*

stabulum, -ī, [√sta (of sto) + bulum], n., *a stall, a stable, a fold, a hive* (of bees).—Less exactly, *a herd, an abode* (of wild beasts), *a dwelling-place, a cover, a den, a shepherd's hut.*

stagnŏ̄, -āvī, -ātum, -āre, [†stagnŏ-], 1. v. n., *stagnate.*—stagnāns, -āntis, p. as adj., *stagnant, standing in pools, standing.*

stagnum, -ī, [?, unc. root + num, n. of -nus, cf. magnus], n., *a pool, a pond, standing water, a cistern* (open, in a house), *a lake, a stream* (flowing slowly), *deep waters, the depths* (of the sea where the water is still), *the deep water, a sluggish stream, sluggish waters.*

statiŏ̄, -ōnis, [as if √sta+tio, prob. through intermediate stem, cf. statim], f., *a standing.*—Concretely, *a position, a situation, a station, a stopping-place, a resting-place, a harbor, a landing-place, a roadstead, a home, an abode.*—In military sense, *a post.*

statuŏ̄, -uī, -ūtum, -uere, [†statu-], 3. v. a., *set up, set in position, place, build, found, throw up* (a mound).—Esp., *set up* (as an offering), *offer.*—In battle (with loco, cf. cedere loco), *stay, rally.*—Fig., *establish, ordain, determine, resolve.*

status, -us, [√sta (in sto) + tus], m., (*a standing*), *a position, a condition, a state.*

stella, -ae, [prob. †stera- (√ster + a) + la], f., *a star, a planet, a shooting-star, a meteor* (prob. not distinguished as such).—Less exactly, *a constellation.*

stellāns, -āntis, [as if (perh. really) p. of stello (fr. †stella-)], adj., *starry.*

stellātus, -a, -um, [p.p., cf. stellans], adj., *studded with stars, studded* (as with stars).

stelliŏ̄, -ōnis, [†stella- (reduced) + io], m., (*spotted*), *a newt, a lizard.*

sterilis, -e, [†sterŏ- (cf. στερεός,

hard) + lis (-lus)], adj., *barren, sterile, unfruitful*.
sternāx, -ācis, [stern (as if root of sterno) + ax, cf. capax], adj., *throwing its rider* (of a horse), *stumbling, floundering*.
sternō, strāvī, strātum, sternere, [√ster, cf. στορέννυμι], 3. v. a., *spread out, lay flat, throw on the ground, strew.* — Esp. of violent overthrow, *lay low, lay prostrate, fell, strike down, bring down, slay, kill, lay waste, sweep away, mow down, overwhelm, overthrow;* — pass., *fall, lie strewn*: sternamur campis (*we may lie dead on the plains*); so, artus sternit humi moriens (*falls with his limbs* &c.). — In pass. or with reflexive, *throw one's self, lie down.* — Also, *level, smoothe.* — Fig., *crush, depress, cast down*: mortalia corda. — With change of point of view, *bestrew, cover with, strew with.* — strātus, -a, -um, p.p. as adj., *outspread, scattered, slain, strewn, calm* (of the sea). — Neut., *bedding, a bed, a couch, a pavement*: stratum ostrum (*a purple couch*).
Steropēs, -is, [Gr. Στερόπης], m., one of Vulcan's smiths.
Sthenelus, -ī, [Gr. Σθένελος], m.: 1. A Grecian warrior, the charioteer of Diomede; 2. A Trojan warrior slain by Turnus. See also Sthenius.
Sthenius, -ī (-iī), [Gr. Σθένιος], m., a Rutulian slain by Pallas (sometimes read Sthenelus and Helenus).
Stimichōn (-ontis), [Gr. prop. name (not found)], m., a shepherd.
stimulŏ, -āvī, -ātum, -āre, [†stimulŏ-], 1. v. a., *spur on, goad.* — Fig., *goad to frenzy, stimulate, excite, urge, incite*.
stimulus, -ī, [†stimŏ- (√stig, in stinguo, + nus, cf. στιγμός) + lus], m., *a goad, a spur.* — Fig., *an excitement, a stimulus, a spur* (with the same fig. in English): stimuli Bacchi (*the frenzy of Bacchus*); stimuli amari (*cruel sting*).
stipātus, -a, -um, p.p. of stipo.
stīpes, -itis, (also stīps), [†stipi- (√stip + i, akin to stipo, stips, cf. στείβω) + tus or -tis (reduced)], m., (*the solid trunk?*), *a trunk, a tree-trunk, a stub* (a tree with the branches lopped).
stīpō, -āvī, -ātum, -āre, [†stip- (cf. stipes, stips)], 1. v. a., *cram, crowd, pack*: carinis argentum (*stow, load*). — Also, *accompany, escort, attend upon.* — stīpātus, -a, -um, p.p., *crowded, dense, thronging;* — *escorted*.
stipula, -ae, [†stip- (as if stipŏ-) + la], f., (*a little trunk*), *a stalk, straw, stubble*: viridis (*the blade, before the ear forms*).
stīria, -ae, [akin to stilla], f., *an icicle*.
stirps, stirpis, [?, apparently akin to stipes], f. and m., *a stock, a stem, a trunk, a root* (with the stock, cf. radix, *root* alone), *a stump*: nova stirps (*a new stock, a growth for propagation,* cf. below). — Fig., *a stock, a race, a lineage, a family.* — Of individuals, *a scion, the progeny.* — ab stirpe, *at the lower end, at the root, by race, from the root.* — cum stirpe (stirpibus imis), proverbial, *root and branch*.
stīva, -ae, [?], f., *a plough-handle*.
stŏ, stetī, statum, stāre, [√sta, cf. ἵστημι], 1. v. n., *stand* (upright). — In descriptions (often with a qualifying word), *stand, stand by, stand there, be.* — Less exactly, of things, *stand, stand erect, stand out, stand firm, be built, be;* also, (*come and*) *stand.* — So, fig., *stand fast, stand firm, rest on, depend on, remain standing, remain.* — So: ratis, and the like (*lie, anchor, land*); lapides (of statues); stabis de marmore (of a divinity); stet dura silex (*stand carved from* &c., or literally); stat gravis Entellus; mare placidum (*lie*); vires so-

lidae; cura (*centre in*); res Ilia; spes (*rest on*); regno incolumis (*stand unharmed in his power*); bene stat gratia (*gratitude remains*); comae (*stand on end*); lumina flammā (*stand out*); ferri acies; stetit ante pedes. — Esp. of fighting and the like: acie; Iupiter hac stat (*is on this side*); stare contra (*withstand, be opposed*). — Also, *stop, stay, halt, be checked.* — Of weapons, *stand fast, stick, stay, be fixed.* — Esp., *cost.* — Also, *be fixed, be determined, one is resolved.* — Phrases: stare loco, *remain in position, stand firm;* stant causae belli, *seeds of war are sown;* caelum pulvere, *the air hangs thick with dust.*

stomachus, -ī, [Gr. στόμαχος], m., *the stomach.*

strāgēs, -is, [√ster, stra (in sterno) + unc. term.], f., *devastation.* — Esp. in battle, *slaughter, havoc, carnage:* confusae stragis acervus (*a confused heap of slain*).

strāmen, -inis, [√ster, stra (in sterno) + men], n., *straw, leaves* (spread for bedding).

strātum, see sterno.

strātus, -a, -um, p.p. of sterno.

strepitō, no perf., no sup., -āre, [†strepito- (p.p. of strepo)], 1. v. n., *make a noise, clamor.*

strepitus, -ūs, [†strepi-(of strepo) + tus), m., *a noise, a din, a sound* (loud and confused), *a roar, a busy hum* (of a city), *a murmur.*

strepō, -uī, no sup., -ere, [?], 3. v. n., *make a confused noise, ring, clash, clang, sound, rattle, be noisy, resound.* — Of animals, *cackle, scream.*

strictūra, -ae, [√strig (in stringo) + tura, but cf. pictura], f., *a pressure. — a wrought bar* (or mass of iron).

strictus, -a, -um, p.p. of stringo.

strīdeō, strīdī, no sup., strīdēre, [†stridŏ- (√strid + us, cf. stridulus and strido)], 2. v. n., *grate, creak, rattle, roar, hiss, whiz, twang, burr, hum:* vulnus (*hiss*); procella (*howl*).

strīdō, strīdī, no sup., strīdere, [√strid-, of unc. kin.], 3. v. n., same senses as strideo.

strīdor, -ōris, [√strid (in strido) + or], m., *a harsh noise, a creaking, a grating, a clanking, a roar, a whirring, a burring, a humming:* acuunt stridoribus iras (*with noisy hum*).

strīdulus, -a, -um, [†stridŏ- (whence strideo) + lus], adj., *grating, harsh sounding, whirring.*

stringō, strinxī, strictum, stringere, [√strig (cf. στραγγίζω)]; 3. v. a., (orig. sense unc., poss. *squeeze), bind, compress.* — Esp. of weapons, *bare, draw, unsheath.* — Also, *graze, wound slightly:* magno strinxit de corpore Turni (*cut away a bit*). — So, fig., *touch* (the heart): ripas (of a river, *wash, wear away*). — Also, *strip, gather, trim, cut away.*

Strophades, -um, [Gr. Στροφάδες], f. plur., *two islands off the Ionian Sea south of Zacynthus.* To these islands the sons of Boreas pursued the Harpies.

structus, -a, -um, p.p. of struo.

struō, struxī, structum, struere, [√stru, remotely akin to sterno], 3. v. a., *pile, heap up.* — Hence, *build, erect, raise.* — Also, *dispose, arrange, prepare:* penum (*set forth*). — Esp. of war, *draw out, array.* — Fig., *arrange, plot, design, purpose, aim at, accomplish.* — With changed point of view, *heap up with:* altaria donis (*pile, load*).

Strȳmōn, -ŏnis, [Gr. Στρυμών], m., *a river of Macedonia, near Thrace, famous for its cranes.*

Strȳmonius, -a, -um, [Gr. Στρυμόνιος], adj., *of the Strymon, Strymonian.*

Strȳmonius, -ī, [same word as preceding], m., *a Trojan.*

studium, -ī, (-iī), [?, √stud (in studeo) + ium], n., *zeal, eager-*

ness, diligence, care, earnestness, interest, desire, a favorite pursuit, a pursuit, a taste, fondness, curiosity (desire to see), *an employment.* — Also (in reference to some object), *party spirit, favor, enthusiasm* (for one side or the other), *applause* (expression of interest): studia contraria (*different parties*).

stultus, -a, -um, [√stol (in **stolidus,** of unc. kin.) + **tus**], adj., *foolish.* — Masc. as subst., *a simpleton, a blockhead.*

stūpa, see **stuppa.**

stupefaciō, -fēcī, -factum, -facere, [†stupe (akin to **stupeo**) -facio, cf. **labefacio**], 3.v. a., *stun, daze, stupefy, astonish, overwhelm* (with surprise).

stupefactus, -a, -um, p.p. of **stupefacio.**

stupeō, -uī, no sup., **-ēre,** [†stupŏ- (√stup+us, akin to **stipes,** etc.), cf. στύπος, **stupidus**], 2. v. n., *be amazed, be dazzled, be dazed, be thunderstruck, be astonished, be charmed, marvel, wonder, gaze with wonder:* hic stupet attonitus rostris (*is dazzled and amazed*); stupet in Turno (*look with amazement upon*).

stupor, -ōris, [√stup (in **stupeo**) + or], m., *amazement.* — Also, *dullness, deadness.*

stuppa (stūp-), **-ae,** [Gr. στύππη], f., *tow, hemp.*

stuppeus, -a, -um, [†stuppa- (reduced) + eus], adj., *of tow, hempen:* flamma (*burning tow,* used as a means of warfare).

Stygius, -a, -um, [Gr. Στύγιος], adj., *of the Styx, Stygian.* — Also, *of the Lower world, of Hades:* Iuppiter, rex (Pluto); vi soporatum Stygia (*from the world below*).

Styx, -ygis, [Gr. Στύξ], f., the river that surrounded the world below. — Less exactly, *the world below,* Hades.

suādeō, suāsī, suāsum, suādēre, [†suadŏ- (√suad + us, cf. **malesuada**), akin to ἥδομαι], 2. v. n. and a., *advise, counsel, persuade, invite, suggest, prompt, impel:* tibi haec litora Delius (*warned you to seek*).

suādus, see **malesuada.**

suāvis, -e, [√suad (in **suadeo**) + us, with added i, cf. in **gravis,** cf. ἡδύς, Sk. *svādu*], adj., *sweet, fragrant.* — Neut. as adv., *sweetly.*

sub (old **subs,** cf. **obs** and **suspendo**), [mutilated case-form, cf. **super,** akin to ὑπό], prep. with abl., *underneath, below, under, beneath.* — In various connections where the English conception is different, *near* (a high object), *close to, just at, just behind, in* (a lower place or of light and night conceived as above); hence, *during, on* (a particular night), *in* (an army, under arms), *under the protection of, at* (of the breast): sub falsa proditione (*under a false charge of treason*); sub sole (*in the sunlight, under the light of the sun*); sub arma (*in arms, under arms*). — With acc. in same senses, also to the position indicated by the prep., *under, beneath, down, towards, up to* (up under), *about:* sub haec (*upon this, in reply*); sub ora (*before the face,* cf. "under the eyes"); sub auras (*to the light of day, up, forth*); sub noctem (*towards night*). — In comp., as adv., *under,* also *up* (cf. **sub auras**), *in the place of* (coming up to take a place), *slightly* (not the highest degree), *by stealth, towards, after.*

subāctus, -a, -um, p.p. of **subigo.**
subditus, -a, -um, p.p. of **subdo.**
subdō, -didī, -ditum, -dere, [subdo, *put*], 3. v. a., *put under, put beneath, thrust down, apply:* subdita flamma (*kindled in, penetrating to*).

subdūcō, -dūxī, -dūctum, dūcere, [sub-duco], 3. v. a., *draw up:* naves (*beach,* technical). —

Also, *take from under, take away, withdraw, rescue.* — Also, *steal, deprive one of* (changing the construction). — Also (cf. **sub**): subducere se colles (*slope down, draw themselves down*); subducta unda (*slipping from beneath*).

subdūctus, -a, -um, p.p. of subduco.

subeō, -īvī (-iī), -itum, -īre, [subeo], irr. v. n. and a., *go under, go beneath, take up, support, bear;* fig., *undergo.* — Also (lit. and fig.), *come up, spring up, come forth, succeed, take the place of, come after, come next, follow, go near, go by, approach, enter, come to, come, come upon, come to one's aid:* subibat nox (*was climbing*); mucronem (*meet, fall upon*). — Fig., *occur, come to one's mind, suggest itself:* subit ira (*the angry desire comes over* &c., *anger prompts* &c.). — subitus, -a, -um, p.p. as adj., (*coming stealthily*), *sudden, unexpected.* — Abl. subitō, as adv., *suddenly, unexpectedly, of a sudden, all at once.*

sūber, -eris, [?], n., *a cork-tree.* — Less exactly, *cork.*

subferō, see suffero.

sūbiciō (subiiciō), -iēcī, -iectum, -icere, [sub-iacio], 3. v. a., *throw under, place under, place beneath, put under;* — hence, *set* (of fire), *kindle:* caudam utero (*hang his tail*, of a dog); cui rubor ignem (*spread like fire in her cheeks*). — Also, *throw up:* se alnus (*spring up*); corpora saltu in equos (*spring upon*). — Also, *throw in:* pauca furenti (*throw in a few words amid her ravings*). — subiectus, -a, -um, p.p. as adj., *lying beneath,* — *rising, shooting up.* — Masc. plur., *subjects, the conquered.*

subiectō, -āvī, -ātum, -āre, [subiacto, cf. subicio], 1. v. a., *throw up, cast up.*

subiectus, -a, -um, p.p. of subicio.

subigō, -ēgī, -āctum, -igere, [sub-ago], 3. v. a., (*force up* or *under*), *impel, shove.* — Also, *subdue, bring under cultivation, till;* — *compel, force, constrain.* — Esp.: in cote secures (*sharpen*, work down): scrobes subactae (*sunken, dug down*).

subitō, see subeo.

subitus, -a, -um, p.p. of subeo.

subiunctus, -a, -um, p.p. of subiungo.

subiungō, -iunxī, -iunctum, -iungere, [sub-iungo], 3. v. a., *yoke.* — Less exactly, *attach;* — hence, *adorn, furnish.* — Also, *subdue, control, subject.*

sublābor, -lāpsus, -lābī, [sub-labor], 3. v. dep., *fall down, fall back, fail, deteriorate.* — Also (cf. **sub**), *glide stealthily, creep on, slip away* (of time).

sublāpsus, -a, -um, p.p. of sublabor.

sublātus, -a, -um, p.p. of suffero.

sublegō, -lēgī, -lectum, -legere, [sub-lego], 3. v. a., *pick up by stealth, catch* (secretly).

sublevō, -āvī, -ātum, -āre, [sub-levo], 1. v. a., *raise up, lift up.*

subligō, -āvī, -ātum, -āre, [sub-ligo], 1. v. a., *bind beneath, bind on, fit on* (of a shield).

sublīme [abl. of sublimus, collat. with sublimis], adv., *on high, aloft, borne aloft.*

sublimen [sub-limen], adv., read by many for sublime, sublimis, which see (Geor. i. 242).

sublīmis, -e, [sub-limis (akin to limen, wh. see)], adj., *high, lofty.* — Esp., *raised high, borne aloft, on high, mounted.* — Fig., *elate, exultant.* — Often like most adjectives in adv. sense.

sublūceō, no perf. no sup., -ēre, [sub-luceo], 2. v. n., *shine dimly, glimmer.*

sublustris, -e, [sub-lustris (unc. stem akin to lux + tris), cf. in-lustris], adj., *dim, glimmering, dimly-lighted.*

submergō (summ-), -mersī, -mer-

sum, -mergere, [sub-mergo], 3. v. a., *drown, overwhelm, sink:* submersae puppes (*foundered*).
submersus (summ-), -a, -um, p.p. of **submergo.**
submissus (summ-), -a, -um, p.p. of **submitto.**
submittŏ (summ-), -mīsī, -missum, -mittere, [sub-mitto], 3. v. a., (*send under*), *put under, let down:* submissi petimus terram (on *our knees*).—'Fig., *subdue, repress, subject:* animos amori (*sacrifice*).—Technical (in breeding), *grow up, raise, keep.*
submōtus (summ-), -a, -um, p.p. of **submoveo.**
submoveŏ (summ-), -mōvī, -mōtum, -movēre, [sub-moveo], 2. v. a., *raise up, raise high.*—Also, *move away, remove, clear away:* si quem tellus, etc. (*keep afar*); submota spelunca (*hollowed out, with the inside cleared away*).
subnectŏ, -nexuī, -nexum, -nectere, [sub-necto], 3. v. a., *bind beneath, tie beneath, bind under, bind around, fasten, bind, confine:* mentum mitra crinemque subnexus (*binding under his chin and confining his locks*).
subnexus, -a, -um, p.p. of **subnecto.**
subnīxus, -a, -um, [sub-nixus], adj., *supported by, resting on.*
subolēs (sob-), -is, [sub-†oles, cf. indoles], f., (*succeeding generation,* in place of the old), *a new race, a new stock, offspring, progeny, increase* (of flocks), *a stock, a breed, a child, an infant.*
subrēmigŏ (surr-), no perf., no sup., **-āre, [sub-remigo],** 1. v. n., *row quietly along.*
subrīdeŏ (surr-), -rīsī, no sup., **-rīdēre,[sub-rideo],** 2.v. n., *smile.*
subrīgŏ (surr-), see **surgo.**
subsidium, -ī (-iī), [†subsidŏ- (or †subsid) +ium, cf. praesidium], n., (*sitting in reserve*), *a reserve.* — Hence, *reinforcement, a reinforcement, aid, assistance.*

subsīdŏ, -sēdī, -sessum, -sīdere, [sub-sido], 3. v. n. and a., *sink down, crouch down.*—Of *things, sink, settle:* Teucri (*be absorbed, be lost*); Acestes galea (*remain at the bottom*).—Fig., *subside, abate:* undae.—Act., *lie in wait for, waylay.*
subsistŏ, -stitī, no sup., **-sistere, [sub-sisto],** 3. v. a., *stop behind, stay behind, stop, halt, stand still, resist, hold out, stand fast, stand in reserve:* aper (*stand at bay*); Tibris (*stay his course*).
subsum, no perf., **-esse, [sub-sum],** irr. v. n., *be under, be behind, underlie:* suberunt vestigia fraudis (*there will remain some lurking traces,* &c.) ; subest solo natura (*there is a secret power in the soil*).
subtēmen, -inis, [subtex (as if root of **subtexo**) + **men**], n., *the woof, the filling, thread.*
subter [sub + ter (cf. **inter**)], adv., *beneath, below, underneath.*—Prep. (with acc. or abl.), *under, beneath.*
subterlābor, -lāpsus, -lābī, (or separate), **[subter-labor],** 3. v. dep., *glide beneath, flow under, flow below.*
subtexŏ, -texuī, -textum, -texere, [sub-texo], 3.v. a., *weave underneath.*—With change of point of view, (*underweave*), *line, cover with a veil, veil.*
subtrahŏ, -trāxī, -tractum, -trahere, [sub-traho], 3. v. a., *withdraw:* subtrahitur solum (*the sea flies behind them*).
subulcus, -ī, [akin to **sus,** cf. **bubulcus**], m., *a swineherd.*
suburgeŏ, no perf., no sup., **-urgēre, [sub-urgeo],** 2. v. a., *force up to, force towards, drive close to.*
subvectŏ, -āvī, -ātum, -āre, [subvecto, cf. **subveho**], 1. v. a., *carry up, bring up.*—Less exactly, *transport, ferry over* (by a regular conveyance).
subvectus, -a, -um, p.p. of **subveho.**

subvehŏ, -vexī, -vectum, -vehere, [sub-veho], 3. v. a., *carry up, bring up.* — Pass., *be borne up, ride up, sail up:* nox bigis subvecta (*driving her two-horse chariot*).

subveniō, -vēnī, -ventum, -venīre, [sub-venio], 4. v. n., *come to one's relief* (cf. subsidium), *aid, help, relieve.*

subvolvō, no perf., no sup., -volvere, [sub-volvo], 3. v. a., *roll up.*

succēdō, -cēssī, -cessum, -cēdere, [sub-cedo], 3. v. n. and a., *go beneath, pass beneath, go down, come under, enter* (beneath). — Also, *go under* (a burden), *take up, bear, draw* (of a chariot drawn by a yoke). — Also, *go up, come up, go aloft to, rise to:* huc succedunt (*go to the top of this*).—Also, *go to, come to, repair to, go into, approach, enter* (into), *reach.* — Also, *come up* (instead of), *take the place of, succeed* (to), *take up* (in place of another), *go instead of, come in* (after something else): succedunt illi servant qui vices (*come up*, in place of the others); cura patrum cadere et succedere matrum (*take its place*); pro me hostili succedere dextrae (*expose himself for me*, &c.). — Also, *prosper, succeed.*

succendō, -cendī, -cēnsum, -cendere, [sub-†cando, cf. incendo], 3. v. a., *set on fire beneath.* — Fig., *fire, inflame.*

succēnsus, -a, -um, p.p. of succendo.

successus, -ūs, [sub-cessus, cf. incessus and succedo], m., *advance, career.* — Also, *success.*

succīdō, -cīdī, no sup., -cīdere, [sub-cado], 3. v. n., *fall down, sink, sink down.*

succīdō, -cīdī, -cīsum, -cīdere, [sub-caedo], 3. v. a., *cut beneath:* succiso poplite (*cutting the hamstrings*, back of the knee); succisus flos aratro (*cut off at the root*).

succinctus, -a, -um, p.p. of succingo.

succingō, -cinxī, -cinctum, -cingere, [sub-cingo], 3. v. a., *bind under, gird about.*—Also of things put on by girding, *clothe, surround, equip.* — Poetically, of Scylla: succincta latrantibus monstris (*girt about*).

succīsus, -a, -um, p.p. of succido.

succumbō, -cubuī, -cubitum, -cumbere, [sub-cumbo], 3. v. n., *fall under.* — Fig., *yield to, give way to.*

succurrō, -currī, -cursum, -currere, [sub-curro], 3. v. n., *run to aid* (cf. subsidium), *come to the rescue of, go to save, rescue, save, help, relieve, succor.* — Also, *occur* (to one's mind): succurrit pulchrum mori in armis (*the thought occurs to me*, &c.).

Sucrŏ, -ōnis, [?], m., a Rutulian.

sūcus (succus), -ī, [√suc (sug?) + us, cf. sugo], m., *juice, vital moisture, sap.*— Less exactly, *juice* (as cause of flavor), *flavor.* — Fig., *strength, vigor.*

†sudis, -is, [?], f., *a stake.*

sūdō, -āvī, -ātum, -āre, [√sud (prob. through adj.-stem †sudo-), akin to ἴδος, ἱδρώς, Eng. *sweat*], 1. v. n. and a., *sweat:* aera (conceived as sweating). — Less exactly, *distil, flow with, be wet with.* — Also, *exude from.* — Fig., *reek with:* sanguine.

sūdor, -ōris, [√sud (in sudo) + or], m., *sweat, perspiration.* — Also, *toil.*

sūdus, -a, -um, [prob. se-udus], adj., *dry, clear, fair:* per sudum (*in fair weather*).

suēscō, suēvī, suētum, suēscere, [†sue- (of sueo) + sco], 3. v. n. and a., *be wont, be accustomed, be used.* — suētus, -a, -um, p.p., *accustomed, used, wont.*

suētus, -a, -um, p.p. of suesco.

suffectus, -a, -um, p.p. of sufficio.

sufferō, sustulī, sublātum, sufferre, [sub (subs)-fero], irr. v. a., *bear up.* — Fig., *withstand, hold out, resist.* — In o*t*her senses the perf. tenses and p.p. are referred to **tollo**, to which *t*heir simple forms belong.

sufficiō, -fēcī, -fectum, -ficere, [sub-facio], 3. v. a. and n., *dip in, dye.* — Also: **suffectus sanguine et igne** (*suffused* &c., *bloodshot and fiery*). — Also, *substitute, produce in place of another, supply* (one af*t*er ano*t*her), *choose* (anew) : **ipsae regem** (of bees, *choose* kings in succession). — Hence, *supply* (from time to *t*ime), *yield, afford, furnish, produce.* — In*t*rans., (*supply itself*), *be sufficient, suffice, be adequate, hold out, be able.*

sufflō, -īvī (-iī), -ītum, -īre, [sub-fio, los*t* verb akin to **fumus**], 4. v. a., *fumigate.*

uffodiō, -fōdī, -fossum, -fodere, [sub-fodio], 3. v. a., *stab beneath, stab* (from beneath) : **suffosso equo** (some read **suffuso**).

suffossus, -a, -um, p.p. of **suffodio.**

suffundō, -fūdī, -fūsum, -fundere, [sub-fundo], 3. v. a., *pour in* or *on* (supply by pouring). — Fig., *spread over, diffuse.* — **suffūsus, -a, -um,** p.p. (cf. **spargo**), *suffused, filled, overflowing.*

suffūsus, -a, -um, p.p. of **suffundo.**

suggerō (sub-), -gessī, -gestum, -gerere, [sub-gero], 3. v. a., *place under, heap beneath.* — Also, *furnish* (cf. **sufficio**), *supply, supply one with* (changing cons*t*ruc*t*ion).

suī, gen. (nom. wan*t*ing), [pron. √sva], reflex. pron. 3d pers., referring to the subjec*t*, *himself, herself, itself, themselves;* — also reciprocal, *one another, each other, one the other.* — Often *t*ransla*t*ed in Eng. by a pers. pron., unless connected immedia*t*ely wi*t*h a verb, *him, her, it, them:* **silvas involvens secum** (*rolling in woods with it*); **Teucros ad sese vocavit** (*called to him*); **inter se** (*with, from, by, &c., each other*). — Often los*t* in Eng. (the corresponding verb being intrans.), or absorbed in another phrase. — Often in subordina*t*e clauses referring to the main subjec*t*, but it may also refer to the subordina*t*e subject, whence it is some*t*imes ambiguous. — Of*t*en referring to an ac*t*ive agent not the gramma*t*ical subject. — Reduplicated, **sese,** wi*t*hout difference of meaning.

sulcō, -āvī, -ātum, -āre, [†sulcŏ-], 1. v. a., *plough.* — Poe*t*ically, *plough* (the sea).

sulcus, -ī, [akin to ὁλκός, ἕλκω], m., *a furrow.* — Less exac*t*ly, *a trench, a row* (where the vines were originally plan*t*ed in a furrow), *a train* (of a me*t*eor). — Also, of the pa*t*h of a vessel, where the same figure may be kept; — also, fig. of genera*t*ion.

Sulmō, -ōnis, [a *t*own in I*t*aly], m., a Rutulian.

sulphur (sulf-), -uris, [?], n., *sulphur.*

sulphureus (sulf-), -a, -um, [†sulphur + eus], adj., *sulphurous.*

sum, fuī, futūrus, esse, [√es and √bhu, cf. εἰμί and φύω], irr. v. n., *be, exist, live.* — Also, *happen, take place, there is,* &c. : **erunt altera bella ; forte fuit tumulus.** — Esp., in perf. *t*enses, *has been* (*is no more, is past*) : **sed fortuna fuit.** — Less defini*t*ely, *be* (in a place) : **hinc adeo media est via** (*just here is the middle of our way*). — Esp. wi*t*h indef. subj. followed by a rela*t*ive, *there are those who,* &c. : **semper erunt quarum mutari corpora malis.** — So : **est quod,** *there is reason why, one has reason to.* — With dat., *there is with one, there is on one's part, there is for one, one has.* — Esp. : **esto,** *be it so* (expression of assent), *what then.* — Impers., *it is possible, it is allowed, one can, one may.* — Fading away to a mere copula, *be.* — So wi*t*h nouns, adjec*t*ives, adverbs, and phrases. — Esp., wi*t*h gen., *be, require, cost, belong to, be the part of,* *be the duty of.*—With dat., *be, cause, work, bring :* mox erat hoc ipsum exitio (*was their destruction*). — Also, in inf., by a Greek usage, *to be, as :* esse dederat monumentum sui. — **fuat,** old subjunctive instead of sit.—**forem,** etc., equivalent to **essem.**—**fore,** equivalent to **futurus,** etc., **esse.**—**futūrus, -a, -um,** p.p. as adj., *future, coming.* — Neut., *the future.*

summ-, in words compounded with **sub,** see **subm-.**

summa, -ae, [f. of **summus,** see **superus**], f., *the main thing, the chief point, the conclusion of the whole, the main point :* belli (*the issue, the chief command*); haec summa est (*the substance of the whole*).

summus, -a, -um, superl. of **superus.**

sūmō, sūmpsī, sūmptum, sūmere, [sub-emo, *take*], 3. v. a., *take, take up, bear, put* on, *wear.* — Fig., *take* on, *assume, take up, adopt.* — Esp. with words of punishment (cf. **poena**), *exact* (the penalty), *inflict, satisfy* (the debt of vengeance due): poenas inimico a sanguine sumit (*satisfy with hostile blood the vengeance due,* as if the blood were taken in payment).

sumptus, -a, -um, p.p. of **sumo.**

suō, suī, sūtum, suere, [√su, cf. κασσύω, Eng. *sew*], 3. v. a., *sew, stitch, stitch together.* — Neut. plur. of p.p., **sūta, -ōrum,** *a corslet, a breastplate* (orig. made by stitching).

supellex, supellectilis, [probably super-†lectis (akin to **lego**) and †supellecti + lis], f., *household furniture, furniture.* — Also, *implements* (of farming), *utensils.*

super [mutilated case-form of **superus,** cf. ὑπέρ], adv. and prep. Adv., *above, over, over all, upon* or *above* (something expressed in the context), *on the top.* — Also, *over and above, remaining, left, besides, further, furthermore, and then* (in addition to something done).—Also, *from above.* — As if connected with verbs in half-composition (sometimes considered as compounded and sometimes not). — Prep. (with acc.), *upon* (oftener of motion to, real or conceived, cf. **in**), *on the top of, above, over :* quos super (*over whose heads*). — Also, *more than, besides, beyond :* super omnia (*above all, especially*) ; (with abl.), *on, upon* (of rest). — Also, *on* (fig.), *concerning, about, for the sake of, for, in regard to, as to.* — Also : nocte super media (*about*).

superadditus, see **super.**

superaddo, see **super.**

superadstō, -stitī, no sup., **-stāre,** [super-adsto], 1. v. a., *light upon.*

superbia, -ae, [†superbŏ- (reduced) + ia], f., *pride, arrogance, insolence, lawlessness, wantonness.*

superbus, -a, -um, [super (as stem) + bus, cf. **morbus** and ὑπέρβιος], adj., *overweening, overbearing, proud, haughty, arrogant, insolent, wanton, lawless :* gentes (*fierce, lawless*); nece spoliisque superbus (*exultant, flushed*) ; bello superbus (as much as *ferocious,* unrestrained by the rights of others).—Also, of things connected with persons, as in Eng.: verba (*arrogant*); vox (*insolent, taunting*); fastidia; iussa; animi; bellum (as much as *unprovoked*); rates. — Transferred, of things to be proud of, *proud, splendid, magnificent, superb, glorious, noble, high, lofty, stately :* genus; coniugium (*high alliance*); postes. The last two divisions constantly run into each other, as is the case with all transferred adjectives, cf. auro spoliisque postes; fores superbae (*the doors of the noble,* and at the same time *noble doors*). —Also, in a good sense, *proud, lofty, high-minded :* anima Bruti. —Of a horse: superbi gressus (*proud, high-stepping*).

supercilium, -ī (-iī), [super-†cilium (*over the eyelids*)], n., *the eyebrow.* — Transferred, *a brow* (of a hill).

superēmĭneŏ, no perf., no sup., -ēre, [super-emineo], 2. v. a., *tower above, rise above.*

superĭacĭŏ, -iēcī, -iectum, -iacere, [super-iacio], 3. v. a., *throw over.*—By change of point of view, *cover:* scopulos undā (*drench*).

superimmĭneŏ, no perf., no sup., -ēre, [super-immineo], 2. v. n., *overhang, stand high above:* pastorem ense sequens (*lean threateningly over*).

superimpōnŏ, see **super**.

superĭnĭcĭŏ, see **super**.

superĭntŏnŏ, no perf., no sup., -āre, [super-intono, but see **super**], 1. v. n., *rattle above:* ingens clipeum (*fall crashing above,* of a falling warrior). The passage, Æn. ix. 709, is sometimes otherwise explained.

supernē [abl. of supernus, cf. **inferne**], adv., *from above, above, in the world above* (on earth).

supĕrŏ, -āvī, -ātum, -āre, [†superŏ-], 1. v. a. and n. Intrans., *rise above, be above, go over.*— Fig., *surpass, be lofty, be elated:* superans animis; superante forma. — Also, *be over and above, be left, be left alone, remain, survive, be safe, be spared:* quo non carior alter (*no one alive is more dear,* &c.). — Hence, *abound, be in excess, be abundant:* gregibus iuventus (*is exuberant*); fetus.— Act., *rise above, ascend, go over, pass beyond, pass:* limen (*cross*); Gyan (*pass by*); saltu viam (*bound over*). — Fig., *overcome, conquer, vanquish, prevail over, prevail upon, surmount, overpower, outvie.*— Absolutely (with obj. implied), *gain the mastery, win* (of a race); — hence, with cogn. acc., *gain, win:* locum priorem.

superstes, -ĭtis, [super-†stes(√sta + tis, reduced)], adj., *standing by.* — Also (cf. **super**), *surviving, alive, a survivor.*

superstĭtĭŏ, -ōnis, [super-statio, cf. **supersto**, *a standing by,* cf. **superstes** (first meaning)], f., *superstition, dread.* —Transferred, *an object of dread.*

superstŏ, no perf., no sup., -stāre, [super-sto], 1. v. n. and a., *stand over.*

supersum, -fuī, -esse, (also separate), [super-sum], irr. v. n., (*be over and above*), *remain, survive, still remain, be left, last, continue;* —hence, *suffice, be sufficient.*— Also, *abound, be in excess:* semper tibi erunt (*there will be enough, you will have enough*); superest deducere terram (*the earth is still to be,* &c.). — Esp.: quod superest, *what alone remains, as to the rest* (so much for that, now, &c.), *furthermore, now.*

supĕrus, -a, -um, [†supŏ- (wh. sub, cf. ὑπό) + rus, cf. **inferus**], adj. (mostly plur.), *being above, upper, above, on high, high:* regna (of heaven, opposed to earth); orae (*the upper world,* opposed to the earth beneath); caelicolum rex (*high*); convexa (*the concave skies*). — Masc. plur. as subst., *the gods above* (opposed to **inferi**), *Heaven, the world above, men on earth* (opposed to Hades).— Neut. plur. as subst., *the world above, the heavens, the sky, Heaven.* — Compar. **superior, -ōris**.—Superl. **suprēmus**, -a, -um, [unc. form of †superŏ+mus, cf. **extremus**], *highest, very high, lofty, noble.* — Also, *last, extreme, last degree of, supreme:* salus (*last hope of safety*); macies; lumen (*fading*); ad supremum (*to the end*).— Neut. plur. as subst., *the last offices, the last sad rites, funeral rites.* — Neut. sing. as subst., *the last time, for the last time:* supremum congemuit (*groaned his last*).—**summus**, -a, -um, [sub (sup)+mus, cf. **imus**], *highest, the top of, uppermost, topmost, the highest part of, upper, the surface of, the end of, the head of, the tip of, the edge of, outmost, outer, high, lofty:* **fastigia rerum** (*principal points*, but the Latin keeps the figure, *salient points*); **summa tempora** (*the forehead*)—Fig., *highest, supreme, most important, chief, main, utmost, greatest, extreme:* **summa res** (cf. **summa,** *the main struggle, the welfare* of the *state, the issue* of a conflict); **summae res** (*momentous, the highest interests, the welfare*); **dies** (*final, supreme moment*).—Neut. sing. and plur., *the top, the summit*

superveniō, -vēnī, -ventum, -venīre, [super-venio], 4. v. n., *come upon, come up, arrive, happen upon.*

supervolitō, -āvī, no sup., **-āre,** [super-volito], 1. v. a. and n., *fly over, flit about.*

supervolō, no perf., no sup., **-are,** [super-volo], 1. v. a. and n., *fly over.*

supīnātus, -a, -um, p.p. of **supino.**

supīnō, -āvī, -ātum, -āre, [†supinŏ-], 1. v. a., *bend back, lay on the back:* **supinatae glebae** (*turned up, laid over,* in ploughing).

supīnus, -a, -um, [†supŏ- (wh. **sub** and **super,** lengthened) + **nus**], adj., *laid on the back, face uppermost.*—Esp. of the hands, *upturned* (in supplication), *suppliant.*—Also, *sloping* (as if bent back).

suppleō, -plēvī, -plētum, -plēre, [sub-pleo], 2. v. a., *supply* (from *time* to *time,* cf. **sub**), *fill up, make good.*

supplex, -plicis, [sub-plex, cf. **duplex**], adj., (*kneeling*), *suppliant, as a suppliant, entreating, on one's knees* (fig.), *in supplication, in suppliant guise.*—Of things, as in Eng.—Often as a subst., *a suppliant.*

suppliciter [†supplic-.(as if -plici-) + **ter,** prob. n. of **-terus** (reduced), cf. **uter**], adv., *as a suppliant, in suppliant guise.*

supplicium, -ī (-iī), [†supplic+ **ium**], n., (*a kneeling*), *supplication.*—Also, *punishment.*—Less exactly, *a penalty* (like **poena**): **dira tegens supplicia** (*traces of punishment, wounds*).

suppōnō, -posuī, -positum (-**postum**), **pōnere,** [sub-pono], 3. v. a., *place beneath, put under, set* (of fire placed under), *apply* (of a sickle cutting below the head)· **cultros** (*apply to the throat,* the head of the victim being drawn down).—Also (cf. **sub**), *place secretly, substitute:* **mater supposita** (*spurious*).

suppositus, -a, -um, p.p. of **suppono.**

suppostus, -a, -um; see **suppono.**

suprā [prob. abl. of **superus,** cf. **extra**], adv. and prep. Adv., *above, over,* on *the upper side, over it* (*him, them,* &c.): **vertice supra est** (*is higher, taller*).—Prep., *above, over.*—Fig., *beyond, superior to, contrary to:* **morem; modum; omnia** (*above everything*).

suprēmus, -a, -um; see **superus.**

sūra, -ae, [?], f., *the calf of the leg, the ankle, the leg.*

surculus, -ī, [?], m., *a shoot, a sprout, a scion:* **nec surculus idem Crustumiis Syriisque** (*shoots = mode of growth*).

surdus, -a, -um, [√**sur** (*heavy?*, cf. Sk. *svaras*) + **dus**], adj., *deaf:* **surdis non canimus auris** (proverbial).

surgō (rarely **subrigŏ, surr**-), **subrexī, subrectum, surgere,** [sub-regŏ], 3. v. a. and n. Act., *raise, erect.*—Intrans., *raise one's self, rise, arise* (in most English senses).—Of heavenly bodies.—Of growth or increase or coming into being, of the winds, of rivers, of sounds, of tall objects, of waves, of excitement:* **animo sententia** (*occur to*); **limina gradibus**

(*stand high*); oleaster (*spring up*); in dies Tisiphone (*come forth*); surgens in cornua cervus (*with towering horns*); irae ductori (*be aroused*).

sūs, suis, [prob. √SU, *produce, strengthened*, as s*t*em, cf. *ŭs*, Eng. sow, swine], comm., *a swine, a boar, a sow, a pig.*

susceptus, -a, -um, p.p. of suscipio.

suscĭpĭŏ (succ-), -cēpī, -ceptum, -cipere, [subs-capio], 3. v. a., *take up, raise up, catch.* — Esp., *bear, beget.* — Fig., *begin, take up.*

suscĭtŏ, -āvī, -ātum, -āre, [subscito], I. v. a., *shake up, stir up.* — Less exac*t*ly and fig., *rouse, stir, provoke, awake, instigate, urge, kindle, inflame:* caedem (*make havoc*); poenas (*reawakens vengeance* quie*t*ed by lapse of time).

suspectus, -a, -um, p.p. of suspicio.

suspectus, -ūs, [subs-spectus, cf. suspicio], m., *a look upward, height* (measured by the eye looking up), *distance* (upward).

suspendŏ,-pendī,-pensum,-pendere, [subs-pendo], 3. v. a., *hang up, hang, suspend:* votas vestes (as a vo*t*ive offering after any great danger); arma (as an offering); ceras (*fasten up*, of bees building from above). — Less exactly, *raise, lift:* sulco (of the ear*t*h, *plough*). — suspēnsus, -a, -um, p.p., *hung up, suspended, floating* (of Camilla), *perched upon, hung in air.* — Fig., *anxious, in suspense, in alarm:* multo suspensum numine (*awed*).

suspensus, -a, -um, p.p. of suspendo.

suspĭcĭŏ, -spexī, -spectum, -spicere, [subs-specio], 3. v. a. and n., *look up at, look up, look* (at any*t*hing high). — Less exac*t*ly, *gaze at, behold, see, notice, observe.* — suspectus, -a, -um, p.p. as adj., *suspected, an object of suspicion, distrusted, in suspicion.*

suspīrŏ, -āvī, -ātum, -āre, [subspiro], I. v. n., *sigh.*

sustentŏ, -āvī,-ātum, -āre,[substentus, cf. sustineo], I. v. a., *hold up, support:* sustentata diu (of a ship on a rock, *kept afloat, kept above the waves*); aciem (*hold the line,* main*t*ain the fight). — Also, *hold out against, keep in check.* — Fig., *support, sustain, keep up.*

sustĭneŏ, -tinuī, -tentum, -tinēre, [subs-teneo], 2. v. a. and n., *hold up, support, bear up, bear, carry, hold.* — Also, *withstand, keep in check, keep off, hold out, bear a shock.* — Also, *support, sustain, feed.*

sustuli, see tollo.

susurro, no perf., no sup., -āre, [†susurrŏ-], I. v. n., *hum, buzz, murmur.*

susurrus, -ī, [redupl. root (perh. from the sound)+ us], m., *a whisper, a murmur.*

sūta, -ōrum; see suo.

sūtilis, -e, [†sutŏ- (of sutus) + lis], adj., *sewn, sewed:* cymba (*patched,* either of hides or papyrus, *barkcanoe?*); balteus(*leather, st*i*tched*).

sūtus, -a, -um, p.p. of suo.

suus, -a, -um, [pron. √SVA + YAS (or -us), cf. ἑός], poss. pron. (of 3d pers. reflex.), *his, her, its, their.* — Often emphatic, *his own,* &c. — Masc. plur., *his* &c. *friends, followers, companions, fellow-citizens, men, race,* &c. — Neu*t*., *his* &c. *affairs, property, interests,* &c. — Also (not necessarily referring to subjec*t*), *one's own, favoring, propitious, favorable, suitable, appropriate, fitting.* — Wi*t*h quisque (best rendered by a change of cons*t*ruc*t*ion), *every man's, each one's:* trahit sua quemque voluptas (*each one's* &c. *draws him*).

Sybaris, -is, [Gr. Σύβαρις], m., *a Trojan.*

Sy̆chaeus (Sī-), -ī, m., *the husband of Dido.*

Symaethius, -a, -um, [†Symaethŏ- (reduced)+ ius, cf. Σύμαιθος], adj., *of the Symæthus* (a river at the east end of Sicily), *Symæthian.*

Syrācosius, -a, -um, [Gr. Συρακόσιος], adj., *Syracusan, of Syracuse* (the chief city of Sicily).

Syrius, -a, -um, [Gr. Σύριος], adj., *of Syria* (the country at the eastern end of the Mediterranean, used loosely for all that region), *Syrian, Assyrian.* From this region came many fruits, spices, and fragrant herbs and gums.

Syrtis, -is, [Gr. Σύρτις], f., **Maior** (*Gulf of Sidra*) and **Minor** (*Gulf of Cabes*), the name of two shallow bays on the northern coast of Libya, held to be most dangerous for mariners, prob. on account of violent seas in shallow waters as well as of shifting sands. — Plur., *the Syrtes,* used loosely of the sandbanks and bars of all that region.

T.

tābeō, no perf., no sup., **-ēre,** [††tabi (or -e, in tabes)], 2. v. n., *waste away, melt away:* tabentes artus (*dripping,* as if melting away); tabentes genae (*wasted, with* care).

tābēs, -is, [prob. √ta (cf. τήκω) + bes (or -bis), cf. plebes], f., *a wasting, pining.*

tābidus, -a, -um, [††tabi- (in tabes, cf. tabeo) + dus], adj., *wasting.*

tabula, -ae, [unc. stem (wh. also **taberna**)+la (f. of -lus)], f., *a plank, a board.*

tabulārius, -a, -um, [††tabulari-(tabula+ris)+us], adj., (*of records,* tabula). — Neut. as subst., *archives, record office, registry.*

tabulātus, -a, -um, [††tabula+tus, cf. armatus], adj., *boarded, floored.* — Neut. as subst., *a floor, a story, an upper story:* iuncturas tabulata dabant (as one story was built upon another). — Also, of trees, *a row, a tier, a layer.*

tābum, -ī, [ta+bum (n. of -bus), cf. tabes], n., *matter, moisture* (of putrefaction), *gore.*—Also, *putrefaction, corruption :* ora tristi pallida tabo; infecit pabula tabo.

Taburnus, -ī, [?], m., a mountain between Samnium and Campania, south of the Caudine pass. The southern slope of it was famous for its fertility, and the mountain was one of the great pasture-grounds.

taceo, -uī, -itum, -ēre, [prob. adj.-stem ††tacŏ- of uncertain kin.], 2. v. n. and a., *be silent, keep silence.* — Of things, *be silent, be noiseless, be still.* — Act., *pass in silence, leave unsung:* tacitam se prodit (*without any words*). — **tacitus, -a, -um,** p.p. as adj., *silent.* — Often transferred, *silent:* lumina (*silent glance*). — Often equal to adv., *silently.* — Of things, *still, noiseless, quiet, silent :* Amyclae (*deserted*). — Also, *secret, unseen, unnoticed.*—per tacitum, *in silence, quietly.*

tacitus, -a, -um, p.p. of taceo.

tactus, -ūs, [√tag (in tango) + tus], m., *a touch, contact:* abstinuit tactu (*refused to touch,* the gates in the context).

tactus, -a, -um, p.p. of tango,

taeda, -ae, [?], f., *a pine tree.* — Less exactly, *pine wood, a pine torch, a torch.* — Poetically (from the use of torches at weddings), *marriage.*

taedet, -uit, (taesum, pertaesum est), **taedēre,** [?], 2.v. impers., *it wearies, it disgusts, one is weary* (*disgusted*), *one loathes.* — With the object of the feeling in the genitive or an inf. clause.

taedium, -ī (-iī), [††taedŏ- (wh. **taedet** and **taedulus**) + ium], n., *weariness, disgust.*

Taenarius,-a, -um, [Gr.Ταινάριος], adj., *of Tænarus* (a promontory

at the southern extremity of Laconia, with a cave fabled to be an entrance to the world below).— Hence, *of Hades.*
taenia, -ae, [Gr. ταινία], f., *a ribbon, a fillet:* taenia vittae (*the band of the fillet,* the material of the ornament).
taeter (tē-), -tra, -trum, [perh. akin to **taedet**], adj., *foul, loathsome, disgusting.*
taetricus, -a, -um, [†taetrŏ+cus], adj., (*repulsive*), *harsh, forbidding.* See also **Tetrica.**
Tagus, -ī, [a river of Lusitania], m., a Latin hero.
tālāris, -e, [†talo- (reduced) + aris], adj., *of the heel.* — Neut. plur., *the talaria,* the winged sandals of Mercury.
talentum, -ī, [Gr. τάλαντον], n., *a talent,* a Greek weight varying from about sixty to about one hundred pounds. Used indefinitely for masses and quantities, as in Eng. "*tons,*" *weight, mass.*
tālis, -e, [pron. √ta (cf. **tam, tó**) + **alis**], pron. adj., *such* (with correlative *as*), *in such guise, so* (equal to an adv.).— Often (without correlative), *of what* follows or goes before, *such, like this, this (that, these,* &c.). — Esp. in neut. plur. **talia,** *like this, words like these, such words as these, such things as these, such as this, thus, in such wise:* tali ore locutus (*these words*). — Or, as is indicated by the context, *such, this (these,* &c.), *like this, in this guise.*—Esp. with emphasis, *such as this* &c., *so great, so important, thus or so* (with adj. to be supplied from the context): non Achilles talis in hoste fuit (*not thus cruel,* as you); nunquam animam talem amittes (*so mean a life as yours*).
Talos, -ī, [?], m., a Rutulian.
talpa, -ae, [?], f. and m., *a mole.*
tālus, -ī, [?], m., *the ankle-bone, the ankle.*
tam [unc. case-form of pron. √ta,

cf. **nam**], adv., *so, so much* (with correl. *as*), *as* (demonstrative), *as much, to such a degree.* — Without correl., *so* (as is indicated by the context, cf. **talis**). — With comparatives (and superlatives in same sense), *the . . . the.* — Esp.: tam . . . quam, *as well . . . as, no less . . . than.* — Often with an adj. where in Eng. *such* is used to modify the whole idea: tam dira cupido (*such dread desire*).
tamen [unc. form. fr. pron. √ta], adv. (opposed *to* a concession), *yet, still, however, nevertheless, none the less, after all, just as well.* Often the concession is only implied in the context.
Tanager, -gri, [?], m., a river of Lucania, in a grazing region.
Tanais, -is, [Gr. Ταναΐς], m.: 1. A river of Scythia (*the Don*); 2. A Trojan in Æneas' expedition.
tandem [tam-dem, cf. **idem**], adv. (orig. sense unc.), *at length, at last, finally.* — With interrogative and imperative clauses indicating impatience, *pray, I pray, tell me:* huc tandem concede (*I entreat*).
tangō, tetigī, tactum, tangere, [√tag, cf. τεταγών], 3. v. a., *touch, take hold of, reach, attain:* dextram (*grasp*); cubile eri (*share the couch*). — Hence, *have to do with, be involved in.* — Fig., *move, touch, affect, come home to one.* — **tactus, -a, -um,** p.p., *touched.* — Esp.: de caelo, *struck by lightning.*
tanquam (tam-), [tam-quam], adv., *as much as.* — With **si,** *just as if.*—Also, without **si,** *just as if, as if.* — Often with irony, *as if forsooth.*
tantus, -a, -um, [for tavantus, pron. √ta + vant (cf. -osus) + us], pron. adj., *so great, so much, such* (in size, &c., with correl. *as*), *as* (demonstrative) *great, such great.* — Often without correl., *so great* (as is indicated by the context, cf. **talis**), *so much, such, like this, this great, that great:* tantae molis

erat (so much as appears in the context). — Also, introducing a clause almost causal, *so great*, &c. (*that* it accounts for the preceding statement): obstupuere animi tantorum terga boum rigebant (they were thunderstruck, and the hides of such huge, &c., as those they saw, accounted for their amazement). — **tantō**, abl., *with* comparatives and the like, *so much the more* ... (*as*), (*the more*) ... *the more*. — **tantī**, gen., *with* **sum**, *it is worth the price, it is worth while*. — **tantum**, acc. as adv., *so much, in such a degree, as much* ... (*as*), *no more* ... (*than*), *thus far, so long;* — also, *so much* (and no more), *only, merely*. — With **modo**, doubling the words without change of sense. — Neut. as subst., *so much*, &c.; — with partitive gen., *so much* (*of*, as adj. in Eng.), *so great* (and similar expressions of degree according *to* the context).

tapēte, -is, (acc. plur. **tapētas**, abl. **tapētis**), [Gr. τάπης], n.(and m.), *hangings, coverings, drapery.* — Also, *housings* (of horses).

Tarchētius, -ī, [?], m., a Rutulian.

Tarchō (-ōn), -ontis (-ōnis), [an Etruscan word], m., an Etrurian ally of Æneas.

tardātus, -a, -um, p.p. of tardo.

tardē [abl. of **tardus**], adv., *slowly:* crescens (*slow-growing*).

tardō, -āvī, -ātum, -āre, [†tardŏ-], 1. v. a., *retard, keep back, impede, hamper, embarrass, enfeeble, dull, make sluggish.* — **tardāns, -antis,** p. as adj., *sluggish* (creeping slow): senectus.

tardus, -a, -um, [perh. akin to traho], adj., *slow, sluggish, tardy, slow-moving, lazy, inactive, dull, impeded, lingering, late.*

Tarentum, -ī, [Gr. Τάρας corrupted], n., a city of Apulia at the northeast corner of the great gulf which indents the southern extremity of Italy. Its territory was one of the most fertile districts of Italy.

Tarpēius, -a, -um, [†Tarpa + ius, of unc. kin.], adj., a Roman gentile name, in some unknown manner connected with the rock of the Capitol. — **arx,** *the Capitol* of Rome.— sedes, *the Tarpeian rock.* — Fem. *Tarpeia:* 1. The maiden who betrayed the Capitol to the Sabines; 2. The name given by Virgil to an attendant of Camilla.

Tarquinius, -a, -um, [Etruscan word (akin to **Tarchon**) Latinized], adj., a Roman gentile name. — Esp., Tarquinius Superbus, *Tarquin,* the last king of Rome. — Plur., *the Tarquins*, the dynasty who were supposed to have come from Tarquinii, and reigned many years at Rome. Also as adj., *Tarquinian.*

Tarquitus, -ī, [akin to **Tarquinius**], m., a Latin hero, slain by Æneas.

Tartareus, -a, -um, [Gr. Ταρτάρειος], adj., *of Tartarus, Tartarean, infernal, hellish* (as in Eng.).

Tartarus, -ī, (plur. **-a, -ōrum**), [Gr. Τάρταρος, -α], m. (n.), (a deep abyss below the infernal world). — Hence, *Tartarus,* the abode of the damned, the lower world (generally).

Tatius, -ī (-iī), [an adj. of unc. kin. (tata?)], m., *Titus Tatius,* a king of the Sabines, with whom Romulus was supposed to have shared his kingdom.

taureus, -a, -um, [†taurŏ- (reduced) + eus], adj., *of a bull:* terga (*bulls' hides*)

taurīnus, -a, -um, [†taurŏ- (reduced) + inus], adj., *of a bull:* vultus (*bull's face*).— Less exactly, *of bull's hide, leathern.*

taurus, -ī, [prob. for STAURUS, cf. ταῦρος, Eng. *steer*], m., *a bull.* — Also, *a bull's hide.* — Also, *the Bull, Taurus* (the constellation).

taxus, -ī, [?], f., *a yew tree, a yew.*

Tāygetē, -ēs, [Gr. Ταϋγέτη], f., one of the Pleiades (used for the constellation).

Vocabulary.

Tāygetus, -ī, also **-a, -orum,** [Gr. Ταΰγετον], m. and n., a mountain-range of Laconia, no/ed for its hun/ing-grounds and its bacchanalian fes/ivi/ies.

tectum, see **tego.**

tectus, -a, -um, p.p. of **tego.**

tēcum, see **tu.**

Tegeaeus(-ēus), -a, -um, [borrowed or imi/a/ed fr. Gr. Τεγέα (as if Τεγεαῖος)], adj., *of Tegea* (a /own of Arcadia). — Less exactly, *Arcadian.* — Masc. (perh. adj.), *god of Arcadia* (epi/he/ of Pan, whose favorite haun/s were in /ha/ coun/ry).

tegmen(tegu-, tegi-), -inis, [√teg (in **tego**) + **men**], n., *a covering, a garb, clo/hing, a defence* (means of defence), *a pro/ec/ion, armor, a shield.* — Also, *shade, a skin* (used as clo/hing).

tegŏ, texī, tectum, tegere, [√teg, akin to στέγω], 3. v. a., *cover, conceal, protect, shelter, surround;* — esp. of escort, *surround (attend).* — Also, *clothe, defend, deck, adorn, veil* (for sacred purposes). — Also, *plan/, sow, bury* (the dead), *close* (the eyes), *shu/ one's self in.* — Fig., *cover, hide, conceal.* — **tectus, -a, -um,** p.p., *covered, concealed, hidden, pro/ec/ed, decked, caparisoned, keeping silence, dissimula/ing* (in mid. sense, *concealing one's self*). — Neu/. (sing. and plur.), *a roof, a ceiling, a house, a hall, an abode, a home* (of men or beas/s), *a palace, a hiding-place, battlements* (the top of a wall): **acies** (*covered column,* the testudo).

tegumen, see **tegmen.**

tēla, -ae, [prob. √tex (in **texo**) + la], f., *a web* (in the loom), *the warp* (perh. the orig. sense), *weaving* (cf. "*the loom*"), *a loom:* **tela curas solabar aniles** (*the loom*).

Tēleboae, -ārum, [Gr. Τηλεβόαι], m. plur., some islands on the Leucadian coast, whence the settlers of Capri were supposed /o have come.

tellūs, -ūris, [?], f., *the earth.* — Esp., *the soil, land, the ground, earth* (as ma/erial). — Personified, *Earth.* — Also, *a land, a region, a country.*

Telōn, -ōnis(?), [?], m., a hero of Capri, fa/her of Œbalus.

tēlum, -ī, [?], n., *a weapon* (missile), *a missile, a javelin, a dart, an arrow, a shaft.* — Less exact/ly, *a weapon* (of any kind, *the cestus, the beam* of Ulysses wi/h which he bored out the Cyclops' eye).

temerātus, -a, -um, p.p. of **temero.**

temerē [abl. of †temerŏ, wh. **temerŏ**], adv., *heedlessly, carelessly, at random, in confusion, without thought, without design, without reason.* — **non** (**haud**) **temere,** *not without a meaning, no accident.*

temerŏ, -āvī, -ātum, -are, [†temerŏ-], 1. v. a., (*treat as of no consequence?*), *profane, pollute, desecrate.*

temnŏ, perf. and sup. not found, **temnere,** [√tem, *cut,* cf. τέμνω], 3. v. a., *despise, scorn, defy, treat with contempt, be disdainful:* **pars belli haud temnenda** (*no despicable, no insignifican/*).

tēmŏ, -ōnis, [perh. akin to **telum**], m., *a pole* (of a chario/, &c.), *the beam* (of a plough).

Tempē, indecl., [Gr. n. plur. Τέμπη], n. plur., a valley in Thessaly, famous for its beau/y. — Less exactly, *a charming valley.*

temperŏ, -āvī, -ātum, -āre, [†temper- (of **tempus,** in orig. sense of *portion*)], 1. v. a. and n., *mix* (in due propor/ion). — Hence, *qualify, temper* (change or dilu/e by mixing): **aera vesper** (*cool*); **scatebris arentia arva** (*refresh,* reduce the parching hea/); **aequor** (*calm*); — so: **iras** (*appease*). — Also (act in due proportion), *restrain one's self, refrain, spare:* **male sibi unda carinis** (*hardly suffer the ships /o live,* keep its hands off them).

tempestās, -ātis, [†tempos- (of **tempus,** prob. as adj.) + tas], f., *a space of time, a season.* — Less exactly, *the weather, weather* (at a particular moment), *state of the weather.* — Esp., *bad weather, a storm, a tempest, a gale.* — Fig. (as in Eng.), *storm, tempest, blast, shower, hail;* — also, where the fig. is not used in Eng., *calamity, misfortune.*

tempestīvus, -a, -um, [†tempestŏ- (cf. **intempestus**) + ivus, cf. **captus, captivus**], adj., *seasonable, timely, in its season.*

templum, -ī, [prob. †temŏ- (√tem, cf. τέμνω + us) + lum, cf. τέμενος], n., (in augury) *a consecrated spot* (marked off by the augur's wand), *a quarter* (of the sky), *a space.* — From consecration, *a temple, a tomb* (as a temple of the manes).

temptāmentum (tentā-), -ī, [†temptā- (of **tempto**) + mentum], n., *an attempt, a solicitation.*

temptō, -āvī, -ātum, -āre, [†tentŏ- (of p.p. of **tendo**)], 1. v. a., *try* (the strength of, lit. and fig.), *attack, assail, disturb, trouble, injure:* **pabula fetas**; **oves scabies**; **pedes** (of wine, *trip up*); — *attempt, try* (a thing experimentally), *venture on, tempt, solicit, search, examine* (*try* to see): **praelia** (*try the issue of*); **auxilium** (*seek*); **se** (*try one's powers*); **temptantum ora** (*those who try it*); **vestes** (*try on, try to wear*); **animum precando** (*try, test*). — Hence, *use, employ, practise:* **patrias artes.**— With inf., *try, endeavor, attempt.*

tempus, -oris, [√tem (cf. τέμνω + us), n., (*a section*), *a time, a point of time, an interval, a season* (of the year), *a period, a moment, time* (as continuous). — Esp., *the time* (the right time), *the best time, time* (with **esse**), *high time, an occasion* (as fitting), *an opportunity.* — Also, *the times, circumstances, state* (of affairs), *an exigency, an occasion:* **pro tempore** (*for the occasion, according to one's circumstances*). — Also, (*the right spot,* cf. **templum,** *the fatal spot,* usually plur.), *the temple, the temples;* — *the face, the head.*

tenāx, -ācis, [√ten+ax, cf. **capax**], adj., *tenacious, clinging* (to something), *greedy, grasping:* **vincla** (*confining*); **Fama ficti** (*persistent in*).—Also, *holding together, clinging* (together), *sticky, firm:* **flos** (*persistent,* not dropping off).

tendō, tetendī, tentum (tēnsum), **tendere,** [√tend, further formation of √ten (in **teneo**)], 3. v. a., *stretch, stretch out, extend, hold out, offer:* **bracchia huc illuc**; **dextram**; **munera**; **caelo manus cum voce** (*stretched out his hands and raised his voice*); **ramos** (*spread*); **illa** (*strain*); — intrans., *extend.* — Esp., *spread* (a tent), *encamp.* — Also, *distend, strain, fill* (of sails), *hold tight, draw in* (of reins), *bend* (a bow): **ubera**; **vela**; **retinacula**; **vim et vincula capto** (*hold fast the captive with,* &c.). — Also, *aim, aim at, direct:* **spicula cornu** (*fit, aim*); **quo tendant ferrum.** — With **gressus iter,** etc., (or intrans. without), *make one's way, hold one's course, turn one's steps, make headway, proceed, advance, come, go, lead* (of a path): **contra** (*reply*).— Hence, with inf., *intend, strive, struggle.*

tenebrae, -arum, [?], f. plur., *darkness, night, gloom.* — Esp., *the Shades, the dim shades, the world below.*

tenebrōsus, -a, -um, [†tenebra- (reduced) + osus], adj., *dark, darkened, dim, gloomy.*

Tenedos, -ī, [Gr. Τένεδος], f., an island in the Ægean, off the Troad.

teneō, tenuī, tentum, tenēre, [√ten- (in **tendo**)], 2. v. a. and n., *hold, hold* (in the hand), *carry, bear, cling to, grasp:* **tela** (*bear arms,* as in Eng.); **arbos poma** (*bear*); **tenenti similis** (*as if he* *had him in his grasp*); in media morte tenetur(*is in the very grasp of death*).—Hence,*occupy,inhabit, possess, hold possession of, control, hold bound, guard, rule, have, be in* (a place), *fill* (merely being there), *reach* (and so, *hold*): altum (*be on*); polum (*cover*); auros (*sail through*); prima (*hold the first place*); metum (*gain*); muros (*reach*); peste teneri (*be overcome*). — Fig., *possess* (of a passion, &c.), *fill:* voluptas silvas.— Also, *hold* (*fast*), *maintain, retain, keep, remember:* se rupes (*hold fast*); vestigia (*keep one's feet, plant firmly*); morem hunc sacrorum. — Also, *hold* (back), *bind, detain, delay, hold* (bound), *confine, restrain, keep in, keep out, surround* (with siege), *encompass:* nox lunam in nube (*hide*); quo te cunque lacus fonte.— Fig., *detain, entice, allure, attract.*— So (in any position), *keep* (*t*his way or tha*t*), *direct, turn:* immota lumina; intenti ora (*held their faces in eager attention*); veteris Dei se more tenens (*living*, &c.).—Also, of a course, *keep, hold:* iter; fugam (*pursue one's flight*); medium iter. — Absolu*t*ely (wi*t*h implied objec*t*): tenent Danai qua deficit ignis (*possess whatever,* &c.).

tener, -era, -erum, [†tene (√ten wi*t*h s*t*em-vowel)+ rus], adj., *delicate, tender, soft, frail, plastic:* orbs mundi (*fluid, plastic,* not yet hardened); umor (*permeating*), *young, youthful, tender, delicate* (from you*t*h). — Masc. plur., *the young, young shoots:* a teneris (*from the earliest age*).

tenor, -ōris, [√ten (in teneo) + or], m., *a course* (cf. tenere iter, etc.), *a character*.

tento, see tempto.

tentōrium, -ī (-iī), [†tentŏ- (p.p. of tendo, reduced) + orium, n. of adj.], n., (*place of tents*), *a tent*.

tenuis, -e, [√ten (in tendo, teneo) + us, cf. gravis and Sk. *tanus*], adj., *thin* (of texture or consis*t*ency), *fine, delicate, slender, fragile, light, airy, substanceless, yielding, shallow* (of a burrow), *narrow, slight, light* (of soil), *permeating, subtle, heady* (of wine): aurum (*thread of*); spiramenta (*fine, minute*). — Fig., *humble, feeble, slight, unimportant, poor:* in tenui labor (*in a trifling matter*).

tenuō, -āvī, -ātum, -āre,[†tenui-], 1. v. a., *make thin, waste away, cause to waste away, reduce*.

tenus [√ten (in teneo) + us, n. acc.], prep., *as far as, up to*.

tepefaciō, -fēcī, -factum, -facere, [stem akin to tepeo-facio], cf. calefacio], 3. v. a., *warm, heat* (modera*t*ely). — tepefactus, -a, -um, p.p., *warmed, heated:* terra (*reeking*); hasta (*steeped*).

tepefactus, -a, -um, p.p. of tepefacio.

tepeō, no perf., no sup., -ēre, [√tep (akin to Sk. √tap, *burn*), prob. *t*hrough adj.-stem †tepŏ-, cf. tepidus], 2. v. n., *be warm:* caede humus (*reek*).

tepēscō, tepuī, no sup., tepescere, [†tepē- (of tepeo)], 3. v. n., *become warm:* ferrum in pulmone (*be steeped*).

tepidus, -a, -um, [as if (or really) †tepŏ- (wh. tepeo) + dus], adj., *warm, heated, simmering, reeking, still warm* (of a body), *not yet cold*.

ter [petrified form of tres], adv., *three times, thrice.* — There was of*t*en a supers*t*i*t*ion connec*t*ed wi*t*h *t*his number. — ter centum, *thrice a hundred, three hundred.*— terque quaterque, *thrice and again,* indefini*t*ely for *three or four times*. — terque quaterque beati, *thrice and four times blest* (of degree).

terebinthus, -ī, [Gr. τερέβινθος], f., *a turpentine tree, turpentine wood*.

terebrō, -āvī, -ātum, -āre, [†terebra-], 1. v. a., *bore, bore into, bore out.*

teres, -etis, [†tere- (of tero) + tis (reduced)], adj., *smooth and round* (cylindrical), *round, smooth, well rounded:* habena (*well rolled?, well twisted?,* not left flat, but worked into a round cord like a shoe-string).

Tēreus, -eī, (acc. -ea), [Gr. Τηρεύς], m.: 1. A king of Thrace whose wife Progne along with her sister Philomela served up his son Itys at his table. All three were changed into birds; 2. A Trojan.

tergeminus (trī-), -a, -um, adj., *having three bodies, threefold, triple.*

tergeō, tersī, tersum, tergēre (also -ō, -ere), [?], 2. (3.) v. a., *clean, polish.*

tergum, -ī, [√terg + um, poss. akin to **tergeo,** orig. *hide?*], n., *the back* (of men and animals): terga resolvit (*body,* of Cerberus). — Less exactly, *a ridge* (of a furrow), *a furrow?, the side* (of a tree, as if it faced the south), *the upper part of the body* (of a serpent). — Also (see above), *a hide,* esp. *a bull's hide,* hence *a shield, a layer* (of a shield no longer made of hide). — a tergo, *from behind, in the rear, behind.* — in tergum, *backward.*

tergus, -oris, [√terg (cf. **tergum**) + us], n., *the back* (only of animals). — Also (cf. **tergum**), *a hide.*

terminō, -āvī, -ātum, -āre, [†terminō-], 1. v. a., *fix bounds to, limit.*

terminus, -ī, [√ter (in trans) + minus, cf. -μενος], m., *a bound, a limit.* — Fig., *a fixed bound, a destined end.*

ternus, -a, -um, usually plur., [†tri + nus], adj., *threefold, three at a time, three each.* — Less exactly, *three.* — Regularly: terna arma, *three sets of arms;* terna hiberna, *three winters.*

terō, trīvī, trītum, terere, [√ter, cf. τείρω (for τεργω)], 3. v. a., *rub, crush, wear, chafe, wear smooth* (by constant use): iter (*wear a path,* of the ant); calcem calce Diores (*tread on the heels*); labore manum (*callous, chafe*). — Esp., *thresh, press* (of olives). — Also, *polish, turn.* — Also, *wear away* (of time), *waste, pass:* otia (*waste the time in idleness*). — In pass. by a change of idiom, *rub against:* alvo balteus (lit., *is rubbed by*).

terra, -ae, [prob. for **tersa,** √tors (in torreo) + a, cf. τέρσω, Eng. *thirst*], f., *dry land* (as opposed to sea), *the earth, the land.* — Also, *the earth* (in all relations), *land, soil, the ground:* semina terrarum (*earth,* as an element). — Personified, *Earth.* — Also, *a land, a country.* — terra marique, *by land and sea;* orbis terrarum, *the circle* (according to earlier notions) *of the lands, the whole world, the world.*

terrēnus, -a, -um, [†terra- (with unc. change of stem) + nus], adj., *earthy, of earth:* artus (of earthy materials).

terreō, -uī, -itum, -ēre, [?, prob. fr. adj.-stem], 2. v. a., *frighten, alarm, affright, scare, terrify;* — *frighten away, scare away;* — *drive in terror, hunt, pursue:* me patris imago (*haunt*); terruit Auster euntes (equal to *deter,* though the orig. fig. is kept); frustra terrebere nimbis (*needlessly fear*).

terreus, -a, -um, [†terra- (reduced) + eus], adj., *of earth.* — Also, *earth-born?* (according to a doubtful reading).

terribilis, -e, [as if (or really) †terrō- (wh. **terreo**) + bilis], adj., *causing terror, dreadful, dread, terrible.*

terrificō, no perf., no sup., **-āre,** [†terrificō-], 1. v. a., *frighten, alarm, terrify.*

terrificus, -a, -um, [†terrō- (wh. **terreo**) -ficus (√fac + us, cf. **magnificus**)], adj., *awe-inspir-*

ing, terrible, dread, dreadful, frightful.
territō, no perf., no sup., -āre,[†terrĭtŏ- (cf. **terreo**)], 1. v. a., *alarm, frighten, affright:* quos bello (equal to *pursue, menace*).
territus, -a, -um, p.p. of **terreo**.
terror, -ōris, [√ter (in **terreo**) + or], m., *terror, alarm;* — also in pl., *alarm, terror, terrors, alarms, signs of terror.* — Concre*t*ely, *a terror, a dreadful sight* (*omen, event,* &c.).
tertius, -a, -um, [†tertŏ- (†tri + tus reduced, cf. τρıτός) + ius], adj., *third.*
tessera, -ae, [Gr. τέσσαρες La*t*inized], f., *a square* (cf. **quadra**). — Esp*:*, a square table*t* on which the wa*t*chword was inscribed and passed *t*hrough the ranks, *a watchword.*
testa, -ae, [√tors (in **torreo**) + ta (f. of tus)], f. (perh. subs*t*. omi*tt*ed), *baked clay, a tile, potsherds.* — Also, *a piece of pottery* (*a jar, a lamp*).
testātus, -a, -um, p.p. of **testor**.
testis, -is, [?, but cf. **antistes** and **superstes**], comm., *a witness* (of an ac*t*ion, a vow, a promise, &c.).
testor, -ātus, -ārī, [†testi- (of **testis**)], 1. v. dep., *call to witness, swear by, protest before:* deos et sidera. — Also, *declare* (calling something to wi*t*ness), *swear, protest, bear witness, asser*ᵖ*, asseverate;* — *give warning* (approve by tes*t*imony a course of conduc*t*), *exhort, bear witness to a thing, testify to* (as a souvenir), *be a witness of.* — Also, *entreat* (calling something to wi*t*ness): accipe,**testor**.
testūdō, -ĭnis, [†testu- (akin to **testa**) + do], f., *a tortoise* (so called from its resemblance to a pot-lid, **testu**). — Less exac*t*ly, *tortoise-shell.* — From its supposed origin, *a lyre, "shell."* — Also, *the testudo,* a column of a*tt*ack in which the shields were overlapped like shingles, forming a continuous roof like the plates of the tor*t*oise.

tēte, see **tu.**
tēter, see **taeter,** the be*tt*er spelling.
Tēthys, -yos, [Gr. Τηθύς], f., a sea-goddess, the *n*urse of Juno and wife of Oceanus. She was held to be the most ancient of the sea divinities and mo*t*her of all waters.
Tetrica (Tae-), -ae, [?, perh. †taetrŏ + ca], f., a mountain or cliff in the Sabine *t*erritory.
Teucer (-crus), -crī, [Gr. Τεῦκρος La*t*inized], m.: 1. A son of Telamon king of Salamis, and half-bro*t*her of Ajax. He fled from home because he came back wi*t*hout his bro*t*her, and se*tt*led in Cre*t*e, founding a new Salamis; 2. A son of Scamander (said by some *t*raditions to be a Cre*t*an) and the *n*ymph Idæa. He figures as the great founder of the Trojan line *t*hrough his daughter Ba*t*ea, who married Dardanus. Their genealogy according to received tradi*t*ions:

```
SCAMANDER IDÆA
    |              ?(JUPITER) ?(ELECTRA)
  TEUCER                |
    |                   |
  BATEA            DARDANUS
                        |
              ILUS      ERICHTHONIUS
                             |
                           TROS
                             |
                   ILUS      ASSARACUS
                    |           |
                 LAOMEDON    CAPYS
                    |           |
                  PRIAM      ANCHISES
```

Teucria, -ae,[f. of adj.fr.†Teucro-], f., *the land of Teucer, the Trojan land, Troy.*
Teucrus, -a, -um, [same word as **Teucer,** decl. as adj.], adj., *Trojan.* — Plur., **Teucri, -orum,** *the Trojans.*
Teuthrās, -antis, [Gr. Τεύθρας], m., a Trojan.
Teutonicus, -a, -um, [†Teutonŏ + cus], adj., *of the Teutones* (a *t*ribe of Germany). — Less exac*t*ly, *German.*

texō, texuī, textum, texere, [√tex (akin to τέκτων)], 3. v. a., *weave, plait.* — Less exac*t*ly (perh. poe*t*ic, perh. in earlier sense), *build, frame.* — Poe*t*ic: **fugas et praelia** (of dolphins, *weave a tangled web in flight and conflict*). — **textum, -ī,** p.p. neut., *a fabric.*
textīlis, -e, [†textŏ- (of p.p. of texo) + ilis], adj., *woven, of woven stuffs.*
textus, -a, -um, p.p. of texo.
Thaemōn, -ontis, [?], m., a Trojan.
thalamus, -ī, [Gr. θάλαμος], m., *a chamber, a room.* — Poe*t*ic, of bees, *a cell.*—Esp., *a chamber* (for sleeping). — Fig., *marriage, wedlock.*
Thalīa, -ae, [Gr. Θάλεια], f.: 1. One of the Muses, regularly assigned to comedy; 2. A sea-nymph
Thamyrus (-is), -ī, [?], m., a Trojan.
Thapsus, -ī, [Gr. Θάψος], f., a city on a promontory of the same name, on the eas*t*ern coast of Sicily.
Thasius, -a, -um, [Gr. Θάσιος], adj., *of Thasos* (an island off the coast of Thrace, famous for its wine), *Thasian.*
Thaumantias, -adis, [Gr. Θαυμαντίς], f. adj., *daughter of Thaumas, Iris.*
Theānō, -ūs, [Gr. Θεανώ], f., a Trojan woman.
theātrum, -ī, [Gr. θέατρον], n., *a theatre* (proper). — Less exac*t*ly, *a place for games, a theatre.*
Thēbae, -ārum, [Gr. Θῆβαι], f., *Thebes,* a famous ci*t*y of Bœo*t*ia.
Thēbānus, -a, -um, [†Theba + nus], adj.: 1. *Of Thebes* (in Bœo*t*ia), *Theban;* 2. Also, *of Thebe* (a ci*t*y in Mysia, whence came Andromache).
Themillās, -ae, [?], m., a Trojan warrior.
Thermōdōn, -ontis, [Gr. Θερμώδων], m., a river of Pontus, famous as being in the region of the Amazons.
Thērōn, -ōnis, [Gr. Θηρῶν], m., a Latin.

Thersilochus, -ī, [Gr. Θερσίλοχος], m., the name of two different Trojans in Hades.
thēsaurus (thēns-), -ī, [Gr. θησαυρός], m., *a hoard, a treasure.* — Also, *a storehouse, a treasure-house.* — Poe*t*ic, of a hive.
Thēseus, -eī (-eos), [Gr. Θησεύς], m., a king of A*t*hens, slayer of the Mino*t*aur. He assis*t*ed Piri*t*hous in carrying off Proserpine from the infernal regions, for which impiety he was forced to sit upon a rock forever. He was honored as a special divini*t*y by the A*t*henians, and is some*t*imes trea*t*ed as the founder of their race.
Thēsīdēs, -ae, [Gr. Θησείδης], m., *son (descendant) of Theseus.* — Poe*t*ic, in plur., *Athenians, sons of Theseus.*
Thessandrus, -ī, [Greek], m., a Greek hero.
Thestylis, -is, [Gr. Θεστυλίς], f., a rus*t*ic woman, wife or slave of a shepherd.
Thetis, -idis, [Gr. Θέτις], f., a sea-nymph, one of the Nereids, mother of Achilles by Peleus. — Also (cf. Ceres), *the sea.*
thiasus, -ī, [Gr. θίασος], m., *the thiasus, a festive dance* in honor of Bacchus.
Thoās, -antis, [Gr. Θόας], m.: 1. A Greek in the wooden horse; 2. A Trojan.
tholus, -ī, [Gr. θόλος], m., *a dome.* — Esp., *a sacred dome,* in a temple where gif*t*s were hung up.
thōrāx, -ācis, [Gr. θώραξ], m., *a breastplate, a corselet.*
Thrāca (Thrae-), -as, [Gr. Θρᾴκη], f. (of adj., cf. **Thrax**), *Thrace.*
Thrācius (Thrae-), -a, -um, [Gr. Θρᾴκιος], adj., *Thracian, of Thrace*
Thrāx (Thraex), -ācis, [Gr. Θρᾷξ], m., *a Thracian.*
Thrēicius, -a, -um, [Gr. Θρηίκιος], adj., *of Thrace, Thracian.* — Fem. plur., *the Thracian women, the women of Thrace.*
Thrēissa, -ae, [Gr. Θρᾴσσα, f. adj.], f., *a Thracian* (woman), *Thracian.*

Thronius, -I, [?], m., a Trojan.
Thūlē (-ȳlē), -es, [Gr. Θούλη], f., a supposed island at the north-eastern extremity of Europe, beyond Britain, discovered by the navigator Pytheas. Its position is doubtful.
thūreus, see **tureus.**
thūricremus, see **turi-.**
thūrifer, see **turi-.**
thūs, see **tus.**
Thȳbrīnus, see **Tiberīnus.**
Thȳbris (Tȳ-), -is, [?], m.: 1. A hero in the Trojan ranks; 2. See **Tiberis.**
Thȳias (Thȳas), -adis, [Gr. Θυιάς], f., *a Bacchante, a Mænad,* one of the women who joined in the frenzied rites of Bacchus. They are often represented in works of art.
Thymber, -brī, [?], m., a Rutulian (Ribbeck).
Thymbra, -ae, [Gr. Θύμβρη], f., a city near Troy famous for its temple of Apollo.
thymbra, -ae, [Gr. Θύμβρα], f., a *fragrant herb, savory*(?), (*Satureia thymbra*).
Thymbraeus, -a, -um, [Gr. Θυμβραῖος], adj., *of Thymbra, Thymbræan.* — Masc. as subst.: 1. The *god of Thymbra* (Apollo); 2. Name of a Trojan.
Thymbris, -is, [Gr. name of the Tiber], m., a Trojan.
Thymoetēs, -ae, [Gr. Θυμοίτης], m., a Trojan at the siege of Troy. — Also one in Æneas' expedition.
thymum (-us), -ī, [Gr. θύμον], n., *thyme* (a fragrant herb whose blossoms are loved by bees).
Thyrsis, -idis, [Gr. Θυρσίς], m., a shepherd.
thyrsus, -ī, [Gr. θύρσος], m., *a plant-stalk.* — Esp., *the thyrsus* (prob. originally a stalk), or wand of Bacchus, wreathed with ivy and vine leaves or other plants, and borne in the festival rites of the god.
tiāra (-ās), -ae, [Gr. τιάρα (-ας)], f. (or m.), *a regal cap* (a head-dress used by Eastern nations), *a head-dress* (equal to **mitra,** wh. see).
Tiberīnus (Tibr-, Thȳ-), -a, -um, [Tiberi + nus], adj., *of the Tiber.* — Masc. as subst., *Tiber* (the river-god). — *the Tiber* (half personified).
Tiberis (Tibr-, Thȳ-), -is (-idis), [?], m.: 1. *The Tiber,* the great river of Rome; 2. The ancient Italian hero from whom the river was supposed to have been named.
tībia, -ae, [?], f., *the leg-bone.* — Also, *a pipe,* the special instrument of shepherds, and in its larger forms of frenzied religious worship. It was blown at the end (the *flute* form being rare), and often two of different pitch were put together and blown at the same time.
Tibur, -uris, [?], n., an old and famous *town* of Latium on the Anio, twenty miles north-east of Rome, situated on a rocky hill. It long defended itself against the Roman power.
Tiburtus, -ī, [†Tibur + tus], m., one of the mythic founders of Tibur, to which he was supposed to have given its name. (Now *Tivoli,* still famous for its waterfall.)
Tiburs, -urtis, [†Tibur + tis, cf. **Quiris**], adj., *of Tiber.* — Masc. plur., *the inhabitants of Tiber, the Tiburtines.*
tignum, -ī, [unc. root + **num,** cf. **magnus**], n., *a beam, a rafter.*
tigris, -is (-idis), [Gr. τίγρις], m. and f., *a tiger, a tigress.* — Also, *the Tiger,* a name of a ship.
Tigris, -idis (-is), [Gr. Τίγρις], m., the river in Asia flowing between Mesopotamia and Assyria, and joining with the Euphrates in the Persian Gulf.
tilia, -ae, [?], f., *the linden, the lime* (corresponding to the American basswood).
Timāvus, -ī, [?], m., a river between Istria and Venetia, flowing from seven rocky sources (between Aquileia and Trieste), makes a short

course as a wide river in*to* the Adriatic.

timeō, -uī, no sup., **-ere,** [as if †timŏ (cf. **timidus**)], 2. v. a. and n., *fear, dread.* — Intransitive, *be alarmed, be in fear.* — Also, *show one's fear.* — **timēns, -entis,** p. as adj., *fearful, alarmed, in one's fear, in fear.*

timidus, -a, -um, [†timŏ (wh. **timeo**)+dus], adj., *fearful, timid, frightened.*

timor, -ōris, [√tim (in **timeo**) + or], m., *fear, dread, alarm.* — Personified, *Fear.*

tinea, -ae, [?], f., *a worm* (moth or the like).

tingō (tinguō), tinxī, tinctum, tingere, [√ting, cf. τέγγω], 3.v.a., *wet, dip* (in wa*t*er), *bathe, plunge.* — Also, of the wet*t*ing subs*t*ance, *wash, bathe.*

tinnītūs, -ūs, [†tinni- (stem of **tinnio**) + tus], m., *a rattling noise, a ring, a jingle.*

Tiphys, -yos, [Gr. Τιφύς], m., the pilo*t* of the Argo.

Tirynthius, -a, -um, [Gr. Τιρύνθιος], adj., *of Tiryns,* an ancien*t* town of Argolis, where Hercules was educa*t*ed. — Masc. as subs*t*., *Hercules.*

Tīsiphonē, -ēs, [Gr. Τισιφόνη], f., one of the Furies.

Titan, -ānis, [Gr. Τιτάν], m., a name of the sun-god as in some way confounded wi*t*h the Titans. See **Titanius.**

Titānius, -a, -um, [Gr. Τιτάνιος], adj., *of the Titans* (a mysterious race of giants, sons of Heaven and Ear*t*h, who warred agains*t* Zeus), *Titanian.* One of the Ti*t*ans was Hyperion, the father of the Sun and the Moon according *t*o the confused my*t*hs, and these la*tt*er are called Ti*t*ans also.

Tīthōnius, -a, -um, [†Tithonŏ + ius], adj., *of Tithonus.*

Tīthōnus, -ī, [Gr. Τιθωνός], m., a son of Laomedon who married Aurora and became the fa*t*her of Memnon. He was changed in*t*o a locust (*cicada*) at his wife's reques*t*, since endowed wi*t*h immor*t*ali*t*y he had not received e*t*ernal you*t*h.

titubātus, -a, -um, p.p. of **titubo.**

titubō, -āvī, -ātum, -āre, [?], 1. v. n. and a., *stumble, reel, totter.* — **titubātus, -a, -um,** p.p. in act. sense, *stumbling, tottering.*

Tityrus, -ī, [Gr. Τίτυρος, Dor. form of Σάτυρος], m., a shepherd's name in bucolic poe*t*ry.

Tityus (-os), -ī, [Gr. Τιτυός], m., a giant of Euboea who offered violence to La*t*ona (or to Diana). He was punished in Tartarus, s*t*re*t*ched out *o*n the ground and having his liver torn by vul*t*ures.

Tmarius, -a, -um, [†Tmaro+ius], adj., *of Tmaros* (see following word). — Also, *of Epirus.*

Tmarus, -ī, [Gr. Τόμαρος (Τμάρος), a moun*t*ain in Epirus], m., a Ru*t*ulian.

Tmōlius, -a, -um, [†Tmolo+ius], adj., *Tmolian, of Tmolus.* — Masc. as subs*t*., *Tmolian wine* (half personified).

Tmōlus, -ī, [Gr. Τμῶλος], m., a moun*t*ain in Lydia famous for its wines.

tōfus (toph-), -ī, [?], m., *tufa.*

togātus, -a, -um, [†toga + tus, cf. **armatus**], adj., *clad in the toga, of the toga* (wearing it).

tolerābilis, -e, [†tolera- (of **tolerŏ**) + bilis], adj., *tolerable, endurable:* non (*unendurable*).

tolerō, -āvī, -ātum, -āre, [†toler- (√tol, in **tollo,** + us), cf. **onus, onero**], 1. v. a., *bear, support.* — Fig., *endure:* vitam (*sustain,* get a subsis*t*ence).

tollō, sustulī, sublātum; tollere, [√tol, perf. and sup. borr. fr. **suffero,** see **fero**], 3. v. a., *lift, raise* (in all Eng. senses): aulaea (*draw up,* but closing ins*t*ead of opening the scene); saxum (*take up*); me humo (*raise up*); bracchia (*put up*); rates (*take up* to launch); caeli sidera (*bear up*, of A*t*las); in astra nepotes (*raise to heaven*, as gods); fluctus (*throw up, stir up*); undam de flumine (*dip up, take up*); sublato pectore (*with lofty neck*); sublatus ensis (*uplifted sword*). — Wi*t*h reflexive or in passive, *raise one's self, rise, spring up, go up :* se ab solio; se adrectum; nimbus arenae tollitur; quae se tollunt (*spring up*, of *t*rees); — so, fig.: se clamor (*go up, arise*, see below). — Also, fig., *raise* (and the like): vocem (*send up, send forth*); clamores; gemitum (*utter*); sublata rebus secundis (*elated, puffed up*); vos in tantum spe (*raise your hopes so high, be inspired with so much hope*); animos (*encourage, exalt, cheer, revive, be inspirited*); praelia venti (*stir up*); ad astra Daphnim (*extol, immortalize*); tollent animos sata; minas (of a snake, *rise menacingly*). — Also (where *raise* is not used in Eng.), *take up and carry away, take away, carry off, bear away, bear off, remove, put away, put an end to, extirpate, destroy, cease, forbear :* tollite me Teucri; dona; certamina; sive est virtus et gloria tollat (*carry it off, have it*); de caespite silvam; minas; sublatis dolis (*without longer concealment*). — In a special sense, *take up* (of a new-born child), hence, *rear, bring up*.

Tolumnius, -ī (-iī), [?], m., an augur of the Ru*t*uli.

tondeō, totondī, tōnsum, tondēre, [?], 2. v. a., *shear* (of the thing sheared and the produc*t*), *clip, crop, trim, strip, pluck :* bracchia (for o*a*rs). — Esp., *mow, reap*. — Of animals, *crop, browse, graze* on, *feed* on *:* campum equi; iecur (of vul*t*ures). — tōnsus, -a, -um, p.p. as adj., *trimmed, mown, cropped, clipped, sheared, shorn :* tonsae valles (*grazing valleys*);

tonsa oliva (*olive leaves*, stripped off); — so: tonsa corona (*leafy garland*). — Fem. as subs*t*., *an oar* (cf. tondere bracchia).

tonitrus, -ūs, [†toni- (weaker s*t*em of tono) + trus, cf. Quinquatrus], m., *thunder, a clap of thunder*.

tonŏ, tonuī, tonitum, tonāre, [?], 1. v. n., *thunder*. — Of o*t*her *noises* as in Eng.: eloquio (of an orator); antra Aetnaea; axis (of a chario*t*); tonat ter centum Deos (*calls with loud voice up*on, *t*hunders the *n*ames of, cogn. acc.).

tōnsus, -a, -um, p.p. of tondeo.

tōphus, see tofus.

tormentum, -ī, [√torqu + mentum], n., *an engine* (for hurling missiles by means of a twis*t*ed rope). — Also, *torture, pain, torment*.

tornus, -ī, [Gr. τόρνος], m., *a lathe :* facilis (*chisel*, transferring, to render facilis).

torpeō, -uī, no sup., -ēre, [†torpŏ- (cf. torpidus) of unc. kin.], 2.v.n., *be benumbed, be stiff*. — Fig., *be sluggish, be enfeebled, be inactive, be idle*.

torpor, -ōris, [√torp- (in torpeo) + or], m., *torpor, numbness, paralysis*.

Torquātus, -ī, [†torqui + tus (cf. armatus)], m., the *n*ame of Titus Manlius Torquatus, given him for slaying a Gaul in single comba*t*.

torqueō, torsī, tortum, torquēre, [√torqu, akin to τρέπω], 2. v. a., *whirl, twist, twirl, turn* (with some violence or has*t*e), *bend :* ter fluctus (of a ship, *spin around*); amenta (*wind up*, of the thong of a javeli*n*); verbera fundae (*twirl* around the head to *t*hrow); axem umero (*whirl*, of A*t*las); tegumen leonis (*fling around*, as a robe); undam (*in a whirling eddy*); ora (*distort, pucker*). — From the spinning motion of a dar*t* (cf. amenta above), *hurl, throw, fling, roll* (of a river): tres Notus in saxa (of ships);

aquosam hiemem (*fling down, let fly*). — Simply, *turn* (but with a poetic conception): **currus** (almost equals *twist*); **vi portam** (*wrench around*); **cornua** (*haul around*); **vestigia**; — so, fig.: **lumina**; **oculos**; **aciem**. — Poetically, *rule, sway, control:* **sidera mundi** (almost lit.); **caelum et terras**; **bella**.—**tortus, -a, -um,** pp. as adj., *twisted, bent, twined:* **cucumis** (*crooked*); **imber** (prob. *hail*); **orbes** (*winding*); **angues** (*writhing*); **quercus**(*a garland*); **vortex** (*whirling*).

torques (-is), -is, [√torqu + es (-is)], m. and f., *a necklace* (twisted round the neck), *a collar.*— Also, *a collar* (for cattle). — Also, *a wreath, a festoon.*

torrens, see **torreo.**

torreō, torruī, tostum, torrēre, [†torrŏ- (√ors + us, cf. **terra** and **torridus**)], 2. v. a., *roast, parch* (lit. and fig.). — **torrēns, -ēntis,** p. as adj. (from fire or *boiling water*), *boiling, roaring, raging.* As subst., *a torrent.*

torridus, -a, -um, [†torrŏ- (wh. **torreo**)+dus], adj., *burning, hot, fiery.*

torris, -is, [√tors (cf. **torreo**) + is], m., *a firebrand.*—Also, *a stake* (burnt at the end for a weapon).

tortilis, -e, [†tortŏ- (p.p. of **torqueo**) + lis], adj., *twisted, encircling* (twisted around).

tortus, -a, -um, p.p. of **torqueo.**

tortus, -ūs, [√torqu (in **torqueo**) + tus], m., *a coil, a writhing coil* (of a snake).

torus, -ī, [?, √star (in **sterno**) + us], m., *a bulge;* plur., *the muscles* (esp. of the neck); *the neck, a cushion, a bed* (perh. orig. sense), *a couch* (for sitting, reclining at meals, or laying out the dead). — Fig., of natural lying-places: **viridans** (*green couch of turf*); **riparum** (*grassy couches*); **arma toro requirit** (equal to *chamber*, where the arms were hung over the bed).

torvus, -a, -um, [√tor (cf. **terebro**)+**vus**, cf. τορός], adj., (*piercing* only of the expression), *piercing* (of eyes), *grim, savage, frowning, wild-eyed, glaring.* — Neut. as adv.: **torvum clamat** (*wildly*, coupled with **torquens aciem**); **torva tuens** (*fiercely*).

tostus, -a, -um, p.p. of **torreo.**

tot [for **toti**, pron. √ta + ti, cf. **quot**], indecl. adj., *so many, as many*(demonstrative), *these many, those many.*

totidem [toti + dem, cf. **idem**], indecl. adj., *just so many, just as many, as many, the same number, a like number.*

totiēns (-ēs), [toti as stem (reduced) + iens, cf. **noviens**], adv., *so many times, as* (cf. **tot**) *many times, so often, as* (cf. **tot**) *often.*

tōtus, -a, -um, [?], adj., *the whole of* (a thing collectively, cf. **omnis**, *all, every*), *all, the whole, entire.* — Often (like all adjs. of quantity, order, and degree) equal to an adv., *entirely, completely, wholly, all over, all.*

trabālis, -e, [†trabi- (of **trabs**, reduced) + alis], adj., *of a beam.* Also, *like a beam:* **telum.**

trabea, -ae, [†trabi- (reduced) + ea, f. of -eus], f., *a trabea, a robe,* woven in stripes, worn by magistrates, &c.

trabs (trabēs), -is, [?], f., *a beam* (hewn), *a timber.* — Less exactly, *a ship.*

tractābilis, -e, [tractā- (of **tracto**) + bilis], adj., *manageable.* — So, of the weather, *fit for navigation.* — Of persons, *yielding, tractable.*

tractim [as if acc. of †tracti- (√trah + tis), cf. **partim**], adv., *draggingly, slowly, gradually, continuously.*

tractō, -āvī, -ātum, -āre, [†tractŏ- (of **tractus**)], 1. v. a., *handle.*

tractus, -a, -um, p.p. of **traho.**

tractus, -ūs, [√trah (of **traho**) + tus], m., *a drawing:* **tractu**

gementem ferre rotam (*as it moves*); tanto tractu se conligit anguis (*so wide a sweep*). — Also (cf. tra̱no, *trace*), *a streak, a stretch* (cf. Eng. use), *a quarter, a region.*

trādō, -didī, -ditum, -dere, [trans-do], 3. v. a., *hand over, give over, give in charge, surrender.*

trādūcō, -dūxī, -dūctum, -dūcere, [trans-duco], 3. v. a., *draw over, transfer, remove.*

trahea, -ae, [†traha- (reduced) + ea, f. of -eus], f., *a drag, a sledge* (used also for threshing).

trahō, traxī, tractum, trahere, [√trah (for -gh), akin to τρέχω], 3. v. a., *drag* (with violence, or with difficulty), *drag on, drag along, drag away, bear on* (of rivers, &c.), *carry with it* (of something falling, &c.), *carry off* (as captive): tractae catenae (*dragging, clanking chains*); nubem (*drive*); armenta cum stabulis(*carry away*); genua aegra; sinus ultimus orbes (of a snake); naves in saxa (of Scylla). — Also (without violence), *draw, draw out, draw in, move on* (slowly or continuously), *trail, lead* (of children, &c.), *draw* (lots): sinum ex alto (*roll*); alvum (*trail,* as hanging low); vela (*take in*). — Fig., *draw, derive, entice, attract, trace,* pass. *be traced* (*extend*), *dissolve* (draw in), *utter with difficulty:* gyros (*trace*); Iris mille colores; a pectore vocem (*utter with difficulty*). — So, also, *drag out, perform* (slowly), *while away, waste* (of time), *dally, delay:* moras (*create*); vitam; noctem sermone; — pass., *draw on* (of future time). — Esp., *absorb, draw in:* per ossa furorem.

trāiciō (trānsiciō, also separate, trāiic-, trānsiic-), -iēcī, -iectum, -icere, [trans-iacio], 3. v. a. and n., *throw across, throw over.* — With change of point of view,

pierce, transfix. — Intrans., *pass across, pass.*

trāiectus (trāns-), -a, -um, p.p. of traicio.

trāmes, -itis, [√mi (in meo) + tis (reduced), cf. comes], m., *a cross-path, a by-way.* — Less exactly, *a path* (lit. and fig.), *a course.*

trānō (trāns-), -āvī, -ātum, -āre, [trans-no], 1. v. a., *swim across, cross* (of rivers), *sail through* or *across* (of birds). — Also, of Mercury as a winged creature.

tranquillus, -a, -um, [?], adj., *quiet, calm, still, tranquil.*—Neut. as subst.: tranquillo, *in calm weather.*

trāns [unc. form √tra, tar (in terebro)], prep., *across, through, over.* — Adv., in comp., in same sense.

trānsabeō, -iī, no sup., -īre, [transabeo], irr. v. a. and n., *pass beyond.* — Also, *pierce, penetrate, pass through* (of a weapon, &c.).

trānsadigō, -ēgī, -āctum, -igere, [trans-adigo], 3. v. a., *thrust through* (with two accs.). — Also, *pierce through, penetrate.*

trānscrībō (trānss-), -scrīpsī, -scrīptum, -scrībere, [transscribo], 3. v. a., *transcribe.*—Also, *make over by writing;* — hence, *assign over, transfer, make over.* — Esp., *enroll* (in a different list, cf. conscribo), *transfer.*

trānscurro, -cucurrī (-currī), no sup., -currere, [trans-curro], 3. v. a. and n., *run across, fly across, shoot across.*

trānseō, -iī (-īvī), -itum, -īre, [trans-eo], irr. v. n. and a., *pass over, cross, pass by, pass, outstrip.* — Also, *pierce, pass through, penetrate.* — Also, *pass over* or *by* (*unmentioned*).

trānsferō, -tulī, -lātum, -ferre, [trans-fero], irr. v. a., *carry over, transfer.*

trānsfīgō, -fīxī, -fīxum, -fīgere, [trans-figo], 3. v. a., *thrust through.*

— Also, *pierce through* (cf. **figo**), *transfix*.

trānsfīxus,-a,-um, p.p. of **transfigo**.

trānsfodiŏ, -fōdī, -fossum, -fodere, [trans-fodio], 3. v. a., *pierce, transfix*.

trānsformō, -āvī, -ātum, -āre, [trans-formo], 1. v. a., *transform, metamorphose;* — with reflexive, *change*.

trānsfossus,-a,-um, p.p. of **transfodio**.

trānsiliŏ (transs-), -uī (-īvī), no sup., **-īre**, [trans-salio], 3. v. a. and n., *leap across, fly over.* — Of things, *fly through*.

trānsmissus, -a, -um, p.p. of **transmitto**.

trānsmittō,-mīsī,-missum,-mittere, [trans-mitto], 3. v. a. and n., *suffer to pass across* (cf. **mitto**, *let go*). — Fig., *transmit, assign over*. — Wi*t*h acc. dep. or **trans**, *pass over:* **campos; cursum** (*cross the passage*).

trānsportō, -āvī, -ātum, -āre, [trans-porto], 1. v. a., *bear across, carry across:* **ripas** (*carry the shades across the stream*).

trānstrum, -ī, [trans + trum], n., *a cross-beam*. — Esp., *a thwart, a bench* (for rowers athwar*t* the ship).

trānsverberō, -āvī, -ātum, -are, [trans-verbero], 1. v. a., *strike through, pierce, transfix*.

transversus, -a, -um, p.p. of **transverto**.

trānsvertō,-vertī,-versum,-vertere, [trans-verto], 3. v. a., *turn athwart*.—**trānsversus, -a, -um**, p.p. as adj., *lying across, running across*.— Neu*t*. plur. as adv., *askance, athwart* one's *course*.

trapētus, -ī, [Gr. τραπητός], m., *an oil-mill*.

trecentī, -ae, -a, [†tri-centum, decl.], adj., *three hundred*.

tremebundus, -a, -um, [†treme- (as of tremo, but cf. rubicundus) + bundus], adj., *trembling, quivering*.

tremefaciō, -fēcī, -factum, -facere, [unc. s*t*em (akin to **tremo**) -facio], 3. v. a., *make tremble, shake*. — **tremefactus, -a, -um**, p.p., *shaken, trembling, quivering, shuddering*.

tremendus, see **tremo**.

tremescō (-iscō), no perf., no sup., **-ere**, [†treme- (of tremo) + sco], 3. v. n. and a. incep*t*., *tremble*. — Wi*t*h inf. and acc., as in Eng.(?), *tremble, shudder*. — Wi*t*h obj., *tremble at, shudder at*.

tremō, -uī, no sup., **-ere**, [√trem, cf. τρέμω (perh. fr. a s*t*em, cf. **terreo**)], 3. v. a., *tremble, quake, quake with fear, shake, quiver:* **cristae** (*nod, flutter*). — Act., *tremble at, shudder at, quake with fear at*. — **tremēns, -entis**, p. as adj., *trembling, quivering, frightened*. — **tremendus, -a, -um**, p. ger., *dreadful, awful, dread*.

tremor, -ōris, [√trem + or], m., *a trembling*.

tremulus, -a, -um, [†tremō- (√trem + us) + lus], adj., *tremulous, quivering, shimmering*.

trepidō, -āvī, -ātum, -āre, [†trepidŏ-], 1. v. n. and a., *tremble, quake with fear, flutter*. — Also, *hurry to and fro, bustle*. — Act. (as verb of fearing), *fear, dread, shrink from*. — **trepidāns, -antis**, p. as adj., *frightened, in a panic, in alarm*.

trepidus,-a,-um,[†trepŏ-(√trep, of unc. kin. + us) + dus], adj., *trembling, agitated, shuddering, quaking, bustling, hurrying, confused, in confusion, in agitation;* — *frightened, fearful, anxious, alarmed, in eager haste*.

trēs, tria, [†tri-, of unc. kin., cf. τρεῖς, Eng. *three*], num. adj. plur., *three*.

trībulum, -ī, [tri (as roo*t* of tero) + bulum], n., *a drag* (for threshing, wi*t*h teeth benea*t*h).

trībulus, -ī, [Gr. τρίβολος], m., *a caltrop* (a poin*t*ed ins*t*rument laid on the ground as a defence agains*t*

cavalry). — Also, *a caltrop.*
tribus, -us, f., *a tribe.*
tricorpor, -oris, [†tri-†corpor- (decl. as adj.)], adj., *three-bodied.*
tridēns, -dentis, [†tri-dens (decl. as adj.)], adj., *three-toothed, three-pronged.* — Masc. as subst., *a trident,* the a*tt*ribu*t*e of Nep*t*une.
trietēricus, -a, -um, [Gr. τριετηρικός], adj., *biennial,* occurring once in *t*hree years according to the notions of the ancien*t*s, who coun*t*ed bo*t*h *termini* of a period.
trifaux, -faucis, [†tri-faux, decl. as adj.], adj., *three-throated, triple-jawed:* trifauci latratus Cerberus (*with the baying of his three throats*).
trīgintā[tri-unc. s*t*em, cf. **vigintī**], indecl. num. adj., *thirty.*
trilix, -licis, [†tri-lix, cf. **bilix**], adj., *three-ply, threefold* (of three thick*n*esses).
Trīnacrius, -a, -um, [Gr. Τρινάκριος], adj., *of Sicily* (called *Trinacria* from its *t*hree promontories), *Sicilian.* — Fem. (cf. Gr. Τρινακρία), *Sicily.* (This word, as is the case wi*t*h most *n*ames of coun*t*ries, serves as adj. of its own fem.).
Triōnēs, -um, [?], m. plur., the Great and Li*tt*le Bears, *Ursa Major and Minor,* or *Charles' Wain* (see also **septemtrio**).
triplex, -icis, [†tri-plex, cf. **duplex**], adj., *threefold, triple:* gens (*in three divisions*).
tripūs, -odis, [Gr. τρίπους], m., *a tripod,* a three-legged s*t*and used by the ancien*t*s, especially for cooking and for sacred rites. — Esp., *the Tripod,* or cauldron on a tripod, at Delphi, on which the pries*t*ess sat when delivering the oracle. — Plur., referring to the same, but almos*t* in sense of *oracles.*
tristis, -e, [?, perh. √ters (in **tereo**] + tis], .adj., *sad, gloomy, mournful, wretched, sorrowful.* — Also of things connec*t*ed wi*t*h persons in the same sense. — Also, as affec*t*ing o*t*hers, *grim, gloomy, sullen, stern.* — Transf., *sad* (causing sadness), *bitter, dreary, mournful, melancholy, ill-omened, wretched, gloomy, dreadful, cruel, harsh, noxious, baneful:* tempus (*disastrous*); Minervae sidus(*stormy*); nihil triste (*there is no sorrow*). — Of *t*aste, &c., *bitter, harsh.* — Neu*t.* as subs*t.*, *the bane.*
trisulcus, -a, -um, [†tri-sulcus, decl. as adj.], adj., *three-forked.*
trīticeus, -a, -um, [†tritico- (of **triticum,** reduced) + eus], adj., *of wheat:* messis (*wheat-harvest*).
Trītōn, -ōnis, [Gr. Τρίτων], m.: A sea-god, son of Nep*t*une, represen*t*ed as blowing a conch-shell. — Plur., *sea-gods.* — 2. A name of a ship.
Trītōnia, -ae, [Gr. Τριτώνιος], f., a name or appella*t*ion of Pallas (Minerva) of uncer*t*ain origin.
Trītōnis, -idis, [Gr. Τριτωνίς], f., same as **Tritonia.**
trītūra, -ae, [√tri(in tero)+tura, but see **pictura**], f., *threshing.*
trītus, -a, -um, p.p. of **tero.**
triumphātus, -a, -um, p.p. of **triumpho.**
triumphō, -āvī, -ātum, -āre, [†triumphŏ-], 1. v. *n.* and a., *triumph* (*t*echnically). — Act., *enjoy a triumph over, lead in triumph, conquer, subdue.*
triumphus, -ī, [prob. corr. fr. Gr. θρίαμβος, a hymn to Bacchus], m., *a triumph* (in the Roman technical sense, where the general wi*t*h his army went in procession to the Capi*t*ol to offer a sacrifice). — Less exac*t*ly, *a triumph* (generally), *a victory.*
Trivius, -a, -um, [†tri-†via, decl. as adj.], adj., *of three ways.* — Masc. and fem., of gods whose *t*emples were built at the junction of *t*hree ways. — Fem., **Trivia,** as subs*t.*; — esp., *Hecate* or *Diana,* on accoun*t* of her *t*hree forms. — Neu*t.*, *a square,* where three ways met, *corners.*

Troas, -adis, [Gr. Τρῳάς], f. adj., *a Trojan woman.*—Plur., *the Trojan women.*
Troia, see **Troius.**
Troiānus, -a, -um, [†Troia+nus], adj., *Trojan.*—As subst., *a Trojan.*
Troilus, -i, [Gr. Τρώιλος], m., a son of Priam killed in the Trojan war.
Troiugena, -ae, [†Troiu- (of unc. form) -gena (cf. **indigena**)], comm., *born in Troy, Trojan.* — As subst., *a Trojan.*
Troius, -a, -um, [†Trō- (of **Tros**) +ius], adj.: A. *Of Tros.*—Fem.: 1. *Troy,* the city of Tros; 2. A city of the same name in Epirus; 3. The game or exercise of the Trojan youths in honor of Anchises. — B. Less exactly (as with most names of countries, &c.), *of Troy, Trojan.* — Masc., *a Trojan.*
tropaeum (-phaeum), -i, [Gr. τρόπαιον], n., *a trophy,* regularly a trunk of a tree arrayed in arms and left standing on the battle-field. — Less exactly, *a trophy* (generally), *a victory.*
Tros, -ōis, [Gr. Τρώς], m., a king of Phrygia (see **Dardanus**). — As adj., *Trojan.* — As subst., *a Trojan.* — Plur., *the Trojans,* said to be named for him.
trucīdō, -āvī, -ātum, -āre, [?, prob. noun-stem akin to **trux**, and **caedo**], 1. v. a., *cut down, slaughter.*
trudis, -is, [√trud (in **trudo**) + is], f., *a boat-hook, a pole* (for boating), said to have a crescent-shaped head, cf. **contus.**
trūdō, trūsī, trūsum, trūdere, [?], 3. v. a., *push, push on, shove, thrust, press against, struggle against.* — Esp., *put forth* (of growth). — In pass. or with reflexive, *sprout.*
truncus, -a, -um, [?], adj., *lopped, stripped, cut off, maimed, mutilated:* pinus (*a pine trunk*); trunca pedum (*destitute of,* of maggots); tela (*broken,* perh. with only the heads off). — Masc., *a trunk* (of a tree, opposed to the branches), *a stock, a main shoot.* — Also, *a headless trunk* (of a man).
trux, trucis [?], adj., *savage, grim, gloomy.*
tū, tuī, [cf. σύ, Eng. *thou*], pers. pron., *thou, you* (according to Eng. idiom). — Plur., **vōs,** *you* (of several); — also apparently (never really) of one, when others are included.
tuba, -ae, [f. of **tubus**], f., *a trumpet* (straight, cf. **cornu,** *a curved horn*).
tueor, tuitus (tūtus), tuērī, [?], 2. v. dep., *look at, gaze at, gaze upon, look, behold.* — Also (lit. and fig.), *protect, defend.* — **tūtus, -a, -um,** p.p. in pass. sense, *protected, safe* (as regards externals, cf. **securus,** as regards one's self), *secure, without danger, in safety, undisturbed, unharmed:* dare tuta vela (*sail safely*).—Fig.: fides (*secure, trustworthy*). — Transferred, *safe* (*protecting*): tegmina capitum. — Like **securus,** *fearless, in security.* — Neut. sing. or plur., *safe places* (i.e. *safety*), *a safe retreat, a safe position,* &c., *safety, security.* — Abl. as adv., *safely, with impunity.*
tugurium, -ī (-iī), [√teg + unc. term.], n., *a hut.*
Tulla, -ae, [f. of **Tullus**], f., an attendant of Camilla.
Tullus, -ī, [?], m., a Roman name. — Esp., *Tullus Hostilius,* the third king of Rome.
tum [n. acc. pron. √ta (in **tam,** etc.), cf. **dum**], adv. demonstrative, *then, at that time.*—With correlative, *at the time, that time, then* (sometimes not expressed in Eng.), *in that case, now* (in Eng. sense of past time), *by and by, meanwhile, just then.*—Also, *thereupon, next, then again, then, besides, and . . . too.* — Esp.: quid tum, *what then* (what follows logically from the preceding?), *what next.*

— **tum iam,** *just then* (but confounded with **iam tum**); **iam tum,** *even then, just then, then already*); **tum vero,** emphatic, introducing the most important point of a narrative.

tumeŏ, no perf., no sup., **-ere,** [†tumō- (√tu + mus, cf. **tumulus,** τύλος)], 2. v. n., *swell, be swollen.*

tumēscō, tumuī, no sup., **-mēscere,** [†tumē-(of **tumeo**)+sco], 3. v. n., *swell, rise* (of the sea or war, &c.).

tumĭdus, -a, -um, [†tumŏ- (wh. tumeo) + dus], adj., *swelling, swollen, rising, huge.*—Fig., *puffed up, swelling.*

tumor, -ōris, [tum (as root of tumeo) + or], m., *a swelling.* — Fig., *anger.*

tumultus, -ūs, [†tumulŏ- (of **tumulus** in earlier meaning, cf. **tumeo,** reduced) + tus], m., *an uproar, a tumult, a noise, a disturbance, a commotion, disorder, confusion.* — Also, of the mind, *anxiety, agitation, excitement:* laetitia mixto tumultu. — Esp., *a domestic war, a war.*

tumulus, -ī, [†tumŏ- (whence **tumeo**) + lus], m., *a mound, a hill.* — Esp., *a tomb.*

tunc [tum-ce, cf. **hic**], adv., *then* (more definite than **tum,** but confused with it), *at that time.* The readings often vary between **tum** and **tunc.**

tundō, tutudī, tūnsum (tūsum), tundere, [√tud, akin to Sk. √tud, with same meaning], 3. v. a., *strike, beat, bruise.* — Esp. of beating the breasts in grief. — Also, *pound, bruise, crush, thresh.* — Less exactly, *tear* (of a vulture), *beat* (of waves), *assail* (by words).

tunica, -ae, [?], f., *a tunic,* the ancient undergarment, a sort of shirt or frock. — Fig., *a coating* (of bark or the like).

tunsus, -a, -um, p.p. of **tundo.**

turba, -ae, [√tur (cf. **turma** and θόρυβος) + ba, cf. **morbus, superbus,** and τύρβη], f., *a disturbance, a tumult, confusion.* — Esp., *a throng, a crowd, a flock* (of birds), *a multitude, the crowd* (as opposed to leaders, &c.).

turbātus, -a, -um, p.p. of **turbo.**

turbĭdus, -a, -um, [†turba+dus], adj., *confused, agitated, wild, turbid, roily, stormy, eddying* (of dust), *whirling* (of rain). — Of persons (cf. **turba**), *wild* (often equals adv. *wildly*), *agitated, impetuous, confused, in a panic.*

turbō, -āvī, -ātum, -āre, [†turba], 1. v. a., *agitate, disturb, throw into confusion, drive in a panic, frighten* (chase), *scatter:* turbatur (*confusion reigns*); globum (*break,* i.e. the order); omnia metu; latratu apros (*rouse*); turbantur arenae (*tossed, driven*). — Less exactly and fig., *alarm, trouble, disturb, strike with a panic, break off* (a truce), *spread alarm* (among, or absolutely). — **turbātus, -a, -um,** p.p. as adj., *agitated, disordered, in a panic, broken, panic-stricken, in confusion* (equal adv.), *frightened, alarmed, disturbed, disordered, angry, troubled, confused, excited.*

turbō, -ĭnis, [†turba- (or -o) + o (-in), cf. **homo**], m., *a whirling; a whirling eddy:* quo turbine adacta (of an arrow, simply *by whose hurling*); venti (*a whirlwind,* see next division). — Esp., *a whirlwind, a hurricane:* nigro circumdata turbine (including the cloud that often accompanies the vortex); ingentis turbine saxi (*like a whirlwind,* making one as it goes); quo turbine torqueat hastam (i.e. force like a whirlwind). — Also, *a top* (perh. nearer the original sense).

tūreus, (thū-), -a, -um, [†tur+eus], adj., *of incense.*

turgeō, tursī, no sup., **turgēre,** [?], 2. v. n., *swell.*

tūricremus, -a, -um, [†tur- (as if turi-) + cremus (cf. **cremo**)],

adj., *incense-burning, smoking with incense.*
tūrifer, -era, -erum, [†tur- (as if turi-) -fer (√fer + us)], adj., *incense-bearing.*
turma, -ae, [√tur (in turba) + ma], f., *a troop* (of horse, technically a tenth of the *ala* or division of about 300 men), *a squadron.* — Also, of the Trojan boys exercising as cavalry. — Less exactly, *a troop* (of other things), *a throng, a band.*
Turnus, -ī, m., the Rutulian king who, as a suitor for the hand of Lavinia, resisted the settlement of Æneas, and was finally slain by him.
turpis, -e, [?], adj., *unseemly, unsightly, foul, ill-formed, misshapen, ugly:* tabum; racemi; Egestas (*squalid,* as emaciated and in rags). — Also, in a moral sense (cf. *foul,* &c.), *unseemly, base, dishonorable, vile, disgraceful.*
turriger, -era, -erum, [†turri-ger (√ges, in gero, + us)], adj., *tower-bearing, crowned with towers* (as cities were usually represented allegorically).
turris, -is, [prob. borrowed, cf. Gr. τύρσις], f., *a tower.* — Esp., a military tower for siege, advanced to the walls on wheels, or one on a wall for defence. — Loosely used of high buildings.
turrītus, -a, -um, [†turri + tus, cf. **armatus**], adj., *armed with towers, crowned with towers* (as Cybele was represented). — Less exactly, *towering, pinnacled* (of cliffs).
turtur, -uris, [?], m., *a turtle-dove.*
tūs (**thūs**), **tūris,** [Gr. θύος], n., *frankincense, incense.*
Tuscus, -a, -um, [?], adj., *of Etruria, Etrurian, Tuscan, Etruscan.* — Plur. as subst., *the Etrurians.*
tussis, -is, [?], f., *a cough.*
tūtāmen, -inis, [†tutā- (of tutor) + men], n., *a protection, a defence.*
tūte, see **tu.**

tūtēla, -ae, [†tutē- (as if stem of tutor) + la, cf. **candela**], f., *guardianship, protection.*
tūtor, -ātus, -ārī, [†tutŏ- (p.p. of tueor)], 1. v. dep., *protect, defend, support.*
tūtus, -a, -um, p.p. of **tueor.**
tuus, -a, -um, [pron. √TVA + YAS], poss. pron., *thy, your* (of one person, according to Eng. idiom), *thine, yours.* — Plur. (less commonly sing.) as subst., *your (friends, men,* &c., *affairs, interests,* &c.).
Tybris, etc.; see **Tiberis.**
Tȳdeus, -eī (-eos), [Gr. Τυδεύς], m., the father of Diomede. He fought in the Theban war.
Tȳdīdēs, -ae, [Gr. patronymic], m., *son of Tydeus, Diomedes.*
tympanum, -ī, [Gr. τύμπανον], n., *a drum, a timbrel,* used especially in the rites of Cybele. — Also, *a wheel* (not with spokes, but solid like a child's truck, cf. **rota,** one with spokes).
Tyndaris, -idis, [Gr. Τυνδαρίς], f., *daughter of Tyndarus, Helen,* as daughter of Leda his wife.
Typhōeus, -eī (-eos), [Gr. Τυφωεύς], m., a giant, also called *Typhon,* the hero of many fables. According to one, he was struck by lightning and buried under Ætna by Jupiter. According to another, it was under Ischia. He seems to have been a type of volcanoes in general.
Typhōeïus, -a, -um, [Gr. adj. fr. preceding], adj., *of Typhon:* tela (*the bolts of Typhon,* by which he was slain).
tyrannus, -ī, [Gr. τύραννος], m., *a king.* — Esp., *a tyrant, a despot.*
Tyrēs, -ae, [?], m., a Trojan (or Arcadian) in the army of Æneas.
Tyrius, -a, -um, [†Tyrŏ- (reduced) + ius], adj., *of Tyre, Tyrian.* — Less exactly, *of Carthage, Carthaginian.* — Plur. masc., *the Tyrians, the Carthaginians.*
Tyros (-us), -ī, [Gr. Τύρος, a Phœnician word], f., *Tyre,* the great city of Phœnicia, from which came

the colony of Dido. It was most famous for its purple dye.

Tyrrhēnus, -a, -um, [Gr. Τυρρηνός], adj., *Etruscan, Etrurian, Tuscan.* — Masc. as subst., *an Etrurian;* — plur., *the Etrurians, the Etruscans.*

Tyrrhēnus, -ī, [m. of preceding],

m., an Etrurian among Æneas' allies.

Tyrrheus (Tyrrhus), -eī, [?], m., the herdsman of King Latinus.

Tyrrhīdae, -ārum, [Gr. patronymic fr. preceding], m. plur., *the sons of Tyrrheus:* **puerī** (*young sons of,* &c.).

U.

1. **ūber, -eris,** [unc. form akin to οὖθαρ, Eng. *udder*, perh. also to **uveo**], n. (oftener plur.), *an udder, the breast.* — Fig., *the bosom* (of the earth, as the source of nourishment), *soil* (as fertile), *fertility:* (tellus) vos ubere laeto accipiet (*in her fertile bosom*); rarum (*light spongy soil*); fertilis ubere campus(*in production*); densum (*a thick planted soil*); ubere glebae (*fertility of the soil*); divitis uber agri (*fertile soil of a rich land*).

2. **ūber, -eris,** [same word as prec. decl. as adj., cf. n. plur. -a], adj., *fertile, productive, rich, abundant, plentiful, luxuriant.*

ubī [held to be pron. √quo + bi, cf. **tibi**, and Umbr. *pufe*], adv.: 1. Interr., *where* (almost always with strong feeling, in despair or irony); 2. Rel., *where* (with expressed or implied antecedent), *in a place where* (without def. antecedent), *wherever.* — Also, *when, whenever, after, as soon as.*

ubīque [ubi-que, cf. **quisque**], adv., *everywhere, on all sides, all around.*

Ūcalegōn, -ontis, [Gr. Οὐκαλέγων], m., a Trojan.

ūdus, -a, -um, [prob. contr. fr. **uvidus**, or formed from shorter stem], adj., *wet, moist, damp, watery:* udae vocis iter (*moist passage of the voice*); venenum(*dank*); liber (*juicy*).

Ūfēns, -entis, [?], m.: 1. A river in Latium; 2. The same word used as the name of a Rutulian.

ulcīscor, ultus, ulcīscī, [√ulc, poss. akin to ἄρκιος], 3. v. dep., *take vengeance on* or *for* (a wrongdoer or a wrong). — Also, *avenge* (the wronged).

ulcus, -eris, [prob. Gr. ἕλκος], n., *a sore, an ulcer.*

ūlīgō, -inis, [?, prob. akin to **uveo**], f., *moisture.*

Ulixēs, -ī (-eī, -is), [dialectic form of 'Οδυσσεύς], m., a Greek hero of the Trojan war famed for his cunning. His wanderings are the theme of the Odyssey.

ūllus, -a, -um, -īus, [†unŏ- (reduced) + lus], pron. adj., only in real or limited negatives, cf. **quisquam**, *any, anyone:* dum amnes ulli rumpuntur (*so long as any* &c., until they do not, foll. by postquam). — With negatives, *not any, no, none, no one.*

ulmus, -ī, [?], f., *an elm, an elm tree.* The vines of the ancients were often trained upon them.

ulna, -ae, [?, cf. ὠλένη, Eng. *elbow*], f., *the forearm, the elbow.* — Also, *an ell* (perh. the distance from the hand to the elbow, but used also of the outstretched arms, hence the length is unc.).

ulter, -tra, -trum, [pron. √ul (of unc. kin., cf. **uls**) + ter (comp. suffix akin to -τερος), cf. **alter**], pron. adj., (*on the farther side*). — Comp., **ulterior, -us,** *the farther.* — Neut. as adv., *farther, further, any more.* — Superl., **ultimus, -a, -um,** [pron. √ul + timus, cf. **intimus**], *farthest, extreme, uttermost, at the end:* auctor san-

guinis (*original, earliest, farthest in the line*). — Of time, *last, final*. — Of degree, *last, extreme:* iussa (*most degrading, most arrogan*t). — Neut. plur., *the end, the farthest point*.
ulterius, see **ulter**.
ultimus, -a, -um; see **ulter**.
ultor, -ōris, [√ulc (in ulciscor) +tor], m., *an avenger*.
ultrā [prob. abl. of **ulter**, cf. **extra**], adv. and prep. Adv., *on the other side, farther, beyond*. — Fig., *further, more, besides*. For **ulterius**, see **ulter**. — Prep., *beyond:* ultra placitum (*above measure*).
ultrīx, -īcis, [√ulc + trix, cf. **ultor**], f., *an avenger* (female). — As adj., *avenging*.
ultrō [dat. of **ulter**], adv., *to the farther side.* — Also, *beyond, furthermore, in addition, besides* (often of something not to be expected, see below). — Also, when nothing is expected of one, or called for, (*more than is required*), *voluntarily, of one's own accord, unprovoked, unaddressed, fir*st (without being spoken to).
ultus, -a, -um, p.p. of **ulciscor**.
ulula, -ae, [akin to ὀλολύζω, prob. an old word made from the sound, originally *a wail*, cf. for the form ἀλαλά], f., *a screech-owl* (a bird of ill-omen).
ululātus, -a, -um, p.p. of **ululo**.
ululātus, -ūs, [†tululā- (of **ululo**) + tus], m., *a howl, a wail, a wailing, a cry, a shriek, a wailing cry*.
ululō, -āvī, -ātum, -āre, [ulula-, cf. ὀλολύζω and ἀλαλά], 1. v. n. and a., *a howl, a wail, a cry, a shriek.* — Poetic, of a place, *resound with wails*, &c. — ululātus, -a, -um, p.p. in pass. sense, *worshipped with cries* (prop. of the name, cog. acc., uttered, &c.); — also, *echoing with cries* (where the object would have been acc. of space).
ulva, -ae, [?], f., *sedge, coarse grass*.
Ulyssēs, see **Ulixes**.
Umber, -bra, -brum, [prob. akin to **imber**], adj., *of the Umbri* (a tribe of Northern Italy between the Rubicon, the Nar, and the Tiber). — Masc., *an Umbrian hound, an "Umbrian"* (cf. Newfoundland).
umbō, -ōnis, [?, akin to **umbilicus**, and ἄμβων], m., (prob. any *protuberance*), *a boss* (of a shield). — Less exactly, *a shield*.
umbra, -ae, [?], f., *a shade, a shadow;* — hence, *darkness, gloom*. — Esp., *a ghost* (of a dead person, as a mere shadow?, but confounded in use with *gloom*), *a shade, an apparition* (of any kind), *a vision, a phantom*. — Also, plur., *the realm of shades, the shades, the world below.* — Poetic, *leaves and branches* (which serve as shade).
umbrāculum, -ī, [as if †umbrā- (of **umbro**) + culum], n., *a bower, an arbor*.
umbrātus, -a, -um, p.p. of **umbro**.
umbrifer, -era, -erum, [†umbra- (weakened) -fer (√fer + us)], adj., *bearing shade, shady*.
Umbrō, -ōnis, [†Umbrŏ+o (on)], m., an ally of Turnus.
umbrō, -āvī, -ātum, -are, [†umbra-], 1. v. a., *shade, overshadow*.
umbrōsus, -a, -um, [†umbra- (reduced) + osus], adj., *shady* (both furnishing shade and being shaded).
ūmectō (hum-), -āvī, -ātum, -āre, [†umectŏ- (of **umeo**)], 1. v. a., *moisten, bedew, bathe, water*.
ūmeō (hum-), no perf., no sup., **-ēre,** [†umŏ- (√u or †uvi + mus], cf. **umifer**], 2. v. n., *be moist, be wet*. — **ūmēns, -ēntis,** p. as adj., *moist, damp, watery, dewy:* umbra (*dewy shades*).
umerus (hum-), -ī, [?, akin to ὦμος], m., *the shoulder*.
ūmēscō (hum-), no perf., no sup., **-ere,** [†tume- (of **umeo**) + sco], 3. v. n., *be moistened, be sprinkled, be spattered*.
ūmidus, -a, -um, [†umŏ- (cf. **umifer**) + dus], adj., *moist, damp, dewy*. — Also, *wet, rainy, liquid, watery*.

Vocabulary. 293

ūmor (hūm-), -ōris, [um (as root of umeo) + or], m., *moisture, juice, fluid, liquor:* gelidus (i.e. *snow*); Bacchi (i.e. *wine*).

umquam, see unquam.

unā [abl. of unus, cf. ea], adv., (*by the same way*), *together, at the same time, along with, at once.*

ūnanimus, -a, -um, (also -is, -e), [†uno-animus (weakened and decl. as adj.)], adj., *of one mind, harmonious, in concert, sympathizing.*

unctus, -a, -um, p.p. of ungo.

uncus, -a, -um, [√unc (cf. ancus, ὄγκος) + us], adj., *bent, hooked, crooked:* manus (*clenched*, on a rock).

unda, -ae, [√und + a, cf. Sk. √ud, Gr. ὕδωρ, and Eng. *water*], f., *a wave, a billow, a sea.* — Poetic, of smoke, *an eddy, a waving column;* —and of persons, *a wave, a stream.* — Also, *the sea, water, the waters.*

unde [held to be quom-de, cf. ubi and inde], adv.: 1. Interr., *whence, from what place, from whence, from what source:* unde hominum genus (*whence comes, what is the origin*); 2. Rel., *from whence.* — Also, *from whom, from which, whence.*

undecimus, -a, -um, [undecim + mus, cf. primus], adj., *eleventh:* alter ab undecimo (*twelfth*).

undique [unde-que, cf. quisque], adv., *from all sides, from every quarter, on all sides* (cf. hinc), *everywhere, all around.*

undō, -āvī, -ātum, -āre, [†unda-], 1. v. n., *wave, flow in waves, roll in waves:* volutus ad caelum undabat vortex (*a whirling eddy rolled to heaven*).—undāns, -āntis, p. as adj., *surging, seething, waving, eddying, streaming:* Cytorus buxo (*waving with woods of box*); Nilus bello (*swelling with a tide of war*).

undōsus, -a, -um, [†unda- (reduced) + osus], adj., *boisterous, wave-washed.*

ungo (unguŏ), unxī, unctum, ungere, [√ung, akin to Sk. *añj*], 3. v. a., *smear, besmear, anoint:* tela manu (of poisoned arrows); corpus (for burning). — unctus, -a, -um, p.p. as adj., *smeared, greased, greasy, oily:* carina (*well-pitched*).

unguen, -inis, [as if √ung (cf. ungo) + en (prob. really †ungi + nus, reduced)], n., *unctuous matter* (perh. a particular kind, now unknown).

unguis, -is, [?, cf. poss. ὄνυξ], m., *a nail* (of the finger or toe); — in (ad) unguem, *perfectly, exactly* (from trying a work with the nail). — Also, *a claw* (of a bird or beast), *a talon.*

ungula, -ae, [†ungui + la], f., *a claw, a hoof.*

unquam (umquam), [held to be cum-quam, cf. ubi and quisquam], adv., *ever* (with negatives, see ullus), *at any time.* — With negatives, *never.*

ūnus, -a, -um, -īus, [old oinus, unc. pron. stem + nus, cf. οἶος and Eng. *one*], num. adj., *one, the same, a like, a single, alone, only, only one, the sole.* — Esp.: haud unus, *more than one, not the same;* ad unum, *to a man;* in unum, *to the same place, together, into one, in one;* venturus in unum, *come face to face with.* — Emphatic, *the one, the very* (with superlatives), *especially, more than all others.* — Also, in plur., *one,* &c.

ūpiliō, -ōnis, [†ovi- unc. stem], m., *a shepherd, a keeper of the flock.*

urbs, urbis, [?], f., *a city* (only of a large fortified place, the capital or chief town of a region). — Poetic, of the citizens. — Also, of a beehive, *colony, city.*

urgeo (-ueō), ursī, no sup., urgere, [√urg, akin to εἴργνυμαι], 2. v. a., *press hard, press close;* — hence, *pursue, attack, overwhelm, drive, drive on, force, urge on, stimulate, hurry on, hasten* (a work), *bear on* (of a crowd, &c.), *urge, press close upon, press on:* amor habendi apes; vicinia Persidis (*crowd close upon*); ad litora fluctus (*roll*); propius urgente caterva (*pressing him closer*); urgens egestas (*compelling need*); urgente ruina (*borne on by the flying throng*); urgens fatum (*overwhelming*); pedem pede (*press on one's heels*); poenis urgentur (*are tormented*). — Also, *weigh down, press upon, keep down, hem in, confine:* utrimque latus nemoris; — so, fig., *weigh down, overcome, worry, pursue, annoy.*

urna, -ae, [?], f., *a jar, an urn.* — Esp. used for drawing lots, and in choosing the judges (jury) in criminal cases, who were drawn by lot as in modern times: urnam movet Minos (i.e. to mix up the names).

ūrŏ, ūssī, ūstum, ūrere, [√us, cf. Gr. αὔω, Sk. √*ush*], 3. v. a, *burn.* — Less exactly, of land, *exhaust, dry up, poison.* — Fig., esp. of the passions, *burn, fire, set on fire, excite, worry, disturb:* me amor; me Daphnis; atrox Iuno (of Venus); uritur Dido (*burns with love*).

ursa, -ae, [f. of ursus], f., *a she-bear.*

ursus, -ī, [?, akin to ἄρκτος], m., *a bear.*

urus, -ī, [a Gallic word], m., *the urus.* — Less exactly, *a wild ox* (the Italian buffalo).

usquam [held to be unc. case (cf. **cis, uls**) of pron. †quŏ+quam, cf. **quisquam**], adv., *anywhere* (in neg. clauses, cf. **ullus**): si quid usquam iustitia est (*if justice counts for something anywhere,* as it would seem not to have thus far); dubitem haud equidem implorare quod usquam est (*what power there is anywhere,* not mine).

usque [unc. stem (same as in **usquam**)+que, cf. **quisque**], adv., (*in every place*), *all the way, even (to), clear (to), as far as:* usque sub (*quite up to, quite into*); ad usque columnas (*to the far columns*); usque ab (*all the way from*); super usque (*away beyond*); quo usque (*how far,* clear up to what point, *how long*). — Also, of time and degree, *all the time, constantly, ever, even, quite:* iuvat usque morari; usque dum (*all the time* that, *always while*); usque adeo (*quite, to such a degree, so very much, so very*); turbatur agris (*so much confusion,* &c.); usque adeone mori miserum est (*so very hard a fate,* &c.).

ūsus, -ūs, [√ut (or stem as root) + tus], m., *use, employment, enjoyment, experience* (continued use): quos indiget usus (*need requires*); usus medendi (*practice of medicine*); pervius usus tectorum (*a much-used passage*); —passing into *service, purpose, use* (purpose or advantage of employment), *usefulness, advantage, profit:* neque erat coriis usus (*nor could anything be done with,* &c.); ipsos ad usus (*for this very purpose*). — — Also, *activity* (changing the point of view). — Esp. as predicate with esse, (*there is use for*), there is need of, something is required.

ut (uti), [held to be case of pron. √quŏ], adv. (conj.): 1. Interr., *how.* — Esp. in indirect questions: aspice laetentur ut omnia (*how,* the beginner should beware of *that*); 2. Rel., *as* (with or without correlative *so,* &c.), *just as,* — so in asseverations, *as sure as.* — Of condition or state (almost of place) passing into *as* of time. — Hence, *when, as soon as, no sooner than, as.* — Also, with subj., *that, in order that, so that, to.*

utcumque (-cunque), [ut-cunque, cf. **quicunque**], adv., *however, in whatever way.*

ūter, ūtris, [?], m., *a bag* (of skin for holding wine), *a skin.*

uterque, utraque, utrumque, utriusque, [uter-que, cf. quisque], pron. adj., *each* (of two), *both;* — in Eng., by a change of point of view, *either.*
uterus, -ī, [?], m., *the womb.*—Less exactly, *the belly.*
utī, see **ut.**
ūtilis, -e, [stem akin to **utor** + lis], adj., *advantageous, useful, adapted, serviceable:* bis pomis utilis arbos (*productive in*).
utinam, [uti-nam, cf. quisnam], conj., (*how pray*), *oh that, would that.*
utor, ūsus, ūtī, (old oitor), [?], 3. v. dep., *use, enjoy,* take advantage of, *employ, show* (in sense of *use,* changing the point of view according to Eng. idiom).

utrimque [unc. case of **uterque,** cf. **hinc**], adv., *from both sides.*— Also (cf. **hinc**), *on each side, on both sides.*
ūva, -ae, [f. of †uvŏ- (cf. **uvidus**) + a], f., *the grape* (collectively, of the bunches of fruit as well as the entire vine), *grapes, the vine.*— Plur., *grapes, clusters* (*bunches,* of grapes). — Poetically (of a cluster of bees), *a grape-cluster.*
ūvidus, -a, -um, [†uvŏ- (real or supposed, wh. **uveo,** cf. **uva**) + dus, prob. √UG, cf. ὑγρος], adj., *soaked, wet, wet through.*
uxor, -ōris, [?], f., *a wife.*
uxōrius, -a, -um, [†uxor + ius], adj., *of a wife.* — Also, *uxorious, devoted to one's wife* (to excess).

V (consonant).

vacca, -ae, [?], f., *a cow, kine.*
vaccīnium, -ī, (-iī), [?, poss. akin to **vacca**], n., *a whortle-berry* (or some similar berry). — Also, a flower of some uncertain kind.
vacŏ, -āvī, -ātum, -āre, [†vacŏ- (cf. **vacuus, Vacuna**)], 1. v. n., *be empty, be free from, be unoccupied:* vacare domos hoste (*the dwellings are vacant, deserted by the enemy*); hic solus locus (*this only means is open*). — Fig., *be at leisure.*— Impersonal, *there is* (*one has*) *time* (for a thing), *there is room:* hactenus indulsisse vacat (*thus far it was open to me,* &c., *it was permitted*).
vacuus, -a, -um, [√vac (in vaco) + uus, cf. **adsiduus**], adj., *vacant, open, unoccupied, empty, deserted, unobstructed, clear:* aurae (as in Eng.); caelum (*free*); orbis (*desolate, without inhabitants*); saltus (*open,* with no trees). — Fig., *unoccupied, idle:* mentes.
vādŏ, perf. and sup. not found, **vādere,** [?, √vad, cf. **vadum** (poss. akin to βαίνω)], 3. v. n., *go, walk, proceed, go on:* vadit discordia

(*stalks abroad*); ille ducem vadentem aequat (*as he walked, moved*). — Esp.: vade age (like Homeric βάσκ' ἴθι), *come go, go on now,* of command, encouragement, or farewell.
vadōsus, -a, -um, [†vadŏ- (reduced) + osus], adj., *shallow.*
vadum, -ī, [√vad (of **vado**) + um], n., *a ford, a shoal, a shallow, a sand-bank.* — Also, *the bottom of the sea, the depths.* — Less exactly, *the sea, the waters, a wave.*
vae [?, cf. Gr. οὐαί], interj., *alas!*
vāgīna, -ae, [unc. stem + na], f., *a scabbard, a sheath.*
vāgītus, -ūs, [†vagi- (of **vagio**) + tus], m., *a crying.*
vagor, -ātus, -ārī, [†vagŏ- (of **vagus**)], 1. v. dep., *move to and fro, roam, rove, wander, stray, fly to and fro* (of birds).—Fig., *spread abroad:* fama.
valeo, -uī, -itum, -ēre, [†valŏ- (√val + us, cf. **validus** and Sk. balas, *strength*)], 2. v. n., *be strong, be stout, be sturdy.*—Esp. of health, *be well.* — Fig., *be strong, have power, have force, avail, have*

*effec*t, *be of use, serve, be worth, be able, can.* — With cogn. acc., *have power to do, can do:* quidquid sive animis sive arte vales (*whatever resources you have*, &c.). — With negatives, *not serve one, be powerless, be useless, fail:* non lingua valet. — Esp. in imperat., *be well, farewell, adieu.* — **valēns, -ēntis,** p. as adj., *strong, stout, sturdy.*

Valerus, -ī, [?], m., a Rutulian.

validus, -a, -um, [†valŏ- (wh. valeo) + dus], adj., *strong, stout, sturdy, stalwart, vigorous.* — Transferred: ictus (*heavy*); pondus (*heavy*). — Often a standing epithet like "*good sword.*"

vallis (-ēs), -is, [?], f., *a valley.*

vallŏ, -āvī, -ātum, -āre, [†vallŏ-], 1. v. a., *entrench, fortify.* — Poetical: moenia vallant, t*hey entrench themselves with walls.*

vallum, -ī, [n. of **vallus**, used collectively], n., *a rampar*t (of stakes filled with earth, the regular Roman entrenchment), *an entrenchment, a wall, a fortification.*

vallus, -ī, [?, cf. ἧλος, *a nail*], m., *a stake.*

vannus, -ī, [?, perh. akin to **ventus**], f., *a basket* (broad and shallow for winnowing). — Also, the shallow basket employed in the rites of Bacchus, the meaning of which is uncertain, but which often appears among his emblems. Sometimes it serves for his cradle.

vānus, -a, -um, [prob. √vac (in vacuus) + nus], adj., *empty.* — Esp. of phantoms, dreams, &c., *empty, bodiless, idle.* — Fig., *baseless, empty, vain, idle, groundless, without foundation, meaningless, ineffectual, fruitless, false, deceitful:* veri vana (*destitute of truth,* with a suspicion of the lit. sense); ne vana putes haec fingere somnum (*invents these idle tales*). — Neut. plur. as adv., *vainly.*

vapor, -ōris, [√vap (of unc. kin., cf. **vapidus**) + or], m., *steam, vapor.* — Less exactly, *heat, fire.*

vapōrŏ, -āvī, -ātum, -āre, [†vapor-], 1. v. a. and n., *steam, smoke.* — Act., *fill with vapor* or *smoke, fumigate:* templum ture (*fill with smoke of incense*).

variŏ, -āvī, -ātum, -āre,[†variŏ-], 1. v. a. and n., *diversify, variegate.* — Also, *change:* vices(*change their posts*). — Intrans., *change, waver, fluctuate.*

varius, -a, -um, [†vărŏ- (varus, *stretched apart*) + ius], adj., *of two things or more, diverse, different, various, different sorts of, opposing, on different sides.* — Also (of one thing in its parts), *varying, varied, changeable, variable, changeful, changing, various, manifold, motley, variegated, party-colored, spotted:* imagorerum(*various thoughts and feelings*); irarum aestus (*ebbing and flowing, fluctuating*). — Sometimes in the sing. to be rendered by the plur.: vario certamine (*in the various rivalries*); dissensu vario (*in many altercations*); fremor (*different murmurs*); vario motu (*with various emotions*).

Vărus, -ī, [varus, *bow-legged*], m., a Roman name. — Esp., *L. Alfenus Varus,* who, as an officer of Augustus, had charge of the confiscation of the lands in Virgil's region. He has as good a title as any to be considered the person to whom Virgil dedicates his tenth Eclogue.

vastātor, -ōris, [†vastā- (of vasto) + tor], m., *a ravager.* — Less exactly, *a destroyer.*

vastŏ, -āvī, -ātum, -āre,[†vastŏ-], 1. v. a., *devastate, lay waste, make desolate, ravage:* agros cultoribus (*despoil*).

vastus, -a, -um, [?, p.p. of lost verb], adj., *desolate, laid waste, desert.* — Also (by an unc. connection), *huge, enormous, immense, far-stretching, vast, wide* (of lands), *measureless,* — Fig., *mighty, fright-*

ful, tremendous, deafening (of noise).

vātēs, -is, [?], comm., *a soothsayer, a diviner, a seer, a prophet, a prophetess.* — Also, *an inspired bard, a bard, a poet.*

ve [prob. pron. √VA, cf. Sk. *vā*], conj. enclit., *or* (not exclusive, cf. **aut**). — Also (as the regular connective with **si** and **ne**), *and* (in Eng. taking the two branches together where the Latin takes the two separately, see **sive** and **neve**). — Also with questions, where English admits *or*.

vectis, -is, [√veh (in **veho**) + tis], m., *a pole* (for carrying or lifting). — From similarity, *a bar* (closing a door).

vectŏ, -āvī, -ātum, -āre, [†vectŏ- (cf. **veho**)], 1. v. a., *carry, transport.*

vector, -ōris, [√veh (of **veho**) + tor], m., *a voyager* (cf. **vehor**), *a traveller, a merchant* (as a sailor, according to ancient usage).

vectus, -a, -um, p.p. of **veho**.

vehō, vexī, vectum, vehere, [√veh (I.-E. VAGH), cf. ὄχος, Eng. *wagon*], 3. v. a., *carry.* — Esp. (of sailing and riding), *bear, convey, carry, bring.* — Also, pass. (almost as dep., cf. **vector**), *be borne, ride, sail, journey.*— Less exactly, *draw, lead, conduct, drive.* — Poetic (or proverbial): **quid vesper serus vehat** (*brings with it*).

vel [prob. imperat. of **volo**], conj., *or* (not exclusive, cf. **aut**); — repeated (or in other combinations), *either ... or.*— Also, *even.* — Esp. with superlatives, *even, the very* (often omitted in Eng.).

vēlāmen, -inis, [†velā- (of **velo**) + men], n., *a veil, a covering, a garment, clothing.*

vēlātus, -a, -um, p.p. of **velo**.

Velīnus, -a, -um, [†Velia + nus], adj.: 1. *Of Velia* (a town of Lucania near which Palinurus was drowned); 2. *Of Velia*, another (unknown) place which gave its name to a lake in the Sabine country. — Masc., *Velinus* (the lake itself).

vēlivolus, -a, -um, [†velo-†volus (√vol + us, wh. **volo,** *fly*)], adj., *winged with sails:* **mare** (i.e. covered with sails like wings).

vellō, vulsī (volsī), vulsum (volsum), vellere, [√vel, akin to ἕλκω], 3. v. a., *pull, pluck:* **aurem** (as a reminder). — Esp., *pull up, pull out, tear out, tear up;* — so of the standards in a camp, as a sign of moving: **castris signa** (*break up and move from camp*); **signa** (*advance the standards*). — Also, *pull down, overthrow, tear away, tear down.*

vellus, -eris, [?, unc. root + us, thought to be √VAR, *cover* (poss. akin to **vello,** as plucking is no doubt earlier than shearing)], n., *a fleece* (on or off the sheep), *a sheep-skin* (fleece and all). — Used also of fleecy clouds and of cotton. — Also, *a lock of wool* (used as a festoon).

vēlŏ, -āvī, -ātum, -āre, [†velŏ-], 1. v. a., *cover* (esp. of the head), *veil, crown, adorn, cover* (more generally), *clothe, surround* (with a garment, &c.). — Pass. (as middle), *cover &c. one's self.* — **vēlātus, -a, -um,** p.p., *crowned, veiled, covered, wearing* (something); — also (cf. **armatus**), *sail-clad* (of a vessel's yards).

vēlōx, -ōcis, [?], adj., *swift, fleet.*

vēlum, -ī, [referred to √veh (in **veho**) + lum, which suits the form, but sense can hardly be the orig. sense], n., *a sail.* — Also (cf. **velo**), *a cloth, a covering.*

velut (-utī), [vel-uti], adv., *just as, as, as when, like, as if, as it were, as though.*

vēna, -ae, [?], f., *a vein, an artery.* — Poetical: **in venis silicis** (supposed to contain fire). — Also (as in Eng.), *a vein* (of metal). — Also, *a stream, a water-course.*

vēnābulum, -ī, [†venā- (of **venor**) + bulum], n., *a hunting-spear.*

vēnātor, -ōris, [†venā-(of **venor**) + tor], m., *a hunter.* — In app. as adj., *hunting:* canis (*hound*).
vēnātrix, -īcis, [†venā-(of **venor**) + trix], f., *a huntress.*
vēnātus, -ūs, [†venā- (of **venor**) + tus], m., *hunting, the chase* (acc. as supine of **venor,** wh. see).
vendō, -didī, -ditum, -dere, [**venum-**(acc. of unc. kin.) -do(*put*)], 3. v. a., *sell.* — Also (as in Eng.), *sell* (*betray*).
venēnum, -ī, [?], n., *poison, venom* (of serpents, &c.). — Less exactly, *a potion* (perh. orig. sense), *a drug, a magic herb.* — Poetic, of dyes.
venerābilis, -e, [†venerā (of **veneror**) + bilis], adj., *venerable, venerated, revered, held in reverence.*
venerātus, -a, -um, p.p. of **venero.**
venerō, -āvī, -ātum, -āre, [†Vener- (of **Venus,** in earlier sense of *grace* or the like)], 1. v. a., *worship, reverence.* — Pass., **veneror** as dep., in same sense.—Also, *adore, pray, supplicate, offer prayers to* or *at.* — **venerandus, -a, -um,** p. ger. as adj., *venerable, adorable, worthy of all homage, revered.* — **venerātus, -a, -um,** p.p. as adj., *reverend, revered.*
venia, -ae, [√ven (cf. **Venus**) + ia, prob. through adj.-stem, cf. **insidiae**], f., *favor, pardon, indulgence, a boon* (concretely). — — Often rendered by a diff. construction: veniam rogantes corpora redderet (*asking that he would graciously,* &c.) ; veniam precari quem finem ferat (*graciously to make known*).
Venīlia, -ae, [prob. akin to **venio,** cf. the use of the word as wife of Janus], f., the mother of Turnus.
veniō, vēnī, ventum, venīre, [√ven, cf. βαίνω, Eng. *come,* Sk. √gam], 4. v. n., *come* (to a place), *come in, arrive, reach;* — also of states or conditions. — Fig., *come in, come around, return, come; arise, rise* (of heavenly bodies), *come forth, appear, succeed* (*come next*), *possess one* (of passions, &c.), *come upon; — spring up, grow:* segetes (*flourish*).—Also, *come* (from a place, without a terminus), *spring from.* — **veniēns, -entis,** p. as adj., *coming, next, future.* — **ventūrus, -a, -um,** f.p. as adj., *to come, future;* neut., *the future.*
vēnor, -ātus, -ārī, [?], 1. v. dep., *hunt* (with acc. or absolutely), *pursue, chase.*
venter, -tris, [unc. root, prob. akin to γάστηρ], m., *the belly.* — Also, of things: in ventrem cucumis cresceret (*fill its paunch*).
ventōsus, -a, -um, [†ventŏ- (reduced)+osus], adj., *windy, stormy, boisterous:* murmuris aurae; folles (*puffing*). — Also, as in Eng., *windy, empty, vain:* lingua ; gloria. — Poetically: alae (*wings of the wind*).
ventus, -ī, [√ven (akin to Sk. va, *blow*) + tus], m., *wind.* — Often of a particular wind ; — so in plur., *winds,* or in poetic plur., *wind.*
Venulus, -ī, [cf. **Venīlia**], m., a messenger of Turnus.
Venus, -eris, [√ven (akin to Sk. √van)+ us, cf. **genus**], f., *grace, beauty.* — Esp., *Venus,* the goddess of love and beauty. — Also (cf. **Ceres,** *corn*), *love* (sexual) ;— so of animals. — Concretely, *a loved one.*
veprēs (-is), -is, [?], m. (or f.), *a bramble, a thorn-bush.*
vēr, vēris, [for vasar, cf. ἔαρ, ἦρ], n., *the spring, spring weather, spring-time.*
verbēna, -ae, [?], f., a plant, *vervain.*—Also, in pl., *sacred branches,* borne by heralds, and used for religious and magic rites.
†**verber** (not found), **-eris,** [?], n. (mostly plur.), *a lash, a whip;* hence, *scourging, a blow.* — Also, *a thong, a rein.* — Less exactly, of other things, *a stroke, flapping.*

Vocabulary. 299

verbero, -āvī, -ātum, -āre, [†ver-ber-], 1. v. a., *lash* (with a whip), *scourge.* — Less exactly, *beat, strike, lash* (generally): **ictibus auras; aethera alis; imber humum; quadrupes calcibus auras** (*paw the air*).

verbum, -ī, [?, perh. √ver (cf. ῥῆμα and Eng. *word*) + **bum** (cf. **morbus**)], n., *a word* (as expressing something), *words* (a statement, a prayer, a vow, &c.): **in verbo** (*at the word*); **verba inter singula** (*with every word*). — Plur., *words, language, discourse:* **has inter voces, media inter talia verba,** *amid these words* (as sounds), *amid such thoughts* (*language*) *as these;* **rerum verborumque,** *in word and deed;* **non replenda est curia verbis** (as opposed to deeds).

vērē, [abl. of **verus**], adv., *truly* (*with truth*), *really.*

vereor, veritus, vererī, [√ver (cf. ὁράω, Eng. *ware*), through adj.-stem (cf. οὖρος)], 2. v. dep. Absolutely, *feel awed, be awed.* — Active, *fear, dread;* — with clause, *be afraid* (that), *fear, be alarmed;* — with indirect question, *be anxious, be concerned;* with complementary inf., *be afraid* (to do anything), *shrink* (from doing). — Less strong than other verbs of fearing, cf. **metuo, timeo.**

Vergilius (the proper Latin spelling, not **Virg-**), **-ī** (**-iī**), [?, cf. **Vergiliae**], m., a Roman gentile name. — Esp., *Publius Vergilius Maro, Virgil* (the established Eng. word, cf. *Horace, Livy, Leghorn*), the poet.

vergō, no perf., no sup., **vergere,** [?], 3. v. a. and n. Act., *bend, turn, incline.* — Intrans., *incline, lie* (of places), *slope, turn:* **vineta ad solem cadentem; quo vergat pondere letum** (*which scale death should turn,* by which weight the balance should be inclined).

verĭtus, -a, -um, p.p. of **vereor.**

vērō [abl. of **verus**], adv., *truly* (*in truth,* cf. **vere**), *doubtless, assuredly.* — Often ironical, *forsooth, indeed.*—Adversative, *however, but, yet.* — **tum vero,** see **tum.**

verrō, verrī, versum, verrere, [?], 3. v. a. (and n.), *sweep* (for clearing). — Less exactly (as in Eng.), *sweep, sweep over, skim:* **caerula nautae; vestigia** (of an animal with its tail). — Without acc., *sweep:* **per auras** (of the winds).

versicolor, -ōris, [†versŏ-color, decl. as adj.], adj., *changeable, party-colored, variegated.*

versō (**vorsō**), **-āvī, -ātum, -are,** [†versŏ- (cf. **verto**)], 1. v. a., *turn* (repeatedly or with violence), *roll, toss, wheel, turn over, wield:* **terram; telum dextera; serpens volumina** (*roll, wind*); **oves** (*drive, pasture*); **currum; se in suo vulnere** (*welter, writhe*). — Less exactly: **animos in pectore** (*bear*); **animum per omnia; ignem in ossibus** (*fire the frame with heat*).—Also, *overturn, overthrow, ruin:* **odiis domos.**—Fig., *turn over, revolve, ponder, meditate:* **omnia secum; dolos.**

versus (**vorsus**), **-a, -um,** p.p. of **verto.**

versus, -ūs, [√vert (of **verto**) + tus], m., *a turn, a turning.* — So, *a furrow* (once across a field), *a line, a row,* and, esp., *a verse* (of poetry, beginning the rhythm anew), *poetry.*

vertex (**vortex**), **-icis,** [†verti- (akin to **verto,** cf. **verticula**) + cus (reduced)], m., *a whirl, an eddy, a whirlpool, a vortex, a whirlwind, an eddying flame.* — From the peculiar growth of hair, *the crown* (of the head), *the head,*— *the top, the summit:* **caeli** (*the heights*). — Also, *the pole* (of the heavens). — Phrase: **a vertice,** *from above, overhead.*

vertō (**vor-**), **vertī, versum, vertere,** [√vert, cf. Sk. √vṛt, *turn,*

Eng. *worth*], 3. v. a. and n., *turn* (lit. and fig. in various relations); —so, *turn around, reverse, invert,*—*turn towards, direct,*—*turn away, drive off, divert, transfer,*—*turn up, upturn, turn over, overturn, overthrow.*—So: **sidera retro**; **terga** (of flight); **versis sagittis** (*with arrows in retreat*, of the Parthians); **versis frontibus** (*changing front*, of the revolving scene); **arma** (*reverse*, in sign of mourning); **aratrum** (*to plough across*); **cardo versus; freta** (in rowing); **puppes versas** (*steering*); **spicula infensa** (*present, level*); **vestigia; iter; lumina** (*roll*); **praedas** (*drive off*); **stimulos** (*ply*); **in viscera vires** (*turn against*); **munera in Aenean**; **crateras** (*drain, tip up*); **morsus** (*use the teeth*); **procellae vocem** (*bear away*); **domos** (*overthrow, ruin*); **versi Aquilones** (*changing*).— Esp. of battle, *turn, put to flight, rout, drive back:* **versi hostes** (*flying*). — Often, *change, alter, change into, transform:* **nomen**; **vestes**; **fata versa** (*changing*). — Also, of thought, *turn* (one's mind), *change* (one's purpose): **quae te sententia** (*what purpose changes you*); **varii pectore sensus** (*alternate*).— With reflexive (often without) and in passive, *turn one's self, turn, change, be changed, transform one's self, revolve, turn out, tend:* **hic victoria** (*hinge on this point*); **aestas septima** (*is rolling on*); **caelum** (*revolve*); **ordo** (*moves on, by fate*); **Turnus vertitur** (*moves to and fro*); **quo se vertant hospitia**; **nec bene vertat** (*turn out ill*). — In special uses: **omnia sub pedibus verti regique** (*be controlled*); **versum fas atque nefas** (*confounded*); **memet in omnia** (*try every resource*).

verū, -ūs, [?], n., *a spit.* — Also, *a dart.*

vērum, see **verus.**

vērus, -a, -um, [?], adj., *true, real,* — Also, *right, fitting, appropriate:* **nomen**(*real, appropriate*).—Neut. (sing. and pl.) as subst., *the truth, things true.* — Neut. as adv., *truly* (*in truth*, cf. **vere**); —also, *but, however, yet, still*; often in a mere transition or interruption, *but:* **verum age.** See also **vero.**

verūtus, -a, -um, [†veru + tus, cf. **auratus**], adj., *armed with darts.*

vēsānus, -a, -um, [vē-sanus], adj., *insane, crazy, mad.*—Transferred, *maddening, mad, furious.*

vescor, no p.p., **vesci,** [?], 3. v. dep., *feed on, eat, subsist on, feast on:* **aura** (*breathe the vital air*).

vescus, -a, -um, [?], adj., *small, meagre, thin.* (A word of uncertain etymology and meaning. In both places in Virgil, and in some other passages, it seems to have the meaning of *meagre food*).

Vesēvus (Vesuvius), -ī, [?], m., *Vesuvius,* the volcano near Naples: **iugum** (*the ridge of Vesuvius*):

vesper, -erī and **-eris,** [?, cf. Ἕσπερος], m., *the evening.* — Also, *the evening star* (perh. orig. sense). — Poetically, *the West.*

Vesta, -ae, [?, cf. ἑστία, poss. √ves, *dwell*? (cf. Sk. √vas and ἄστυ, but also **ver**) + ta], f., the goddess of household fire (cf. **Vulcan** of fire in general, esp. destructive or mechanical). She is the emblem of household purity and family life (**cana Fides et Vesta**). Her effigy and her fire were carried away from Troy by Æneas, as a sacred charge, and her fire was kept constantly burning in her temple as the hearth of the State considered as a family. She is often represented sitting with covered head and holding in her hand a Palladium. — Also, *the household fire, the hearth.*

vester, -tra, -trum, [pron. †vas + ter, cf. **alter**], pron. adj., *your, yours.*

vestibulum, -ī, [?], n., *a porch, a*

portico, a vestibule, an entrance. — Fig., *a beginning, an opening.*
vestigium, -ī, [?, adj.-stem wh. **vestigo**], n., *a track, a trace, a footprint, a sign, a vestige, a token:* hederae pandunt vestigia (*give indications*).—Less exactly, *a step, a footstep* (of walking, as in Eng.), *the feet, a course* (on foot, or even of inanimate things), *the fetlocks* (or *feet* of a horse).
vestīgō, -āvī, -ātum, -āre, [?, adj.-stem wh. **vestigium**], 1. v. a., *track, trace.* — Less exactly, *examine, search for.*
vestiō, -īvī (-iī), -ītum, -īre, [†vesti-], 4. v. a., *clothe.* — Fig. (as in Eng.), *clothe, cover, invest, deck:* aether campos lumine (*clothe, fill,* with a different fig.).
vestis, -is, [√ves (cf. ἐσθής, Sk. √vas, *clothe*) + tis], f., *a garment, a robe, covering, clothing.* — Also, *a fabric* (generally), *stuffs, hangings, cloth, drapery, housings.*
Vesulus, -ī, [?], m., a mountain of Liguria.
veternus, -a, -um, [†veter- (of vetus) + nus], adj., *old.* — Masc. as subst. (prob. subst. omitted), *lethargy, sluggishness, heaviness, inactivity.*
vetitus, -a, -um, p.p. of **veto.**
vetō, -uī, -itum, -āre, [prob. rudely formed from **vetus**, as if †vetŏ-], 1. v. a., (prob. political, *keep the old,* vote against the new), *forbid, prohibit.* — **vetitus, -a, -um,** p.p. as adj., *forbidden, unlawful.* — Neut. as subst., *a prohibition, an order* (of prohibition).
vetus, -eris, [unc. root + us (cf. ἔτος), prob. orig. noun (cf. acc. plur. in -a)], adj., *of long standing* (cf. **antiquus**), *old, aged, ancient, former.*—Masc. plur., *the ancients.*
vetustās, -ātis, [†vetus (with orig. s) + tas], f., *age, antiquity, lapse of time:* aevi (*long lapse of time*).

vetustus, -a, -um, [†vetus (with orig. s) + tus (cf. **honestus**)], adj., *ancient* (cf. **vetus**).
vexātus, -a, -um, p.p. of **vexo.**
vexō, -āvī, -ātum, -āre, [†vexŏ- (as p.p. of **veho**)], 1. v. a., *shake.* — Fig., *harass, worry.*
via, -ae, [√veh (of **veho**) + a (or -ia)], f., *a road, a way, a path, a street.* — Less exactly, *a passage, a course.* — Fig., *a way, a means, a mode, a fashion, a course.* — Plur. equals *journeys, journeyings, wanderings.* — Special: quos ipse via sibi repperit usus, *in course of time, by practice.*
viātor, -ōris, [†via- (as if of **vio**, perh. really) + tor], m., *a wayfarer, a traveller.*
vibrātus, -a, -um, p.p. of **vibro.**
vibrō, -āvī, -ātum, -āre, [†vibrŏ- (of lost adj. of unc. kin.)], 1. v. a. and n., *agitate, swing, brandish.* — Intrans., *quiver, wave:* vibranti cuspis transverberat ictu (*quivering with the blow,* the force was so great). — **vibrātus, -a, -um,** p.p., *curled, frizzled* (of hair), *forked* (*quivering,* of the lightning).
vīburnum, -ī, [?, poss. akin to **vibro**?], n., *the viburnum* (a low shrub of uncertain identity).
vice, see **vicis.**
vicia, -ae, [?], f., *a vetch* (a kind of leguminous plant).
vīcīnia, -ae, [†vicinŏ- (reduced) + ia], f., *nearness, close proximity:* Persidis (*neighboring Persia*).
vīcīnus, -a, -um, [†vicŏ- (reduced) + inus], adj., (*of the same quarter*), *near, neighboring, in the vicinity, close by.* — Masc. as subst., *a neighbor.*
vicis (gen., no nom. found), [?], f., (orig. sense unc.), apparently, *change, interchange:* hac vice sermonum; in vicem (*in turn, alternately*).—Also, plur., *changes, chances, fortune.* — Also, *a post* (perh. as held by soldiers in succession), *a place, a duty, a function.*

vicissim [acc. adv., same root as **vicis**], adv., *alternately, in turn.*

victima, -ae, f., *a victim.*

victor, -ōris, [√vic (of **vinco**) + **tor**], m., *a victor, a conqueror.* — As adj., *victorious, triumphant.*

victōria, -ae, [†victor + ia], f., *victory, triumph, success.*

victrīcia, see **victrix.**

victrix, -īcis, [√vic (in **vinco**) + **trix**], f., *a conqueror* (female). — Also, as adj. in f. and n., *victorious, conquering, of victory;* — also, *successful.*

victus, -a, -um, p.p. of **vinco.**

victus, -ūs, [root of **vivo** (wh. see) + **tus**], m., *a living, a sustenance, support* (of life), *food:* facilis victu gens (*gaining an easy subsistence*).

vidĕn', see **video** and **ne.**

videō, vīdī, vīsum, vidēre, [†vidŏ- (cf. **providus**)], 2. v. a. and n., *see* (with the eye or mind).—Pass., *be seen, seem, appear;* — esp., *seem best, seem good, be determined.* — Also, *see* (*experience*), *live to see, meet.* — **vidēns, -entis,** p., *seeing, awake, with the eyes open.* — See also **visum.**

viduātus, -a, -um, p.p. of **viduo.**

viduō, -āvī, -ātum, -āre, [†viduŏ- (of **viduus**)], 1. v. a., *deprive, rob, strip.* — **viduātus, -a, -um,** p.p. as adj., *destitute, free from.*

vigeō, no perf., no sup., **-ēre,** [†vigŏ- (cf. **vigil**)], 2. v. n., *thrive, flourish, be in vigor, be powerful, gain strength.*

vigil, -ilis, [†vigŏ- (wh. **vigeo**) + **lis**], adj., *wakeful, awake, watchful, sleepless, unsleeping.* — Fig., also *of things.* — As subst., *a watchman, a sentinel, a guard:* vigilum excubiae (*posts of sentinels*).

vigilāntia, -ae, [†vigilant + ia], f., *watchfulness.*

vigilō, -āvī, -ātum, -āre, [†vigil-], 1. v. n. and a., *be awake, wake, wake up, watch.* — With acc., *look out for, watch for.*

vīgintī [†dvi (of **duo**) + unc. form, cf. **triginta**], indecl. adj., *twenty.*

vigor, -ōris, [√vig (in **vigeo**) + **or**], m., *activity, vigor, strength, force.*

vīlis, -e, [?], adj., *cheap, poor.*

villa, -ae, [?], f., *a farm-house.*

villōsus, -a, -um, [†villŏ- (reduced) + osus], adj., *shaggy, hairy.*

villus, -ī, [?, cf. **vellus**], m., *a coarse hair, hair* (of animals), *a fleece* (plur.), *wool* (coarse).

vīmen, -inis, [√vi (in **vieo**) + **men**], n., *a twig* (flexible), *osier.* — Also, *a shoot.*

vīminĕus, -a, -um, [†vimin + eus], adj., *of wicker, plaited, woven.*

vinciō, vinxī, vinctum, vincīre, [prob. akin to **vinco** through adj.-stem], 4. v. a., *bind, tie up.* — Esp. of garlands, *twine, encircle.* — Fig., of wine, *tie, hamper:* linguam.

vinclum, see **vinculum.**

vincō, vīcī, victum, vincere, [√vic, of unc. kin.], 3. v. a. and n. Of battle, *conquer, defeat, subdue.* — Also, of rivalry, *surpass, outvie, conquer, excel, gain one's point, beat, prevail;* — so: ea vincam verbis (*master*); fata (*outlive*). — Also, of things, *overcome, outlast, prevail against, wear out, rise above.* — With cogn. acc.: hoc vincite (*gain this victory*).—**victus, -a, -um,** p.p. as adj., *conquered, broken, shattered.*

vinctus, -a, -um, p.p. of **vincio.**

vinculum, -ī, [as if †vincŏ- (akin to **vincio**) + lum], n., *a bond, a fetter, a band, a shoe-lacing, a strap, a thong.* — Fig., *a bond, an obligation, a binding force, a tie* (esp. of marriage).

vindēmia, -ae, [†vinŏ- †demia (lost stem akin to **demo**, cf. **praemium**)], f., *a vintage.* — Also, concretely (as in Eng.), *the vintage, crop of grapes, grapes.*

vindicō, -āvī, -ātum, -āre, [†vindic- (of unc. orig.)], 1. v. a., *set free, release.*

vīnētum, -ī, [†vĭnŏ- (reduced) + etum, cf. **dumetum**], n., *a vineyard.*

vīneus, -a, -um, [†vĭnŏ- (reduced) +eus], adj., *of vines.*—Fem. (some noun omitted), *a vineyard.*

vīnitor, -ōris, [†vĭnŏ + tor, cf. **viator**], m., *a vine-dresser, a vine-pruner.*

vīnum, -ī, [poss. borrowed, cf. οἶνος, but cf. **vitis** and **vieo**], n., *wine.*

viola, -ae, [†vĭŏ- (akin to ἴον) + la], f., *a violet* (probably several kinds of flowers more or less like our violets).

violābilis, -e, [†violā- (of **violo**) + bilis], adj., *to be violated.*

violārium, -ī(-iī), [†viola+arium (n. of -arius)], n., *a bed of violets, a violet-bed.*

violentia, -ae, [†violent + ia], f., *violence, fury, ferocity.*

violentus, -a, -um, [?, perh. akin to **vis**, perh. to **violo**], adj., *violent, ferocious, boisterous, rapid.*

violō, -āvī, -ātum, -āre, [?, poss. akin to **vis** (cf. **violentus**), poss. to **viola** (cf. μιαίνω, and see below)], 1. v. a., *do violence to, outrage* (lit.), *injure, mar, ravage.*—Also, *profane, sully, stain* (fig.), *violate, outrage* (fig.).—Also, *stain* (imitating μιαίνω, but perh. orig. sense).

vīpera, -ae, [†vīvŏ- (or stem akin) -para (akin to **pario**), cf. **puerpera**], f., *a viper, a snake.*

vīpereus, -a, -um, [†vipera- (reduced) + eus], adj., *of snakes, snaky;* —*venomous, poisonous.*

vir, virī, [?, cf. Sk. viras, *hero*], m., *a hero, a man* (opposed to woman), *a husband.*—Also, of animals, *the male, the leader, the lord.*

virāgō, -inis, [†vir (as if virā-, cf. **imago**) + go], f., *a masculine woman, a virago:* **Iuturna** (the "Amazon" Juturna).

Virbius, -ī, [?], m., a name of Hippolytus.—Also of his son, an ally of Turnus.

virectum, see **viretum.**

vireō, no perf., no sup., **virēre,** [†virŏ- (cf. **viridis**)], 2. v. n., *be green, flourish, grow, put forth leaves.*

virēscō, no perf., no sup., **virēscere,** [vire- (of **vireo**) + sco], 3. v. n., *grow green, be green.*

virētum (-ectum), -ī, [n. p.p. of **vireo**], n., *a grassy spot, a green thicket.*

virga, -ae, [?, perh. √vir (in **vireo**), perh. √virg (cf. Sk. √vṛj)], f., *a shoot, a twig, a sapling, a rod, a wand.*

virgātus, -a, -um, [†virga + tus, cf. **auratus**], adj., *striped.*

virgeus, -a, -um, [†virga- (reduced) + eus], adj., *of twigs, of shoots, osier.*

virgineus, -a, -um, [†virgin+eus], adj., *of a maiden, maiden, maidenly.*

virginitās, -ātis, [†virgin- (as if virgini-) + tas], f., *maidenhood, virginity, chastity.*

virgō, -inis, [stem akin to **virga** + o, cf. **propago**], f., *a maiden, a maid, a virgin.*— Esp., *the Virgin,* Astræa, or Justice, who lived on the earth in the golden age, but fled to heaven in the more corrupt ages.

virgultum, -ī, [†virgula-(reduced) + tum (cf. **salictum**)], n., *a thicket.*

viridāns, -antis, [p. of **virido**, fr. †viridi-], adj., *green.*

viridis, -e, [†virŏ- (wh. **vireo**) + dus (weakened)], adj., *green:* Aegyptus (*clad in verdure, flowery, blooming*); litus (*grassy*); antrum (*mossy*); umbra (*leafy*). —Fig., *green, fresh, vigorous.*

virīlis, -e, [†virŏ- (of **vir**) + ilis], adj., *manly, masculine, heroic, male.*

virōsus, -a, -um, [†virŏ-(reduced) + osus], adj., *odorous, fetid.*

virtūs, -ūtis, [†virŏ- (reduced) + tus], f., *manliness, manhood, bravery, heroism, courage, virtue, excellence.*— More concretely, *a virtue,* *a good quality:* mea virtus (*consciousness of virtue*); socium virtus omnis (*valiant souls*).

virus, -ī, [unc. root, cf. Sk. *vishas, ĭós,* perh. akin to **viola**], n., *poison, venom:* lentum distillat ab inguine (*an excretion*).

vīs, vīs, [?, cf. **īs**], f. sing., *power, strength, might, virtue, effectiveness.*—Also, *force, violence.*—Plur., *strength* (usually active, cf. **robur**), *power, force, energy, might, ability, vigor, powers, forces:* vim viribus exit (*escapes violence by main force*); vires occultae (*a secret virtue*). — Also, *a multitude, a quantity.*

viscum, -ī, [?, poss. akin to **virus**, from its slimy, sticky nature], n., *mistletoe.*

viscus, -eris, (generally plur.), [?], n., *the flesh* (or soft parts inside the skin), *the inwards, the body* (as opposed to the skin and bones). — Esp., *the viscera* (the lungs, liver, &c., used for divination), *the entrails.* — Less exactly and fig., as in Eng., *bowels* (of a mountain), *the vitals* (of one's country).

vīsō, vīsī, vīsum, vīsere, [old desiderative for **vividso**, from √vid (in **video**), reduplicated with -so, (akin to Gr. fut. ending)], 3. v. a., *go to see, visit.* — Less exactly, *examine, see.*

vīsum, -ī, [n. p.p. of **video**], n., *a sight, a spectacle, a portent, a prodigy.*

vīsus, -a, -um, p.p. of **video**.

vīsus, -ūs, [√vid (of **video**) + tus], m., *the sight* (power or act of seeing, cf. **visum**), *vision, the gaze, a look.* — Also, *a sight, an omen.* — Also, *appearance, aspect.* — Abl. as supine of **video**, wh. see.

vīta, -ae, [root or stem of **vivo** + ta], f., *life* (existence, also the conditions of life, *nature*), *life* (the vital principle), *the breath of life, the vital spark;* — hence, *the soul, the shade, a spirit.* — Also, *a mode of life, life* (course, history of life).

vītālis, -e, [†**vita** + **lis**], adj., *of life, vital.*

vīteus, -a, -um, [†**viti-** (reduced) + **eus**], adj., *of the vine:* pocula (*of wine*).

vitiōsus, -a, -um, [†**vitiō-** (reduced) + **osus**], adj., *faulty, blemished, unsound:* ilex (*decaying*).

vītis, -is, [√vi (of **vieo**) + tis], f., *a vine* (esp. of the grape). — — Less exactly, *grapes.*

vītisator, -ōris, [†**viti-sator**], m., *a vine-planter.*

vitium, -ī (-iī), n., *a flaw, a blemish, a defect.* — Also, *an injurious principle* (of the earth or air): terrae; aeris (*effect*).—vitiō, abl., *by the fault of, through the influence of, caused by.*

vītō, -āvī, -ātum, -āre, [?], 1. v. a., *avoid, shun.*

vitreus, -a, -um, [†**vitro-** (reduced) + **eus**], adj., *glassy, sea-green* (the color of glass).

vitta, -ae, [akin to **vieo**], f., *a fillet, a band.* — Esp. as worn in sacred observances, and by suppliants, wound around sacred objects, and hung on the hands or on the olive-branches carried as signs of supplication.

vitula, -ae, [?, f. of **vitulus**], f., *a heifer.*

vitulus, -ī, [?, akin to ἰταλος, perh. to **vetus,** as *yearling,* cf. ἔτος], m., *a bullock.*

vīvāx, -ācis, [stem of **vivo** (reduced) + **ax**, cf. **capax**], adj., *long-lived, enduring.*

vīvidus, -a, -um, [†**vivŏ** (of **vivus**) + **dus**], adj., *lively, vigorous, active.* — Also, fig. in same senses.

vīvō, vīxī, victum, vīvere, [√viv (orig. form unc., but with a g, cf. *quick,* and Sk. √jiv), cf. βίος], 3. v. n., *live, be alive, pass one's life.* — Also, *subsist, live* (on anything). — Also, of things, *live, remain, grow, keep alive:* vitium tegendo (*thrive*); sub pectore vulnus; stuppa (as being on fire). — Esp. in imperat., *may you*

Vocabulary. 305

live, farewell, I wish you well, adieu.

vīvus, -a, -um, [√viv (in vivo) + us, cf. *quick*], adj., *alive, living:* vivus per ora feretur (*undying*); — so : vultus (*living*, made like life). — Also, of plants, *living, growing.* — Also, of things as partaking of the life of nature, *living, natural, flowing, perennial, solid* (of rock): sulphura (*native*). — As subst., *the living, living creatures.* — Phrase : ad vivum, *to the quick.*

vix [?], adv., *with difficulty, hardly, scarcely.* — Also, of time, *hardly, just, no sooner* (with a new incident immediately following).

vocātus, -a, -um, p.p. of voco.

vocātus, -ūs, [†vocā- (of voco) + tus], m., *a call, a demand, a request, an invocation, a prayer.*

vōciferor, -ātus, -ārī, [lost †vociferō- fr. †voc, of vox (as if voci-) -fer], 1. v. dep., *cry out, shout, cry, exclaim.* — With the words in direct discourse.

vocŏ, -āvī, -ātum, -āre, [†vocŏ- (√voc + us, cf. aequivocus)], 1. v. a. and n., *call* (in every shade of invitation and command), *call to, call for, pray for, call upon, invoke, pray to, invite, summon, call together, rally, call by name, speak of, proclaim, direct:* ad poenam (*bring to justice*); in artes (of trees, *try to turn, demand of them*); me ad fata (*ask to share*); pugnas (*proclaim*); cornix pluviam (as if the bird had power to bring it); ventis vocatis (*having invoked the winds*, but also of Mercury, *summon*); concilium (*convene*). — Also, of things more or less personified, *call, summon, challenge, rival, bid to go, direct, demand, await:* Zephyri; Cithaeron; ipsa res (*bid*); lux ultima (*summon*); aurae vela (*invite*); cursus vela (*direct*); cursum ventus (*guide*). — Esp., *call* (by name), *name.*

volaema, -ae, [†vola- (*palm of the hand*)], f., name of a large kind of pears.

volātilis, -e, (†volatō- (p.p. of volo) + lis], adj., *flying, winged.* — Poetically, of missiles.

Volcēns, -entis, [?], m., a Latin.

volēma, see **volaema,** the better authenticated reading.

volitŏ, -āvī, -ātum, -āre, [as if †volitŏ- (supposed p.p. of volo), cf. domito], 1. v. n., *flit about, fly to and fro, flit, fly abroad, fly.* — Less exactly, *rush to and fro:* milite Volsci (*scour the fields*); victor volitare per ora (*fly*). — — Of things, *float, whirl, fly:* turbo (*spin*). — volitāns, -antis, p. as subst., *an insect.*

volnus, see **vulnus.**

volō, voluī, no sup., **velle,** [√vol, akin to βούλομαι and Sk. √vṛ], irr. v. a. (with obj. implied), *wish, will, be willing, consent, allow, choose, design :* hunc laetum diem esse velis (*graciously make*). — Also, (*wish for one's self*), *intend, purpose, have in view, mean.* — With acc. and inf., *claim, will have it that.* — volēns, -entis, p. as adj., *propitious, gracious, willing, cheerful, glad.*

volō, -āvī, -ātum, -āre, [?], 1. v. n., *fly, fly about, flit.* — Less exactly and fig., *fly* (as in Eng.), *whirl along, skim, rush, speed, dart, be hurled, be flung, wave, shoot* (of stars), *roll up* (of smoke, &c.). — volāns, -antis, p. as subst., *flying creatures, winged creatures, birds.*

Volscēns, see **Volcens.**

Volscus, -a, -um, [?], adj., *of the Volsci* (a people of Latium, between the Pomptine marshes and Campania, who waged a stubborn warfare against the Romans, but were finally conquered about B.C. 325), *Volscian.* — Plur. as subst., *the Volsci* (the people themselves), *the Volscians.*

volūbilis, -e, [†volvi- (of volvo) + bilis], adj., *whirling.*

volucer (-cris), -cris, -cre, [†volŏ- (cf. **velivolus**) + cris, cf. †ludi- crŏ-], adj., *flying, winged.* — Less exactly, *flying, rapid, fleet, winged* (fig.). — Also, *fleeting:* Somnus. — Fem. (rarely m.) as subs., *a winged creature, a bird.*

volūmen, -inis, [†volvi- (of **vol- vo**) + men], n., *a roll, a coil, a fold, a band* (wound around). — Less exactly, *a joint* (the folding of the legs).

voluntās, -ātis, [†volent- (earlier volont-, of **volens**) + tas], f., *wish, will, desire, pleasure* (desire).

voluptās, -ātis, [†volupi- (reduced, cf. **volup**) + tas], f., *pleasure, de- light, enjoyment, joy.* — Concretely, as in Eng., of the source of delight.

Volusus, -ī, [?], m., a Rutulian.

volūtābrum, -ī, [†volutā- (of **vo- luto**) + brum], n., *a wallow, a slough.*

volūtō, -āvī, -ātum, -āre, [†vo- lutŏ- (cf. **volvo**)], 1. v. a. and n., *roll.* — Less exactly, *roll back, send echoing, make echo, echo, make re- sound.* — Esp. with reflexive (or without) and in pass., *roll, writhe.* — Fig., *revolve, turn over, ponder, meditate.*

volūtus, -a, -um, p.p. of **volvo**.

volvō, volvī, volūtum, volvere, [√volv, cf. ἐλύω], 3. v. a. and n. Act., *roll.* — Pass. (as middle), *be rolled, roll:* volvitur Euryalus leto (*writhe*); — and fig., *turn over, revolve* (in the mind), *pon- der:* sub pectore sortem. — Esp., of the eyes, *turn, roll.* — Also, in pass., rarely act., of regular revolu- tion, *revolve, run round, roll round:* volvitur annus (*roll round*); volvenda dies; volvun- tur sidera (*are gliding on*); ca- sus (*run the round of*); vices (*turn on, roll on*); saecula (of an oak, *live the round of*). — Gener- ally with motion onwards, *roll on, roll down;* — pass., also, *pour, glide, wind:* volvimur undis (*are tossed*); volvunt ad litora fluctus (of the winds); lacrimae volvun tur inanes (*pour down, are shed*); incendia aestus (*the fire rolling brings the heat,* &c.); lapis volu- tus (*whirling*); sic volvere Par- cas (*turn the wheel of destiny*); rotam volvere per annos (*run the round*); — esp., *unroll* (of a scroll): arcana; monimenta (*un- roll, study*). — Also, *roll up, roll forth, pour forth, send forth, send rolling up;* — pass. as mid.: ignis ad fastigia volvitur; saxa (of Ætna); sub naribus ignem equus (*breathe forth*); volvitur ater odor tectis (*pour through,* from the fire). — Also, *roll over, throw headlong, send whirling, throw rolling, precipitate, go whirling* (pass.). — Also, intrans., *roll, re- volve.*

vōmis (**vōmer**), -eris, [?], m., *a ploughshare.*

vomō, -uī, -itum, -ere, [√vom, akin to ἐμέω, Sk. √vam], 3. v. a. and n., *vomit, vomit forth, belch forth, throw up, send forth, emit.*

vorāgō, -inis, [†vorā- (of **vorŏ**) + go, prob. through intermediate stem, cf. **imago**], f., *an abyss, a whirlpool, a vortex, a yawning chasm.*

vorō, -āvī, -ātum, -āre, [†vorŏ- (cf. **omnivorus**), akin to βιβρώ- σκω, Sk. √gar], 1. v. a., *devour.* — Fig., of the sea, *swallow up, engulf.*

vortex, see **vertex**.

vōsmet, see **tu**.

vōtum, see **voveo**.

vōtus, -a, -um, p.p. of **voveo**.

voveō, vōvī, vōtum, vovere, [?], 1. v. a., *vow, devote, dedicate.*

vōtus, -a, -um, p.p. as adj., *vowed* (promised in a vow), *votive.* — Neut. as subst., *a vow, a prayer* (usually accompanied by a vow). — Also, *a votive offering* (the thing vowed).

vōx, vōcis, [√voc (in **voco**, etc.) as stem (akin to ἔπος and Sk.

√vach)], f., *a voice* (as sound, cf. **verbum**), *the voice:* nec vox nec verba sequuntur (*articulate sound nor intelligible words*). — Less exactly, *a voice* (of other living things), *a note, a tone, a sound, a cry, a song:* septem voces (*the seven tones* of the scale). — Also, *words, language, speech*, often rendered *voice* also in Eng.: vox excidit ore (*these words*, &c.); voce magister (*in song*); prodere voce sua (*by his words*); rumpit vocem (*utter a voice, break silence*); vocem volutant (*roll their voices*). — voce, abl., may often be absorbed in some other word, or rendered *lips,* or *aloud,* or by some similar device: compellat voce Menoeten (*aloud*); sic voce precatur (*with these words*); nostrā voce (*from my lips*); qua voce (*with what prayer*); voce lacessit (*with taunting words*).

Vulcānius (Vol-), -a, -um, [†Vulcanŏ- (reduced) + ius], adj., *of Vulcan, Vulcanian.* — Less exactly, *of fire.*

Vulcānus (Vol-), -ī, [?], m., *Vulcan,* the god of fire in its destructive and mechanical forms. He was fabled to have a forge beneath the Lipari islands, where he wrought the thunderbolts of Jupiter. — Fig., *fire.*

vulgātus, -a, -um, p p. of vulgo.
vulgō (volgō), [abl. of vulgus], adv., *generally, commonly, everywhere.*

vulgō (vol-), -āvī, -ātum, -āre, [†vulgŏ-], (of vulgus)], 1. v. a., *spread abroad, publish, make known, make common:* omnia vulgata (*trite themes*).

vulgus, -ī, [√vulg (cf. Sk. vargas, *a crowd*) + us], n. (sts. m.), *the populace, the common mass, the crowd, the people* (generally). — Also, of animals, *the mass, the flock, the swarm.*

vulnerō (vol-), -āvī, -ātum, -āre, [†vulner- (of vulnus)], 1. v. a., *wound.* — Also fig., as in Eng.

vulnificus (vol-), -a, -um, [stem of vulnus (as if vulnŏ-) -ficus (√fac + us)], adj., *wounding, destructive, cutting.*

vulnus (vol-), -eris, [?], n., *a wound* (given or received), *a stroke, a blow.* — Less exactly, *a weapon* (inflicting a wound). — Also, of the mind, *a wound, a blow, a pang, a pain.*

vulpēs (vol-), -is, [?], f., *a fox.*
vulsus (vol-), -a, -um, p.p. of vello.
vultur (vol-), -uris, [?], m., *a vulture.*

Vulturnus (Vol-), -ī, [†vultur + nus], m., *a river of Campania* (*Volturno*).

vultus (vol-), -us, [√vol (of volo) + tus], m., *an expression* (of the face), *the countenance, the aspect.* — Also, of things, *appearance, look, aspect.*

X.

Xanthō, -us, [Gr. Ξανθώ], f., one of the Nereids.

Xanthus, -ī, [Gr. Ξάνθος], m., a common name of rivers: 1. A river of the Troad; 2. A stream in Epirus, named for the first; 3. A river in Lycia, a favorite haunt of Apollo.

Z.

Zacynthus, -ī, [Gr. Ζάκυνθος], f., an island in the Ionian sea (now *Zante*).

Zephyrus, -ī, [Gr. Ζέφυρος], m., *Zephyrus* (*the West wind*). — Less exactly, *wind* (from any quarter).

zōna, -ae, [Gr. ζώνη], f., *a belt.* — Also, *a zone* (of the earth).

Press of
Berwick & Smith,
Boston.

GREEK BOOKS.[2]

Allen	Medea of Euripides	$1.00
College Series of Greek Authors .... See D'Ooge, Dyer, Humphreys.		
D'Ooge	Sophocles' Antigone: *Text and Notes*	95
	Text only	45
Dyer	Plato's Apology and Crito: *Text and Notes*	.95
	Text only	45
Flagg	Hellenic Orations of Demosthenes	1.00
	Anacreontics	.35
	Seven against Thebes	1.00
Goodwin	Greek Grammar	1.50
	Greek Reader	1.50
	Greek Moods and Tenses	1.50
	Selections from Xenophon and Herodotus	1.50
Goodwin & White:	Anabasis	1.00
	Anabasis (*with Vocabulary*)	1.50
Humphreys	Aristophanes' Clouds: *Text and Notes* ...	95
	Text only	45
Keep	Essential Uses of the Moods	.25
Kendrick	Greek at Sight	.15
Leighton	New Greek Lessons	1.20
Liddell & Scott..	Abridged Greek-English Lexicon	1.90
	Unabridged Greek-English Lexicon	9.40
Seymour	Selected Odes of Pindar	1.40
Sidgwick	Greek Prose Composition	1.50
Tarbell	Philippics of Demosthenes	1.00
Tyler	Selections from Greek Lyric Poets	1.00
White	First Lessons in Greek	1.20
	Schmidt's Rhythmic and Metric of the Classical Languages	2.50
	Œdipus Tyrannus of Sophocles	1.12
	Stein's Dialect of Herodotus	.10
Whiton	Orations of Lysias	1.00

Copies sent to teachers for examination, with a view to Introduction, on receipt of Introduction Price given above.

GINN & COMPANY, Publishers.

BOSTON.   NEW YORK.   CHICAGO.

Latin Text-Books

		INTROD. PRICE.
ALLEN & GREENOUGH:	Latin Grammar	$1.12
	Latin Composition	1.12
	Caesar (four books, with vocabulary)	1.12
	Sallust's Catiline	.60
	Cicero, 13 orations (or 8 orations with vocabulary)	1.12
	Cicero de Senectute	.50
	Ovid (with vocabulary)	1.40
	Virgil (Bucolics and 6 Books of the Æneid)	1.12
	Preparatory Course of Latin Prose	1.40
ALLEN	Latin Primer	.90
	New Latin Method	.90
	Introduction to Latin Composition	.90
	Latin Reader	1.40
	Latin Lexicon	.90
	Remnants of Early Latin	.75
	Germania and Agricola of Tacitus	1.00
BLACKBURN	Essentials of Latin Grammar	.70
	Latin Exercises	.60
	Latin Grammar and Exercises (in one volume)	1.00
CROWELL	Selections from the Latin Poets	1.40
CROWELL & RICHARDSON:	Brief History of Roman Lit. (BENDER)	1.00
GREENOUGH	Virgil:—	
	Bucolics and 6 Books of Æneid (with Vocab.)	1.60
	Bucolics and 6 Books of Æneid (without Vocab.)	1.12
	Last 6 Books of Æneid, and Georgics (with notes)	1.12
	Bucolics, Æneid, & Georgics (complete, with notes)	1.60
	Text of Virgil (complete)	.75
	Vocabulary to the whole of Virgil	1.00
GINN & HEATH:	Classical Atlas and Geography (cloth)	2.00
HALSEY	Etymology of Latin and Greek	1.12
	Classical Wall Maps (three or more), each	3.50
KEEP	Essential Uses of the Moods in Greek and Latin	.25
KING	Latin Pronunciation	.25
LEIGHTON	Latin Lessons	1.12
MADVIG	Latin Grammar (by Thacher)	2.25
PARKHURST	Latin Verb	.35
PARKER & PREBLE:	Handbook of Latin Writing	.50
SHUMWAY	Latin Synonymes	.30
STICKNEY	Cicero de Natura Deorum	1.40
TETLOW	Inductive Latin Lessons	1.12
TOMLINSON	Manual for the Study of Latin Grammar	.20
WHITE (J. W.)	Schmidt's Rhythmic and Metric	2.50
WHITE (J. T.)	Junior Students' Latin-English Lexicon (mor.)	1.75
	English-Latin Lexicon (sheep)	1.50
	Latin-English and English-Latin Lexicon (sheep)	3.00
WHITON	Auxilia Vergiliana; or, First Steps in Latin Prosody	.15
	Six Weeks' Preparation for Reading Cæsar	.35

Copies sent to Teachers for Examination, with a view to Introduction, on receipt of Introduction Price.

Send for description of our new Illustrated Caesar (seven books).

GINN & COMPANY, Publishers,
BOSTON, NEW YORK, AND CHICAGO.

Mathematical Books

		INTROD. PRICE.
Byerly	Differential Calculus	$2.00
	Integral Calculus	2.00
	Syllabus of Plane Trigonometry	.10
	Syllabus of Analytical Geometry	.10
	Syllabus of Analytical Geometry, *adv. course*	.10
	Syllabus of Equations	.10
Ginn	Addition Tablets { Pocket size	.25
	{ Large size	3.00
Halsted	Mensuration	1.00
Hardy	Quaternions	2.00
Hill	Geometry for Beginners	1.00
Peirce	Three and Four-Place Logarithms	40
	Tables, chiefly to Four Figures	.40
	Elements of Logarithms	50
	Tables of Integrals	10
Waldo	Multiplication and Division Tables: —	
	Folio size	.50
	Small size	.25
Wentworth	Elements of Algebra	1.12
	Complete Algebra	1.40
	Plane Geometry	.75
	Plane and Solid Geometry	1.25
	Plane and Solid Geometry and Trigonometry	1.40
	Plane Trigonometry. *Paper*	.30
	Plane Trigonometry and Tables. *Paper*	.60
	Plane and Spherical Trigonometry	.75
	Plane and Spherical Trigonometry, Surveying, and Navigation	1.12
	Plane and Spherical Trig. and Surveying, with Tables	1.25
	Surveying. *Paper*	.25
	Trigonometric Formulas	1.00
Wentworth & Hill :	Five-Place Log. and Trig. Tables (7 *Tables*)	.50
	Five-Place Log. and Trig. Tables (*Comp. Ed.*)	1.00
	Practical Arithmetic	1.00
	Examination Manuals. I. Arithmetic	.35
	II. Algebra	.35
	Exercise Manuals. I. Arithmetic	
	II. Algebra	.70
	III. Geometry	
Wheeler	Plane and Spherical Trig. and Tables	1.00

Copies sent to Teachers for Examination, with a view to Introduction, on receipt of Introduction Price.

GINN & COMPANY, Publishers,
BOSTON, NEW YORK, AND CHICAGO.

Books on English Literature.

		INTROD. PRICE.
Allen	Reader's Guide to English History	$ .25
	History Topics	.25
Arnold	English Literature	1.50
Carpenter	Anglo-Saxon Grammar	.60
	English of the XIVth Century	.90
Church	Stories of the Old World	.40
	(Classics for Children.)	
Craik	English of Shakespeare	.90
Garnett	Beówulf (*Translation*)	1.00
Harrison & Sharp : Beówulf (Text and Glossary)		1.12
Hudson	Harvard Edition of Shakespeare: —	
	20 Vol. Edition. *Cloth, retail*	25.00
	10 Vol. Edition. *Cloth, retail*	20.00
	Life, Art, and Characters of Shakespeare. 2 vols. *Cloth, retail*	4.00
	New School Shakespeare. *Cloth.* Each play	.45
	Old School Shakespeare, per play	.20
	Expurgated Family Shakespeare	10.00
	Essays on Education, English Studies, etc.	.25
	Three Vol. Shakespeare, per vol.	1.25
	Text-Book of Poetry	1.25
	Text-Book of Prose	1.25
	Pamphlet Selections, Prose and Poetry	.20
	Classical English Reader	1.00
Hudson & Lamb : Merchant of Venice		.25
	(Classics for Children.)	
Hunt	Exodus and Daniel	.60
Lambert	Robinson Crusoe	.35
	(Classics for Children.)	
	Memory Gems	.30
Lounsbury	Chaucer's Parlament of Foules	.50
Minto	Manual of English Prose Literature	2.00
Sprague	Selections from Irving { *Cloth*	.35
	{ *Boards*	.25
	Two Books of Paradise Lost, and Lycidas	.45
Thom	Two Shakespeare Examinations	.45
Yonge	Scott's Quentin Durward	.40
	(Classics for Children.)	

Copies sent to Teachers for Examination, with a view to Introduction, on receipt of Introduction Price.

GINN & COMPANY, Publishers,
BOSTON, NEW YORK, AND CHICAGO.

University of California
SOUTHERN REGIONAL LIBRARY FACILITY
405 Hilgard Avenue, Los Angeles, CA 90024-1388
Return this material to the library
from which it was borrowed.